Macworld®
FileMaker® Pro 3 Bible, 2nd Edition

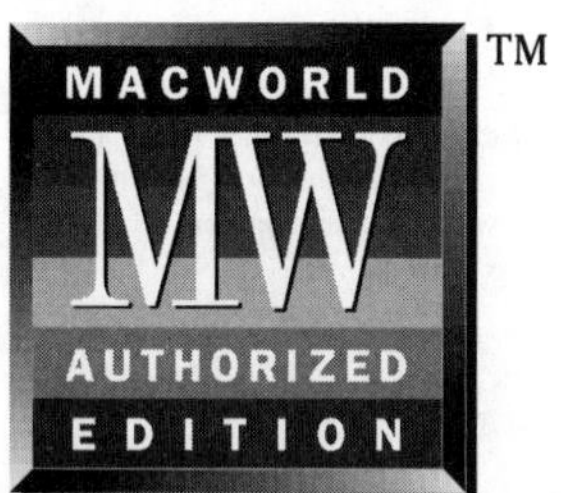

Macworld® FileMaker® Pro 3 Bible, 2nd Edition

by Dr. Steven A. Schwartz

IDG Books Worldwide, Inc.
An International Data Group Company

Foster City, CA ♦ Chicago, IL ♦ Indianapolis, IN ♦ Southlake, TX

Macworld® FileMaker® Pro 3 Bible, Second Edition

Published by
IDG Books Worldwide, Inc.
An International Data Group Company
919 E. Hillsdale Blvd.
Suite 400
Foster City, CA 94404
http://www.idgbooks.com (IDG Books Worldwide Web site)

Copyright © 1996 IDG Books Worldwide, Inc. All rights reserved. No part of this book, including interior design, cover design, and icons, may be reproduced or transmitted in any form, by any means (electronic, photocopying, recording, or otherwise) without the prior written permission of the publisher.

Library of Congress Catalog Card No.: 96-75407

ISBN: 1-56884-728-9

Printed in the United States of America

10 9 8 7 6 5 4 3

2B/RZ/RR/ZW/FC-IN

Distributed in the United States by IDG Books Worldwide, Inc.

Distributed by Macmillan Canada for Canada; by Contemporanea de Ediciones for Venezuela; by Distribuidora Cuspide for Argentina; by CITEC for Brazil; by Ediciones ZETA S.C.R. Ltda. for Peru; by Editorial Limusa SA for Mexico; by Transworld Publishers Limited in the United Kingdom and Europe; by Academic Bookshop for Egypt; by Levant Distributors S.A.R.L. for Lebanon; by Al Jassim for Saudi Arabia; by Simron Pty. Ltd. for South Africa; by Pustak Mahal for India; by The Computer Bookshop for India; by Toppan Company Ltd. for Japan; by Addison Wesley Publishing Company for Korea; by Longman Singapore Publishers Ltd. for Singapore, Malaysia, Thailand, and Indonesia; by Unalis Corporation for Taiwan; by WS Computer Publishing Company, Inc. for the Philippines; by WoodsLane Pty. Ltd. for Australia; by WoodsLane Enterprises Ltd. for New Zealand. Authorized Sales Agent: Anthony Rudkin Associates for the Middle East and North Africa.

For general information on IDG Books Worldwide's books in the U.S., please call our Consumer Customer Service department at 800-762-2974. For reseller information, including discounts and premium sales, please call our Reseller Customer Service department at 800-434-3422.

For information on where to purchase IDG Books Worldwide's books outside the U.S., please contact our International Sales department at 415-655-3172 or fax 415-655-3295.

For information on foreign language translations, please contact our Foreign & Subsidiary Rights department at 415-655-3021 or fax 415-655-3281.

For sales inquiries and special prices for bulk quantities, please contact our Sales department at 415-655-3200 or write to the address above.

For information on using IDG Books Worldwide's books in the classroom or for ordering examination copies, please contact our Educational Sales department at 800-434-2086 or fax 817-251-8174.

For press review copies, author interviews, or other publicity information, please contact our Public Relations department at 415-655-3000 or fax 415-655-3299.

For authorization to photocopy items for corporate, personal, or educational use, please contact Copyright Clearance Center, 222 Rosewood Drive, Danvers, MA 01923, or fax 508-750-4470.

LIMIT OF LIABILITY/DISCLAIMER OF WARRANTY: AUTHOR AND PUBLISHER HAVE USED THEIR BEST EFFORTS IN PREPARING THIS BOOK. IDG BOOKS WORLDWIDE, INC., AND AUTHOR MAKE NO REPRESENTATIONS OR WARRANTIES WITH RESPECT TO THE ACCURACY OR COMPLETENESS OF THE CONTENTS OF THIS BOOK AND SPECIFICALLY DISCLAIM ANY IMPLIED WARRANTIES OF MERCHANTABILITY OR FITNESS FOR A PARTICULAR PURPOSE. THERE ARE NO WARRANTIES WHICH EXTEND BEYOND THE DESCRIPTIONS CONTAINED IN THIS PARAGRAPH. NO WARRANTY MAY BE CREATED OR EXTENDED BY SALES REPRESENTATIVES OR WRITTEN SALES MATERIALS. THE ACCURACY AND COMPLETENESS OF THE INFORMATION PROVIDED HEREIN AND THE OPINIONS STATED HEREIN ARE NOT GUARANTEED OR WARRANTED TO PRODUCE ANY PARTICULAR RESULTS, AND THE ADVICE AND STRATEGIES CONTAINED HEREIN MAY NOT BE SUITABLE FOR EVERY INDIVIDUAL. NEITHER IDG BOOKS WORLDWIDE, INC., NOR AUTHOR SHALL BE LIABLE FOR ANY LOSS OF PROFIT OR ANY OTHER COMMERCIAL DAMAGES, INCLUDING BUT NOT LIMITED TO SPECIAL, INCIDENTAL, CONSEQUENTIAL, OR OTHER DAMAGES.

Trademarks: All brand names and product names used in this book are trade names, service marks, trademarks, or registered trademarks of their respective owners. IDG Books Worldwide is not associated with any product or vendor mentioned in this book.

is a trademark under exclusive license to IDG Books Worldwide, Inc., from International Data Group, Inc.

About the Author

In 1978, Dr. Steven Schwartz bought his first microcomputer, a new Apple II+. Determined to find a way to make money with it, he began writing software reviews, BASIC programs, and user tips for *Nibble* magazine. Shortly thereafter, he was made a contributing editor.

Over the past 18 years, Steven has written hundreds of articles for more than a dozen computer magazines. He currently writes for *Macworld* and *Multimedia World.* He was also a founding editor of *Software Digest*, as well as Business Editor for *MACazine.* From 1985 to 1990, he was the Director of Technical Services for Funk Software.

Steven is the author of more than 25 books, including *Macworld Guide to ClarisWorks 2, Macworld ClarisWorks 2.0/2.1 Companion, Macworld ClarisWorks 3.0 Bible, Macworld ClarisWorks 4.0 Bible, Macworld FileMaker Pro 2.0/2.1 Bibl*e (IDG Books Worldwide); *The 9–to–5 Mac* (Hayden Macintosh Library); *Help! The Mac Answer Book* (Alpha Books); and a series of popular game strategy guides from Prima Publishing, COMPUTE Books, and others.

Steven has a Ph.D. in psychology and currently lives in Arizona, where he writes books and reviews, consults on game development issues, and complains about the heat.

ABOUT IDG BOOKS WORLDWIDE

Welcome to the world of IDG Books Worldwide.

IDG Books Worldwide, Inc., is a subsidiary of International Data Group, the world's largest publisher of computer-related information and the leading global provider of information services on information technology. IDG was founded more than 25 years ago and now employs more than 8,500 people worldwide. IDG publishes more than 275 computer publications in over 75 countries (see listing below). More than 60 million people read one or more IDG publications each month.

Launched in 1990, IDG Books Worldwide is today the #1 publisher of best-selling computer books in the United States. We are proud to have received eight awards from the Computer Press Association in recognition of editorial excellence and three from *Computer Currents*' First Annual Readers' Choice Awards. Our best-selling *...For Dummies®* series has more than 30 million copies in print with translations in 30 languages. IDG Books Worldwide, through a joint venture with IDG's Hi-Tech Beijing, became the first U.S. publisher to publish a computer book in the People's Republic of China. In record time, IDG Books Worldwide has become the first choice for millions of readers around the world who want to learn how to better manage their businesses.

Our mission is simple: Every one of our books is designed to bring extra value and skill-building instructions to the reader. Our books are written by experts who understand and care about our readers. The knowledge base of our editorial staff comes from years of experience in publishing, education, and journalism — experience we use to produce books for the '90s. In short, we care about books, so we attract the best people. We devote special attention to details such as audience, interior design, use of icons, and illustrations. And because we use an efficient process of authoring, editing, and desktop publishing our books electronically, we can spend more time ensuring superior content and spend less time on the technicalities of making books.

You can count on our commitment to deliver high-quality books at competitive prices on topics you want to read about. At IDG Books Worldwide, we continue in the IDG tradition of delivering quality for more than 25 years. You'll find no better book on a subject than one from IDG Books Worldwide.

John Kilcullen
President and CEO
IDG Books Worldwide, Inc.

Eighth Annual Computer Press Awards 1992

Ninth Annual Computer Press Awards 1993

Tenth Annual Computer Press Awards 1994

Eleventh Annual Computer Press Awards 1995

IDG Books Worldwide, Inc., is a subsidiary of International Data Group, the world's largest publisher of computer-related information and the leading global provider of information services on information technology. International Data Group publishes over 275 computer publications in over 75 countries. Sixty million people read one or more International Data Group publications each month. International Data Group's publications include: **ARGENTINA:** Buyer's Guide, Computerworld Argentina, PC World Argentina; **AUSTRALIA:** Australian Macworld, Australian PC World, Australian Reseller News, Computerworld, IT Casebook, Network World, Publish, Webmaster; **AUSTRIA:** Computerwelt Osterreich, Networks Austria, PC Tip Austria; **BANGLADESH:** PC World Bangladesh; **BELARUS:** PC World Belarus; **BELGIUM:** Data News; **BRAZIL:** Annuário de Informática, Computerworld, Connections, Macworld, PC Player, PC World, Publish, Reseller News, Supergamepower; **BULGARIA:** Computerworld Bulgaria, Network World Bulgaria, PC & MacWorld Bulgaria; **CANADA:** CIO Canada, Client/Server World, ComputerWorld Canada, InfoWorld Canada, NetworkWorld Canada, WebWorld; **CHILE:** Computerworld Chile, PC World Chile; **COLOMBIA:** Computerworld Colombia, PC World Colombia; **COSTA RICA:** PC World Centro America; **THE CZECH AND SLOVAK REPUBLICS:** Computerworld Czechoslovakia, Macworld Czech Republic, PC World Czechoslovakia; **DENMARK:** Communications World Danmark, Computerworld Danmark, Macworld Danmark, PC World Danmark, Techworld Denmark; **DOMINICAN REPUBLIC:** PC World Republica Dominicana; **ECUADOR:** PC World Ecuador; **EGYPT:** Computerworld Middle East, PC World Middle East; **EL SALVADOR:** PC World Centro America; **FINLAND:** MikroPC, Tietoverkko, Tietoviikko; **FRANCE:** Distributique, Hebdo, Info PC, Le Monde Informatique, Macworld, Reseaux & Telecoms, WebMaster France; **GERMANY:** Computer Partner, Computerwoche, Computerwoche Extra, Computerwoche FOCUS, Global Online, Macwelt, PC Welt; **GREECE:** Amiga Computing, GamePro Greece, Multimedia World; **GUATEMALA:** PC World Centro America; **HONDURAS:** PC World Centro America; **HONG KONG:** Computerworld Hong Kong, PC World Hong Kong, Publish in Asia; **HUNGARY:** ABCD CD-ROM, Computerworld Szamitastechnika, Internetto online Magazine, PC World Hungary, PC-X Magazin Hungary; **ICELAND:** Tolvuheimur PC World Island; **INDIA:** Information Communications World, Information Systems Computerworld, PC World India, Publish in Asia; **INDONESIA:** InfoKomputer PC World, Komputek Computerworld, Publish in Asia; **IRELAND:** ComputerScope, PC Live!; **ISRAEL:** Macworld Israel, People & Computers/Computerworld; **ITALY:** Computerworld Italia, Macworld Italia, Networking Italia, PC World Italia; **JAPAN:** DTP World, Macworld Japan, Nikkei Personal Computing, OS/2 World Japan, SunWorld Japan, Windows NT World, Windows World Japan; **KENYA:** PC World East African; **KOREA:** Hi-Tech Information, Macworld Korea, PC World Korea; **MACEDONIA:** PC World Macedonia; **MALAYSIA:** Computerworld Malaysia, PC World Malaysia, Publish in Asia; **MALTA:** PC World Malta; **MEXICO:** Computerworld Mexico, PC World Mexico; **MYANMAR:** PC World Myanmar; **NETHERLANDS:** Computer! Totaal, LAN Internetworking Magazine, LAN World Buyers Guide, Macworld Netherlands, Net, WebWereld; **NEW ZEALAND:** Absolute Beginners Guide and Plain & Simple Series, Computer Buyer, Computer Industry Directory, Computerworld New Zealand, MTB, Network World, PC World New Zealand; **NICARAGUA:** PC World Centro America; **NORWAY:** Computerworld Norge, CW Rapport, Datamagasinet, Financial Rapport, Kursguide Norge, Macworld Norge, Multimediaworld Norge, PC World Ekspress Norge, PC World Nettverk, PC World Norge, PC World ProduktGuide Norge; **PAKISTAN:** Computerworld Pakistan; **PANAMA:** PC World Panama; **PEOPLE'S REPUBLIC OF CHINA:** China Computer Users, China Computerworld, China InfoWorld, China Telecom World Weekly, Computer & Communication, Electronic Design China, Electronics Today, Electronics Weekly, Game Software, PC World China, Popular Computer Week, Software Weekly, Software World, Telecom World; **PERU:** Computerworld Peru, PC World Profesional Peru, PC World SoHo Peru; **PHILIPPINES:** Click!, Computerworld Philippines, PC World Philippines, Publish in Asia; **POLAND:** Computerworld Poland, Computerworld Special Report Poland, Cyber, Macworld Poland, Networld Poland, PC World Komputer; **PORTUGAL:** Cerebro/PC World, Computerworld/Correio Informático, Dealer World Portugal, Mac*In/PC*In Portugal, Multimedia World; **PUERTO RICO:** PC World Puerto Rico; **ROMANIA:** Computerworld Romania, PC World Romania, Telecom Romania; **RUSSIA:** Computerworld Russia, Mir PK, Publish, Seti; **SINGAPORE:** Computerworld Singapore, PC World Singapore, Publish in Asia; **SLOVENIA:** Monitor; **SOUTH AFRICA:** Computing SA, Network World SA, Software World SA; **SPAIN:** Communicaciones World España, Computerworld España, Dealer World España, Macworld España, PC World España; **SRI LANKA:** Infolink PC World; **SWEDEN:** CAP&Design, Computer Sweden, Corporate Computing Sweden, Internetworld Sweden, it.branschen, Macworld Sweden, MaxiData Sweden, MikroDatorn, Nätverk & Kommunikation, PC World Sweden, PCaktiv, Windows World Sweden; **SWITZERLAND:** Computerworld Schweiz, Macworld Schweiz, PCtip; **TAIWAN:** Computerworld Taiwan, Macworld Taiwan, NEW ViSiON/Publish, PC World Taiwan, Windows World Taiwan; **THAILAND:** Publish in Asia, Thai Computerworld; **TURKEY:** Computerworld Turkiye, Macworld Turkiye, Network World Turkiye, PC World Turkiye; **UKRAINE:** Computerworld Kiev, Multimedia World Ukraine, PC World Ukraine; **UNITED KINGDOM:** Acorn User UK, Amiga Action UK, Amiga Computing UK, Apple Talk UK, Computing, Macworld, Parents and Computers UK, PC Advisor, PC Home, PSX Pro, The WEB; **UNITED STATES:** Cable in the Classroom, CIO Magazine, Computerworld, DOS World, Federal Computer Week, GamePro Magazine, InfoWorld, I-Way, Macworld, Network World, PC Games, PC World, Publish, Video Event, THE WEB Magazine, and WebMaster; online webzines: JavaWorld, NetscapeWorld, and SunWorld Online; **URUGUAY:** InfoWorld Uruguay; **VENEZUELA:** Computerworld Venezuela, PC World Venezuela; and **VIETNAM:** PC World Vietnam. 10/22/96

Acknowledgments

I am grateful to the many people who offered their encouragement and support throughout the writing of this update, including Nancy Dunn, Ken Brown, and Kathie Duggan at IDG Books Worldwide; Jay Lee; Kevin Mallon at Claris Corporation; and my agent and friend, Matt Wagner.

The following individuals were kind enough to provide materials that are included on the disk that accompanies this book:

- Mark Wall, Green Mountain Software, at `http://www.hsv.tis.net/~greenmtn/`
- Bill Taube, Database Associates, Inc., at `DBA1@aol.com`
- Steve Abrahamson, Ascending Technologies, at `Steve@asctech.com`
- Dave Applegate at `Apple5@aol.com`

Credits

Senior Vice President and Group Publisher
Brenda McLaughlin

Acquisitions Editor
Nancy E. Dunn

Managing Editor
Terry Somerson

Editorial Assistants
Suki Gear
Jean Leitner

Production Director
Andrew Walker

Supervisor of Page Layout
Craig A. Harrison

Development Editor
Kenyon Brown

Copy Editor
Kathryn Duggan

Technical Editor
Jay Lee

Project Coordinators
Phyllis Beatty
Ben Schroeder

Layout and Graphics
Elizabeth Cárdenas-Nelson
Laura Carpenter
Stephen Noetzel
Chris Pimentel
Andreas Schueller
Elsie Yim

Proofreader
Mary C. Oby

Indexer
Steve Rath

Production Administration
Tony Augsburger
Todd Klemme
Jason Marcuson
Jacalyn L. Pennywell
Leslie Popplewell
Patricia R. Reynolds
Theresa Sánchez-Baker
Melissa Stauffer
Bryan Stephenson

Book Design
Beth Jenkins
Shelley Lea

Cover Illustration
Stuart Bradford

Contents at a Glance

Table of Contents

Chapter 15: Automating FileMaker Pro ... 447

Part V: Mastering FileMaker Pro 561

Chapter 19: Linking Databases: Relationships and Lookups 563

Chapter 20: Sharing and Protecting Data 591

Preface

FileMaker Pro is a mature database product. We're not talking about some company's latest brain child that is being foisted — bug-laden — onto an unsuspecting public. In its various incarnations and from its various publishers, it has been known as FileMaker, FileMaker 2, FileMaker IV, FileMaker Pro, FileMaker Pro 2, and now FileMaker Pro 3. FileMaker Pro has been around the block — and I've been in lock-step with it.

Why FileMaker Pro?

Unlike many computer products that are periodically "redefined" by having drastic changes made to the *user interface* (the way you interact with the program and perform different procedures) or to the program's *focus* (such as changing a simple text editor into a desktop publishing program), FileMaker Pro's versions have all shown a steady progression forward. This means that if you've used any version of FileMaker Pro — even one that is several years old — the information and experience you've gained has not been a waste of time. Much of your knowledge can be applied directly to the current version of the program.

Although I've reviewed computer programs for more than 18 years for magazines such as *Macworld, Multimedia World, Mac Home Journal, MACazine, Macintosh Business Journal,* and *Software Digest,* surprisingly few products exist that impress me so much that I've stuck with them over the years. FileMaker Pro is such a program. Apparently, much of the Macintosh community agrees with my assessment, because FileMaker Pro currently owns about 70 percent of the Mac database market (and it's making steady inroads into the world of Windows, too). Because it's safe to assume that you own a copy of FileMaker Pro, you're in excellent company.

What's So Special About FileMaker Pro 3?

I'm glad you asked.

In addition to its continuing improvements in ease-of-use, FileMaker Pro 3 represents a major leap forward in terms of power features. At long last, FileMaker Pro now offers full *relational* capabilities. Now — in addition to being the best flat-file database program around — developers and businesses who formerly had to look elsewhere for solutions to their corporate database problems can now turn to FileMaker Pro. (Of course, the rest of us home and business users can also take advantage of the new relational features. The nice thing, though, is that we don't *have* to. If you're comfortable using FileMaker Pro as a flat-file database, you don't have to change the way you use the program. The relational capabilities are there for whomever wants to use them, but can safely be ignored by those who don't.)

New scripting features make it possible to perform complex activities, such as conditional tests and loops, as well as to dial phone numbers and exert greater control over the document window. Improved formatting commands and the new text ruler bar make it simple to format selected text and paragraphs. And the Button tool enables anyone to easily create attractive buttons for their databases.

In short, FileMaker Pro 3 is a *major* update to the program. This book is intended to help you use it to the max.

About This Book

The *Macworld FileMaker Pro 3 Bible* is a different kind of computer book. First, it's not a manual. Many people don't like computer manuals — perhaps because they feel obligated to read them from cover to cover to avoid missing something important, or because manuals are designed to explain how features work rather than how to put a program to work for you. The *Macworld FileMaker Pro 3 Bible* is not a book that you *have* to read. It's a book that I hope you'll *want* to read — because it provides easy-to-find, easy-to-understand explanations of the common tasks for which you bought FileMaker Pro in the first place. When you want to know how to use a particular program feature, you can use the extensive table of contents or index to quickly identify the section of the book that you need to read.

Second, although I hope that you'll find some of the material in this book to be entertaining, the primary mission of the *Macworld FileMaker Pro 3 Bible* is to inform. I want you to really understand how FileMaker Pro works and to be able to make it do exactly what you want it to do. No matter where you turn in this book, if you find yourself with a puzzled look on your face after reading a section, I haven't done my job.

Finally, the philosophy of this book — as well as the other books in the IDG *Macworld* Bible series — is that you don't want or need a handful of books to learn all about a computer program; one book should suffice. The *Macworld FileMaker Pro 3 Bible* is an all-in-one book that gives you a well-rounded knowledge of FileMaker Pro. You don't just learn *how* to perform an action; you also learn *when* and *why* you would perform that action. You can find almost anything you want to know about FileMaker Pro in this book.

Who Can Use This Book

The *Macworld FileMaker Pro 3 Bible* is for anyone who uses version 3 of FileMaker Pro:

- If you're a beginning FileMaker Pro user, step-by-step instructions help you get up to speed quickly with explanations of how to perform common (and not so common) FileMaker Pro features and procedures.
- If you're an intermediate or advanced FileMaker Pro user — someone who doesn't need much hand-holding — tips and insights in each chapter help you get the most from FileMaker Pro. You'll find the information provided in the notes, tips, and sidebars to be handy tools for your FileMaker Pro toolbox.

How This Book Is Organized

Each chapter is self-contained. When you need to perform a particular FileMaker Pro task, scan the table of contents to locate the chapter that addresses your needs. You can also flip through the pages of the book to quickly find the chapter you need. The *Macworld FileMaker Pro 3 Bible* is divided into six Parts.

Part I: The Fundamentals

This section is a gentle introduction to database concepts, essential FileMaker Pro concepts and procedures, and relational databases.

Part II: Learning Database Design Basics

This section instructs you in using the various design tools to construct databases and to design different types of layouts.

Part III: Working with Databases

In this section, I explain what you need to know when you're ready to start working with a database: entering and editing data, searching for particular records, sorting, designing reports, and printing.

Part IV: Putting FileMaker Pro to Work

This section covers material that helps you make more productive use of FileMaker Pro. It isn't essential to learn about these features immediately, but you will want to tackle them after you're comfortable with the FileMaker Pro basics.

Part V: Mastering FileMaker Pro

Material in this section will interest more experienced FileMaker Pro users and would-be developers, including using relationships and lookups to link databases and tips for creating databases that you'd like to share (or sell) to others.

Part VI: Appendixes

The section includes instructions for using the *Macworld FileMaker Pro 3 Bible* disk that's conveniently packaged with the book. I've also included keyboard shortcuts and a listing of resources that'll help you get the most from using FileMaker Pro.

Icons Used in This Book

The chapters in this book contain the following icons:

Highlights time-saving shortcuts or quick techniques that will help you work smarter.

Identifies new features found in FileMaker Pro 3.

Alerts you that the action or operation being described can cause problems if you're not careful.

Highlights a special point of interest about the topic under discussion — information that is not necessarily vital to performing a task. Look here if you're interested in achieving a more well-rounded knowledge of FileMaker Pro .

How to Use This Book

Far be it from me to tell you how to read this book. Reading and learning styles are all very personal. When I get a new computer program, I frequently read the manual from cover to cover before even installing the software. Of course, I'll be flattered if you read the *Macworld FileMaker Pro 3 Bible* the same way — but I'll be *surprised* if you do, too.

This book is written as a reference to "all things FileMaker Pro." When you want to learn about defining fields, there's a specific chapter to which you can turn. If you just need to know how to use the spelling checker, you can flip to the table of contents or the index and find the pages where it's discussed. Most procedures are explained in step-by-step fashion, so you can quickly accomplish even the most complex tasks. You can read this book as you would a novel, read just the chapters that interest you, or use it as a quick reference when you need to learn about a particular feature or procedure.

For those who prefer a little more direction than "whatever works for you," some general guidelines are suggested in the following paragraphs — arranged according to your level of Mac expertise and previous FileMaker Pro experience.

However, I do have one general suggestion: *If at all possible, read this book with FileMaker Pro on-screen.* Sure, you can read about editing a user dictionary for the spelling checker while relaxing in the tub, but — unless you have exceptional recall — what you read will be more meaningful if you're sitting in front of the computer.

For the Beginner

Like the manuals for most computer programs, this book assumes that you have a general grasp of the procedures necessary to use your computer, such as using the mouse, choosing commands from menus, and printing documents. If FileMaker Pro is your first Mac program and you have not yet taken the time to work through the owner's manual that came with your Macintosh, Performa, or Macintosh-compatible computer, stop reading now. It's time to drag out the manuals for your computer, printer, and system software. Once you fill in the gaps in your Mac education, you'll feel more confident and comfortable tackling FileMaker Pro and any other programs you eventually purchase.

If you're relatively new to FileMaker Pro, start by reading all of Part I. This will acquaint you with database concepts and the FileMaker Pro basics. Next, work through the tutorial presented in Chapter 4. This chapter gently leads you through the process of creating your first database, a full-featured Address Book in which you can record your business and personal contacts. Finish up by reading the remaining chapters of Part II (Chapters 5 through 7) and at least the first three chapters of Part III (Chapters 8 through 10). This will provide you with a sufficient grounding in FileMaker Pro concepts and features to enable you to tackle basic database projects. Then, as you find it necessary to explore additional program features, such as printing or creating calculations, you can just jump to the appropriate chapter.

The more advanced stuff is saved for Part IV and Part V. Although you'll eventually want to check out the material in those parts, too, you'll note that I've purposely separated the advanced matters from the basics in order to keep new users from being overwhelmed.

For the More Experienced User

If you're familiar with databases, you can safely skip Chapters 1 and 2. The material in these chapters is very basic and is probably second-hand to you. If FileMaker Pro is your first database program, however, you should at least skim through the material in Chapter 1.

Chapter 3 is essential for every FileMaker Pro user. Many FileMaker Pro tasks, such as using the tools, are discussed here.

Parts II and III are the real meat-and-potatoes chapters for new FileMaker Pro users. Many of the topics covered in these parts are at least touched upon in Chapter 4. After completing this tutorial chapter, you may feel sufficiently confident to tackle some of your own database projects. You can treat the remainder of the book as reference material to be read as needed.

For an Owner of a Previous Version of FileMaker

As mentioned earlier, FileMaker (in its various incarnations) has always worked basically the same. Through the years, however, new features and capabilities have been added. If you are familiar with an older version of FileMaker, you should pay particular attention to material in the following chapters:

- Chapter 15 discusses ScriptMaker and explains how to create auto-entry data fields.
- Chapter 16 explains the procedures for moving data between FileMaker Pro and other programs.
- Chapter 19 discusses FileMaker Pro's relational and lookup capabilities, enabling you to automatically bring data from an external database into the current database.
- Chapter 20 tells how FileMaker Pro works on a network and explains how Publish & Subscribe (a feature introduced with System 7) is used.

Macworld FileMaker Pro 3 Bible Disk

Packaged with this book is the *Macworld FileMaker Pro 3 Bible* disk, a collection of ready-to-run FileMaker Pro templates, example databases, demos, and FileMaker-related utilities. Whether you just want to get up and running quickly, need some help with the more advanced topics covered in the book, or are looking for new ways to use FileMaker Pro, you're strongly encouraged to check out the disk.

Note: *The Macworld FileMaker Pro 3 Bible disk is neither a product of nor is it endorsed by Claris Corporation.*

The Fundamentals

This section contains an introduction to database concepts. Other topic include essential FileMaker Pro concepts and procedures, and relational databases.

CHAPTER 1

What Is a Database?

In This Chapter

- Understanding essential database terminology
- Comparing paper databases and computer databases
- Looking at the differences between flat-file and relational databases
- Understanding important FileMaker Pro concepts and terms
- Learning some of the potential uses for FileMaker Pro

Before exploring FileMaker Pro 3.0, you need to understand what a database is. A *database* is an organized collection of information, usually with one central topic. In a computer database (as opposed to a paper database), the program that you use to enter and manipulate the data is called a *database program* or a *database management program.*

The word *organized* is a key part of this definition. Otherwise, a shoe box stuffed with business receipts might be considered a database. In general, if you need to manually look at every scrap of data before finding the one for which you're searching, you don't have a database. You just have a shoe box full of stuff.

Even if you have never used a computer database, you're already familiar with many examples of paper databases:

- Address books and business card files
- Employee records
- Recipe card files

- Telephone books
- Holiday greeting card lists

Every database — whether on paper, in a hand-held electronic organizer, or in a computer — is composed of records. A *record* contains all the information that has been collected on one individual or entity in the database. In the preceding examples, a record holds all the address data on one friend or business associate (address book or business card file); the employment information on one employee (employee records); the ingredients and cooking instructions for one recipe (recipe card file); the name, street address, and phone number for one person or business in the area (telephone book); and the name of one person or family whom you previously received a card from or intend to send a card to (holiday greeting card list).

Records are divided into fields. A *field* contains a single piece of information about the subject of the record. In an address database, for example, the fields may include first name, last name, address, city, state, ZIP code, and phone number. Figure 1-1 shows the relationship among the components of a database.

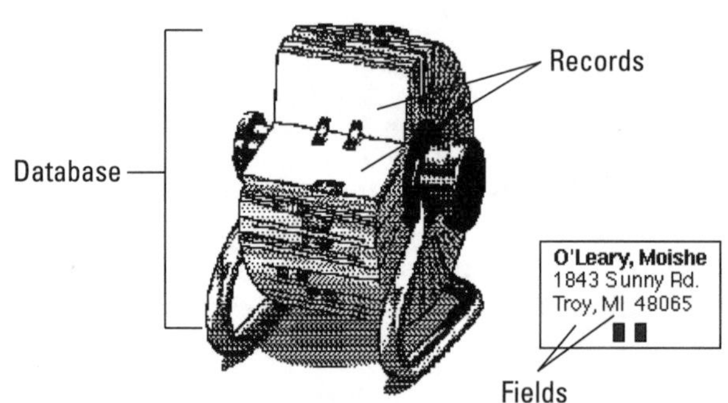

Figure 1-1: Every database is composed of records that contain fields. [Card file image from EPS Business Art, part of the ClickArt software series, courtesy of T/Maker Company.]

What distinguishes a database from any old hodgepodge of information is that the data within each record is *organized.* Fields are responsible for this organization. The fields appear in the same place on every record and are reserved for a particular type of information. In the example in Figure 1-1, the field for the last name is always in the upper-left corner of the address card, and it always contains a person's last name. No matter which address card you pull, you can be assured of finding a last name at that spot on the card.

Of course, in some paper databases, maintaining this level of organization can be difficult. When you are writing or typing an address card, for example, you may occasionally reverse the order of the last and first names or enter a company name in that location. Organization in informal paper databases comes exclusively from your own consistency — or lack of it.

When consistency is critical, such as when you are recording information on employees or filling out a customer invoice, records are often designed as forms. Spaces on the form have labels so that you always know which piece of information belongs where. You can still type a phone number in the space labeled "Social Security number," but at least the labels make catching and correcting mistakes easier. Forms help organize the data in much the same way that a computer-based database does. In fact, this type of paper database is frequently the basis for a computer database.

Paper Databases Versus Computer Databases

So what's wrong with paper databases? Many homes and businesses depend heavily on them. The following sections discuss some of the shortcomings of paper databases and explain how computer databases can avoid these limitations.

Limitations of Paper Databases

First, consider some of the shortcomings of paper databases:

- *It's easy to make data-entry errors.* Even when you are using a typeset form, nothing prevents you from entering the wrong data in a field or forgetting to fill in a critical field, such as the hire date or medical history.
- *Maintenance can be difficult.* For records to be easy to locate, they must be in some rational order. Whenever you return or add a record to a folder or the filing cabinet, you have to be careful to place it in the correct spot. If you put the vendor file for Alpha Gamma Corp. in the *Q* folder, you may never find it again!
- *Updating records can be time-consuming.* Because of changes in information, such as addresses, phone numbers, and salaries, few databases are static. Updating a paper record may require several steps, including finding the record, erasing the old information, writing in the new information (or typing a whole new record), and returning the form to the filing cabinet. Making an across-the-board change — such as granting an incremental salary increase to all employees — can take a long time.
- *Sorting records, selecting subgroups of records, and creating reports are cumbersome tasks.* Your boss walks into your office and says, "We're thinking about putting in a day-care center. How many of our 149 employees have kids under

the age of five?" Or you may be thinking of sending a direct-mail piece to your local customers. To determine printing and postage costs, you need to know how many customers are in the target ZIP code or are within a particular range of ZIP codes.

In either case, you have to examine every record in the paper database. Whenever a task requires sorting, organizing, or summarizing the data in a different way, you can look forward to a nightmare of paper shuffling. And when you're through, you'll have to restore all the records to their original order!

- *Sharing records is difficult.* When a supervisor borrows some employee records, for example, the office manager no longer has easy access to those records. (They're no longer in the file drawer.)
- *Information is hard to reuse.* If you want to use the information in a paper database for any purpose other than just reading it (addressing envelopes, for example), someone has to drag out the typewriter. Photocopying an address and then taping it onto a letter is considered bad form — unless you're creating a ransom note.

Advantages of Computer Databases

Computer databases, on the other hand, offer the following benefits:

- *Entering error-free information is easier.* Most database programs have many features that speed data entry. Setting *default values* for some fields can save an incredible amount of typing time and ensure that information is entered consistently. (Using *CA* as the default entry for a State field, for example, ensures that you don't end up with records that variously contain *CA, Calif.*, and *California* in the same field.)

  Other useful data-entry features include *auto-incrementing fields* (which automatically assign invoice or record numbers to new records), *field types* (which, for example, can prevent you from entering alphabetic information in a field that was designed to record salary data), *range checking* (which accepts only numbers within a particular range), and *required fields* (which warn you if you do not fill in a critical field).
- *You can easily add, delete, or change data.* Making a change to a record involves merely bringing the record up on-screen, editing it, and then closing the file. Because you make all changes on a computer, you don't need to search through file drawers or hunt for an eraser. And if you need additional copies of a record, you can quickly print them. As you can see, the ease with which you can *manage data* is one of the key reasons for buying and using a database program such as FileMaker Pro.

- *Finding records is simple.* A Find feature enables you to jump directly to the record or records of interest.
- *You can specify criteria for sorting data.* Arranging records in a different order is as simple as issuing a Sort command. You can rearrange records in order of salary, record creation date, or any other field that is in the database. Most database programs also enable you to simultaneously sort by multiple fields. For example, you can sort a client database by city within each state.
- *You can work with discrete groups of records.* Using the database program's record selection tools, you can select a subgroup of records that is based on any criteria that you want. You may, for example, want to organize recipes according to their main ingredient or group employee records according to salary ranges or by department.
- *Database programs can perform calculations.* Database programs frequently offer many of the same calculation capabilities that spreadsheet programs offer. Instead of using a hand calculator to compute the sales tax and total for an invoice, you can have a database program automatically make the computations for you. In addition to performing computations within individual records, database programs can also generate summary statistics across all records or for selected groups of records. For example, you can easily summarize the efforts of different sales teams by calculating sales totals and averages by region.
- *Many people can simultaneously access the database.* If several people in a company need to view or modify the information in a database, you can use a database program on a network.
- *You can readily use information for multiple purposes.* For example, you can use the address information in records to print mailing labels, envelopes, or a pocket-sized address book, as well as to create personalized form letters.
- *You can create custom reports.* Only you are in a position to decide which reports are essential to running your business, department, bowling league, or home. In most database programs, you can create your own reports and lay them out in any format that meets your information needs. Because you can save report formats on disk, you can reuse a format whenever you want to generate a current report.
- *You can use data from one program in another program.* Most database programs can import and export data.

  Importing enables you to bring information into the database from other programs. For example, you may already have an address book program, desk accessory, or HyperCard stack in which you've recorded the addresses of friends and business associates. Rather than retyping those addresses in your database program, you can export them from the original program (creating a file that your database program can read) and then import them into a database.

Exporting, on the other hand, enables you to use fields and records in a database to create a file that other programs can read. For example, you can easily export numeric data so you can graph it with a spreadsheet program.

When Should You Use a Database Program?

Although the list of reasons why computer databases are superior to paper databases is lengthy, you also need to recognize that not every database is a good candidate for computerization. Specifically, when you are deciding between using a paper database and using a computer database, you need to ask yourself the following questions (the more *yes* answers you give, the more reasons you have for using a database program):

- *Will the contents of individual records change frequently?* If the information for each record is not static and editing is often necessary, choose a computer database.
- *Is much of the information repetitive?* As mentioned previously, database programs enable you to create default entries for fields. If much of the information that you'll enter is repetitive, using a database program can help you avoid unnecessary typing.
- *Will the records need to be grouped or sorted in different ways?* Database programs can quickly sort and select records for even very large collections of data.
- *Will calculations be necessary?* The more complex the calculations, the more you need a database program.
- *Will printed output be required?* Unless photocopies are satisfactory, use a database program.
- *Will reports be necessary?* Summarizing information is a task at which database programs excel. If your reports go beyond simple record counts, a database program may be the best choice.

Flat-File and Relational Databases

You can roughly classify every database program as either *flat file* or *relational,* according to the program's relational capabilities; that is, its ability to simultaneously draw information from more than one database on the basis of shared fields.

That explanation is quite a mouthful, isn't it? A couple of definitions and an example may make it easier to swallow:

- A *flat-file database* always consists of a single file. All fields that are required have to be contained within that data file.
- A *relational database* consists of two or more interrelated data files that have one or more key fields in common.

  Instead of designing a single customer database that contains all your customer information (as you would in a flat-file database program), you might create several smaller databases. For example, you could create one database called "Addresses" to contain just customer addresses, and another called "Orders" to hold information about the customers' previous orders. To link the records in the two databases, you could assign a unique identification number to each customer. By placing the I.D. field in both data files, you can *relate* the two sets of information. For example, you can generate a statement from the Orders database and instruct the program to pull the customer's mailing address from the Address database after finding the record that contains the matching I.D. number, as shown in Figure 1-2.

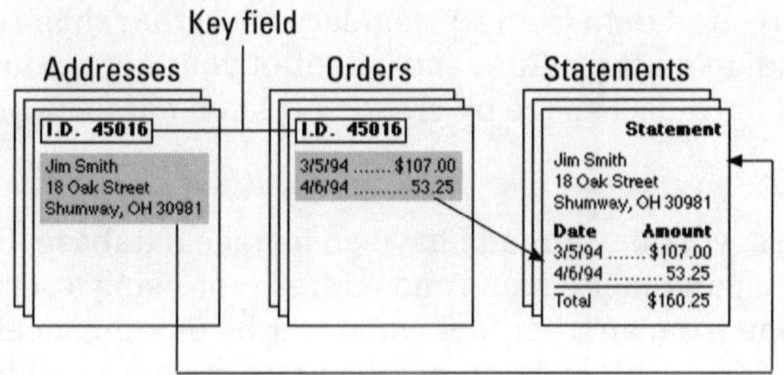

Figure 1-2: Relational database programs can create a report by extracting information from several files.

Both types of database programs have advantages. Conceptually, flat-file database programs are easier to understand and to learn to use. All the important data is in a single file. If you need to record additional information, you just add more fields.

Because of the multi-file approach that relational database programs use, the files tend to be smaller and, hence, faster to work with for common tasks such as sorting and searching. Because of their power and flexibility, relational database programs are frequently used for large record-keeping projects or projects that have complex requirements.

Learning to use a relational database program can be difficult, however, because of the complexity of the relational concept and the fact that much of the program's power frequently comes from a programming language that you need to use to create advanced databases. In addition, designing relational databases often requires substantial planning. You must usually decide on the relational (or key) fields ahead of time and determine what data will be collected in each file. Unlike a flat-file database, a relational database is not easy to toss together.

Introducing FileMaker Pro

Because this book is about FileMaker Pro, you may well be asking yourself where it fits into the "relational versus flat file" classification scheme. Up through FileMaker Pro 2.1, FileMaker Pro was a flat-file database program with some relational capabilities. Specifically, you could use its Lookup feature to look up information in a secondary file and then copy that information into the current file.

FileMaker Pro 3.0, on the other hand, has *full* relational capabilities. In addition to lookups (which are still supported), you can define relationships between files that merely *display* the related data from a secondary file rather than *copy* it into the primary file. Depending on the nature and extent of your data, you can save substantial amounts of hard disk space by creating related databases instead of relying on lookups.

If you run a business, you may already have an invoice database, for example. Instead of retyping a customer's name and address (or using a series of lookups to copy this information from another file) whenever he or she places another order, you can store the address information in a separate customer address database and then merely *reference* it in the invoice file. No matter how many invoices you create for a customer, the name and address information is only recorded once.

FileMaker Concepts

Even before you sit down to try out FileMaker Pro, it's important that you understand a few key concepts and features. Although all database programs have much in common with each other (as explained earlier in this chapter), FileMaker Pro has distinct ways of doing things that clearly distinguish it from other programs. (These differences explain — at least partially — why FileMaker Pro has long been the database program of choice for Macintosh users and is making great strides in the Windows world.) The remainder of this chapter provides an introduction to these key concepts and an explanation of how you can use FileMaker Pro to tackle many database needs — both in the business and home user arenas.

Understanding Layouts

Much of FileMaker Pro's power comes from a feature called layouts. A *layout* is an arrangement of a set of database fields for a particular file. Every layout is a view or window into the contents of a database, and different layouts present different views (frequently using different groups of fields). You can create individual layouts for doing data entry, generating reports (on-screen or printed), and printing labels or envelopes. And you can have as many layouts for each file as you need.

Whenever you create a new database and define its fields, FileMaker Pro automatically generates a layout that is a standard arrangement of all the fields that you have defined (see Figure 1-3). If a quick-and-dirty database is all you need, you can use this standard layout to start entering data immediately.

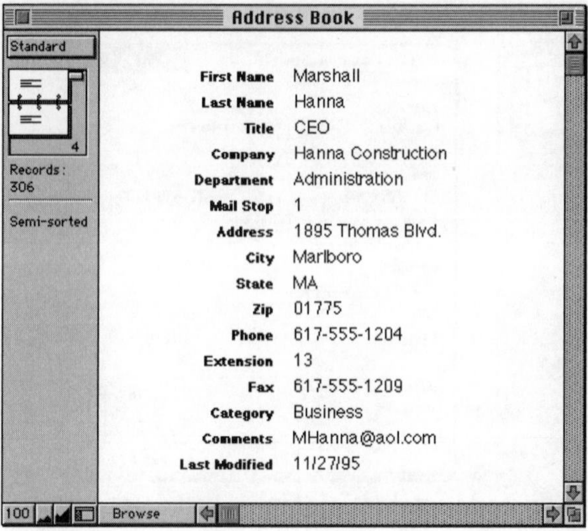

Figure 1-3: A standard database layout

On the other hand, you can customize a database layout by doing any of the following:

- Changing the placement of fields (to create a columnar report, for example)
- Eliminating fields from the layout that you do not want to display (while still being able to use them in other layouts where they *will* display)
- Removing some or all of the field labels or moving the labels to different positions (field labels are not attached to fields)
- Embellishing the layout by adding text and graphics and by modifying the font, style, color, pattern, or border for fields
- Eliminating layout parts (which are explained later in this chapter) that are not needed or adding parts that display summary statistics or present information that repeats on every page

Figure 1-4 shows a custom layout for the same database as the one previously shown in Figure 1-3. The data-entry screen is more attractive because of the rearrangement of the fields, changes in font sizes and styles, and the addition of color and graphics. The ability to produce custom layouts is one of the many features that attracts users to FileMaker Pro.

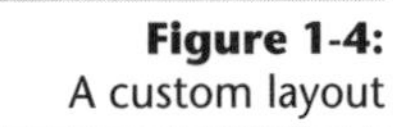

Figure 1-4: A custom layout

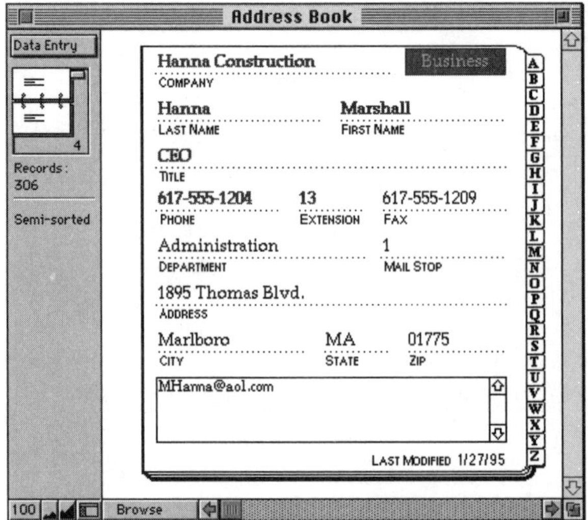

Every layout that you create for a database is separate from every other layout, but it draws from the same set of fields. When you design a new layout, you select only the fields that you need. In a customer database, for example, you can use one layout to display invoice information, such as the customer's name, address, items or services purchased, and a total. A second layout may contain only name and address information that is formatted as a mailing label. You can create a third layout to print or display a client phone book or monthly client purchase totals. Figure 1-5 shows three different layouts for the same database.

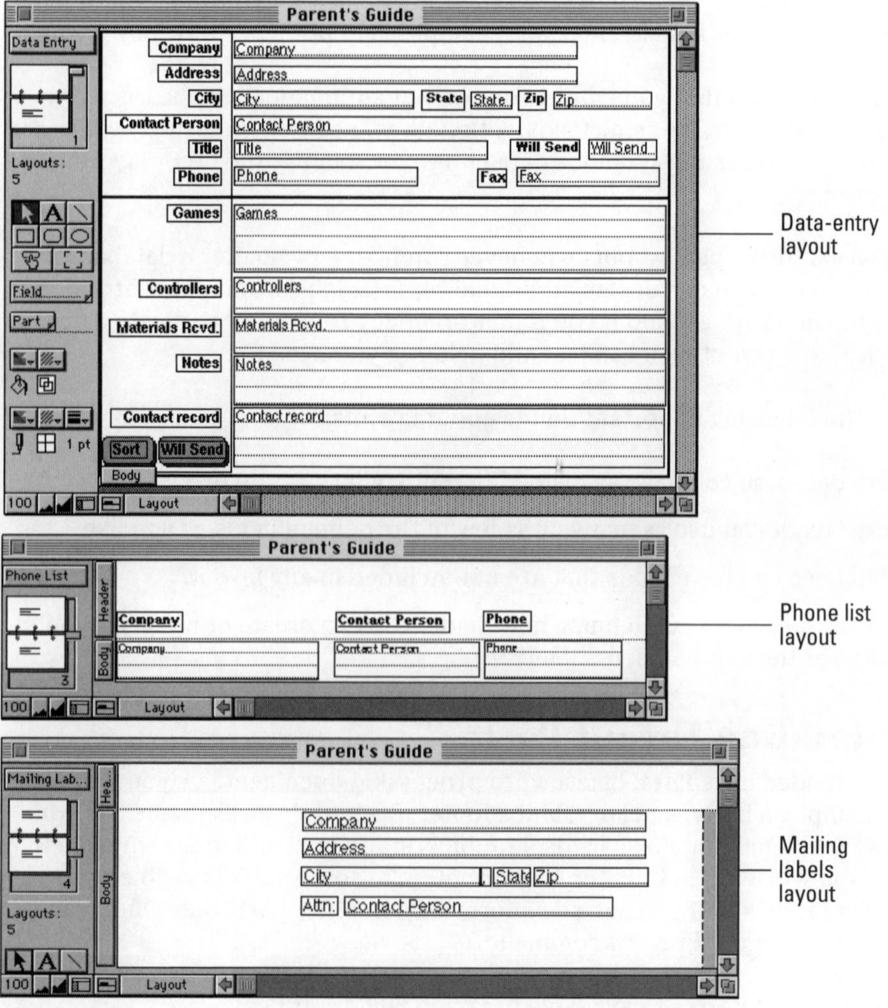

Figure 1-5: Layouts for data entry, a phone book, and mailing labels

No practical restrictions limit the number of fields you can use in a layout. Data-entry screens, for example, frequently have many fields so that you can easily enter all important information for a record in a single layout. At the other extreme, a Help screen or menu layout may contain only static text — no fields at all.

As you design layouts for a database, you may need to create additional fields that are specific to a single layout. For example, a field that shows a total for each customer order is important in an invoice layout but unnecessary (or pointless) in an address label layout. Conversely, you do not have to include every field that you define. You may want to create a field to use only as a test for a calculation (determining whether another field is blank, for example) and not place it on *any* layout.

Keep in mind that data that you enter in one layout automatically appears in any other layouts that use those same fields. Although you can — and usually will — create an all-encompassing layout for data entry, you can use the other layouts for data entry, too.

Because you can make new layouts whenever you like — even after a database contains records — you can design additional reports, labels, and data-entry screens as the need arises. And if you didn't originally remember to create a field that is critical to a layout, you can just add fields as you need them.

Remember the following important points about layouts:

- Every database can have as many different layouts as you need.
- Every layout can use as many or as few of the defined fields as you like.
- A database can have fields that are not included in any layout.
- As with the process of defining new fields, you can create or modify layouts whenever the need presents itself.

Understanding Layout Parts

Layouts are divided into parts. Like a word processing document, a layout can have, for example, a body, a header, and a footer. Each of these elements is a *part*. Every part can contain database fields, graphics, static text, and other embellishments. (As you will learn in Chapter 5, information in some parts is visible both onscreen and in reports, but you can see information in other parts only when you print a report or use the Preview command.)

The following layout parts are available to you in FileMaker Pro:

- *Title header and title footer:* This special header or footer appears only on the first page of a report, and substitutes for any other header or footer part that has been defined for the layout.

- *Header and footer:* Headers and footers appear at the top or bottom, respectively, of every page of a report or other type of layout. (If you create a title header or footer, it takes precedence on the first page of the report.) Page numbers, logos, and the current date are popular items to place in a header or footer.
- *Body:* Unlike the other layout parts, information in the body appears in every record in the database. For this reason, you normally place most fields in the body.
- *Sub-summaries:* You use sub-summary parts to summarize groups of related records after you have sorted the database by the contents of a particular field. For example, after sorting an address database by city, you can use a sub-summary field to display a count of records in each city. Sub-summaries can appear above or below each group of records, and they are visible only in Preview mode and in printed output. (Preview and other FileMaker Pro modes are discussed in the next section.)
- *Grand summaries:* Statistics that appear in a grand summary apply to all records that are currently visible (that is, they are being *browsed*). A grand summary can appear at the beginning (leading grand summary) or end (trailing grand summary) of a report, and it is visible only in Preview mode and in printed output.

When you first create a layout, it starts with only a body, header, and footer. You can remove unnecessary parts and add other parts as you like. Figure 1-6 contains a layout that has several parts. The figure illustrates the relationship between the layout and an on-screen preview of the report.

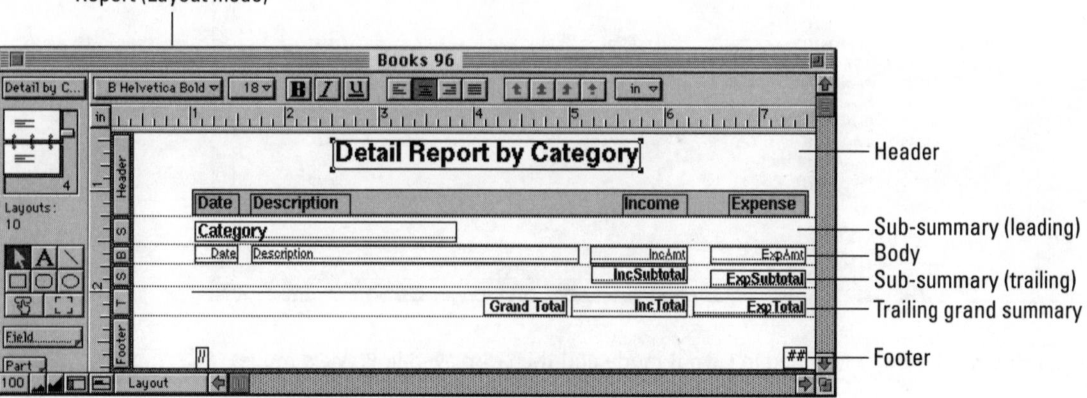

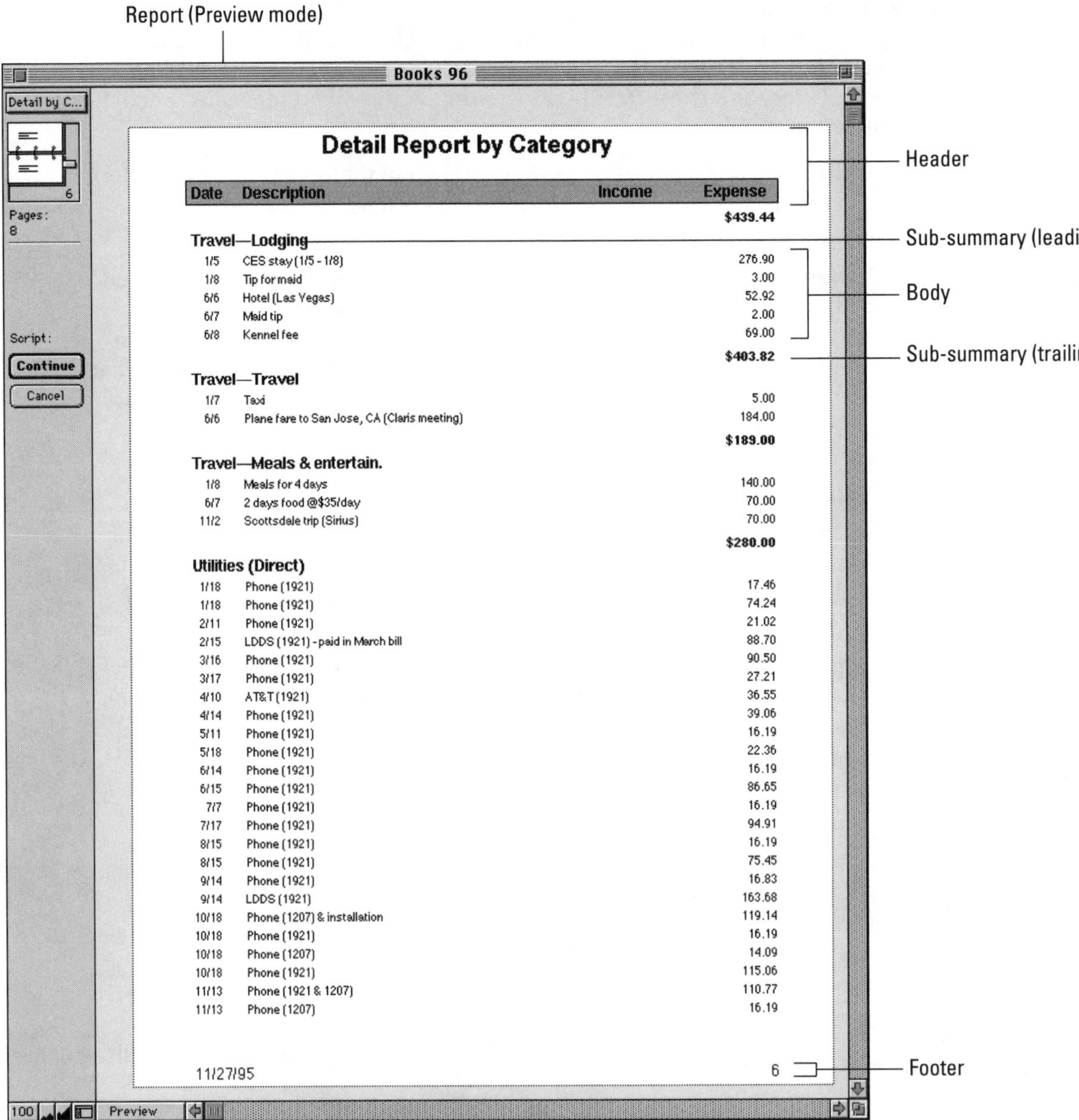

Figure 1-6: Layout parts (as defined in Layout mode and then displayed in Preview mode)

Understanding Modes

FileMaker Pro has four modes of operation: Browse, Layout, Find, and Preview. The mode that you are in at any given moment governs the types of activities that you can perform:

- *Browse mode:* You use this mode to create and delete records, as well as to enter and edit data. (You perform all data entry in Browse mode.)
- *Layout mode:* You design, edit, or delete database layouts in Layout mode.
- *Find mode:* You can search for or hide records, which meet criteria that you specify, in Find mode.
- *Preview mode:* Preview a report or layout on-screen (usually prior to printing) in Preview mode.

Thus, when you want to enter a new record, you first need to switch to Browse mode. To modify any portion of a layout (to add or resize a graphic, for example), you have to be in Layout mode. If you're not sure what mode you're in, check the Mode indicator at the bottom of the database window.

Preview Your Documents Before Printing

When examining any type of layout in Preview mode, whatever is shown on the preview screen is precisely what will be sent to the printer. Thus, you can save considerable time and paper by using Preview mode to check the layout of labels and reports, for example, before printing them.

Getting "The Big Picture"

Now that you understand what a database program is and does, and how to determine when it's the right tool for the job, you may be facing a problem common to anyone who buys a new type of program. You probably wonder what *you* can do with FileMaker Pro. (Yes, many of us often purchase software solutions before clearly defining the problems they were intended to solve.)

Although FileMaker Pro is a wonderful piece of technology, it's only as useful as you make it. And, like so many other things in life, understanding how something works is not the same as knowing *when* to use it. If you've ever taken an advanced math or statistics course, you understand what I mean. Memorizing formulas is not the same as knowing when they should be applied.

If you've already experimented with the sample files and templates that are included with FileMaker Pro 3.0, it should be obvious that they are not meant to serve all your database needs. (Neither are the templates included with this book, by the way.) Before long, you will be faced with the prospect of designing and using your *own* databases. And if you're new to databases, your biggest initial problem will not be learning how to use the program, but rather what to use it for.

To get you into the proper mind set, this chapter concludes with a list of some uses to which FileMaker Pro can be put — some general and some very specific. Hopefully, these examples will give you ideas for databases that you may want to create, moving you from the thinking stage to the doing stage.

Business Uses for FileMaker Pro

Because of the ease with which you can create functional, useful databases (regardless of your prior database experience), FileMaker Pro has long been a favorite program among business users. Here are a few of the things you can do:

- *Automate business forms.* Most businesses rely on forms, and many of these forms are perfect targets for databases. A petty cash voucher system is one example. Rather than just fill out a slip of paper that gets tossed into a cash box or drawer, you can duplicate the voucher as a FileMaker Pro data-entry form. Features such as date-stamping and assigning serial numbers can be automatically applied to each new voucher. And by creating appropriate report layouts, you can break down disbursements by time periods, departments, or individuals.
- *Improve shipping records.* Rather than frantically search for a shipping receipt or bill of lading whenever a shipment goes awry, FileMaker Pro can help you

keep track of incoming and outgoing shipments. The program's search capabilities make it easy to locate any shipment documentation that normally might be tucked away in a file drawer. FileMaker Pro can also help you organize your receipts and create appropriate reports — grouping them and showing total shipments to each customer, for example.

- *Reuse existing customer data.* For many businesses, the customer list is its most valuable asset. Sadly, many businesses — both small and large — still attempt to maintain their customer records on paper only. Entering customer information into a database makes it possible to do mass mailings to announce sales, easily update and correct customer information (a change of address, for example), examine customer buying patterns, and determine when an additional sales call or purging from your list is necessary.
- *Track rental information.* Small businesses that do rentals are excellent candidates for FileMaker Pro. By creating appropriate formulas, scripts, and reports, you can instruct the program to find all rentals that are late, calculate late charges, and determine who your best customers are, for example.
- *Examine employee performance.* Although not the best choice for project tracking (there are many programs designed specifically for this task), you can certainly create a simple assignment-oriented database that records each assignment you hand out, including its due date, progress notes, and completion date. By adding fields for "quality of work," the database can help you perform (and document) the dreaded annual salary review.
- *Schedule company resources.* Conference rooms, audio-visual equipment, and other limited company resources are often in high demand. If you're the office manager, you may want to create a database of resource requests. You can then sort by resource, date, and time to quickly flag duplicate requests.

Home Uses for FileMaker Pro

FileMaker Pro isn't just for business. In fact, home users make up a substantial portion of those who have purchased and use FileMaker Pro for their data recording needs. Here are some ways you can use FileMaker Pro for your own record-keeping:

- *Maintain a home inventory.* If you know anyone who has had a large casualty loss due to a burglary, fire, or natural disaster, you understand the pressing need for documenting everything you own. An inventory database can be used to conveniently list your possessions along with their serial numbers, purchase date, and cost. A similar database that lists insurance policies, credit cards, and other important documents (and their locations) can also be very useful.

- *Track a collection.* A database program is ideal for recording purchases and catalog values for any set of collectables, such as stamps, coins, baseball cards, comic books, paintings, books, and wines. If you have a scanner or digital camera, you can also include graphic images of the items in the database.
- *Record credit card and checking account activity.* If you don't already have a home accounting program, you can use FileMaker Pro to create one for yourself. Every transaction (a check, deposit, charge, or payment) can be treated as a separate record.
- *Never a lender be.* Do you have neighbors, friends, and relatives that are great at borrowing, but not so hot at returning items? Use a database to track what was lent, when, and to whom. By including a simple date calculation, you can automatically determine how long it has been since each item was lent, too. (Even if you don't throw this information in the borrowers' face — as in, "Bill, you borrowed my hedge clippers 47 days ago!" — at least you'll always know where your stuff is.)
- *Get a handle on your investments.* Let's say you just sold some stock and you don't remember what you paid for it. The IRS expects you to record this information in order to determine capital gains. FileMaker Pro can help you keep track of your buy and sell costs. And with all its calculation capabilities, you can also use FileMaker Pro to calculate gains and losses (in dollars and percentages), the number of days that an investment was held, and so on.

Summary

- Every database is composed of records — one per person or entity in the database. Records are divided into fields, which are each designed to hold one particular piece of information.
- A database program, such as FileMaker Pro, enables you to store information for rapid retrieval and organize the data in ways that are extremely cumbersome and time-consuming if attempted with a paper database.
- Paper databases are most useful when the data collected is relatively static. A database program is a better choice when data frequently changes, when you need to use the information for multiple purposes, or when you want to be able to print the information. A database program is also a better choice when you want to perform calculations or you need summary information or reports.

FileMaker Pro Basic Operations

CHAPTER 2

In This Chapter

- Starting up and quitting FileMaker Pro
- Performing common file-handling procedures
- Issuing commands
- Using FileMaker Pro's tools and palettes

In Chapter 1, you learned that FileMaker Pro is a mode-oriented program. That is, the mode that you're in (Browse, Layout, Find, or Preview) determines the types of operations that you can currently perform. Now that you understand the fundamental FileMaker Pro concepts of modes and layouts, you're ready to explore the basic — yet essential — program procedures for performing common operations:

- Running and quitting the program
- Handling files
- Issuing commands
- Using the layout and status tools

Starting Up

You can start up FileMaker Pro using one of two basic methods. The method that you use depends on whether or not you also want to simultaneously open one or more databases.

When books, magazines, or manuals discuss *starting up* a program, they sometimes use the terms *run* and *launch*. All three terms mean the same thing.

To launch FileMaker Pro without opening an existing database, do the following:

1. Locate the FileMaker Pro icon on the desktop (see Figure 2-1).

   If the program is stored on a disk whose window is closed, double-click the disk icon to open its window. Similarly, if the program is stored in a folder that is not presently open, double-click the folder to display its contents. Continue opening folders as necessary until you see the FileMaker Pro icon.

If you don't feel like double-clicking to open disks or folders, you can also open them by selecting them and then choosing Open from the File menu or by pressing ⌘-O.

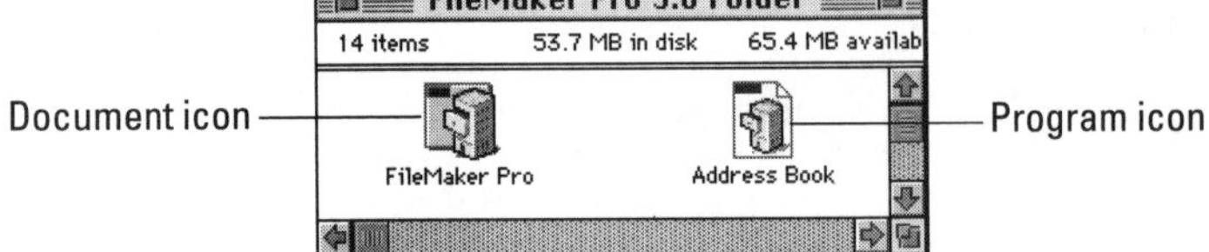

Figure 2-1: The FileMaker Pro program icon and a document icon

2. Double-click the FileMaker Pro program icon.

— or —

2. Click once to select the FileMaker Pro program icon and then choose Open from the File menu or press ⌘-O.

   FileMaker Pro loads into memory and presents you with the New Database dialog box (see Figure 2-2).

New Database

CLARIS®

FileMaker PRO® 3.0

Create a new file using a template:

Create a new empty file...

Open an existing file...

No longer show this dialog

Template Info... Register...

Business

Asset Management
Bid Comparison
Business Cards
Buy versus Lease
Cash Receipts
Club Membership
Employee Leave Forms
Equipment Rental & Usage
Expense Report

Cancel OK

Figure 2-2: This dialog box appears when the program starts.

3. Click the appropriate radio button in the New Database dialog box:
   - To create a new database from one of the included templates, click the radio button labeled "Create a new file using a template," choose a category from the pop-up menu, and choose a database template from the list that is presented.
   - To create a new database from scratch, click the radio button labeled "Create a new empty file."
   - To open an existing database, click the radio button labeled "Open an existing file."
4. Complete your choice by clicking OK.
   - *If you chose "Create a new file using a template,"* FileMaker Pro automatically generates a new, empty copy of the chosen database file.
   - *If you chose "Create a new empty file,"* a standard file dialog box appears, like the one shown in Figure 2-3. Type a name for the new file, select a location on disk in which to store the database, and click Save. The Define Fields dialog box appears, enabling you to complete the initial database definition.

     Define the necessary fields and click Done. A standard layout is created for you, the first record of the database is displayed, and you are switched into Browse mode where you can begin entering data for the first record. (The details of defining fields and designing layouts are covered in Chapters 5 and 6.)
   - *If you chose "Open an existing file,"* a standard file dialog box appears. Navigate to the drive and folder that contains your database, choose its name in the file list, and click Open.

Figure 2-3: This file dialog box is presented when you create a new database.

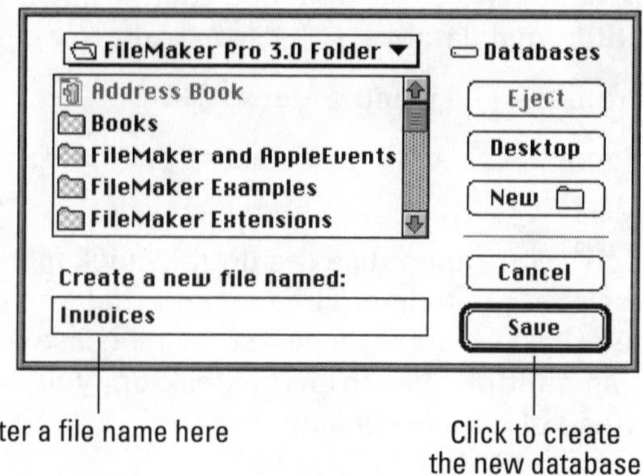

If you prefer, you can just dismiss the New Database dialog box by clicking the Cancel button. You can then use commands from the File menu to create new databases (New) or open existing databases (Open). Note that the New and Open options work the same whether you select them in the New Database dialog box or choose their commands from the File menu.

Dealing with the New Database dialog box can be a nuisance — and totally unnecessary if the database you want to work with already exists. You can simultaneously launch FileMaker Pro and open a database file by following these steps:

1. Locate the file icon of the database you want to open.
2. Double-click the database file icon.

— or —

2. Click once to select the database file icon and then either choose Open from the File menu or press ⌘-O.

   FileMaker Pro launches, and the database is automatically opened.

If you want, you can simultaneously launch FileMaker Pro and open *several* databases, as follows:

1. Locate the file icons of the databases you wish to open.

   To simultaneously open more than one database, all of the database files have to be on the same disk and in the same folder (or in the root directory of the same disk).

2. Drag to select all the databases of interest.

— or —

2. Click one of the databases to select it and then, while holding down the Shift key, click the additional databases that you want to open.
3. Choose Open from the File menu or press ⌘-O.

   FileMaker Pro launches, and all the selected databases are automatically opened.

Try as you might, you cannot use the double-click method to open several database files at the same time. The moment that you double-click a file icon, all of the other previously selected icons cease to be selected. When you are opening multiple files from the desktop, you have to use the Open command instead of double-clicking.

FileMaker Pro and Memory Usage

When you launch FileMaker Pro and open a database, the entire database is not always loaded into memory. FileMaker Pro uses a *disk-caching* scheme, loading only the data that it requires at the moment (based on your Find requests, the layout in use, and so on). When the program needs to display additional records or a different layout, it reads the information in from the disk, replacing the data that was previously in memory with the new data. This way, you can open a 10MB FileMaker Pro database with a Mac that only has 5MB of *RAM* (Random Access Memory), for example. Disk caching is common to many database programs.

An important consequence of this disk-caching scheme can be seen if you are using FileMaker Pro with a portable computer, such as a PowerBook. With large databases, you can expect more disk accesses than normal, which will quickly use up the current battery charge. Unless you can plug your portable computer into a wall outlet (rather than run it from its battery), you are well-advised to restrict your work to smaller databases or use larger databases sparingly — closing them as soon as you've accomplished the task at hand.

Quitting

When you're ready to end a FileMaker Pro session, choose Quit from the File menu (or press ⌘-Q). Any open data files are closed as part of the Quit process. Because FileMaker Pro automatically saves changes to files as you work with them, you don't need to issue any Save commands. (For more information on how FileMaker Pro saves data, see "Saving Files," later in this chapter.)

FileMaker Pro and the Power Switch

Just as it's a bad idea to shut down your Mac by simply cutting the power instead of using the Shut Down command, turning off the juice is also a poor substitute for using a program's Quit command. Although FileMaker Pro does indeed save your work automatically and even has a command that can be used to recover a damaged database file, don't take unnecessary risks with your data. Unless circumstances beyond your control prevent doing so (your system crashes, lightning strikes, or your puppy yanks out the Mac's power cord), you should always use the Quit command to conclude a FileMaker Pro session.

File-Handling Procedures

While you are working in FileMaker Pro, you may want to open additional database files, create new files, close files, or make a backup copy of a database that you are using. The information in this section explains how to perform these common procedures.

Opening, Creating, and Closing Databases

You use the File menu or a keyboard shortcut to open a database, create a new database, or close a database. To open an existing database, follow these steps:

1. Choose Open from the File menu (or press ⌘-O).

   A standard file dialog box appears, as shown in Figure 2-4.

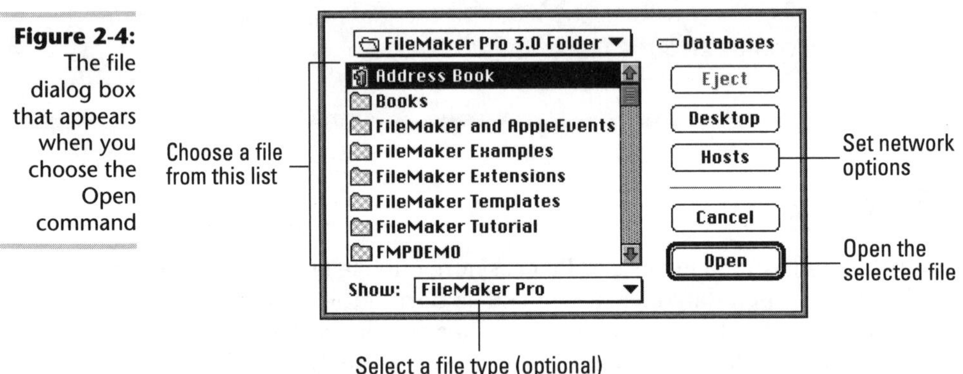

Figure 2-4: The file dialog box that appears when you choose the Open command

2. Navigate to the drive and folder where the database file is stored.
3. Open the file by double-clicking its file name or by selecting the file name and then clicking the Open button.

   As mentioned previously, you can have several FileMaker Pro databases open at the same time, if you like. To open additional databases, simply repeat these steps.

FileMaker Pro 3.0's Open dialog box includes a new Show pop-up that enables you to filter the file list to display only particular types of files. By default, FileMaker Pro is selected — showing only current (3.0) or older (pre-3.0) databases. Select a different file format, such as Tab-Separated Text, only when you want to convert an existing file into a FileMaker Pro 3.0 database. The procedure for doing this is described in Chapter 16.

To create a new database file from scratch or from a Claris-provided template, choose New from the File menu. A modified version of the New Database dialog box appears, as previously shown in Figure 2-2. (The "Open an existing file" option has been eliminated.) Follow the instructions presented earlier in this chapter for working with the New Database dialog box.

When you're through working with a database, you can close its file by performing any one of the following actions:

- Choose Close from the File menu (or press ⌘-W).
- Click the file's close box, which is in the upper-left corner of the document window.
- Choose Quit from the File menu (or press ⌘-Q). Quitting automatically closes any open database files and records any unsaved changes.

When you are working in FileMaker Pro, remember that you do not have to close *any* files. You can have as many open files as will fit in your computer's available memory.

Saving Files

In most Macintosh programs, the procedure for saving a new file or for saving changes that you've made to an older file is to choose the Save or Save As command from the File menu. In FileMaker Pro, however, you do not use these methods. In fact, if you examine the File menu (see Figure 2-5), you'll note that it does not have Save and Save As commands. These commands are missing because FileMaker Pro automatically saves changes as you work with a file. And when you close a file or quit the program, you never see a dialog box asking whether you want to save your changes — the program has already saved them.

Figure 2-5: FileMaker Pro's File menu

File
New...
Open... ⌘O
Close ⌘W
Define Fields... ⇧⌘D
Define Relationships...
Access Privileges ▸
Single-User
Page Setup...
Print... ⌘P
Import/Export ▸
Save a Copy As...
Recover...
Quit ⌘Q

You can, however, exert some control over *when* FileMaker Pro saves files. Choose the Preferences command from the Edit menu and then choose Memory from the pop-up menu in the Preferences dialog box. You can instruct FileMaker to save only during idle time or every so many minutes. The latter option is most useful if you are a PowerBook user. By setting the minutes between saves to a relatively high number, you can conserve battery power by reducing the frequency of "hits" on the internal hard disk or floppy drive. Select a setting with which you're comfortable. For instance, if you set 15 minutes as the save period, you are risking up to 15 minutes worth of data in the event that your Mac crashes before the data is saved. Don't worry about quitting before the time is up, however. As mentioned earlier, FileMaker Pro automatically saves all data when you quit.

Because the integrity of your data is of paramount importance, FileMaker Pro's approach to saving goes a long way toward reducing the risk of data loss. The only negative side to auto-saving is that FileMaker Pro saves *all* changes — both good and bad — that you make to a database. For example, if you experiment with a layout, FileMaker Pro records the changes. Two options are available for recovering from inadvertent changes:

- Immediately choose the Undo command from the Edit menu (or press ⌘-Z).
- Create a backup of the file before you make any major changes (as discussed in the next section, "Making a Backup Copy of a File").

The Undo command has two limitations. First, you can undo only the most recent modification that you have made to the database. (The wording of the Undo command automatically changes to reflect the most recent action that you can undo.) For example, if you delete some text from a field and then type information into another field, you cannot undo the deletion. (You can, however, use the Revert Record command — found in the Mode menu — to undo *all* changes made to an individual record.)

Second, some commands simply cannot be undone. When you can't use the Undo command, it changes to Can't Undo. Actions that cannot be undone include using most of the Delete commands, such as Delete Record, Delete All, Delete Layout, and the Delete command in the Define Fields dialog box.

The moral is that relying on the Undo command to save you from major mistakes can *be* a major mistake. The only safe approach is to keep backups of important files to ensure that you can recover from even the most horrendous mistake or computer calamity.

Making a Backup Copy of a File

Don't trust computers! Do I have your attention now? Although you may have spent thousands of dollars on your Macintosh and programs, they are not infallible. Regardless of how many times they hear this, most new computer users appear to feign deafness. Then they wake up one morning to find that their hard disk has bit the dust, the kids threw out the folder that contained the family's financial records, or a thief has walked off with the Mac. Without a backup of your important data, you're right back at square one.

Because your data and layouts are important to you, FileMaker Pro provides several ways to make backup copies. In the event that something happens to the original file, you can use the backup copy to get the database up and running again. In addition to using the backup procedures provided by FileMaker Pro, you can make copies by using the Finder or a commercial backup program, such as DiskFit Direct or Retrospect from Dantz Development.

In particular, you may want to make a backup copy of a file for the following reasons:

- As a general precaution against data loss due to user error, hardware failure, or software problems (a crash, for example)
- When you are planning to make a major change to a database, such as deleting records or modifying a layout
- When you want to create a database template, either to give to someone else or to save for your own use

You can make an exact duplicate of a database file (containing all the data and layouts) from the Finder, using a commercial backup program or from within FileMaker Pro. However, you can make *templates* (databases without data) only from within FileMaker Pro.

To duplicate a FileMaker Pro database file from within FileMaker Pro, do the following:

1. In FileMaker Pro, open the database that you wish to copy.
2. Choose Save a Copy As from the File menu.

   A file dialog box appears, as shown in Figure 2-6.

Figure 2-6: This dialog box enables you to save a copy of a FileMaker Pro database in any of three formats.

3. Click the Type: pop-up menu and select the type of file that you want to create:
    - *copy of current file:* Use this choice when you want an exact duplicate of a database, including all the layouts and data that it contains.
    - *compressed copy (smaller):* This choice produces a usable copy of a database, but the copy is compressed to save disk space. This option is particularly useful when you are *archiving* a database (storing it for posterity or as a backup) or when a database is a bit too large to fit on a floppy disk.
    - *clone (no records):* Select this option when you want to create a template from the database. All formulas, field definitions, and layouts are retained in the new file, but it contains no records.
4. Enter a new file name for the copy in the "Create a copy named" text box or leave the displayed default name as is.

    The default name that FileMaker Pro presents is one of the following, depending on the type of file you selected in step 3:
    - *Current file name* Copy (if you chose "copy of current file" or "compressed copy")
    - *Current file name* Clone (if you chose "clone")
5. Using standard file dialog box procedures, navigate to the disk and folder in which you want to save the copy.
6. Click Save (or press Enter or Return).

    The copy is saved in the format that you selected.

More About Clones

A FileMaker Pro *clone* is the equivalent of a template or stationery file that you create in most other programs. It's an empty database, ready for you to begin adding records. Unlike icons for templates or stationery files that you create in other programs, however, the icon for a clone looks exactly like the icon for any other FileMaker Pro database file, so recognizing that it's a clone is difficult. And because it's not a *real* template or stationery file, when you open a clone, you aren't opening a copy of it — you're opening the actual file. Any data that you add to the clone is automatically saved as part of the file. If you want to preserve the clone, make a copy of it (or make a second clone) and make changes to the copy rather than to the original.

Clones are particularly useful when you have databases that you routinely need to start over from scratch (for example, a bookkeeping database that you clear monthly or annually), when you want to experiment with a layout, or when you want to provide a template for other users but don't want them to have your data.

When you open a clone for the first time, it will not contain any records. To begin using the file, choose New Record (⌘-N) from the Mode menu.

Automatic Backups

If you're worried about making inadvertent changes to a database or concerned that something catastrophic may happen to it, you can create a FileMaker Pro script that automatically creates a backup every time you open the database. A copy of the script is added to the Script menu so that you can instantly create backups during a session, too.

To create an automatic backup script, follow these steps:

1. Launch FileMaker Pro and open the database.
2. Choose ScriptMaker from the Script menu.

   The Define Scripts dialog box appears (see Figure 2-7). The dialog box displays all scripts that have been defined for the database.

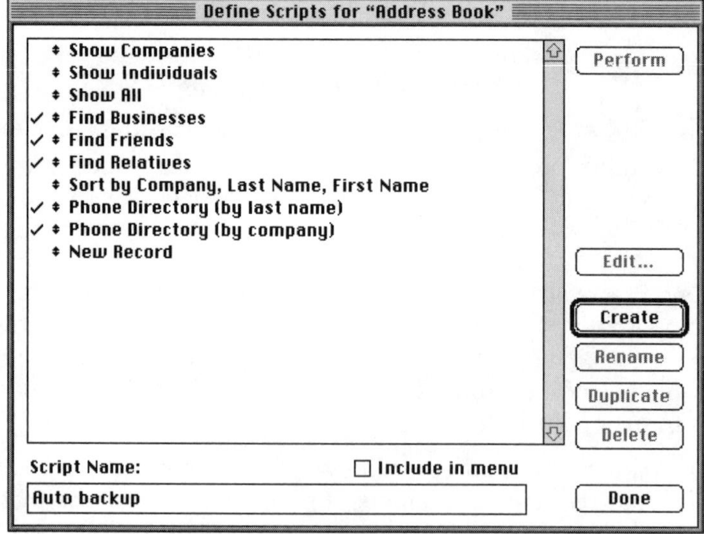

Figure 2-7: The Define Scripts dialog box

3. Type a name for the script in the Script Name box.

   If the Include in menu check box does not contain a check mark, click once in the box to add the check mark.

4. Click Create to define the script.

   The Script Definition dialog box appears, as shown in Figure 2-8.

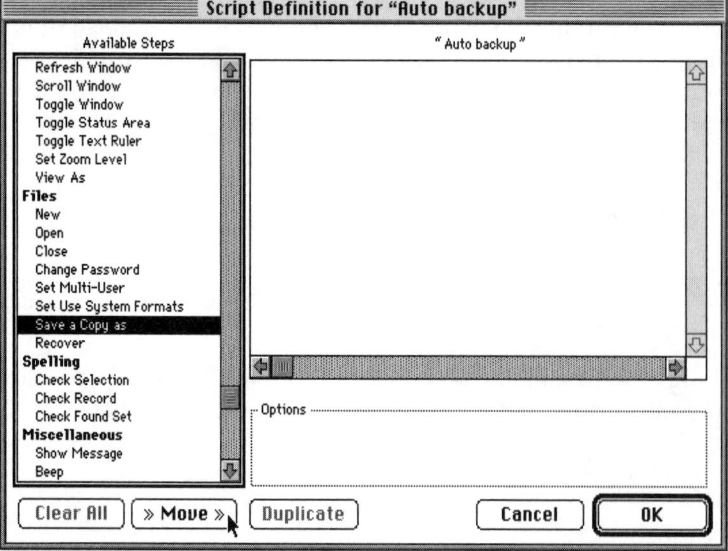

Figure 2-8: The Script Definition dialog box

5. Click Clear All to clear the script definition list on the right side of the dialog box.
6. Scroll down the Available Steps list until the choice "Save a Copy as" appears.
7. Select "Save a Copy as" and then click the Move button.

   The script step is copied to the script list on the right.
8. Click the Specify File button.

   A standard file dialog box appears, as shown in Figure 2-9.

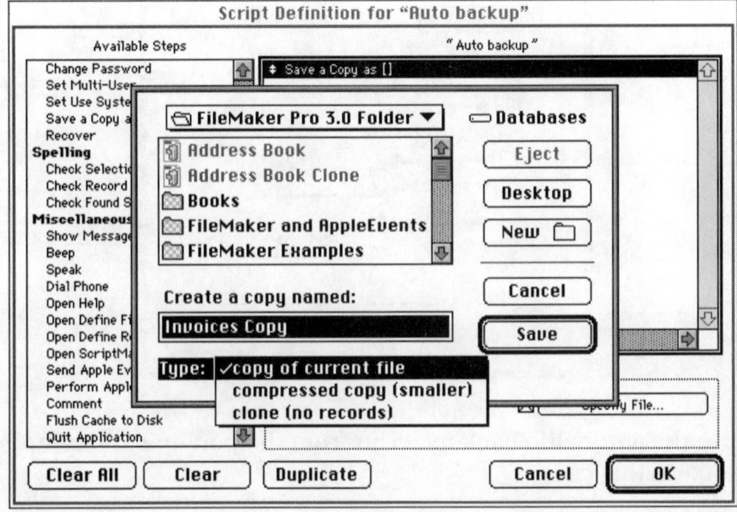

Figure 2-9: You specify the name, location, and type of backup file in this dialog box.

9. Navigate to the drive and folder where you intend to store the backup files made by the script.

   By default, FileMaker Pro offers to name the backup file *filename* Copy, but you can change the name of the file using normal editing techniques.
10. At the bottom of the dialog box, click the Type: pop-up menu and choose either "copy of current file" or "compressed copy (smaller)."

    Either option will save a complete copy of the database, including all records, layouts, and field definitions. If disk space is at a premium, you may prefer to use the compressed copy option.
11. Click the Save button.
12. To complete the script, click OK and then click Done in the dialog boxes that appear.

    A backup copy is created, and the script is added to the bottom of the Script menu.

13. To make the script execute automatically whenever you open the database file, choose Preferences from the Edit menu.

    The Preferences dialog box appears.

14. Choose Document from the Preferences dialog box's pop-up menu (as shown in Figure 2-10). Click the Perform script check box in the "When opening" section of the dialog box.

Figure 2-10: The Preferences dialog box

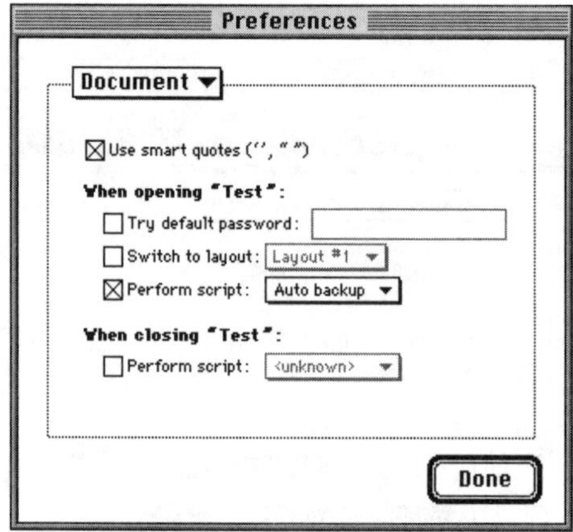

15. Choose the automatic backup script from the pop-up list that appears ("Auto backup," in this case).

16. Click Done.

    The changes are recorded, and the dialog box disappears.

Keep the following in mind when you are using this backup script:

- Each time a new backup is created, it writes over the previous backup file. If you need to keep multiple generations of backups, you should return to the desktop and manually rename the backup before or at the end of each FileMaker Pro session.

- Remember that the backup file is an exact copy of the original. Thus, it also contains the automatic backup script. If you ever need to use the backup file, be sure to rename it before opening it in FileMaker Pro. Otherwise, an error dialog box will appear, informing you that FileMaker was unable to create a backup (because the script is attempting to make a copy of the currently open database, using its own name).

Issuing Commands

Issuing commands in FileMaker Pro is no different from issuing them in any other Macintosh program. For those of you who are new Mac users, the following discussion will be helpful.

To issue a command in FileMaker Pro — to create a new record or add formatting to a field, for example — you can use the mouse to choose the command from a menu or, if the command has a *keystroke equivalent*, you can press a special combination of keys. Figure 2-11 shows an example of selecting a command from a menu.

Figure 2-11: Selecting a command from a menu

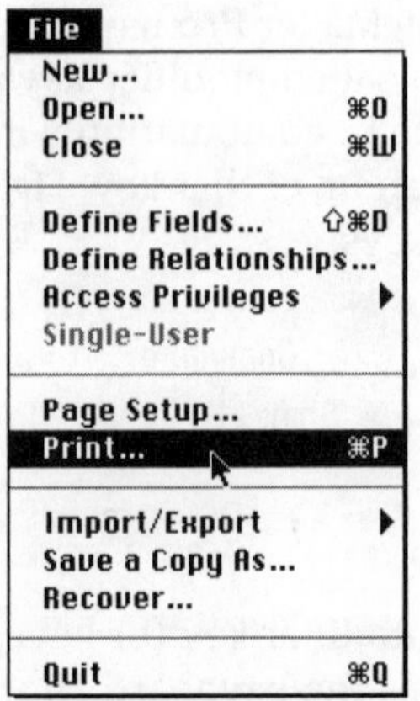

Some menu commands may be gray. These *grayed-out* commands are not presently available, usually because they are not relevant to the operation that you are attempting to perform. For example, when you're in Browse mode and a field is not currently selected, text-formatting commands in the Format menu are grayed-out. This is because the formatting commands can only be executed when something is selected that you can format. Grayed-out commands become available only when they are relevant to the current state of the database and what you are doing at the moment.

To choose a menu command, do the following:

1. Click the menu title that contains the command that you want to issue.

   The menu drops down, exposing the commands within it.

2. While continuing to hold down the mouse button, drag the pointer until the command that you want to issue is highlighted (turns black).

3. Release the mouse button.

   The command executes.

A propeller-shaped symbol and a letter follow some menu commands. The ⌘ symbol represents the Command key (shown on most keyboards as ⌘ or). You can issue any menu command that is followed by a letter, number, or symbol without using the mouse or the menus. Such a command is said to have a *keyboard shortcut*, a *keyboard equivalent*, or a *Command-key equivalent* (all three terms mean the same thing).

To issue a keyboard shortcut, follow these steps:

1. Press and hold the modifier key (or keys) that precedes the letter, number, or symbol in the menu.

   The modifier keys that FileMaker Pro uses include the Shift, Option, and Command keys. They are called modifier keys because they have an effect only when you press them in combination with a letter, number, or symbol key. They modify the meaning of that key. Figure 2-12 shows the symbols used to represent these keys.

Figure 2-12: Modifier key symbols as displayed in FileMaker Pro menus

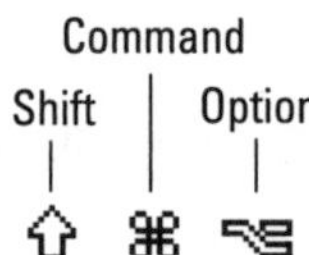

2. While holding down the modifier key (or keys), press the letter, number, or symbol key that completes the keyboard shortcut.

   The command executes.

A complete list of the keyboard shortcuts available in FileMaker Pro 3.0 can be found in Appendix B.

Commands with Ellipses and Arrows

If you browse through FileMaker Pro's menus, you'll notice that two unusual elements are tacked onto the end of some commands: ellipses and triangles.

An *ellipsis* is a series of three dots. They indicate that the command displays a dialog box to which you have to respond (see the second set of Format menu commands in the figure below). In contrast, menu commands that do not have ellipses are executed immediately.

A right-facing triangle that follows a menu command (see the top set of Format menu commands in the figure below) indicates that the command is accompanied by a *hierarchical menu* (also called a *pop-up menu* or *submenu*). When the mouse pointer slides over one of these menu commands, another menu pops out to the side of the original menu. You need to continue to hold down the mouse button while you move the pointer and highlight the appropriate command in the submenu. Then release the mouse button to choose the command.

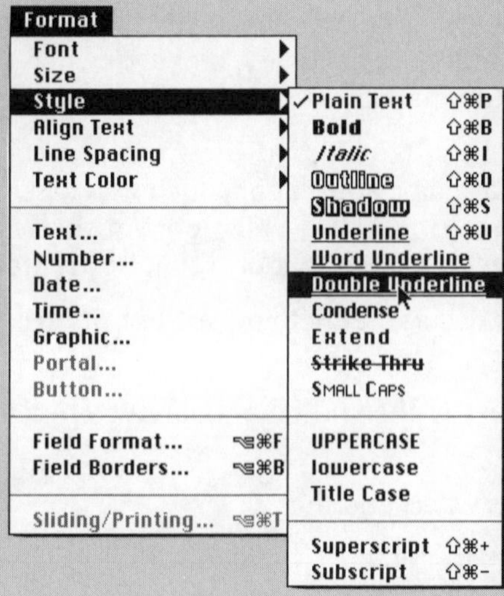

Overcoming Keystroke Conflicts Caused by Utilities

If using a keyboard shortcut produces an unusual effect (a dialog box appears that seems to have nothing to do with FileMaker Pro, for example), you probably have a utility running in the background that is conflicting with FileMaker Pro. Many background programs are constantly scanning for the particular key combination that activates them. On my system, for example, attempting to execute the keyboard shortcut for Define Fields (Shift-⌘-D) results, instead, in the launching of DiskTop — a file-manipulation utility.

Several options are available for overcoming conflicts of this sort:

- Reconfigure the utility so that it responds to a different key combination.

  See the utility's manual for instructions. Assuming that reconfiguration is possible, this is the best solution. To avoid additional conflicts, try to choose key combinations that are unlikely to conflict with your main programs. You can avoid many conflicts by using the Control key as the modifier key rather than the Command, Option, or Shift keys.

- If you cannot reconfigure the utility, turn it off when you are using FileMaker Pro. Again, see the manual for details.

  No matter how helpful utilities are, few of them are as critical as the work that you do in a major application, such as a database, word processing program, or spreadsheet. If a utility gets in the way, temporarily shut it down. If you can't reconfigure it or shut it down, get rid of it.

- When a conflict occurs, restrict yourself to using FileMaker Pro's menus to select the command.

  This solution is better than nothing, but not by much. It may remind you of this old joke:

  Patient: "It hurts when I do this."

  Doctor: "Well, then don't do that!"

Using Tools and Palettes

This section provides a brief introduction to the tools and palettes that are available in FileMaker Pro 3.0. Later chapters describe them in detail.

Figure 2-13 shows FileMaker Pro in Layout mode. This figure shows all tools except the few that are specific to Find mode.

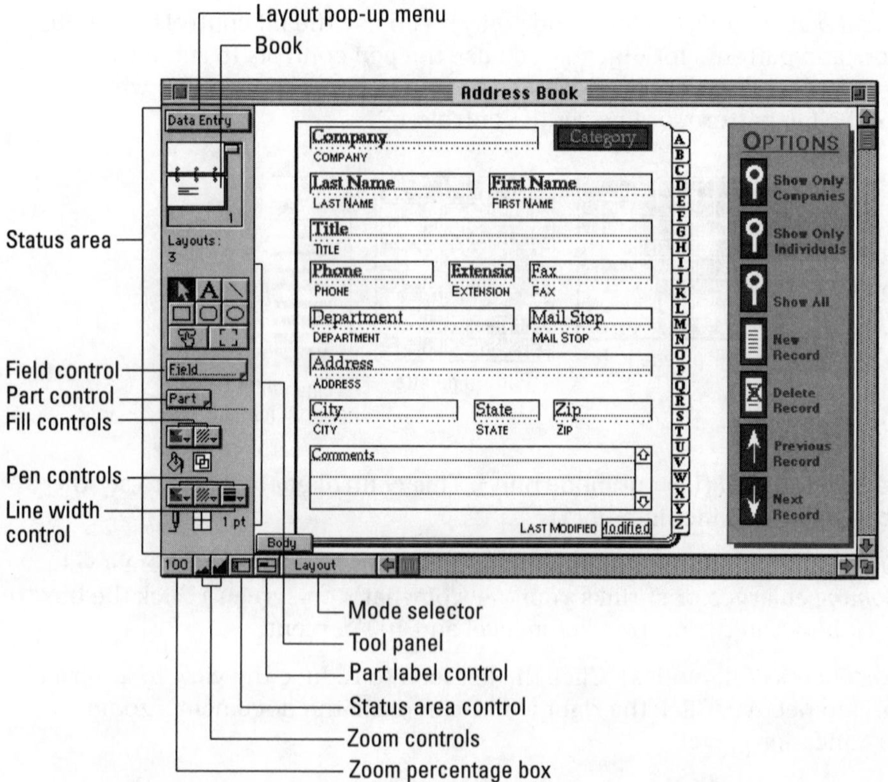

Figure 2-13: The FileMaker Pro tools and palettes

The following list briefly describes the basic FileMaker tools and palettes:

- *Layout pop-up menu* (available in all modes): Click this icon to display a menu of the names of all layouts that have been created for the current database. Selecting a different layout from the menu switches to that layout.
- *Book:* In Browse mode, you use the Book tool to switch to different records. In Layout mode, you use it to switch to different layouts. In Find mode, you use it to switch between multiple find requests.

- *Tools palette* (Layout mode only): From the top left, these tools are used to select objects (the Pointer tool), add or edit text (the A tool), draw lines (the Line tool), draw rectangles and squares (the Rectangle tool), draw rounded rectangles and rounded squares (the Rounded Rectangle tool), draw ovals and circles (the Oval tool), create buttons, and create portals to display fields from a related database.
- *Field and part tools* (Layout mode only): These tools enable you to place additional fields and parts on a layout.
- *Fill and pen controls* (Layout mode only): You use the fill controls to set fill colors and patterns for objects. You use the pen controls to set line and border colors. Figure 2-14 shows the pop-up palettes that appear when you click the fill, pattern, or line width controls.

Figure 2-14: Select a color, pattern, or line width by clicking in these palettes.

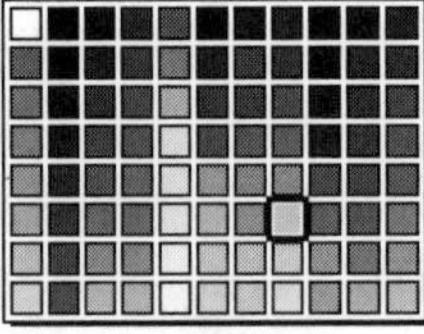
Fill palette

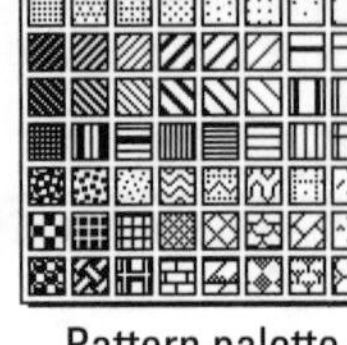
Pattern palette

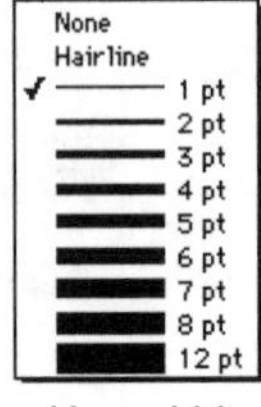

Line width pop-up menu

- *Line width control* (Layout mode only): This control enables you to set the thickness of any line (in points).
- *Zoom percentage box* (all modes): This box shows the current zoom level. (*Zooming* enlarges or shrinks your view of what's on-screen.) Click the box to switch between the current zoom level and 100 percent.
- *Zoom controls* (all modes): Click the left icon to reduce the view to a "bird's eye" perspective. Click the right icon to increase the document's zoom (magnification) level.
- *Status area control* (all modes): Click this control to show or hide the entire status area, including all tools.
- *Part label control* (Layout mode only): Click this control to switch between displaying layout part labels horizontally and displaying them vertically.
- *Mode selector* (all modes): This displays the current mode. Click the mode selector to display a pop-up menu (see Figure 2-15) that enables you to switch between the four program modes: Browse, Layout, Find, and Preview.

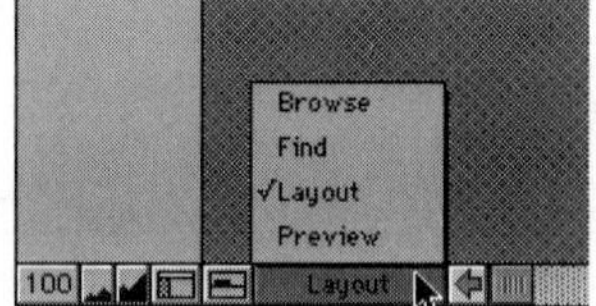

Figure 2-15: The Mode pop-up menu

In addition to these tools, a few special tools are introduced in Find mode, as shown in Figure 2-16.

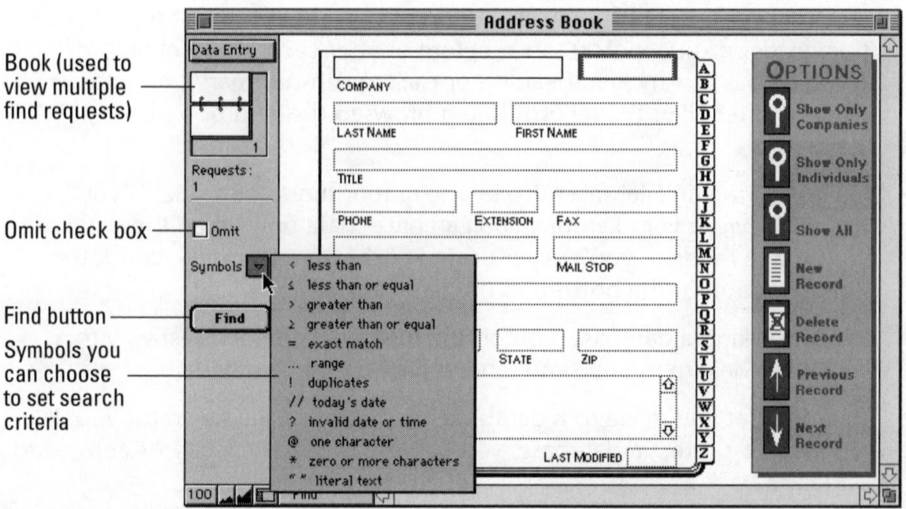

Figure 2-16: The tools in Find mode

You use these Find tools as follows:

- *Omit check box:* Check this box to exclude records from the found set that match the find criteria. For example, if the criterion is Sales > 100000, you can create a found set of records that includes everyone *except* salespeople with sales of more than $100,000.
- *Symbols pop-up menu:* Instead of typing conditional symbols and special characters when you are entering find criteria, you can select them from this pop-up menu.
- *Find button:* Click this button when you are ready to execute a find request (or multiple find requests).

Summary

- Layouts are arrangements of database fields. Different layouts enable you to view and present information in different ways. You can have as many layouts for a database as you like.
- Layouts are divided into sections called *parts*. Depending on the parts in which you place fields, text, and objects, they will be printed once for every record in the database (body), only at the top or bottom of each report page (header or footer), only at the top or bottom of the first report page (title header or title footer), once before or after each group of records sorted on the sort-by field (leading or trailing sub-summary), or once before or after all of the records being browsed (leading or trailing grand summary).
- You do all work in FileMaker Pro in one of four modes: Browse, Layout, Find, or Preview. For example, you can enter data only when the database is in Browse mode. If you're ever unsure of the current mode, check the Mode indicator at the bottom of the database window.
- Double-clicking a database icon on the desktop is the quickest way to launch FileMaker Pro and simultaneously open the database.
- Changes that you make to a database are automatically saved for you. If you want to protect a database, you can use the Save a Copy As command to make a backup copy.
- You can issue commands by choosing from menus and, in some cases, by pressing keyboard shortcuts.

What's New in FileMaker Pro 3.0?

3 CHAPTER

In This Chapter

- Learning about the new relational features
- Understanding the global, programmatic changes introduced in FileMaker Pro 3.0
- Learning about the new field types and field options
- Using the new layout features and data entry enhancements
- Using the powerful additions to ScriptMaker, such as looping and conditional script steps
- Controlling data storage

As it has in the past, FileMaker Pro 3.0 builds upon the capabilities and features of previous versions of the program. If you've used FileMaker Pro in any of its earlier incarnations, this chapter will help smooth your transition to FileMaker Pro 3.0 by pointing out the changes and additions that you'll have to learn about. The sections in this chapter briefly describe the new features and how to use them in your own databases.

Relational Features

This section explains the new relational capabilities — unquestionably the most important change introduced in FileMaker Pro 3.0.

Fully Relational Databases

Previous versions of FileMaker Pro were only semi-relational. You could use lookups to combine information from other files with the current database, but the lookup data was copied into the records of the current database. Now that FileMaker Pro is fully relational, you can easily combine the information in multiple files without duplicating data.

To use this feature, choose Define Relationships from the File menu. The Define Relationships dialog box appears, as shown in Figure 3-1. Click New and select a FileMaker Pro database to relate to the current database. In the Edit Relationship dialog box, define the relationship by selecting a pair of match fields from the two databases. Click OK and then Done. Related fields can either be placed directly onto layouts in the primary database or displayed within a portal (created with the Portal tool). See Chapter 19 for additional information about creating and working with relational databases and lookups.

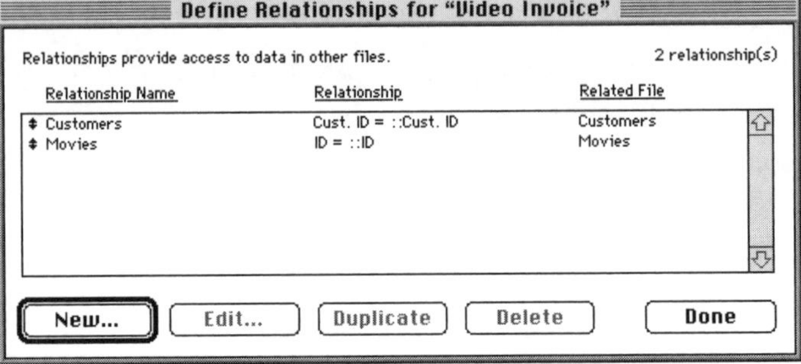

Figure 3-1: Two relationships have been defined for the Video Invoice database.

Portals

Placing a *portal* in a layout enables you to view data from multiple matching records in a related file. For example, if a relationship is based on an area code, you could use a portal to display the name, address, and phone number of all records that contain that area code.

You must be in Layout mode to create a portal. Select the Portal tool and drag to draw a rectangle on the desired layout. When you release the mouse button, the Portal Setup dialog box appears. Set options and click OK. Drag one or more related fields that you want to view into the portal rectangle.

Global Program Changes

The following general features represent major changes that are not specific to any single mode or portion of FileMaker Pro 3.0.

Power Mac Native Version

On the Macintosh, FileMaker Pro 3.0 can be installed as a "Fat Binary" version that will run on any Macintosh, a Power Macintosh-specific version, or a 680x0-specific version (for non-Power Macintoshes). The version is selected when you run the installation program.

New Database Dialog Box

When you launch FileMaker Pro 3.0, the New Database dialog box is immediately displayed. (Note that you will also see a modified version of this dialog box that excludes the Open option when you choose New from the File menu.) From this dialog box, you can either create a new file using any one of over 40 customized templates, create a new file from scratch, or open an existing file.

Drag and Drop Support

Macintoshes equipped with the Drag Manager extension can drag FileMaker Pro field data and layout objects into other applications that support drag and drop. Similarly, text from other applications that support drag and drop can be dragged into FileMaker Pro fields. (Drag and drop is a direct procedure; it does not use the Mac's Clipboard as a temporary storage place for the data or object.)

To enable drag and drop, choose Preferences from the Edit menu. In the Preferences dialog box that appears, choose General from the pop-up menu, and then click in the check box for "Enable drag and drop text selection." Click OK to save the changes and dismiss the Preferences dialog box.

TCP/IP Support

FileMaker Pro 3.0 provides cross-platform network support via TCP/IP and is Open Transport compatible.

To use this feature, choose Preferences from the Edit menu. Choose General from the pop-up menu in the Preferences dialog box, and then choose TCP/IP from the Network protocol pop-up menu. Quit FileMaker Pro and restart the program to put the network protocol change into effect.

Default Passwords

This feature enables developers to specify a default password for a database that will automatically be used whenever that database is opened. Assigning a default password shields the user from the password dialog box, while effectively restricting access to the feature set assigned to that password by the developer.

You can set one or more passwords for the database by choosing Define Passwords from the Access Privileges submenu of the File menu. Then choose Preferences from the Edit menu. In the "When opening…" portion of the Document section of the Preferences dialog box, click the check box for "Try default password" and type a password to use, as shown in Figure 3-2.

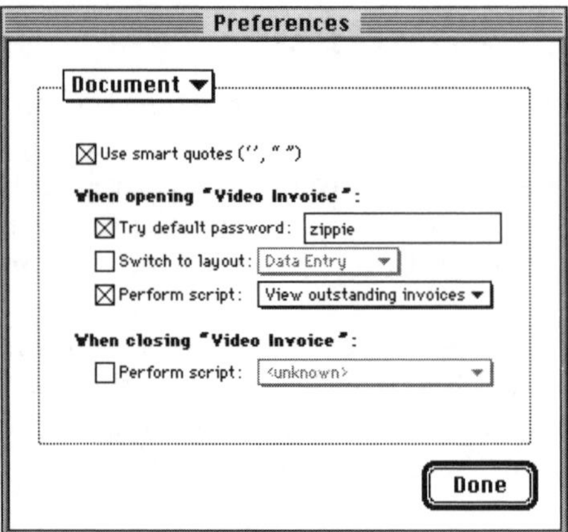

Figure 3-2: Specifying a default password for a database

Databases Created from Templates in the New Database Dialog Box

As an added convenience, you can create a new database from any of the Claris-provided templates listed in the New Database dialog box.

From the New Database dialog box (shown when the program launches or New is chosen from the File menu), click "Create a new file using a template," choose a category from the pop-up menu, select a template, and click OK.

If a template list is not presented in the New Database dialog box, choose Preferences from the Edit menu, choose General from the pop-up menu, and then click the check box labeled "Show templates in New dialog."

Foreign Files Used to Automatically Create New Databases

FileMaker Pro 3.0 can read many types of text, spreadsheet, and database files and automatically convert them to new FileMaker Pro databases.

To use this feature, choose Open from the File menu. In the Open file dialog box, choose the appropriate file type from the Show pop-up menu, select the file, enter a file name for the file you're about to create, and click Save. The file is created, and temporary names (f1, f2, and so on) are assigned to each field.

Support for Larger Files and Maximum Number of Open Files

As many as 50 files can be open at the same time. (The previous limit was 16.) Databases can now be significantly larger — up to 2GB in size.

No special commands or procedures are required to use this feature.

Field Types and Options

FileMaker Pro 3.0 introduces a new field type (Global), renames an existing field type (from Picture/Sound to Container field), and includes several new field data validation and auto-entry options.

Global Fields

A Global field is used to hold the same value for all records in the database (a state sales tax percentage, for example). It can also be used to temporarily store script results. Each Global field is stored only once for the entire database. If placed in a layout, a Global field shows the same value for every record.

To create a Global field, choose Define Fields from the File menu and set a field's type to Global. Select a data type for the field, such as Number or Date, to indicate the kind of information that will be stored in the field.

Container Fields

The Picture/Sound field type has been replaced by the Container field type. A Container field can store a picture, sound, or QuickTime movie. When importing an element into a Container field, you can now elect to store only the element's file reference (a pointer) rather than the element itself, saving disk space in the file as a result.

To create a Container field, choose Define Fields from the File menu and set a field's type to Container. Storage options for a Container field can be set individually for each imported element via the Import dialog box (when you import each picture, sound, or movie).

Merge Fields

Rather than having to create a merge document (such as a form letter) in a word processing program, you can now generate merges entirely within FileMaker Pro. This new feature allows for easier text integration and is much more efficient than sliding fields.

To add a merge field to a layout, switch to Layout mode, set the text insertion point in a new or existing text block, choose Merge Field from the Paste Special submenu of the Edit menu, and choose the merge field. A reference to the merge field is pasted into the layout in the form <<*field name*>>. For example, a salutation in a letter might appear as Dear <<First Name>> as shown in Figure 3-3.

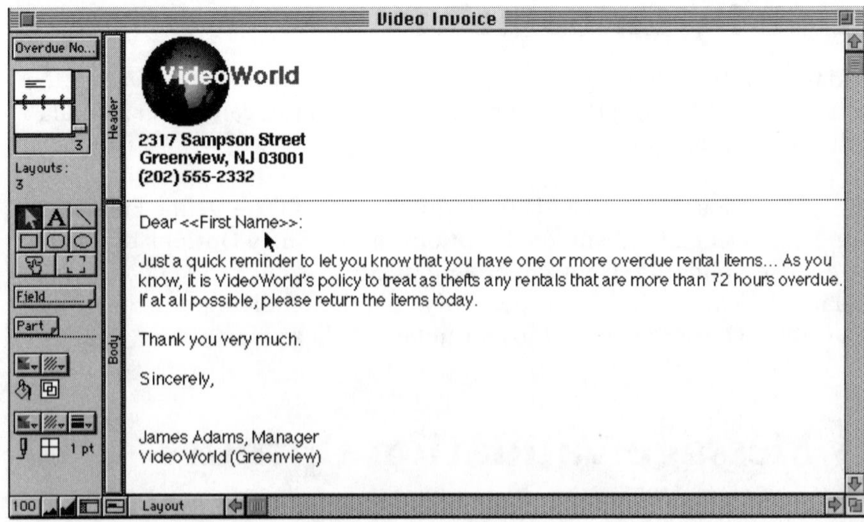

Figure 3-3: A merge field is used in this form letter layout to address each person by her or his first name.

Auto-Entered Calculations

In previous versions of FileMaker Pro, calculations could only be performed in Calculation fields. Now data can be automatically placed in new records based on any calculation expression. Note that unlike data in a Calculation field, you can edit data that has been auto-entered via a calculation.

To use this feature, select a field in the Define Fields dialog box, and click Options. The Entry Options dialog box appears. Choose Auto Enter from the pop-up menu, and then click the "Calculated value" radio button. Enter the formula and click OK.

Auto-Entered Value from a Previous Record

You can instruct FileMaker Pro 3.0 to automatically insert the value from the most recently created or edited record.

To use this feature, choose Define Fields from the File menu. The Define Fields dialog box appears. Select a field and click Options. In the Entry Options dialog box that appears, choose Auto Enter and click the "Value from previous record" radio button. Click OK.

Validation by Calculation

This field validation option allows you to specify a Boolean formula as a validation criterion, such as Age > 18. (Note that the field specified in the validation formula need not be the current field.)

To use this feature, choose Define Fields from the File menu. The Define Fields dialog box appears. Select a field and click Options. In the Entry Options dialog box that appears, choose Validation from the pop-up menu, and click the check box marked "Validated by calculation." In the Specify Calculation dialog box that appears, enter a Boolean (true/false, yes/no) formula and click OK.

Display Message Validation Option

If a validation criterion that has been set for a field is not satisfied by the current entry, a user-specified message can be displayed.

To specify a validation message for a field, choose Define Fields from the File menu. The Define Fields dialog box appears. Select a field and click Options. In the Entry Options dialog box that appears, choose Validation from the pop-up menu, and select validation criteria. Click in the check box marked "Display custom message if validation fails," and enter the message in the text box. Click OK.

New Calculation Functions

FileMaker Pro 3.0 adds dozens of new functions that can be used in formulas. Of particular interest to many users and developers are the GetRepetition, GetSummary, and Status functions. Using these functions, it is possible to address specific elements in repeating fields and summary calculations, as well as determine environmental information — anything from the current record count to the current platform (Macintosh or Windows).

To use these new calculation functions in a formula, define a Calculation field, specify that a calculated value should be auto-entered into the field, or specify that the field should be validated by a calculation. In the Specify Calculation dialog box, select any of the new functions.

Custom Date Formats

You can define a custom format for any Date field.

To use this feature, you must be in Layout mode. You can then select a Date field, and choose Date from the Format menu. The Date Format dialog box appears (see Figure 3-4). Click the Custom radio button, and select components for the date.

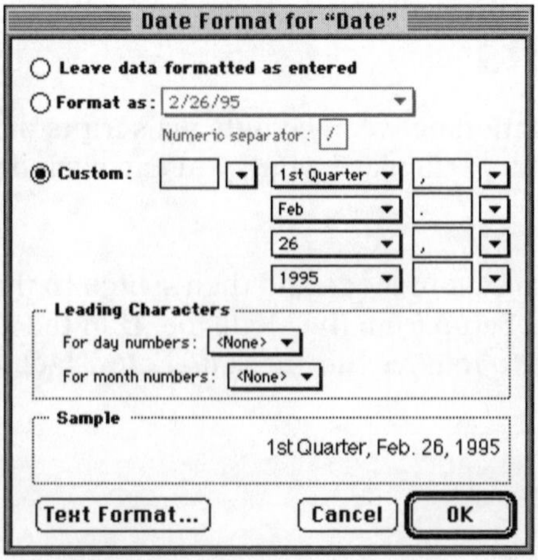

Figure 3-4: Components for a custom date format can be chosen from pop-up menus.

Layout Features

When designing and working with layouts, you can now create 3D buttons with a Button tool, hide layouts (preventing them from being listed in the layouts pop-up menu), and display a text ruler at the top of the database window.

Button Tool

The Button tool enables you to easily create basic buttons (see Figure 3-5). (In previous versions, buttons had to be created manually via a multi-step procedure.) Inclusion of the Button tool puts button creation in the hands of all users.

To use this feature, switch to Layout mode, select the Button tool, and drag to create a button. When you release the mouse button, the Specify Button dialog box appears. Choose a button action and then click OK. Type a label for the button. (Note that you can set the preferred button shape to rounded or rectangular in the Preferences dialog box.)

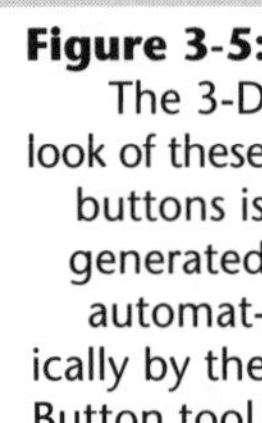

Figure 3-5: The 3-D look of these buttons is generated automatically by the Button tool.

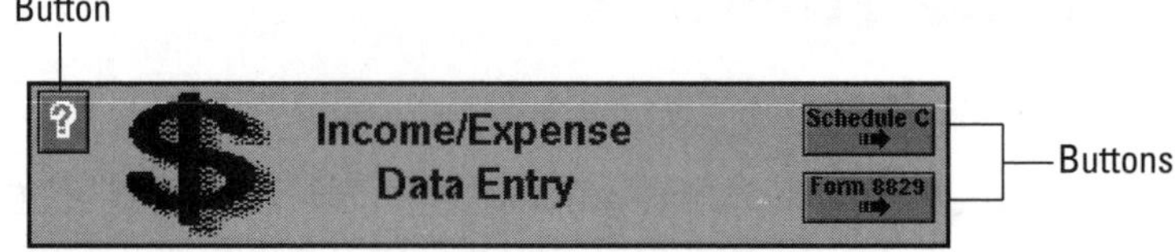

Hidden Layouts

If you want to control navigation between layouts via scripts or don't want users to be able to view or switch to a particular layout, you can exclude the layout from the pop-up layouts menu.

To use this feature, switch to Layout mode and then switch to the layout that you want to hide. Choose Layout Setup from the Mode menu. In the Layout Setup dialog box that appears, click once to remove the check mark for "Include in layouts menu."

Text Ruler

To make it easy to assign default formats to fields in a layout, FileMaker Pro 3.0 provides a text ruler. The ruler bar includes icons and pop-up menus for major formatting options, such as font, size, alignment, and character styles.

To access the text ruler in Layout mode, choose Text Ruler from the Show menu.

Data Entry Enhancements

FileMaker Pro 3.0 offers several enhancements that make it easier to enter and edit data, such as a text ruler bar and paragraph formatting commands similar to those found in major word processing programs.

Text Ruler Bar

A text ruler can be displayed to simplify field formatting when entering or editing data (see Figure 3-6). The ruler bar includes icons and pop-up menus for major formatting options, such as font, size, alignment, tab stops, and character styles.

To access the text ruler in Browse mode, choose Text Ruler from the Format menu.

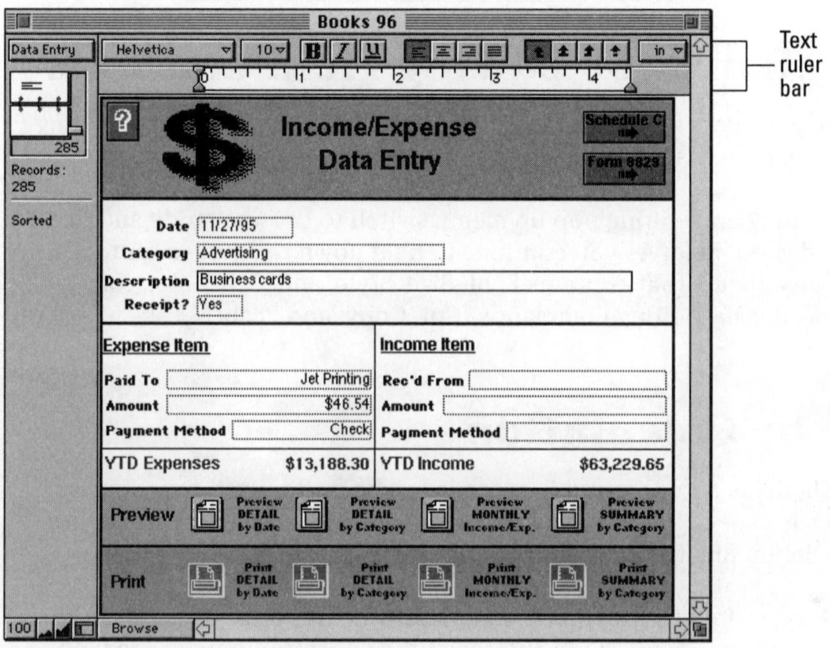

Figure 3-6. The new text ruler and ruler bar make it simple to format data.

Paragraph Formatting Options

Paragraph formatting commands (similar to those found in word processing programs) have been added to FileMaker Pro 3.0.

To access the paragraph formatting commands, switch to Browse mode, select text that you want to format, and then choose Text from the Format menu. The Default Text Format dialog box appears. Click the Paragraph button. In the Paragraph dialog box (shown in Figure 3-7), you can set alignment, indents, and line spacing (line height, as well as space above and below). To set tab stops for the paragraph, click the Tabs button.

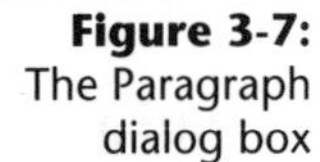

Figure 3-7: The Paragraph dialog box

Pop-Up Menus for Editing Field Contents

In FileMaker Pro 3.0, every field has its own hidden pop-up formatting and editing menu, providing easy access to field formatting options.

To use the formatting and editing pop-up menu, switch to Browse mode and Control-click in the desired field. As you continue to hold down the mouse button, a tiny pop-up menu appears that contains Font, Size, Style, and Text Color commands, as well as normal editing commands (Cut, Copy, and Paste).

Replace by Calculation

Replacing data in fields across multiple records can be customized based on a calculation. This is especially effective in Text fields when you use the new word and string calculation functions.

To use this feature, switch to Find mode and identify the records you want to replace. Then switch to Browse mode and select the entire contents of the field whose values you want to replace. Choose Replace from the Mode menu. In the Replace dialog box, choose "Replace with calculated result," click Specify, and define the replacement expression.

Tabs Within Text Fields

In previous versions of FileMaker Pro, the Tab key was used exclusively for moving from field to field within a record. Now you can also use tabs to format Text fields by holding down the Option key and pressing the Tab key.

Revert Record Command

Revert Record works like an Undo command for an entire record. Selecting Revert Record reverses all editing done for the current record, restoring its previous contents.

To use this feature, switch to Browse mode and choose Revert Record from the Mode menu.

Value Lists

Value lists are now separate from field definitions, providing greater flexibility and ease of use. Now even value lists from related files can be displayed as a pop-up list.

To use this feature, switch to Layout mode, select the field to which you want to attach a value list, and then choose Field Format from the Format menu. In the Field Format dialog box, click the second radio button and choose Pop-up list, Pop-up menu, Check boxes, or Radio buttons from the pop-up menu. Choose an existing value list or define a new one by choosing the appropriate option from the second pop-up menu.

Scripting Features

Scripting capabilities have been greatly enhanced in FileMaker Pro 3.0. Scripts can now include loops, conditional tests, and phone dialing steps, for example.

Conditional Scripting and Loops Scripting

FileMaker Pro 3.0 scripts can employ conditional tests (IF..THEN and IF..THEN..ELSE) and loops.

In ScriptMaker, you can choose any of the following steps: If, Else, End If, Loop, Exit Loop If, or End Loop.

Relational Steps

Several steps were added to provide support for the relational aspects of FileMaker Pro 3.0, such as navigation within portals.

You access these steps from ScriptMaker by choosing Go to Related Record, Go to Portal Row, or Open Define Relationships.

Script Control Steps

New steps enable developers or end-users to halt or pause the execution of a script.

In ScriptMaker, you can choose from the following script control steps: Halt Script, Allow User Abort, and Set Error Capture.

Closing Scripts

In addition to specifying a script that automatically executes each time a database is opened, you can specify a closing script that executes when a database is closed. (You may, for example, want to sort the database or export a selected set of records.)

To set a closing script, choose Preferences from the Edit menu, choose Document from the pop-up menu in the Preferences dialog box, and click the "Perform script" check box in the "When closing" section of the dialog box. Choose an existing script from the pop-up menu and then click Done.

Phone Dialing

Phone numbers can be dialed based on specific values or the contents of a database field. You can also set preferences to adjust phone numbers based on different locations (home, office, car, and so on).

To prepare FileMaker Pro for dialing, choose Preferences from the Edit menu. Choose Modem from the pop-up menu and specify the port through which you'll dial: modem or speaker. If you have special dialing requirements, you can set them in the Dialing section of the Preferences dialog box.

You can then add the Dial Phone step to a script (see Figure 3-8). Click the Specify button to set dialing options. (You can either dial a number found in a particular field or dial the same number every time.) Click the Use Dialing Preferences check box if you have dialing requirements that are addressed by the Dialing section of the Preferences dialog box.

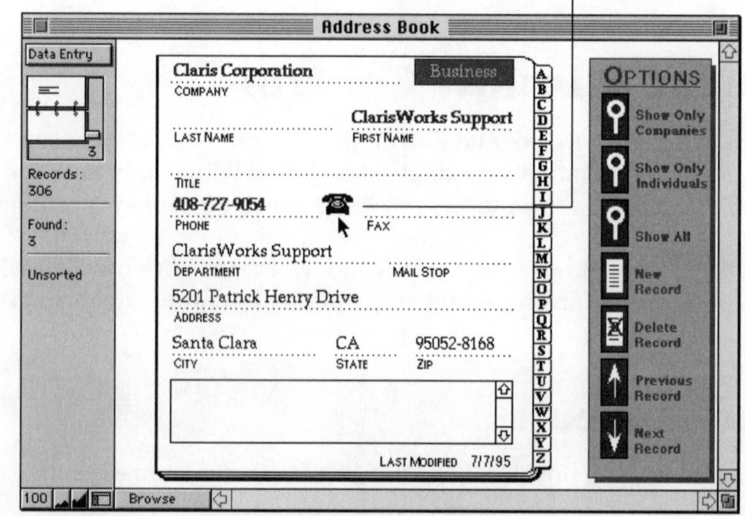

Figure 3-8: Attaching the Dial Phone script step to a button makes it easy to dial phone numbers through a modem or the computer's speaker.

Flush Cache to Disk Step

By using the Flush Cache to Disk step in scripts, you can instruct FileMaker Pro to write to disk all data changes that are currently held in memory.

You can add this feature to a script by choosing the Flush Cache to Disk step.

Set Field and Paste Result Steps

It is now simple to modify the contents of chosen fields via scripts. The Set Field step can replace the contents of a field with the result of a calculation. This step is particularly useful for setting values for Global fields. The Paste Result step pastes the contents of a field or the result of a calculation into another field on the current layout.

These steps can be added to a script by choosing the Set Field or Paste Result step.

Record Copying

Using Copy Record or Copy All Records, you can copy an entire record or all records to the Clipboard as tab-delimited text (which can be pasted into many programs).

You can copy the current record or all records by adding the Copy Record or Copy All Records step to a script.

Document Window Control

The Home, Page Up, Page Down, and End steps from previous versions of FileMaker Pro have been combined into a new single step: Scroll Window. In addition, you now can freeze or refresh the window, as well as specify a zoom percentage.

In ScriptMaker, you can choose the Scroll Window, Freeze Window, Refresh Window, or Set Zoom Level step and select step options from the ones presented.

Comment Step

To document scripts, you now have the option of including non-executing comment lines.

To use this feature, choose the Comment step in ScriptMaker.

PlainTalk Support

Macintoshes equipped with the PlainTalk system extension can be instructed to speak a message or the contents of a selected field.

To add speech capabilities to a script, select the Speak step. Then click the Specify button to choose a field or message to be spoken, as well as a voice for the speech.

AppleScript and Apple Events Support

In addition to sending Apple Events (supported in FileMaker Pro 2.1), FileMaker Pro 3.0 can execute AppleScripts.

To use this feature, choose Perform AppleScript in ScriptMaker.

Miscellaneous New Script Steps

In support of the new features and commands, other new script steps include Revert Record/Request, Exit Record/Request, Toggle Text Ruler, Change Password, Set Multi-User, Set Use System Formats, Recover, Show Message, and Beep.

Data Storage Control

In addition to the new Flush Cache to Disk script step, FileMaker Pro 3.0 offers several field options that enable database designers to exert greater control over how data is stored for individual fields.

Indexing Control

In previous versions of FileMaker Pro, all fields were automatically indexed. Now you can specify indexing options on a field-by-field basis.

To use this feature, choose Define Fields from the File menu. Select a field in the Define Fields dialog box, click Options, and then click Storage Options. Set indexing off or on for the field by clicking the appropriate radio button, as shown in Figure 3-9. (When indexing for a field is off, FileMaker Pro can still index the field if necessary, as long as “Automatically turn indexing on if needed” is checked.)

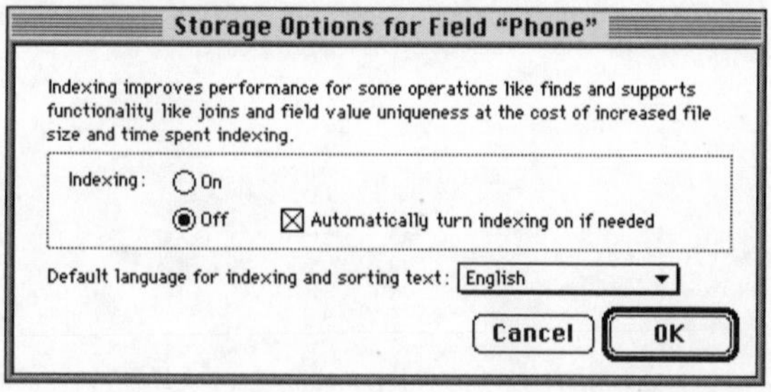

Figure 3-9: Indexing options are set individually for each field in the Storage Options dialog box.

Stored and Unstored Calculation Results

For any Calculation field, the result can be stored with each record or only calculated as needed.

To use this feature, choose Define Fields from the File menu. The Define Fields dialog box appears. Select a Calculation field, click Options, and then click Storage Options. To prevent FileMaker Pro from storing the calculations for the chosen field, click in the check box marked "Do not store calculation results — calculate only when needed."

Summary

- FileMaker Pro 3.0 is a major update to the most popular database application for the Macintosh. New features include full relational capabilities, dozens of additional calculation functions, looping and conditional tests in scripts, and greater control over features that were formerly under program control (such as indexing and data storage).

Learning Database Design Basics

This section shows you how to use FileMaker Pro's design tools to construct databases and to design different types of layouts.

Creating Your First Database: Address Book

In This Chapter

- Setting field types and choosing field options
- Creating pop-up menu fields, required fields, auto-entry fields, and scrolling text fields
- Adding formatting to text, including fonts, sizes, styles, alignments, and colors
- Creating field borders
- Using layout tools to size and place fields, field labels, and other objects precisely
- Using graphics in layouts and grouping and ungrouping objects
- Creating a report layout that has automatic date-stamping and page number-stamping in the footer
- Designing scripts and assigning them to buttons or to the Script menu

When I first conceptualized this chapter, I imagined walking you through the steps of creating a simple FileMaker Pro database. But the more I thought about it, the more pointless that approach seemed. The purpose of this book is to give you a solid understanding of FileMaker Pro's features and capabilities, not just a quick glimpse of them. So the chapter took a dramatic turn.

Instead of helping you design a simple database, this chapter steps you through the creation of a full-featured database called Address Book, a database that has graphics, multiple layouts, buttons, scripts, and reports. Figure 4-1 shows the data entry layout for the completed database and points out some of its features.

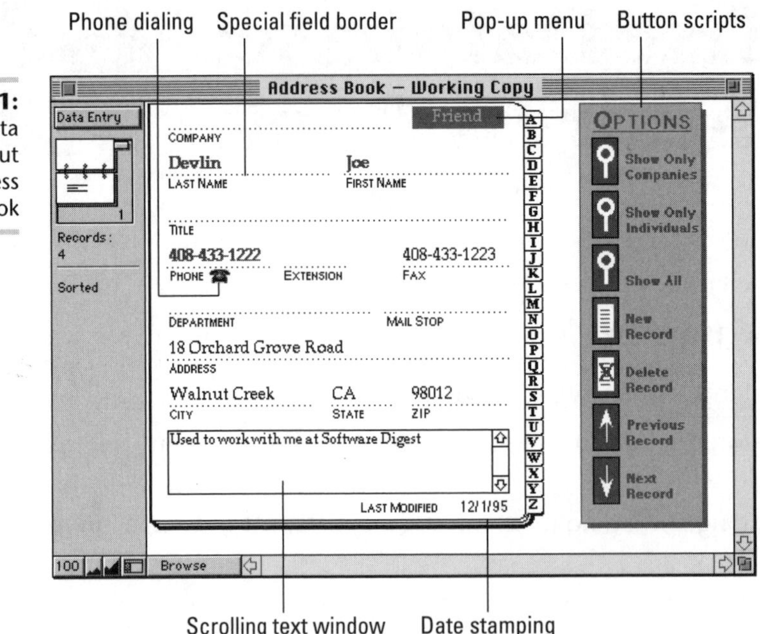

Figure 4-1: The data entry layout for Address Book

The purpose of this extended exercise is to help you become familiar with many of the important functions of FileMaker Pro while you create a database that you may actually want to use. After you finish making the database, you will have at least a passing familiarity with how FileMaker Pro works and what its many capabilities are. Later chapters provide in-depth instructions on using the program features that this chapter discusses.

The *Macworld FileMaker Pro 3.0 Bible Disk* includes two templates for the database: Address Book and Address Book — Graphics. Address Book is the finished database. Before launching into this tutorial, you may want to play with Address Book to see what you are going to accomplish. Address Book — Graphics contains the background graphics that you use to make the database more attractive. If you haven't already done so, install the database templates on your hard disk. (See Appendix A for instructions.)

Designing a database that does exactly what you want it to do (collecting the proper data and presenting it in ways that meet your specific needs) is seldom a linear process. Unless you spend an inordinate amount of time planning a database before you begin the actual construction work in FileMaker Pro, you are likely to add more fields, delete some fields that — in retrospect — you didn't really need, design additional reports, and tweak the layout (trying out different fonts and alignments, for example). In the design process, you'll repeatedly bounce between Layout, Browse, and Preview modes, as well as in and out of ScriptMaker.

Like most tutorials, this one is in a format that is step-by-step and linear. But don't be fooled. This relatively simple database took me a full day to construct, and the process was far from linear. Thus, don't be surprised if the process that *you* go through in designing your own databases doesn't match the Step 1⇨Step 2⇨Step 3 approach that you find in this chapter. (Of course, planning does help. The more time you spend deciding which fields, reports, and scripts you need; how to format fields; and what you want the layouts to look like, the faster the creation process will go.)

Step 1: Create a New Database

If FileMaker Pro isn't already running, double-click the FileMaker Pro icon to launch the program. To begin the process of creating the database, choose "Create a new empty file" from the New Database dialog box, and click OK.

— or —

If FileMaker Pro is already running, choose New from the File menu. The New Database dialog box appears. Choose "Create a new empty file," and then click OK.

In either case, the file dialog box shown in Figure 4-2 appears.

Figure 4-2: Creating a new database

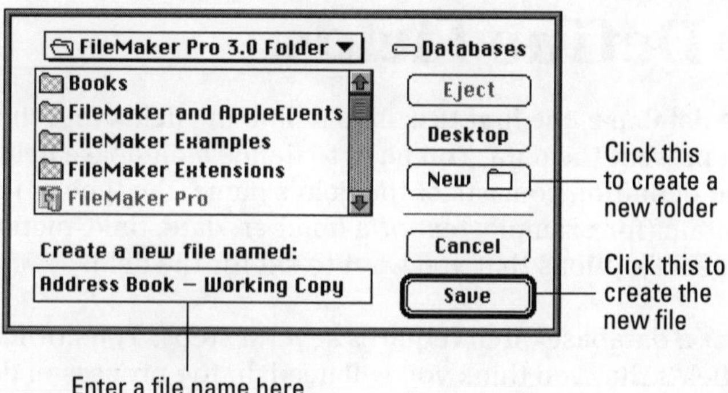

Select the disk drive and folder in which you want to store the new database, enter a name for it (**Address Book — Working Copy**, for example), and click Save. The Define Field dialog box appears, as shown in Figure 4-3.

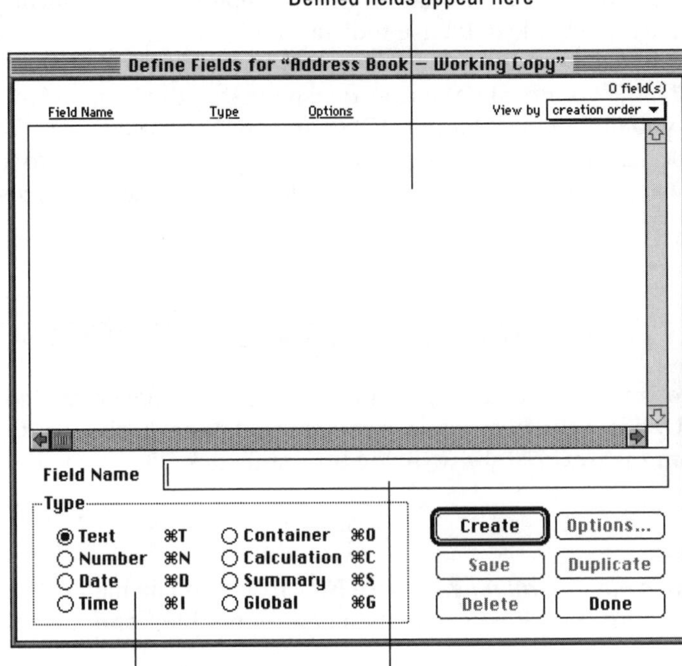

Figure 4-3: The Define Fields dialog box

Step 2: Define Fields

As with any new database, the first task is to define the fields that the database will use to store and present the data. You need to define a database field before you can use it. A field definition consists of the field's name, the type of information that the field will contain (for example, text or a number, date, time, picture, or calculation), and any special options that you want to set for the field.

Defining fields for a database often requires several steps. You normally begin by defining all the fields that you think you will need. In the process of designing the database, however, you often discover that you should have created additional fields or find that you don't need some of the fields that you have defined. Making a change in the fields is not a problem. You can add or remove fields as the need arises, even after you create records and enter data.

To keep things simple, there are only two field types used in the Address Book database: Text and Date. Table 4-1 lists the database fields that you need to define.

Table 4-1
Field Definitions for Address Book

Field Name	*Type*	*Options*	*Field Contents*
First Name	Text		First name of contact
Last Name	Text		Last name of contact
Title	Text		Person's title
Company	Text		Company affiliation
Department	Text		Department
Mail Stop	Text		Mail stop
Address	Text		Street address
City	Text		City
State	Text		State
ZIP	Text		ZIP code
Phone	Text		Area code and phone number
Extension	Text		Phone extension
Fax	Text		Area code and fax number
Category	Text	By Value List, Strict, Required Value, Message	Classification for the record
Comments	Text		Notes
Last Modified	Date	Modification Date	Date the record was last altered

Although the Phone, Extension, Fax, and ZIP fields contain numbers, these fields are defined as Text fields rather than Number fields in Address Book. In FileMaker Pro, you define a field as a Number field for the following reasons:

- You intend to use the contents of the field in a calculation.
- You want to restrict the contents of the field to numbers only.

Because you are not going to base a calculation on any of these four fields and because they can legitimately contain letters or special characters — such as (619) 443-5555, 1-800-SUCCESS, and N9B 3P7 (a Canadian Postal Code) — it makes better sense to treat them as text than to define them as numbers.

You need to set options for only two fields, Category and Last Modified. Although you can set field options when you are defining the field, for this example you define all the fields first and then set the field options.

To define the first field, type **First Name** in the Field Name text box of the Define Fields dialog box. Because Text is already chosen as the field type and you are not assigning any options to the field, click the Create button. The field is added to the scrolling list at the top of the dialog box (see Figure 4-4).

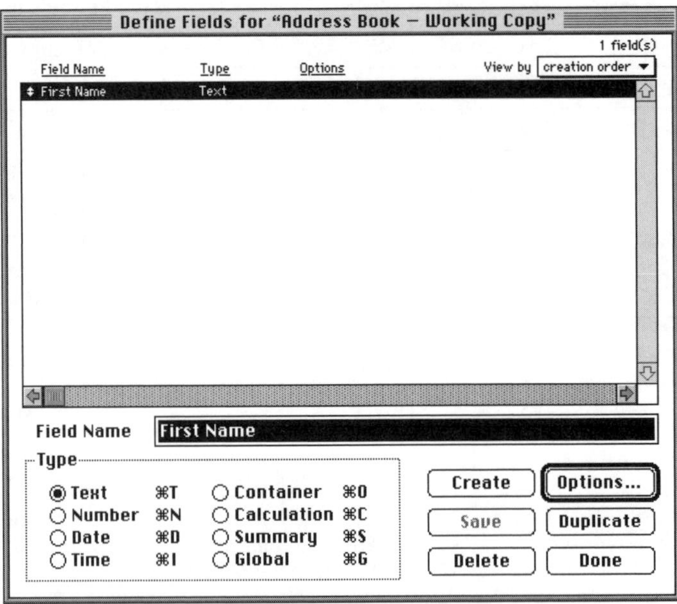

Figure 4-4: Defining the first field

To create the Last Name field, type **Last Name** in the Field Name text box and click Create again. Continue this process, defining every Text field in Table 4-1 (the First Name field through the Comments field).

Finally, create the Last Modified field. Type **Last Modified**, choose Date as the field type, and click Create. The Last Modified field will automatically store the date that each record was last modified, giving you an idea of how current the information is.

You can make the field definition process go faster by pressing Return or Enter immediately after you type each field name. Whenever the Create button, or any other button in a dialog box, is surrounded by a thick line, you can choose it by pressing Return or Enter. Of course, you can still click the button with the mouse, if you prefer.

Step 3: Set Field Options

You can use various FileMaker Pro field options to help you automatically enter information (such as the current date or a serial number), verify that only appropriate data has been entered, create repeating fields (line items in an invoice, for example), or present a pop-up list of values for a field. To give you a sample of these capabilities, this section shows you how to define options for two fields: Last Modified and Category.

With the Last Modified field still selected, click the Options button. The Entry Options for Field "Last Modified" dialog box appears, as shown in Figure 4-5.

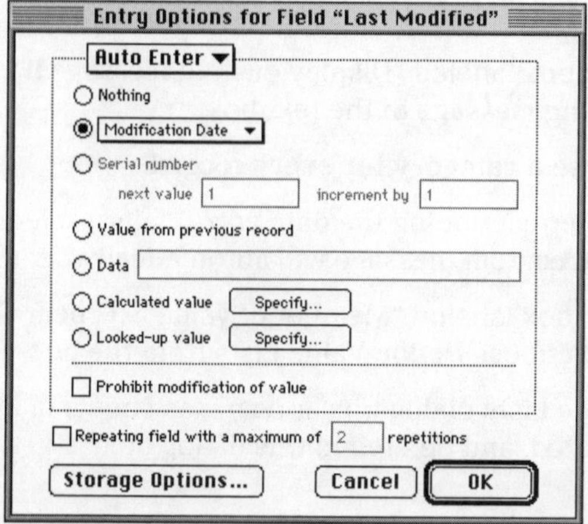

Figure 4-5: Setting an option for the Last Modified field

Regardless of the field for which you are setting options, the dialog box always looks the same. The name of the dialog box changes, however, to reflect the name of the field for which you are setting options.

Choose Auto Enter from the large pop-up menu at the top of the dialog box, and then choose Modification Date from the smaller pop-up menu, as shown in the figure. Click OK to return to the Define Fields dialog box.

When the database is finished, you will use the Category field to assign a general classification to every record: Business, Friend, or Relative. (Even if you would prefer other classifications, please use these for the example. You can change them to something more appropriate later.)

We will make Category a *required field* — one that cannot be empty. This ensures that when you are entering data, FileMaker Pro displays a warning if you attempt to leave a record without first making a Category choice. To set this and other validation options for the Category field, follow these steps:

1. In the Define Fields dialog box, select the Category field and then click Options.

   The Entry Options for Field "Category" dialog box appears.

2. Choose Validation from the large pop-up menu at the top of the dialog box. Click the check box labeled "Not empty."

3. To make sure that this requirement is enforced, click the check box labeled "Strict: Do not allow user to override validation."

4. Click the check box labeled "Display custom message if validation fails," and type the following message in the text box:

   You must choose a category for every record.

   If you (or another user doing the data entry) fail to select a category for a new record, the custom message will automatically be presented.

5. Click the check box labeled "Member of value list" near the middle of the dialog box, and choose Define Value Lists from the pop-up menu to the right.

   The Define Value Lists dialog box appears, as shown in Figure 4-6. Value lists are created, edited, and deleted in this dialog box.

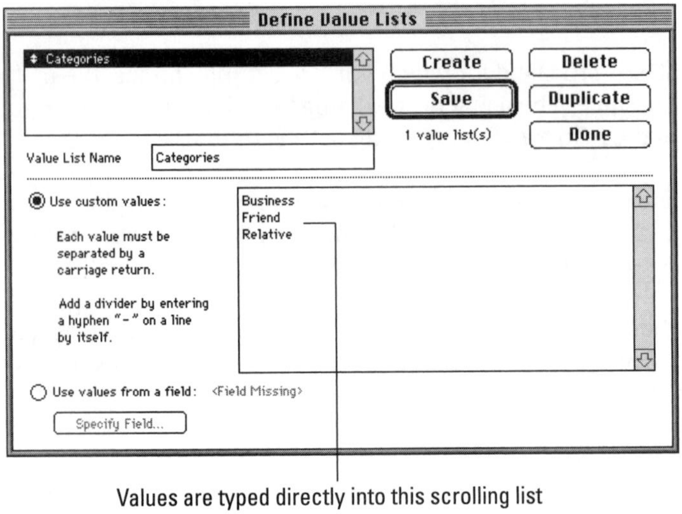

Figure 4-6: Creating a Categories value list

Values are typed directly into this scrolling list

6. Type a name (such as Categories) for the new value list in the Value List Name text box, and then click Create.

   Any values that you enter in this dialog box will appear as a pop-up menu or list when you click or tab into the Category field. The order in which you type the values is the order in which they will appear.

7. Type the three lines of text that are shown in the Define Value Lists dialog box in Figure 4-6, pressing Return after typing the first and second values.

8. After you enter the values, click Save to accept them and click Done. Then click OK to return to the Define Fields dialog box.

After you have defined all the fields and set their options, click Done. A *standard layout* is automatically created for you, as shown in Figure 4-7. As you can see, a standard layout is a vertical arrangement of all the database fields. Each field includes a label that matches whatever you named the field in the Define Fields dialog box.

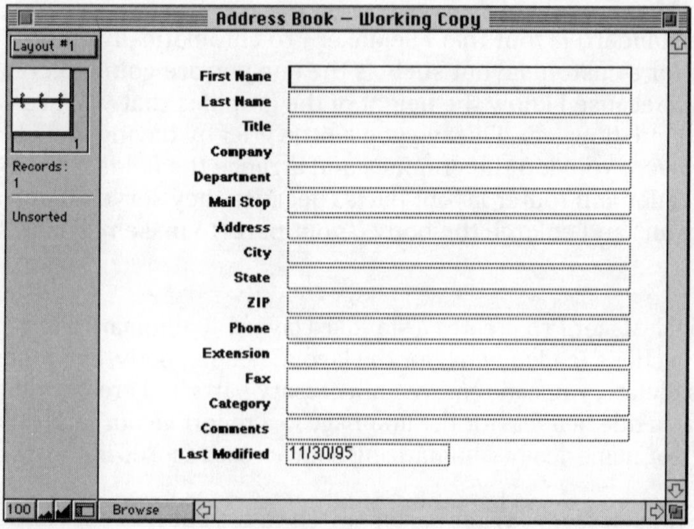

Figure 4-7: The initial database arranged in a standard layout

If you were interested in only a quick-and-dirty database, you could stop right here. Address Book — Working Copy is ready to receive data. However, in keeping with the goal of this chapter — teaching you how to create a *full-featured database* — in the next step, you rearrange the fields, add field formatting, and include some graphics to make this layout more visually appealing.

When you'd like to learn more about defining fields and setting field options, see Chapter 5.

Step 4: Design the Data Entry Layout

If you want to take the data entry layout beyond the functional stage — all the way to attractive and pleasant to use — you may find that you spend more time on this task than on any other database development task. Frankly, however, not every database is worth the extra effort required to "pretty it up." Many databases, such as those intended only for your personal use, need never evolve beyond the functional stage. A database that you use daily or one that you intend to distribute to others, on the other hand, should look good and contain scripts that make it easy to perform common tasks. In this step, you do some of the work that's required to create an attractive layout.

Altering the Layout Parts

Normally, the standard layout that FileMaker Pro automatically creates is a good starting point for a custom layout such as the one you are going to create for Address Book. Because I know the height of the graphics that you are going to place in the background, however, I'll save you a little grief by having you change the size of the layout *before* you add the graphics and arrange the fields. Specifically, you'll remove the header and footer layout parts (because they serve no purpose in the Data Entry layout) and enlarge the body layout part (to make room for the graphics and fields).

When FileMaker Pro creates a standard layout, it automatically generates three basic sections (called *parts*) for the layout: header, body, and footer. As your needs dictate, you can remove unnecessary parts and create additional parts, such as a title header (for the first page in a report layout) and sub-summary parts (for numerically summarizing data across records in the database).

To delete the unnecessary layout parts, switch to Layout mode by choosing Layout from the Mode menu and then choose Part Setup from the Mode menu. The Part Setup dialog box appears (see Figure 4-8). To remove the header part, select Header and click the Delete button. Then delete the footer part in the same manner. Finally, click Done to close the dialog box and return to the layout. Notice that it now contains only one part — the body.

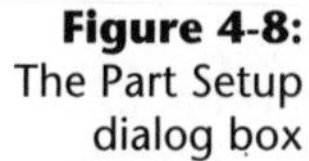

Figure 4-8: The Part Setup dialog box

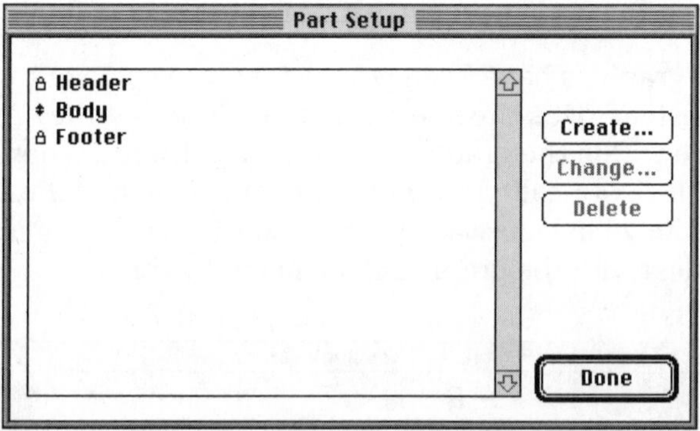

The body needs to be about 5.5 inches high. If you don't see a ruler down the left side of the layout, choose the Graphic Rulers command from the Show menu. To increase the height of the body, drag the Body part indicator (labeled with the word "Body") down until you reach the 5.5-inch mark.

Adding Graphics

Next, add the background graphics. They're stored in the file named Address Book — Graphics. Having the graphics in place enables you to more easily arrange the fields so they fit correctly. (After you begin to create your own databases, you can design your own graphics in any graphics program, buy ready-made graphics called clip art, or — if you don't intend to resell or distribute the databases — you can copy graphics from files that you obtain from user groups and online information services.)

Follow these steps to transfer graphics from Address Book — Graphics to Address Book — Working Copy (or whatever you named the database you are creating):

1. If your copy of the Address Book — Working Copy database isn't already open, choose Open from the File menu, choose the Address Book — Working Copy database, and click Open.
2. Switch to Layout mode by choosing Layout from the Mode menu.
3. Open the database that contains the graphics by choosing Open from the File menu and then selecting the Address Book — Graphics file.
4. Switch to Layout mode by choosing Layout from the Mode menu.

   Note that because the database opens in Browse mode, you can see the graphics when you open the file, but you can't select them. You have to be in Layout mode to copy or otherwise manipulate elements in a layout.

5. In Address Book — Graphics, click to select the graphics.

   Because the graphics have been *grouped* (so you can work with them as a single unit instead of as the mass of little images that they really are), clicking anywhere within the graphics selects everything. (When an object is selected, a black dot called a *handle* appears at each of the object's four corners, as shown in Figure 4-9.) Later you will use the Ungroup command so you can deal with the graphic elements individually.

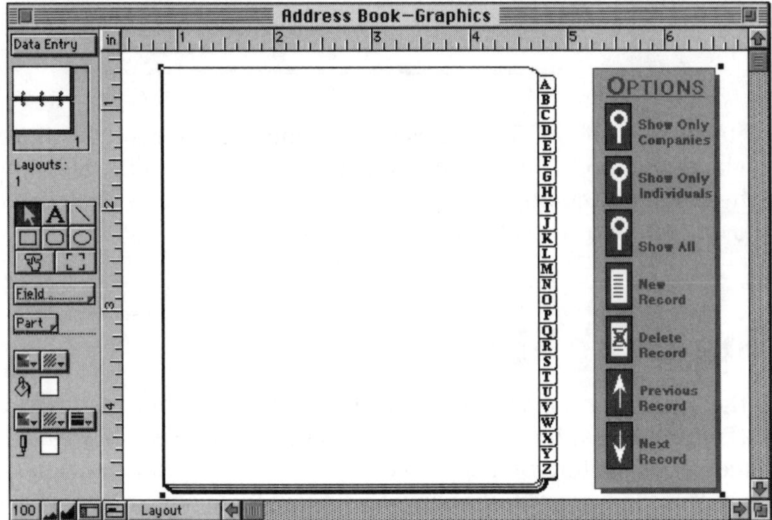

Figure 4-9: The Address Book — Graphics database

6. If drag and drop are enabled on your Macintosh, drag the graphics into the current layout in Address Book — Working Copy.

   A copy of the graphics is transferred. Now close Address Book — Graphics by choosing Close from the File menu, and go to step 9.

— or —

6. Choose Copy from the Edit menu (or press ⌘-C).

   A copy of the graphics is stored in memory (in the Macintosh Clipboard).

7. Choose Close from the File menu (to close Address Book — Graphics).

8. Choose Paste from the Edit menu (or press ⌘-V).

   The graphics are pasted onto the layout in Address Book — Working Copy.

9. Because you want the graphics to appear behind the data fields instead of obscuring them, choose Send to Back from the Arrange menu (or press Shift-⌘-Option-J).

10. Drag the graphics so they approximately match the placement shown in Figure 4-10.

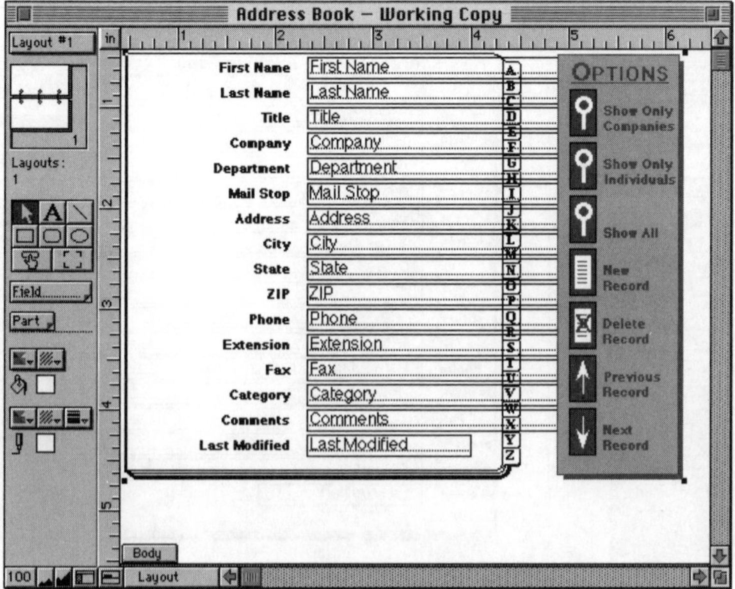

Figure 4-10: Address Book — Working Copy, with the graphics in place

Setting Field Attributes

Instead of immediately moving the fields and labels to their final resting place on the layout, we'll use the initial stacked format to select the fields and assign text attributes (font, size, style, alignment, and color) and field borders to them, as described in the following sections.

Text Attributes

All the field labels are displayed in the finished database with the same font and format, so start by selecting them. To select multiple objects, first select the Pointer tool by clicking its icon in the Tools palette. Then do either of the following:

- Drag a selection rectangle that completely surrounds the objects of interest.
- Hold down the Shift key and click every object that you want to include in the selection.

You can also combine the two approaches. In this case, though, because the field labels are all stacked in a nice, neat column, the first approach is simplest. The selected labels should look like the ones in Figure 4-11.

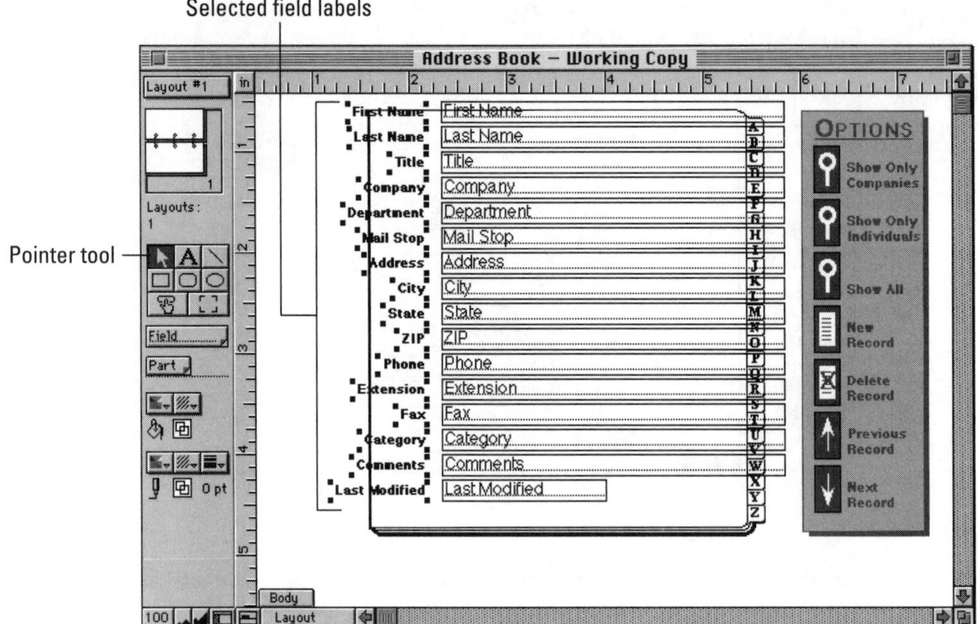

Figure 4-11: Selecting the field labels

Another way to select multiple items on a layout is to hold down the ⌘ key as you drag the selection rectangle. Rather than having to *surround* the objects you're selecting, it's sufficient to merely *touch* them with the selection rectangle.

The format for each of the field labels is left-aligned, 9-point Helvetica, with small caps. With the field labels still selected, choose the following commands from the appropriate submenus of the Format menu:

- Choose Helvetica from the Font submenu. (If Helvetica does not appear as a choice in the Font submenu, choose another font.)
- Choose 9 from the Size submenu.
- Choose Bold or Plain Text from the Style submenu. (Either command will remove the boldface that was assigned by default to the field labels.)
- Choose Small Caps from the Style submenu.
- Choose Left and Top from the Align Text submenu.

Next, format the fields. In the layout, each field appears as a rectangle surrounding a field name. As you apply different formatting attributes to a field, the formatting of the field name automatically changes to reflect the new attributes.

Select individual fields or groups of fields as described in Table 4-2 and apply the designated formats. Each column in the table corresponds to a text attribute command in the Format menu. Working with a single row of the table at a time is easiest.

Table 4-2
Field Text Attributes

Field Name(s)	*Font*	*Size*	*Style*	*Align Text*	*Text Color*
First Name, Last Name, Title, Company, Phone, Extension	Palatino	12	Bold	Left, Top	Dark blue
Department, Mail Stop, Address, City, State, ZIP, Fax	Palatino	12	Plain	Left, Top	Black
Category	Palatino	12	Plain	Center, Top	Faint blue
Comments	Palatino	10	Plain	Left, Top	Black
Last Modified	Helvetica	10	Plain	Right, Top	Black

Showing you which colors to use for the field text is easier than making you guess. Figures 4-12 and 4-13 illustrate the process of picking a text color, as well as the specific colors that you should choose.

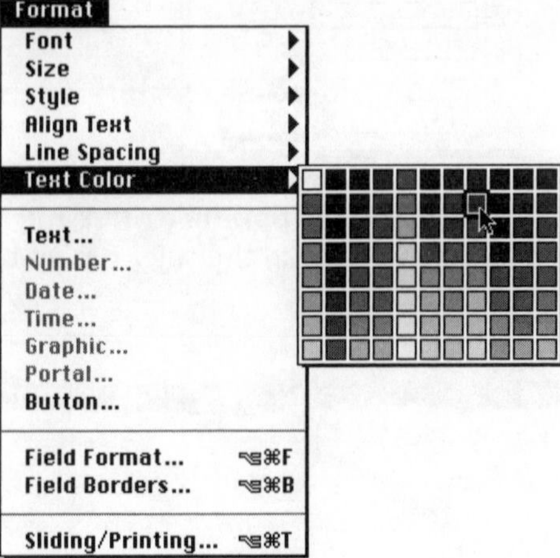

Figure 4-12: Select this color for the First Name, Last Name, Title, Company, Phone, and Extension fields.

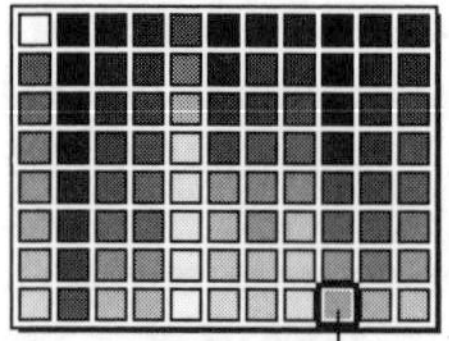

Figure 4-13: Select this color for the Category field.

Simultaneously Choosing Several Text Format Options

Try the following shortcut when making multiple Format menu selections: After you select each field or group of fields, choose Text from the Format menu. In the Text Format dialog box that appears (see the accompanying figure), you can simultaneously set all the text formats for the selected fields.

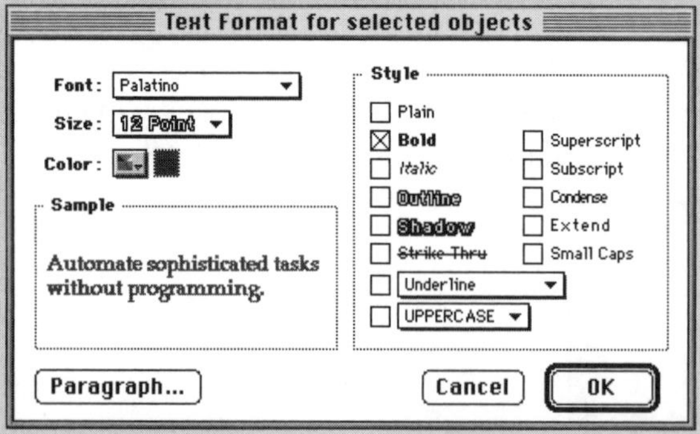

You may also find it helpful to use the pop-up menus and icons on the text ruler bar to select formatting options. To make the ruler bar visible, choose Text Ruler from the Show menu.

Field Borders

If you take another peek at the finished version of Address Book shown in Figure 4-1, you'll note that many fields have a dotted line as a bottom border. Although FileMaker Pro does not have a specific feature for creating dotted lines, you can use the trick described in the following steps:

1. Select all fields except Category, Comments, and Last Modified. (Be sure to select only the fields — *not* the field labels.)
2. Choose Field Borders from the Format menu.

   The "Field Borders for selected objects" dialog box appears, as shown in Figure 4-14.

Figure 4-14: Selecting a pattern for a bottom border

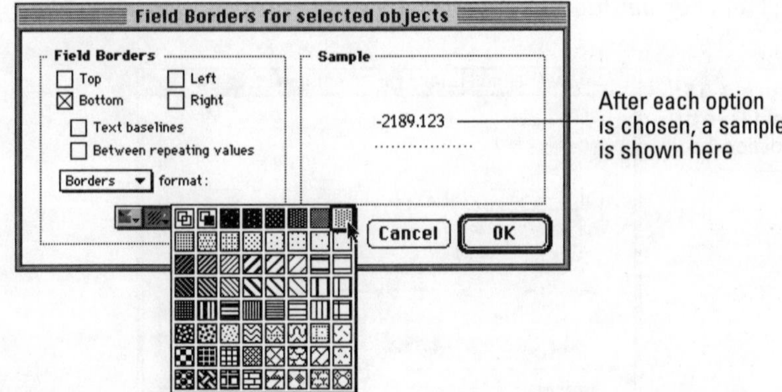

3. Click the Bottom check box.
4. At the bottom of the dialog box, click the pattern pop-up menu (the second icon from the left) and choose the pattern shown on the right side of the pop-up menu in Figure 4-14.

   You'll note that as you are choosing the new pattern, the previous pattern (the solid fill on the left side of the pattern pop-up menu) is still selected. When you release the mouse button, a sample showing the dotted-line pattern appears in the Sample box — replacing the former pattern (a solid line, in this instance).
5. Click OK.

   The new border settings are accepted, and the dialog box closes.

To ensure that the Comments field is always visible, we will surround it with a border. To create the border, switch to Layout mode and select the Comments field; choose Field Borders from the Format menu; place a check mark in the Top, Bottom, Left, and Right check boxes of the Field Borders dialog box; and click OK.

Field Formats

The Format menu has a few commands that you haven't used in the Address Book database. The final option that you are going to use is the Field Format command. You use it in this database to make the Comments field into a scrolling text window. This feature is particularly useful when you want to store a lot of text in a relatively small area on a layout.

Follow these steps to create a scrolling text window for the Comments field:

1. Select the field on the layout (in this case, the Comments field).
2. Choose Field Format from the Format menu.

   The Field Format for "Comments" dialog box appears, as shown in Figure 4-15.

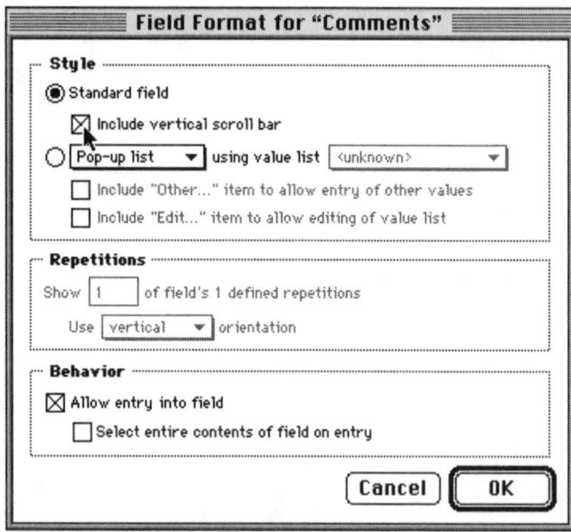

Figure 4-15: The Field Format dialog box

3. Be sure that the "Standard field" radio button at the top of the dialog box is selected and then click the check box labeled "Include vertical scroll bar."
4. Click OK.

   The dialog box closes, and a vertical scroll bar is added to the right side of the Comments field.

Setting Field Dimensions and Placement

The last two major field-arrangement tasks are resizing the fields and placing them in their proper places on the layout. You can alter the size of fields, field labels, and graphics objects on a layout in two ways:

- Manually — by selecting an object and dragging one of its handles in the appropriate direction
- Precisely — by entering one or more dimensions in the Size windoid

A *windoid* is a tiny, special-purpose window provided by many programs to display options that you need to use frequently, such as color, pattern, and other palettes. Windoids float freely on-screen and can be moved (by dragging the title bar) or closed (by clicking the close box) whenever you wish. Windoids have a look that immediately distinguishes them from normal windows.

To see the tiny Size windoid (see Figure 4-16), choose Size from the Show menu.

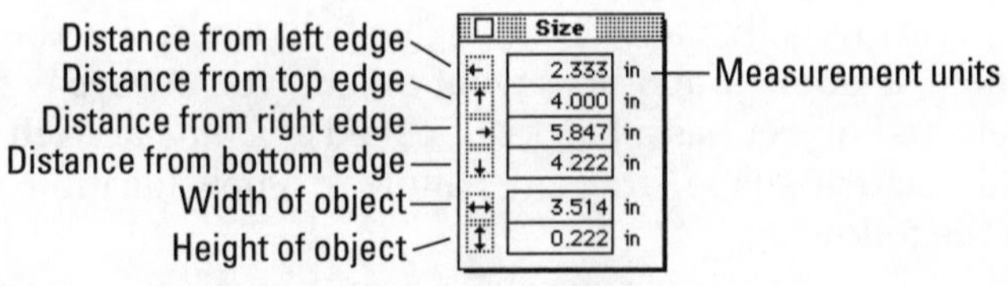

Figure 4-16: The Size windoid enables you to see and change the dimensions and location of any selected object.

Because your task in this tutorial is to *duplicate* the layout shown in Figure 4-1 — rather than make a rough approximation of it — you can use the Size windoid to avoid all the manual dragging and resizing. However, because most of the databases that you'll design from scratch won't have a template that you're attempting to match, you also need to explore the manual method.

Manually Sizing and Placing Objects on the Layout

So that you'll have some fields with which to work, start by selecting the following fields and their field labels: First Name, Last Name, and Title. Choose Duplicate from the Edit menu. (Duplicate is a shortcut for the normal Copy and Paste procedure.) Duplicates of these fields and labels appear on the layout. With these objects still selected, drag them to the right until they cross the vertical dashed line that marks the page break. Moving the objects to this area gives you plenty of room to experiment without fear of disturbing the "real" fields, labels, and graphics.

When you finish trying out the manual sizing and placement procedures, be sure to select the duplicate fields and labels that you created and remove them by pressing the Delete key.

Before modifying any of the duplicate objects, you may want to turn on some of the helpful tools in the Show and Arrange menus. For example, the AutoGrid command (in the Arrange menu) simplifies creating equal-sized fields and arranging them in a uniform manner by restricting field movements and adjustments to those that coincide with grid coordinates. The T-Squares tool (in the Show menu) can help you make sure that fields are properly aligned with one another — in straight rows and columns. You may also want to choose Text Boundaries from the Show menu. This command places a bounding box around every field label and text object on the layout and enables you to more easily determine visually whether these objects are correctly positioned and in alignment with other objects. Finally, the graphic rulers (choose Graphic Rulers from the Show menu) are an enormous help when placing and aligning objects. As you drag any object, its exact position is shown on the horizontal and vertical rulers.

Next you can experiment with manually changing field sizes. Whether you're working with a field, a label, or another layout object, you always begin by selecting the object. (A selected object has a black dot called a *handle* at each of its corners.) To change a field's size or shape, drag any handle to a new location. Dragging options include the following:

- *Dragging:* The normal dragging procedure enables you to change the height, width, or both dimensions as you drag. (If the AutoGrid feature is on and you're reasonably careful, it is fairly easy to make sure that only one dimension changes.)
- *Shift-dragging:* If you press the Shift key as you drag, you restrict size changes to one dimension — horizontal or vertical. When you want to keep all text fields the same height, for example, this technique is ideal for ensuring that only the field's width changes.
- *Option-dragging:* Depending on the shape of the object you're resizing, pressing the Option key as you drag restricts the object's final shape to a square, a square with rounded corners, or a circle.

Manually *placing* an object is also a simple task. Click anywhere within the center of the object and drag it to a new spot on the layout. As you drag, FileMaker Pro displays an outline of the object so that you can easily see the object's precise location before you release the mouse button.

You can "nudge" any selected field, label, or other object slightly by pressing any arrow key. This technique works even when the AutoGrid command is in effect.

After resizing and rearranging the fields and labels, you may also want to try out FileMaker Pro's alignment commands. To keep things nice and uniform, you can use Align and Set Alignment to align the edges of any group of fields or to align fields and their labels, for example. These commands are especially helpful when you have nudged several objects with the arrow keys or have been aligning objects by using the "eyeball method" — as in: "Hmm . . . Looks like the First Name and Last Name fields are lined up now."

The following steps describe how to align selected objects:

1. Select the objects that you want to align with each other by selecting the Pointer tool and then drawing a selection rectangle around the objects, Shift-clicking the objects, or using a combination of the two selection methods.
2. Choose Set Alignment from the Arrange menu.

   The Set Alignment dialog box appears, as shown in Figure 4-17.

Figure 4-17: The Set Alignment dialog box

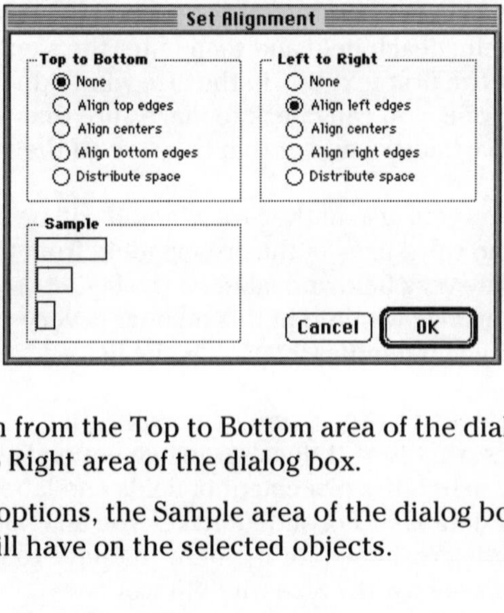

3. Select an option from the Top to Bottom area of the dialog box and an option from the Left to Right area of the dialog box.

   As you choose options, the Sample area of the dialog box shows what effect your choices will have on the selected objects.
4. Click OK.

   The dialog box closes, and FileMaker Pro executes the alignment options. If the result is not what you intended, you can restore the objects to their previous locations by immediately choosing Undo Align from the Edit menu (or pressing ⌘-Z).

The options that you choose in the Set Alignment dialog box remain in effect until you choose new options or until you quit the program. These options are also the ones that will be used when you choose the Align command from the Arrange menu (or press ⌘-K). Unlike the Set Alignment command, Align is immediately executed on the selected objects. No dialog box appears.

If you want to become more familiar with the process of manually sizing and placing fields, refer to Figure 4-1 and attempt to match the field widths and placements as best you can. When you're done, you can use the information in Tables 4-3 and 4-4 in the next section to see how well you have done and to correct any mistakes you have made.

Using the Size Windoid to Size and Place Layout Objects

You can use the Size windoid (shown previously in Figure 4-16) to perform the following functions:

- Determine the exact location and dimensions of any object on a layout
- Move an object to a precise location
- Change the dimensions of an object

Instead of using the Align command to arrange several fields in a perfect column, for example, you can select each field and then enter the same distance from the left edge of the page in the first text box in the Size windoid. Also, by clicking several objects one-by-one, you can check to make sure that they are all exactly the same distance from a particular edge or that they are all the same height or width.

In this tutorial, however, your use of the Size windoid will be a bit unorthodox. You combine the second and third uses of the Size windoid from the preceding list to precisely size and place every field and label on the layout — and you do both at the same time. Using the Size windoid in this manner is very much like having a robot slave who happily and mindlessly pushes the fields around the page for you.

Although this exercise doesn't have a practical application — after you start designing your own databases, that is — it does serve two important purposes. First, it enables you to quickly match the placement of fields and labels with those in the finished Address Book database. Second, it makes you an expert on using the Size windoid. When you have a real need for it, you won't have to flip through the manual or this book to see how the Size windoid works.

To resize and place the fields and labels, read the following instructions for using the Size windoid and then, using the information in Tables 4-3 and 4-4, enter the appropriate numbers in the windoid's text boxes to size and place the fields and field labels, respectively.

1. If the Size windoid is not visible, choose Size from the Show menu.

   The Size windoid appears (as previously shown in Figure 4-16). If you want to change the measurement units for the Size windoid, click one of the units to the right of any number entry in the windoid. Each mouse click chooses one of the three possible measurement units: inches, centimeters, or pixels. Note that visible text or graphics rulers will simultaneously change to reflect the chosen unit.

2. Select the object whose placement or size you want to modify.

   Handles (black dots) appear at the object's corners to show that it is selected.

3. To change the position of the selected object, type numbers into any of the top four text boxes in the Size windoid.

   In order, these boxes represent the object's distance from the left, top, right, and bottom edges of the layout area. To execute the changes, press Tab or Return to move to the next text box, press Enter to stay in the same text box, or use the mouse to click in a different text box.

   You can precisely set the location of any object by specifying any pair of vertical and horizontal figures, such as the distance from the left and distance from the top, or the distance from the right and distance from the bottom. As you make changes to the chosen pair of figures, the numbers in the other pair automatically change to reflect the object's new location.

4. To change the dimensions of the selected object, type numbers into the bottom two text boxes: width and height.

5. To execute the changes, press Tab or Return to move to the next text box, press Enter to stay in the same text box, or use the mouse to click in a different text box.

As an example of using the Size windoid, you can set the size and location of the First Name field and the other fields in the database by following these steps:

1. Using the Pointer tool, select the First Name field.
2. In the Size windoid, type the numbers shown in the First Name row of Table 4-3.

   Move from one text box to another by pressing Tab or Return or click in each box with the mouse.

3. Next, without closing the Size windoid, individually select each additional field and — one-by-one — enter the appropriate settings from Table 4-3.

Table 4-3 lists the size and placement for the fields in the Address Book database. Note that the Height dimension remains constant for most of the fields. This consistency is natural, because most fields contain data that is formatted with the same font and size.

Table 4-3
Field Size and Placement (in inches)

Field Name	*Left Edge*	*Top Edge*	*Width*	*Height*
First Name	2.472	.944	1.681	.222
Last Name	.639	.944	1.681	.222
Title	.639	1.403	3.514	.222
Company	.639	.486	2.347	.222
Department	.639	2.319	2.097	.222
Mail Stop	2.889	2.319	1.264	.222
Address	.639	2.778	3.514	.222
City	.639	3.236	1.514	.222
State	2.319	3.236	.681	.222
ZIP	3.139	3.236	1.014	.222
Phone	.639	1.861	1.097	.222
Extension	1.833	1.861	.681	.222
Fax	3.056	1.861	1.097	.222
Category	3.181	.486	.931	.222
Comments	.639	3.694	3.514	.639
Last Modified	3.472	4.375	.681	.194

Table 4-4 contains the data that you need to position all the field labels. It does not include Width and Height dimensions because every label is already the correct size. Because neither the Comments nor the Category field has a field label in the final layout, remove these two labels by selecting them and pressing Delete. Then, one-by-one, select each field label listed in Table 4-4 and enter its pair of placement figures in the Size windoid.

Table 4-4
Field Label Placement (in inches)

Field Label	*Left Edge*	*Top Edge*
First Name	2.472	1.167
Last Name	.639	1.167
Title	.639	1.625
Company	.639	.708

Field Label	Left Edge	Top Edge
Department	.639	2.542
Mail Stop	2.889	2.542
Address	.639	3.000
City	.639	3.458
State	2.319	3.458
ZIP	3.139	3.458
Phone	.639	2.083
Extension	1.833	2.083
Fax	3.056	2.083
Last Modified	2.611	4.389

Adding the Finishing Touches

In designing the data entry layout, a few small tasks remain:

- Naming the layout
- Setting the final size of the layout
- Completing the formatting of the Category field
- Ungrouping the background graphics
- Importing a phone icon (to be used as a dialing button)

Naming the Layout

Layout #1 is the default name assigned by FileMaker Pro to the first layout created for a database. Because this database will have more than one layout, giving each layout a more descriptive name is preferable. The following steps describe how to assign a name to a layout:

1. Choose Layout from the Mode menu.
2. If the database has more than one layout, switch to the layout that you want to rename by choosing its current name from the layout pop-up menu in the upper-left corner of the document window. (At this point, Address Book has only a single layout, so this step is unnecessary.)
3. Choose Layout Setup from the Mode menu.

   The Layout Setup dialog box appears (see Figure 4-18). The current name of the layout is shown in the Layout Name text box.

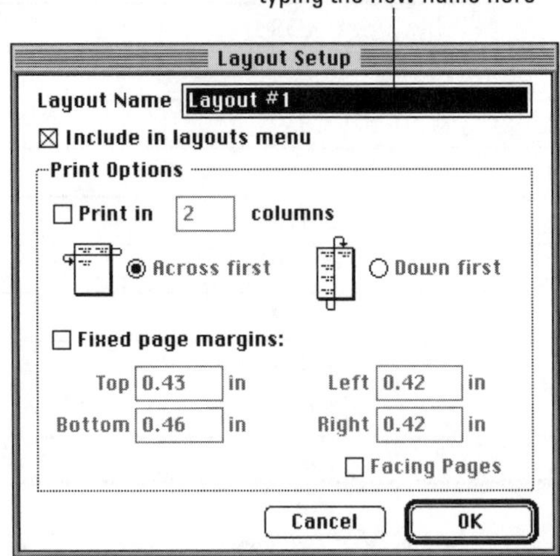

Figure 4-18: The Layout Setup dialog box

4. Type the new name for the layout and then click OK. In this example, type **Data Entry**.

You do not have to assign a name to a layout at any specific time. You can assign and change layout names whenever the mood strikes you. However, because some FileMaker Pro scripts refer to layouts by name, setting layout names early in the design process — and certainly before you begin to create any scripts — is the best method.

Setting the Final Size of the Layout

Because you will use the Data Entry layout only for data entry, and you will never use it to view more than one record at a time, the layout will look better if you eliminate all unnecessary white space that surrounds the graphics. To eliminate the unnecessary white space, do the following:

1. Change to Layout mode (choose Layout from the Mode menu or press ⌘-L).
2. Choose Select All from the Edit menu (or press ⌘-A).

   This command selects all the objects on the layout (in this case, the fields, field labels, and the background graphic).
3. Drag the objects so that their edges are closer to the top and left edges of the layout.
4. Click the Body part indicator and drag it upward to remove any unnecessary space.

5. If you like, you can drag the window's size box (in the bottom-right corner of the window) to match the size of the Data Entry layout.

   Your version of the Data Entry layout should now look similar to the one shown in Figure 4-19.

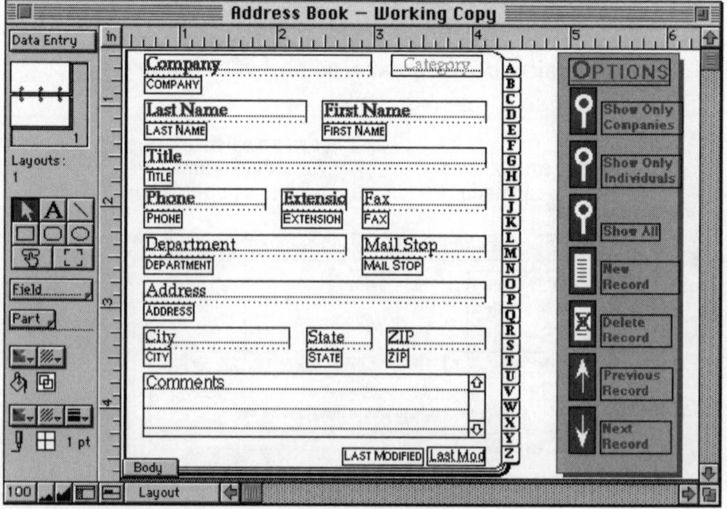

Figure 4-19: The resized Data Entry layout

Formatting the Category Field

Because the text for the Category field is set in a light-colored font, adding a fill color to the field enables you read the text easily and makes the field stand out. To add a fill color, follow these steps:

1. Switch to Layout mode (choose Layout from the Mode menu or press ⌘-L).
2. Select the Category field.
3. In the fill color pop-up palette, select the color shown in Figure 4-20.

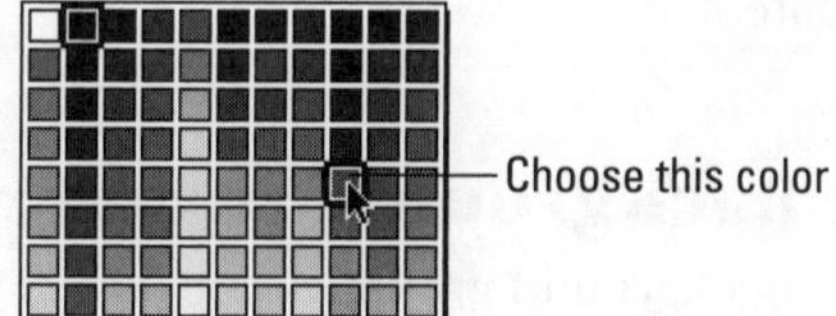

Figure 4-20: Choose this color (the one the cursor is pointing to) for the fill color.

Although we created and attached the Categories value list to this field, we have not yet specified a format for the list. FileMaker Pro can present any value list as a pop-up list, pop-up menu, check boxes, or radio buttons. For this example, we'll make it a pop-up list, as follows:

1. In Layout mode with the Category field still selected, choose Field Format from the Format menu.

   The Field Format dialog box appears, as shown in Figure 4-21.

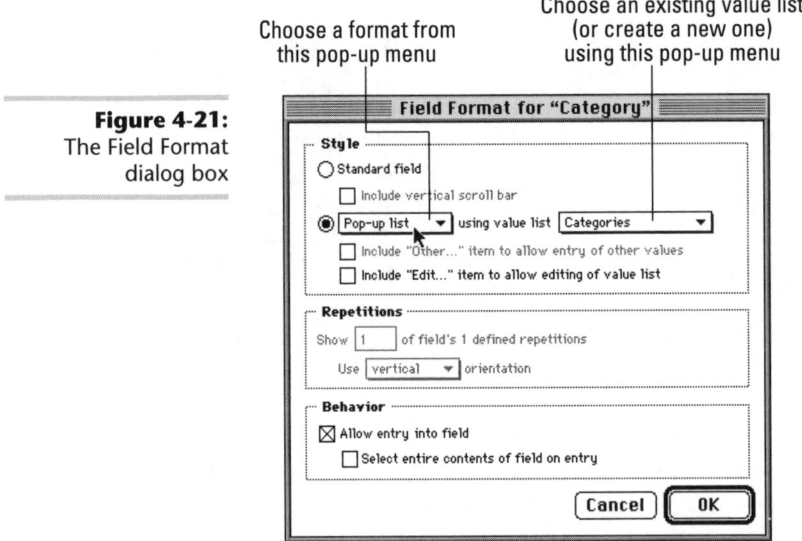

Figure 4-21: The Field Format dialog box

2. Choose "Pop-up list" from the pop-up menu in the Style section of the dialog box, and choose the Categories value list from the pop-up menu to the right.
3. Click OK to dismiss the dialog box.

Now when you switch to Browse mode and tab into the Category field, the pop-up list is automatically presented.

Ungrouping the Background Graphics

To make manipulating the background graphics safer when you were in the design phase of creating the Data Entry layout, the graphics were initially *grouped.* (To group objects, you switch to Layout mode, select the graphic elements to be grouped, and then choose the Group command from the Arrange menu). Grouping enables you to treat two or more individual graphic elements as a single entity. As a result, you can move the graphics without fear of leaving some elements behind, and you can apply a formatting command that simultaneously affects all the graphic elements in the group.

After you *ungroup* the graphics, you can treat each graphic element, such as the buttons in the control palette, individually. You can move, format, or assign a script to just one element, for example.

Follow these steps to ungroup previously grouped objects (in this case, the background graphics):

1. Change to Layout mode by choosing Layout from the Mode menu (or pressing ⌘-L).
2. Select the graphic element that you want to ungroup.

   Because all the graphics form a single group, click anywhere in the background graphic (the control palette on the right, for example). Handles appear at the corners of the graphic to show that it is selected.
3. Choose the Ungroup command from the Arrange menu (or press Shift-⌘-G).

   Every element in the selected object that was previously grouped is now displayed with its own handles, showing that it is ungrouped.

Importing an Icon for a Phone Dialing Button

One of the hot new features of FileMaker Pro 3.0 is its support for phone dialing through a modem or the computer's speaker. Rather than add an ordinary button that says "Dial" or "Phone," it's much cooler to use an icon. (You must install the contents of the enclosed *Macworld FileMaker Pro 3.0 Bible Disk* to use this feature.)

To import the phone dialing icon, follow these steps:

1. Change to Layout mode by choosing Layout from the Mode menu (or pressing ⌘-L).
2. Choose Import Picture from the Import/Export submenu of the File menu.

   A standard file dialog box appears.
3. Navigate to the drive and folder that contains the graphics file named Phone.

   You'll find Phone in the same folder as Address Book — Graphics (the file that contained the background graphics for this database).
4. Select Phone in the file list and click Open.

   A copy of the phone icon appears in the layout.
5. Drag the phone icon just to the right of the Phone field label.

   If you prefer, you can place the phone icon using the Size windoid: distance from left = 1.056 in.; distance from top = 2.083 in.

Although you will later assign scripts that interact with the Data Entry layout, the design work is now done. The layout that you just created should look very much like the one shown in Figure 4-22. For more information on designing and modifying layouts, see Chapter 6.

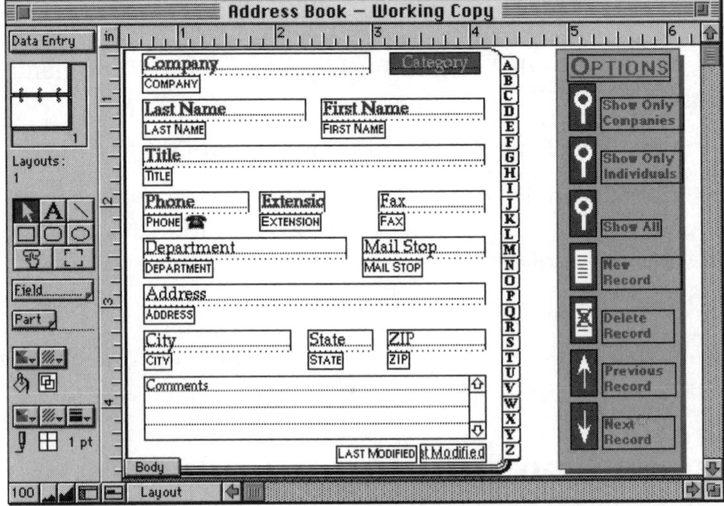

Figure 4-22: The finished Data Entry layout

Step 5: Design a Report Layout

Although the Data Entry layout is excellent for its intended purpose (entering address and contact information), most users wouldn't have much interest in using this layout to create reports.

If you're curious, open the finished Address Book database, make sure that the Data Entry layout is selected, and then choose Preview from the Select menu. Preview mode shows what you would get if you were to print the current layout. As you can see, only two records fit on a page, and the information in each record is arranged in exactly the same way as it looks when you're in Browse mode — pretty, but hardly functional.

Unless you have designed an all-purpose layout for a database, you're usually better off creating one layout for data entry and other layouts for reports. As an example of the kinds of reports that you can produce from the Address Book database, you will now create a layout for a phone directory. The Phone Directory layout is a columnar report layout. As with most such layouts, you can print reports that you generate from it or view them on the monitor. The finished layout looks like the one in Figure 4-23.

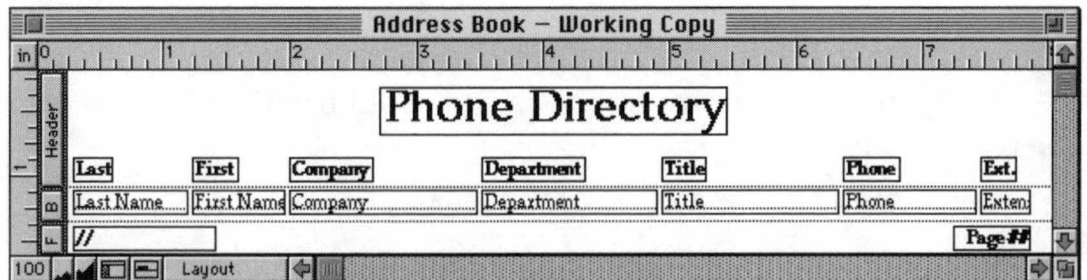

Figure 4-23: The completed Phone Directory layout

Preselecting Text Formatting Settings

Whenever you enter Layout mode and set a new font, style, color, or so on without first selecting a field or object to which the formatting will be applied, those formatting options become the new defaults. The next field, label, or object that you create will automatically use those preselected settings. Thus, you can use this trick to preselect the text formatting for the fields and save yourself the trouble of having to manually reformat each field after FileMaker Pro generates the layout. (Pressing ⌘ and clicking on a field or object also changes the default setting.)

To preselect the text formatting for the Phone Directory layout, enter Layout mode, make sure that no field or object is selected in the current layout (Data Entry), and choose the following settings in the Format menu:

- Font: Palatino
- Size: 10
- Style: Plain Text
- Align Text: Left, Top
- Text Color: Black

Finally, set the fill and pen colors in the Tools palette to white.

To create the preliminary Phone Directory layout, follow these steps:

1. Change to Layout mode by choosing Layout from the Mode menu (or pressing ⌘-L).
2. Choose New Layout from the Mode menu (or press ⌘-N).

   The New Layout dialog box appears, as shown in Figure 4-24.

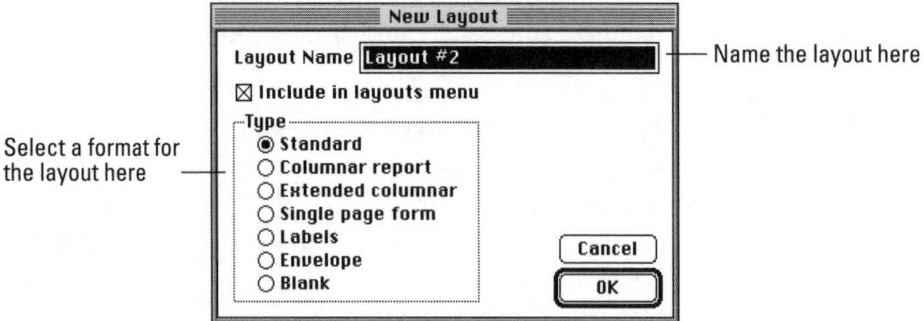

Figure 4-24: The New Layout dialog box

3. Type a name for the layout in the Layout Name text box. (In this case, type **Phone Directory**.)

   Instead of accepting the default name for the layout (Layout #2, in this example) or naming it later in the process as you did with the Data Entry layout, you can name this layout when you create it. Only the *first* layout created for a database is automatically named Layout #x.

4. Click the radio button labeled "Extended columnar."

   FileMaker Pro 3.0 can automatically generate two types of columnar reports: columnar report and extended columnar. The only difference between the two layouts is the manner in which FileMaker places the fields when it creates the layout.

   In a *columnar report* layout, the arrangement of fields will not exceed the width of a single page. If the fields don't initially fit, FileMaker automatically wraps them into as many rows as are needed. In an *extended columnar* layout, FileMaker assumes that you don't care how wide the layout is and simply arranges all the field columns in a single continuous row. Because this format is going to be the final format for the report (you'll change the size of the fields as necessary to make them fit), the extended columnar layout is the best format to choose.

5. Click OK.

FileMaker presents the Specify Field Order dialog box, as shown in Figure 4-25.

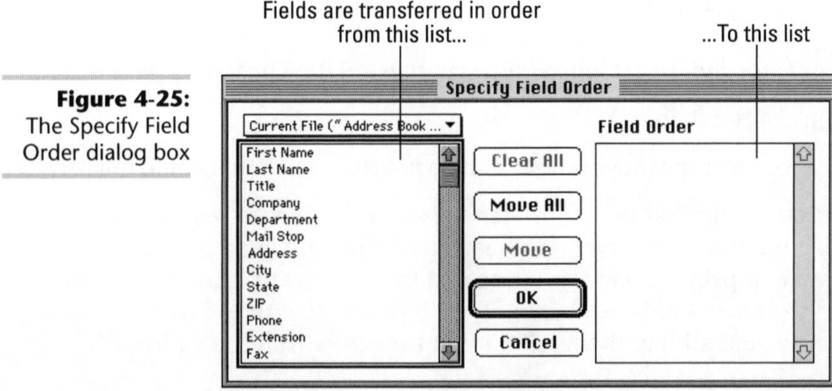

Figure 4-25: The Specify Field Order dialog box

6. Select fields in the left side of the dialog box, click Move to transfer them to the Field Order list on the right, and when you have finished, click OK.

   The Specify Field Order dialog box has two functions. You use it to select the initial set of fields that you want to appear in the layout, as well as to set the order in which the fields appear. For the Phone Directory layout, select and move the following fields (in order): Last Name, First Name, Company, Department, Title, Phone, and Extension.

   The report layout is generated, as shown in Figure 4-26.

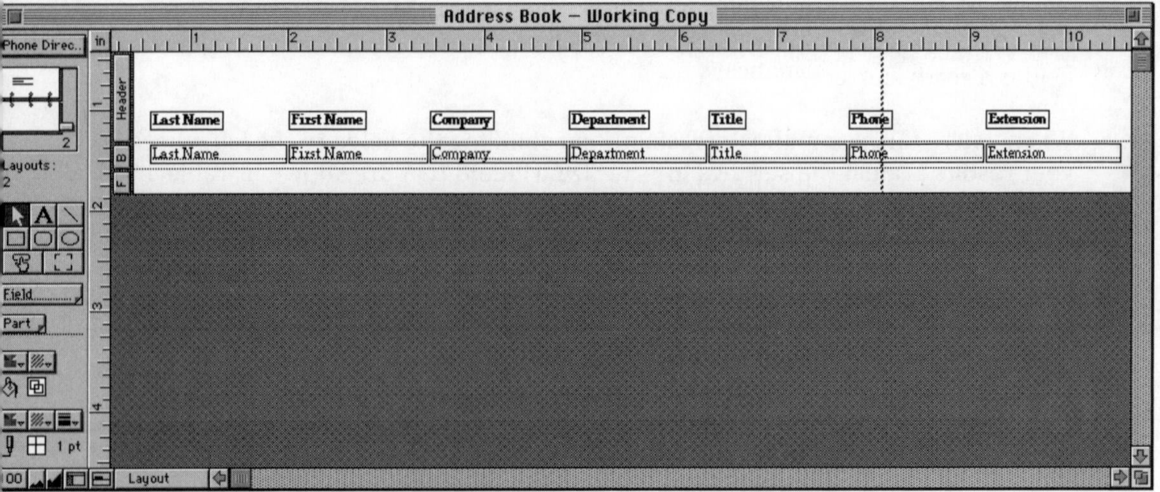

Figure 4-26: The tentative layout for the phone directory report

If you scroll the Phone Directory layout from side-to-side, you see that it extends beyond the current page width by more than two inches. Several possible solutions are available for handling this problem:

- Set the printing for *landscape mode* (sideways) using the Page Setup command.
- Remove some of the fields.
- Change the layout by reducing the size of some fields and sliding them to the left.

Although using either of the first two approaches is an easy way to resolve the width problem, assume that you have your heart set on producing a phone directory report that you can print in portrait mode and that you want it to include every one of the originally chosen fields. In this case, we'll proceed with the third option — reducing field sizes and sliding them left so that they fit within the width of a single page.

Resizing the Fields

Try using the "eyeball" (best approximation) approach to manually resize and move the fields so they fit on the layout. You can use Figure 4-23 as a rough guideline to how wide the fields should be. (Unless you're feeling adventuresome, though, leave the column headings and field labels where they are. In the next section, you'll learn an easy way to move them.)

When you alter the width of each field, hold down the Shift key as you drag. Doing so assures that only one dimension of the field will change — the width, in this case. Because you pre-specified the font to be used in every field, the *height* of each field is already correct.

When you're through manually resizing and shuffling the fields to the left, check your results against the settings for the Size windoid that are shown in Table 4-5. Please note that no settings are right or wrong. As long as you have left sufficient room for each field to display its intended contents, the layout is fine. However, if the data from any record doesn't fit within a field's new dimensions (the database may contain an extra-long company name, for example), the extra characters will be *truncated* (chopped off) when the report is printed. When setting field widths, err on the plus side if possible.

As before, to examine or alter the dimensions or placement of any field, select the field on the layout and then check its size and location in the Size windoid.

Table 4-5
Field Dimensions (in inches)

Field Name	*Distance from Left Edge*	*Field Width*
Last Name	.458	.917
First Name	1.403	.736
Company	2.167	1.486
Department	3.681	1.403
Title	5.111	1.403
Phone	6.542	1.069
Extension	7.639	.403

Formatting the Header

In a columnar report, the field labels for the columns are normally placed in the header layout part rather than in the body layout part. That way, when you scroll the report on-screen or print it, you can be assured that the column headers (the field labels) are always visible. To format the field labels, you need to do the following:

- Move the field labels downward, placing them closer to the body of the report (because I think they look better that way)
- Align each field label with its matching field

To move the field labels closer to the body, drag a selection rectangle around all of them and then press the down arrow key five or six times. This technique moves all the field labels exactly the same distance.

To align each label with its matching field, follow these steps:

1. Select a field and its matching label by Shift-clicking the two elements.
2. Choose Set Alignment from the Arrange menu.
3. Set options in the Set Alignment dialog box, as shown in Figure 4-27. (In the Top to Bottom area, choose None; in the Left to Right area, choose Align left edges.)

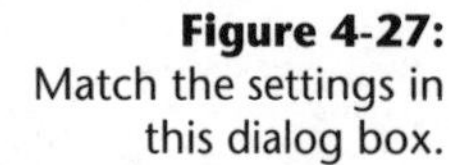

Figure 4-27: Match the settings in this dialog box.

4. Click OK.

   The dialog box closes, and the two fields are aligned.

After you set the proper alignment options, you can quickly align the remaining fields and labels by selecting each pair and pressing ⌘-K (the keyboard shortcut for the Align command).

The labels now have only one thing wrong with them: some of them are too long or too close to the next label. Select the Text tool (the uppercase *A*) from the Tools palette and change the wording of the three labels that are too long:

- Change Last Name to Last
- Change First Name to First
- Change Extension to Ext.

Finally, the report could use a label of its own — a title, that is. Select the Text tool again, click near the top center of the header part, and type **Phone Directory**. Then select the Pointer tool, click the Phone Directory text to select it, and — using commands in the Format menu — set the text to 24-point Palatino Bold. As the last step, drag the text and place it near the top center of the header.

Formatting the Footer

Like every other layout generated by FileMaker Pro, this one already has space reserved for a footer. Although the Data Entry layout doesn't need a footer, footers are often useful in report layouts, such as Phone Directory. They can be used to present any information that you want to see on every page, such as the page number, date, name of the database, or name of the user who created the report. To complete the Phone Directory layout, you will add a date-stamp and a page number placeholder to the footer.

To add the date-stamp, choose Date Symbol from the Paste Special submenu of the Edit menu. The date symbol, a pair of slashes (//), appears in the layout. Select the Pointer tool and drag the date symbol to the left edge of the layout inside the footer area, moving it directly under the Last Name field. Widen it to ensure that there's sufficient room to display a complete date.

To add automatic page-numbering to the footer, select the Text tool and type **Page** followed by a space somewhere in the footer. Then choose Page Number from the Paste Special submenu of the Edit menu. The page number symbol, a pair of pound signs (##), appears at the end of the text string. Using the Pointer tool, drag the Page text to the right edge of the layout. To make sure that the page numbers never get clipped on the right-hand side, set a new alignment for the Page text by choosing Right from the Align Text submenu of the Format menu.

Finally, to make the information in the footer stand out from the body of the report, we'll display it all in boldface. If the footer items aren't already formatted with boldface, use the Pointer tool to select all footer elements and press Shift-⌘-B (the keyboard shortcut for making text boldface). When you print the Phone Directory layout or view it in Preview mode, the date and page number symbols will automatically be replaced by the current date and the appropriate page numbers.

For more information on working with layout parts, see Chapter 6.

Step 6: Create the Scripts

Strictly speaking, you could quit right here and still have an extremely functional database. But by adding scripts that automate many of the database operations, you can transform this functional database into an easy-to-use, time-conserving database. Carefully chosen scripts can eliminate an enormous amount of wasted effort. What's the point of constantly re-creating a particular find request or set of sort instructions, for example, when all you have to do is design a small script that performs these actions at the touch of a button?

Because the term *script* smacks of programming, many users shy away from the ScriptMaker feature. The simple but powerful scripts presented in this section show you what you have been missing and demonstrate just how easy ScriptMaker is to use. And no programming is required!

Address Book uses scripts in two ways: some are assigned to buttons, and others are available only as commands in the Script menu. Furthermore, some of the scripts contain several steps, and some execute only a single command. By looking at the ways in which scripts are incorporated into this database, you can get a good idea of the kinds of things that you can do with scripts in your own databases.

Revealing a Script's Sort and Find Instructions

You can easily reveal the sort and find instructions that are used in scripts contained in other people's databases. Perform the script and then immediately choose the Sort (⌘-S) and Modify Last Find (⌘-R) commands.

When you are examining the sort and find requests, *performing* the sort or find isn't necessary or desirable. You simply use these commands to determine what options the creator of the database set for the scripts. You can exit the Sort dialog box by clicking Done and exit the find request by choosing Browse mode from the Mode menu (or by pressing ⌘-B).

The Script Definition Process

When creating a script, the first step is to use menu commands to perform all the actions that the script will eventually handle. Doing so "sets up" the database so that all necessary command options are already selected. That is, while you are executing the steps that you intend to include in the script, you set, for example, the correct Sort, Find, Page Setup, Print, Export, and Import options. Setting these options is essential because you cannot specify sort fields, find logic, print options, or settings for other commands as you create the script. In fact, the following methods are the *only* ones that you can use to set options for commands used in scripts:

- Instruct the script to present a dialog box that enables the user to verify the settings or enter different ones.
- Instruct the script to use the command settings that were in effect at the moment when the script was created.

If you are creating a generic sort, find, or export script, the first approach works well. Each time the script step is executed, the user can enter the appropriate settings in the dialog box that appears.

In many cases, though, you want scripts to perform steps that have preset options. For example, you may create a script that switches to a particular layout, finds only the records of employees who have arrived late for work more than three times in the last month, sorts the found records by salary, sets printing for landscape mode, and then prints the resulting report. Although you can instruct FileMaker Pro to present a dialog box for each of the last four actions (Find, Sort, Page Setup, and Print), doing so is a waste of time. Because you intend to use the same options every time you execute this script, incorporating the command options within the steps of the script is much simpler. Doing so adds consistency to the script's performance, and it ensures that no matter who runs the script (such as a temporary worker or an assistant who is sitting in for you), the result will always be the same.

After creating the necessary scripts in the following sections, you'll assign some of the scripts to the buttons in the background graphics. Other scripts will be available only as commands in the Script menu.

The Address Book Scripts

Address Book contains 10 scripts. Some are attached to buttons, others appear in the Script menu, and one is a special-purpose script that is used only as a step in another script. Each script is described in detail in the pages that follow. The first script, Show Companies, contains a complete walk-through of the script creation process. After creating the Show Companies script, you should have little difficulty creating the other scripts.

Before you start creating scripts, spend a few minutes entering some sample records for the database. You can more easily determine whether your scripts are working correctly if you have records in the database. (To create a new record, enter Browse mode and choose New Record from the Mode menu.) Be sure that your records contain a sample of all three Categories (Business, Friend, and Relative) and that some records include a Company name and some do not. When you're ready to use your own data with the copy of Address Book that you have created (or with the finished template that's on the *Macworld FileMaker Pro 3.0 Bible Disk*), you can delete the dummy records.

The Show Companies Script

This script limits visible records to those that have an entry in the Company field. Because FileMaker Pro does not have a Find symbol that enables you to search for a field that is not empty, the find request has to do things the hard way. That is, it checks to see whether the Company field is blank and then omits all such records. The result is that only records that contain something in the Company field are displayed.

We are interested in looking at records sorted by company, so Company is selected as the first sort field. Because you may have several records for the same company, the records are further sorted by Last Name. Thus, all the personnel from a particular company will be listed in alphabetical order according to last names.

Follow these steps to create a script that sorts records by companies and last names:

1. If the Data Entry layout isn't currently displayed, choose Data Entry from the layout pop-up menu in the upper-left corner of the document window.
2. Choose Find from the Mode menu (or press ⌘-F).

   A find request form appears, as shown in Figure 4-28.

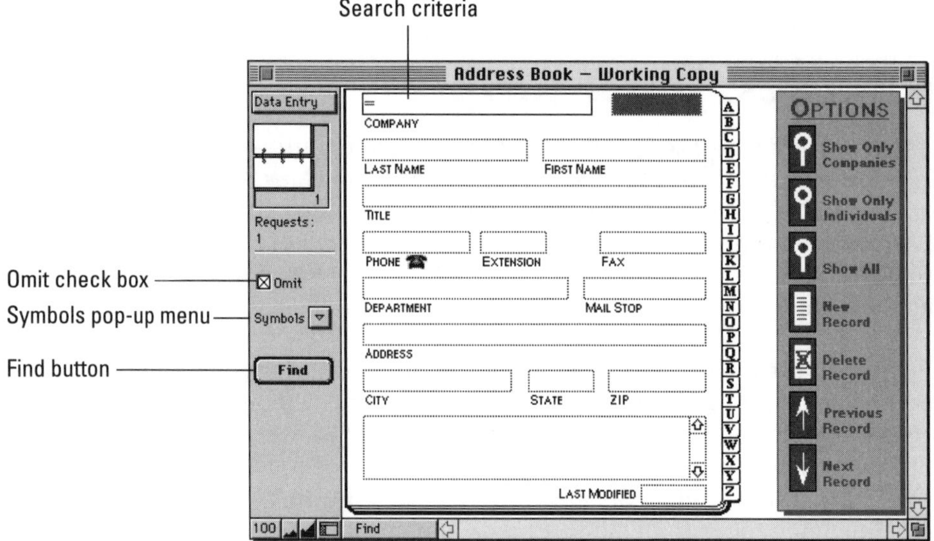

Figure 4-28: A find request form

3. Enter an equal sign (=) in the Company field, as shown in the figure, and click the Omit check box.

   The equal sign stands for "exact match." No characters follow the equal sign, so you are looking for records that contain nothing in the Company field (that is, records in which this field is blank). You can type the equal sign or choose it from the Symbols pop-up menu.

4. Click Find.

   The search executes.

5. Choose Sort from the Mode menu (or press ⌘-S).

   The Sort Records dialog box appears, as shown in Figure 4-29.

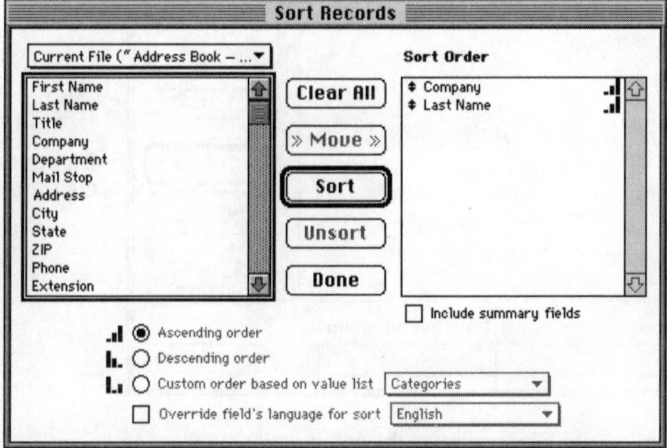

Figure 4-29: The Sort Records dialog box

6. In the field list, choose Company as the first sort field and then click Move to add the field to the Sort Order list.

7. Choose Last Name as the second sort field and then click Move to add the field to the Sort Order list.

8. Click Sort.

   The database is sorted by the two fields.

   You have completed the preparatory steps for creating the Show Companies script. Next, you build the actual script.

9. Choose ScriptMaker from the Script menu.

   The Define Scripts dialog box appears, as shown in Figure 4-30.

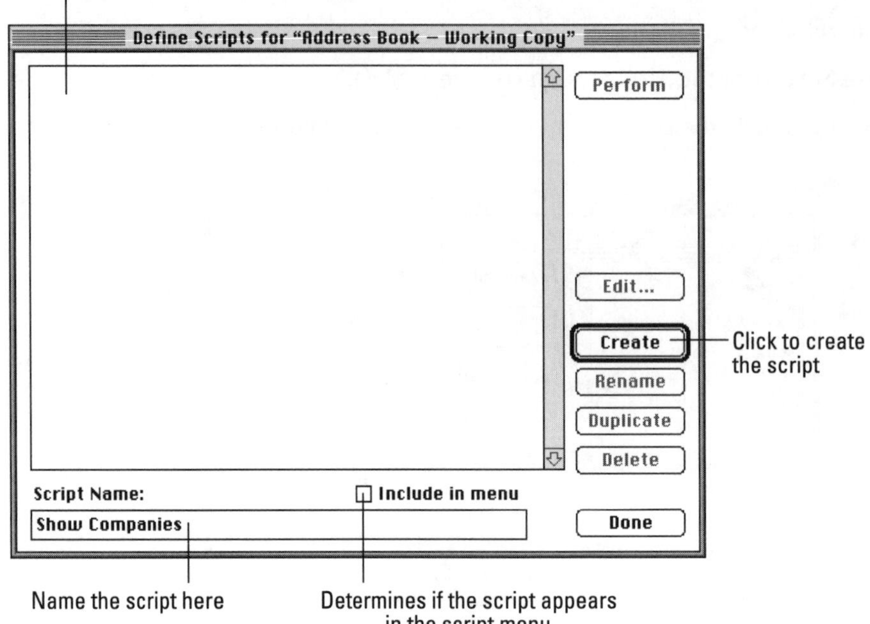

Figure 4-30: To create a new script, enter a name for it in the Define Scripts dialog box and then click Create.

10. Type **Show Companies** in the Script Name text box, click the check box labeled "Include in menu" to remove the check mark, and then click Create.

Because this script will be attached to a button, there is no need to also list it in the Script menu.

The Script Definition dialog box appears, as shown in Figure 4-31, listing FileMaker Pro's best guess at the steps that will be needed.

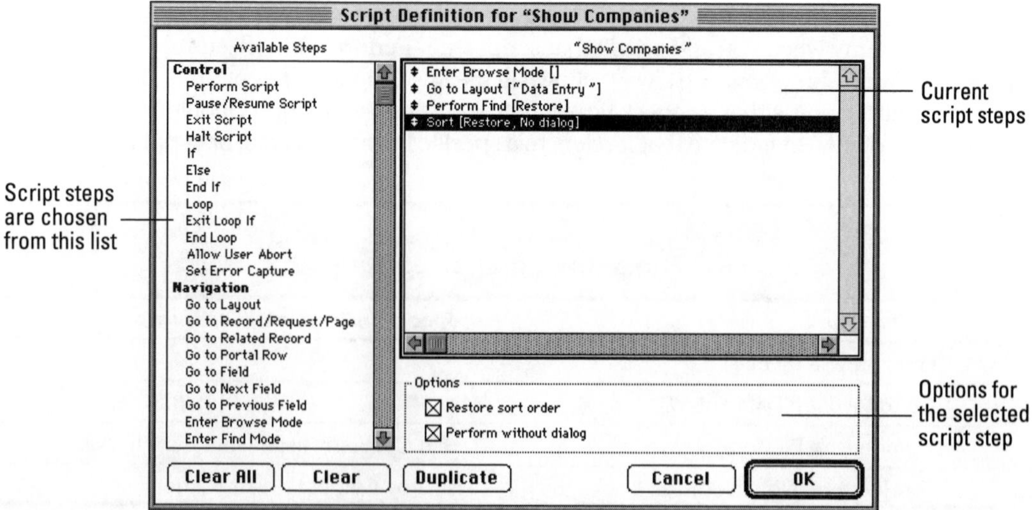

Figure 4-31: The Script Definition dialog box

11. In the list of included script steps (on the right side of the dialog box), select the Page Setup step and then click the Clear button to remove this step.
12. Select the Print step from the list of included steps and click the Clear button to remove this step.

Because this script has nothing to do with printing, you can eliminate both the Page Setup step and Print steps. Although the Page Setup step can affect the on-screen and printed appearance of the layout, this database is always used with the standard portrait-mode Page Setup options. Because you are not going to change the Page Setup, you do not need to restore these settings each time you execute the script.

13. Click OK to accept the script definition.
14. When the Define Scripts dialog box reappears, click Done to return to the database.

Table 4-6 shows the final steps in the Show Companies script. Details for some of the steps are listed in the second column (Special Instructions/Comments). You will create the remaining scripts for the database by following the instructions presented in the explanatory text and the tables.

Any text in brackets that is shown as part of a script step is an option that you specify when you add or edit that script step (Perform Find [Restore], for example.) Available options are always shown in the lower-right corner of the Script Definition dialog box, either as check boxes, buttons, or pop-up menus. Quotation marks around text indicate that it refers to a specific layout, file, field, or script name.

Table 4-6
The Show Companies Script

Script Step	*Special Instructions/Comments*
Enter Browse Mode []	
Go to Layout ["Data Entry"]	
Perform Find [Restore]	= in Company field; Omit box checked
Sort [Restore, No dialog]	Sort by Company, Last Name

Script steps can be reordered, if necessary. To change the position of any step, move the mouse pointer into the list of currently selected steps. As the pointer passes over the double-arrow symbol at the beginning of any step, the pointer changes to a larger version of the double-arrow symbol. Click to select the step, and then drag it up or down in the steps list. When you release the mouse button, the step is fixed in its new position in the list.

The Show Individuals Script

Table 4-7 shows the steps in the Show Individuals script. The find request in this script is very straightforward, particularly when you compare it to the find request used in the Show Companies script. To find records of *individuals* (records that have no entry in the Company field), you search for Company fields that are empty (=).

Table 4-7
The Show Individuals Script

Script Step	*Special Instructions/Comments*
Enter Browse Mode []	
Go to Layout ["Data Entry"]	
Perform Find [Restore]	= in Company field
Sort [Restore, No dialog]	Sort by Last Name

Sorting is done by the Last Name field only. Because these records are for people who have no company affiliation, sorting by company is pointless. If you expect that the database will contain records for several individuals who share the same last name, you can modify the Sort request by adding First Name as a second sort field.

The Show All Script

Table 4-8 shows the steps in the Show All script. The purpose of this script is to make all of the records visible (the same as issuing a Find All command) and then sort them by Company and Last Name. Note that the Find All command does not use a Find layout to perform a search. Choosing the Modify Last Find command will *not* display instructions relevant to a Find All command. Instead, Modify Last Find shows the most recent *regular* find request performed for the database — which has absolutely nothing to do with the Find All command.

Table 4-8
The Show All Script

Script Step	*Special Instructions/Comments*
Enter Browse Mode []	
Go to Layout ["Data Entry"]	
Find All	
Sort [Restore, No dialog]	Sort by Company, Last Name

The Find Businesses Script

Table 4-9 shows the steps in the Find Businesses script. This script finds all records for which you have chosen Business in the Category field pop-up menu. Although the Find Businesses script serves a purpose similar to that of the Show Companies script, it finds all records that you have identified as being a business, rather than relying on the contents of the Company field. Many self-employed people, for example, operate a business out of their home but have no company name. Similarly, you may also have records that list home addresses of your business contacts. (Although the records may not contain a company name, you still consider them business contacts.) The Find Businesses script will locate all of these records.

Table 4-9
The Find Businesses Script

Script Step	*Special Instructions/Comments*
Enter Browse Mode []	
Go to Layout ["Data Entry"]	
Perform Find [Restore]	"Business" in Category field
Sort [Restore, No dialog]	Sort by Company, Last Name

The found records are sorted by the Company field and then by the Last Name field. Because your business contacts may or may not have a company name, also sorting them by company is important. Records without a company name (the Company field is blank) will appear first in the sorted database.

You can later execute this script by selecting it from the Script menu. To do so, the script must have the "Include in menu" option associated with it in the Define Scripts dialog box. (Make sure that this option is set when defining the script.) Because this script is the first one added to the Script menu, FileMaker Pro assigns it a keyboard shortcut of ⌘-1.

The Find Friends Script

Table 4-10 shows the steps for the Find Friends script. This script finds all records for which you have chosen Friend in the Category field pop-up menu. The found records are sorted by last name only. Although you can also sort by company name, you have identified the individuals in these records as being personal friends rather than business contacts, so you'll be able to locate them more easily if they're alphabetized by last name rather than by company.

Table 4-10
The Find Friends Script

Script Step	*Special Instructions/Comments*
Enter Browse Mode []	
Go to Layout ["Data Entry"]	
Perform Find [Restore]	"Friend" in Category field
Sort [Restore, No dialog]	Sort by Last Name

You can later execute this script by choosing it from the Script menu (place a check mark in the check box labeled "Include in menu" in the Define scripts dialog box), and you can execute it by pressing ⌘-2.

The Find Relatives Script

Table 4-11 shows the steps for the Find Relatives script. This script works exactly like the Find Friends script described in the preceding section, but it finds only the records for which you have chosen Relative in the Category field pop-up menu. The found records are sorted by last name only.

Table 4-11
The Find Relatives Script

Script Step	*Special Instructions/Comments*
Enter Browse Mode []	
Go to Layout ["Data Entry"]	
Perform Find [Restore]	"Relative" in Category field
Sort [Restore, No dialog]	Sort by Last Name

You can later execute this script by choosing it from the Script menu (place a check mark in the check box labeled "Include in menu" in the Define scripts dialog box), and you can execute it by pressing ⌘-3.

The Sort by Company, Last Name Script

This utility script performs just one action: sorting the database by company and last name. Its only purpose is to be part of the Phone Directory (by Last Name) script that is described in the next section. (A script that is executed by another script is known as a *sub-script*). Thus, you will neither assign it to a button nor place it in the Script menu.

Follow these steps to create the script that will sort the database by the Company and Last Name fields:

1. Perform a sort, using Company and Last Name as the sort fields.
2. Choose ScriptMaker from the Script menu.
3. Type **Sort by Company, Last Name** in the Script Name text box, click to remove the check mark in the check box labeled "Include in menu," and then click Create.
4. Click the Clear All button.
5. In the Available Steps list, double-click the Sort step.
6. Accept the default settings: Sort [Restore, No dialog].
7. Click OK and then click Done.

The Phone Directory (by Last Name) Script

Table 4-12 shows the steps for the Phone Directory (by Last Name) script. This script prints a phone directory that is alphabetized by last name only. As in the Show Individuals script, if your database will contain records for several individuals who share the same last name, you may want to modify the sort instructions by adding First Name as the second sort field.

Table 4-12
The Phone Directory (by Last Name) Script

Script Step	*Special Instructions/Comments*
Enter Browse Mode []	
Go to Layout ["Phone Directory"]	Switch to the Phone Directory layout
Find All	Use all records
Sort [Restore, No dialog]	Sort by Last Name
Page Setup [Restore, No dialog]	
Print [No dialog]	
Go to Layout ["Data Entry"]	
Perform Script [Sub-scripts, "Sort by Company, Last Name"]	Sort by Company, Last Name

When printing, this script uses the Page Setup and Print options that were in effect when the script was created and prints without displaying a dialog box. Thus, it is important to turn the printer on before you execute the script.

Just before creating the script, choose both the Page Setup and Print commands from the File menu and make sure that they are set for normal defaults: Portrait mode (right-side up); U.S. Letter paper; 1 copy; Pages: All; and Records being browsed. (If you are using a dot-matrix printer rather than a laser or ink-jet printer, you may need to change the options to indicate an appropriate paper type for your printer.)

After printing the phone directory, the script automatically returns to the Data Entry layout, finds all records, and then performs the Sort by Company, Last Name script (sorting the records by company and last name).

You can later execute this script by choosing it from the Script menu (place a check mark in the check box labeled "Include in menu" in the Define scripts dialog box), and you can execute it by pressing ⌘-4.

The Phone Directory (by Company) Script

Table 4-13 shows the steps for the Phone Directory (by Company) script. This script and the Phone Directory (by Last Name) script are different in two small ways. First, this script sorts by the Company and Last Name fields rather than only by the Last Name field. Thus, the list is alphabetized by company and, within each company, employees are listed alphabetically according to their last names. Second, because the Sort command arranges the database in the same order that it needs to be in after the script is finished, you don't need to perform another sort as the final script step.

When creating this script, see the instructions presented for the Phone Directory (by Last Name) script to set the Page Setup and Print options.

Table 4-13
The Phone Directory (by Company) Script

Script Step	*Special Instructions/Comments*
Enter Browse Mode []	
Go to Layout ["Phone Directory"]	Switch to the Phone Directory layout
Find All	Use all records
Sort [Restore, No dialog]	Sort by Company, Last Name
Page Setup [Restore, No dialog]	
Print [No dialog]	
Go to Layout ["Data Entry"]	

You can later execute this script by choosing it from the Script menu (place a check mark in the check box labeled "Include in menu" in the Define scripts dialog box), and you can execute it by pressing ⌘-5.

The Dial Script

Since we've gone to the trouble of importing a telephone icon into the Data Entry layout, we can change it into a button by creating a simple dialing script and then attaching it to the icon. The Dial script consists of only one script step: Dial Phone.

To set up the Dial script, follow these steps:

1. Choose ScriptMaker from the Script menu, and enter **Dial** as the name of the script.

   Because we do not want to list this script in the Script menu, remove the check mark from the check box labeled "Include in menu."

2. Click Create to define the script.
3. Click Clear All to eliminate the predefined steps.
4. Select the Dial Phone step, and click Move to add it to the script.
5. Click the check box labeled "Perform without dialog," and then click the Specify button.

   The Dial Phone dialog box appears, as shown in Figure 4-32.

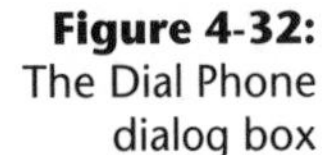

Figure 4-32: The Dial Phone dialog box

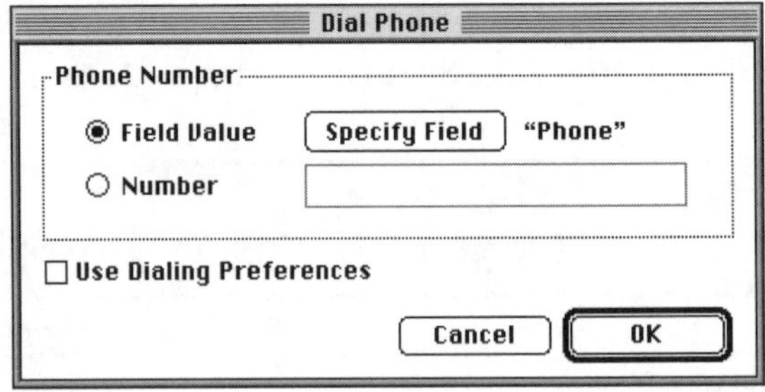

6. Click the Field Value radio button in the Dial Phone dialog box. Select Phone as the field to be dialed.

   If you have set (or intend to set) dialing preferences, click the Use Dialing Preferences check box. (To set your dialing preferences, choose Preferences from the Edit menu.)
7. To exit from ScriptMaker, click OK, OK, and then Done.

In the next section, we will attach the script to the telephone icon. For more help with designing and editing scripts, see Chapter 15.

Assigning Scripts to Buttons

After defining all the scripts, you can attach several of them to the graphic buttons in the Data Entry layout. (Any object on a layout can be made into a button by simply attaching a script or script step to the object.) Whenever a button is clicked, the attached script or script step is instantly performed. Many users find it more convenient to click a button than to pull down the Script menu and select a script. (Note, however, that there is nothing to prevent you from attaching the same script to a button *and* adding the script to the Script menu.)

Follow these steps to assign a script to a button:

1. Switch to Layout mode (choose Layout from the Select menu or press ⌘-L).

2. Using the Pointer tool, select the button or object to which you want to attach the script.
3. Choose Button from the Format menu.

   The Specify Button dialog box appears, as shown in Figure 4-33.

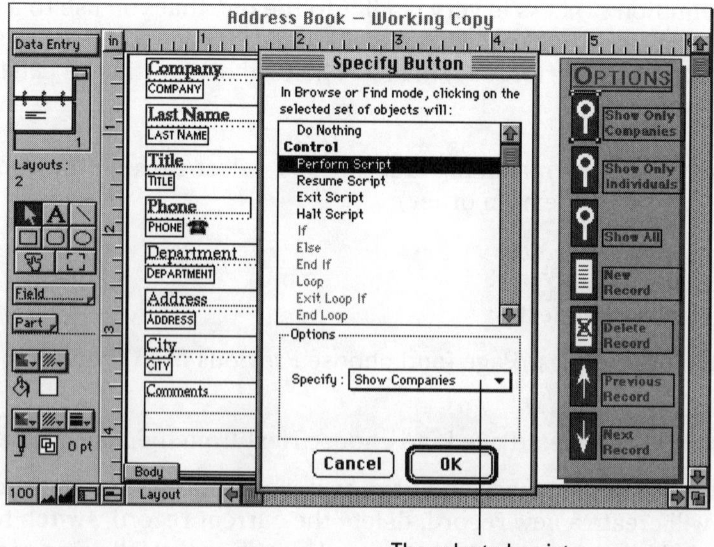

Figure 4-33: The Specify Button dialog box

4. Select Perform Script and choose the specific script in the Specify pop-up menu.
5. Click OK.

   FileMaker Pro assigns the script (or action) to the button that you selected.

Use this procedure to attach scripts to the top three buttons in the Data Entry layout, as indicated in Figure 4-34. Finally, using the same procedure, select the phone icon on the layout, and assign the Dial script to it.

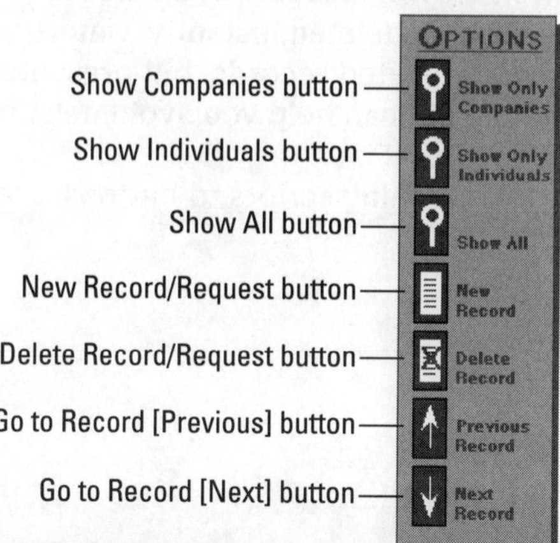

Figure 4-34: Attach the Show Companies, Show Individuals, and Show All scripts to the buttons shown.

You have not yet created scripts for the other four button icons (New Record, Delete Record, Previous Record, and Next Record) because you can control each button by a single script step. Instead of using ScriptMaker to design a script for each button, you can simultaneously create and assign the scripts by using only the Button command.

The button definition process is very similar to the one that you use to assign scripts to the first three buttons. The only difference is that you select a specific FileMaker Pro function (script step) in step 4 instead of choosing an existing script to be performed.

To assign functions to the remaining four buttons, select each button and assign the following actions to them (in order):

- New Record/Request
- Delete Record/Request
- Go to Record/Request/Page [and choose Previous from the Specify pop-up menu]
- Go to Record/Request/Page [and choose Next from the Specify pop-up menu]

When you later use the database and have switched to Browse mode, clicking these four buttons will create a new record, delete the current record, switch to the previous record in the current sort order, and switch to the following record in the current sort order, respectively. Of course, you can also perform these actions by choosing menu commands (New Record or Delete Record), pressing keyboard shortcuts (⌘-N or ⌘-E), and clicking book pages in the status area. Because these functions are common, however, providing them as buttons is a thoughtful touch.

Note that the Delete Record/Request script step has an option that enables you to delete records without having to respond to a dialog box that asks whether you are sure that you want to delete the record. Unless you're a very careful computer user, however, you should not set this option. If, in a moment of carelessness, you click the Delete Record button when you meant to click the New Record or Previous Record button, the record will be deleted instantly. Unfortunately, you cannot use the Undo command to restore deleted records, but presenting the Delete dialog box (as will be done in Address Book) can help you avoid deleting records by mistake.

For more information about attaching scripts to buttons, see Chapter 15.

The Button Tool

FileMaker Pro 3.0 includes a new feature specifically designed to create buttons: the Button tool. By switching to Layout mode, selecting the Button tool from the Tools palette, and then drawing, you can create attractive 3-D buttons. Although this feature is not used in the Address Book database, you can learn all about it in Chapter 6.

Step 7: Set Document Preferences

To complete the Address Book database, you can add one last option to make the database even easier to use. You can specify *start-up actions* that will occur whenever you open the database. For example, you can make the Data Entry layout automatically appear, regardless of the layout you last used.

Follow these steps to set database start-up actions:

1. Choose Preferences from the Edit menu.

   The Preferences dialog box appears (see Figure 4-35).

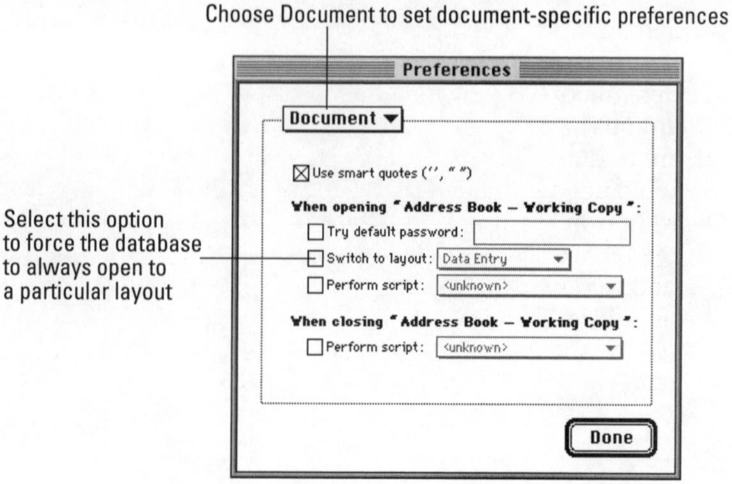

Choose Document to set document-specific preferences

Preferences

Document

Use smart quotes (‘’, “ ”)

When opening "Address Book – Working Copy":

Try default password:

Switch to layout: Data Entry

Perform script: <unknown>

When closing "Address Book – Working Copy":

Perform script: <unknown>

Done

Select this option to force the database to always open to a particular layout

Figure 4-35: The Preferences dialog box

2. To set preferences for the current database, choose Document from the pop-up menu in the Preferences dialog box.

   Only preferences relevant to the current document are displayed.

3. Set document preferences.

   In this instance, click the check box labeled "Switch to layout" in the "When opening 'Address Book—Working copy'" section of the dialog box and choose Data Entry from the pop-up layout menu.

4. Click Done.

   The Preferences dialog box closes, and the changes are recorded.

By choosing Data Entry from the "Switch to layout" pop-up menu, you ensure that the database will automatically open in the Data Entry layout, regardless of the layout that you were in when you last closed the database. Because the primary purpose of Address Book is entering, editing, and viewing address records, you can save a little time and effort by making sure that the Data Entry layout always appears when you first open the database.

For additional information on setting preferences, see Chapter 7.

Summary

- Creating a database can be as simple as defining fields and then using the default (standard) layout that FileMaker Pro provides. However, taking the time to enhance the database by creating custom layouts, adding graphics, and designing scripts can greatly improve a database's functionality and ease of use.
- Each field in a database is a specific type. The field type determines the kind of information that the field can contain, such as text, numbers, dates, or pictures.
- You can resize and move fields as necessary. You can also apply different formatting options to fields, such as fonts, styles, sizes, and colors.
- A database can have as many different layouts as are needed to collect and display the data in the ways that you want. For example, it is not unusual to create one layout specifically for entering and editing data and other layouts for generating reports and mailing labels. Every layout draws on the same information contained in the database; it simply arranges the data in a different way.
- Scripts enable you to automate common and not-so-common database procedures. ScriptMaker sets many script options for you by "watching" the actions that you perform.
- You can use graphic or text objects on a layout as buttons, or you can use the Button tool to create 3-D buttons. When you click a button, it executes the script or script step that has been attached to it.

Defining Fields

CHAPTER 5

In This Chapter

- Learning about field types
- Setting field options
- Changing field definitions and options

As explained in Part I of this book, fields are the building blocks from which databases are constructed. In this chapter, you learn all about defining fields, selecting types for them, and setting field options. You should note that FileMaker Pro 3.0 has added a new field type (Global); changed field indexing from a mandatory, automatic feature to an optional one; and added several useful data validation and auto-entry options.

Setting Field Definitions

Until you define fields for a database, you cannot store data in the database. (Technically, it isn't even a database until fields have been defined.) After you select the disk drive and folder in which you want to store the new database and give the database a name, the next step is to define the fields. The process of defining a field includes the following:

- Naming the field
- Setting a *type* for the field (the type of information that the field will store)
- Setting options for the field (data validation procedures, auto-entry options, value lists, lookups, and so on)

The first two steps, naming the field and selecting a data type for the field, are required. Setting options, naturally enough, is optional. You create all fields in the Define Fields dialog box, shown in Figure 5-1.

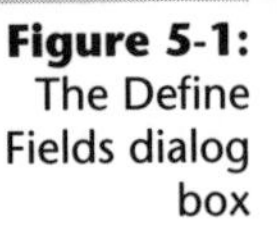

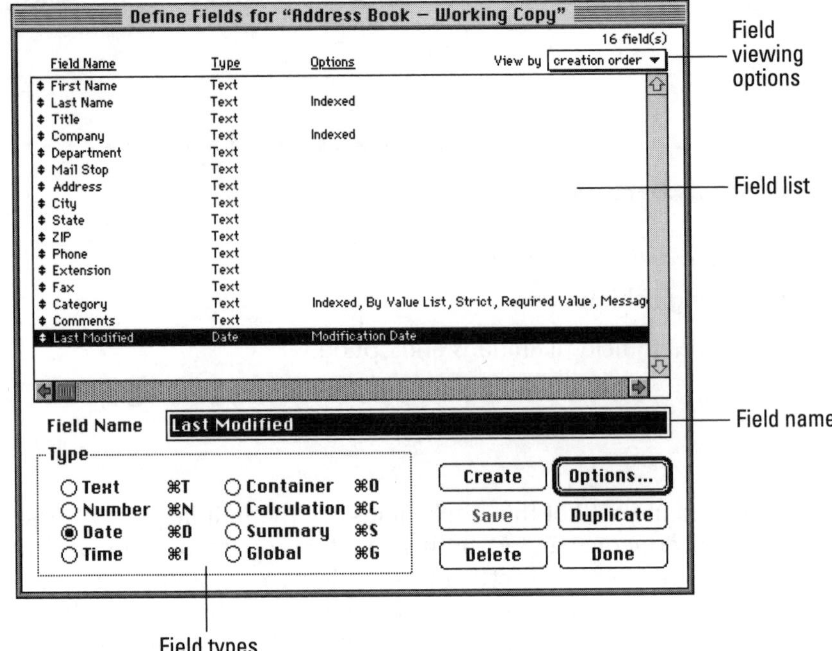

Figure 5-1: The Define Fields dialog box

You can reach the Define Fields dialog box in one of two ways:

- *Create a new file.* When you create a new database file (by choosing "Create a new empty file" from the New Database dialog box or by choosing New from the File menu), the Define Fields dialog box automatically appears after you name the new database.
- *Choose Define Fields from the File menu (or press Shift-⌘-D).* When you want to create new fields or examine, edit, or delete existing field definitions, choose the Define Fields command.

Follow these steps to define a field:

1. To create a new database when launching FileMaker Pro, choose "Create a new empty file" from the New Database dialog box. Enter a file name for the database in the standard file dialog box that appears and click Save.

— or —

1. To create a new database when FileMaker Pro is already running, choose New from the File menu (⌘-N), and then choose "Create a new empty file" from the New Database dialog box. Enter a file name for the database in the standard file dialog box that appears and click Save.

— or —

1. For an existing database, choose Define Fields from the File menu (or press Shift-⌘-D).

   In all of these cases, the Define Fields dialog box then appears.

2. Type a name for the new field (up to 60 characters long) in the Field Name box.

   If you think that you may want to use the field in a calculation formula, be sure that the name does not contain a number, period, comma, quotation mark, math symbol, or a logical keyword (AND, OR, NOT). In addition, the name cannot be the same as any of the FileMaker Pro built-in functions. (Refer to Chapter 14 for the names of FileMaker Pro functions.) Such symbols and words will be improperly interpreted as being part of the formula. To prevent such occurrences, FileMaker Pro routinely warns you if you enter an improper name, as shown in Figure 5-2.

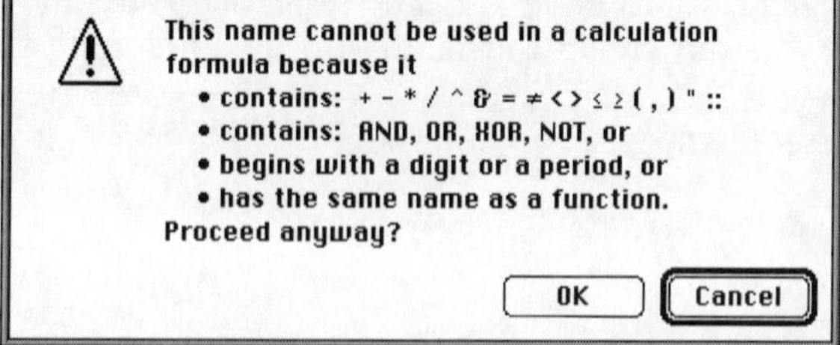

Figure 5-2: This warning appears if you enter an improper field name.

3. Click a radio button to select a data type for the field.

   As Figure 5-1 shows, a field type can also be selected by pressing the keyboard equivalent, such as ⌘-D for a Date field. Field types are explained in "All About Field Types," later in this chapter.

4. Click Create.

   If you select Calculation, Summary, or Global as the field type, another dialog box appears in which you specify additional required settings (such as a formula). For any other field type, the basic definition process ends when you click Create.

5. To define additional fields, repeat steps 2 through 4. Click Done when you are through defining fields.

After you create a field, you can set options for it, as described in "Setting Field Options," later in this chapter.

When you create a database, you normally begin by defining all its fields. You should note, however, that you are not locked in to this set of fields. You can later add new fields, delete fields, set and change field options, or even change field types (from Number to Text, for example). You can change field definitions at any time by choosing Define Fields from the File menu (or pressing Shift-⌘-D). For additional information, see "Modifying Field Definitions, Names, and Options," later in this chapter.

Breaking Up Complex Fields

When you are defining fields for a database, think seriously about dividing complex fields into their logical components. For example, instead of defining a single Name field, you may want to define Title, First Name, and Last Name fields. This approach makes sorting by last name simple. If you attempt to sort a single Name field, on the other hand, FileMaker Pro will list everyone alphabetically by their first name or — worse yet — by their title, such as Mr., Dr., or Ms.

Using different fields for Title, First Name, and Last Name also makes doing a mail merge easy. You can create the salutation by combining the Title and Last Name fields, as in

```
Dear <<Title>> <<Last Name>>:
```

rather than

```
Dear <<Name>>>:
```

Thus, instead of saying "Dear Dr. John Abrams:," the form letter would read "Dear Dr. Abrams:".

As you can see, combining several specific fields is much easier than attempting to dismantle and work with a single general field. Plan ahead.

All About Field Types

Every field in a FileMaker Pro database must have a field type. The *field type* determines the kind of data you can enter and store in a field. Number fields, for example, store numeric data. Because Number fields contain numbers, you can use them to perform calculations, such as SALE * .05 for a field that computes a commission.

FileMaker Pro 3.0 has eight field types from which you can choose: Text, Number, Date, Time, Container, Calculation, Summary, and Global. Each field must be defined as being one — and only one — type.

In order to improve the speed of executing find requests, FileMaker Pro can keep track of data that has been entered in any field and maintain an index for that field. Depending on the field type that you assign to a field and the indexing option you select, FileMaker Pro indexes all data for that field, only part of the data, or no data at all, as Table 5-1 summarizes and the following sections describe.

In previous versions of FileMaker Pro, indexing was automatic. In FileMaker Pro 3.0, on the other hand, indexing is optional. To turn on indexing for a field, you must select the field in the Define Fields dialog box, click Options, and then click Storage Options. You'll learn more about indexing options in "Setting Field Options," later in this chapter.

Table 5-1
Field Type Specifications

Field Type	***Field Content and Restrictions***	***Indexed Information***
Text	Up to 64,000 characters of any type	Every word
Number	Up to 255 characters (must be on one line)	First 122 numeric characters (non-numeric characters are ignored)
Date	One date between year 1 and 3000 (8 characters — month, day, and year — plus separators)	Entire date
Time	One time (8 characters — hours, minutes, and seconds separated by colons)	Entire time

(continued)

Table 5-1 *(continued)*

Field Type	*Field Content and Restrictions*	*Indexed Information*
Container	One picture, QuickTime movie, or sound	Not indexed
Calculation	One formula with a text, numeric, date, time, or container result	Calculation result (the amount of data indexed corresponds to the result type chosen)
Summary	Result of one summary function	Not indexed
Global	A text string, number, date, time, or container item, depending on the data type chosen	Not indexed

In addition, field data used in any of the following manners is automatically indexed (unless you specifically turn indexing off for the affected fields):

- Finding duplicates
- Using a value list
- Validating fields that have the unique or existing value validation criterion set for them
- Matching fields in a lookup, related, or master file (based on a relationship)

Text Fields

A Text field can store any type of information: text, numbers, and other characters. With a maximum of 64,000 characters, Text fields are ideal for handling large amounts of information, such as comments and notes. If indexing has been turned on for a given Text field, searching for any word in the field is easy because FileMaker Pro automatically indexes every word — not just the first one. Because you can enter any type of data in a Text field, a majority of database fields are defined as Text fields.

Number Fields

Although its name implies otherwise, you can also enter anything in a Number field — text and symbols, in addition to numeric characters. Number fields, however, have greater restrictions than Text fields have. They can contain a maximum of only 255 characters, and you must enter data as a single line. If you attempt to press Return when you are typing an entry in a Number field, FileMaker Pro beeps and ignores the Return. Because the numeric information in Number fields is readily accessible for use in formulas and computations, the contents of Number fields are frequently used as the basis for Calculation fields, which are discussed later in this chapter.

When indexing is turned on for a Number field, only the first 122 numeric characters (numbers, decimal points, or signs) are indexed. Text and other characters are ignored. If you enter both text and numbers in a Number field, individual numbers in the field are combined to form a single number. As an example, suppose that you have entered the following address in a Number field:

```
23 East Elm Street, Apt. #7
```

For indexing purposes, FileMaker Pro treats this field as though it contains the number *237*. (It appends the *7* to the end of the number *23*.) This method of operating also affects searches (performed with the Find command). If you enter 23 or 7 as the Search string, the search will fail. Similarly, because the text in a Number field is not indexed, searching for Elm also fails. On the other hand, searching for 237 — the concatenated numbers — successfully finds this record.

This discussion of concatenation leads to an important point. If you think that you will need to enter both text and numeric information in a field, you may be happier if you define it as a Text field rather than as a Number field. If you're just interested in making sure that only legitimate numbers can be entered into a numeric field, you have to set the "of type Number" option for the field. See "Setting Field Options," later in this chapter, for instructions.

Date Fields

Date fields are reserved for dates. Each date can contain up to eight characters plus separators (MM/DD/YYYY), and the entire date is indexed as a single string (when indexing is turned on for the field). When you type dates, you must use only numbers and the following separators: slash (/), hyphen (-), period (.), or space. Thus, all the following dates are proper FileMaker Pro dates: 3/14/96, 3-14-96, 3.14.96, and 3 14 96. Leading zeroes (as in 03/09/96) are optional. The year portion of the date must be between 1 and 3000.

When you enter the month or day part of a date, you can use one or two digits. You can enter any year in the current century with either two or four digits (4-15-*96* or 4/15/*1996*, for example). Table 5-2 describes how to enter other years.

Table 5-2
Entering Other Years

For a year in the range . . .	*Enter this . . .*
1 – 9	A single digit in the year's place (**4**, for example)
10 – 99	Four digits (the year preceded by two zeroes, as in **0057**)
100 – 999	Three or four digits (**756** or **0756**, for example)
1000 – 1899	Four digits — the actual year (**1847**, for example)
1900 – 1999	Two or four digits (**94** or **1994**, for example)
2000 – 3000	Four digits (**2017**, for example)

The manner in which the date is *displayed*, on the other hand, is determined by the format that you have set for the field using the Date command in the Format menu (see Chapter 6). Note that when you base a find request on the contents of a Date field, you have to enter a date that is in keeping with the restrictions listed in Table 5-2 for entering a date.

Here's a way to avoid some typing. When you enter a date for the current year, you don't have to include the year at all. If you type **4/17**, for example, FileMaker Pro fills in the current year for you.

Time Fields

Like Date fields, a Time field can hold one time (up to eight characters in length), and it is indexed as a single string (if indexing is turned on for the field). You can enter times as hours (5); hours and minutes (5:12); or hours, minutes, and seconds (5:12:43). When you enter data in a Time field, you have to separate the parts of the time with colons (see Figure 5-3). Leading zeros are optional (both 5:07 and 5:7 are acceptable, for example). You can also append AM or PM to the end of a time string. You can set a display format for a Time field by using the Time Format command (see Chapter 6).

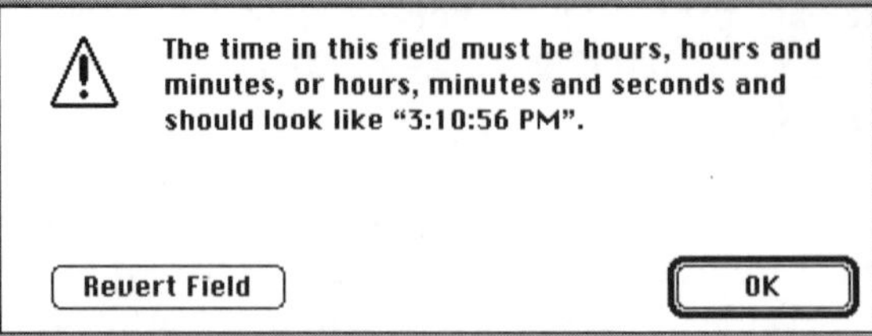
The time in this field must be hours, hours and minutes, or hours, minutes and seconds and should look like "3:10:56 PM".
Revert Field
OK

Figure 5-3: This message shows the correct way to enter a time. You can click Revert Field to restore the previous contents of the current Time field.

Container Fields

A Container field (called a Picture/Sound field in previous versions of FileMaker Pro) can store one of three types of material: a picture, a QuickTime movie, or a sound.

In the Windows version of FileMaker Pro 3.0, a Container field can also store OLE (Object Linking and Embedding) objects.

You can play movies and sounds from within a database by double-clicking a field in which either type of data is stored. You can copy pictures and QuickTime movies and paste them into the field, or you can import them by using the Import/Export submenu in the File menu. (See Chapter 16 for instructions.) You can copy and paste sound clips into a Container field, or you can record them directly into the field if you have the necessary hardware. Figure 5-4 shows a record that contains a movie.

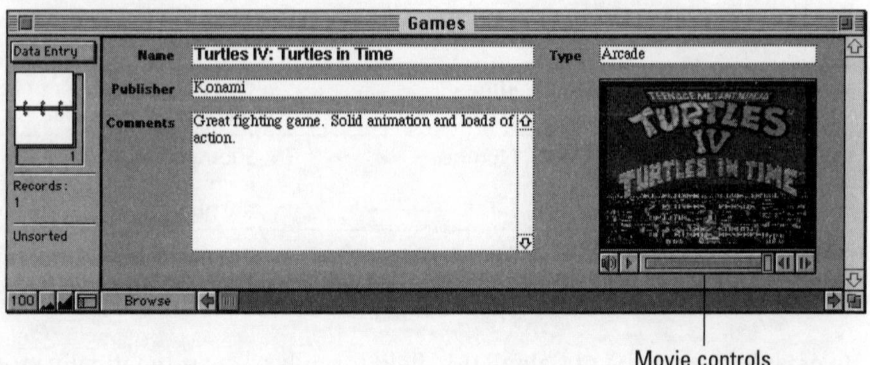

Figure 5-4: A QuickTime movie in a Container field

Information in a Container field is not indexed, so you cannot perform a find operation based on the contents of the field. Of course, this limitation makes sense because the information in the field isn't labeled in any way — there's nothing to search for. If you want to search for a particular picture, sound, or movie, you can create a separate Text field to store a title or set of keywords that describe the picture, sound, or movie, and then base your find request on the contents of the Text field.

Calculation Fields

Calculation fields perform numeric, text, date, or time calculations within each record. A calculation can include constants, any of FileMaker Pro's built-in functions, and references to other fields, as well as any combination of these items. The ability to perform calculations elevates a database from a nicely arranged stack of note cards to a powerful provider of information. For example, you can use any word processing program to type an invoice. But an invoice database that has Calculation fields can automatically total the purchases, compute the sales tax, and show you the number of days that a payment is overdue, for example.

You specify the formula for a Calculation field in the Specify Calculation dialog box, which appears automatically when you select Calculation as the field type. You need to specify the result type for each Calculation field. A result can be text, a number, a date, a time, or a container. Table 5-3 describes other types of calculations you can perform.

Table 5-3
Examples of Calculations

Formula	***Result Type***	***Explanation***
SalesTotal * .08	Number	Multiply the value in the SalesTotal field by 0.08 to compute the salesperson's commission.
First & " " & Last	Text	Concatenate each person's first and last name to show the full name. (First and Last are separated by a space.)
EndTime - StartTime	Time	Compute the amount of time spent on a particular task.
DueDate - Today	Number	Subtract today's date (Today) from the due date to determine the number of days that remain.
If(State="CA", Picture 1,Picture 2)	Container	If the state is California, display Picture 1; otherwise, show Picture 2.

By default, the results of Calculation field formulas are automatically stored on disk as part of the file's data. For calculations that change frequently, you can turn off the storage setting for the field — thereby instructing FileMaker Pro to calculate the formulas only as needed. For example, if a project management database has a field that computes the number of days until each project is due, it might be preferable to turn off automatic storage for the field (since the field will have to be recalculated whenever you open the database).

To avoid erroneous results, FileMaker Pro will not let you modify the contents of a Calculation field. To emphasize this fact, Calculation fields are automatically skipped when you tab from field to field. However, if you want to copy the contents of a Calculation field, you can click the field and then choose Copy from the Edit menu (or press ⌘-C).

You cannot edit the results in a Calculation field, but you can auto-enter a calculation in any Text, Number, Date, Time, or Container field. Unlike a result in a Calculation field, auto-entered calculations *can* be edited. Whenever you create a new record, the auto-enter calculation is used to create a default value for the field. You might, for example, want to use today's date plus one day as a default entry in a Homework Due Date field. See "Setting Field Options," later in this chapter, for details.

Chapter 14 presents the details of creating formulas for Calculation fields, as well as descriptions of FileMaker Pro's built-in functions. Additional instructions for defining a Calculation field can be found in the section "Defining Calculation, Summary, and Global Fields," later in this chapter.

Global Fields

Global fields are a new feature introduced in FileMaker Pro 3.0. A Global field is used to hold the same value for all records in a database (a state sales tax percentage, for example). It can also be used to temporarily store script results. Each Global field is stored only once for the entire database. If placed in a layout, a Global field shows the same value in every record.

After defining a field as Global, the Options for Global Field "*field name*" dialog box appears (as shown in Figure 5-5). At a minimum, you must select a data type for the field by choosing Text, Number, Date, Time, or Container from the Data type pop-up menu. You can also make it a repeating field by clicking the Repeating field check box and entering a number for maximum repetitions that the field will require. Additional instructions for defining a Global field can be found in the section "Defining Calculation, Summary, and Global Fields," later in this chapter.

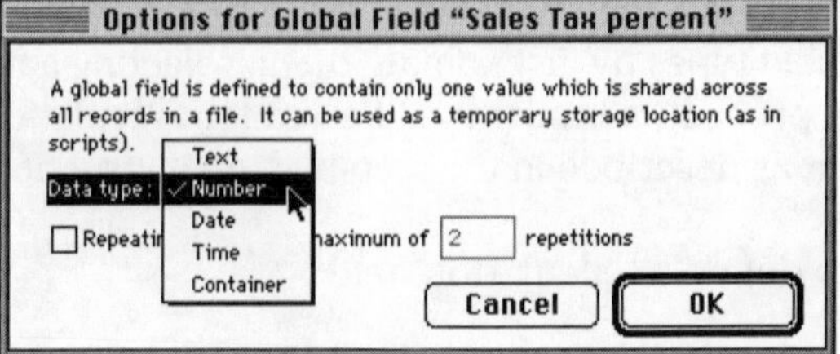

Figure 5-5: Setting options for a Global field

Summary Fields

Instead of performing calculations within each record as Calculation fields do, Summary fields perform calculations *across* records. For example, in a database that tracks customer purchases, you could define a Summary field named Grand Total to total all the purchases by all customers.

A Summary field is based on the contents of a single Number, Date, Time, or Calculation field, and it summarizes the records that you are currently browsing. When all records are visible, the Grand Total field provides the total of all purchases by all customers. If, on the other hand, you issue a find request to restrict the visible records to only customers from Boston, the Grand Total field shows total purchases by Boston customers rather than by the entire database.

You can place Summary fields in any layout part: header, body, footer, and so on. If you place a Summary field in a sub-summary part and you sort the database by a particular field, you can generate group statistics, such as computing the average rainfall for cities in country A, country B, and so on. (Chapter 6 discusses the sub-summary and other layout parts.)

FileMaker Pro automatically recalculates Summary fields whenever necessary. When you change the contents of a field on which a summary is based or when the set of browsed records changes, the summary figure is recalculated.

Functions for Summary fields include Total, Average, Count, Minimum, Maximum, Standard deviation, and Fraction of total. Defining Summary fields is discussed in the next section.

As it does with Calculation fields, FileMaker Pro prevents you from tabbing into a Summary field. However, you can click a Summary field and copy its contents. Summary fields are not indexed, nor can you base a find operation on the contents of a Summary field.

Defining Calculation, Summary, and Global Fields

You normally define field types by just naming them, selecting a field type, and clicking Create. The definition procedure is slightly different for Calculation, Summary, and Global fields, however, as described in the step-by-step instructions in this section.

Follow these steps to define a Calculation field:

1. In the Define Fields dialog box, type a name for the new field (up to 60 characters) in the Field Name box.
2. In the Type section of the dialog box, click the Calculation radio button (or press ⌘-C).
3. Click Create.

   The Specify Calculation dialog box appears , as shown in Figure 5-6.

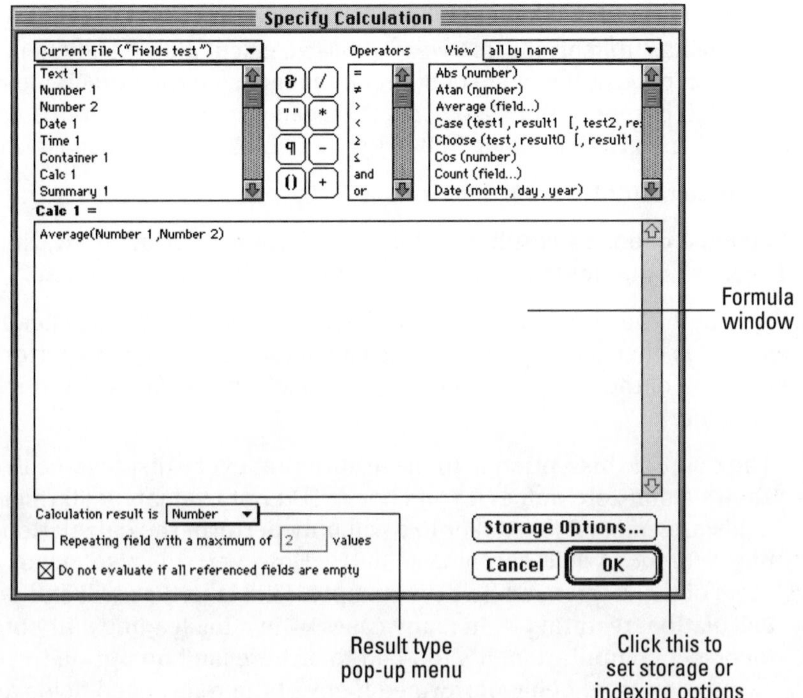

Figure 5-6: Create a formula for the Calculation field in this dialog box.

4. Enter the formula for the field in the scrolling text box in the center of the dialog box.

   You can select field names, special symbols, operators, and functions by clicking the appropriate items in the upper part of the dialog box. You can also type directly into the formula definition box.

   To make it easier to find the appropriate formula in the list on the right side of the dialog box, you can set a different viewing preference by clicking the View pop-up menu, as shown in Figure 5-7.

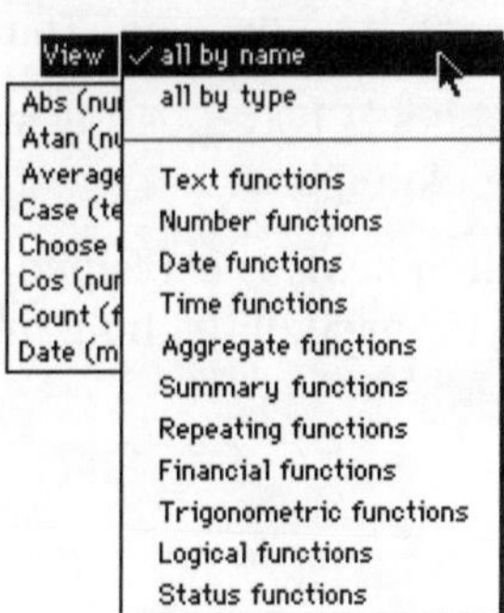

Figure 5-7: The View pop-up menu

By default, FileMaker lists the fields from the current file. If you have defined relationships for this file and want to base a calculation on a field in a related database, choose the name of the relationship from the pop-up menu in the upper-left corner of the dialog box. (You can also create relationships from this dialog box by choosing Define Relationships from the same pop-up menu.)

5. Choose a result type for the formula.

   You must choose a result type for every formula. Choose Text, Number, Date, Time, or Container from the "Calculation result is" pop-up menu.

6. By default, the check box labeled "Do not evaluate if all referenced fields are empty " is checked. If you want the calculation to always be performed — even if all of the referenced fields are blank — click the box to remove the check mark.

The point of this option is to make sure that every displayed calculation shows a non-zero value. If you choose "Do not evaluate if all referenced fields are empty," FileMaker Pro will only perform the calculation if at least one referenced field contains an entry. However, this also means that if *some* of the referenced fields are empty, FileMaker Pro will still perform the calculation, resulting — in many cases — in a misleading and potentially incorrect computation. It's too bad that there isn't an option to keep the calculation from being performed if *any* of the referenced fields are blank.

7. *Optional*: If you want this field to be a repeating field, click the check box labeled "Repeating field with a maximum of" and type a number for the maximum number of repeats that you want the field to have.

   See "Repeating Fields," later in this chapter, for more information.

8. *Optional*: To set indexing or storage options for the results of the calculation, click Storage Options.

9. Click OK.

   FileMaker Pro evaluates the formula and reports any errors that it detects. When the formula is correct, it returns you to the Define Fields dialog box.

10. You can define additional fields by repeating steps 1 through 9, or you can click Done to dismiss the dialog box.

The process of creating Calculation fields is explained in greater detail in Chapter 14, where definitions and examples for each of the built-in functions are also provided.

Follow these steps to define a Summary field:

1. In the Define Fields dialog box, type a name for the new field (up to 60 characters) in the Field Name box.
2. In the Type section of the dialog box, click the Summary radio button (or press ⌘-S).
3. Click Create.

   The Options for Summary Field "*field name*" dialog box appears, as shown in Figure 5-8.

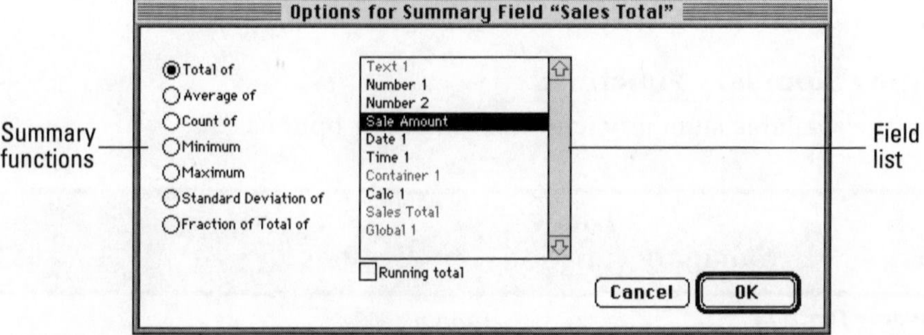

Figure 5-8: Select a field and a summary function in this Options dialog box.

4. Choose a summary function by clicking the corresponding radio button.

   See the next section for a description of the available summary functions and their options.
5. From the scrolling field list, select a field on which to base the summary.
6. *Optional*: At the bottom of the dialog box, many of the summary functions provide an option that you can select by clicking the check box and, if required, choosing a field from the new list that appears (see Figure 5-9).

The type of option displayed in this dialog box depends on the particular summary function.

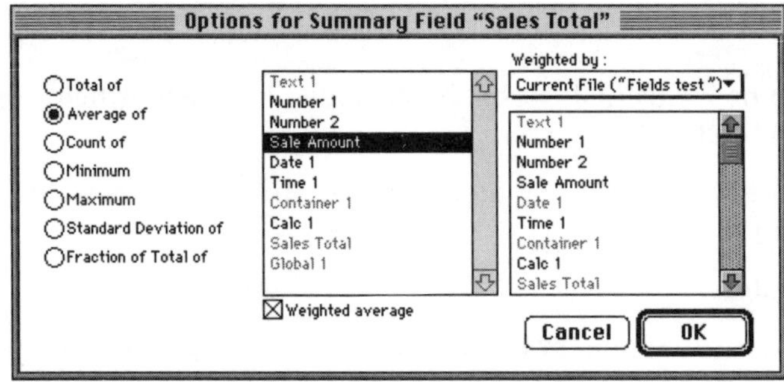

Figure 5-9: If you choose a weighted average summary function, for example, you must also choose a field that contains the weighting information.

7. Click OK to accept the definition or Cancel to ignore the settings that you have selected.

Understanding Summary Functions

Table 5-4 lists the available summary functions and their options.

Table 5-4
Summary Functions and Options

Summary Function	*Option*
Total	Running total
Average	Weighted by field name
Count	Running count
Minimum	None
Maximum	None
Standard deviation	By population
Fraction of total	Subtotaled when sorted by field *x*

The following descriptions of the summary functions and their options can help you select the most appropriate function for any Summary field:

- *Total/Running total:* The Total function totals a selected field across all records that are being browsed.

  Example: In a database in which you record household expenses, you can create a Total Summary field that shows total expenses for the entire database. You can place the Total Summary field in a sub-summary part and then sort by Expense Category to calculate separate totals for each type of expense.

Select the "Running total" option if you prefer to see a cumulative total for the field as you flip from one record to another. To calculate subtotals for groups of records, place this Summary field in a sub-summary part and then sort by the appropriate field.

- *Average/Weighted by* field name: The Average function calculates a simple numeric average of a selected field for the records being browsed. Place this Summary field in a sub-summary part if you want to calculate group averages.

  Example: If bowling scores of 112, 142, and 175 were being summarized, the average displayed would be 143 — the sum of the scores (429) divided by the number of scores (3).

  If you check the "Weighted by *field name*" option, the statistic is weighted by another field of your choice (instead of being calculated as a simple average).

  Example: In the Want List on the *FileMaker Pro 3.0 Bible Disk*, one Calculation field displays the percentage of the catalog value at which each stamp was purchased. If you were to use the Average summary function to compute the average percentage, the result would have little meaning because, from a monetary standpoint, purchases for hundreds of dollars would be treated the same as purchases for pennies. Weighting the average by the purchase price, on the other hand, gives greater importance to the more expensive purchases.

- *Count/Running count:* Placed in any part other than a sub-summary, the Count function shows the number of records that contain any value in the selected field across the records that are currently being browsed. This function is considerably more useful when placed in a sub-summary part, however, where it shows how many qualifying records are in each group (after being sorted by the appropriate field).

  Example: To determine how many records have an entry in an Address field, place a Count Summary field in any layout part other than a sub-summary. The Count Summary field then shows the number of records from which you can create usable mailing labels. If you create a Count Summary field based on a field that is always filled in, place it in a sub-summary part, and then sort by the appropriate field, you can get an accurate count of the number of members in each subgroup.

  The "Running count" function is also more informative when you place it in a sub-summary part, where it shows the cumulative number of records in each group (after being sorted by the appropriate field). When you place a Running count Summary field in another layout part, it simply matches the record numbers — as in 1, 2, 3, 4, and so on.

- *Minimum:* When placed in any part other than a sub-summary, the Minimum function shows the smallest value for the chosen field across all records being browsed. When you place it in a sub-summary part, this function shows the smallest value for the chosen field for each group of records being browsed.

  Example: In a software inventory database, a Minimum Summary field can show you the cheapest program in the lot. If you perform a find operation on a particular software category, the field displays the least expensive program of that type. Placed in a sub-summary part and then sorted by software category, the Summary field shows the least expensive program for each type of software, on a category-by-category basis.

- *Maximum:* When placed in any part other than a sub-summary, the Maximum function shows the largest value for the chosen field across all records being browsed. When placed in a sub-summary part, this function shows the largest value for the chosen field for each group of records being browsed.

  Example: In a software inventory database, a Maximum Summary field can show you the most expensive program in the lot. If you perform a find operation on a particular software category, the field displays the most expensive program of that type. Placed in a sub-summary part and then sorted by software category, the Summary field shows the most expensive program for each type of software, on a category-by-category basis.

- *Standard deviation/by population:* This function computes a statistic called a *standard deviation* for the chosen field across all records being browsed. The "Standard deviation" function shows how widely the values summarized vary from one another.

  If you check "by population," the formula used to compute the standard deviation is a population — rather than a sample — formula.

  Example: You can use a "Standard deviation function" in a student database to see how much the students' grades vary. Place the same field in a sub-summary part and then sort by age, grade level, or teacher name, for example, to get the same information separately for each group.

- *Fraction of total/Subtotaled when sorted by field* x: When placed in any part other than a sub-summary, this function shows the portion of the total for a field that can be accounted for by each record. When placed in a sub-summary part, the function shows the portion of the total for a field that can be accounted for by each group rather than each record. If you check the "Subtotaled when sorted by field" option, and you sort the database by the selected field, the "Fraction of total" figures are fractions of each group rather than of all visible records; that is, the "Fraction of total" figures within each group will add up to 1.0 (or 100 percent).

Example: In a household expense database, place this field in any layout part other than a sub-summary to determine the fraction of total expenses that each transaction accounted for. Place the same field in a sub-summary part and then sort by Expense Category to see the fraction of the category that can be attributed to each expense item.

More Help with Summary Functions

If you're having trouble making sense of Summary fields, how the different functions work, and when you should use them, the quickest path to understanding is to create a test file and try out the various options. You can use Summary File Tester, a sample file on the *Macworld FileMaker Pro 3.0 Bible Disk*.

Summary File Tester contains only six records and consists of the following four fields:

- City — a Text field
- Age — a Number field
- Salary [in thousands] — a Number field
- Summary — a Summary field

The same Summary field appears in two places in the database — in the body and in a trailing sub-summary part (at the bottom of each record). That way, you can determine the correct layout part in which to place your *own* Summary fields. The following figure shows a record from Summary Field Tester in which City is the Sort field.

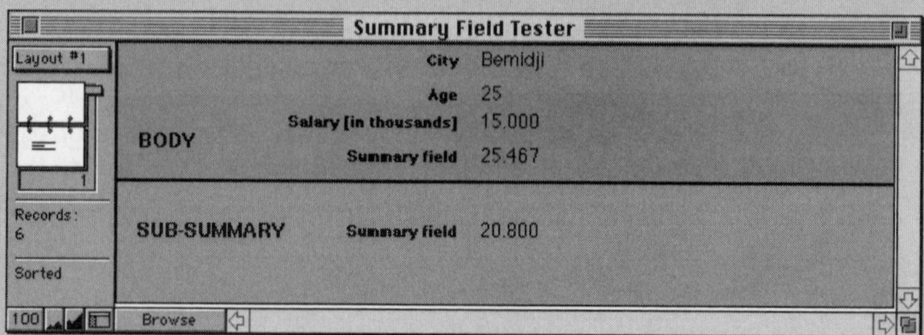

To see how each summary function and option works, open Summary Field Tester and do the following:

1. Choose the Define Fields command from the File menu (or press Shift-⌘-D).

   The Define Fields dialog box appears (as previously shown in Figure 5-1).

(continued)

(continued)

2. Select Summary field in the list of defined fields and click Options.

   The Options for Summary Field "*field name*" dialog box appears.

3. Choose a different option from the summary function pop-up menu or alter the status of the check box, if one appears at the bottom of the dialog box.

   Leave the field list pop-up menu alone (reading "Salary [in thousands]").

4. To dismiss the dialog boxes, click OK and then Done.

   If the status area shows that the records are Unsorted or Semi-Sorted, choose the Sort command from the Mode menu (or press ⌘-S). The Sort dialog box should show that the database will be sorted by City, which is the Sort field set for the sub-summary part. Click Sort or press Return or Enter to execute the sort.

Repeat these steps as often as you like, testing a different summary function or option each time. After each definition has been completed, flip through the records to see what the Summary field is summarizing, both in the body and in the sub-summary part.

Changing the Field Order

A field list appears in several FileMaker Pro dialog boxes, such as the Define Fields and Sort dialog boxes. By default, fields appear in the list in the order in which you created them. Working with this list can often be easier if you establish a new order for fields. To change the order for all field lists, choose one of the following options in the View by pop-up menu in the upper-right corner of the Define Fields dialog box (see the accompanying figure):

- *creation order:* Fields are listed in the order in which they were defined.
- *field name:* Fields are sorted alphabetically by field name.
- *field type:* Fields are grouped by type (Text, Number, and so on). Within each type, the fields are presented in creation order.
- *custom order:* You can manually drag one or more fields to a new position in the list. This process is described in the following step-by-step instructions.

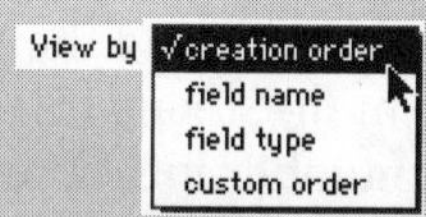

The following steps describe how to create a custom field order:

1. In the Define Fields dialog box, move the pointer over the name of the field that you want to move.

   When the pointer moves over the beginning of a field name, it changes to a two-headed arrow.

2. With the two-headed arrow visible, click to select the field, drag the field up or down in the list, and release the mouse button when the field is where you want it to be.

   As soon as you move a single field, the View by pop-up menu automatically shows that the custom order setting has been selected.

3. Repeat these steps for any additional fields that you want to move. Note that even if you switch back and forth between several different field order views, when you next choose the custom order view, all the manual modifications that you made to the field order are restored.

Setting Field Options

The types of options that can be set for a field vary with the field type. Options for Global, Calculation, and Summary fields have already been discussed. The options that can be set for Text, Number, Date, Time, and Container fields are as follows:

- *Data auto-entry:* When a new record is created or an existing record is modified, you can have FileMaker Pro automatically enter the creation or modification date or time for each record, the name of the user who created or last modified the record, a serial number, the value from the previous record, a calculated value, a value looked up in another database, or a default value into the chosen field.

- *Data validation:* Depending on the options chosen, you can require that a field not be left blank, that the value entered must be unique, that the value already exists in another record, that the data must be of a particular type, that the data is restricted to entries in a value list, or that entries fall within a specific range.

- *Look up data values in another file:* When data is entered into a lookup field, FileMaker Pro automatically looks up information in another file and then copies selected data into one or more fields in the current file. Using this option in an inventory database, you could enter a part number into a field. FileMaker Pro would then open the second database file that you specified; find the part name, description, color, and unit cost for the part; and then transfer a copy of that information to the first database. Because of the complexity of this concept, lookups are covered separately in Chapter 19 — along with relationships.
- *Repeating values:* This option enables you to enter multiple values in what normally would be considered a single field. In an invoice database, for example, you can define Quantity, Item Description, Price, and Extended Price fields as repeating, each of which can receive up to ten values. (*You* determine the maximum number of values.)
- *Present a list of values from which to choose:* This option causes a user-defined list of values to appear when someone tabs into or clicks the field. For example, you can create a value list that lists all the payment methods (such as specific credit cards, checks, cash, and traveler's checks) that your store accepts as payment for services and goods. In addition to speeding data entry for the field with which it is used, this option helps ensure that each entry is spelled correctly and worded consistently. Depending on the formatting option selected (choose Field Format from the Format menu), value lists can be presented as pop-up lists, pop-up menus, check boxes, or radio buttons.

The following steps describe the general procedure for setting options for a Text, Number, Date, Time, or Container field. Instructions for setting specific kinds of field options are in the sections that follow.

1. Choose Define Fields from the File menu (or press Shift-⌘-D).

   The Define Fields dialog box appears (as previously shown in Figure 5-1).

2. In the field list, select the Text, Number, Date, Time, or Container field for which you want to set options.

   — or —

2. If the field doesn't already exist, define the field by following the instructions for defining fields, presented earlier in this chapter.

3. Click Options (or double-click the name of the field in the field list).

   The Entry Options for Field "*field name*" dialog box appears, as shown in Figure 5-10. Note that the title of the Entry Options dialog box changes to reflect the name of the selected field. The specific options that you can set also vary with the data type of the field. For example, the only data validation options available for a Container field are "Not empty" and "Validation by calculation."

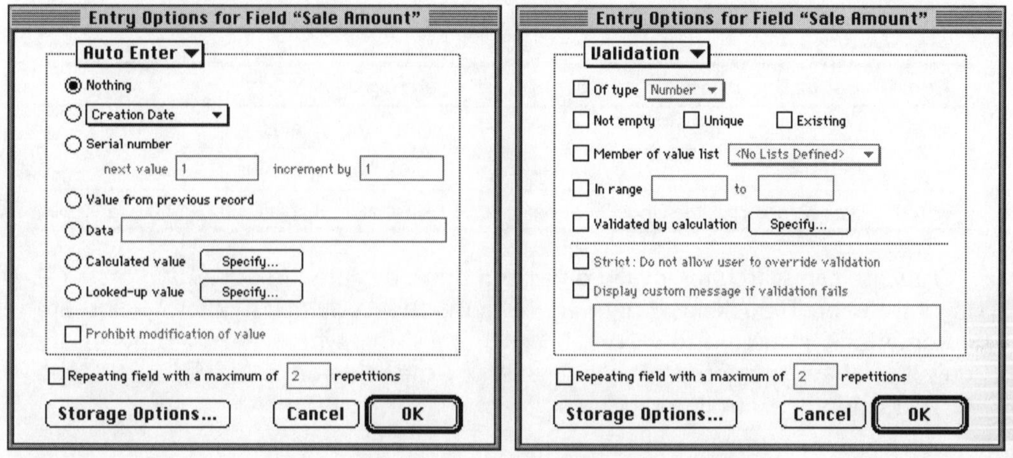

Figure 5-10: The Entry Options dialog box contains auto-entry options (left) and validation options (right) , depending on which you choose from the pop-up menu.

4. Choose Validation or Auto Enter from the pop-up menu at the top of the dialog box and set options as desired.
5. If you want to set other options, choose the other setting (Validation or Auto Enter) from the pop-up menu at the top of the dialog box and set the options as desired.
6. Click OK to return to the Define Fields dialog box.
7. To set options for additional fields, repeat steps 2 through 6. Click Done when you are through setting options.

Problems with Setting Field Options After-the-Fact

You should note that setting entry options for a field after the field contains data for some records can cause problems. FileMaker Pro does not warn you about existing records that, as a result of the new field options, now contain invalid data. You have to find and correct them yourself. The following table lists find request symbols that are helpful in performing this task.

Find Symbol or Operation	*Action*
=	Find empty fields
!	Find duplicate values
value1 . . . value2, and click the Omit check box	Find values that fall outside of the range

You also can search for invalid dates and times by entering a question mark (?) in a Date or Time field. However, because the contents of these fields are automatically restricted to valid dates and times, this type of search is necessary only if you have converted a field to a Date or Time field from some other field type (a Text field, for example).

Auto Enter Options

When Auto Enter is chosen from the pop-up menu at the top of the Entry Options dialog box, you are shown options that provide for the automatic entry of several types of information in a field when you initially create or later modify a record. The various auto-entry options are discussed in the following sections.

Creation Date, Creation Time, Modification Date, Modification Time, Creator Name, and Modifier Name

Choose Auto Enter from the pop-up menu at the top of the Entry Options dialog box, click the second radio button, and choose an option from the pop-up menu to the right (see Figure 5-11). The specific choices that can be selected in the pop-up menu depend on the type of the field for which you are setting options. If you are defining options for a Date field, for example, you can select only the Creation Date and Modification Date options. Other options are grayed-out (dimmed).

Figure 5-11: Setting an automatic date, time, creator, or modifier stamp for a field

Selecting Creation Date or Creation Time causes FileMaker Pro to automatically enter the appropriate data as each new record is created. When these options are set, you can tell how old each record is, so you have an idea of whether the record is up-to-date.

If you define a Creation Date, Creation Time, or Creator Name field *after* the database already contains records, the field will be blank in existing records. You may want to manually enter this information for the old records.

Modification Date and Modification Time show when any field in a record was last changed. FileMaker Pro automatically enters the appropriate value when you finish editing a record (by pressing Enter or switching to a different record). If you're interested only in how current a record is — as opposed to when it was originally created — use the Modification Date option. When a new record is created, the Modification Date is the *same* as the Creation Date.

Creator Name and Modifier Name show who created or last modified the record, respectively. These field options are extremely helpful in a multi-user environment to help determine who is creating or modifying records.

The Creator Name and Modifier Name are read from information entered in the Sharing Setup control panel (System 7). If the Creator and Modifier Name fields in your database are always blank, you need to identify yourself to your Mac, as described in the following steps:

1. Choose Control Panels from the Apple menu.

   The folder in which your control panels are stored appears on the desktop.

2. Double-click the icon named Sharing Setup.

   The Sharing Setup control panel opens.

3. Type your name or other identifying information in the Owner Name box in the Network Identity section of the window, as shown in Figure 5-12.

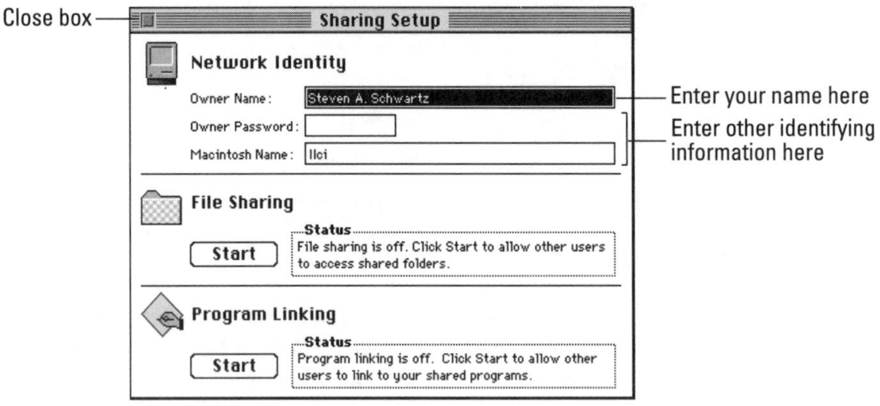

Figure 5-12: Identifying yourself (System 7)

4. To close the window and save your changes, click the close box in the upper-left corner of the Sharing Setup control panel.

Performing Automatic Time Calculations

If you do time billing, you can use the Creation Time and Modification Time auto-entry options to track time spent on the phone with a client or time spent working on a project. For example, you can create a simple database like Time Billing (shown in the figure at the end of this sidebar). When a client calls, you immediately create a new record. The Creation Date (Date), Creation Time (Start Time), and Modification Time (End Time) values are automatically filled in for you. The Total Time is calculated by subtracting the Start Time from the End Time. When the record is created, the result of this formula is initially zero (0).

Then enter the client's name. When the call ends, press Enter to complete the record. The Modification Time is then automatically updated to reflect the current time, and the Total Time is recalculated to show the actual length of the call.

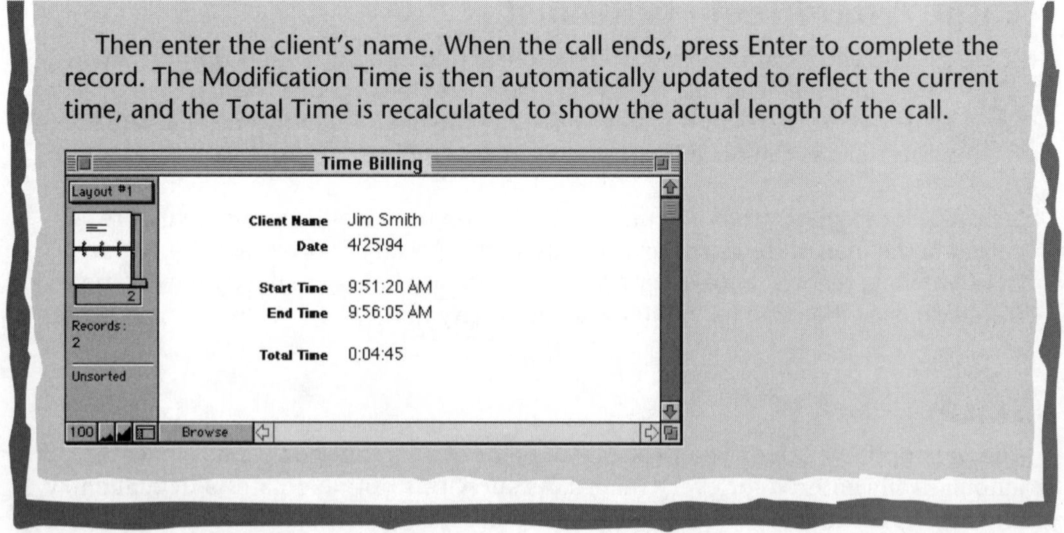

Serial Number

You use this option to automatically enter a number that increments by a set amount for each new record. For example, you can use this option to create invoice and statement numbers.

The following steps describe how to create a field in which FileMaker Pro automatically enters serial numbers using the increment that you specify:

1. Select a Number or Text field in the Define Fields dialog box and click Options.
2. Choose Auto Enter from the pop-up menu at the top of the Entry Options dialog box and then click the radio button labeled "Serial number."
3. In the "next value" text box, enter the starting serial number.

   This number will be assigned to the next new record that you create.
4. In the "increment by" text box, enter a number for the amount that you want each new serial number to increase over the previous serial number.
5. Click OK to return to the Define Fields dialog box.

You should note that a serial number does not have to be a simple number. For example, you can set the starting serial number ("next value") as A27B-1000. In a mixed text-and-number entry such as this one, FileMaker increments the serial number by using the right-most number string and ignoring other numbers in the string. In this example, assuming that the increment was 1, the next serial numbers would be A27B-1001, A27B-1002, and so on.

Value from Previous Record

If you enter data in pre-sorted batches, this new auto-entry option can be very helpful. Selecting the "Value from previous record" option instructs FileMaker Pro to automatically display the most recently entered data for this field as the default entry in each new record.

Suppose, for example, that you must enter information from warranty cards received in the mail. If the cards are already sorted by city and you set the "Value from previous record" auto-entry option for the City field, you'll only have to type the city name when you encounter a different city in the card stack.

Data

The Data option enables you to specify a piece of data that you want to have automatically entered for every record. As such, this option creates a default entry for a field. For example, in an employee database, employees often live in the same city. By using the name of this city as auto-entry data, you can save some typing. If you create a record for an employee who lives in a *different* city, you can edit the name of the city in that record.

Calculated Value

This new auto-entry option enables you to use a formula to set a default value for any Text, Number, Date, Time, or Container field. Unlike formulas entered for Calculation fields, auto-entered formulas *can* be edited.

When you click the radio button labeled "Calculated value" (or click its Specify button), a modified version of the Specify Calculation dialog box appears (as shown previously in Figure 5-6). Create the formula and click OK. You'll note that the result type of the formula must match the data type of the field. Optionally, you can remove the check mark from the "Do not evaluate..." check box at the bottom of the dialog box.

Looked-Up Value

This auto-entry option instructs FileMaker Pro to look up information in a second database (or in the same database) and copy it into the current database. When you create several databases that share some common element, such as address information, you can minimize the amount of duplicate data entry that is required by instructing each of these databases to automatically extract the address information from a separate Address database.

A *lookup* is a one-way function in which data is copied from another file into the current file (much like importing field information but affecting only the current record rather than the entire database). To learn more about lookups and the new relational capabilities of FileMaker Pro 3.0, see Chapter 19.

The following steps describe how to create a lookup field:

1. Choose Define Fields from the File menu (or press Shift-⌘-D).

   The Define Fields dialog box appears.

2. Select or create a field to receive the copied (lookup) data, and then click Options or double-click the field name in the field list.

   The field type of the selected field must be Text, Number, Date, Time, or Container.

3. Choose Auto Enter from the pop-up menu at the top of the Entry Options dialog box and then click the radio button labeled "Looked-up value."

   The Lookup for Field *"field name"* dialog box appears, as shown in Figure 5-13.

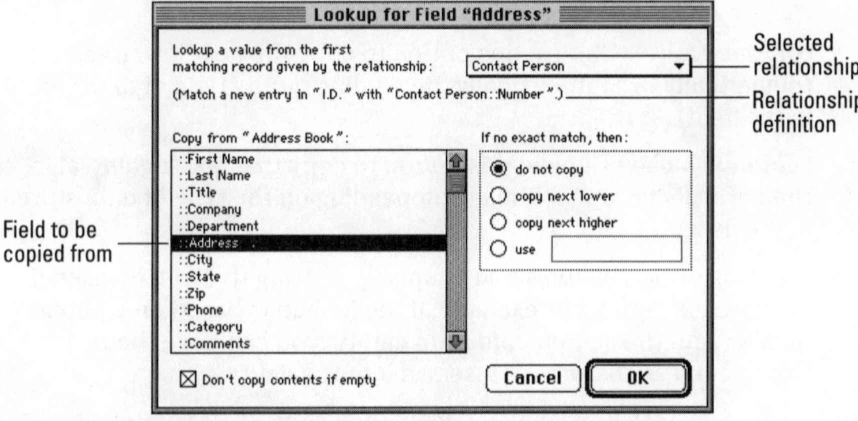

Figure 5-13: The Lookup for Field dialog box

4. From the pop-up menu, choose the relationship from which you intend to extract the lookup information.

   If a relationship that links the two files does not already exist, choose Define Relationships from the pop-up menu and then define the relationship.

Whenever a lookup is performed, the second file is automatically opened for you as part of the lookup process.

5. In the "Copy from" section of the dialog box, select the name of the field that you want to copy into the current database.

   When the lookup is executed, the contents of the selected field are copied into the current field, whose name is shown in the title of the dialog box. (In the example shown in the previous figure, Address will be copied from the lookup file into the Address field in the current file.)

6. In the section of the dialog box labeled "If no exact match, then," select from the following options to tell FileMaker Pro what to do if it doesn't find an exact match:

   - *do not copy*: This option is the default and, in most cases, it is what you want. Rather than copying erroneous data, the field is left as is.

After a lookup executes, you can still edit the contents of the field into which data was copied. If you ever edit the *trigger field* (the field in the current database that initiates the lookup), however, the lookup will be executed anew. If a match is found, your edited data will be replaced.

   - *copy next lower:* Choose this option to copy the next lower value (numerically or alphabetically, depending on the type of data stored in the field).
   - *copy next higher:* Choose this option to copy the next higher value (numerically or alphabetically, depending on the type of data stored in the field).
   - *use:* This option enables you to specify a string that will be used if no match is found. For example, if the lookup is based on a phone number and the search comes up empty, you can have the text, "Not a current customer," inserted into the field.

7. *Optional:* Click the check box labeled "Don't copy contents if empty" to avoid copying information from a blank field into the current file.

   In the example shown in the previous figure, if you had hand-entered an address in the Address field, selecting this option would prevent the address from being replaced by a blank address from the external file.

8. Click OK to accept the options you have just set or click Cancel to ignore the new settings.

9. Repeat steps 2 through 8 to define additional lookup fields, as desired. Click Done when you're ready to close the Define Fields dialog box and return to the database.

Choose the Match Field Wisely

When you are selecting a field on which to base a lookup, you'll be much happier if you choose one whose contents will be unique to each entry, such as a customer ID number, Social Security number, or telephone number. If, for example, you use the contents of the Last Name field as what you're attempting to match, you will run into problems if you have several people who share the same last name. No matter how many times you execute the lookup, you'll find only the first person who has that particular last name.

Here are some other important factors to keep in mind when you are creating and using lookups:

- To determine whether a match has been found, FileMaker Pro compares only the first 20 characters in the match fields. It ignores word order, punctuation, and capitalization, as well as any text that is contained in a Number field.
- If the data in the external database changes, a lookup that you previously performed may now contain data that is incorrect. To correct this situation, you can instruct FileMaker Pro to perform the lookup again by tabbing into the field that is used to trigger the lookup and choosing the Relookup command from the Edit menu.

Unlike a regular lookup, which is performed for only the current record, a relookup is performed for all records that are being browsed. To perform a relookup for only the current record, the easiest method is to cut the data from the trigger field, paste it back into the field, and then tab to the next field. Editing the data in the trigger field automatically causes the lookup to be executed.

- You can select any FileMaker Pro file in which to do a lookup, including the current file. This technique can be extremely useful with any database that contains multiple records for the same customer, client, or subject. As an example, an invoice database can look for a customer ID among the existing records and then, if a match is found, fill in the fields of the mailing address for you.

Using Lookups to Fill in Multiple Fields

At first glance, you may not think that you can trigger a lookup that will copy *multiple* fields to the original database. As the example in the instructions for creating a lookup field shows, when a match is located, the lookup copies the contents of only one external field into one field in the current database.

The solution is to individually define a lookup for every field that you want to copy, using the same trigger field for each lookup. For example, to copy an entire address, begin by identifying a unique field, such as the Social Security number, phone number, or a customer ID number. Then create a separate lookup for each field in the address (First Name, Last Name, Address, City, State, and ZIP) using the same trigger and match fields in each lookup definition (the Social Security number, for example). When you enter the information in the trigger field during data entry, FileMaker will perform all the lookups simultaneously. Although FileMaker will appear to be doing only one lookup, in fact, it will perform half a dozen of them — pulling all the data from the same record in the lookup file.

Protecting Auto-Entered Values

To protect auto-entered values, you may want to check the "Prohibit modification of value" option in the bottom section of the Entry Options dialog box. Setting this option prevents you and other users of the database from inadvertently altering the contents of an auto-entry field.

You need to set this option for each field that you want to protect (a serial number field, for instance). If you later discover that you need to edit one or more of the auto-entered values for a particular field, return to this screen, remove the check mark from the "Prohibit modification of auto-entered values" option, edit the field as necessary, and then restore the check mark.

Data Validation Options

Choose Validation from the pop-up menu at the top of the Entry Options dialog box to set or view data validation options. These options govern the types of information that must, may, or may not be entered in a chosen field.

You need to keep two important things in mind when you create a validation option for a field. First, you can set validation options only for Text, Number, Date, Time, and Container fields. Second, even with a validation option set, unless you also set the new option labeled "Strict: Do not allow user to override validation," FileMaker Pro gives you (or any other person who may be using the database) the option of overriding the validation requirements. If you leave a required field blank, for example, you see a dialog box like the ones shown in Figure 5-14.

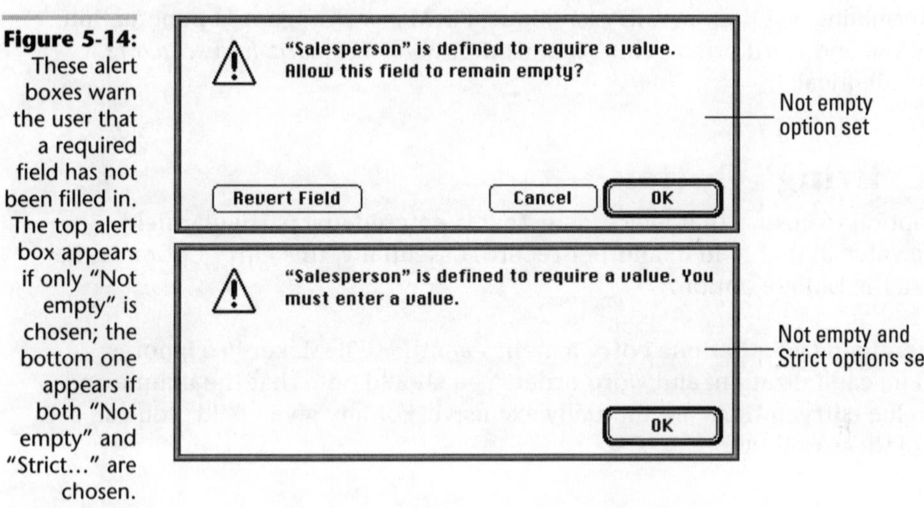
"Salesperson" is defined to require a value.
Allow this field to remain empty?
Revert Field
Cancel
OK
Not empty option set
"Salesperson" is defined to require a value. You must enter a value.
OK
Not empty and Strict options set

Figure 5-14: These alert boxes warn the user that a required field has not been filled in. The top alert box appears if only "Not empty" is chosen; the bottom one appears if both "Not empty" and "Strict..." are chosen.

The following sections describe the validation options.

The "Of type" Option

Use this option to indicate that only a number, date, or time is an acceptable entry for the field. Assigning this option is the way to ensure that only numbers are entered in Number fields, for example. (A number can include a decimal separator, thousands separator, sign, and parentheses.)

As with the other data validation options, the user can still override the warning dialog box that appears when the wrong data type is entered — unless you also set the "Strict: Do not allow user to override validation" option.

The "Not empty" Option

Click this check box to create a *required field* (one that must not be empty). In many databases, you will have essential fields that render a record worthless if their data is left blank. In a customer database, for example, you cannot send out bills if the Name, Address, or City field for a customer is blank. If you attempt to switch to another record without filling in a required field, FileMaker Pro displays a warning.

The "Unique" Option

This option requires every record in the database to have a different value for the field. FileMaker Pro warns you if you enter a value that already exists in another record. Often, customer or record ID numbers must be unique.

When determining whether an entry is unique, FileMaker Pro ignores punctuation, capitalization, and word order. Thus, it considers *Steve Schwartz* and *schwartz, steve* to be identical.

The "Existing" Option

Use this option to ensure that every value that is entered in a particular field matches a value in that field in another record. Essentially, this entry option is the opposite of the Unique option.

When determining whether one entry matches another, FileMaker Pro ignores punctuation, capitalization, and word order. You should note that the unique and existing value entry options are mutually exclusive. For any given field, you can set only one of these options.

When to Use the "Existing" Option

From the explanation of the Existing option, you may think that you should add it only after a database contains many records. In fact, the opposite is true. This option causes a warning dialog box to appear if you enter a value that has never been used for the field, and, as usual, you can override the warning and accept the value. Thus, if you add this entry option when you first create the database, you can specify the allowable entries as you enter records. If you set this option for a Company Name field, for example, you can ensure that every company name is always entered exactly the same way. (However, sorting the database periodically to check the accuracy of your mental notes concerning the companies that you've already entered is still a good idea.)

The "Member of value list" Option

Select this option to restrict data to the items in a value list. For example, you may have a Payment Method field that includes all allowable forms of payment in a value list (such as cash, VISA, MasterCard, and Discover). Linking the validation options to this value list prevents your salespeople from entering (and — presumably — accepting) other forms of payment, such as personal checks.

If a suitable value list hasn't already been created for the database, choose Define Value Lists from the pop-up menu to the right and create the value list. (See "Value Lists," later in this chapter, for instructions.)

Value lists in FileMaker Pro 3.0 are no longer treated as though they are linked to a specific field. Any value list that you define for a database can be associated with any field in the database — or with *several* fields, if you like. For example, you could create a single value list that contained the choices: "Yes," "No," and "Don't know," and use this value list with every Yes/No question in a survey database.

The "In range" Option

Select this option to specify an allowable range for a Text, Number, Date, or Time field. Enter the lowest acceptable value in the first text box and the highest acceptable value in the second ("to") text box. Since text is handled alphabetically, you can enter the letters *A* and *F* to restrict acceptable entries to text strings that begin with the letters *A*, *B*, *C*, *D*, *E*, and *F*, for example.

Using the "Of type Number" Option with a Numeric Range

For numeric ranges, you may want to set the "Of type Number" option as well as the "In range" option. This ensures not only that the value will be in range, but also that it will be the proper data type — a number.

In order to get precisely the type of validation you require, it is not uncommon to select two or more validation options that work in concert with each other.

The "Validated by calculation" Option

If necessary, any Text, Number, Date, Time, or Container field can be validated by a Boolean (true/false) formula. As an example, the formula Age ≥ 18 could be used to determine whether the entry in Age is a legitimate one (≥18) or should be flagged (<18).

To set the validated by calculation option, select the field name in the Define Fields dialog box and then click the Validated by calculation check box. A slightly modified version of the Specify Calculation dialog box appears. Enter a Boolean formula (one that returns a true or false result), check or remove the check mark from the check box labeled "Validate only if field has been modified," and click OK.

The "Strict: Do not allow user to override validation" Option

When set in combination with one or more other validation options, the Strict… option prevents you or other users from overriding validation warnings (previously shown in Figure 5-14). Thus, if you have specified "Of type Number" as a validation setting for a field and have also chosen the Strict option, users will be prevented from entering anything other than a legitimate number in the field — rather than simply being warned of their error and allowed to override the warning.

I consider this to be one of the most useful changes introduced in FileMaker Pro 3.0. If you are serious enough about maintaining valid data to assign a validation option to a field, you can now easily enforce the validation.

The "Display custom message if validation fails" Option

This option enables you to present a dialog box with a custom message if the validation fails (see Figure 5-15). (This option can only be checked if you have also chosen at least one other validation option.) Rather than rely on FileMaker Pro's standard validation error messages, you may prefer to display a detailed explanation of what you expect from the user, for example.

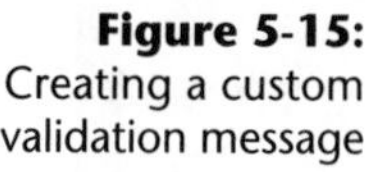

Figure 5-15: Creating a custom validation message

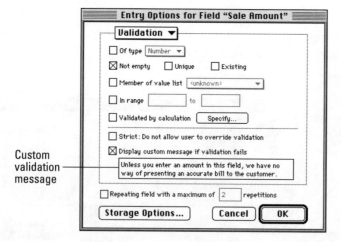

Repeating Fields

Although most fields are intended to handle only one piece of data, you may sometimes want to use a single field to handle multiple bits of information. This type of field is called a *repeating field.*

In older, less capable database programs, you often had to handle repeating fields the hard way. For example, to create an eight-line invoice, you had to define eight separate Quantity, Item Description, Unit Price, and Extended Price fields. Calculations based on these fields were cumbersome to create, as in *ExtPrice1* + *ExtPrice2* + *ExtPrice3*. . . . The FileMaker Pro invoice shown in Figure 5-16, on the other hand, was created by defining a single field for each of the following: Quantity, Item Description, Unit Price, and Extended Price. Then the repeating field option was assigned to each field. You can set any type of field to repeat, except for Summary fields.

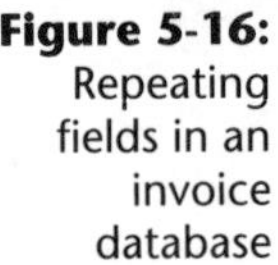

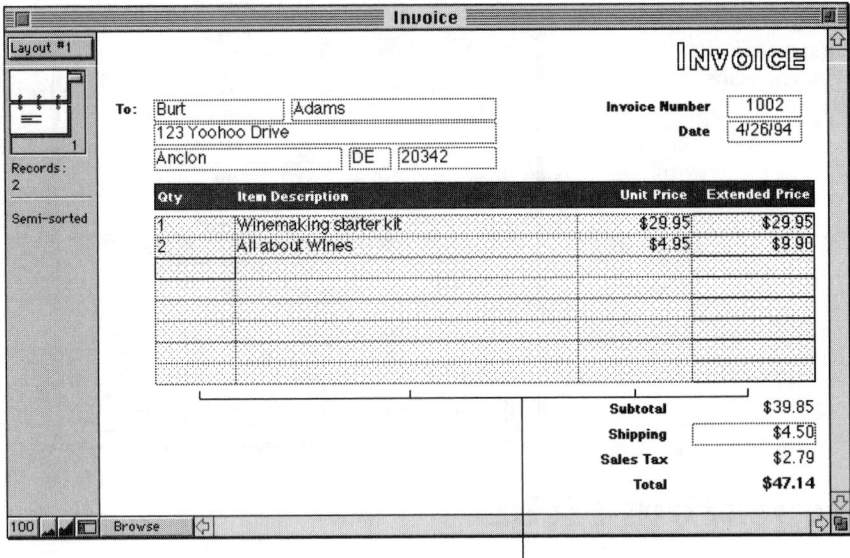

Figure 5-16: Repeating fields in an invoice database

Follow these steps to set the repeating field option for a field:

1. Choose the Define Fields command from the File menu (or press Shift-⌘-D).

   The Define Fields dialog box appears.

2. From the scrolling field list, select the Text, Number, Date, Time, Container, Calculation, or Global field that you want to define as a repeating field.

3. Click Options.

   An Options, Entry Options, or Specify Calculation dialog box appears. (The specific dialog box that appears depends on the type of field that you chose in step 2.)

4. Click to place a check mark in the option marked "Repeating field with a maximum of *x* repetitions" and enter the maximum number of repetitions in the text box.

   The number is simply the upper limit of repetitions that the field can store. You set the number of repetitions that are *displayed,* on the other hand, by switching to Layout mode and choosing the Field Format command from the Format menu (described in Chapter 6).

5. Click OK to return to the Define Fields dialog box.

6. Repeat steps 2 through 5 for additional fields that you want to define as repeating fields.

7. Click Done to record the changes and return to the database.

Several built-in functions are provided expressly for the purpose of performing computations on repeating fields. You are already familiar with many of them, such as Total and Average, from the discussion in this chapter concerning summary functions (see "Defining Calculation and Summary Fields"). For calculation purposes, you can use the Extend built-in function to treat a nonrepeating field as though it repeats.

You need to be aware of several important facts about repeating fields:

- Regardless of the number of repetitions that are visible on the current layout, FileMaker Pro uses *all* repetitions in calculations.

  For example, if you alter an invoice layout that was originally designed to show eight line items so that it now shows only five, FileMaker Pro will also consider the other three line items when it calculates the Sum (repeating field) function. If you really want to keep the additional entries from being included in the calculation, you must delete them.
- When conducting a sort that is based on a repeating field, FileMaker Pro uses only the first entry in the sort.
- Other database programs may not correctly handle a FileMaker Pro export that contains repeating fields.

Value Lists

If you have been impressed by the pop-up menus used in many programs, you will be equally impressed to learn that FileMaker Pro enables you to create the same type of choice lists for your database fields.

You determine the values that appear in the list. Depending on the format that you select for a field, the list is presented as a pop-up menu, a pop-up list, a set of check boxes, or a set of radio buttons. When you tab into a field that is formatted as a pop-up list, the list automatically appears. When you click a field that is formatted as a pop-up list or a pop-menu, the list or menu appears. Even if a field has an associated value list, you can still type different information in the field (unless you also set the "Member of value list" validation option, as described previously in this chapter).

There are two ways to create a value list for a field. The first — setting "Member of value list" as a validation option — was described earlier in this chapter. While that approach enables you to create a value list, it does not attach it to the field. The second method of creating value lists has the advantage of both defining the list *and* attaching it to the field. To use this method, follow these steps:

1. Switch to Layout mode (⌘-L), select the field to which you want to attach a value list, and choose Field Format from the Format menu.

The Field Format dialog box appears, as shown in Figure 5-17.

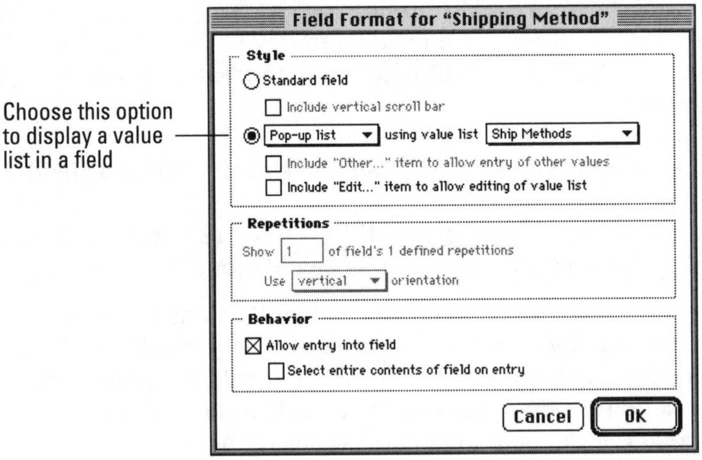

Figure 5-17: The Field Format dialog box

Choose this option to display a value list in a field

2. To define the format for the field as a value list, click the second radio button in the Style section of the dialog box (as shown in the figure) and choose a format for the list from the first pop-up menu (Pop-up list, Pop-up menu, Check boxes, or Radio buttons).

3. If an appropriate value list has already been defined, choose it from the pop-up menu to the right. Go to step 7.

–or–

3. To define a new value list that you intend to use with this field, choose Define Value Lists from the pop-up menu to the right.

   The Define Value Lists dialog box appears, as shown in Figure 5-18.

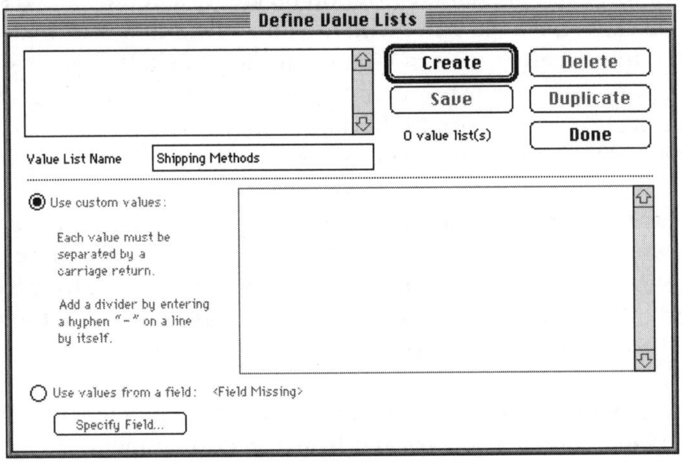

Figure 5-18: The Define Value Lists dialog box

4. Type a name for the new list in the Value List Name text box, and click Create.
5. Click the "Use custom values" radio button (if it is not already selected), and type entries for the value list, pressing Return after each entry except the last one. (If you press Return after the final entry, you will end up with an extra blank line at the end of the list.)

   You can type a hyphen (-) on any line to generate a dashed line in pop-up menus and lists or a blank space between radio buttons and check boxes.

FileMaker Pro does not have an option to alphabetize the values in a value list. If you want them in a particular order, you have to type them in that order. However, you can change their order by cutting and pasting them.

— or —

5. Click the radio button labeled "Use values from a field."

   The Specify Fields for Value List dialog box appears, as shown in Figure 5-19.

Figure 5-19: The Specify Fields for Value List dialog box

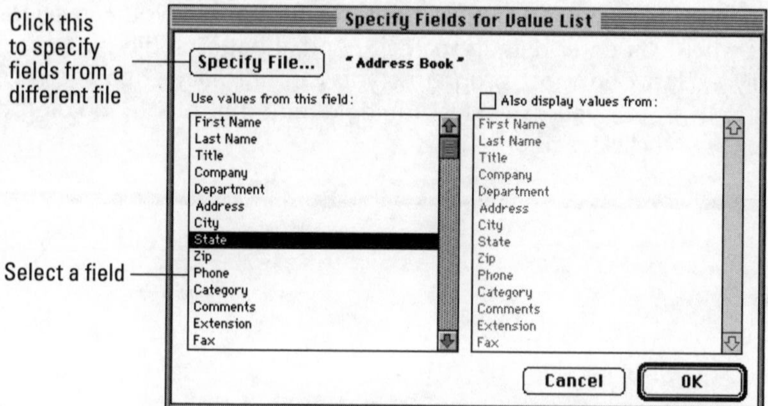

   Choosing this option instructs FileMaker Pro to create a value list based on the contents of another field — in this or in another database. By default, FileMaker Pro lists all fields in the current file. Choose a field on which to base the value list from the scrolling list on the left. (Optionally, you can select a second field from the list on the right.)

   On the other hand, if you want to base the value list on the contents of a field in a *different* database, click the Specify File button and select the database from the file dialog box that appears. Then choose the one or two fields from the scrolling lists. Click OK to leave the Specify Fields for Value List dialog box.

6. Click Done when you are finished creating the value list.

7. *Optional:* If you select any format other than Pop-up list, you can click the check box for "Include 'Other...'" item to allow entry of other values. This adds a choice marked "Other..." to the pop-up menu, check boxes, or radio buttons.

   An Other... choice facilitates the entry of data that is not present in the field's value list.

8. *Optional:* If you have created a custom value list by typing its entries and then choose either of the pop-up formats, you can click the check box for "Include 'Edit...' item to allow editing of the value list." This adds a choice marked "Edit..." to the pop-up list or pop-up menu.

9. Click OK to record the changes or Cancel to leave the field formatting the way it was.

Selecting Multiple Radio Buttons or Check Boxes

If you format a value list field as a set of check boxes, you can select multiple options when you enter data in the field. And although radio button options are mutually exclusive in most programs (you can normally choose only one radio button from a set), you can select multiple radio buttons by holding down the Shift key as you click each one.

Indexing and Storage Options

NEW TO 3 VERSION

In FileMaker Pro 2.1 and earlier, field indexing was done automatically, and data storage was an issue over which you had no control. In FileMaker Pro 3.0, *you* determine whether any or all fields are indexed, as well as whether calculation results are stored with the data file or are calculated only as needed.

Indexing improves the speed with which find and sort operations are performed. Any fields that you regularly sort the database by or use as the basis of Find commands are good candidates for indexing.

Indexing options can be set for any Text, Number, Date, Time, or Calculation field. (Indexing options *cannot* be set for Container, Global, or Summary fields.) In addition to indexing options, you can also set *storage* options for Calculation fields.

To set indexing options for a Text, Number, Date, or Time field, follow these steps:

1. Choose Define Fields from the File menu (or press Shift-⌘-D).

   The Define Fields dialog box appears.

2. Select the field for which you'd like to set storage options and click Options. (If the field has not yet been created, create it first and *then* click Options.)

   An Entry Options dialog box appears.

3. Click the Storage Options button.

   The Storage Options for Field "*field name*" dialog box appears, as shown in Figure 5-20.

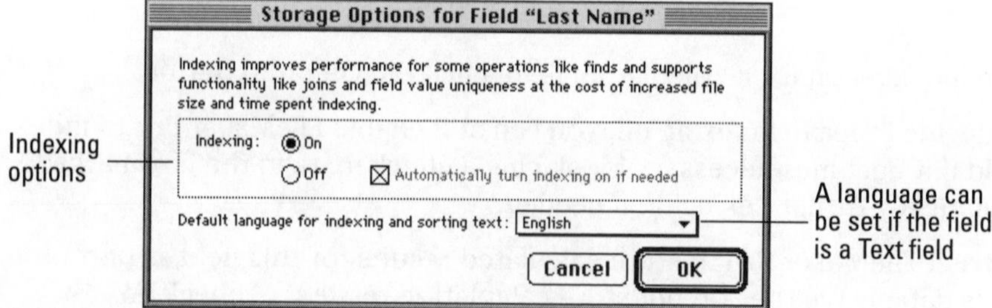
Storage Options for Field "Last Name"
Indexing improves performance for some operations like finds and supports functionality like joins and field value uniqueness at the cost of increased file size and time spent indexing.
Indexing: On
Off
Automatically turn indexing on if needed
Default language for indexing and sorting text: English
Cancel
OK
Indexing options
A language can be set if the field is a Text field

Figure 5-20: The Storage Options dialog box for a Text, Number, Date, or Time field

4. To turn indexing on for a field, click the On radio button.

   If you decide to leave indexing off, you can still enable FileMaker Pro to index the field if it becomes necessary by placing a check mark in the box marked "Automatically turn indexing on if needed."

5. *Optional (for Text fields only):* You can set a particular language to be used to determine sort and index orders by choosing the language from the pop-up menu at the bottom of the dialog box.
6. Click OK to return to the Define Fields dialog box.

To set indexing or storage options for a Calculation field, follow these steps:

1. Choose Define Fields from the File menu (or press Shift-⌘-D).

   The Define Fields dialog box appears.
2. Select the Calculation field for which you'd like to set storage options and click Options. (If the Calculation field has not yet been created, create it first and *then* click Options.)

   A Specify Calculations dialog box appears.
3. Click the Storage Options button.

   The Storage Options for Field "*field name*" dialog box appears, as shown in Figure 5-21.

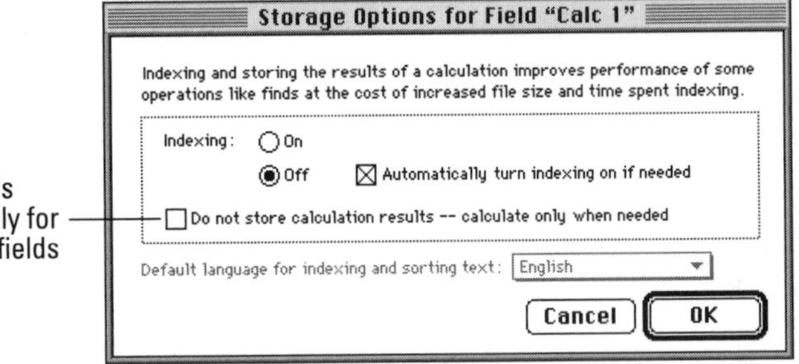
Storage Options for Field "Calc 1"
Indexing and storing the results of a calculation improves performance of some operations like finds at the cost of increased file size and time spent indexing.
Indexing:
On
Off
Automatically turn indexing on if needed
Do not store calculation results -- calculate only when needed
Default language for indexing and sorting text:
English
Cancel
OK
This option is available only for calculation fields

Figure 5-21: The Storage Options dialog box for a Calculation field

4. To turn indexing on for a Calculation field, click the On radio button.

   If you decide to leave indexing off, you can still enable FileMaker Pro to index the field if it becomes necessary by placing a check mark in the box marked "Automatically turn indexing on if needed."
5. To instruct FileMaker Pro to store calculated results for this field as part of the file's data, leave the "Do not store calculation results..." check box unchecked (this is the default setting). If you want to reduce storage requirements for the database (at the expense of increased time to perform recalculations), place a check mark in the check box.
6. Click OK to return to the Define Fields dialog box.

Modifying Field Definitions, Names, and Options

A few capabilities of the Define Fields dialog box still remain unexplored (and unexplained). As previously mentioned, FileMaker Pro 3.0 enables you to add, change, or delete field definitions and options whenever you like. You can also rename fields. And to speed the process of creating fields, FileMaker Pro lets you duplicate existing field definitions. The step-by-step instructions in the following sections explain how to perform these tasks.

Changing Field Names

Unless you give a great deal of thought to field names when you design databases, you'll find that the names you choose for some fields can sometimes stand a little improvement. Feel free to change them to names that are more appropriate. FileMaker Pro 3.0 automatically corrects field labels, sort instructions, and other references to the field (in formulas and scripts, for example).

Follow these steps to give a field a different name:

1. Choose Define Fields from the File menu (or press Shift-⌘-D).

   The Define Fields dialog box appears.

2. Select the field that you want to rename.

   The field name appears in the Field Name text box.

3. Type a new name in the Field Name box and click Save.

   FileMaker Pro renames the field and automatically adjusts any references to the field in Calculation field formulas, Summary fields, and scripts to reflect the new field name. If, when you originally created the field, you accepted and placed the default label for the field in a layout, FileMaker Pro also changes the label to match the new field. Field labels that you have manually edited or typed from scratch, on the other hand, are unaffected.

4. To rename additional fields, repeat steps 2 and 3. Click Done when you are through renaming fields.

Actually, field names aren't all that important. As long as the field name clearly indicates to you what each field is meant to hold, it doesn't matter whether you name a field Sale Amount, Sale, Amount, Amt, or S1. Because each field's default label is identical to the name, however, you may well want to edit the *label* for the field (as it appears in the various layouts) to something more descriptive. Remember, a field label is just a piece of static text and can be changed as you like, whenever you like.

Deleting a Field and Its Data

The more you work with a particular database, the more familiar you become with the data it was designed to collect. If you decide that you no longer need a particular field (or perhaps that you should never have included it in the first place), follow these steps to delete the field and the data it contains:

1. Choose Define Fields from the File menu (or press Shift-⌘-D).

   The Define Fields dialog box appears.

2. Select the field that you want to delete and then click the Delete button.

   One of three dialog boxes appears:

   - The normal dialog box simply asks whether you're sure you want to delete the field and its contents (see Figure 5-22, top).
   - If the field is referenced in a Calculation or Summary field, another dialog box appears (see Figure 5-22, middle), explaining that you cannot delete the field. To delete such a field, you first have to edit the appropriate Calculation and Summary field formulas and options so that they no longer reference the field that you want to delete.
   - If the field defines a current relationship with another database, it cannot be deleted unless you first delete the relationship definition (as shown in Figure 5-22, bottom).

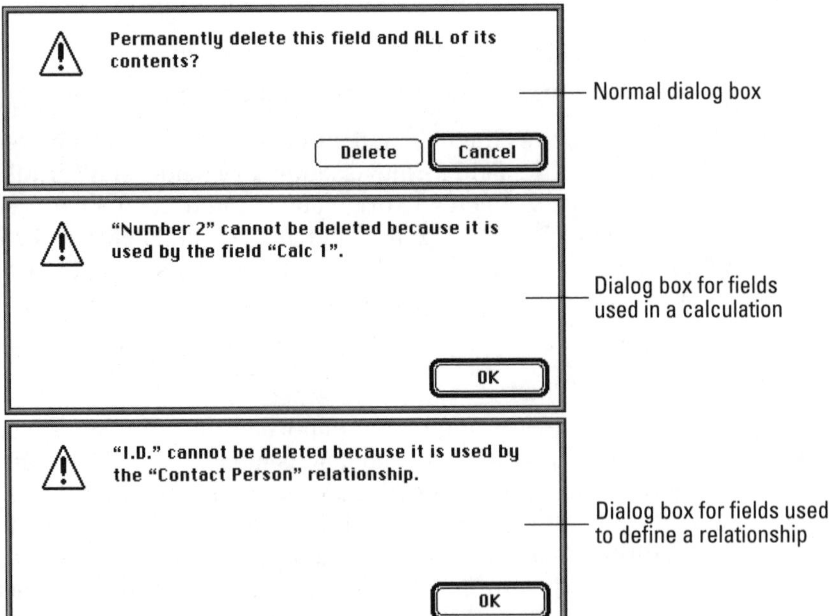
Permanently delete this field and ALL of its contents?
Delete
Cancel
Normal dialog box
"Number 2" cannot be deleted because it is used by the field "Calc 1".
OK
Dialog box for fields used in a calculation
"I.D." cannot be deleted because it is used by the "Contact Person" relationship.
OK
Dialog box for fields used to define a relationship

Figure 5-22: Any of these dialog boxes may appear when you attempt to delete a field.

3. Click the Delete button in the dialog box to delete the field or click Cancel if you change your mind.

4. To delete additional fields, repeat steps 2 and 3. Click Done when you are ready to return to the database.

As the dialog box in Figure 5-22 warns, *deleting a field eliminates the field and all the data for the field.* You cannot undo a field deletion. If there is a chance that you may later need the data, you should first make a backup copy of the file by choosing the Save a Copy As command from the File menu before you delete the field.

An Alternative to Deleting a Field

Instead of deleting a field, you can simply remove it from all layouts. Removing a field in this manner does not delete it. All data previously entered in the field remains intact. To be able to see the data, all you have to do is add the field back onto a layout. This approach makes the database larger than necessary, however, because it is still storing information that you may never use again. If you're *certain* that you no longer need to continue collecting the data for a field, the *best* approach is to make a backup copy of the original database, delete the field in the current version of the file, and then move on.

Duplicating Fields

To save time, you may want to duplicate some existing fields — particularly fields that have complex options that you want to avoid having to recreate. After you duplicate a field, editing and renaming the new field is a simple matter (see the instructions for renaming a field, earlier in this section).

For example, in an invoice or statement database, you might have a series of repeating fields that you use to record each line item (such as Quantity, Description, Unit Cost, and Extended Cost). You'd use separate Calculation fields to compute the total for each of the cost fields. After defining a formula for the first Calculation field as *Sum (Unit Cost)*, you could duplicate the field definition and, in the formula, simply replace *Unit Cost* with *Extended Cost.*

To duplicate an existing field, follow these steps:

1. Choose Define Fields from the File menu (or press Shift-⌘-D).

   The Define Fields dialog box appears.

2. Select the field that you want to duplicate and click the Duplicate button.

   FileMaker Pro creates an exact duplicate of the field and appends the word "Copy" to its name. For example, if the field to be duplicated is named Comments, the duplicate is named Comments Copy. Additional duplicates of the same field are named Comments Copy2, Comments Copy3, and so on.

3. *Optional*: To rename the duplicate field, select the field in the scrolling field list, type a new name in the Field Name box, and click Save.

4. *Optional*: To change any of the options for the duplicate field, select the field and click Options.

5. To duplicate additional fields, repeat steps 2 through 4. Click Done when you are through duplicating fields.

Replacing One Field with Another

Has this ever happened to you? After carefully selecting, placing, resizing, and setting attributes for fields on a layout, you discover that one of the fields wasn't the right one. Rather than deleting the errant field and then adding the correct one, you can use the following trick to redefine the field as a different field:

1. Switch to Layout mode, hold down the ⌘ key, and double-click the field you want to redefine.

   The Specify Field windoid (listing the defined fields for this database, as well as those specified in any existing relationships) appears.

2. Select a replacement field and click OK.

Redefining the field preserves its original placement on the layout, as well as its dimensions and formatting attributes.

Setting Field Options for Existing Fields

You do not have to set field options when you first define a field. You can set them later as the need arises. (However, if you enter data before setting options for a field, you may need to go back and correct some of the earlier entries for the field.)

Follow these steps to set options for fields that you have already defined:

1. Choose Define Fields from the File menu (or press Shift-⌘-D).

   The Define Fields dialog box appears.

2. Select the field for which you want to set options and click the Options button. (You can also double-click any field in the list to move directly to the Options dialog box for that field.)
3. In the dialog box that appears, set options as described in "Setting Field Entry Options," earlier in this chapter.
4. To accept the new options, click OK. To ignore the options you have selected, click Cancel.
5. To set options for other fields, repeat steps 2 through 4. Click Done when you are through setting options.

Changing a Field Definition

The following steps describe how to change a field definition:

1. Choose Define Fields from the File menu (or press Shift-⌘-D).

   The Define Fields dialog box appears.

2. Select the field you want to change.

3. To change the field's type, select a new type and click Save.

   If changing to the new field type involves any potential problems, FileMaker Pro presents a dialog box, such as the ones shown in Figure 5-23. (The *particular* box that you see is related to the type of change that you want to make.) This warning box contains information that you should consider before proceeding with the conversion. If such a warning box appears, you may want to use the Save a Copy As command to make a backup copy of the database before you proceed.

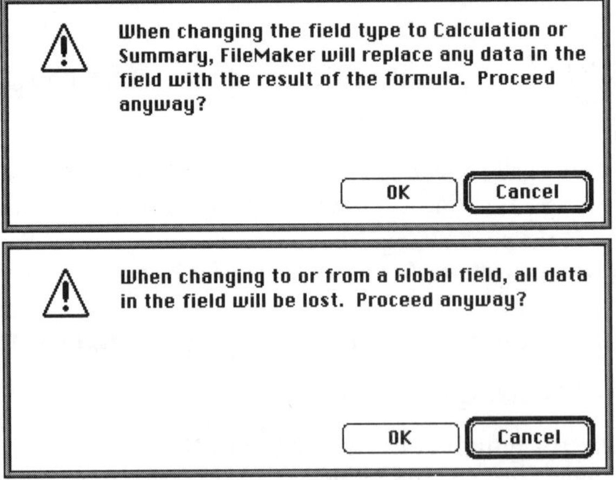
When changing the field type to Calculation or Summary, FileMaker will replace any data in the field with the result of the formula. Proceed anyway?
OK
Cancel
When changing to or from a Global field, all data in the field will be lost. Proceed anyway?
OK
Cancel

Figure 5-23: Warning boxes like these may appear when you are changing a field type.

— or —

3. If you are changing the field to a Summary or Calculation field, click the Options button, select a summary function or create the formula for the Calculation field, and click OK to accept the changes or Cancel to revert to the original settings. Similarly, if the change is to a Global field, choose a data type for the field (in the Options dialog box that appears) and then click OK.

4. To change additional field definitions, repeat steps 2 and 3 for each field. When you are through, click Done to leave the Define Fields dialog box.

Changing or Deleting Options for a Field

To change or delete options for a field, follow these steps:

1. Choose Define Fields from the File menu (or press Shift-⌘-D).

   The Define Fields dialog box appears.

2. Select the field whose options you want to change and then click the Options button or double-click the field name in the field list.

   An Options dialog box appears, appropriate to the data type of the field that you selected.

3. Change the options that you want to modify and then click OK to return to the Define Fields dialog box.

   The means of changing options is always obvious. You can add or remove options by clicking check boxes, clicking buttons, making selections from pop-up menus, and using normal editing techniques (to change value lists and formulas, for example).

4. To change options for other fields, repeat steps 2 and 3. Click Done when you are through changing field options.

Summary

- FileMaker Pro 3.0 includes eight field types: Text, Number, Date, Time, Container, Calculation, Summary, and Global. The type that you choose for a field determines the kinds of information that you can enter in the field.
- The new Global field type enables you to record a single value that is used for every record for the current database. A Global field value is stored only once the entire database (rather than storing a separate copy of the value for every record).
- You can set auto-entry options for a field to instruct FileMaker Pro to automatically enter a value for a field whenever you create a new record or, in some cases, when you edit a record. By selecting the option labeled "Prohibit modification of value," you can protect the auto-entered data from inadvertent (or deliberate) modification.
- Rather than associate each user-defined value list with a particular field (as was done in previous versions of FileMaker Pro), any value list that has been defined for a database can now be associated with *many* fields in the database.
- Data validation options help ensure that only acceptable values are entered for a field. By selecting the option labeled "Strict: Do not allow user to over-ride validation," you can protect the integrity of the field's data and ensure that only the *right* kind of information is accepted.
- You can alter the fields for a database at any time by changing their names, definitions, or options. You can also add new fields or delete existing fields.

CHAPTER 6

Layouts

In This Chapter

- Creating standard and special-purpose layouts
- Understanding and using the different layout parts
- Adding and removing elements from layout parts
- Formatting fields and other items in a layout

If you have previously used other database programs — particularly any of the simpler ones, such as Retriever or HyperCard — before you switched to FileMaker Pro, you may have gotten used to routinely creating every field that was needed for a database and then dutifully arranging them all on a single form. That, however, is *not* the way that FileMaker Pro works.

Although you may create dozens or even hundred of fields for a FileMaker Pro database, it's unlikely that you'd ever want or need to display them all on the same form. To print envelopes or mailing labels, for example, you only need the name and address fields for each client in your database (you don't need information about the products that each client has ordered). If you're preparing a summary of recent sales figures, client address information is of little importance. Even though all this data may be collected in the same database, you only need to display it where it's appropriate. The FileMaker Pro feature that makes this possible is called the layout.

A *layout* is a particular arrangement of all or a subset of the fields that have been defined for a database. You choose the fields that are included in each layout — as many or as few fields as you like. You can arrange the fields in each layout to address a specific need (such as printing labels, entering data, or presenting a report); you can add layout parts, such as a header and footer, to make some information repeat on every page, for example; and you can include special items to help identify your layouts or make them more attractive (such as titles, graphics, and buttons). *You can have as many layouts for a given database as you like — one to suit every need.* (For a quick introduction to creating and modifying layouts, see Chapter 4.)

Users of previous versions of FileMaker Pro have two new layout tools to learn about in FileMaker Pro 3.0. First, there is now a Button tool with which you can make attractive 3-D buttons. Second, the Tools palette includes a Portal tool that enables you to create a window into any related database. (The new relational capabilities of FileMaker Pro 3.0 are discussed in greater detail in Chapter 19.)

Layout Basics

A FileMaker Pro layout is composed of layout parts (the sections of the layout, such as the body, header, and footer), fields (in which data is entered and displayed), and static objects (such as graphics, titles, and field labels).

When you design a new database and define its initial set of fields, FileMaker Pro automatically creates a default layout for you (named Layout #1). The default layout is a one-column arrangement of all fields that have been defined for the database in the order that they were defined. To create the initial layout for a new database, follow these steps:

1. To create a new database when launching FileMaker Pro, choose “Create a new empty file” from the New Database dialog box that automatically appears.

— or —

1. If FileMaker Pro is already running, choose New from the File menu. Then choose “Create a new empty file” from the New Database dialog box that appears.

   The Define Fields dialog box appears.

2. Define the initial fields for the database by following the procedures outlined in Chapter 5. Click Done when you are finished.

A default layout entitled Layout #1 appears (see Figure 6-1), ready for you to begin entering data. The first record is automatically created for you, and the database switches to Browse mode.

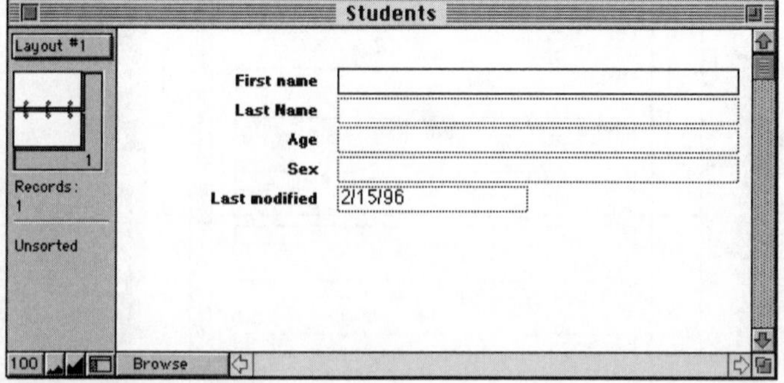

Figure 6-1: A new, default layout

For many data collection purposes, the initial layout is all you'll need. If you have other layout requirements, such as printing labels or generating reports, you will want to create additional layouts that present the data in other ways.

You aren't locked into using Layout #1 as is — or at all, for that matter. You may find that it can serve as the basis for a custom layout. You just change the formatting and arrangement of its fields. On the other hand, if you don't even want to use it as the starting point for a custom layout, you can delete it. Modifying and deleting layouts are explained later in this chapter.

You create new layouts and modify existing ones in Layout mode, which is one of FileMaker Pro's four operational modes. (The others are Browse, Find, and Preview.) Switch to Layout mode, and you'll see a screen similar to Figure 6-2, which shows the Address Book database that you created in Chapter 4 in Layout mode.

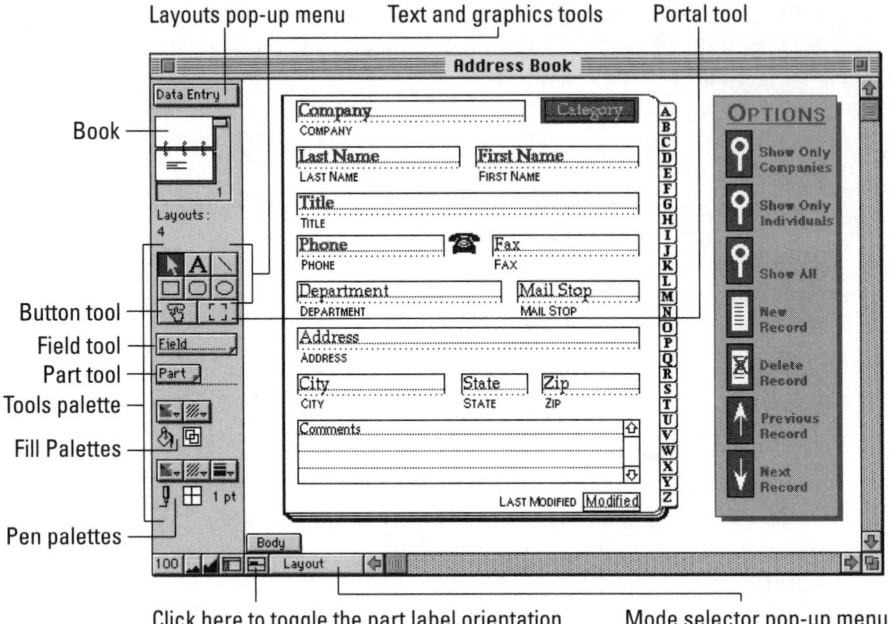

Figure 6-2: The Address Book database in Layout mode

At the upper-left corner of the Address Book database is a pop-up menu, listing the layouts that have been defined. This menu enables you to choose an existing layout to edit. Below the pop-up menu is a book icon that also gives you access to available layouts. You click the book to page up and down through the available layouts. Below the book icon are the tools that you use to add or modify elements on a layout. You use the field and part icons to create new layout parts and to add fields to the layout.

Important Layout mode features and options can be found in the Mode, Show, Arrange, and Format menus. These menus contain commands to add items to layouts, arrange them, and specify how to display them. To switch to Layout mode, follow these steps:

1. Launch FileMaker Pro, if it isn't already running.
2. Open the database in which you want to add, modify, or view layouts.
3. Choose Layout from the Mode menu (or press ⌘-L) or choose Layout from the mode selector pop-up menu at the bottom of the document window (as shown previously in Figure 6-2).

4. From the layouts pop-up menu in the upper-left corner of the window, choose the layout you want to view.

— or —

4. Click the book icon to page through the available layouts until the one you want appears.

Creating New Layouts

As previously explained, after you define fields for a new database, FileMaker Pro creates your first layout for you. You can immediately use this layout for data entry and browsing, if you like.

To view data in other ways, you must add more layouts. FileMaker Pro includes seven predefined layout styles that you can use as starting points. The supported layout styles are described in Table 6-1.

Table 6-1
FileMaker Pro Predefined Layout Styles

Layout Name	*Purpose*
Standard	Shows one record per screen, with all fields displayed in the order in which they were defined; same as the default layout used when creating a new database.
Columnar report	Fields are displayed left to right in columns with one record per line. Fields that don't fit on one line are wrapped to the next line.
Extended columnar	Same as the Columnar report layout except that the fields aren't wrapped. All fields are displayed on one line, no matter how long.
Single page form	One record per screen with no header or footer.
Labels	Fields are formatted for use with mailing labels.
Envelope	Fields are formatted for use with business envelopes.
Blank	A blank layout that you can use to create custom layouts.

Follow these steps to create a new layout based on any of the predefined layout styles:

1. Determine what sort of layout you want to use and what fields you need to display.

2. With the appropriate database open in FileMaker Pro, switch to Layout mode by choosing Layout from the Mode menu (or by pressing ⌘-L).
3. Choose New Layout from the Mode menu (or press ⌘-N).

   The New Layout dialog box appears, as shown in Figure 6-3.

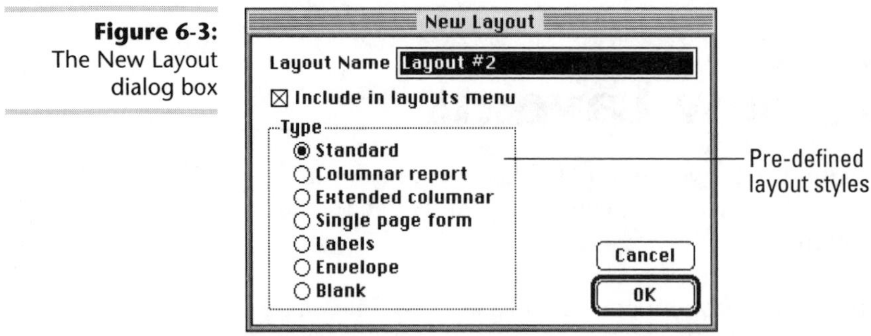

Figure 6-3: The New Layout dialog box

4. Type a name for the new layout.
5. Choose the layout style you want to use by clicking the appropriate radio button in the Type box. (Do not choose the Blank type unless you want to create a layout from scratch, as described later in this chapter.)
6. Determine whether the layout should appear in the layouts pop-up menu by leaving or removing the check mark in the "Include in layouts menu" check box.
7. Click OK to create the layout.

If you choose the Standard, Single page form, or Blank layout type, FileMaker Pro creates your layout immediately. The Standard and Single page form layouts include all fields that have been defined for the database; the Blank layout contains *no* fields (that is, it consists of just a blank page).

The other layout types use a limited set of the fields (such as the Labels and Envelope layouts). When you choose a Columnar report, Extended columnar, Labels, or Envelope layout, a dialog box appears where you must select which fields to use, as explained in the following sections.

Hiding Layouts

Being able to display the name of a layout in the layouts pop-up menu or hide it can be very useful. For example, if you are distributing a shareware template, you may want to reveal certain layouts only after users have paid the shareware fee. Similarly, there may be some layouts that you *never* want users to see. Hiding a layout by removing the check mark from the "Include in layouts menu" check box (previously shown in Figure 6-3) makes it impossible to see the layout in Browse mode. (It can still be seen in Layout mode, however.) Hiding the layout in this manner and setting appropriate access options can make it *completely* invisible to the user.

You can also hide any layout to which you don't want users to be able to switch. In a database that is entirely script controlled, for example, you might list only the layout for the main menu or the data-entry screen, and leave the task of switching to other layouts to scripts attached to navigation buttons. This way, you can keep users from inadvertently messing up the database by directly selecting layouts that should normally be reached only as part of a script.

Regardless of the type of layout you choose, the sections included in the layout (called layout *parts*) are restricted to a body (where the fields are generally placed) and, in some cases, a header and a footer part. You'll learn all about adding, removing, and modifying layout parts in "Working with Layout Parts," later in this chapter.

Standard and Single Page Form Layouts

A Standard layout is the same one that FileMaker Pro creates as the default data-entry layout (Layout #1) when you define fields for a new database. All the fields in your database are automatically included in a Standard layout and they appear, top to bottom, in the order in which they were defined. Fields are labeled with their field names. Figure 6-4 shows a Standard layout.

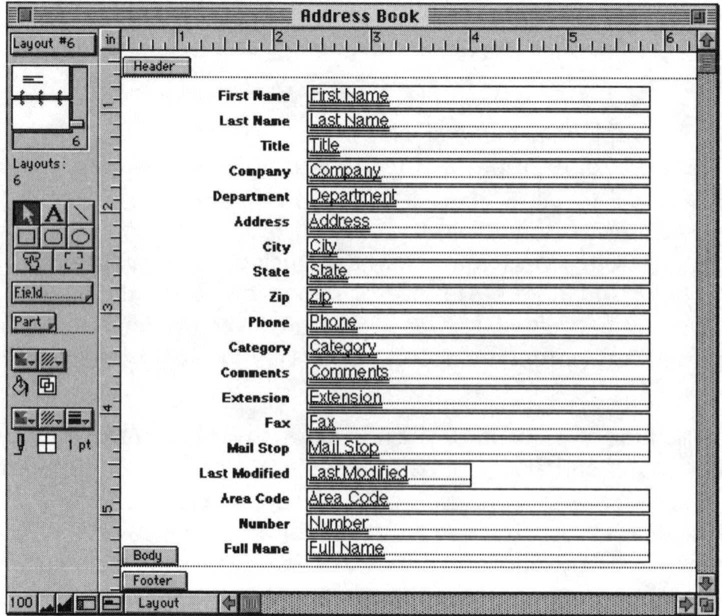

Figure 6-4: A Standard layout for the Address Book database

In this type of layout, one record is displayed at a time. In addition to the body area, where the fields are displayed, the layout includes blank header and footer parts.

The Single page form layout is exactly same as the Standard layout, except that it doesn't have a header or footer part. It contains only a body in which all the defined database fields are displayed in a single column.

Columnar Layouts

FileMaker Pro offers two kinds of *columnar* layouts (in which fields are displayed in columns across the page). In a Columnar report layout, FileMaker Pro attempts to fit all fields on a single line but wraps excess fields to the next line. In an Extended columnar layout, FileMaker Pro displays all fields on a single line, no matter how wide the line is. Columnar and Extended columnar layouts are frequently used to produce reports. Figure 6-5 shows an Extended columnar layout for the Address Book database.

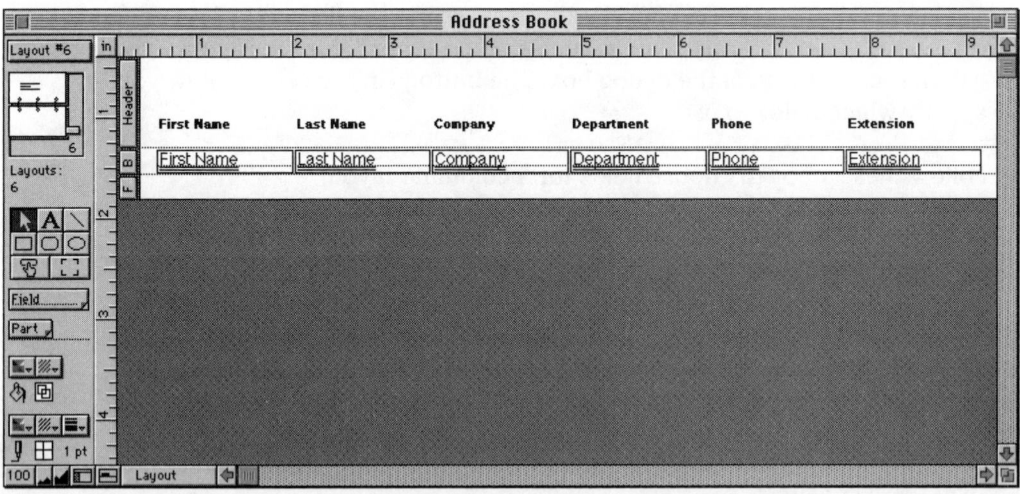

Figure 6-5: An Extended columnar layout for the Address Book database

Only the fields that you specify appear in a columnar layout. When you create a columnar layout, the Specify Field Order dialog box appears (see Figure 6-6). In this dialog box, you specify which fields should appear in the layout and in what order across the page.

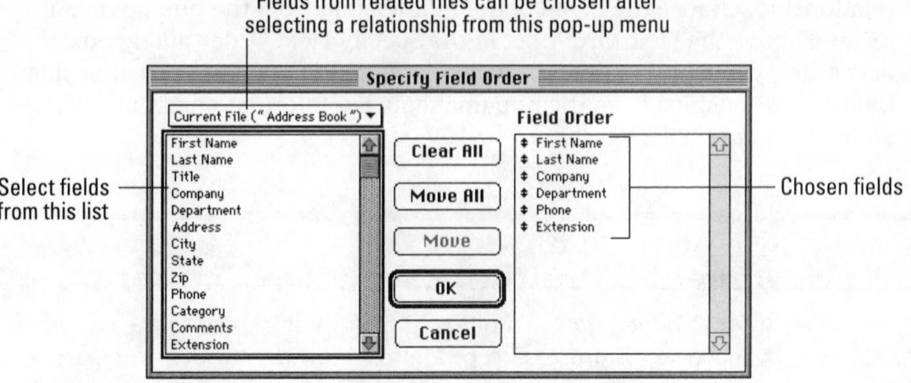

Figure 6-6: The Specify Field Order dialog box

The names of the fields in your database appear in the list on the left side of the dialog box. The currently selected fields and their order in the layout appear in the list on the right side of the dialog box. The buttons in the center allow you to specify which fields to use.

Follow these steps to choose fields for a columnar layout:

1. In the Specify Field Order dialog box, click the name of the field that you want to appear first in the layout (as the leftmost column).
2. Click the Move button to move this field to the Field Order list.
3. Repeat steps 1 and 2 for all fields that you want to use in the layout.
4. When you finish adding fields, click OK.

   FileMaker Pro creates the layout with the fields you specified in the order you specified.

After fields have been moved into the Field Order list, you can change their order by dragging a field's name up or down to another position. To remove a selected field from the Field Order list, select its name in the list and then click Clear. (The Move button changes to Clear when you select a field in the Field Order list.) To remove all fields and start over, click Clear All.

Because FileMaker Pro 3.0 is a relational database program, you can also add *related* fields to layouts. To choose fields from any currently defined relationship, choose the name of the relationship from the pop-up menu located above the Field Order list in the Specify Field Order dialog box. If necessary, you can also define a new relationship at this time by choosing Define Relationships from the pop-up menu. For information about relationships, see Chapter 19.

Previewing and Printing Layouts in Columns

If you merely want to *print* data in a multi-column format (similar to the column formatting in advanced word processing programs), you don't need to create a separate columnar layout. Using the Layout Setup command, you can instruct FileMaker to print or preview *any* layout in two or more columns. The columns are visible only in Preview mode or when you print the database; Browse mode still shows the original layout.

Choosing Layout Setup from the Mode menu brings up the Layout Setup dialog box, as shown in the Figure 6-7.

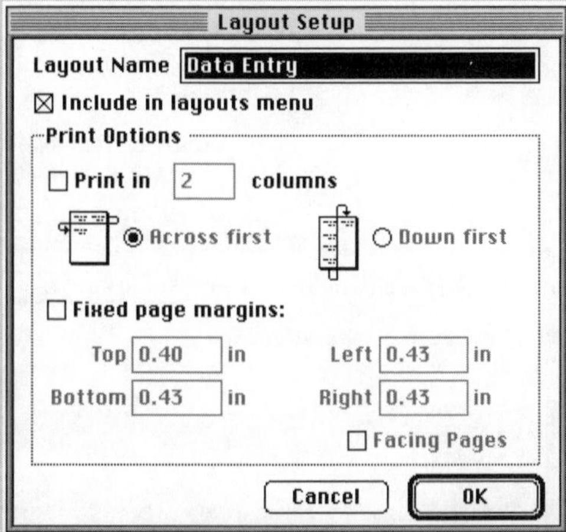

Figure 6-7: The Layout Setup dialog box

Click the "Print in" check box to choose to display columns and then indicate how many columns you want to use by typing a number in the text box. Finally, specify how records will fill the columns by clicking the radio button that corresponds to the desired option:

- Across first: Fills each column across the page before proceeding to the next row. This option is good for printing labels and whenever you want to conserve paper.
- Down first: Fills an entire column on a page and then moves to the top of the next column. This option is appropriate for phone directory listings, for example.

If you use Apple's LaserWriter 8 printer driver, you can create a similar effect in the Page Setup dialog box. From the Page Setup's Layout pop-up menu, choose either 2-Up or 4-Up. Instead of printing a single record per page, either two or four records will now appear on every page.

Label Layouts

FileMaker Pro's predefined Labels layout style is designed specifically for printing labels. You can specify any of the supported Avery label formats, or you can create your own label format.

When you choose the Labels layout style to create a new layout, the Label Setup dialog box appears (see Figure 6-8). You use this dialog box to specify a label format.

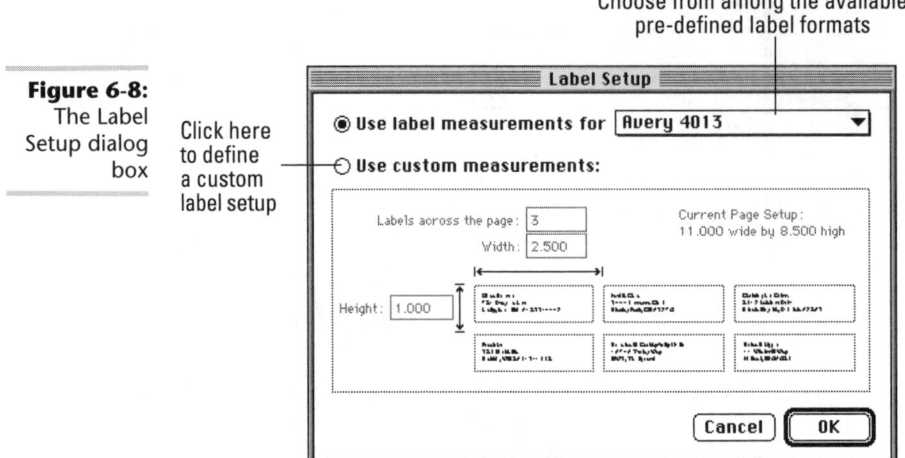

Figure 6-8: The Label Setup dialog box

The Label Setup dialog box contains two radio-button options: one for using the predefined Avery label formats, and another for entering custom measurements. The latter procedure can be tricky if you don't have much experience working with label stock.

Using a Predefined Avery Label Format

Follow these steps to use any of the predefined Avery label formats in your Labels layout:

1. In the Label Setup dialog box (previously shown in Figure 6-8), click the "Use label measurements for" radio button.
2. Select the Avery label part number for the label stock that you want to use from the pop-up menu.

3. Click OK.

   The Specify Layout Contents dialog box appears, as shown in Figure 6-9.

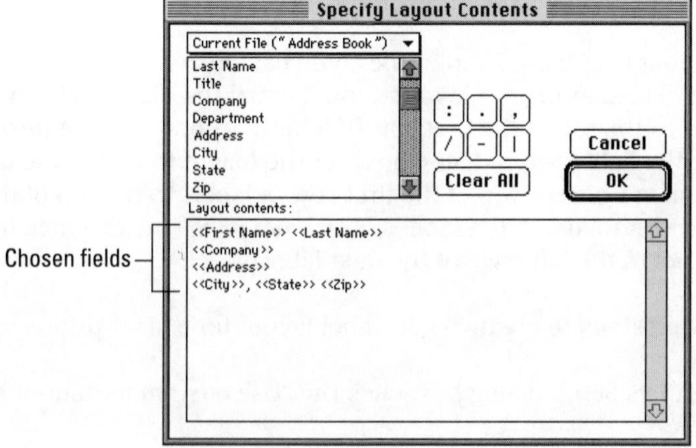

Figure 6-9: The Specify Layout Contents dialog box

4. Select fields for the label layout by double-clicking them.

   Add space between fields and punctuation marks, as necessary. Be sure to press Return to end each label line (except the last one).

5. Click OK to finish defining the label layout.

If you've used other versions of FileMaker Pro, you'll notice that the process of creating a label layout has changed considerably. When creating a label layout in previous versions of the program, you only had to choose the fields that would be included in the layout. Then you returned to the layout and made any necessary changes to the fields, such as altering their size, placement, or formatting.

In FileMaker Pro 3.0, the arrangement of fields (including the line each one is on, as well as the spacing and punctuation that separates fields) is set in the Specify Layout Contents dialog box. In addition, rather than place normal fields on the layout, FileMaker Pro now places the entire label as a block of merge fields. (Merge fields are surrounded by bracket symbols, as shown previously in Figure 6-9.) Unlike a normal field, a merge field does not have to be resized; it automatically expands as needed to handle the data it must contain. In fact, when you finally see the layout that has been generated, the only thing you may want to change is the formatting (selecting a different font or size, for instance).

Creating Custom Label Formats

If you buy labels from a company other than Avery and don't know which, if any, Avery label is compatible, you can choose the "Use custom measurements" option in the Label Setup dialog box to create your own label format.

If you know a couple of fairly simple rules, you can create labels from scratch. First, the height of the header in your layout should equal the distance from the top of the label sheet to the top of the first row of labels. Second, when entering the dimensions in the Label Setup dialog box, set the height to match the label's *vertical pitch* (the distance from the top of the first row of labels to the top of the second row). Set the width to match the label's *horizontal pitch* (the distance from the left edge of one label to the left edge of the next label).

Use the following steps to create a new label layout for a laser printer:

1. In the Labels Setup dialog box, click the "Use custom measurements" radio button.

   The dimmed area at the bottom of the dialog box becomes active.

2. Enter the height and width for the labels, as well as the number of labels across, and then click OK.

   If the dimension entered for the label height does not divide evenly into the length of the label page, an alert message appears. Click OK to use the currently entered label height or Cancel to enter a different height.

   The Specify Layout Contents dialog box appears, as shown previously in Figure 6-9.

3. Select the fields to be placed on the labels.

   Add space between fields and punctuation marks, as necessary. Be sure to press Return to end each label line (except the last one).

4. Click OK when you are finished.

   The label layout appears.

5. Choose the Size command from the Show menu.

   The Size windoid appears.

6. Click the Header part label to select it. Then in the Size windoid (shown in Figure 6-10), click the bottom value to select it and enter the header height (the distance from the top of the label sheet to the top of the first row of labels).

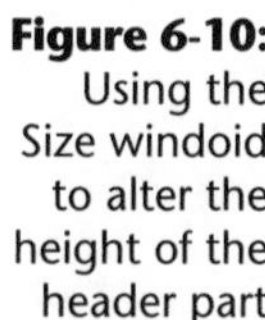

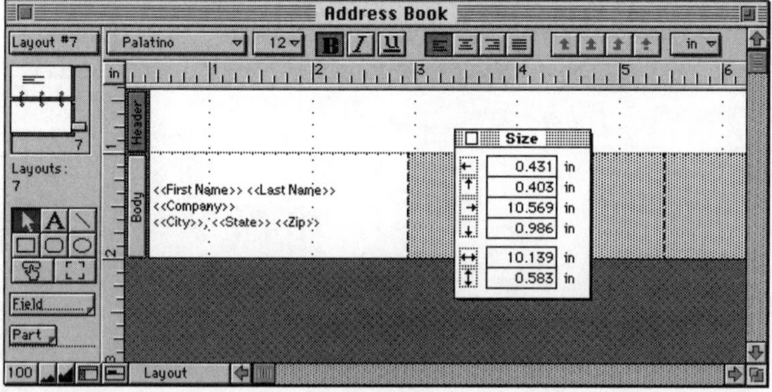

Figure 6-10: Using the Size windoid to alter the height of the header part

7. *Optional:* Format the fields in the layout as needed.

   After using the Text tool to select a field name and its surrounding brackets, you can apply formatting commands, such as choosing a different font, style, or size. If you want to apply the same formatting to *all* fields, use the Pointer tool to select the entire block of fields and then choose formatting commands.

Envelope Layouts

The process of creating an Envelope layout is very similar to that of creating a label layout. Just follow these steps:

1. Switch to Layout mode and choose New Layout from the Mode menu (or press ⌘-N).

   The New Layout dialog box appears.

2. Enter a name for the layout, click the Envelope radio button, and then click OK.
3. Click OK again.

   The Specify Layout Contents dialog box appears (as shown previously in Figure 6-9).

4. Select fields for the envelope layout by double-clicking them.

   Add space between fields and punctuation marks, as necessary. Be sure to press Return to end each address line (except the last one).

5. Click OK to finish defining the layout.

   The new envelope layout appears, as shown in Figure 6-11.

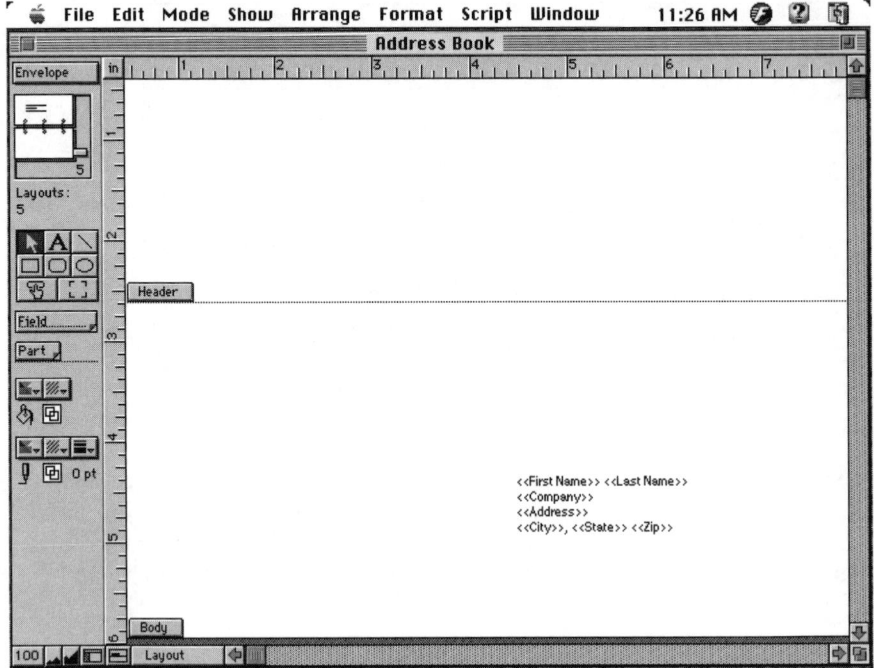

Figure 6-11: An Envelope layout prepared for use with the Address Book database

Like a Labels layout, FileMaker Pro 3.0 uses its new merge fields to format the body of an Envelope layout. Rather than place normal, resizable fields on the layout, the entire envelope address is a single text object with the field names embedded in it. (If you attempt to click on any of the address information, you'll see that the field is surrounded by four *handles* — black dots.) If you want to change the formatting of the address, you can use the Text tool to select individual field names and their surrounding brackets (<< >>) and then choose commands from the Format menu.

As with any other type of layout, you can add static graphic and text items (such as your logo or the return address), if you wish. These operations are detailed in the section called "Designing Your Own Layouts."

Blank Layouts

As its name suggests, the Blank layout style presents you with a blank form — devoid of fields and field labels. The layout contains header, body, and footer parts. Choose the Blank layout style when you want to create a layout entirely from scratch.

As an alternative, you will sometimes find it easier to edit an existing layout (a Standard layout, for example) or to duplicate an existing layout and then edit the duplicate.

Designing Your Own Layouts

There's often more to creating layouts than just cloning a template and tossing in a few fields. For example, you may want to put fields in different positions in the layout; or you may want certain fields to print only at the top or bottom of a page or only after a group of sorted records. Further, you may want to apply formatting to different fields and to add extra objects, such as field labels and graphics. FileMaker Pro's Layout mode has tools and commands that enable you to do all these things and more.

Understanding Layout Parts

All FileMaker Pro layouts are divided into *parts* that control how and when data appears. When you change to Layout mode, each layout part is labeled. Figure 6-12 shows many of the available layout parts as they appear when you're in Layout mode and Preview mode. The various layout parts are described in the following sections.

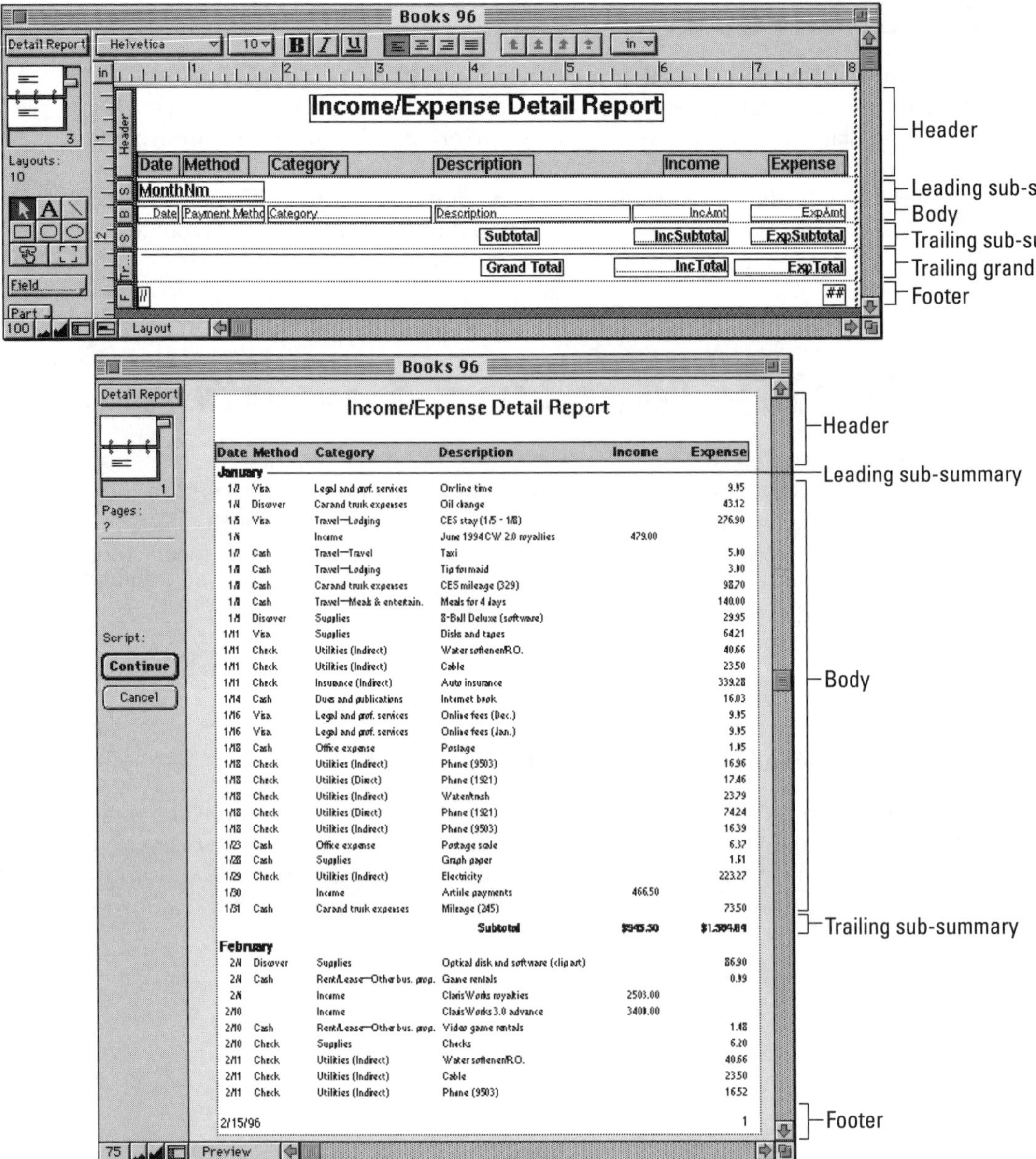

Figure 6-12: Layout parts as they look in Layout mode (top) and in Preview mode or when printed (bottom)

Body

Every layout normally has a body. The layout body is displayed once for each record. If you have fields that you want to see in every record you view, you should put those fields in the layout body. If you open several databases from the *Macworld FileMaker Pro 3.0 Bible Disk* and then switch to Layout mode, you'll note that the bulk of the fields usually appear in the body of the layout. (If you don't want to see detailed data for each record, you can remove the body from the layout, as long as you leave some other part — such as a sub-summary or summary part.)

Header

FileMaker Pro displays the header at the top of every page. The header is visible in all modes. At printing time (or in Preview mode), the header is printed (or shown) at the top of each page. You can use headers for column headings, report titles, logos, and so on. Layout navigation buttons are commonly placed in the header area, too. You can also create a *title header* part that is visible only on the first page of a printed or previewed report.

Footer

FileMaker Pro displays the footer at the bottom of every page. The footer is visible in all modes. At printing time (or in Preview mode), the footer is printed (or shown) at the bottom of each page. You can also create a special *title footer* part that prints only on the first page of a report.

Sub-summary and Grand Summary Parts

Sub-summary and grand summary parts are used to print information that summarizes the found set of records; that is, the current subset of records that you are browsing. You use these parts to display information calculated by Summary fields that have been placed in these parts. A *Summary field*, in effect, computes a statistic (such as a total or average) across all records in the found set.

Sub-summary parts are used to display or print a summary of values for records sorted by a specific field. A sub-summary of total sales by salesperson, for example, would show the sales subtotal for each salesperson in the current found set. In this example, the database must first be sorted by the Salesperson Name field. The field on which the database is sorted is also referred to as a *break field* (it breaks the database into groups). You must select a break field when you create the sub-summary part.

A grand summary part is used to display or print summary figures for the entire found set (rather than for each sub-group in the found set, as is done in a sub-summary part), regardless of their sort order. For example, you could display the grand total of sales for all salespeople in a database.

You can place a sub-summary or grand summary part before or after the body. The former is called a *leading* sub-summary or grand summary, and the latter is called a *trailing* sub-summary or grand summary. To learn more about using Summary fields and summary parts, see Chapter 5.

The report layout previously shown in Figure 6-12 includes two sub-summary parts. Each uses the Month field as the break field; that is, the database must first be sorted by the Month field in order to generate a report that groups records by month. The leading sub-summary part is used to display a single field containing the name of the month. The trailing sub-summary part displays the summary data (income and expense totals for each month). A trailing grand summary is used to display the total income and expense amounts for the entire found set.

Adding a Layout Part

You use the Part Setup command to add a part to a layout. The Part Setup dialog box appears, as shown in Figure 6-13.

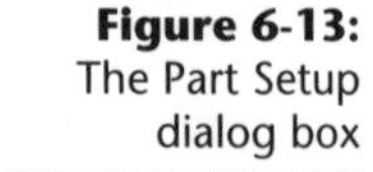

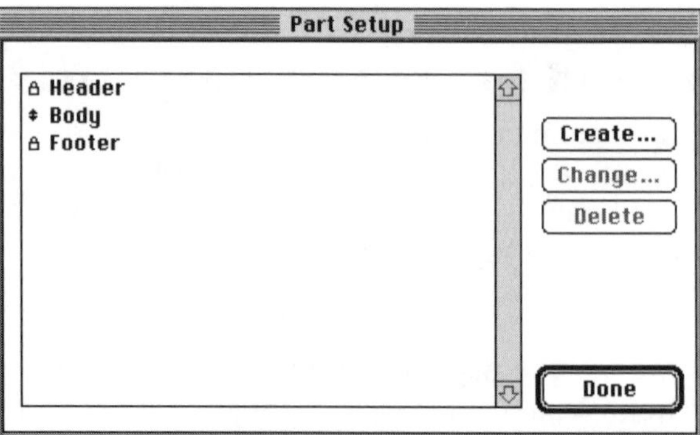

Figure 6-13: The Part Setup dialog box

This dialog box shows all parts that are currently used in the layout. To add a new part, click the Create button. The Part Definition dialog box appears, as shown in Figure 6-14.

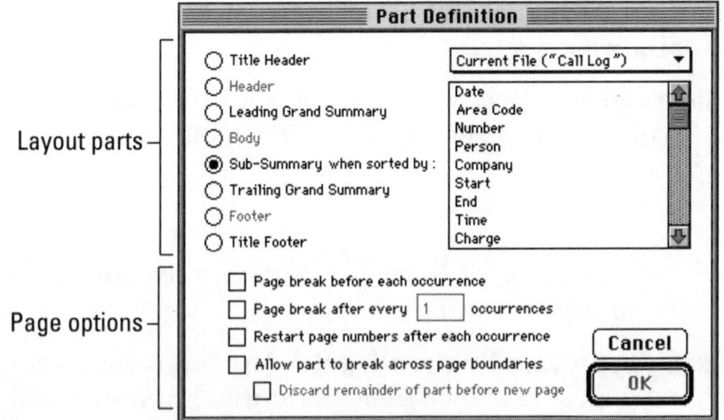

Figure 6-14: The Part Definition dialog box

You can go *directly* to the Part Definition dialog box — without seeing the Part Setup dialog box first — by clicking the part icon in the Tools palette and dragging it onto the layout.

To specify the type of part you're creating, click the appropriate radio button. (Buttons are dimmed for parts that already exist or that aren't appropriate for the type of layout that you're modifying.) Below the radio buttons are check box options for page numbering and page breaks. The specific options that can be set vary with the type of part you're creating.

Follow these steps to add a new part to a layout:

1. In Layout mode, choose the appropriate layout from the layouts pop-up menu.
2. Choose Part Setup from the Layout menu and, when the Part Setup dialog box appears (as previously shown in Figure 6-13), click Create.

   — or —

2. Drag the Part tool across to the layout.

   In either case, the Part Definition dialog box appears (as previously shown in Figure 6-14).
3. Click the radio button for the part you want to add.

   If the button is dimmed, the part already exists or isn't appropriate to the layout that you chose.
4. *Optional:* Choose page-numbering and page-break options.

5. If the part is a sub-summary, choose the sort field from the field list on the right side of the dialog box.

   The sort field can also be selected from any file that is related to the current database. To display these fields, choose the name of the relationship from the pop-up menu.

6. Click OK.

   If you began this process by dragging a part onto the layout, you are immediately returned to Layout mode.

   If you began this process by choosing the Part Setup command, you return to the Part Setup dialog box. Click Done to return to Layout mode.

Modifying Parts

You can change existing parts in several ways. For example:

- You can change a part's size.
- You can change the order in which parts appear on a page — within limits. (You can't put a header below the body or a footer above it, for instance.)
- You can change the part types and options.
- You can move the part labels out of your way.
- You can delete a part.

These procedures are explained in the following sections.

Resizing Layout Parts

To change the height of a part, you drag its label. Part labels appear on the left side of the layout area. The name of the part appears in its label.

Follow these steps to make a layout part larger or smaller:

1. Switch to Layout mode and choose the appropriate layout from the layouts pop-up menu.
2. Locate the label for the part that you want to resize. (The label contains the part's name.)

3. Click and drag the part label in the appropriate direction: up to make the part smaller or down to make it larger.
4. Release the mouse button when the part is the size you want.

FileMaker Pro allows you to drag a part until you come to some other object — a field in another part, for example. To drag past an object (text, a graphic, or a field), hold down the Option key as you drag.

You can also set the height of a part by choosing the Size command from the Show menu. This command allows you to set the part's height precisely. Choosing the Size command brings up a small window (called a *windoid)* like the one shown in Figure 6-15.

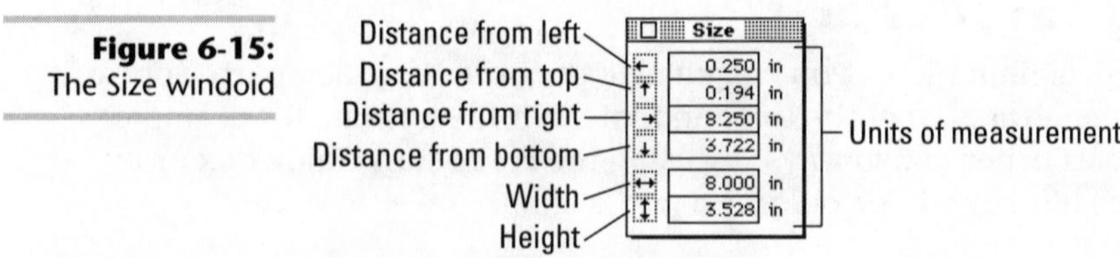

Figure 6-15: The Size windoid

The Size windoid includes dimensions for the top, bottom, left and right margins of a part and for the part's width and height.

To specify a part's size precisely, follow these steps:

1. In Layout mode, choose the appropriate layout from the layouts pop-up menu.
2. Choose the Size command from the Show menu.

   The Size windoid appears.
3. Click the label of the part that you want to resize.

   The part label turns dark to show that it is selected.
4. Enter the desired height for the selected part in the bottom text box. Press Tab, Enter, or Return to put the new height into effect.

Multi-Page Layouts

If you like, you can extend a single layout body over two or more pages. To do so, you simply make the body very long, changing its length by dragging its part name (Body) downward on the layout. FileMaker Pro then displays a dashed line to show where the page breaks. Place the fields that you want to appear on the first page above the dashed line; put fields for the second page below the dashed line. Of course, pages can be broken right to left (the wide way) as well.

Reordering Layout Parts

Within certain logical limitations, you can change the order in which parts appear in a layout. Headers always go at the top and footers at the bottom, for example. You can change part order in two ways: by using the Part Setup dialog box or by holding down the Shift key while you drag a part's label.

To use the Set Layout Order command to change the order of parts, follow these steps:

1. In Layout mode, switch to the appropriate layout.
2. Choose Part Setup from the Mode menu.

   The Part Setup dialog box appears, as shown in Figure 6-16.

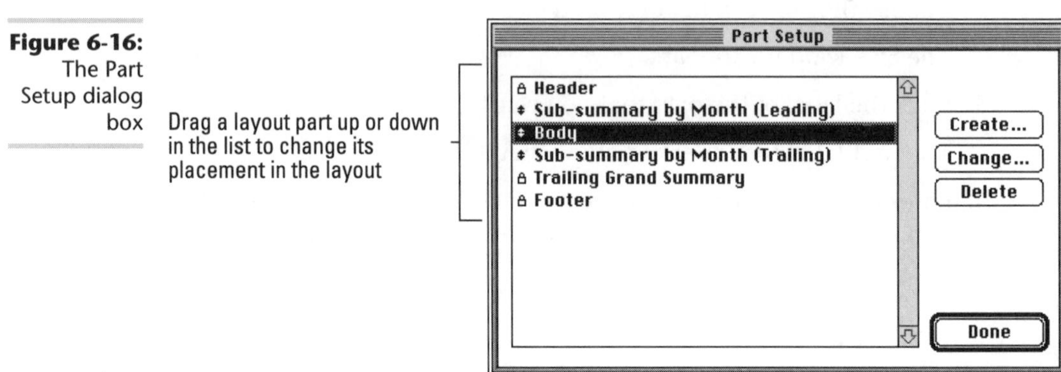

Figure 6-16: The Part Setup dialog box

3. Drag part names up or down in the part list to set their new order.

A part name with a lock icon next to it (such as a trailing grand summary) cannot be moved.

4. Click Done.

Changing Part Types and Options

You can change a part's type, and you can reset certain options for the parts. (For example, you might want to choose a different break field for a sub-summary part.) You do both of these in the Part Definition dialog box. Follow these steps to change a part's type and/or options:

1. In Layout mode, switch to the layout that contains the part you want to modify.
2. Double-click the label for the part you want to change.

— or —

2. Choose Part Setup from the Mode menu, select the part name, and click the Change button.

   In either case, the Part Definition dialog box appears for the chosen part (as previously shown in Figure 6-14).

3. Click options to make the necessary changes.

Options that are dimmed are not available or are not allowed.

4. Click OK.

   If you began this process by double-clicking a part label on the layout, you are immediately returned to Layout mode.

   If you began this process by choosing the Part Setup command, you return to the Part Setup dialog box. Click Done to return to Layout mode.

Deleting Layout Parts

The method you use to delete a layout part depends on whether the part already contains objects (fields, labels, or graphics). If the part is empty, you can drag it upward on the layout until it disappears. Otherwise, you can select the part's label and press the Delete key. You can also delete a part from the Part Setup dialog box in Layout mode by choosing Part Setup from the Mode menu, selecting the name of the part, and clicking the Delete button.

If a part contains objects, you'll see an alert box when you try to delete it, because any objects in the part will be deleted with the part. Any fields that are removed from the part when you delete it can be added back to the layout using the Field tool. However, other objects, such as graphics or static text, will have to be recreated if you find that you still need them.

To recover a part that you deleted with the Delete key, choose Undo from the Edit menu (or press ⌘-Z) immediately after deleting it. Part deletions accomplished within the Define Parts dialog box, on the other hand, *cannot* be recovered with the Undo command.

Adding Items to a Layout Part

You now know enough about layout parts to create neat, well-ordered, appropriately sized, *blank* layout parts. However, the purpose of a layout part is to display information rather than blank space. You must add objects to the parts. *Objects* include fields, field labels, text, graphics, portals, and buttons. To add objects, you use the tools in the Tools palette on the left side of the document window. Additional options for placing, arranging, and formatting objects are available in the Show, Arrange, and Format menus.

Adding Fields

The most important objects in any layout are usually the fields. You have seen how to add fields at layout-creation time. The Standard layout automatically places every field that has been defined for the database. With the Labels, Envelope, and columnar layouts, you specify which fields to place, as well as the order in which they are placed. You can also add a field to any layout at *any* time, even if the field didn't exist when you created the layout.

Toggling the Positions of Part Labels

Part labels are used in Layout mode to resize, move, or modify parts. These labels may get in your way, however, obscuring the fields and labels beneath them. To switch labels to a vertical position, click the part-label control at the bottom of the Layout window. You'll find this control just to the left of the mode selector pop-up menu, as previously shown in Figure 6-2.

You add fields by using the Field tool. This tool appears in the center of the layout tool palette and is labeled *Field.*

Follow these steps to add a field to a layout part:

1. In Layout mode, switch to the layout to which you want to add the field.
2. Click the Field tool and drag the field object into the appropriate layout part and approximate position.

   The Specify Field dialog box appears, as shown in Figure 6-17.

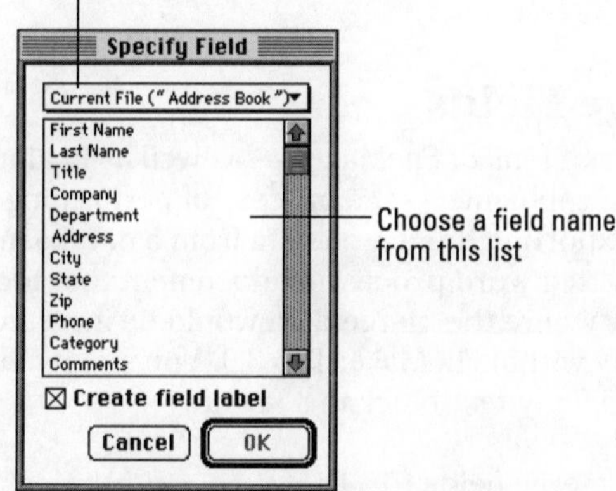

Figure 6-17: The Specify Field dialog box

3. Click the name of the field you want to add.

   You can choose any field that has been defined for the database, as well as any field in a related file. To view fields in related files, choose the name of the relationship from the pop-up menu at the top of the Specify Field dialog box.
4. If you want a matching field label to be created, make sure there is a check mark in the "Create field label" check box. (If you don't want a label, remove the check mark.)
5. Click OK.

   The field appears in the layout part in which it was placed.
6. Move and resize the field as necessary.

   To move a field within a layout, select the Pointer tool, click once within the field to select it, and then drag the field to a new location. To resize a field, select the Pointer tool, click once within the field to select it, and then drag any of the field's *handles* — the black dots in the four corners of a field.

To delete a field from a layout, click to select it and then press the Delete key.

If you find that you've simply added the wrong field to a layout, there's a better approach to correcting this problem than just deleting the errant field and then adding the right one. You can swap one field for another. In Layout mode, hold down the ⌘ key while double-clicking the field. The Specify Field dialog box appears and presents a list of all fields that have been defined for the database. Choose the replacement field from the field list. All formatting options that were set for the old field are automatically applied to the new field.

You can use a similar technique to quickly duplicate the formatting of an existing field. Just Option-drag the field (press Option as you drag the field). When you release the mouse button, the Specify Field dialog box appears. Choose a field from the field list.

Adding Merge Fields

In previous versions of FileMaker — as well as in almost any other database program you can name — the process of performing a mail merge involved two steps: exporting the merge data from a database program and then merging it with a word processing document that included field placeholders (to show where the merge data would be inserted). Merges can now be done entirely within FileMaker Pro 3.0. You simply embed one or more *merge fields* in any text block in a layout.

Follow these to add merge fields to a layout:

1. In Layout mode, switch to the layout to which you want to add the merge fields.
2. Create or select an existing text element in the layout, and then set the text insertion point by clicking or using the arrow keys.
3. From the Paste Special sub-menu of the Edit menu, choose Merge Field (or press ⌘-M).

   The Specify Field dialog box appears (as previously shown in Figure 6-17).
4. Choose a field to insert by selecting it and clicking OK.

   The merge field is added at the current text insertion point. A merge field is always surrounded by bracket symbols, as in <<Last Name>>. Figure 6-18 shows a form letter that contains two merge fields. As illustrated in the figure, merge fields can also be selected from any related file, as well as from the current database. To view the fields in a related file, choose the name of the relationship from the pop-up menu at the top of the Specify Field dialog box.

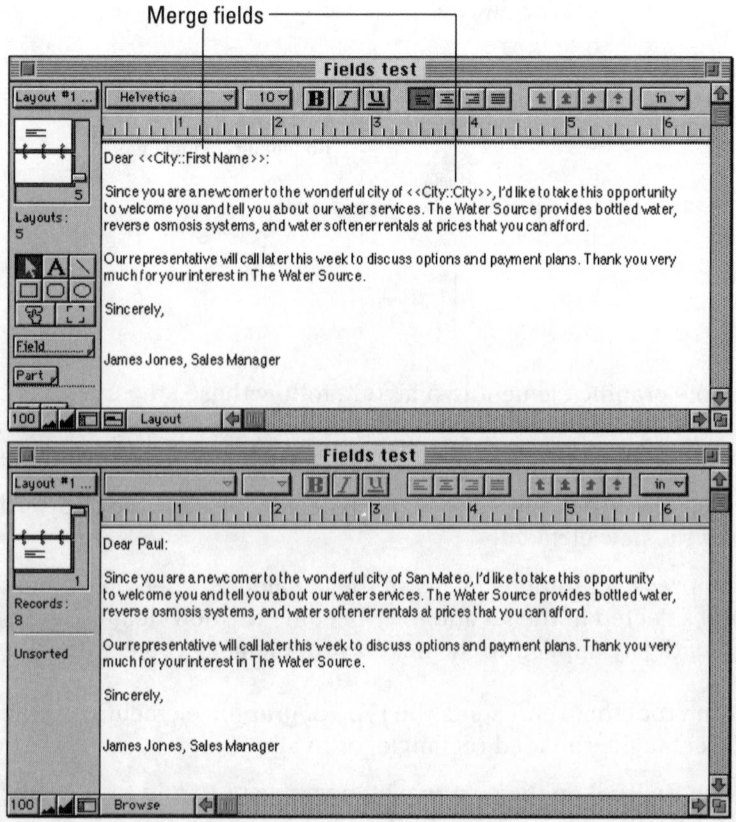

Figure 6-18: A layout with two merge fields in Layout mode (top) and Browse mode (bottom)

Like any other text, merge fields can be formatted by changing the font, style, size, color, and so on. When formatting a merge field, be sure to apply the formatting to the surrounding brackets, too.

Adding Graphics

FileMaker Pro offers several ways to add graphic elements to layouts. You can create simple graphics — including ovals, squares, and lines — directly in the program by using the Line, Rectangle, Rounded Rectangle, and Oval tools in the Tools palette (see Figure 6-19). Each tool is identified by an icon that shows the result of using that tool.

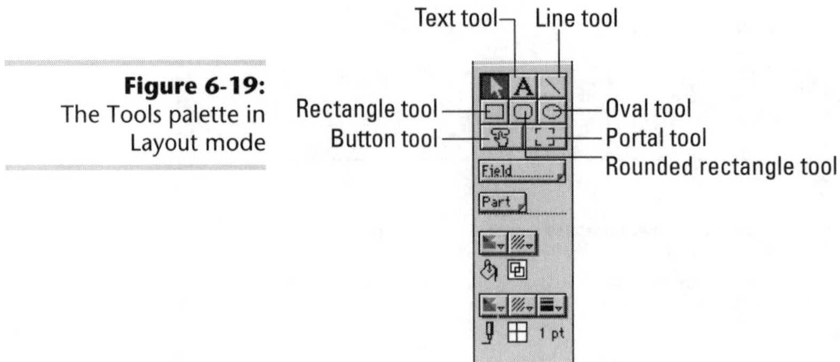

Figure 6-19: The Tools palette in Layout mode

To add a simple graphic element to a layout, follow these steps:

1. In Layout mode, switch to the layout to which you want to add the element.
2. Use the Fill, Border, and Line Width palettes to select the appropriate formatting for the new element.

If you preselect options in any of these palettes when no element is currently selected in the layout, they become the new default settings and are automatically applied to the next layout element you create.

3. Click the tool that represents the type of graphic element you want to add (line, rectangle, rounded rectangle, or oval).
4. Position the tool on the part to which you want to add the graphic, and then drag until you create an element that's the desired size.

You can create special objects by holding down the Option key as you drag with any of the tools. When Option is pressed, the Rectangle and Rounded Rectangle tools create squares; the Oval tool creates circles; and the Line tool is restricted to straight horizontal, vertical, or 45-degree lines.

To change the formatting for an object, click the object to select it and then choose options in the Fill, Border, and Line Width palettes. You can also drag an object to change its position and drag its handles to change its size.

Complex graphics, such as logos or elaborate illustrations, are better created in a dedicated graphics program. To bring graphics in from other programs, use the Import/Export command as follows:

1. In Layout mode, switch to the layout to which you want to add the graphic.

2. Choose Import/Export from the File menu, and then choose Import Picture from the submenu.

   A modified file dialog box appears, as shown in Figure 6-20.

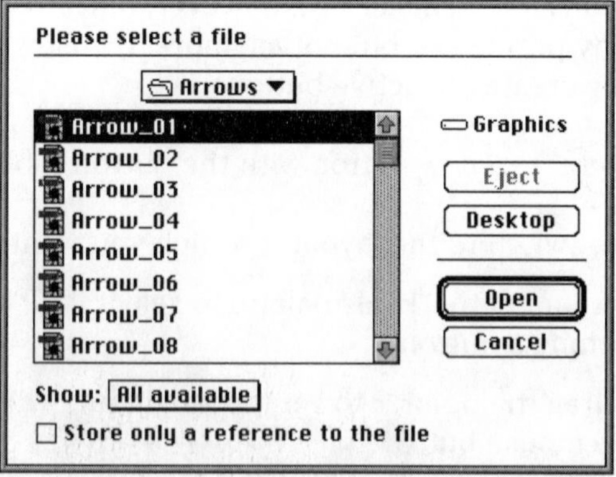

Figure 6-20: Select a graphic file to import.

3. *Optional:* To limit the file list to only those graphic images saved in a particular format, choose a format from the Show pop-up menu.
4. Find the graphic's name in the list and click to select it.
5. *Optional:* To store a reference to the graphic file in the database (rather than the actual graphic), click the check box at the bottom of the dialog box.
6. Click Open.

   The graphic appears in the current layout.

7. Drag the graphic to the appropriate position in the layout. Drag the graphic's handles to change its size, if necessary.

Of course, graphics can also be added to a layout via the Mac's copy and paste routine. Simply open the graphic file in its original program, select it, issue the Copy command, and then — in FileMaker Pro — issue the Paste command.

To remove any graphic on a layout, select it with the Pointer tool and press the Delete key.

FileMaker Pro 3.0 supports a new system software feature called *drag and drop*. Using drag and drop, you can move a graphic or text object from one program to another by simply selecting it in the original program's document and then dragging it to the other program's document. If you have a graphics program that supports drag and drop (ClarisWorks 4.0, for example), you can drag a graphic directly onto a FileMaker Pro layout.

Adding Buttons

Ever since scripting was introduced in FileMaker Pro, you could make the program perform special tasks for you in response to a button click. Any object — text or graphic — could be made to function as a button. In previous versions of FileMaker Pro, however, button creation was often a tedious, lengthy process — but not anymore. By using the new Button tool, you can *quickly* create attractive buttons.

Follow these steps to create a new button with the Button tool:

1. In Layout mode, switch to the layout to which you want to add the button.
2. Click the Button tool in the Tools palette to select it. (The Button tool looks like a finger pushing a button.)
3. On the layout, drag the pointer to set the height and width of the button, and then release the mouse button.

   The new button becomes visible and the Specify Button dialog box appears, as shown in Figure 6-21.

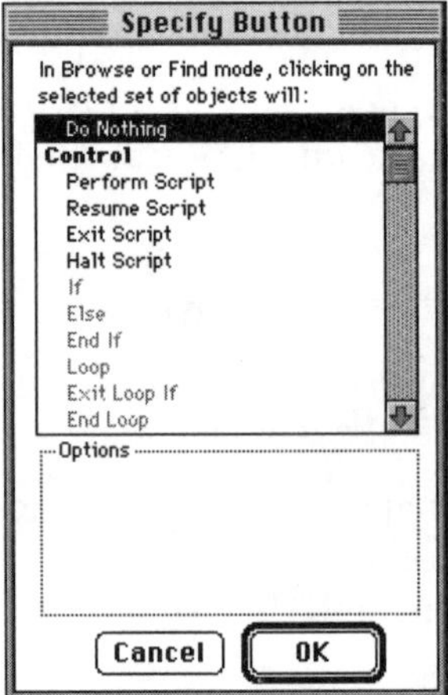

Figure 6-21: The Specify Button dialog box

4. Select the script step to be assigned to the button and set any necessary options.

   If you want to associate an existing script with the button (rather than just a single script step), choose the Perform Script step. For more information about scripting, see Chapter 15.
5. Click OK.

More About Buttons

When choosing an action for the button (step 4 in the button creation procedure), you can select Do Nothing for any button for which a final script doesn't already exist. To later assign a permanent action to the button, simply select the button and choose the Button command from the Format menu.

Also, because a button is like any other object in a FileMaker layout, you can change its formatting if you wish. Features that you may want to alter include the button label (changing its font, size, style, or color); the button's fill color, pattern, or border; and the size of the button. Note that you can create two styles of buttons: rectangles or round rectangles. To switch from one button style to the other, choose Preferences from the Edit menu, choose Layout from the pop-up menu at the top of the dialog box, click the appropriate radio button ("create rounded buttons" or "create rectangular buttons"), and then click Done.

The Specify Button dialog box is removed and a text insertion point appears in the center of the blank button.

6. Type a name for the button.
7. Press Enter or click anywhere outside of the button to end the button-definition process.

To remove a button from a layout, select it with the Pointer tool and press the Delete key. If you simply want to move the button to a different layout in the same database, select it, choose the Cut command from the Edit menu, switch to the target layout, and then choose Paste from the Edit menu.

Adding Portals

Fields from related databases can be put directly onto a layout (as described previously in "Adding Fields"). Related fields placed in this manner, however, can show only the value from a single matching record. If you want to display values from a *series* of matching records, you must place the related fields in a portal.

A *portal* is best thought of as a window into a related file. All fields placed within a portal must be from a previously defined relationship. Any record that meets the requirements of that defined relationship will display its data in the portal.

For example, Figure 6-22 shows a portal that contains the full names and phone numbers of a series of people (the fields placed in the portal were First Name, Last Name, and Phone). The relationship was defined as matching the City fields in the current and the related database. Thus, when I enter **San Mateo** in the City field of the current record, the portal displays the names and phone numbers of all records in the related file that also have San Mateo in the City field.

First Name	Last Name	Phone
Paul	Baldwin	415-513-8929
Dany	Brooks	415-513-7436
Dave	Dempsey	415-513-7481
Marci	Galea	415-513-7541
Lisa	Higgins	415-513-7396
Fiona	Murphy	415-513-7661

Figure 6-22: A portal that displays three fields from a related file

To create a portal in a layout, follow these steps:

1. If you haven't already done so, define the relationship that will be used for the portal's data by choosing Define Relationship from the File menu. (See Chapter 19 for information about defining relationships.)
2. In Layout mode, switch to the layout to which you want to add the portal.
3. Click the Portal tool in the Tools palette to select it. (The Portal tool looks like a square that is missing the center section on each of its sides.)
4. On the layout, drag the pointer to indicate the height and width of the portal, and then release the mouse button.

   The portal becomes visible and the Portal Setup dialog box appears, as shown in Figure 6-23.

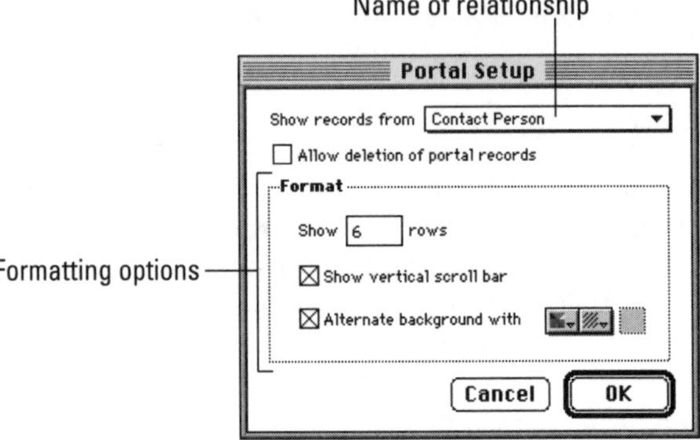

Figure 6-23: The Portal Setup dialog box

5. Choose a relationship from the pop-up menu at the top of the dialog box.
6. In the "Show rows" text box, enter the number of rows that the portal will display.
7. Change any of the other options that you wish to as follows:
   - Click the check box labeled "Allow deletion of portal records" if you want to be able to delete records in the related file by selecting them in the portal.
   - If you think that the number of records will sometimes exceed the number of portal rows set in step 6, click the check box for "Show vertical scroll bar." Doing this will enable you to scroll through all the records in the portal.
   - To make it easier to distinguish each portal record from the next, click the check box labeled "Alternate background with" and then choose a color and/or fill pattern. When you switch to Browse mode, you'll see that the portal row colors alternate between white and the selected color/pattern combination (much like "green bar" printer paper or some types of ledger paper).
8. Click OK to dismiss the Portal Setup dialog box.
9. Click the Field tool in the Tools palette and drag a field into the portal.

   When you release the mouse button, the Specify Field dialog box appears.
10. Choose a related field and then click OK.

    The field and its label appear in the portal.
11. Drag the field into the top row of the portal. Move the field's label so that it is above the field's position (outside of the portal) or, if you prefer, you can delete the field label.
12. Repeat steps 9 through 11 for additional related fields that you want to display in the portal.

Fields inside the portal, as well as the portal itself, can be resized as needed. If you later need to modify the portal settings, you can select the portal and choose Portal from the Format menu or simply double-click the portal. In either case, the Portal Setup dialog box appears.

For more information about portals and relationships, see Chapter 19.

Formatting Fields and Other Objects

Newly-placed fields are seldom exactly as you want them. The field may be too small or too large, or it may be in the wrong position. The field's formatting — text attributes, borders, and so on — may not display the field in the manner you had intended. Other objects, such as buttons and graphics, may also be in the wrong place, be the wrong size, or need additional formatting. Fortunately, you can easily correct these problems. FileMaker Pro includes a wide variety of tools that make the placement and formatting of fields and other objects as simple as possible.

Although this section concentrates on the size, placement, and formatting of *fields*, the majority of the commands and procedures apply to *any* object on a layout, such as buttons, field labels, graphics, and static text.

Using the Measurement and Alignment Tools

The Show menu (shown in Figure 6-24) includes many tools that make it easy to accurately place or arrange fields, labels, graphics, and other objects on the layout — even when you're doing it manually by dragging the objects.

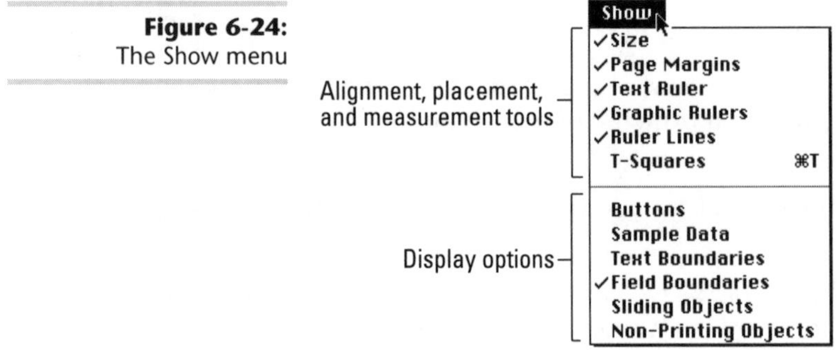

Figure 6-24: The Show menu

The measurement and alignment tools listed in the upper-half of the Show menu provide the following functions:

- *Size:* As described previously in this chapter, you can type entries in any of the Size windoid's six text boxes to change the dimensions and location of the currently selected object in a layout. To display the Size windoid (illustrated previously in Figure 6-15), choose Size from the Show menu.

- *Page Margins:* Choose the Page Margins command from the Show menu to determine where layout objects will appear in printouts in relation to the page margins.

- *Text Ruler:* FileMaker Pro 3.0 includes a text ruler and an associated ruler bar that can be displayed at the top of the document window. Although the main purpose of the text ruler is for formatting fields and text objects (such as field labels), it is also useful for showing and checking an object's horizontal location on the layout. Choose the Text Ruler command from the Show menu to toggle this ruler on and off.
- *Graphic Rulers:* Graphic rulers can be shown at the top and left edges of the layout area. Choose the Graphic Rulers command from the Show menu to toggle these rulers on and off. When you select and drag any object, its dimensions and location are indicated on the rulers.
- *Ruler Lines:* You can display dotted lines that correspond to lines on the rulers. You can use these lines to check layout spacing and positioning of objects. Choose Ruler Lines from the Show menu to toggle the lines on and off.
- *T-Squares:* These are solid vertical and horizontal lines. You use these T-square lines to precisely position an object relative to the rulers. (You can drag the lines to move them.) Choose T-Squares from the Show menu or press ⌘-T to toggle the T-square lines on and off.

The bottom of the Show menu contains additional options to make objects visible or stand out while in Layout mode. You can choose any of the following helpful options:

- *Buttons:* Surrounds all buttons in the layout with a gray border.
- *Sample Data:* Displays sample data of the correct type in each field, rather than the field name.
- *Text Boundaries:* Surrounds all static text in the layout (such as field labels and titles) with a black border.
- *Field Boundaries:* Surrounds each field in the layout with a black border.
- *Sliding Objects:* Shifts the remaining objects if any of the objects originally defined in the layout are missing. Sliding objects — commonly found in label layouts — are indicated by tiny left-pointing and upward-pointing arrows to indicate the direction that they will be shifted. In an address label, for example, you normally want fields to move up to remove blank lines if an entire record line (such as a company name or department) is missing.

- *Non-Printing Objects:* Surrounds all objects that have been designated as non-printing with a gray border; that is, these objects are visible only on-screen and will not appear in printouts or in Preview mode.

FileMaker Pro also maintains an invisible grid that corresponds to current ruler settings. If the grid is on, objects being moved or resized move in increments, snapping to the nearest grid intersection. Choose Autogrid from the Arrange menu to toggle the grid on and off.

To change the spacing and units for the grid and rulers, choose Set Rulers from the Mode menu and choose new settings in the Set Rulers dialog box, as shown in Figure 6-25.

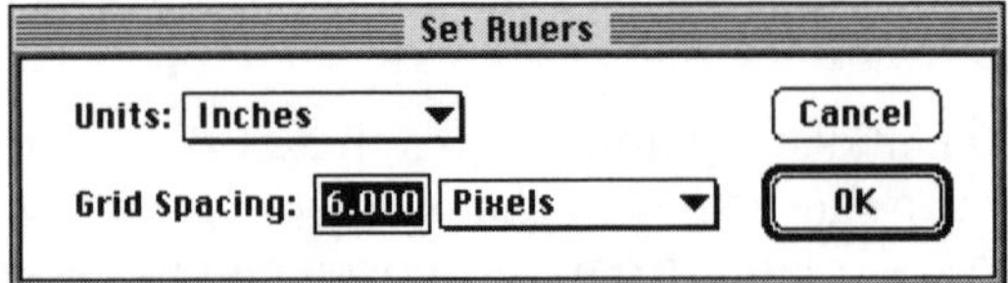

Figure 6-25: The Set Rulers dialog box

You can also quickly change the units by clicking the Units box in the upper-left corner of the document window. Each time you click it, it switches to a different measurement unit, such as inches or centimeters. (The Units box is only visible when text and/or graphic rulers are displayed.)

Moving and Resizing Fields and Objects

One of the simplest things to change is a field or object's position on a layout. Just click to select it, and then drag it where you want. (The tools described in "Using the Measurement and Alignment Tools" can be very helpful in this task.)

It's often necessary to alter a field's *size*, too. If a Text field is too small, part of the text is hidden until you click on or tab into the field. A Number field that is too small to completely show its contents will display only a question mark. On the other hand, the default size for some fields, such as a State field that is designed to hold a two-letter abbreviation, may be much too long.

To change a field's size or position, follow these steps:

1. In Layout mode, switch to the layout that contains the field that you want to modify.
2. Choose the Pointer tool from the Tools palette.
3. To move the field, click and drag the field to the desired location.

   To restrict the movement of the field to straight horizontal or vertical, hold down Shift as you drag.
4. To change the field's size, click to select it and then click and drag a handle (any of the four black dots) until the field is the desired size.

   You can press Shift as you resize any field to restrict changes to only the vertical or horizontal size of the field.

Setting Field Formatting

When you define fields for a database (in the Define Fields dialog box), you must specify a *type* for each field, such as Text, Date, Time, or Number. Although the field type determines the kind of data that the field will store, it does *not* determine how that field's data will be displayed in a layout. To set a display format for a field, you change to Layout mode and do either (or both) of the following:

- Choose formatting options from the Format menu.
- Choose settings from the fill, pen, or line palettes in the Tools palette.

Any formatting options that you set for a field while in Layout mode will be applied to the field and its data when viewed in Browse mode, as described in the following sections.

Using the Format Menu

To set formatting options for a field, switch to Layout mode, select a field, and then choose commands from the Format menu (see Figure 6-26). Regardless of the type of the selected field, these commands at the top of the Format menu can be selected: Font, Size, Style, Align Text, Line Spacing, and Text Color.

Figure 6-26: The Format menu (in Layout mode)

The commands that are available in the second section of the Format menu depend on what is currently selected: a graphic object, a field of a particular type, a field label, and so on.

For example, if a Date field is selected, the Text, Date, and Button formatting commands are available in the Format menu. Text can be chosen because the field contains alphabetic characters, as do most field types; Date can be chosen because the field is a Date field; and Button can be chosen because virtually any object on a layout can be made into a button.

The Text Command

As shown in Figure 6-27, choosing the Text command from the Format menu is an easy way to assign multiple text formatting commands to a field, field label, or piece of static text. Rather than having to select multiple commands from the Format menu, you can set all text formatting options in the Text Format dialog box. (The Paragraph button is grayed out unless you are currently formatting a Text field.)

Figure 6-27: The Text Format dialog box

The Date and Time Commands

When formatting a Date or Time field, choose Date or Time from the Format menu. The Date Format or Time Format dialog box appears, as appropriate (see Figure 6-28). Rather than enabling you to set text attributes for the fields — as the Text Format dialog box does — these dialog boxes let you assign a particular date or time display format for the field. You can either display the dates and times as they were typed into the field (by clicking the "Leave data formatted as entered" radio button), or format them by setting options for the field (such as leading characters and separators). The Sample box at the bottom of the dialog box shows the effects of your choices.

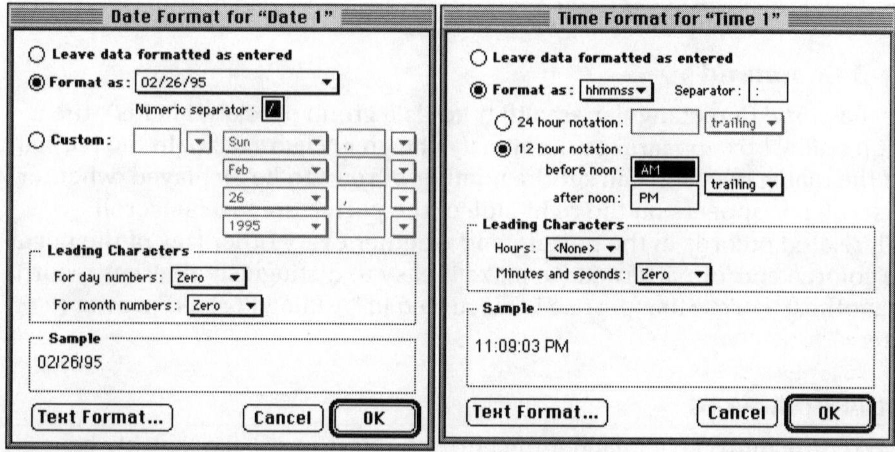

Figure 6-28: The Date Format and Time Format dialog boxes

If you also want to set general text formatting options for a Date or Time field, you can click the Text Format button at the bottom of the Date Format or the Time Format dialog box.

The Graphic Command

When you select a graphic or a Container field on a layout, you can choose the Graphic command from the Format menu. The Graphic Format dialog box appears, as shown in Figure 6-29. By choosing the appropriate options in the dialog box, you can change the size of the graphic or its alignment.

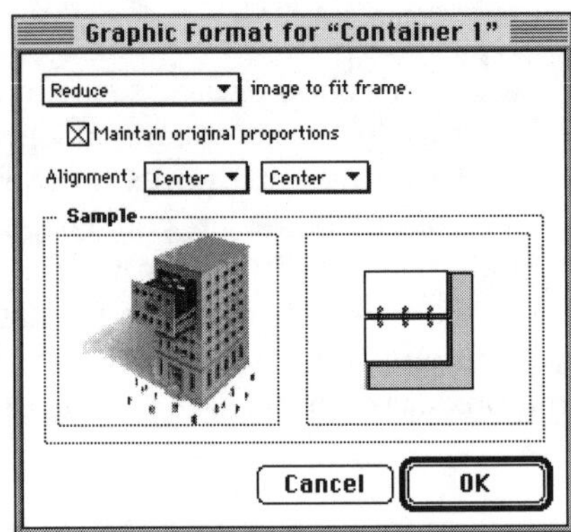

Figure 6-29: The Graphic Format dialog box

The Portal Command

If you select a *portal* (a rectangular area that holds a group of related fields), the Portal Setup dialog box appears (as previously shown in Figure 6-23). In the Format portion of the dialog box, you can set the number of rows to be displayed, whether a vertical scroll bar appears on the right side of the portal (so you can scroll through all related records in the portal), and whether every other row of the portal should be colored and/or patterned (to make it easy to distinguish different records from one another). Formatting portals is discussed in "Adding Portals," earlier in this chapter.

The Button Command

You can select the Button command if the current object could conceivably be defined as a button. Since virtually every element on a layout can be made into a button — including normal fields — the Button command is always present.

When you choose Button from the Format menu, the Specify Button dialog box appears (as previously shown in Figure 6-21). To define the object as a button, simply choose the script or script step that will execute whenever the button is clicked. Options (when available) can be set at the bottom of the dialog box.

If you hold down the Option key as you double-click fields and other objects on a layout, the appropriate Format dialog box is automatically presented to you.

Adding Borders

Although fields are frequently displayed in Layout mode with boxes around them, these boxes appear only for your convenience in moving and resizing the fields. If you want borders to appear around a field when you browse or print (that is, when you are actually *using* the database), you must create the borders by using the Field Borders command.

Follow these steps to add borders to a field:

1. In Layout mode, switch to the layout that contains the field to which you want to add borders.
2. Click to select the appropriate field.

   If there are additional fields to which you'd like to apply the same border options, you can select them all by Shift-clicking them.
3. Choose Field Borders from the Format menu (or press Option-⌘-B).

   The Field Borders dialog box appears, as shown in Figure 6-30.

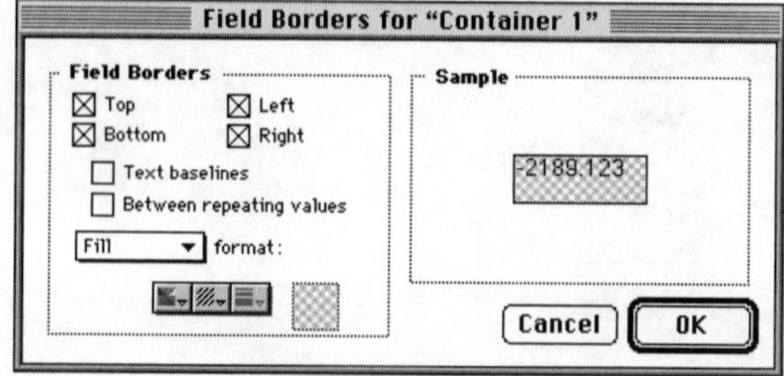

Figure 6-30: The Field Borders dialog box

4. Click the appropriate check boxes for the borders you want to add.
5. Choose Borders from the dialog box's pop-up menu.
6. Choose the desired color, pattern, and line width for the borders from the pop-up menus at the bottom of the dialog box.

   The effects of your choices appear in the Sample box on the right side of the dialog box.
7. Click OK.

Adding Baselines

You may want the contents of a field to be underlined. FileMaker Pro refers to such an underline as a *baseline*. As with borders, you add baselines by using the Field Borders dialog box (previously shown in Figure 6-30).

Choose Baselines from the Field Borders dialog box's pop-up menu. Then choose the desired color, pattern, and line width for the baselines from the pop-up menus at the bottom of the dialog box. The effects of your choices appear in the Sample box on the right side of the dialog box.

Setting Fill Colors and Patterns

You can add a fill color and/or pattern to a field — whether the field has a border or not. In Browse mode, the color and/or pattern appears behind the field's data.

You can specify fill colors and patterns in two ways. The first way is to use the Fill tools (the two pop-up palettes above the bucket icon in the Tools palette, as shown in Figure 6-31). If no field is currently selected when you choose a color or pattern with these tools, the color and pattern become the default fill color and pattern. If you now add a field, it is automatically formatted with the selected fill pattern and color.

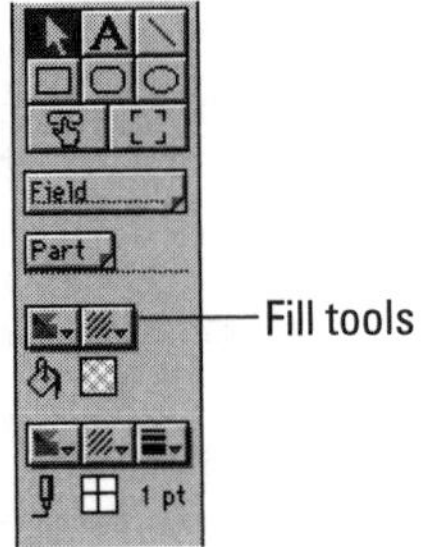

Figure 6-31: The Tools palette (in Layout mode)

You can also set default formatting options by simply pressing ⌘ and clicking on any field or object. Then whenever you create a new field or text object, these format settings will automatically be applied.

Alternatively, you can use the Field Borders command to select a fill for a field. Choose Fill from the dialog box's pop-up menu and then choose the desired color and pattern for the fill from the pop-up menus at the bottom of the dialog box. The effects of your choices appear in the Sample box on the right side of the dialog box.

Adding Scroll Bars

If you don't make a field large enough initially, the entire contents of the field may not always be visible. Although you could simply make the field bigger, this method may not produce the effect you want — especially if the available space in your layout is limited, such as when you're designing a layout for use only on-screen. To make it possible to view the additional contents of a field, you can add scroll bars to the field. These scroll bars enable you to scroll a field and view its additional contents — just as you can with many document windows. You add scroll bars by using the Field Format dialog box.

To add scroll bars to a field, follow these steps:

1. In Layout mode, switch to the layout that contains the field to which you want to add scroll bars.
2. Click to select the field.
3. Choose Field Format from the Format menu (or press Option-⌘-F).

   The Field Format dialog box appears, as shown in Figure 6-32.

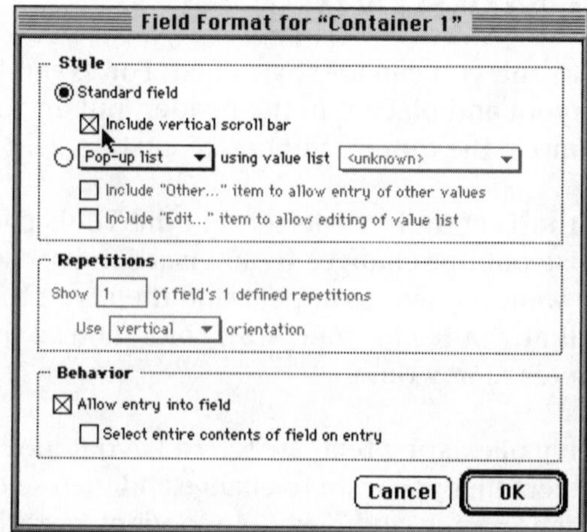

Figure 6-32: The Field Format dialog box

4. Click the "Include vertical scroll bar" check box.
5. Click OK.

Formatting Repeating Fields

As you learned in Chapter 5, some fields can contain more than one entry. These fields are called *repeating fields*. In an invoice database, for example, you might have a repeating field named Price that contains a series of prices — one for each item in an order. Use the Field Format dialog box to set options for repeating fields, as follows:

1. In Layout mode, select the field you want to format.
2. Choose Field Format from the Format menu (or press Option-⌘-F).

   The Field Format dialog box appears (as shown previously in Figure 6-32).

3. Enter the number of repetitions to show for the field.
4. Choose an orientation from the pop-up menu as follows:
   - Choose Vertical to display repetitions in a single column.
   - Choose Horizontal to display repetitions in a row.
5. Click OK.

Adding and Modifying Text

To identify items in a layout, you can add extra text. For example, you can add text as a title for a report layout and place it in the header, put an automatic page number and a date stamp in the footer, and create custom field labels for fields.

You add text by using the Text tool (the letter *A* in the Tools palette). When you click this tool, the mouse pointer changes to an insertion bracket. Click to position the bracket where you want the text to appear and then type the text. Text appears with the current default attributes for font, size, color, and so on, but you can change all these attributes at any time.

To change the formatting of existing text, switch to Layout mode, use the Pointer tool to select the text object that you want to change and then select the desired Font, Size, Style, Align Text, Line Spacing, and Text Color options from the Format menu.

To edit existing text, use the Text tool to select the text, position the insertion point inside the text box, and use the standard editing keys to modify the text.

Besides adding standard text items, you can paste special items onto a layout, such as the current time and date, an automatic page number, or your user name. To insert special text of this type, follow these steps:

1. In Layout mode, click the Text tool.
2. Click to position the insertion point where you want the special text to appear.
3. From the Paste Special submenu of the Edit menu, choose one of the following options: Current Date, Current Time, Current User Name, Date Symbol, User Name Symbol, Page Number, or Record Number.

Applying the Finishing Touches

Even after adding all the desired elements to a layout, the layout may still need minor adjustments. If object alignment is a problem, you can easily correct it. You can also group objects so that you can move or format them as a unit. You can even set the order in which fields are filled during data entry.

Aligning Objects

The Align and Set Alignment commands in the Arrange menu enable you to align objects with other objects on the layout. If you have a vertical list of fields, you can use this command to perfectly align one edge of each of the fields and field labels, for example.

Follow these steps to align two or more objects:

1. In Layout mode, select the objects that you want to align. (You can hold down the Shift key to select additional objects after the first.)
2. Choose Set Alignment from the Arrange menu (or press Shift-⌘-K).

   The Set Alignment dialog box appears, as shown in Figure 6-33.

Figure 6-33: The Set Alignment dialog box

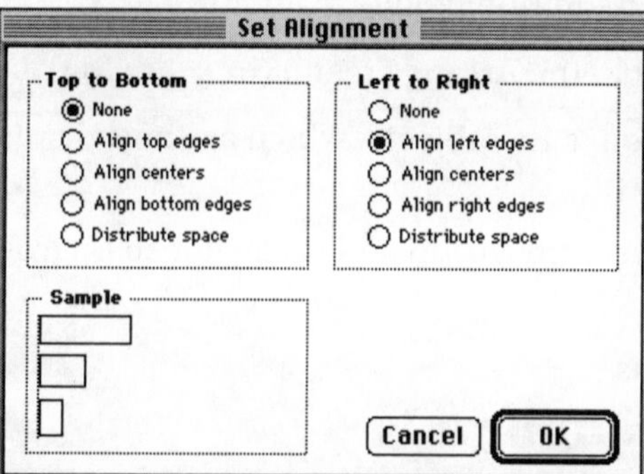

3. Choose the Top to Bottom and Left to Right options that you want to use.

   The effects of your choices appear in the Sample box in the lower-left corner of the dialog box.
4. Click OK.

The alignment settings are applied to the selected objects. If you find that you have made an error, you can correct it by immediately selecting the Undo Align command from the Edit menu.

If you later want to apply the same alignment settings to a different group of objects, just select the objects and choose the Align command from the Arrange menu (or press ⌘-K).

You can also have FileMaker Pro snap objects to a grid automatically by choosing AutoGrid from the Arrange menu (or pressing ⌘-Y). This option makes field and label placement extraordinarily simple because each placed or moved object snaps to the nearest grid intersection.

Grouping Objects

To make it easier to move several aligned objects to a new position without messing up their alignment, you can group the objects. FileMaker Pro treats grouped objects as though they were a single object.

To group several objects, follow these steps:

1. In Layout mode, select the objects that you want to group. (Hold down the Shift key to select additional objects after the first.)
2. Choose Group from the Arrange menu (or press ⌘-G).

   FileMaker Pro groups the objects, which are now displayed with a single set of handles.

To ungroup objects, select the group and then choose Ungroup from the Arrange menu (or press Shift-⌘-G).

Other Object Commands

You can also change the layering order in which objects are displayed (back to front) with the Bring to Front (Shift-Option-⌘-F), Send to Back (Shift-Option-⌘-J), Bring Forward (Shift-⌘-F), and Send Backward (Shift-⌘-J) commands in the Arrange menu. These commands are particularly useful for placing background graphics behind fields or other graphics.

If you want to make sure that a particular object isn't moved by mistake, you can lock it in place by choosing the Lock command from the Arrange menu (or pressing ⌘-H). To unlock an object (so you can change its size, position, and attributes, for example), choose Unlock from the Arrange menu (or press Shift-⌘-H).

Setting the Tab Order for Data Entry

You can set the order in which you move from field to field on a layout when you press the Tab key. Although this has no effect on the *appearance* of the layout, it can often be the difference between an easy-to-use layout and one that is annoying to use. The default order is left to right and top to bottom. You can change this order and even omit fields from the tab order, if you want.

To change the tab order, you use the Set Tab Order command as follows:

1. In Layout mode, choose Set Tab Order from the Mode menu.

   The Set Tab Order dialog box appears, as shown in Figure 6-34. Each field in the layout is marked by a numbered arrow.

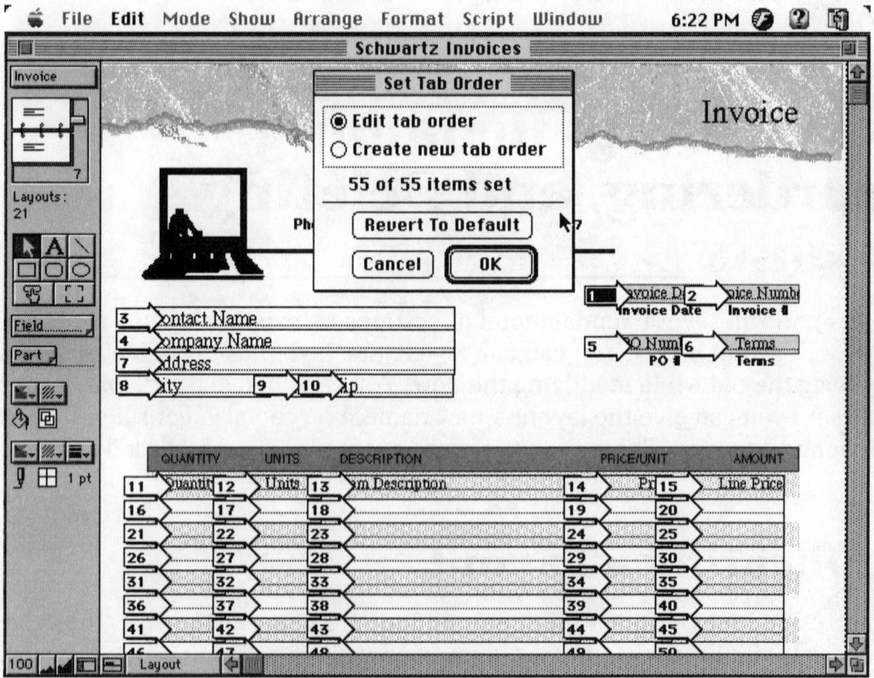

Figure 6-34: The Set Tab Order dialog box

2. Click the appropriate radio button to specify whether you want to edit the existing tab order or create a new one.

3. To specify the tab order for fields, edit the numbers in the arrows that appear next to each field in the layout. Enter **1** in the arrow for the field that is to be first, and so on.

— or —

3. Select New Tab Order to remove all the arrow numbers and then click the arrows in the order in which you want the related fields to appear.

To omit a field from the tab order, leave its arrow blank. When the user presses the Tab key, the omitted fields will be skipped.

4. Click OK to save the new tab order or click Cancel if you change your mind.

At any time during this process, you can revert to the tab order that FileMaker Pro originally set for the layout by clicking Revert to Default.

Duplicating, Renaming, Reordering, and Deleting Layouts

You can perform several fundamental operations on existing layouts so that they meet your current needs. You can use an existing layout as the basis for a new one, preserving the old while modifying the new. You can change the display order in a layout, and you can give the layout a new name. You can also get rid of layouts that are no longer required. These layout operations are discussed in the following sections.

Duplicating a Layout

To create a new layout that differs only slightly from an existing one, the easiest method is to duplicate the existing layout and make small changes to the copy. As an example, when you write letters, you may at times use pre-printed envelopes that include your return address and at other times use plain, unprinted envelopes. If you already have a layout for printing on one type of envelope, you can duplicate the layout, make a couple of small changes, and handle the other type of envelope, too.

To duplicate a layout, switch to Layout mode, choose the layout you want to duplicate by selecting it from the layouts pop-up menu, and choose Duplicate Layout from the Mode menu.

Reordering Layouts

In the layouts pop-up menu, layouts are displayed in the order in which you created them. This order, however, may not be what you want. For example, you may want to display the layouts you use most frequently at the top of the layouts pop-up menu.

To change the order in which layouts are displayed in the pop-up menu, follow these steps:

1. In the appropriate FileMaker Pro database, switch to Layout mode.
2. Choose Set Layout Order from the Mode menu.

   The Set Layout Order dialog box appears, as shown in Figure 6-35.

Figure 6-35: The Set Layout Order dialog box

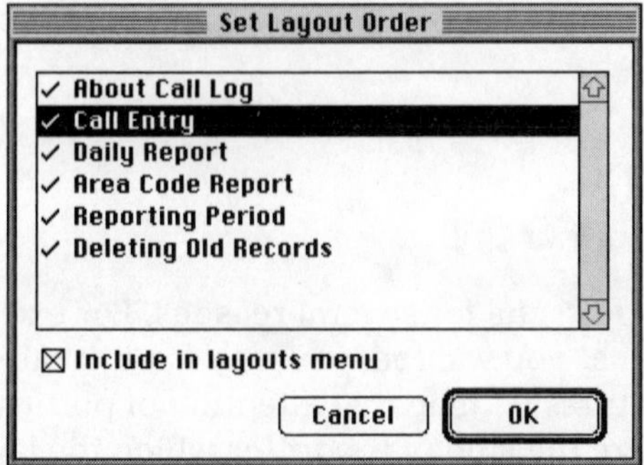

3. Drag layout names into the desired order.

   To make a layout first in the list, for example, click and drag its name to the top of the list.
4. Click OK to put the new order into effect.

   You return to the Layout Options dialog box.

As Figure 6-35 shows, you can also change whether a layout's name appears in the layouts pop-up menu. A check mark in front of a layout name signifies that it will be listed in the layouts pop-up menu. The check mark works as a toggle — you can click in front of any layout name to add or remove the check mark.

Renaming a Layout

The default names assigned to new and duplicated layouts (such as Layout #1 and Data Entry Copy) aren't very informative. However, you can use the Layout Setup dialog box to give a layout a new name.

Follow these steps to rename a layout:

1. In the appropriate FileMaker Pro database, switch to Layout mode.
2. Choose the layout that you want to rename from the layouts pop-up menu.
3. Choose Layout Setup from the Layout menu.

   The Layout Setup dialog box appears.
4. Type a new name for the layout in the Name text box.
5. Click OK.

Deleting a Layout

A layout may no longer be useful for several reasons. For example, the layout may not have been exactly what you wanted, you may have created it just to test certain FileMaker Pro layout features with no real intention of putting the layout to use, or you may no longer require the kind of report for which the layout was designed.

You can eliminate layouts that you no longer need by following these steps:

1. In the appropriate FileMaker Pro database, switch to Layout mode.
2. Choose the layout you want to delete from the layouts pop-up menu.
3. Choose Delete Layout from the Mode menu (or press ⌘-E).

   An alert box appears, asking you to confirm that you want to delete the layout.
4. Click the Delete button in the alert box.

   FileMaker Pro removes the layout from your database.

Summary

- FileMaker Pro supports the use of multiple layouts, allowing you to specify what fields to display and how to format them.
- Layouts can be based on any of seven predefined layout styles, including layouts for columnar reports, Avery labels, and business envelopes.
- Layouts can have multiple sections (called parts), including headers, footers, a body, sub-summaries, and a grand summary.
- Layout parts can include fields, text, and graphics. Objects of any type can be aligned and moved as a group.
- FileMaker Pro includes a large number of tools that enable you to precisely size and place fields and objects on a layout. Powerful formatting commands can be applied to fields and objects to make them look just like you want them to.

Setting Preferences

CHAPTER 7

In This Chapter

- Customizing FileMaker Pro's operation by setting preferences
- Setting startup and closing actions for a database
- Setting Memory preferences to optimize the use of batteries in a portable Macintosh
- Preparing FileMaker Pro for phone dialing

Not everyone likes to work the same way (some of us are morning people, and others are night owls, for example). The same holds true for using FileMaker Pro. The way that you prefer to create database layouts, enter data, and work with a database may differ significantly from the way that your neighbor performs the same tasks. Fortunately, you can set preferences to customize the way that you work with the program in general and the way that you work with individual databases in particular. If you work on a portable Macintosh, you can also conserve battery power by setting a preference that specifies the time interval for automatically saving changes.

It's important for you to know that these preferences exist, how to set them, and how to change them when necessary. For example, you may find yourself working on someone else's computer or with a database that another person created. If the other person's computer or setup behaves differently from yours, you benefit from knowing that the differences are likely due to alternative preferences and that you can easily change them to match your normal way of working. (Be considerate, though. If you change the preferences on someone else's Mac, put them back as you found them when you're through.)

Preference options have expanded greatly in FileMaker Pro 3.0. If you intend to use the program's new phone dialing capabilities, set a default password for a database, or use drag and drop, you should be certain to explore the revised Preferences dialog box. Also, setting document window control options is no longer a startup preference. You must now add such steps to a startup script instead.

Working with the Preferences Dialog Box

You set all preferences from the Preferences dialog box (shown in Figure 7-1). To access this dialog box, choose the Preferences command from the Edit menu.

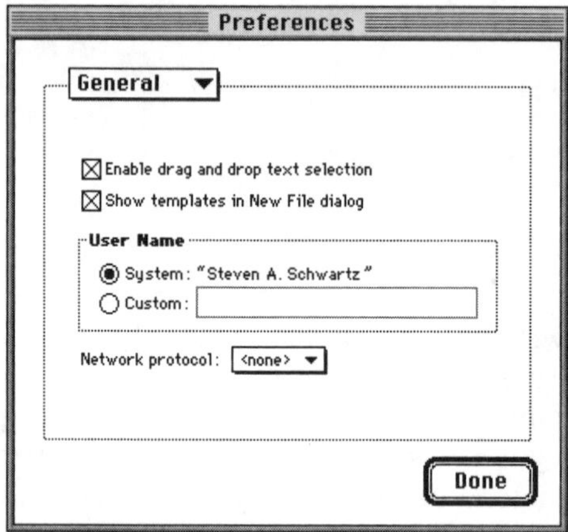

Figure 7-1: The Preferences dialog box

At the top of this dialog box is a pop-up menu containing the six preference categories:

- *General preferences* refer to those that govern how FileMaker Pro behaves as a whole and enable you to specify a network protocol, if appropriate.
- *Document preferences* apply only to the current database document. You can set these preferences differently for every database.
- *Layout preferences* have an effect only on actions that occur in Layout mode.
- *Memory preferences* enable you to adjust the frequency with which FileMaker Pro saves data to disk.
- *Modem preferences* enable you to configure FileMaker Pro to work with a modem.

- *Dialing preferences* enable you to specify prefixes and suffixes to use when dialing phone numbers from various locations.

Follow these general steps to set preferences:

1. Choose Preferences from the Edit menu.

   The Preferences dialog box appears (as previously shown in Figure 7-1).
2. Determine which category of preferences you want to set and choose the corresponding option from the pop-up menu.

   The preference settings change to those appropriate to the selected category.
3. Make the desired changes by clicking and/or by selecting options from pop-up menus.
4. Choose another category for which you want to make changes.

— or —

4. Click Done to put changes into effect and dismiss the Preferences dialog box.

Unlike many dialog boxes in which you make choices, the Preferences dialog box doesn't have a Cancel button. Normally, pressing Cancel discards all changes and dismisses the dialog box. If you select some options in the Preferences dialog box and then change your mind, you have to manually restore the options to their previous settings.

The following sections discuss the specific options that you can set in each category.

Setting General Program Preferences

The General preferences category (previously shown in Figure 7-1) provides options that govern overall program behavior. The General preferences options are as follows:

- *Enable drag and drop text selection:* FileMaker Pro 3.0 supports System 7.5's drag-and-drop feature, enabling you to select and drag information from one field to another, from one FileMaker Pro database to another, and between FileMaker Pro databases and documents created in other programs (such as word processors, spreadsheets, and graphics programs).

To drag text or objects between FileMaker Pro and another application, the other application must also support drag and drop.

- *Show templates in New File dialog:* FileMaker Pro 3.0 includes over 40 business, home, and educational templates that you can use to create a variety of ready-to-use databases. Check this option if you want these templates to be listed and selectable in the New Database dialog box that appears when you launch FileMaker Pro as well as when you choose New from the File menu.

- *User Name:* This option governs whether FileMaker Pro uses the system user name or a name that you supply in the Preferences dialog box. (The user name can be used as an auto-entry option for Text fields or pasted into a field with the Paste Special command.) The default is to use the system name (System), which is set in the Sharing Setup control panel in System 7. Click the System button to use the name that appears in quotes, or click the Custom button and enter another name in the text box. (Note that if the system name is currently blank — shown as an empty pair of quotation marks — you haven't identified yourself to the Mac. Step-by-step instructions in Chapter 5 tell you how to set the system user name.)

  You can paste the user name into a field with the Paste Special command, automatically enter it in a field by setting an appropriate auto-entry option, or use it in scripts. A networked database, for example, could be designed so that the current user's name is automatically entered as the person who created or most recently modified each record.

You can also create scripts that employ the custom user name. For example, you may want to create a script that finds data specific to a given individual, such as all telephone orders taken by a particular telemarketer. Instead of creating a separate script for every user, you can have FileMaker Pro use the custom user name. To find information for a different person (another telemarketer, for instance), you merely change the custom user name in the Preferences dialog box before running the script. (See Chapter 15 for more information about scripts.)

- *Network protocol:* If you are going to be using FileMaker Pro over a network, choose the appropriate network protocol from this pop-up menu. (If you aren't sure of the correct choice, ask your network administrator.)

Setting Document-Specific Preferences

In addition to setting preferences for FileMaker Pro as a whole, you can set Document preferences (shown in Figure 7-2) individually for each database. For instance, you can set a startup action for a given database by setting a preference that directs it to automatically open to a particular layout or run a special script. Obviously, you wouldn't want all databases to run a sort script when they're opened, but you certainly might want *some* of your databases to do so.

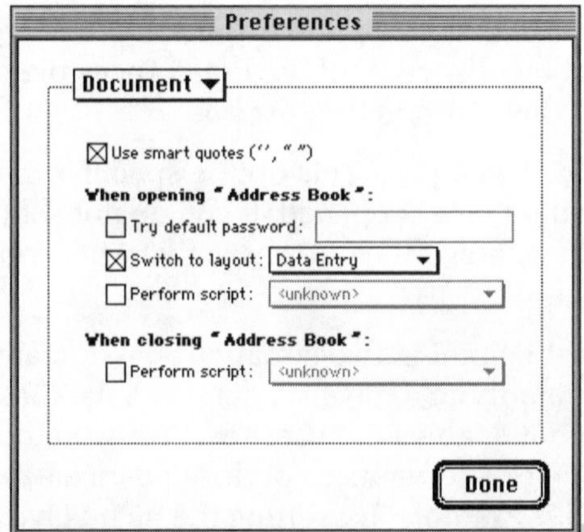

Figure 7-2: Document preferences

Every database can have different Document preferences. As with other FileMaker Pro preferences, you can change these preferences whenever you like. The five Document preferences that you can set are as follows:

- *Use smart quotes:* This option instructs FileMaker to use curved open and closed quotation marks rather than straight quotation marks (‘ ’ and “ ” versus ' ' and " "). The former characters are commonly referred to as curly or "smart" quotes and are generally favored — mainly because they look more professional.

  FileMaker Pro 3.0 contains a set of rules that determines when it uses a left quote and when it uses a right quote. When the "Use smart quotes" option is selected, the appropriate curly quote character is typed each time you press the single or double quotations mark key. Note that this preference option has no effect if the font that you're using doesn't contain symbols for the curved quotes — straight quotes will be used instead.

- *When opening, try default password:* In addition to normal and blank passwords (discussed in Chapter 20), FileMaker Pro now lets you specify a default password that is automatically tried when a user opens a particular database. You can associate specific privileges with the default password (such as allowing the user to only browse through records, but not edit, create, or delete them). One advantage of establishing a default password rather than using an ordinary password is that the user is never confronted with a request to enter a password. The database opens automatically (just like most other databases), and only the FileMaker Pro features specified by the person who developed the database are enabled.

  You set the default password option by clicking the "Try default password" button in the Document section of the Preferences dialog box and then typing the default password in the text box.

- *When opening, switch to layout:* This option specifies a particular layout to display when the database is opened. If you do not set this option, the database opens to whatever layout was active when you last closed the database.

  This option is most helpful in two situations. First, many databases are menu-driven. Instead of a normal data-entry screen, a database might contain a menu of buttons that enables the user to select which portion of the database or function he or she wants to perform: data entry, report printing, or label generation, for example. By setting the menu layout as the opening screen, you can ensure that new users won't be confused by starting in a different (possibly foreign) section of the database each time.

  Second, many databases are designed so that they revolve around one basic screen. For example, the Address Book database discussed in Chapter 4 has a data-entry layout as the central screen. Since most of the work a user will do is on that layout, it makes good sense to open automatically to that particular layout.

- *When opening, perform script:* This option automatically performs the selected script when the database is opened. For instance, you can perform a script that opens to a particular record (other than the first one), sets a particular display option, and so on.

FileMaker Pro 2.1 included separate Document preferences for the initial settings of the status area (shown or hidden) and zoom options. If you still wish these options to be set automatically when opening a database, you can do so by including them as steps in an opening script. See Chapter 15 for more information about scripts.

- *When closing, perform script:* This option automatically performs the selected script when the database is closed (when you click the document's close box, choose Close from the File menu, press ⌘-W, or quit from FileMaker Pro while the database is still open). For example, you may want to execute a script that performs a general sort or automatically prints a daily report. Setting this as a closing action — rather than an opening action — enables you to avoid a lengthy delay at the very beginning of your work session.

Manually Entering Curly Quotes

In some databases (ones that refer to measurements in feet or inches, for example), using smart quotes may not be to your advantage. If the "Use smart quotes" option is selected, you cannot type straight quotations marks (' and "). If you find that you frequently need to use straight quotes in a particular database, the best approach is to remove the check mark from the "Use smart quotes" setting. When you need curly quotes, you can enter them manually, as explained in the following table. (As a bonus, you can also use the instructions in the table to produce curly quote characters in other programs that don't provide a smart quotes option.)

Type this . . .	*To produce this curly quote character . . .*
Option-[	“ (double left quote)
Shift-Option-[	” (double right quote)
Option-]	‘ (single left quote)
Shift-Option-]	’ (single right quote)

Setting Layout Preferences

Layout preferences (shown in Figure 7-3) are concerned solely with actions that can take place while you're in Layout mode — either designing a new layout or editing an existing one. Settings chosen in the Layout section of the Preferences dialog box affect *all* databases, not merely the one that is active when the Preferences command is chosen.

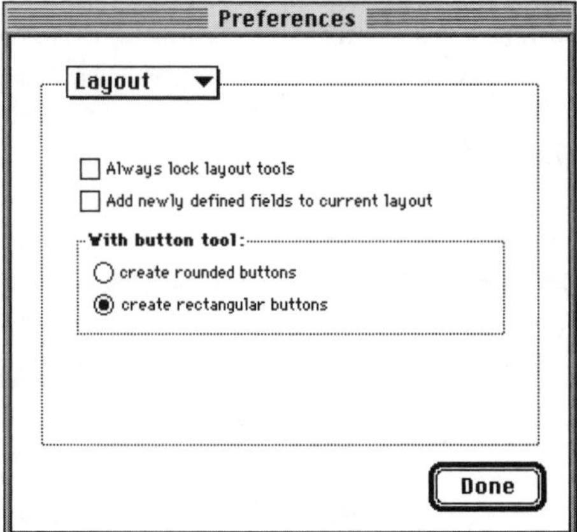

Figure 7-3: Layout preferences

The Layout preferences perform the following functions:

- *Always lock layout tools:* This option determines how tools behave when you're designing or modifying layouts. By default, FileMaker Pro automatically switches back to the Pointer tool after you perform an operation with any other tool. Although this way of operating enables you to quickly select an item after you modify it, this feature can be annoying if you routinely perform several operations in a row with the same tool. When the "Always lock layout tools" box is checked, FileMaker Pro keeps the same tool selected until you choose a different tool or press the Enter key.
- *Add newly defined fields to current layout:* This option determines whether new fields that you define will automatically be added to the current layout. By default, FileMaker Pro is set to add them. To be able to define new fields without automatically placing them on the current layout, click to remove the check mark from this option. You will then have to add newly defined fields manually (by dragging them onto the layout).

- *Button shape:* The new Button tool is used to draw attractive buttons on layouts. (Scripts or individual script steps can be attached to any button to make it perform one or more actions when clicked.) Choose a preferred button shape by clicking one of the two options: "create rounded buttons" or "create rectangular buttons." In order to design buttons of the other shape, simply change this setting. The new button shape will be in effect for all new buttons created in this or any other database.

Using Memory Preferences to Set a Save Interval

Memory preferences control the manner in which FileMaker Pro saves data to disk. As you work, FileMaker Pro saves data in two ways: by using the memory cache and by copying new data to the disk that contains the original database document. The *cache* is a special part of RAM (Macintosh memory) that is set aside for FileMaker Pro's use. Changes are accumulated in the cache until it is full or until an opportune moment arises (that is, when the system is idle). At this point, changes are flushed from the cache and saved to disk.

This way of operating is fine for desktop computers. On laptops, however, it can waste battery power. One of the most energy-consuming aspects of laptop operation is powering up and running the disk drives. For this reason, the drives on a laptop are frequently powered down and kept idle when data isn't being read from or written to them. If FileMaker Pro is set to save all changes to disk during idle time, however, it can keep the drives running more often and longer than normal and thus decrease the amount of work time that you get from a battery charge. To prevent such power waste, you can specify that FileMaker Pro save only after a given interval — perhaps once every 30 minutes.

Setting a save interval involves a significant trade-off. The longer the interval you choose, the less battery power is consumed, but the more data you put at risk. If you suffer a crash between saves, you may lose everything that is in the cache. This problem is not significant if you're just using the database to look up information or if you're making only limited changes. Note, however, that even if you set a relatively long save interval, FileMaker Pro will still save if the cache fills before the interval is reached.

To set a save interval in the Memory section of the Preferences dialog box (as shown in Figure 7-4), click the button labeled "every . . . or when necessary" and choose the desired interval from the pop-up menu. Remember that longer intervals are riskier to data, but they save more power.

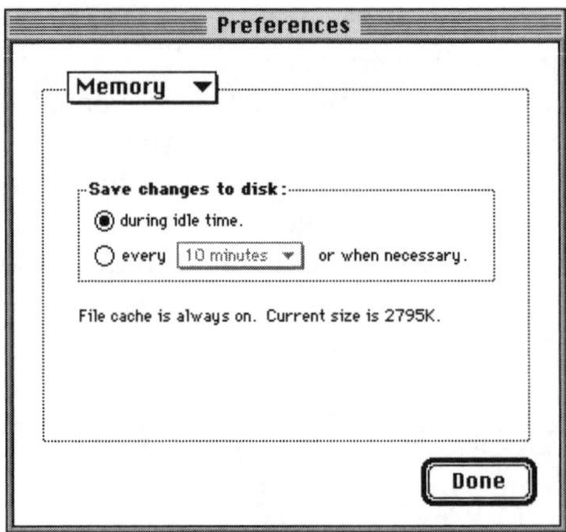

Figure 7-4: Setting Memory preferences

If you later change your mind and want to set a different save interval, simply repeat these steps. If you decide that you'd rather just save new data as soon as possible, choose the Memory icon again and click the button labeled "during idle time" (the default).

ScriptMaker includes a new step that you can use to directly control the cache: Flush cache to disk. To learn about this step, see Chapter 15.

Setting Modem and Dialing Preferences

The Modem and Dialing preferences work together to enable FileMaker Pro scripts to dial telephone numbers through a modem or the Mac's speaker.

Modem Preferences

The Modem preferences (shown in Figure 7-5) enable you to configure a modem to work with FileMaker Pro. If you do not have a modem, you can configure the Modem preferences to use the Mac's speaker for dialing. (When dialing a number, you'll have to put your telephone handset up to the speaker.)

Figure 7-5: Modem preferences

Preferences

Modem

Modem Commands
Setup: ATQ0V1E1S0=0
Prefix: DT
Hang up: +++ATH

Connection
Output: Speaker
Speed: 2400 baud

Defaults

Done

The Modem Commands portion of the dialog box is used to specify a setup string for the modem. It includes a command prefix (*DT* means to dial using touch-tone) and a command to hang up the modem. For most modems, the default entries for these commands can be left alone. If you decide to change them, refer to your modem manual for the appropriate commands.

The Connection section of the dialog box is used to specify the port to which your modem is connected and the speed with which the modem should operate. In the Output pop-up menu, choose the port to which your modem is attached (Modem or Speaker). Generally, Modem is the correct choice. Choose Speaker if you don't have a modem or if you don't want to use it for dialing.

The Speed pop-up menu is used to set the modem speed for dialing. (Since you will not be using the modem for telecommunication tasks, the particular speed chosen isn't important — select any speed that is supported by your modem.)

If — after experimenting with the Modem preferences — you want to return to FileMaker Pro's original settings, simply click the Defaults button at the bottom of the dialog box (refer to Figure 7-5).

Dialing Preferences

The Dialing preferences (see Figure 7-6) are used to create sets of dialing configurations based on your current location (Home, Office, Road, and Other). You can create different preferences for each of the four locations.

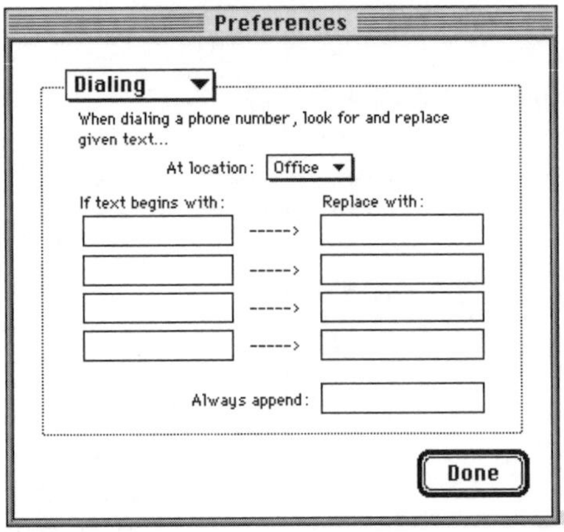

Figure 7-6: Dialing preferences

In the Dialing preferences, you can establish substitution strings to be dialed, depending on the composition of different phone numbers. Table 7-1 gives some examples of Dialing preferences when the local area code is 617.

Table 7-1
Substitution Strings for Dialing Preferences

If text begins with:	*Replace with:*	*Comments*
617		If your area code (617) is found, do not dial the area code as part of the number.
617	9,	Dial local calls by replacing the area code with 9, followed by a 2-second pause (represented by a comma).
	1	Regardless of the number found, treat it as long distance by preceding it with a 1.

Optionally, you can also specify a dialing suffix in the "Always append" text box. Some long-distance services can track different types of calls (various business projects, for example) if you append extra digits to the phone number.

To set the Dialing preferences for this and future sessions, select a location from the "At location" pop-up menu. When you are at another location (taking your PowerBook on the road, for example), choose a different location.

To dial from a FileMaker Pro database, you must use a script that contains the Dial Phone step. Also, unless the script step enables the "Use dialing preferences" option, the Dialing preferences are ignored.

The Power User's Guide to Preferences

Setting a startup script with the Perform script preference option is the best way to exert control over a database. Scripts enable you to have FileMaker Pro automatically perform any of the following actions when the database is opened or closed:

- Make sure that the database is sorted in a particular order.
- Select a subset of records with which to work or make certain that all records are visible.
- Perform a Relookup procedure so that all lookup fields contain current data.
- Open to a report layout and automatically print a current copy of the report.

As an example, here's a startup script that you can use to automatically create a backup file each time you open a particular important database:

1. Launch FileMaker Pro and open the database.
2. Choose ScriptMaker from the Script menu.

   The Define Scripts dialog box appears. The dialog box displays all scripts that have been defined for the database.
3. Type a name for the script in the Script Name box, such as Auto Backup.

   If the "Include in menu" check box does not contain a check mark, click once in the box to add the check mark.

(continued)

(continued)

4. Click Create to define the script.

   The Script Definition dialog box appears, as shown in the following figure.

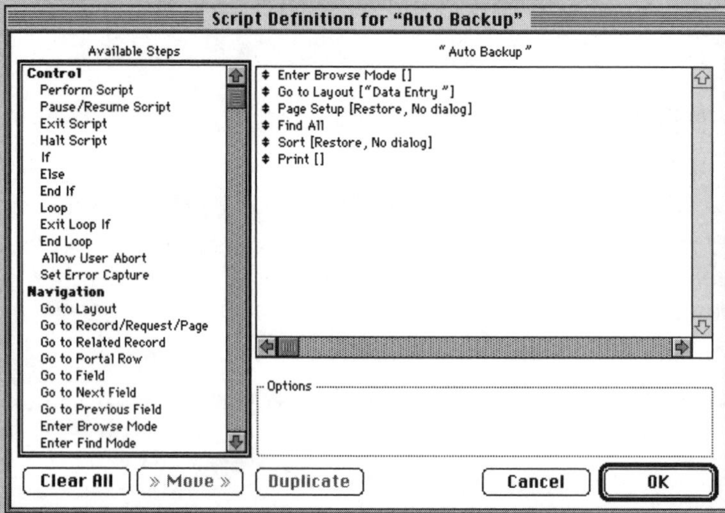

5. Click Clear All to clear the script definition list on the right side of the dialog box.
6. Scroll down the Available Steps list until the choice "Save a Copy as" appears.
7. Select "Save a Copy as" and then click the Move button.

   The script step is copied to the script list on the right.
8. Click the Specify File button.

   A standard file dialog box appears.
9. Navigate to the drive and folder where you want to store the backup files made by the script.

   By default, FileMaker Pro offers to name the backup file "Copy of *filename*," but you can change the name of the file.
10. At the bottom of the dialog box, click the Save: pop-up menu and choose either "copy of current file" or "compressed copy (smaller)."

    Either option will save a complete copy of the database, including all records, layouts, and field definitions. If disk space is at a premium, you may prefer to use the latter option.

11. Click the Save button.
12. To complete the script, click OK and then click Done in the dialog boxes that appear.

    A backup copy is created, and the script is added to the bottom of the Scripts menu.

To make the script execute automatically whenever you open the database file, select the script as the one to be performed when opening the database in Document preferences, as shown previously in Figure 7-2.

Keep the following in mind when using this backup script:

- Each time a new backup is created, it writes over the previous backup file. If you need to keep multiple generations of backups, you should return to the desktop and manually rename the backup before or at the end of each FileMaker Pro session.
- Remember that the backup file is an exact copy of the original. Thus, it also contains the automatic backup script. If you ever need to use the backup file, be sure to rename it before opening it in FileMaker Pro. Otherwise, an error dialog box will appear, informing you that FileMaker was unable to create a backup (because the script is attempting to make a copy of the currently open database, using its own name).

Summary

- You can customize how FileMaker Pro operates, as well as the startup and closing actions of individual databases, by using the Preferences command in the File menu.
- Selecting the "Use smart quotes" option instructs FileMaker Pro to automatically substitute curved left and right quotation marks for straight quotation marks. However, using this option makes entering foot and inch symbols (straight quotation marks) difficult.
- You can save battery power on a portable Macintosh (a PowerBook, for example) by specifying the frequency with which FileMaker Pro saves data to disk.
- To prepare FileMaker Pro for scripts that use the Dial Phone step, choose settings from the Modem and Dialing preferences.

Working with Databases

PART III

This section covers what you need to know when you're ready to start working with a database: entering and editing data, searching for records, sorting, using the spelling checker, designing reports, and printing.

Using Browse Mode: Viewing, Entering, Editing, and Deleting Records

CHAPTER 8

In This Chapter

- Switching to Browse mode
- Working in different layouts
- Navigating among and viewing records
- Adding and deleting records
- Entering and editing data in records
- Restrictions on entering data in different types of fields
- Entering data in fields that present a value list
- Reusing data from previously entered records

As a FileMaker Pro user, you will spend most of your time in Browse mode, one of the four FileMaker Pro operational modes discussed in Chapter 1. Whenever you want to view, enter, or edit data, add new records, or delete records, you must first switch to Browse mode.

Browse Mode Basics

As the name suggests, you can use Browse mode to flip through a database record-by-record, examining, creating, and modifying records as you go. You also have to be in Browse mode to *omit* records (temporarily hide them) or to sort records. Because you usually omit records in conjunction with a find request, this topic is discussed in Chapter 9. Sorting is covered in Chapter 10.

You can be in only one mode at a time. Determining which mode you are in is easy. In the Mode menu, the current mode has a check mark next to it, as shown in Figure 8-1. The name of the current mode also appears in the mode selector pop-up menu at the bottom of the database window (also shown in Figure 8-1).

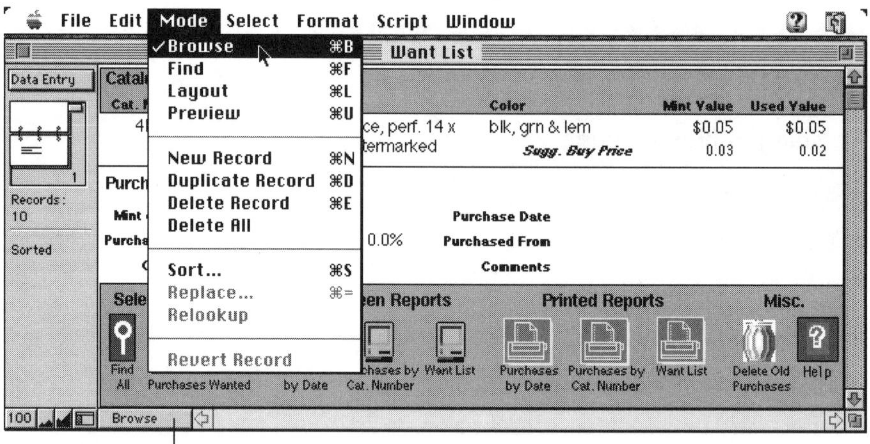

The mode selector pop-up menu also shows the current mode

Figure 8-1: The current mode is indicated both in the Mode menu and in the mode selector pop-up menu.

Switching to Browse Mode

Regardless of the mode you're currently in, you can switch to Browse mode in two ways:

- By choosing the Browse command from the Mode menu (or pressing ⌘-B)
- By choosing Browse from the mode selector pop-up menu at the bottom of the database window

You also switch to other modes (Find, Layout, and Preview) by selecting the mode from one of these menus.

When you first open a database, FileMaker Pro automatically displays it in Browse mode. This is convenient, since browsing is what you do most.

Using Browse Mode Controls

As shown in Figure 8-2, fewer controls are available in Browse mode than in Layout mode — the mode in which database layouts (arrangements of fields, graphics, and static text) are designed. Available controls are all related to record navigation and data viewing.

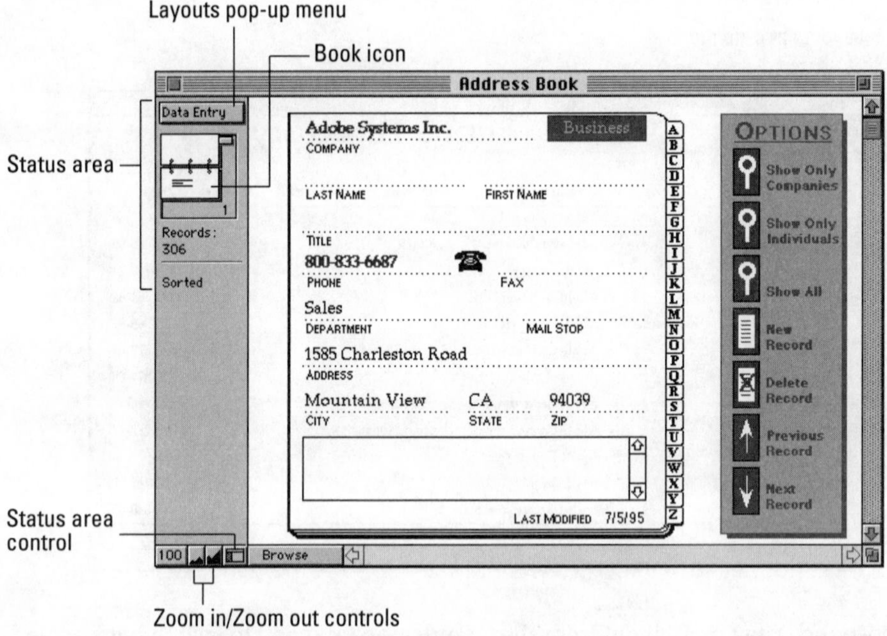

Figure 8-2: Browse mode controls

Using the Layouts Pop-Up Menu to Switch Layouts

The importance of layouts in FileMaker Pro is stressed throughout this book. As you will recall, a *layout* is a particular arrangement of database fields. Because no single way of displaying fields is equally useful for all tasks, many databases have multiple layouts. For example, a layout that makes it easy to enter data may not be the best one for displaying data when you want to look something up or generate a report. You can change layouts in Browse mode at any time.

In the upper-left corner of the window, above the status area, is the layouts pop-up menu (previously shown in Figure 8-2). You use this menu to determine which layout is currently displayed and to switch between available layouts for the database (by selecting a layout from the menu). For example, you use the following steps to switch the Address Book database from one layout to another and then back again:

1. With the Address Book database displayed, choose the Phone Directory layout from the layouts pop-up menu.

   The display changes to show the Phone Directory layout (see Figure 8-3). The layouts pop-up menu shows that you have changed to a new layout.

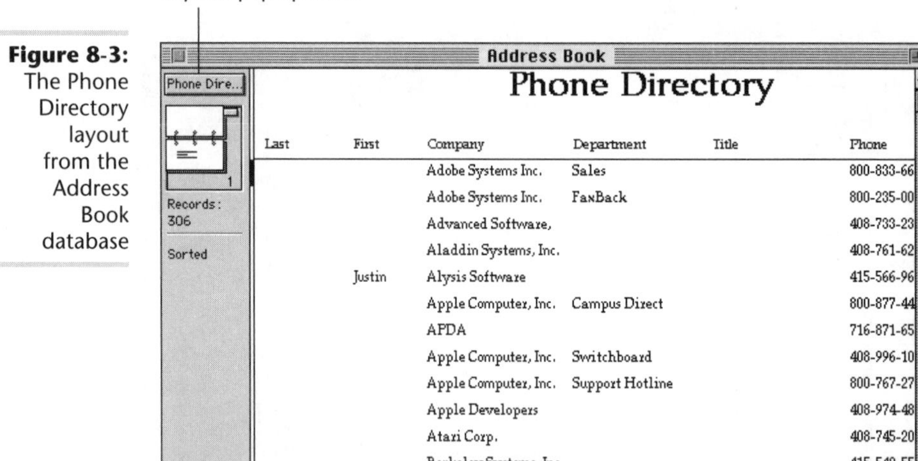

Figure 8-3: The Phone Directory layout from the Address Book database

2. Choose the Data Entry layout from the layouts pop-up menu to switch back again.

Keep in mind that different layouts may require different amounts of screen space in order to be fully displayed. When changing from one layout to another, you may sometimes need to resize the database window.

If you want, you can specify an opening layout for each database. Instead of opening to the layout that was displayed when you last closed the database (which is the default), FileMaker Pro displays the opening layout that you set in the Preferences dialog box. For instructions on setting an opening layout, see Chapter 7.

Using the Book Icon to Navigate Among Records

Below the layouts pop-up menu is the book icon (see Figure 8-4). In Browse mode, you use the book to navigate among records in order to select the next one you want to work with or view.

Figure 8-4: The book icon

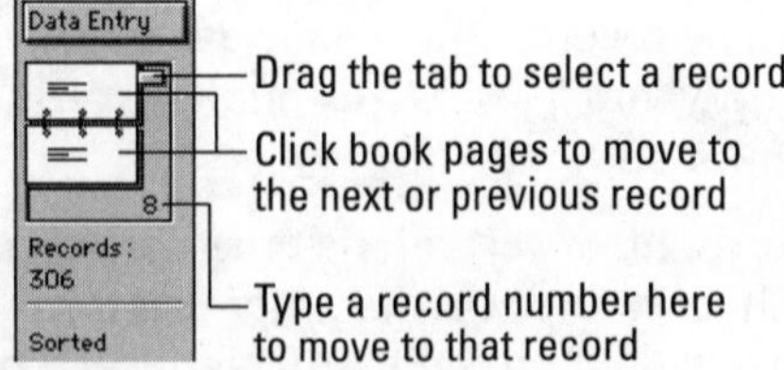

The book has different functions in other modes. In Find mode, you use it to switch between multiple find requests. In Layout mode, each book page represents a different layout. In Preview mode, you click the book to view different report pages.

In Browse mode, the navigation operations that you can perform by using the book include the following:

- Flipping from one record to the next or the previous record (by clicking the bottom or top pages of the book, respectively)
- Quickly moving to the first or last record (by dragging the tab on the side of the book to the top or bottom)
- Moving to an approximate position in the database (by dragging the tab on the side of the book)
- Moving to a specific record (by typing a record number in the area below the book)

The tab on the side of the book shows the approximate position in the database of the record that is currently displayed. The number below the book shows the exact position of the current record. The first record in the database is record number 1, the second is record number 2, and so on. The area below the book shows the total number of records that are currently in the database, the number of records that are being browsed (if all records aren't presently visible), and whether the database has been *sorted* (arranged in a particular order). In the example previously shown in Figure 8-4, the eighth record out of 306 is currently displayed, and the database is in sort order.

Browsing Suggestions

One common thing to do with a database is to look up individual records. After all, the purpose of a database is to store information for later retrieval. Although you can locate and examine records in several ways (many of which are discussed in later chapters), frequently you'll just flip through records one at a time until you find the one you want.

Flipping through records, however, can be time-consuming when working with a large database. (See Chapter 9 for quicker, more efficient search methods.) One thing that you can do to make this process easier is to switch to a layout that shows more than one record at a time, such as the Phone Directory layout for the Address Book database, or to display the records in the current layout as a list (see the sidebar, "Browsing Without Using the Book," later in this chapter).

The following sections explain the various methods of navigating through the database. If you want to experiment with the different methods, you can use the Address Book database or any other database that's handy.

Moving to the Next or Previous Record in a Database

You can use the book icon or keyboard shortcuts to move forward and backward in a database one record at a time. Follow these steps:

1. To move forward in a database, click the lower half of the book.

   Each click switches to the next record in the current sort order, making it the current record. The book tab moves down slightly, and the new record is displayed.

— or —

1. To move backward through a database, click the upper half of the book.

   Each click switches to the previous record in the current sort order, making it the current record. The book tab moves up slightly, and the new record is displayed.

2. Continue clicking until the desired record appears.

FileMaker Pro 3.0 also provides keyboard shortcuts that you can use to move to the next or previous record. To go to the next record, press ⌘-Tab. To go to the previous record, press Shift-⌘-Tab or Option-⌘-Tab.

Moving to the First Record in a Database

Follow these steps to move to the first record in a database:

1. Click the book tab and drag upward until it reaches the top of the book.
2. Release the mouse button.

— or —

1. Click the record number indicator directly below the book to select it.
2. Type **1** and then press Return or Enter.

   You can type any number to move directly to a particular record. Although you normally won't know specific record numbers, you will always know the first one.

   The first record in the database becomes the current record.

You can tell when you're at the first record of a database because the top half of the book icon is blank. As usual, the record number (1, in this case) is displayed below the book.

If the current layout displays one record per screen (such as the Data Entry layout in the Address Book database), only the first record is visible. If you have chosen View as List from the Select menu, as is often done in reports, a small vertical bar marks the current record in the list (as previously shown in Figure 8-3).

Moving to the Last Record in a Database

Follow these steps to move to the last record in a database:

1. Click the book tab and drag downward until it reaches the bottom of the book.
2. Release the mouse button.

   The last record in the database becomes the current record.

— or —

1. Click the record number indicator directly below the book to select it.
2. Type a large number and press Return or Enter.

   As long as the number is greater than or equal to the number of records that are currently being browsed, the last record is displayed, and it becomes the current record.

When the last record is selected, the bottom of the book is blank — showing that no records follow the current one. As always, the record number is displayed immediately below the bottom book page.

Regardless of the record navigation method that you use, if you attempt to move up past the first record or down past the last record, nothing happens.

Who's on First?

The particular database record that is displayed as first and the one that is last depends on whether the database has been sorted, and if so, by which field or fields. For example, the first record originally entered in Address Book may have been the one for Don Smith.

If you sort the database by the Last Name field, the new first record may be that of Jim Abrams. See Chapter 10 for more information on sorting and how it affects a database.

Moving to a Specific Record in a Database

You can also move to a specific record number if you happen to know, for example, that the desired record is the fourth one down.

Follow these steps to move to a specific record number:

1. Click the record number indicator below the book to select it.

   — or —

1. If no record is currently selected, press the Escape key (Esc).

   In either case, the record number indicator changes to inverse video to show that it is selected.

2. Type the number of the record that you want to examine, and press Return or Enter.

   The corresponding record appears on the screen and becomes the current record.

When you are browsing a database, you usually have all of its records at your disposal. Sometimes, however, you may want to view only a subset of the records. To view a subset, you can issue a find request. A find request restricts visible records to those that match the find criteria (Salary < 50000, for example). For more information about searching for record subsets, see Chapter 9.

Browsing Without Using the Book

You can completely bypass the book when you are browsing records by choosing View as List from the Select menu. In list view, all records are displayed as a continuous scrolling list. You use the scroll bar at the side of the database window to change the view of the records. Reports and data-entry screens that have limited fields are often displayed and worked with in list view. If you have an Apple Extended keyboard (or an equivalent keyboard from another manufacturer), you can also use the following keys to move through the database in list view:

Key	*Effect*
Home	Move to the first record
End	Move to the last record
Page Up	Move up one screen
Page Down	Move down one screen

Note that these keys are purely for navigation and *looking* at records. If you want to add data to or edit the current data in a record, you must *select* the record by clicking somewhere inside it.

If list view isn't the view you normally use for the current layout, choose View as Form from the Select menu. The display reverts to one record per screen.

Changing the Magnification Level

Below the status area (at the bottom of the database window) are three tools that enable you to change your view of the database: the magnification level, zoom out, and zoom in controls. For example, you can decrease the magnification (or zoom out) to get a bird's-eye view of a layout or report (as shown in Figure 8-5); and you can increase the magnification (or zoom in) to concentrate on a particular section of a record. Although these tools are more useful in Layout mode, you can use them in Browse mode, too.

Figure 8-5: Address Book zoomed to 75 percent

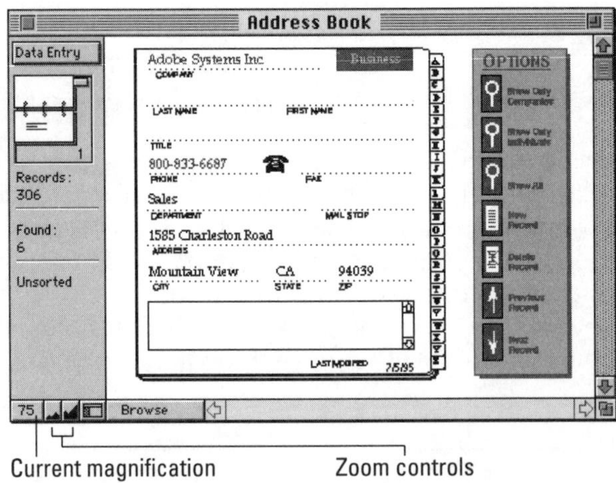

The current magnification is shown as a percentage: 100 means that the database is shown actual size, 200 means that it's twice the normal size, and so on. Clicking the number toggles the display between 100 percent and the most recently selected zoom level. You use the pair of buttons to the right of the magnification percentage to zoom out (decrease magnification) and zoom in (increase magnification), respectively. Each time you click one of the buttons, the magnification is decreased or increased.

Showing and Hiding the Status Area

To the right of the zoom controls is the status area control (previously shown in Figure 8-2). This button, which works as a toggle, enables you to hide or show the status area. Hiding the status area gives you more room in which to display the database. When you click the status area control to hide the status area, the current layout fills the entire window. Click the status area control again to display the status area and regain access to the tools.

Finally, to the right of the status area control button is the mode selector pop-up menu. As mentioned earlier in this chapter, you can use this menu to switch from one FileMaker Pro operational mode to another.

Data Entry and Editing

Perhaps the most important uses of Browse mode are entering and editing data. As you work with FileMaker Pro, you'll discover that a wealth of commands and techniques have been provided to make data entry and editing as simple as possible.

Creating New Records

Few databases are static entities that you just browse through now and then. Whether you've just finished designing a database or are working with one that you've had around for years, you'll want to add new records to it at some point. For example, a new business or personal contact requires a new record in your Address Book database. After you add the new record, you can enter the appropriate information in each of the record's fields.

The exact way in which you add a record to the database can sometimes depend on the way in which the database was designed. For example, in the Data Entry layout for Address Book (previously shown in Figure 8-2), you can click a New Record button to activate a script that adds a new record to the database. Most database layouts, however, don't have such a button. Instead, you switch to Browse mode and choose the New Record command from the Mode menu (or press ⌘-N).

The new record appears on-screen, and it is added in the database immediately after the current record. Unless you have set auto-entry options for some fields (see Chapter 5), the record is blank.

If adding the new record disrupted an existing sort order (the indicator below the book icon reads "Semi-sorted"), you can restore order to the database by sorting again, as discussed in Chapter 10.

Entering Data

A blank record isn't very useful. After adding a record, you need to enter appropriate information in it — usually by typing it. First, however, you need to select the field in which you want to enter data, either by clicking in the field or tabbing into it.

You enter information one field at a time. The *current field* is the one in which you can immediately enter and edit data. The current field is surrounded by a solid border; borders around all other fields are dotted. The current field also contains the *insertion point*, a blinking vertical line that is sometimes called the cursor. Figure 8-6 shows a new record's current field and insertion point.

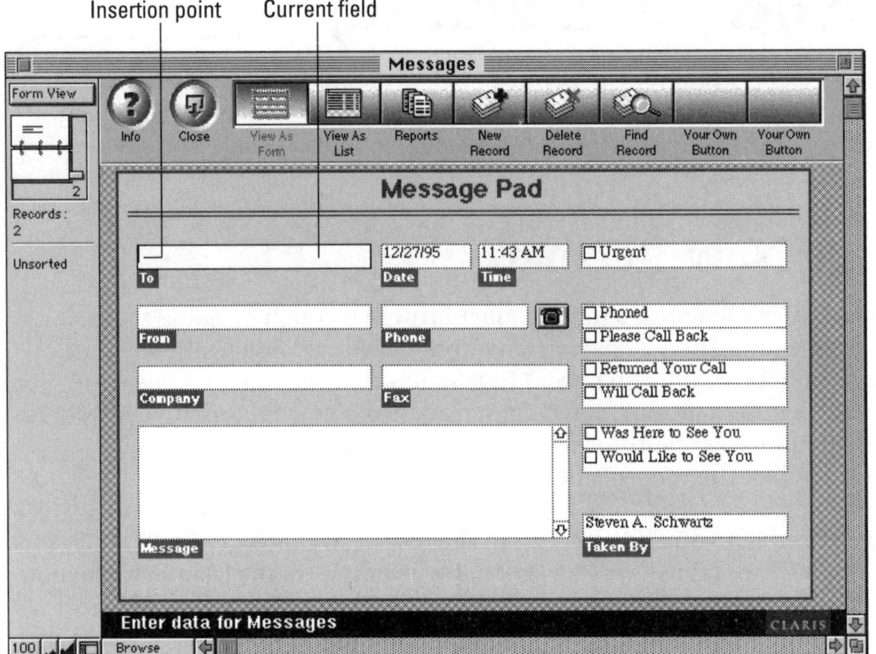

Figure 8-6: A new record

The position of the insertion point in a blank field is determined by the alignment that has been set for the field (using the Align Text submenu of the Format menu). When a field is left-aligned, the insertion point appears on the left side of the field. When a field is right-aligned — as Number fields frequently are — the insertion point is on the right side of the field.

To enter data in another field, you first need to make it the current field. You can either click the field with the mouse or tab into the field by pressing the Tab key. Pressing Tab moves you forward through a record one field at a time. Pressing Shift-Tab moves you back to the previous field.

By default, when you press the Tab key, the insertion point moves through the fields from left to right and top to bottom. However, you can create a custom tab order by changing to Layout mode and choosing the Set Tab Order command from the Mode menu. See Chapter 6 for details.

You cannot tab into a Summary or Calculation field because you cannot edit or manually enter data in these types of fields. (The only permissible action in these fields is copying the contents.) To select a Summary or Calculation field for copying, you must click the field with the mouse.

When you are finished entering data in the record, press the Enter key, choose New Record again, or use the book icon to switch to a different record. The record is immediately evaluated by FileMaker Pro and examined for data validation failures (such as leaving a required field blank). If you have committed any errors, FileMaker Pro will let you know.

Keep in mind that you can enter data in *any* layout in which fields are displayed — including layouts for reports or mailing labels, for example. Of course, because some layouts show different sets of fields, data entry is more convenient in some layouts than in others. Regardless of which layout you use when entering or editing data, the new data for a field is recorded in all layouts in which that same field appears. For example, the Address Book database has two layouts: Data Entry and Phone Directory. Adding or changing the text in a record's Company field in the Phone Directory layout simultaneously changes the text in the Company field in the Data Entry layout. (Remember — every layout is simply a different arrangement of the data contained in the database.)

Using the Data-Entry and Cursor-Control Keys

As you're entering data, some keys actually enter data (*data-entry keys*) and others merely move the insertion point (*cursor-control keys*) — either within a field or between fields. The differences between the data-entry and cursor-control keys are explained in the following sections.

The Data-Entry Keys

Data-entry keys do what their name suggests. When you press a data-entry key, a corresponding character is entered in a field at the insertion point. The data-entry keys consist of the letters *a* through *z*, the numerals *0* through *9*, and the punctuation keys, as well as these same keys pressed in combination with Shift, Option, and Shift-Option. Return also acts as a data-entry key. Pressing Return ends the current line and adds a new line to the field.

Number fields do not accept a Return. You need to enter all numbers on a single line within the field.

In previous versions of FileMaker Pro, the Tab key was used exclusively to move from field to field within a record. In FileMaker Pro 3.0, you can embed a tab character within any Text field by pressing Option-Tab. By default, tab stops are set every half inch. To set different stops for a Text field, choose Text Ruler from the Format menu, click the icon for the type of tab you want to set (left, center, right, or decimal), and then click the appropriate position on the ruler.

The Cursor-Control Keys

You use the cursor-control keys to move within and between fields. As the name suggests, a cursor-control key merely moves the cursor. Table 8-1 lists the cursor-control keys and their functions.

Table 8-1
Cursor-Control Keys

Key or Key Combination	*Function*
Tab	Move to the next field
Shift-Tab	Move to the previous field
Up arrow	Move up one line in the current field, if possible; otherwise, do nothing
Down arrow	Move down to the next line in the current field, if possible; otherwise, do nothing
Left arrow	Move one character position left in the current field, if possible; otherwise, do nothing
Right arrow	Move one character position right in the current field, if possible; otherwise, do nothing

After you master the cursor-control keys, entering data is relatively straightforward. FileMaker Pro supports the text-entry, cursor-control, and editing functions that you have already learned in other programs (such as pressing Delete to remove the previous character and using the Cut, Copy, and Paste commands). Keep in mind, however, that some field types and definitions may restrict the range of acceptable data that you can enter, as described in the next section.

Typing Special Characters

You use the Option and Shift-Option key combinations to type special characters, such as symbols and foreign language characters. For example, to type a bullet (•), you press Option-8. If you want to find out where those special characters are hiding — the ones that aren't visible on the keyboard — you can use a desk accessory such as Key Caps from Apple Computer (included with every copy of the system software) or a more advanced utility such as KeyFinder. (KeyFinder was formerly a part of the Norton Utilities for Macintosh from Symantec Corporation.)

As you hold down Shift, Option, or Shift-Option, Key Caps shows the characters that you can type by pressing a particular letter, number, or punctuation key in combination with the modifier key or keys that you're holding down. A *modifier key* is any key that changes the meaning of a normal key. In regular typing, the modifier keys are Shift and Option. The Control and Command modifier keys — if supported — are under program control and are usually reserved for issuing commands from the keyboard and similar functions. You can copy any character created in Key Caps and then paste it into the current document.

KeyFinder is much easier to use and more powerful than Key Caps. It shows, at a glance, every character that's available in a particular font. After you click the desired symbol, KeyFinder tells you what keys to press to create that symbol in your document. Undefined characters are shown as boxes. As with Key Caps, you can copy any character created in KeyFinder and paste it into the current document.

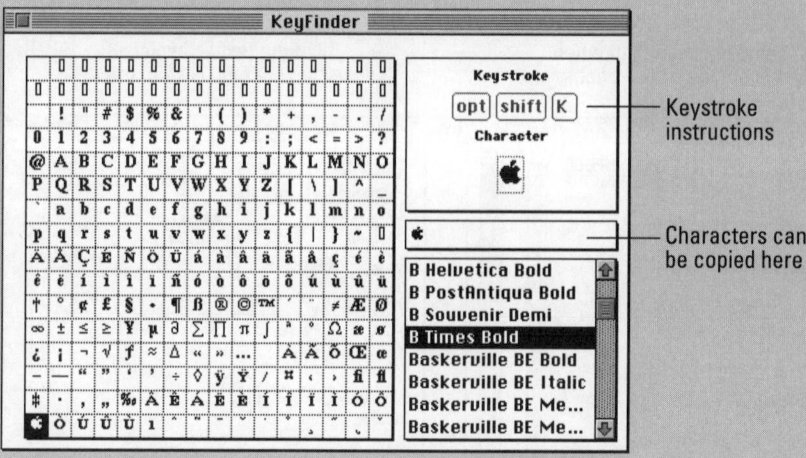

If you need to move a database between the Macintosh and Windows versions of FileMaker Pro or if you are using a database on a mixed PC and Mac network, be sparing with your use of special characters. In most cases, these characters will not translate appropriately from one platform to the other. See Chapter 16 for details.

Entering Different Types of Data

In FileMaker Pro, each defined field is one of eight different data types: Text, Number, Time, Date, Global, Container, Calculation, and Summary. You can neither enter nor edit data in Calculation and Summary fields. The following sections describe data entry and editing in the other six types of fields. (If you need additional help in determining what kinds of information can and cannot go into the different field types, see Chapter 5.)

Any formatting that you set for a field is applied *after* you enter the data and move to another field.

Text Fields

Text fields can contain any kind of character data, including text, numbers, and other characters. A single Text field can accept up to 64,000 characters of text.

If you exceed the size of a Text field (as designed in Layout mode) when entering information into it, the field automatically expands downward to accommodate the excess text. When you leave the field, it reverts to its original size, and the extra text is hidden from view. To see all the information that's stored in the field, you have to click or tab into the field (see Figure 8-7). If you want to use the field's contents in a printed report, be aware that whatever you normally see on-screen is also what will appear in the report. If the contents of the entire field are not visible, you are well-advised to expand the field in Layout mode or edit the field's contents before printing.

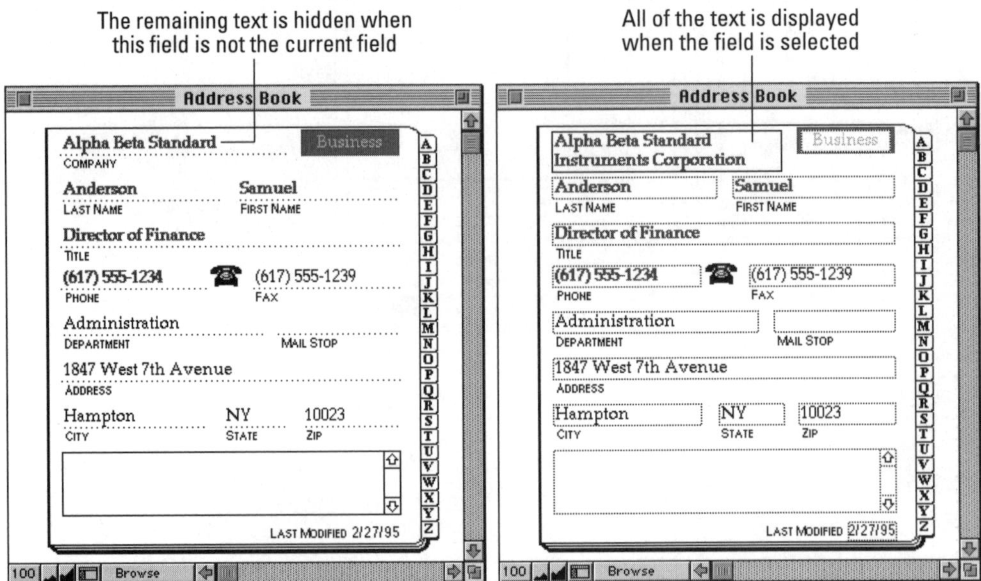

Figure 8-7: Text overflow in a field

Creating Multi-Word Index Entries

As part of its record-keeping routine, FileMaker Pro creates a separate index for each database field for which the indexing storage option has been turned on. The index consists of every word or value entered in each Text, Time, Date, Number, and Calculation field. If you want an entire phrase from a Text field to serve as an index entry (such as "Jim Knowles"), press Option-spacebar between each word in the phrase. See Chapter 5 to learn about field indexing.

Number Fields

FileMaker Pro ignores non-numeric data in a Number field when it is performing calculations based on the field, executing find requests based on the field, and recording index entries for the field. Number values can consist of up to 255 characters, typed on a single line (no Returns are allowed). Any numeric formatting that you have set for the field (with the Number command from the Format menu) is applied only to the numeric parts of data within the field.

If a number exceeds the width of its field, it displays as a single question mark. (This same restriction applies to Global fields of type Number.) You can see the entire number by clicking the field or tabbing into it. A question mark also appears in a Calculation or Summary field if the formula cannot be evaluated or if it results in a divide-by-zero error.

Although you can enter any kind of character in a Number field, restricting the field to numeric data may be helpful — particularly if someone else will be doing the data entry. To restrict the field to numeric data, set the option labeled "Verify that field is of type Number" when you are defining the Number field. (See Chapter 5 for instructions on how to set field validation options.)

You use the Number command from the Format menu (in Layout mode) to set a particular display format for the field.

Time Fields

When entering data in a Time field, you can use either the standard 12-hour format or the 24-hour military time format. When you type values, you need to use colons to separate the hours, minutes, and seconds (for example, 1:00 PM or 13:00:00). In 12-hour format, if you leave off the AM or PM designation, FileMaker Pro assumes that you mean AM. If you simply enter the number **7**, for example, FileMaker interprets it as 7:00 AM.

Unlike with Number fields, you must leave any extraneous, non-time related data out of a Time field. FileMaker Pro accepts only legitimate times.

You use the Time command from the Format menu (in Layout mode) to set a different display format for the date. However, this command affects only how the time is displayed in the record, not how you enter it.

Date Fields

Date fields are similar to Time fields. The maximum length of a Date field is ten characters — up to eight characters for the month (2), day (2), and year (4), plus two separators. You can separate the parts of the date with any non-numeric character, such as a slash or dash. If you enter only two digits for the year, FileMaker assumes that you mean the current century. If you omit the year altogether, FileMaker assumes that you mean the current year (per the system clock).

You use the Date command from the Format menu (in Layout mode) to set a different display format for the date. However, this command affects only how the date is displayed in the record, not how you enter it. Regardless of the date format, leading zeroes (as in 04/07/95) are optional. As with Time fields, you must leave any extraneous, non-date related data out of a Date field. Only legitimate dates are accepted.

If the database was created on a Macintosh that uses U.S. date formats, you enter dates in month-day-year format (12/31/95, for example). If the database was created on a system that uses an international format for dates (day-month-year, for example), you have to use that same format when you enter dates.

In Time and Date fields, you can edit auto-entry times or dates (information that's taken from the system clock) unless the option labeled "Prohibit modification of auto-entered values" is selected as part of the field's definition. (See Chapter 5 for details on setting auto-entry options for fields.)

With recent versions of System 7, you can use the Date & Time control panel to set an international date or time format for programs such as FileMaker Pro to use.

Global Fields

Global fields are used to store a single value that is shared across all records ina database. For example, in an invoice database, you might use a Global field to record the state sales tax percentage or a flat-fee shipping charge that is added to all orders. Global fields are also useful in scripts.

When creating a Global field, you have to decide whether it will hold text, number, date, time, or container (sound, picture, or movie) data, as shown in Figure 8-8. The data type selected for the field determines the type of information the field can hold, as well as the rules that apply to entering data in the field (as described in this chapter).

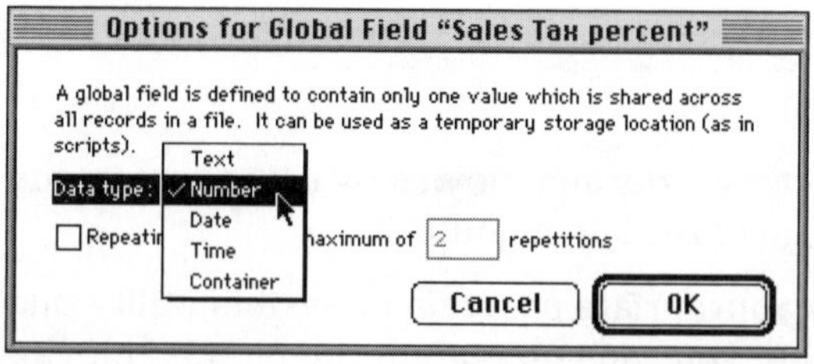

Figure 8-8: Setting the data type for a Global field

Container Fields

Container fields can contain still images, sounds, or movies. (In the Windows version of FileMaker Pro, Container fields can also store OLE objects.) Working with Container fields is a little more complicated than working with Text or Number fields. In the case of movies and sounds, the Macintosh needs to have special capabilities that are provided in the software, hardware, or a combination of the two (described later in this section).

Table 8-2 lists and explains the graphics and sound file formats that FileMaker Pro 3.0 supports. (A *format* is a specific method for storing a particular kind of data.)

Table 8-2
Supported Graphics and Sound Formats

Format	*Description*
TIFF (Tag Image File Format)	A still graphics format. Images can be color or grayscale. Compressed versions are supported, but they may not be compatible with all programs. TIFF is also supported by other computer systems, such as IBM. (Between the Mac and PC, there are many varieties of TIFF, but not all are supported.)
PICT	A Macintosh-specific graphics format. (This is perhaps the most common format available for the Mac.)
MacPaint	An older Macintosh black-and-white graphics format, now falling into disuse.
EPS or EPSF (Encapsulated PostScript)	A graphics format for detailed drawings that is favored by illustrators. The quality of the graphic depends on the output device.
SND 1 and SND 2	Macintosh sound formats. These formats require a microphone (to record sounds) and the Sound control panel.
MooV	QuickTime movie format. It requires System 6.0.8 or higher and the QuickTime extension.

You can use a variety of methods to insert pictures, sounds, and movies into a Container field:

- You can import pictures and movies by using commands in the Import/Export submenu of the File menu.
- If you have an appropriate program or system utility that can open a picture, movie, or sound, you can copy or cut the picture, movie, or sound to the Clipboard and then paste it into the Container field. Current versions of Apple's Scrapbook desk accessory, for example, can be used to store all three types of material.
- If your Mac has a microphone, you can use the Sound control panel to record sounds directly into the field.

The remainder of this section describes how to use each of these methods to insert data into a Container field.

Follow these steps to import a picture or a movie into a Container field:

1. Switch to Browse mode by choosing Browse from the Mode menu (or by pressing ⌘-B).
2. Make the Container field the current field by clicking or tabbing into it.
3. Choose the Import/Export submenu from the File menu and then drag across to select the appropriate command: Import Picture for a still graphic or Import Movie for a QuickTime movie.

   One of the dialog boxes in Figure 8-9 appears.

Figure 8-9: Importing a movie (top) and a picture (bottom)

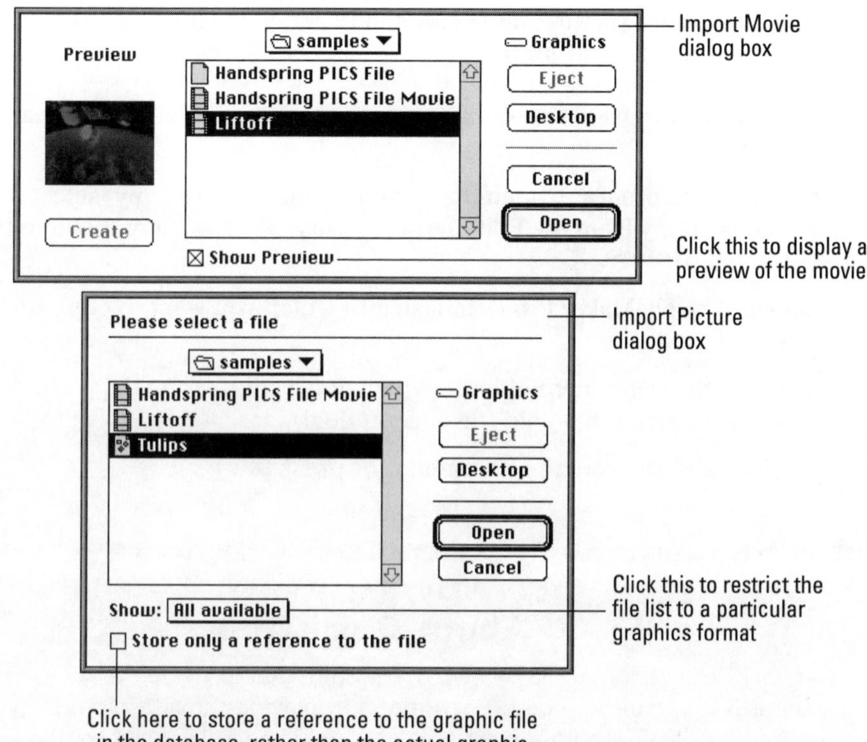

If the desired picture or movie isn't shown in the file list, use normal navigation techniques to move to the appropriate disk and folder. For help with file navigation, see Chapter 2.

4. Select the picture or movie that you want to insert.

If you are inserting a movie, you can click the Show Preview check box in the Import Movie dialog box to see a frame of the movie before you import it.

5. Click Open to place the picture or movie in the field.

When a movie is imported into a Container field, only a *reference* to the movie file is actually stored in the database (rather than the movie itself). When importing a picture, on the other hand, the actual picture is stored in the database — unless you check the check box labeled "Store only a reference to the file" (as previously shown in Figure 8-9). The ability to store graphic references is a new space-saving feature of FileMaker Pro 3.0.

You can also copy a picture, movie, or sound and paste it into a Container field, as described in the following steps:

1. Open the program that contains the picture, sound, or movie that you want to copy.
2. Within the program, open the item that you want to copy, select it, and then choose Copy from the Edit menu (or press ⌘-C) to copy the item to the Clipboard.
3. Open the FileMaker Pro database into which you want to copy the picture, sound, or movie.
4. Select the Container field into which you want to copy the picture, sound, or movie (making that field the current field).
5. Choose Paste from the Edit menu (or press ⌘-V).

About QuickTime

QuickTime is an Apple system extension that provides a set of tools and standards for creating, editing, storing, and playing moving pictures with sound on the Macintosh. An important part of QuickTime is its ability to play movies on *any* Mac. The more recent versions of QuickTime even support Macs that have black-and-white displays.

QuickTime movies require a great deal of disk space. For example, a 19-second movie that I created occupies over 6MB of space! Getting video data into a Macintosh requires special hardware, such as a video capture card. Although you can use simple utility programs to capture and edit movies, serious QuickTime work requires serious software, such as Adobe Premiere. Because of the storage, hardware, and software requirements, movie making is out of the reach of many users. If you don't want to create your own movies, many prerecorded QuickTime movies are available as commercial products.

Dealing with Lost Movies

When you copy or import a QuickTime movie into a Container field in FileMaker Pro, a link is created to the original movie. The actual movie data is not copied into the database. Using this method saves disk space, but it also has important consequences. If you delete the original movie or move the database to another Mac without also supplying a copy of the movie, the link will be broken, and FileMaker Pro won't be able to play the movie. However, you will be given an opportunity to insert the disk that contains the movie.

If you think that the movie is on a disk that is already *mounted* (displayed on the desktop), you can tell FileMaker Pro where to find the movie or ask the program to search for the movie. If the movie is nowhere to be found, the contents of the Container field are changed to a still picture. If you eventually locate the movie or transfer a new copy of it to your hard disk, the next time you open the database that references the movie, the link is reestablished.

You can record sounds directly into a Container field if you have a Macintosh that is equipped with a microphone and have the Sound control panel installed and properly configured. (The Sound control panel is part of the Macintosh system software.)

Follow these steps to record a sound directly into a field:

1. Double-click the Container field into which you want to record.

   The Sound Record dialog box appears, as shown in Figure 8-10.

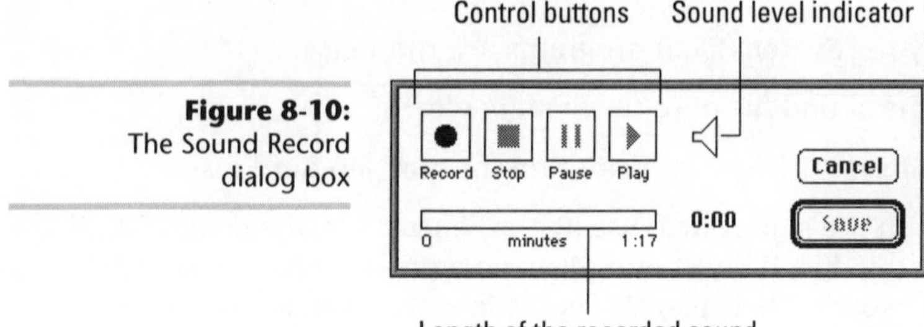

Figure 8-10: The Sound Record dialog box

You click the control buttons at the top of the dialog box to record, stop recording, pause the recording, and play back the recording. A bar below the buttons indicates the length of the recording. The icon that looks like a speaker indicates the sound level.

2. When you are ready to record, click Record.
3. Speak or otherwise direct sound into the microphone.
4. When you are done recording, click Stop.
5. Click Play to listen to the sound that you recorded.

Playing back stored sounds or movies is simple. To play back a sound, just double-click the field in which it is stored. To play back a movie, click the Play/Stop button on the movie's frame (see Figure 8-11) or double-click the movie itself. To stop playback, click the movie once or click the Play/Stop button again. Other movie controls enable you to change the playback volume and step forward or backward through the movie one frame at a time.

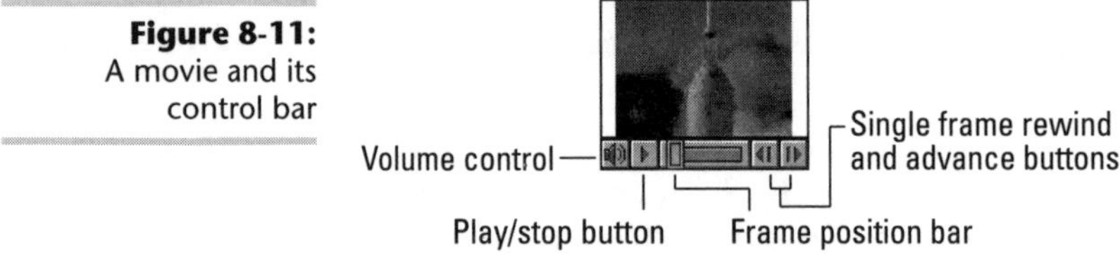

Figure 8-11: A movie and its control bar

If you already have sound files that you'd like to add to a Container field, you can use your Mac's System file as a temporary repository for them (enabling you to copy the sounds without having any special audio software). The following steps describe how to accomplish this:

1. Close all programs that are currently running.

   You cannot modify the System file if programs are running.

2. Drag the icon for the sound file onto the System file.

   The System file is inside the System Folder on the start-up hard disk.

   If the sound file is on the same hard disk as the System file, the sound file is *moved* into the System file. If the sound file is on a different hard disk than the System file, the sound file is merely *copied* into the System file.

3. Open the Sound control panel, as shown in Figure 8-12.

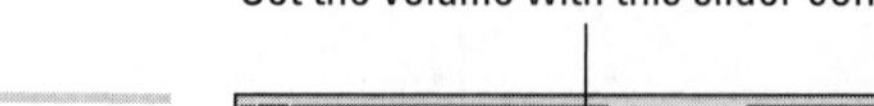

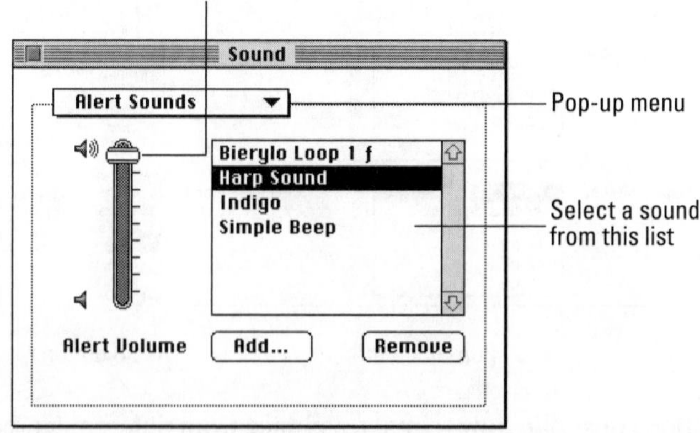

Figure 8-12: The Sound control panel

The Alert Sounds portion of the Sound control panel lists the names of all sounds that are currently installed in the System file. (If Alert Sounds is not displayed, choose it from the pop-up menu.)

4. Select the sound that you want to copy and choose Copy from the Edit menu (or press ⌘-C).

   A copy of the sound is placed on the Clipboard.

5. Close the Sound control panel by clicking its close box in the upper-left corner.
6. Open the FileMaker Pro database in which you want to paste the sound.
7. Select the Container field in the desired record and choose Paste from the Edit menu (or press ⌘-V).

   The sound is pasted into the field.

8. If you want to paste additional sounds into the database, leave the database open, open the Sound control panel again, and continue to copy and paste.
9. To remove the sound and restore the System file to its original condition, double-click the System file icon and drag the sound resource to the Trash or to its original location on disk. Then close the System file.

Working with Value Lists

Not all data has to be typed or imported. Using the Field Format command (in Layout mode), you can format fields to display as pop-up lists, menus, radio buttons, and check boxes (see Figure 8-13). These formats help speed data entry by providing a list of user-defined choices from which you can select. The list of choices is called a *value list.* Any of these formats except pop-up lists can also have an Other choice appended to it. (For information on creating value lists and attaching them to fields, see Chapter 5.)

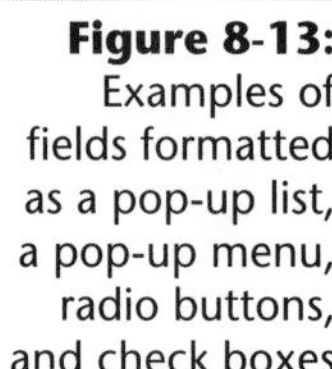

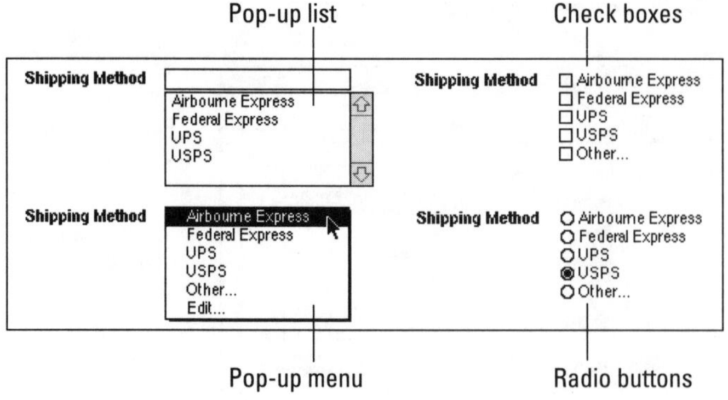

Figure 8-13: Examples of fields formatted as a pop-up list, a pop-up menu, radio buttons, and check boxes

The following sections describe how to make a choice from different kinds of value lists.

Choosing an Item from a Pop-Up List

When you click or tab into a field formatted as a pop-up list, a scrolling list of values appears, similar in appearance to a list that you'd find in most dialog boxes. To choose an item from a pop-up list, follow these steps:

1. Click or tab into the field that contains the pop-up list.

   The list automatically expands.

2. Select the item of interest by clicking it once.

   The choice is registered and the insertion point moves to the next field.

   — or —

2. If you want to enter a response that is not included in the value list, ignore the list and click once in the field, type a different response, and then press the Tab key to move to the next field.

You can also use the arrow keys to choose a particular item. The up arrow and left arrow move up in the list; the down arrow and right arrow move down in the list. In addition, you can type the first letter or two of a value to quickly select that item. Complete your selection by pressing Return.

A pop-up list can also have an Edit choice. Include such a choice when you want the user to be able to edit the value list on which the field choices are based. (See Chapter 5 for instructions.)

Choosing an Item from a Pop-Up Menu

When you click a field formatted as a pop-up menu, a traditional pop-up menu appears. Unlike using a pop-up list, you cannot manually enter a value that is not in the menu unless you have included an Other menu choice. To choose an item from a pop-up menu, follow these steps:

1. Click or tab into the field that contains the pop-up menu.

   Initially, the field is blank.

2. Click the blank box to expose the pop-up menu and then drag to select your choice.

— or —

2. If an Other value was included in the original field format, you can record a choice that is not listed in the menu by choosing Other from the pop-up menu. Type your choice in the Other dialog box that appears (see Figure 8-14) and click OK.

   To clear an Other choice from a record, choose Other again and then delete the text that you previously entered in the Other dialog box.

Figure 8-14: The Other dialog box

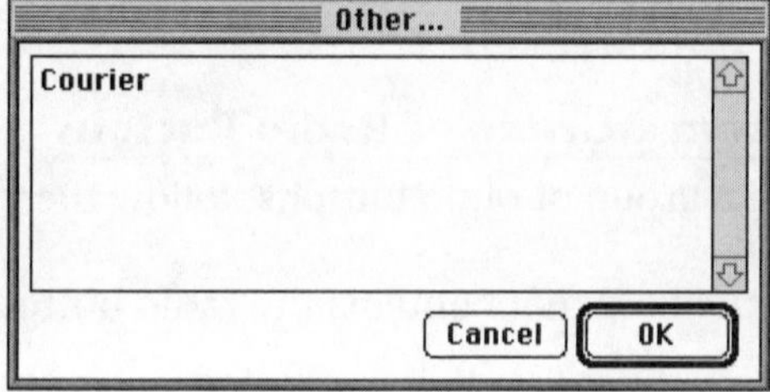

As Figure 8-13 illustrated, a pop-up menu can also have an Edit choice. Include such a choice when you want the user to be able to edit the value list on which the field choices are based. (See Chapter 5 for instructions.)

Choosing an Item from a Group of Check Boxes

Check boxes can be used to enable users to choose multiple options from a value list. To choose an item from a group of check boxes, follow these steps:

1. Click or tab into the field that contains the check boxes.
2. To select a particular check box, do one of the following:
   - Click the check box once.
   - Select the check box by using the arrow keys and then press Return or the spacebar.

- Select the check box by typing the first letter or two of the check box label and then press Return or the spacebar.

When selected, a check box is marked with an *X.*

— or —

2. If an Other value was included in the original field format, you can record a choice that is not listed as an option by clicking or otherwise selecting the Other check box. Type your choice in the Other dialog box (previously shown in Figure 8-14) and click OK.

   To clear an Other choice from a record, click the Other check box again and then delete the text that you previously entered in the Other dialog box.

   Although an alternate choice is recorded, you cannot see it on the layout. You just see that Other has been selected. To determine the exact wording of the choice, click the Other check box again. The Other dialog box appears, showing what you originally typed as your choice.

Multiple choices are frequently found in market research surveys. It's common to see a set of check boxes preceded by the statement: "Check all that apply." No special procedure is necessary to check several check boxes; simply click all the ones that you want. Note, however, that sorts, calculations, and summaries that are based on a field with multiple choices can produce unusual results.

Choosing an Item from a Group of Radio Buttons

To choose an item from a group of radio buttons, follow these steps:

1. Click or tab into the field that contains the radio buttons.
2. To select a particular button, click the button once or select the radio button by using the arrow keys, and then press Return or the spacebar. Or, you can select the radio button by typing the first letter or two of the button's label, and then press Return or the spacebar.

   When selected, the radio button blackens.

— or —

2. If an Other value was included in the original field format, you can record a choice that is not listed as an option by clicking or otherwise selecting the Other radio button. Type your choice in the Other dialog box (previously shown in Figure 8-14) and click OK.

   To clear an Other choice from a record, click the Other radio button again and then delete the text that you previously entered in the Other dialog box.

   Although an alternate choice is recorded, you cannot see it on the layout. You just see that Other has been selected. To determine the exact wording of the choice, click the Other radio button again. The Other dialog box appears, showing what you originally typed as your choice.

Although radio buttons are normally used in most Macintosh programs to present mutually-exclusive choices, you can select multiple radio buttons if you want. Just press Shift as you make your selections. Note, however, that sorts, calculations, and summaries that are based on a field with multiple choices can produce unusual results.

Changing a Value in a Value List

To change a value that you have previously selected from a value list, use the following procedures:

- *Pop-up lists and pop-up menus:* Select a different item from the pop-up list or menu.
- *Radio buttons:* Click a different radio button. The previously selected button or buttons become deselected.
- *Check boxes:* Each check box works as a toggle. Click to reverse the state of any given check box.

To change a value that you have manually typed in a pop-up list field or an Other choice that you've selected in a pop-up menu, radio button, or check box field, use normal editing techniques.

Copying and Reusing Data

If you have already typed a particular piece of data somewhere else — either within or outside the current database — you can use it again without having to retype it. The simplest method is to select the data that you want to use from another record, another field, or another program (such as a word processor or graphics program), copy it to the Clipboard, and then paste it into the database field where you want it. (If you'd rather *move* data from one field or record to another, use the Cut command rather than the Copy command.)

You can also copy the contents of a field that is formatted as a value list (a pop-up list, a pop-up menu, radio buttons, or check boxes). Simply select the field and choose Copy from the Edit menu. Then, in the field where you want the value to appear, choose Paste (⌘-V). The appropriate information will appear in the field.

Copying Data from a Field Index

You can reuse data that you have previously typed in the database by selecting it from the index that FileMaker Pro maintains for the field. (This assumes, of course, that you have turned on the indexing storage option as part of the field's definition, as explained in Chapter 5.) Each index consists of all of the words and numbers that you have entered in that field. You can use the index to make sure that a particular value is always entered in the same form in every record in which it appears. In a customer database, for example, you can use this technique to ensure that you don't have half a dozen different entries for the same company name (such as Apple, Apple Inc., Apple Computer, and Apple Computer Inc.).

To enter data from a field index, follow these steps:

1. Select the field into which you want to enter data, making it the current field.

   If the field is currently empty, skip to step 3.

2. If the field currently contains data, you can either replace all or part of that data or append the new information to the existing data as follows:

   - To replace the existing data, select the data.
   - To append the new information to the existing data, click in the field to position the insertion point where you want the new data to be pasted.

3. Choose the Paste Special submenu from the Edit menu and drag across to the From Index command (or press ⌘-I).

   The View Index dialog box appears, as shown in Figure 8-15.

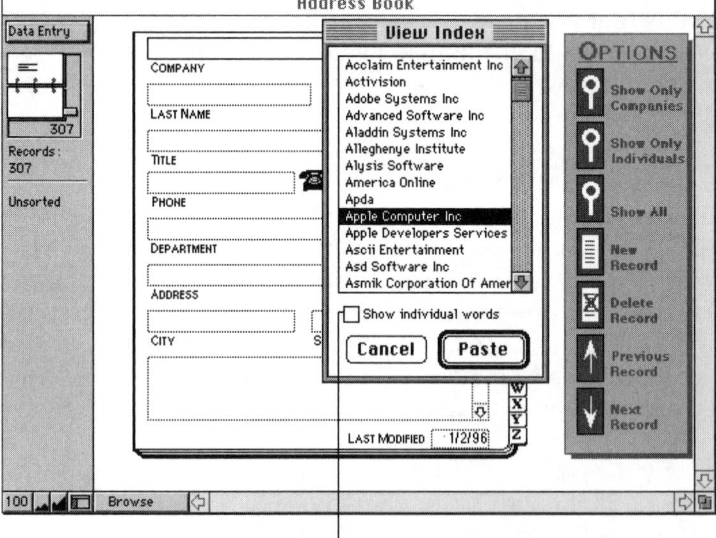

Figure 8-15: The View Index dialog box

4. Select the item that you want to insert by typing the first few characters of the item's name, using the arrows and other navigation keys (Home, End, Page Up, Page Down), or using the mouse to select the item directly.

5. Click Paste to insert the item in the current field.

The View Index dialog box now has a check box at the bottom that determines whether individual indexed words are listed or multi-word text strings are displayed as they were originally typed. As Figure 8-15 illustrated, removing the check mark is preferable when working with some fields, such as the

Company field from the Address Book database. Note, too, that punctuation is *not* recorded in the index and every indexed word is capitalized, so you may still have to do some minor editing after pasting from the index.

Duplicating a Field from the Previous Record

If data in the current field will be exactly the same as in the corresponding field in the last record you entered or edited, you don't have to retype it. You can copy it directly into the new field by using the Paste Special From Last Record command. (Think of this as a "ditto" command.)

To duplicate a field from a previous record, follow these steps:

1. Make sure that the last record that you entered or changed has the data you want to copy.
2. Select the field in the new record into which you want to copy the data.
3. Choose the Paste Special submenu of the Edit menu and drag across to From Last Record (or press ⌘-' [apostrophe]).

   The data from the corresponding field in the last record that you modified is immediately entered in the current record.

Creating a Duplicate Record

Sometimes working with a duplicate record is preferable to creating a whole new record and copying fields, especially if you want to enter a new record that is very similar to an existing one. In the Address Book database, for example, you may have a new contact at a company that is already in the database. Your previous contact still works there, so you don't want to modify that person's record. Instead, you can duplicate the record and then edit the duplicate.

To create a duplicate record, follow these steps:

1. Select the record that you want to duplicate.
2. Choose Duplicate Record from the Edit menu (or press ⌘-D).

   A duplicate record is added to the database and becomes the current record. You can now edit the duplicate.

Entering the Current Date, Time, or User Name

You can insert the current date, current time, or the current user's name into a field by choosing the appropriate menu command. Follow these steps:

1. Select the field into which you want to insert data, making it the current field.

2. Choose the Paste Special submenu from the Edit menu and then drag across to the appropriate option as follows:
   - Choose Current Date (or press ⌘ -- [hyphen]) to insert the current system date.
   - Choose Current Time (or press ⌘-; [semicolon]) to insert the current system time.
   - Choose Current User Name (or press Shift-⌘-N) to insert the name of your Macintosh (set with the Chooser in System 6 or the Sharing Setup control panel in System 7). If you have set a custom user name in FileMaker Pro's Preferences dialog box, the custom name is used instead. (See Chapter 7 for information on setting preferences.)

Editing Records

No one would claim that, once entered, a given record's data will be valid forever. Information needs to be updated from time to time. In the case of the Address Book database, for example, people move, change jobs, and get new titles or phone numbers. You can edit the records for these individuals to keep them up to date. You can also eliminate records if you no longer need the data they contain.

In a nutshell, editing an existing record involves locating the record, moving into the first field that you want to edit, changing the data in it, and then repeating this process until you have made all desired changes. The procedures discussed previously in this chapter, as well as the way that the data-entry and cursor-control keys work, apply to the process of editing data, too.

You can also edit data that is entered automatically, such as the date, time, or a default value, unless you have set the option for "Prohibit modification of auto-entered values" as part of the field's definition. See Chapter 5 for details.

The normal editing keys that are supported in most Mac programs are also supported in FileMaker Pro. In addition to the data-entry keys discussed previously, you can use the keys, commands, and procedures listed in Table 8-3 while entering and editing data.

Table 8-3
Editing Techniques

Key, Command, or Procedure	*Function*
Delete	Deletes the character to the left of the insertion point or, if text is selected, deletes the selection; also deletes contents of Container fields
Del (Apple Extended or equivalent keyboards only)	Deletes the character to the right of the insertion point or, if text is selected, deletes the selection; also deletes contents of Container fields
⌘-X or Cut (Edit menu)	Deletes the current selection within a field and places a copy of it on the Clipboard
Clear (Edit menu)	Deletes the current selection within a field without placing a copy of it on the Clipboard
⌘-C or Copy (Edit menu)	Copies the current selection within a field and places a copy of it on the Clipboard
⌘-V or Paste (Edit menu)	Pastes the contents of the Clipboard into a field at the current insertion point
⌘-A or Select All (Edit menu)	Selects the entire contents of the current field
Double-click	Selects the current word within a field
Triple-click	Selects the current line within a field
Quadruple-click	Selects all text within the current field

The following steps describe the general procedure for modifying a record:

1. With the database open, find the record that you want to modify and make it the current record.
2. Tab into or click to select the first field that you want to modify.
3. Edit the data using normal editing procedures.
4. Tab into or click the next field that you want to modify, and edit the data. Continue editing in this manner until you have made all changes that you want to make.

   As you edit and move from field to field, FileMaker Pro evaluates the changes. If it discovers an error, it notifies you.
5. When you have finished editing the current record, press Enter or switch to another record.

If you make an inadvertent change to a field, you can often correct it by choosing the Undo command from the Edit menu (or by pressing ⌘-Z). The wording of the Undo command changes to reflect the most recent "undoable" action, such as "Undo Typing." Undo, however, is available only for the most recent action you performed. For example, if you type some text and then press the Delete key to remove a character, you can only undo the single character deletion — not the typing.

FileMaker Pro 3.0 adds a powerful new form of Undo. To undo *all* changes made to the record since it was last worked on, choose Revert Record from the Mode menu.

Changing the format of a field is also editing (applying italic or boldface to a word for emphasis, for instance). If you can't remember the keyboard shortcuts or don't feel like dragging the mouse pointer all the way to the top of the screen to choose the appropriate menu command, you can take advantage of the following new FileMaker Pro feature.

Within any field, select the characters of interest and then press the Control key. A miniature pop-up menu appears from which you can choose character formatting commands and standard editing commands, as shown in Figure 8-16.

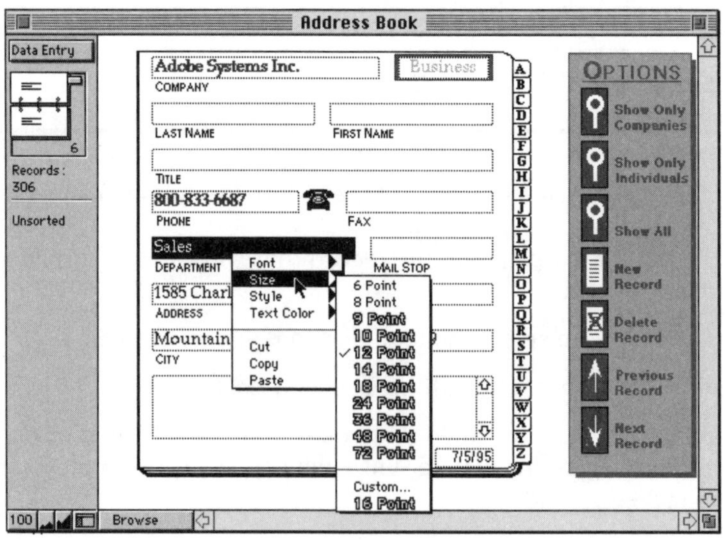

Figure 8-16: A pop-up menu for choosing field formats and editing commands

Replacing Data in Multiple Records

You can replace data in several records at the same time with the Replace command. One handy use of this command is to reorder and renumber serialized records that have gotten out of order after records have been imported from other sources. Because the Replace command is best used on a limited group of records, rather than on a whole database, coverage of this topic is postponed until the next chapter, where finding and selecting groups of records are discussed.

Deleting Records

Here's how to get rid of old and unneeded records:

1. Locate the record that you want to delete and make it the current record.
2. Choose Delete Record from the Mode menu (or press ⌘-E).

   An alert box appears, asking you to confirm that you want to delete the record.
3. Click Delete to remove the record or click Cancel to dismiss the alert box without deleting the record.

Before you delete a record, think carefully about whether you need the information it contains. After you delete the record, it is gone for good. You cannot get it back by using Undo. The best rule is to make certain that the data is useless before you delete the record.

Mass deletions are often performed on *found sets*, which are groups of records that are identified by one find request or a series of find requests. For example, in a client database, you may want to delete records for any person or company that hasn't done any business with your firm in the last several years. After performing the appropriate find operation, you can choose the Delete All command from the Mode menu to eliminate those records. (In earlier versions of the program, this command was named Delete Found Set.) The Delete All command is also discussed in Chapter 9.

If you plan on wholesale deletions (via the Delete All command), making a backup copy of the database before you delete the records is a good idea. Old data is sometimes useful, so erring on the conservative side is often best.

Using the Spelling Checker

Depending on the type of database with which you are working, FileMaker Pro's spelling checker may be helpful. You can instruct the program to check spelling as you type or to check it on command (to examine a particular layout, record, group of records, or a text selection). You access the spelling checker and spelling options by choosing the Spelling submenu of the Edit menu. The spelling checker is covered in detail in Chapter 11.

Summary

- You use Browse mode to view records within an existing database, to enter new records, and to modify or delete existing records.
- Databases can have different layouts to serve different purposes, such as data entry and data retrieval. You select layouts in Browse mode by using the layouts pop-up menu.
- You can display the records within a database one per screen or as a continuous scrolling list. The book icon enables you to move from one record to another, to an approximate position within the database, or to a specific record number. When a database is displayed in list form (View as List), the scroll bar functions in much the same way as the book icon.
- You use data-entry keys and cursor-control keys to enter and edit character data. The former enter alphanumeric characters; the latter determine the location where newly-typed characters are inserted.
- FileMaker Pro supports the use of still-picture, sound, and moving-picture data in several file formats. Only one copy of a given sound or picture is stored in the particular database's library, no matter how many records contain that sound or picture. For each sound or picture, you can specify whether it is stored within the database or whether only a pointer to the element's location on disk is recorded.
- FileMaker Pro 3.0 maintains an index for each database field in which the indexing storage option has been turned on. (In previous versions of the program, *all* fields were automatically indexed.) The index contains every word and number that has been entered in the field. Entries can be made into fields directly from the index to ensure the consistency of the database.

Searching for and Selecting Subsets of Records

CHAPTER 9

In This Chapter

- Searching a database for specific information
- Using Find mode to create find requests
- Using multiple find requests to do AND and OR searches
- Searching for special information, such as the current date, invalid data, and duplicate records
- Working with found sets of records
- Using the Omit and Omit Multiple commands to remove records from the found set

In the last chapter, you learned about using Browse mode to flip through records in a database. By now you should agree that this method works reasonably well when you're browsing within a small database, but that it is tedious and cumbersome when you are dealing with a database that contains many records. What's more, Browse mode is no help at all when you want to identify *groups* of records. In working with the Address Book database, for example, you may want to examine all your business contacts, excluding friends and relatives. At best, Browse mode will show your records displayed in a list.

FileMaker Pro's Find mode provides a more efficient way to locate individual records, as well as to group records that share some specific characteristic. Within Find mode, you can quickly search all records in a database for information that matches the contents of a field (such as a particular last name or a known telephone number). You can also have FileMaker Pro create groups of records that share a characteristic (such as all your business contacts or everyone within a certain ZIP code). Going well beyond simple searches, Find mode provides powerful tools for locating and working with individual records and groups of records.

Find Mode Basics

Find mode does much more than make browsing through records easier. The immediate effect of a find request is to change the set of records that you're currently browsing (that is, the ones that are visible). When you want to see only one particular record, you can search using a field that contains unique data, such as a Social Security number, phone number, inventory code, or customer ID number. You will also discover that performing a find operation is often an important part of preparing reports. For example, in a prospective customer database, you may want to see only your successes or clients for whom you have scheduled a follow-up. To produce such a list, you execute a find request prior to printing the report.

Switching to Find Mode

As with Browse mode, you can switch into Find mode in two ways — regardless of the mode you're currently in:

- You can choose the Find command from the Mode menu (or press ⌘-F).
- You can choose Find from the mode selector pop-up menu at the bottom of the database window.

Using Find Mode Tools and Functions

Figure 9-1 shows the Address Book database (discussed in Chapter 4 and provided on the *Macworld FileMaker Pro 3.0 Bible Disk*) in Find mode. As you can see, Find mode has more tools available than Browse mode, but fewer tools than Layout mode.

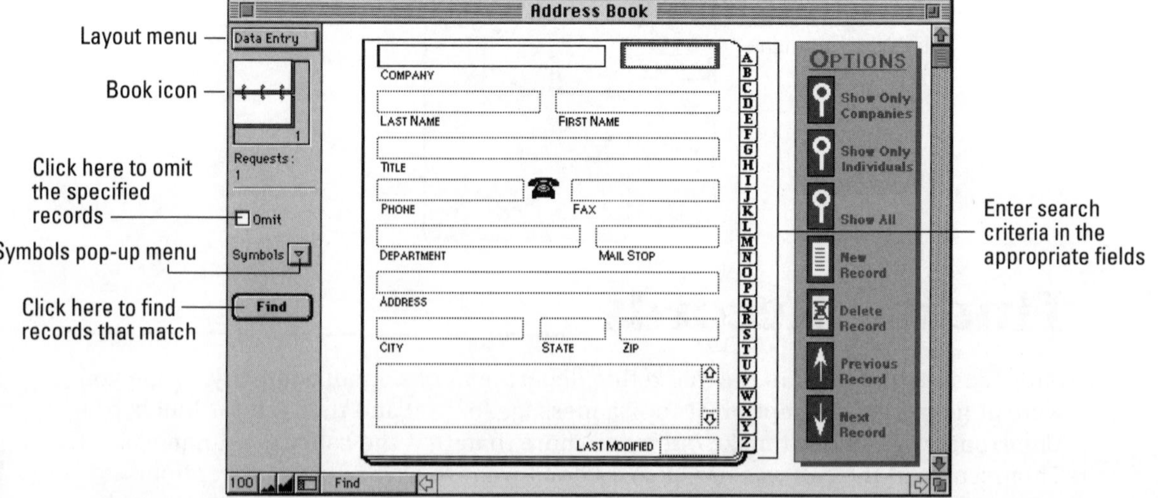

Figure 9-1: The Address Book database in Find mode

The Browse mode tools are also available in Find mode. You can switch to a different layout by using the layouts pop-up menu in the upper-left corner of the window, above the status area. You can change the current magnification at which the database is displayed by using the Zoom in and Zoom out buttons that are below the status area. You can also toggle the status area display itself by using the status area control button to the right of the Zoom in and Zoom out buttons. All of these controls work as they do in Browse mode (described in Chapter 8).

The Symbols pop-up menu (see Figure 9-2) plays an important role in Find mode. It contains special symbols that enable you to easily execute custom searches. Using these symbols, you can search for values that are less than, equal to, or greater than a specified value, for example. For instance, you can search for all records that have an entry in the Last Name field that begins with the letter *H* or later in the alphabet. You can also look for ranges of values and for invalid values. (You'll learn more about using these symbols in "Matching All Criteria," later in this chapter.)

Figure 9-2: The Symbols pop-up menu

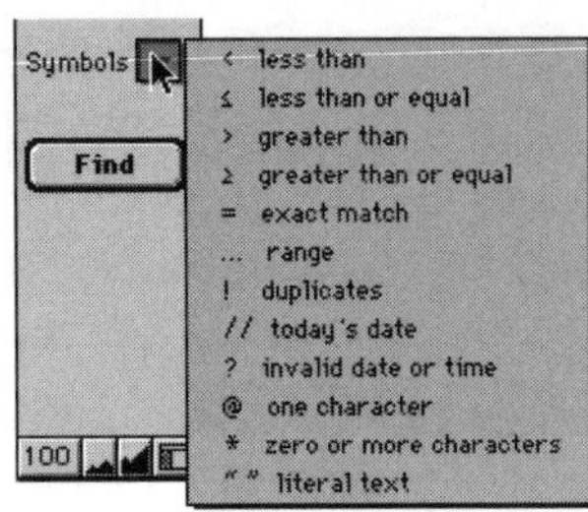

Finding Records

Suppose that you work in the marketing department of a small company. While you were at lunch, your receptionist took a message for you and then left for lunch, too. Unfortunately, you can't make out much more than that the caller's last name is Thompson and the call was urgent. You don't want to wait until the receptionist returns from lunch to find out who called and what the phone number is. What do you do?

Using FileMaker Pro and your Address Book database, you can search through all your contacts for a Thompson. An examination of the found records ought to give you an idea about who this anxious person is. Here's how you do it:

1. First, launch FileMaker Pro and open the Address Book database.

   The Data Entry layout appears, showing names and phone numbers. (If the database opens to a different layout, use the layouts pop-up menu to switch to the correct layout.)

2. Switch to Find mode by using the mode selector pop-up menu, choosing the Find command from the Mode menu, or pressing ⌘-F.

   A blank record called a find request appears on the screen (as previously shown in Figure 9-1). You enter search criteria into the find request.

3. Type **Thompson** in the Last Name field.

4. Click the Find button.

   FileMaker Pro searches for all records having a last name that begins with the letters *Thompson* and locates one record with that last name.

   Because only one record was found that matched your criteria, you call Mr. Thompson back to discover that he needs to place a large rush order with you and would have called a competitor if you hadn't responded so quickly.

This example of using Find mode shows the basic steps involved in locating specific records within a database. With the database open, you switch to Find mode and choose a layout that shows the information for which you want to search. You then enter the search criteria into fields on the layout and click the Find button. Finally, you examine the *found set* (the set of all records that are identified as the result of a find operation).

Searches are performed on the contents of one or more fields in every record in a database. You can look for an exact match in a given field, such as all records that contain Thompson entries in the Last Name field. You can also look for records that contain only partial matches (matching one set of criteria or another), as well as for records that contain specific pieces of information in two or more fields.

As soon as you click the Find button, FileMaker Pro locates any matching records and then switches to Browse mode, displaying only the found set. The number of records in the found set is shown beneath the book icon. The rest of the records in the database are temporarily hidden from view. You then browse (as well as sort or print) the found set as you would browse the entire database. To make all of the records visible again, choose the Find All command from the Select menu (or press ⌘-J).

Matching All Criteria

The simplest kind of find operation consists of searching for records that match all of one or more specific criteria. The preceding scenario — in which you combined a single-field search with manual browsing of the found set — is an example of using a single search criterion. You can also conduct multiple-field searches — all you need to do is enter information in each field on which you want to search.

For example, to locate all Thompsons in the state of Washington, you would use *two* criteria: You would enter **Thompson** in the Last Name field and **WA** in the State field before you clicked Find. To narrow the search even further, you can enter information in as many fields as you like.

Techno-trivia: This type of multi-field search is called an *AND* search. When you type search instructions in multiple fields, you are asking FileMaker Pro to identify only those records that match *all* the criteria (Last Name = Thompson AND State = WA, for example).

When you enter search criteria by simply typing some text or numbers into a field, FileMaker Pro not only locates records that exactly match the specified information, but also finds records that contain the search string at the beginning of any word within the field. Thus, if you enter **Smith,** FileMaker Pro finds not only Smith, but also Smithy, Smithers, and Buddy Joe Smith. You can restrict searches to exact matches if you want to (only a real Smith, for example). Refer to the section on "Matching Text Exactly," later in this chapter.

If FileMaker Pro doesn't locate any records that satisfy all of your search criteria, a dialog box appears that informs you of this fact (see Figure 9-3). You can click Modify Find to return to the find request and enter different criteria, or click Cancel to return to Browse mode.

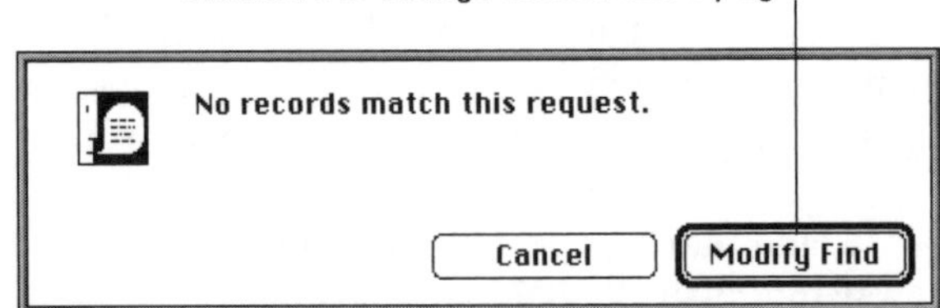
Click here to change criteria and try again
No records match this request.
Cancel
Modify Find

Figure 9-3: No matches were found.

Using Symbols in Search Criteria

To help narrow a search, you can include special symbols in any or all of the search criteria. Symbols can either be selected from the Symbols pop-up menu (in the status area), or they can be typed directly into the appropriate fields on a find request. As Table 9-1 illustrates, some symbols must precede the search string, others must surround it, and still others must be embedded within it. The proper use of each kind of search symbol is discussed later in this chapter.

Table 9-1
Find Symbols

Symbol	*Meaning*	*Example*
<	Less than	<50000 (finds persons who make less than $50,000 per year, for example)
≤	Less than or equal to	≤5 (finds cities with annual rainfall that is less than or equal to 5 inches, for example)
>	Greater than	>6/4/94 (finds any date after June 4, 1994)
≥	Greater than or equal to	≥10:43 (finds any time that is equal to or later than 10:43 AM)
=	An exact match	=Kennedy (finds only records that exactly match this data)
. . .	Data within a range	80210. . .80218 (finds ZIP codes that fall within that range)
!	Duplicate values	! (entered in an ID field, selects all records with duplicate ID numbers)

Symbol	Meaning	Example
//	Current date	// (selects all records with today's date in the chosen field)
?	Invalid dates or times	? (entered in a Date or Time field, finds all records with invalid dates or times)
@	Wildcard for a single character	B@nd (finds Band, Bend, Bind, and Bond)
*	Zero or more characters	B*S (finds BS, bus, bats, and BUSINESS, for example)
" "	Literal text anywhere	"Homer" (finds Homer Simpson, Homer's Iliad, and Hi there, Homer! within the field)

Matching One Criterion or Another

At times, you may want to search for all records that match any of two or more criteria. This kind of search is known as an *OR* search — as in "Find all records that match this set of criteria OR that set." For example, you may want to find all Smiths who live in either California or New York. Such a search is quite different from trying to match all of several criteria (that is, an AND search). For an OR search, you must fill out a separate find request for each criterion by choosing New Request from the Mode menu before clicking the Find button. FileMaker Pro combines all the results of two or more find requests into a single found set. This set combines all records that match any of the search criteria.

Use the following steps to perform a search for data that satisfies the criteria of at least one of several find requests (an OR search):

1. In the database that you want to search, switch to a layout that shows all the fields that you want to use for the search.
2. Switch to Find mode by using the mode selector pop-up menu, choosing Find from the Mode menu, or pressing ⌘-F.

   A blank find request appears.
3. Enter the first criterion into the appropriate field.
4. If you want to use additional criteria for this find request (Last Name = Jones and Salary < 25000, for example), tab to the appropriate fields and enter the criteria.
5. Choose New Request from the Mode menu (or press ⌘-N).

   The database window is cleared and a new blank find request form appears.

6. Enter the criteria for this find request into the appropriate field or fields.
7. Repeat steps 5 and 6 until you have created all necessary find requests.
8. Click the Find button or press Return.

   All find requests are evaluated, and the found set is presented.

Whenever you click Find, all previous searches are cleared. If you want to repeat the most recent search, choose the Modify Last Find command from the Select menu. You will learn more about performing multiple find requests later in this chapter.

Individual Finds Aren't the Same as Multiple Find Requests

Each time you switch to Find mode and issue one or more find requests, two important things happen. First, regardless of which records are currently visible, FileMaker Pro considers *all* records in the search. Second, if you have created multiple find requests (to conduct an OR search), all requests are carried out at the same time.

Every find request starts from square one; the effects are not cumulative. For example, if you conduct *two separate find* operations — the first searching for Smiths from California and the second searching for Smiths from New York — when you execute the second search, only the Smiths from New York appear in the found set. On the other hand, if you conduct *a single find operation that contains two find requests* — one for California Smiths and another for New York Smiths — the found set shows you *all* Smiths who are from California *or* New York.

Matching Different Kinds of Text

By using one of the special symbols that the Find command supports (previously listed in Table 9-1), you can make FileMaker Pro do more than locate matches for single words. You can look for a specific text string, accepting no substitutes (Smith, but not Smithers, for example). You can also look for text that *contains* certain words or phrases. As an example, you can search an Address field for all instances of the word *Drive* — regardless of where the word falls within the field. You can also use this technique to look for pieces of text that aren't contained in the database's index, such as consecutive groups of letters (*mith,* for example). However, such non-index searches can take much longer to perform, especially in large databases. (You may recall from Chapter 5 that in FileMaker Pro 3.0, only fields for which indexing has been turned on are now indexed.)

Matching Text Exactly

In a find request, using the equal sign (=) in a field tells FileMaker Pro to look only for an exact match to the text that you have entered. For example, to find all customers whose last name is Schwartz, you enter **=Schwartz** in the Last Name field. To locate an exact match to a phrase, you enter the phrase but precede each word by an equal sign (for example, **=Sinbad =Schwartz**).

Finding Text Alphabetically Above or Below a Value

You can also look for records that contain values that are less than, less than or equal to, greater than, or greater than or equal to a given value by using the appropriate mathematical symbols. For example, entering **≥Schwartz** in a Last Name field makes FileMaker Pro search for all last names that are either Schwartz or come alphabetically after Schwartz. To identify only those records for persons with a last name greater than but not including Schwartz (that is, those that come after Schwartz), you use the greater than symbol instead — as in **>Schwartz.**

Using Wildcard Characters for Partial Matches

You can search for records that contain a specific group of letters. To do so, you use wildcard characters to represent the missing letters. FileMaker Pro supports @ and * as wildcards. The former symbol (@) stands for a single character, and the latter symbol (*) represents a group of characters that is any length — including zero characters.

If, for example, you want to find all seven-letter names that begin with *John*, you use three @ signs in the last three positions of the search criterion (**John@@@**). Searching for this string of letters finds Johnson and Johnley but not Johnston (because it contains eight letters rather than seven). To find all values that start with a particular group of letters (such as *John*), you merely need to enter the exact group without any wildcards following it. Searching using **John** will find John, Johnson, Johnley, and Johnston.

You can also use wildcard characters in the middle of a word. For example, to find all last names that begin with *Smith* and end with the letter *n*, you enter **Smith*n** in the Last Name field. FileMaker Pro finds Smithson, Smithsonian, and so on. To find words that differ only by a single character, use the @ sign. For example, searching for **Sm@th** finds both Smith and Smyth.

Searching for Nonindexed (Literal) Text

The preceding text search methods find only indexed text items. You will recall that the *index* is a special part of a FileMaker Pro database in which the program keeps a record of each word or value in a given field. If you want to look for information that isn't part of the field's index (including phrases whose component words aren't separated by Option-Space characters), you have to enclose the search text in double-quotes. (When entering data, you can press Option-Space between words to force FileMaker Pro to index a phrase rather than the individual words that make up the phrase.) You can type the quotation marks directly if you want, but FileMaker Pro provides a simpler method. You need only choose literal text from the Symbols pop-up menu in the Find mode status area. Doing so immediately enters both a pair of quotation marks and the insertion point between them.

More About Find Requests

Whenever you switch to Find mode and enter information on the blank form that appears, you're creating a find request. FileMaker Pro enables you to manipulate find requests in several ways. You can delete requests or repeat requests, perhaps editing them slightly to alter the search criteria. For example, if you looked for all Smiths from California one time, you could repeat the request and change **CA** to **NY** to find all Smiths from New York.

Creating Find Requests

Creating a new find request is easy. FileMaker Pro creates a find request automatically when you first switch to Find mode so that you can use the request to enter search criteria. You may want to create additional requests, however, as in searching for information that matches one of several criteria (an OR search).

You have two options when you are creating additional find requests. You can create an entirely new find request from scratch (by choosing New Request from the Mode menu or pressing ⌘-N), or you can duplicate the current find request and edit its contents (by choosing Duplicate Request from the Mode menu or pressing ⌘-D). Until you click the Find button to execute the find requests, you can use the book icon to page through all current find requests — just as you use it in Browse mode to leaf through records and in Layout mode to view multiple layouts that you have designed.

Repeating and Editing Find Requests

When you finish entering all the criteria for a find request and then click the Find button, FileMaker Pro attempts to locate all matching records and then displays them to you in Browse mode as the found set. (If FileMaker Pro does not find any records, you can either modify and repeat the search, or you can cancel the search and return to Browse mode.)

If you switch to Find mode again, FileMaker Pro presents you with a new blank find request form. However, if you are immediately switching back to Find mode, your intent may be to use your previous find requests as the basis for a new search. For example, if a search for Smiths in California doesn't yield results, you may want to go back and look for Smiths in Oregon. By using the Modify Last Find command, you can repeat the last search, preserving all find requests that you defined within it. You can edit any or all of these find requests to match any new search requirements that you have.

To repeat or modify the previous set of find requests, follow these steps:

1. Choose the Modify Last Find command from the Select menu (or press ⌘-R).

In previous versions of FileMaker Pro, this command was called Refind.

FileMaker Pro displays the previous set of find requests.

2. To simply repeat the last find request (or set of find requests), go directly to step 6.

— or —

2. If there are multiple find requests, use the book icon to move to the request that you want to edit.
3. Use normal editing procedures to change the search criteria.
4. Repeat steps 2 and 3 until all find requests match your new requirements.
5. *Optional*: You can also add more requests to the set, duplicate any of the requests, or delete requests (as long as at least one still remains) by choosing the appropriate command from the Mode menu (New Request, Duplicate Request, or Delete Request, respectively).
6. Click the Find button or press Return.

   The find request or requests are executed.

Deleting Find Requests

If one or more requests within the current set of find requests don't meet your needs, you can get rid of them entirely.

To delete find requests, use one of the following methods:

- To start a find request from scratch (effectively deleting all current find requests), choose Find mode again (or press ⌘-F).
- To delete a specific find request, use the book icon to move to the request that you want to delete and choose Delete Request from the Mode menu (or press ⌘-D). Repeat this procedure for each request that you want to delete.

If you think you'll be using a particular find request over and over again, you can create a script that "remembers" your find request and performs the find automatically. This is good for finds with multiple requests or other significant entries. See Chapter 15 for more details on writing scripts.

Matching Special Items

As mentioned earlier in the chapter, you can enter special symbols as part of your search criteria by selecting them from the Symbols pop-up menu (as previously shown in Figure 9-2 and described in Table 9-1). By using these symbols, you can find all records that have values between two extremes, such as two dates, times, or salaries. You can also use symbols to perform database maintenance by searching for erroneous or duplicate values and then eliminating the records that contain them.

Matching Values in a Range

You use the ellipsis symbol (...) to indicate values within a range. You can look for alphabetic values between two text strings, numeric values between two calculated or numeric items, or chronological values between two times or dates. For example, you can search for all records that have last names between Smith and Zane or for all records created between January 1 and December 31, 1996. In the former case, you enter **Smith...Zane** in the Last Name field; in the latter case, you type **1/1/96...12/31/96** in the Date field.

To enter a range in a search field, separate the two values by typing three periods, by pressing Option-; (semi-colon), or by choosing the ... symbol from the Symbols pop-up menu.

Matching the Current Date

Assuming that the system clock in your Macintosh is set correctly, you can easily search for records that match the current date, even if you don't happen to know it yourself. This feature is especially handy in scripts because you don't need to enter specific information. Instead of having to recreate the script each time (changing the date from 4/5/96 to 4/18/96, for example), you can just instruct the script to find *today's* date — whatever the date happens to be. (See Chapter 15 for more information on scripts and their uses.)

To check your Mac's system clock, choose the Alarm Clock desk accessory from the Apple menu or examine the Date & Time control panel.

To find all values that contain the current date, follow these steps:

1. Within Find mode, move the cursor to the Date field in which you want to search.
2. Choose the "today's date" option from the Symbols pop-up menu or type a pair of slashes (//) directly into the field.
3. Click Find or press Return to execute the search.

Searching for Empty Fields

Occasionally, errors creep into a database. For example, you may create extra records and forget to fill them in, or you may get interrupted and neglect to complete the current record. FileMaker Pro provides a way for you to look for all records that have no information in one or more fields. You simply enter an equal sign (=) — and nothing else — in that field. You can then correct or delete the errant records, as you like.

If you want to find all records that contain one or more blank fields, you need to create a separate find request for each potentially blank field and then click Find. If you enter all potentially blank fields in a single find request, FileMaker Pro will find only records in which *all* of these fields are blank. (Remember, when you specify multiple criteria in one find request, you are conducting an AND search. All criteria must be satisfied in order for the record to be found.) Thus, records that have some fields blank and other fields filled in will not be identified.

The correct procedure is to create multiple find requests — one for each field that you want to check for blanks. Although this procedure may sound as if it requires a great deal of work, it usually doesn't. In most cases, you want to search for blanks in a small set of *critical* fields — those that, if left blank, would render the record useless.

Searching for Values Exceeding or Less than a Given Value

In the discussion of text searches, you saw that you can use the <, ≤, >, and ≥ symbols to find text that is alphabetically greater or less than a particular value. You can also use these symbols to find numeric, date, or time values. For example, to find all records dated on or after January 1, 1996, you enter **≥1/1/96.**

To find values that exceed or are less than a given value, follow these steps.

1. Switch to Find mode.
2. Move to the field that you want to use in the search.
3. Choose the appropriate symbol from the Symbols pop-up menu (or type it directly into the field):

   > (greater than) to find all items that exceed the value entered

   ≥ (greater than or equal to) to find all items that exceed or are exactly equal to the value entered

   < (less than) to find all items that are smaller than the value entered

≤ (less than or equal to) to find all items that are smaller than or exactly equal to the value entered

To type the ≤ or ≥ symbols, press Option-, (comma) or Option-. (period), respectively.

4. Following the symbol that you entered in step 3, type the search value.
5. Click Find or press Return to execute the search.

Searching for Duplicate Records

Find mode can also be used to help you perform another form of database maintenance. You can use it to identify records that have the same information in several fields. Although some people do have the same last names, for example, some of these records may be duplicates. If you have checked your mail recently, you have probably noticed that some direct mail firms are sending you more than one copy of their catalog or marketing literature. They have a problem with duplicate database records — the ones that contain *your* name. FileMaker Pro has a special symbol that enables you to find all records that have duplicate information in one field. You can then browse these records and eliminate any exact duplicates.

To search for records that have identical contents in a given field, follow these steps:

1. Switch to Find mode in the appropriate database.
2. Move to the field that you suspect is shared by two or more records.
3. Choose "duplicates" from the Symbols pop-up menu or type a single exclamation point (!).
4. Click Find or press Return to execute the Find.

As when looking for empty fields (discussed previously), if you want to find all records that have duplicate values in one or more of several different fields, you need to create a separate find request for each of these fields. Otherwise, you will find only records that match in all potential fields. (Check those catalog mailing labels again. In most cases, you will find that the labels aren't *exactly* the same. Your name or address may be slightly different on them, for example.) As a rule, you should include only one "duplicates" criterion in each find request.

Searching for Invalid Information

Sometimes, you may find that time or date calculations do not yield valid results, particularly when you work with data that you have imported into a database from another program. FileMaker Pro provides a way to search for records that have invalid dates or times. In the appropriate field on the find request form, enter a question mark (?) or choose "invalid date or time" from the Symbols pop-up menu.

Finding Records that Don't Match the Criteria

When you are trying to narrow down a search for very specific kinds of records, you may find that a little "negative logic" is easier to apply than the conventional kind. For example, suppose you want to find all your contacts in every state *except* California. You can create a separate find request for each of the other 49 states, but doing so is a lot of work. As an alternative, you can enter **California** in the State field and then elect to omit from the found set all records that contain California. FileMaker Pro makes this task easy. Find mode has an Omit check box in the status area (as previously shown in Figure 9-1). You click this check box to turn a conventional find request into one that hides the found records and shows only the records that are left.

In a *series* of find requests, if you use the Omit option in some but not in others, you should put all find requests that include the Omit option at the end of your list. FileMaker Pro works through all find requests in the order that you specify. If you put Omit requests first, later find requests will tend to wipe out their results. For example, if you want to find all records of employees who are older than 25, or have a salary greater than $27,000, or are not from Houston, you create the following three find requests, making sure that you create the request that uses the Omit option last:

```
>25 (in Age field)
>27000 (in Salary field)
=Houston (in City field) and Omit check box checked
```

Remember that whenever you issue multiple find requests, you are conducting an OR search — looking for records that satisfy any one or more of the find requests.

You can also omit records *after* conducting a find request, as described in "Omitting Records from a Found Set," in the next section.

Working with Found Records

You can do many things besides just browsing through a found set. Some of the operations that you can perform are directly related to the reason that you searched for the records in the first place. For example, if you searched for duplicate records, you likely did so because you wanted to delete the duplicates. Another thing that you can do with found records is to copy them to the Clipboard and then paste them into another database or even into another program.

Omitting Records from a Found Set

When working with a found set, you may sometimes want to temporarily hide some of the found records. For example, if you have just done a search to identify duplicate records, the found set contains both the original records that you want to keep and the duplicates. Before you can delete the duplicate records, you need to omit the originals from the found set by using the Omit or Omit Multiple commands. (*Omitting* records merely hides them from view, removing them from the found set. The records still remain in the database, however, and can be revealed with the Find All command.) After omitting the originals from the found set, you can delete the duplicates using the Delete All command (discussed in "Deleting Found Sets from a Database," later in this chapter).

To omit a specific record from a found set, follow these steps:

1. Use the book icon to select the record that you want to omit.

   If the layout is displayed in list view (View as List), you can click in any record to select it.

2. Choose the Omit command from the Select menu (or press ⌘-M).

   The current record is removed from the found set; that is, it is hidden.

3. Repeat steps 1 and 2 for each additional record that you want to omit from the found set.

If a found set contains several consecutive records that you want to omit from the found set, you can omit all of them with one command — Omit Multiple. Here's how:

1. *Optional*: If the records to be omitted are not grouped consecutively, you may be able to use a Sort command (⌘-S) to group them in the desired manner. See Chapter 10 for information on sorting.

2. Use the book icon to select the first record that you want to omit from the found set.

   If the layout is displayed in list view (View as List), you can click in any record to select it.

3. Choose the Omit Multiple command from the Select menu or press Shift-⌘-M.

   The Omit Multiple Dialog box appears, as shown in Figure 9-4.

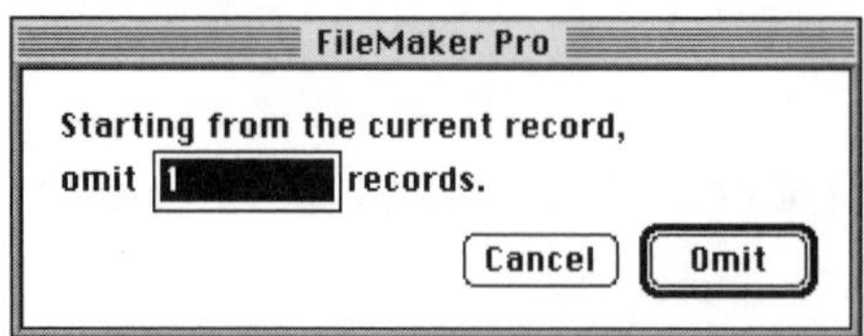

Figure 9-4: The Omit Multiple dialog box

4. Enter the number of consecutive records to omit.

5. Click the Omit button.

   The records are omitted; that is, they are hidden from view.

If you want to restore all records omitted from a found set, simply use the Modify Last Find command to repeat the last find request. You cannot restore omitted records directly (there is no Reveal or "Un-omit" command), but you can use other methods to get them back, as you will learn in the next section.

Omit Can Be Used With or Without a Found Set

Although the Omit command is most frequently used with a found set (following a find request), you can use it at any time to temporarily hide records. In effect, such use of the Omit command manually creates the equivalent of a found set. Suppose, for example, that you are using a database to prepare a list of stamps that you want to purchase from a mail-order dealer. After preparing the want list, you can use the Omit command to selectively eliminate several stamps — either because buying them will put you in the poorhouse or because you think that they are currently overpriced.

Swapping Found Sets with Omitted Records

In the want list example presented in the sidebar "Omit Can Be Used With or Without a Found Set," you learn that you can use the Omit command to hand pick records that you want to remove from a found set. On the other hand, these omitted records may be the ones that really interest you at the moment. Suppose, for example, that you want to prepare a list of all stamps that you have no interest in buying. Perhaps you want to take the list to stamp shows and to meetings with dealers to prevent yourself from buying something that you don't want or need. By using a special FileMaker Pro command called Find Omitted, you can make the omitted records the new found set. Find Omitted swaps the remaining records in the found set with all omitted ones. The omitted records then become the new found set.

Follow these steps to swap a remaining found set with records omitted from it:

1. Use the Omit or Omit Multiple commands to mark records in a found set that you actually want to keep.
2. Choose the Find Omitted command from the Select menu.

   Omitted records become the new found set, and the remaining records are omitted in their place.

Find Omitted can also be used after issuing a normal find request. For instance, after examining the records of all club members whose dues payments are delinquent, you can use Find Omitted to quickly display the records of the members whose payments are up-to-date.

Copying Found Sets

You can copy an entire found set of records to the Clipboard. From there, you can paste the data elsewhere — into documents from other applications, for example. Each field is separated from the next by a Tab character. Consecutive records are separated by Return characters. (This is commonly known as a *tab-delimited* text file.) To copy a found set to the Clipboard, press Option-⌘-C.

This procedure is a quick-and-dirty version of the Export command with "tab-delimited" as the selected format. The main difference is that you have less control over the particular fields that are copied and the order in which they are copied. Whatever layout is in effect when you issue the command determines the selected fields and their order.

Deleting Found Sets

As mentioned previously, one major use for Find mode is to locate records that you want to delete from a database. After you have omitted records that you want to save from a found set, removing the remainder of the records from the database is simple.

Follow these steps to delete records in a found set:

1. Enter Find mode (⌘-F) and create the find requests that are necessary to identify the records that you want to delete.
2. *Optional*: Examine the found set and use the Omit command to leave out records that you do not want to delete from the database.

The Delete All command that you use in this procedure affects only the visible (browsed) records, not all of the records in the database.

3. Choose Delete All from the Mode menu.

   An alert box appears, asking you to confirm that you want to delete the records in question.
4. Click Delete to proceed or click Cancel (or press Return) to dismiss the alert box without deleting the records.

As with other Delete commands in FileMaker Pro, you cannot use the Undo command to undo the Delete All command. Because you risk significant data loss if you make a mistake when using this command, you may want to make a backup copy of the database by using the Save a Copy As command (described in Chapter 2) before you use the Delete All command.

Replacing Values in a Found Set

Another thing you can do with a found set is replace the contents of a single field in all found records at once (in much the same way as you use a word processor's Find and Replace commands). After using find requests to locate the particular records in which you want to make the replacement, you can use the Replace command to replace the contents of any single field with data that you specify.

This global replacement procedure is often useful. For example, either of the following situations would be prime candidates for the Replace command:

- A company that is included in one of your databases has recently changed its name or moved to a new address. Search for the original name of the company and then use Replace to enter the new name or the new address in all found records. If the company has changed *both* its name and address, use two Replace procedures on the same found set: first the company name and then the address. (You can use this same procedure to ensure consistent wording for text in selected fields. By identifying all records that contain Apple in the Company field, for instance, you can use Replace to change all entries to read "Apple Computer, Inc.")

- A major kennel association reclassifies a particular breed of pooch as a "working dog." Search for all instances of that breed and then use Replace to change the classification for each of the found dogs.

Use the following procedure to replace the contents of one field in all records in the found set:

1. Switch to Find mode (⌘-F), and use one or more find requests to select the group of records whose contents you want to replace.

   This creates the found set.

2. In Browse mode, select the field you want to replace by tabbing into or clicking in the field.

   It does not matter what record is currently displayed; any record in the found set will suffice.

3. Type the replacement text or value in the field.

4. Choose Replace from the Mode menu (or press ⌘-=).

   The Replace dialog box shown in Figure 9-5 appears.

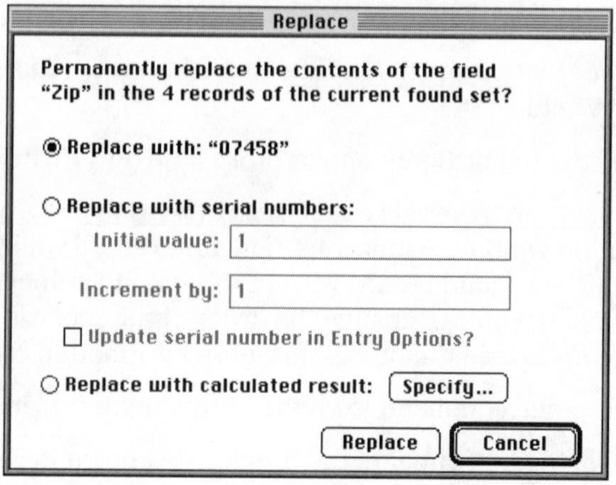

Figure 9-5: Use this dialog box to replace the contents of a field with a single text string or value.

Replace

Permanently replace the contents of the field "Zip" in the 4 records of the current found set?

◉ Replace with: "07458"

○ Replace with serial numbers:

Initial value: 1

Increment by: 1

☐ Update serial number in Entry Options?

○ Replace with calculated result: Specify...

Replace Cancel

5. Select the "Replace with:" option.

   The replacement text or value is shown within quotes. (For example, the replacement string is "07458" in Figure 9-5.)

6. Click Replace.

   The contents of the current field are replaced with the specified text string or value in all records in the found set.

Replacing the Contents of a Field with a Serial Number

As you can tell from looking at the dialog box previously shown in Figure 9-5, you can also use the Replace command to replace the contents of a field in the found set with serial numbers. This option is useful when, for example, you've imported records into a database and have left gaps or otherwise thrown off the existing numbering scheme.

You can also use the Replace command to *create* a record-numbering system where none existed before. Simply define a new field to hold the serial numbers, add it to a layout, issue a Find All command (⌘-J), sort the records (if necessary), select the field, and then issue the Replace command.

To replace the contents of a field in a found set with serial numbers, do the following:

1. Switch to Find mode (⌘-F), and use one or more find requests to select the group of records that you want to renumber.

   This creates the found set.

2. In Browse mode, select the field that you wish to reserialize by tabbing into or clicking the field.

3. *Optional*: Sort the database by one or more appropriate fields.

   When the records are reserialized, numbers are assigned according to each record's position within the found set. The first record will get the first new serial number, the second record will get the second number, and so on. Using the Sort command, you can change the order of the records to a more meaningful arrangement. (See Chapter 10 for more information on sorting records.)

4. Choose the Replace command from the Mode menu (or press ⌘-=).

   The Replace dialog box appears (as previously shown in Figure 9-5).

5. Click the "Replace with serial numbers" radio button.

6. In the "Initial value" text box, enter the value for the new first serial number for the found set. In the "Increment by" text box, enter the value by which each successive serial number should increase over the previous number.
7. Click Replace.

A serial number can contain more than just numbers. If your serial number is a mix of numbers and text, only the numeric portion of the field will change when the field is reserialized. Also, if the selected field was initially defined as an auto-entry field that would receive a serial number, you may wish to click the "Update serial number in Entry Options?" check box. After you reserialize the found set, checking this option instructs FileMaker Pro to note the last serial number used and to make sure that the next new record created continues the serialization sequence. (It updates the Next Value figure in the Entry Options dialog box for the serial number field.)

Replacing the Contents of a Field with a Calculated Result

FileMaker Pro 3.0 adds a powerful new Replace option that enables you to replace the contents of a field with a calculated result. Suppose, for example, that you want to increase the salary of a group of employees by five percent. After using a find request to select the set of employees, you would choose the Replace command, click the radio button for "Replace with calculated result", and — in the Specify Calculation dialog box that appears — enter either of these formulas:

```
Salary + (Salary * .05)
Salary * 1.05
```

The result type for the Replace formula must be the same as the replaced field's type (as set in the Define Fields dialog box when the field was created). If the field is a Text field, for instance, only a formula that returns a text string as a result is allowed.

To learn about defining fields, refer to Chapter 5.

When defining a replacement formula, the Specify Calculation dialog box that appears works exactly the same as when you are defining a formula for a Calculation field. See Chapter 5 for more information.

Working with All Records Again

When all is said and done, you will probably want to go back to working with all the records in the database. To do so, switch to Browse mode (⌘-B) and choose Find All from the Select menu (or press ⌘-J). All records that were previously hidden or omitted will instantly become visible again.

Some "Live" Examples

I realize that after you move beyond a simple one-field search, you can easily get confused. Remembering how to do AND and OR searches, how to look for duplicates, and so on may be difficult for you. Reading about Find mode isn't necessarily the best way to learn about it. You may find this mode easier to understand if you play with it by creating a series of find requests and seeing what happens. The *Macworld FileMaker Pro 3.0 Bible Disk* contains a Find Examples database where you can see examples of many typical find requests, each prepared as a script that you can execute with a button-click.

To use the Find Examples database, click any of the text buttons on the menu screen.

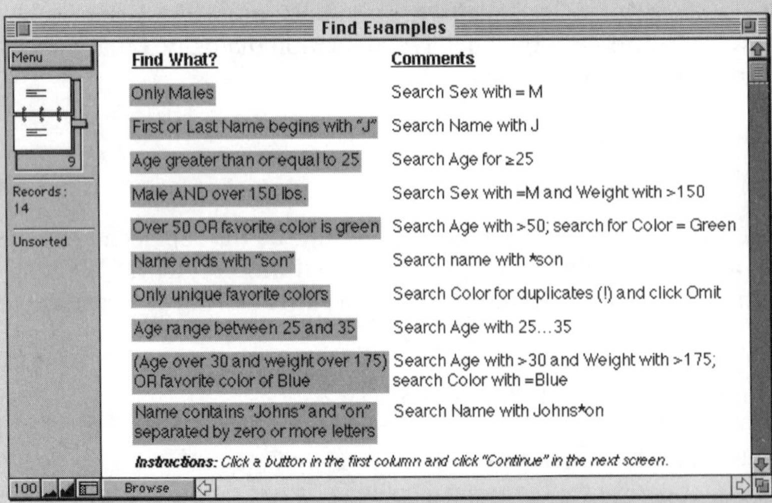

FileMaker Pro enters Find mode and displays another screen that shows the appropriate find request. (The list of find requests is titled "Find Results".) Because the requests are displayed in list view (each line represents a separate find request), you can see all the necessary requests on this single screen. After examining the requests, click the Continue button in the status area. The find requests execute, and the results are displayed. To return to the menu screen, click the Go to Menu button at the bottom of the page.

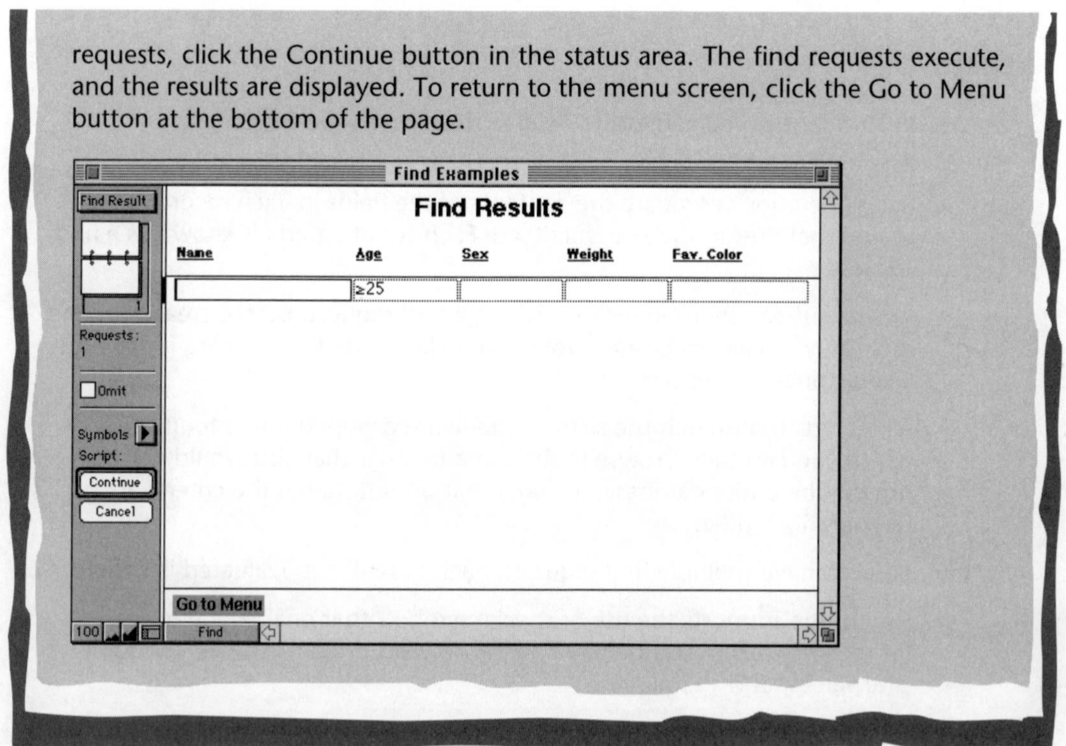

Summary

- In Find mode, you can locate records that match specific criteria.
- FileMaker Pro performs Find operations on one or more fields in a database. Such operations compare the contents of the fields in each record in order to find matches to the search criteria. Each set of criteria is known as a find request.
- Any layout can be used when creating a find request. Before creating a find request, you can select the layout you'd like to use by choosing it from the layouts pop-up menu.
- All records that match the search criteria are grouped into a found set, which you can then browse in the same manner that you would normally browse the entire database. Records that do not match the criteria are temporarily hidden.
- You can have multiple find requests, each of which is evaluated in order.
- Find mode supports the use of special symbols that enable you to search for records within a range of values, for invalid or blank values, for duplicate values, and so on.
- A request to find records that match certain criteria can be changed to a request to omit these records from the found set. To do so, you click the Omit check box on the appropriate find request.
- Other useful activities that you can perform with a found set include manually omitting certain records, swapping the omitted records for those that remain in the found set (creating a found set from just the omitted records), and deleting the found set. You can also copy a found set to the Clipboard for use outside the original database.

Sorting Records

CHAPTER 10

In This Chapter

- Sorting by one or several database fields
- Specifying a sort order for a field
- Choosing an alternate language for a sort field
- Modifying sort specifications
- Restoring a database to its original order

Issuing find requests (discussed in Chapter 9) is one way to locate information in a FileMaker Pro database, but it isn't always the most convenient way. And although flipping through records to find information is easy, it can be very time consuming when working with a large database. The primary reason that this method takes so long is the way that FileMaker stores records. *Records are stored in the order in which they are entered.* Unless you are importing or hand entering data from an existing database (as described in Chapter 16), your records may be in no discernible order whatsoever.

About Sorting

Consider the Address Book database that we created in Chapter 4. On the first day, you record the information for James Johnson when he sends you a letter. Your next few contacts are with Susan Brown, Tom Ziegler, and Paula Short. If you create records for every new person in the order in which the contact is made, the records are stored in that order. What is needed is a way to change the order of the records so that browsing through them is easier and you do not need to issue a find request every time you want to locate a specific record. You can change the order of the records by *sorting* the database. Sorting imparts an order to the records in a database.

In life, we are used to seeing information in a particular order. Phone books are organized alphabetically, entries in check registers are arranged by the date of transaction, and so on. In FileMaker Pro, sorting is the process of ordering the records that are being browsed, according to the values contained in one or more of the database fields. Both the fields used and the kind of sort order imposed on each field (ascending or descending, for example) are up to you. For instance, you can sort the Address Book database in *ascending* order by the Last Name field. After FileMaker Pro completes the sort, the database is arranged so that records with last names beginning with *A* appear first in the database, those beginning with *H* are near the middle, and records with last names beginning with *Z* are at the end. If you choose *descending* order, last names beginning with *Z* appear first, and so on.

Even if you have never performed a sort in a database program before, you have probably done so in the Finder. The View menu (see Figure 10-1) provides a number of commands that enable you to sort the files and folders in any window by name, size, kind, label, or date. Each time you choose a different command from the View menu, the files and folders are sorted according to the new criterion.

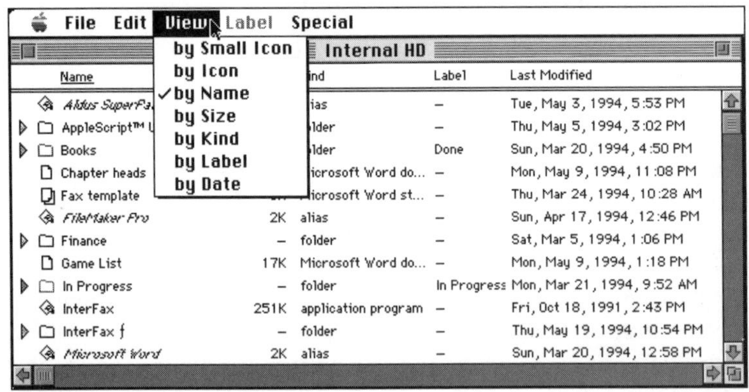

Figure 10-1: The View menu

Sorting in FileMaker Pro works in much the same way that sorting in the Finder works. Depending on your needs at the moment, you may decide to sort by last name and then later re-sort by ZIP code. Just as you can change your choice in the View menu whenever you like, you can sort any FileMaker Pro database as often as you want and by any field or fields that currently interest you.

When people first use sorting, they usually keep it simple, restricting each sort to a single field. They might sort an employee list by last name only, for example. Unfortunately, an important limitation of single-field sorts is that *ties* (cases in which more than one record has the same value for the sort field) *are not broken.* If you sort only by last name, all the people who share the same last name are listed in whatever order their records were originally entered into the database, perhaps as follows:

```
Jones, Evan
Jones, Marcia
Jones, Bubba
Jones, Abbie
```

FileMaker Pro, however, can sort by more than one field, solving the problem of what to do when two or more records contain identical information in the sort field. In the example just mentioned, you can have FileMaker Pro sort the database by the Last Name *and* First Name fields. Records with identical last names are then arranged in order according to their first name. Thus, performing an ascending sort on the Last Name and First Name fields would arrange the Jones records like this:

```
Jones, Abbie
Jones, Bubba
Jones, Evan
Jones, Marcia
```

As you can see, adding First Name as the second sort field re-sorts all records that have the same Last Name.

After you apply the proper sorting options, browsing the database can be much easier — just as the alphabetic ordering of entries makes finding words in a dictionary or names in a phone book easier. In this chapter, you learn how to sort a database, set sorting options, and — if need be — restore the records to their original order.

Sorting in FileMaker Pro 3.0 hasn't changed a great deal from previous versions. The main differences in 3.0 are:

- Custom sorts can be based on any value list that has been defined for the database, not just on a value list that you are using with the chosen sort field.
- Rather than choose an alternate language for all fields in a sort, the language must be set on a field-by-field basis.
- In addition to fields in the current database, you can also choose sort fields from any database that is related to the current database.

More About Sorting

All computer systems contain data that has to be located from time to time. The rapidity with which this information can be found is of critical importance to the system's overall speed and efficiency. Because searching through ordered information is easier than searching through random information (both for the computer and for the computer's human users), the process of sorting has been and continues to be an important topic in computer science research.

One of the simplest sorting methods — frequently taught to beginning computer science students — is the *bubble sort*. In this sort method (or *algorithm)*, each record is compared with the first record. If the two records are out of order, they are swapped, which causes the record that was being compared with the first record to become the new first record. After all records have been compared with the first record, the sort moves on to the second record and repeats the process. Every subsequent record is then compared with the second record. Swapping occurs if the two records are found to be out of order. The procedure continues for the third and every subsequent record down to the next-to-last record. Records are said to *bubble up* into the correct order (hence, the name of the algorithm).

The bubble sort works, but it consumes copious amounts of computing power and is very slow, especially when used with a large database. A more efficient method is the *binary sort,* which involves making comparisons within increasingly small subdivisions of the list that is being sorted. The binary sort uses far fewer steps for large databases than does the bubble sort. Other sort methods also exist.

You should note that the true storage order for a database is rarely (if ever) changed by a sort operation. Physically moving records to reflect a new database order is inefficient and unnecessary. Instead, the current sorted order of the database is often maintained within a separate list. This list shows which record is currently first, second, and so on. Normally, only this list (or *index*) is physically changed when a database is sorted.

Improving Sorts by Indexing

In versions of FileMaker Pro prior to 3.0, data in most types of fields was automatically indexed. That is, FileMaker Pro made a record of the contents of each field and created an ordered list of that data. Because each field was automatically indexed, the speed at which sorts and finds were performed was greatly enhanced. However, the indexing process itself consumed time and the index lists increased the size of the databases.

In FileMaker Pro 3.0, indexing is now optional rather than mandatory. In fact, the default is to index *nothing*. If you want to index a particular field, you must specifically set that option for the field (choose a field in the Define Fields dialog box, click Options, and then click Storage Options, as described in Chapter 5). Fields that are the best candidates for indexing are those on which sorts or finds will be based, as well as those for which you intend to use the Paste Special From Index command to fill the field.

Creating a Sort Order

Prior to sorting a database, you need to make three basic decisions:

- *Whether to sort the entire database or only part of it:* By using find requests, Omit commands, Omit Multiple, or Find Omitted commands (see Chapter 9), you can restrict the visible portion of any database to a selected set of records. As with most FileMaker Pro commands, sorting affects only records that are currently visible.
- *The field or fields on which to sort:* Which fields you sort on depends on how you want to use the database. Use the field or fields that are presently of the greatest importance to you as the sort fields. For example, in a customer database, you may be concerned with sales totals. Sorting on the Total field enables you to easily see which customers are big buyers and which ones have recently bought little or nothing from you.

In FileMaker Pro 3.0, you can also sort on fields from another *related* database; that is, one for which a relationship with the current database has been defined.

- *Whether records should be arranged in ascending, descending, or a custom order:* Text data is usually more useful when you sort it in ascending order. That is, you normally want to see the *A* entries first, rather than the *Z* entries. Numeric information, on the other hand, is frequently more useful when you view it in descending order. When you examine file sizes or cost figures, for example, your primary interest will often be in the largest files or the biggest dollar amounts.

If you have defined one or more value lists for the database, you can sort according to the order set in any of these value lists. This is a great approach for organizing records in a specific order that is neither alphabetic nor numeric. For example, you may have a value list that consists of the department names of your company organized in a specific order. When you sort according to this value list (rather than alphabetically, as you normally might), you can assure that people in Administration will be listed before those in Accounting, for instance. See the section, "Additional Sorting Options," at the end of this chapter, for details.

In previous versions of the program, custom sorts could only be based on the selected field's own value list. Now custom sorts can be performed based on *any* value list that you have defined for the database.

No matter how you organize a database's records, you sort by choosing the Sort command from the Mode menu (or by pressing ⌘-S). The Sort Records dialog box appears, in which you can specify sorting options, as shown in Figure 10-2.

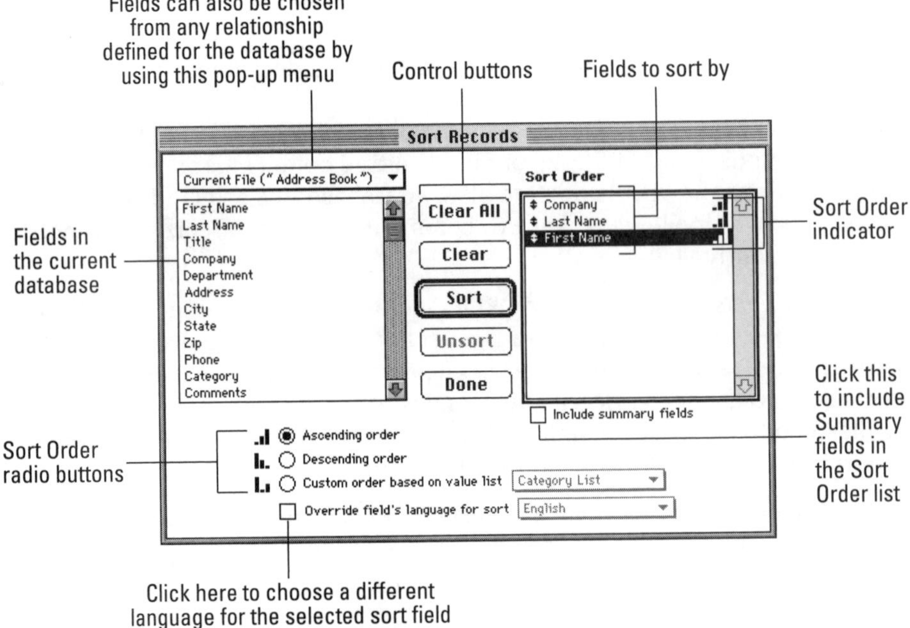

Figure 10-2: The Sort Records dialog box

In the field list area (on the left side of the Sort Records dialog box) is a list of the fields by which you can sort the database. Eligible sort fields include all fields that you have defined for the database — not just the ones that appear on the current layout. By choosing a previously defined relationship from the pop-up menu at the top of the field list, you can sort the database by any field in a *related* file, if you prefer. (If no relationships have been defined for the current database, you can create them by choosing Define Relationships from the same pop-up menu.) For information about relationships, see Chapter 19.

You also can use Summary fields as sort fields if you check the "Include summary fields" check box. For details, see the "Sorting by Summary Fields" section, near the end of this chapter.

In the Sort Order area on the right side of the dialog box is a list of the currently chosen sort fields. The order in which the fields appear corresponds to the order in which the database will be sorted. In Figure 10-2, for example, the database will first be sorted by the Company field. Within each company, records will be re-sorted by each person's last name and then by first name. An icon next to each field name in the Sort Order list indicates the sort order (ascending or descending). The meanings of the icons are shown at the bottom of the dialog box.

The buttons in the center of the dialog box enable you to control the Sort Order list. At the bottom of the dialog box are three radio buttons that you can use to specify, for each sort field, whether you want an ascending sort, a descending sort, or a sort based on a value list. The check box and associated pop-up menu at the bottom of the dialog box enable you to specify an international sorting convention, if desired, for any selected field. (See "Setting an International Sort Order," later in this chapter.)

The following is a brief explanation of the other components in the Sort Records dialog box:

- *Clear All:* Click this button to remove all fields from the current Sort Order list. Use Clear All when you want to define a sort order from scratch and ignore any fields that are presently selected.
- *Move:* Click this button to copy the selected field from the field list to the Sort Order list. Use Move to choose each field by which you intend to sort.
- *Clear:* When you select a field in the Sort Order list, this button replaces the Move button. Click Clear when you want to remove the selected field from the Sort Order list. (Clear enables you to *selectively* remove fields from the Sort Order list. Use Clear All to simultaneously remove *all* fields from the Sort Order list.)
- *Sort:* Click this button to sort the database according to the current specifications and options.

- *Unsort:* This command "undoes" any current sort operation and restores the records to their original order; that is, the order in which you entered them into the database. You seldom need to restore records to the original order — unless, of course, you created or imported the records in some meaningful order that you cannot duplicate by using a Sort command.
- *Done:* This command dismisses the Sort Records dialog box without sorting but preserves any changes that you have made to the sort specifications.
- *Include summary fields:* This check box specifies whether Summary fields are listed as eligible sort fields. If it is not checked, Summary field names are grayed out (dimmed) — meaning that you cannot use them as part of the sort settings.
- *Ascending order:* Click this radio button to sort the selected field from the lowest value to the highest value (from *A* to *Z*, for example).
- *Descending order:* Click this radio button to sort the selected field from the highest value to the lowest value.
- *Custom order based on value list:* If you have prepared one or more value lists for the database (see Chapter 5), click this radio button and select the name of the value list from the pop-up menu. This instructs FileMaker Pro to use the order of the value list as the sort order for the field. (If an appropriate value list doesn't already exist, you can choose Define Value Lists from the pop-up menu.)

  As an example, the days of the week in chronological order might constitute a value list. Using this value list, records sorted according to the list would appear in the order Sunday, Monday, Tuesday, and so on, rather than in ascending or descending alphabetical order.

Sorting on One Field

The simplest and most common kind of sort is one that is based on a single field — sorting only by the ZIP Code, Invoice Total, Age, or Grade Point Average field, for example. Depending on the complexity of their databases, many users find that the majority of their sorts use only a single sort field. The following steps describe how to sort on one field:

1. Decide whether you want to sort the entire database or only selected records.
2. Use the Find, Omit, Omit Multiple, and related commands and options to select the records of interest (see Chapter 9 for instructions).

FileMaker sorts only those records that are currently *visible* (those that are being browsed).

— or —

2. If you are currently browsing only a subset of records and want to sort the entire database, choose Find All from the Select menu (or press ⌘-J).
3. Choose Sort from the Mode menu (or press ⌘-S).

   The Sort Records dialog box appears (as previously shown in Figure 10-2).
4. If the Sort Order list includes fields you don't want to use in this sort operation, click Clear All to remove them all or individually select each field and click Clear.

If you have not sorted the database before, the Sort Order list will already be clear. Otherwise, it will contain the fields used in the most recent sort.

5. In the scrolling field list (on the left side of the dialog box), click the name of the field by which you want to sort.
6. At the bottom of the dialog box, click the radio button that corresponds to the sort order you want to use for the field:
   - Click "Ascending order" to start with the smallest numeric value and end with the largest, to sort words alphabetically (from *A* to *Z*), or to arrange times and dates chronologically.
   - Click "Descending order" to start with the largest numeric value and end with the smallest, to sort words in reverse alphabetic order (from *Z* to *A*), or to arrange times and dates from the most recent to the oldest.
   - Click "Custom order based on value list" to use a value list that you have defined for the database.
7. Click Move to transfer the field to the Sort Order list.

— or —

7. Double-click the field name to simultaneously select it in the field list and move it to the Sort Order list.
8. Click Sort to sort the database in the specified order by the selected field.

When the sort is finished, the status area changes to show that the database has been sorted, as shown in Figure 10-3. The new first record in the sorted database appears in the document window.

Figure 10-3: The status area for a sorted database

Canceling a Sort Operation

Sometimes in the middle of a sort operation, you may decide that you want to sort on fields other than the ones you have chosen. Instead of waiting for FileMaker Pro to finish sorting the database, you can cancel the sort by pressing ⌘-. (period). This feature is especially helpful when the database is large and the sort operation is lengthy.

Sorting on Several Fields

As mentioned earlier in the chapter, sorting by a single field isn't always sufficient, particularly in a database in which several records may have the same value in the sort field. In such a case, you may want to further organize the records by specifying additional sort fields.

As an example, you may have several records for people who have the same last name. Sorting only by the Last Name field will leave the first names in whatever order the records were in when you created them. (Can you imagine what a mess a metropolitan phone directory would be in if it were sorted only by last name? Try finding Jake Johnson in a 20-page listing of Johnsons!) Selecting First Name as the second sort field is often a smart move. And if you believe (or know) that some people have the same last names and the same first names, you can consider adding a third sort field, such as Middle Initial, Phone Number, Address, or Age.

When specifying multiple sort fields, select them in the order of their importance. Fields further down in the Sort Order list are merely tie-breakers, as illustrated in Figure 10-4. Working with the Address Book database, you may decide that your main interest is in companies, rather than in people, and choose Company as the first sort field. If you have multiple contacts at various companies, you can use Last Name or Department as the second sort field. If the companies are very large, you may also want to select a third sort field, such as First Name.

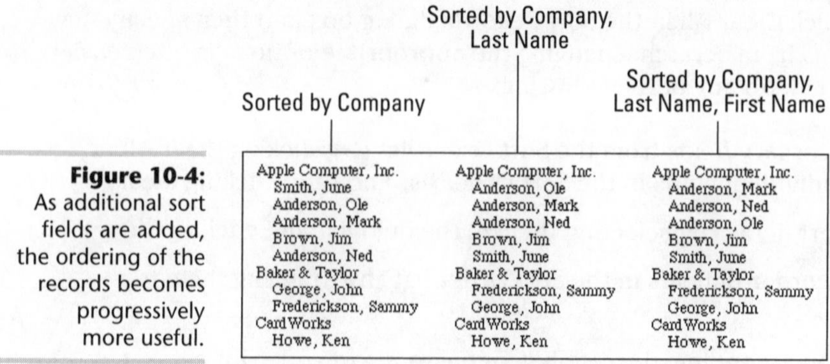

Sorted by Company	Sorted by Company, Last Name	Sorted by Company, Last Name, First Name
Apple Computer, Inc.	Apple Computer, Inc.	Apple Computer, Inc.
Smith, June	Anderson, Ole	Anderson, Mark
Anderson, Ole	Anderson, Mark	Anderson, Ned
Anderson, Mark	Anderson, Ned	Anderson, Ole
Brown, Jim	Brown, Jim	Brown, Jim
Anderson, Ned	Smith, June	Smith, June
Baker & Taylor	Baker & Taylor	Baker & Taylor
George, John	Frederickson, Sammy	Frederickson, Sammy
Frederickson, Sammy	George, John	George, John
Card Works	Card Works	Card Works
Howe, Ken	Howe, Ken	Howe, Ken

Figure 10-4: As additional sort fields are added, the ordering of the records becomes progressively more useful.

The only difference between sorting by one field and sorting by multiple fields is the presence of the additional fields in the Sort Order list. (For instructions, refer to the steps previously presented in "Sorting on One Field.")

If you discover that the fields in the Sort Order list are in the wrong order, you don't have to clear them and start over. You can rearrange the fields by simply dragging them to new positions in the list. To do this, move the pointer over the field you want to relocate in the Sort Order list. When the pointer changes to a double-headed arrow, click and drag the field to its new position in the list, and then release the mouse button.

Sorting on Multiple Fields Versus Performing Multiple Sorts

Performing a sort that includes multiple sort fields is not the same as performing several successive sorts that use those same fields. Every sort always starts from the original record order — not from the order that is currently displayed on-screen.

For example, if you sort a database by the Company and Last Name fields, the records are arranged in order according to company. Within every company, records are further arranged alphabetically by the employees' last names. On the other hand, if you perform two sorts — the first by the Company field and the second by the Last Name field — each sort works independently of the other; that is, the effects are not cumulative. The first sort arranges records in company order. The second merely arranges the records according to last names, completely ignoring the results of the initial sort.

Modifying Sort Specifications

After you define a sort for a database and set options, you may later decide that you want to change some of the options or perhaps sort on different fields. Although you can click Clear All in the Sort Records dialog box and then specify new sorting instructions from scratch, changing the appropriate options is often easier. For example, you can do any of the following:

- Clear unnecessary fields from the Sort Order list (by clicking Clear All or selecting individual fields in the Sort Order list and then clicking Clear)
- Add new sort fields (by selecting them in the field list and clicking Move)
- Change the order of fields in the Sort Order list (by dragging them to new positions)
- Change to an ascending, descending, or custom sort order for a field (by selecting the field in the Sort Order list and then clicking a different sort order radio button)

The Need for Re-Sorting

FileMaker Pro tries to maintain the current sort order for a database, even when you add new records to a previously sorted database. Because it doesn't do a perfect job, however, you see "Semi-sorted" (rather than "Sorted") in the status area. To ensure that all records are correctly sorted, you need to use the Sort command again after you add new records. FileMaker Pro records the last set of sort instructions that you use, so re-sorting the database is as simple as choosing the Sort command and then immediately pressing Return (the equivalent of clicking the Sort button).

Executing a find request, on the other hand, has a more profound effect on the current sort order: It obliterates it. The new condition of the database is reported as "Unsorted" in the status area. Thus, you will usually want to re-sort the database following a find request.

Additional Sorting Options

You can sort a database in more than one way. The Sort command offers additional capabilities, many of which are useful for tasks such as preparing reports. You can sort a database in the order defined in a value list, sort by Summary fields, sort in a way that makes the organization of records more useful for individuals in a different country, and restore the records to the order in which they were entered in the database.

Using a Value List for a Sort

Ascending and descending sorts aren't always appropriate. For example, if you sorted the months of the year in ascending order, you would end up with an alphabetized list that started with April and August and ended with September — probably not what you had in mind. Sorting according to the order defined in a value list offers a way around such problems.

A *value list* displays the acceptable values for a field in a preset order. You can sort the database by any value list that has been defined for the database, substituting the order defined in the value list for the normal alphabetic, numeric, and chronological orders used by ascending and descending sorts.

To sort according to a value list, click the "Custom order based on value list" radio button in the Sort Records dialog box (previously shown in Figure 10-2). Then select an appropriate value list from the pop-up menu — in most cases, a value list that has been defined for use with the chosen sort field. (FileMaker Pro 3.0, however, does not impose this restriction. You could, for example, use a value list composed of credit card names to define a custom order for a First Name field, but I can't imagine why.)

When you select this option, the order used for the sort matches the order in which the various values (entry options) appear in the value list. As shown in the example in Figure 10-5, a value list for a Payment Method field may list various payment methods according to their frequency of use. When the field is sorted, cash transactions will appear first, checks will follow next, and individual credit card charges will be last.

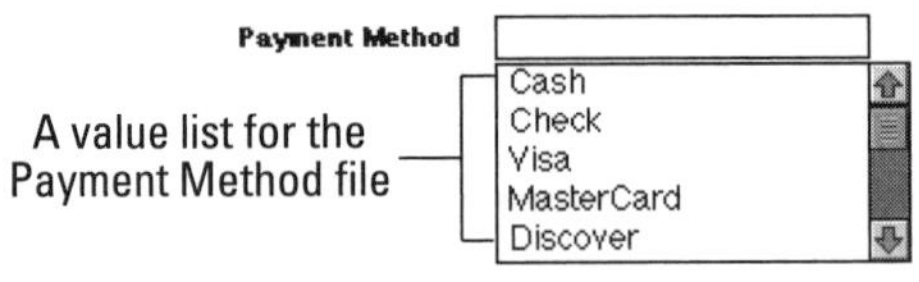

Figure 10-5: Sorting by a field's value list is appropriate when you want records sorted in a special, predetermined order, rather than alphabetically, numerically, or chronologically.

The Handling of "Other..." Choices

When you create a value list, providing an "Other..." choice as a catchall is often helpful. In a value list to be used with a Shipping Method field, for example, you might list choices for Federal Express, UPS, and USPS. Because your company occasionally uses other carriers, you can add an "Other..." choice to the value list so they, too, can be recorded.

In performing an ascending or descending sort on such a field, FileMaker Pro arranges the records in which the "Other..." choice was selected according to the actual contents of the field (Yellow Cab, Jimmy's Messenger Service, and so on). That is, it does not group all of the records together as though they all contained the same value ("Other"). On the other hand, when FileMaker Pro performs a custom sort that is based on a value list (rather than a simple ascending or descending sort), all "Other..." choices *are* grouped together at the end of the database, followed only by records in which nothing at all was chosen or entered for the field. (The procedure for adding an "Other..." choice to a value list is explained in Chapter 5.)

Setting an International Sort Order

Different countries follow different conventions for sorting information. Many countries use a non-Latin alphabet, for example, and some differences also exist between countries that use the Latin alphabet. FileMaker Pro enables you to select an international sorting convention for any field by choosing a language. The available languages appear in a pop-up menu at the bottom of the Sort Records dialog box, as shown in Figure 10-6.

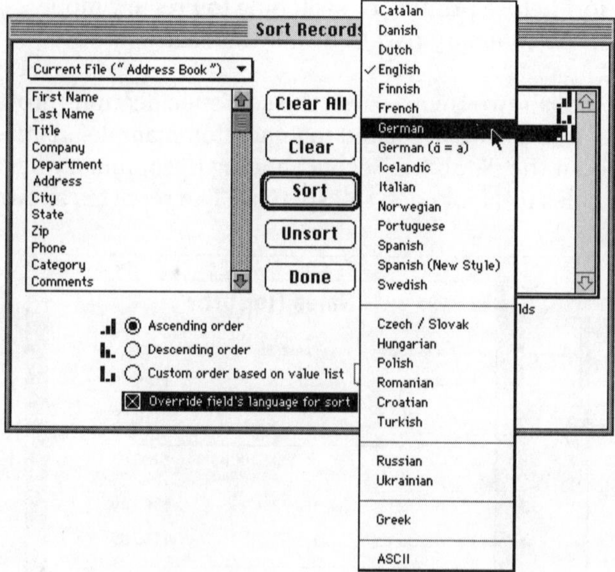

Figure 10-6: Setting an international sort order for a field

To choose a sorting convention for a field, select the field in the Sort Order list, click the check box for "Override field's language for sort," and choose a language from the pop-up menu. The sort language affects only the selected field. To sort additional fields by the same *or a different* language, repeat this procedure for those fields.

Sorting by Summary Fields

As you may recall from Chapter 5, a *Summary field* summarizes information from a single field across a series of records. For example, a Sale Total field may combine individual orders into one sales figure for all records that you are currently browsing.

When placed in a data-entry layout, the data in many Summary fields is the same, no matter which record you're currently viewing. For example, any Total or Average Summary field always shows the same total or average, regardless of which record is currently visible. For this reason, sorting by a Summary field makes more sense in a report layout than in a data-entry layout.

Here's a concrete example. Suppose you want to create a report that shows total sales for each member of your company's sales force. To accomplish this task, all you need to do is create a layout that contains a sub-summary part, define the part as "Sub-summary when sorted by Salesperson," and then place the Sale Total Summary field in the sub-summary part. When you want to see the summary figures, sort by the Salesperson field and then print or preview the report. (As explained in Chapters 5 and 6, you must sort before printing or switching to Preview mode if you want the information in the sub-summary part to display correctly.)

These steps accomplish two things. First, the sort specifications group sales by salesperson. All of Bob's sales are listed together, for example, instead of being scattered throughout the database. Second, adding the Summary field enables you to see an individual sales total for each salesperson. The report is shown in Figure 10-7.

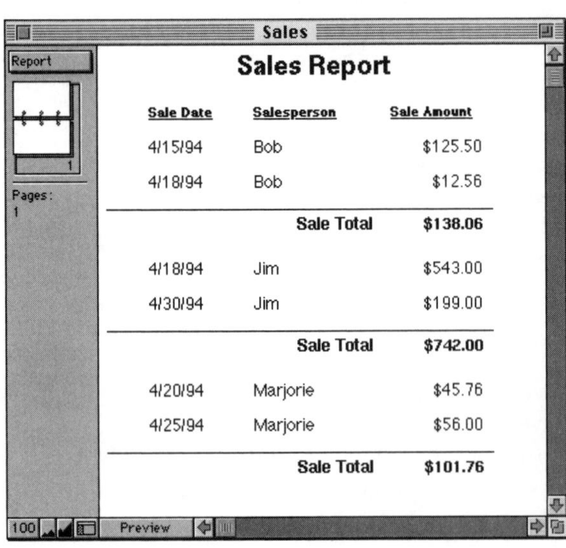

Figure 10-7: This report is generated when the database is sorted by the Salesperson field.

Note, however, that what you have accomplished so far has been done without sorting by the Summary field. Although the salespeople are effectively grouped (for example, all of Marjorie's sales are listed together), arranging the groups in alphabetical order is not necessarily the most informative manner of presenting the data. If you add the Sale Total Summary field to the Sort Order list and sort the database again, the report becomes even more useful. As Figure 10-8 shows, not only are the records still grouped by salesperson, but they are arranged in order of increasing sales (Marjorie, Bob, and Jim).

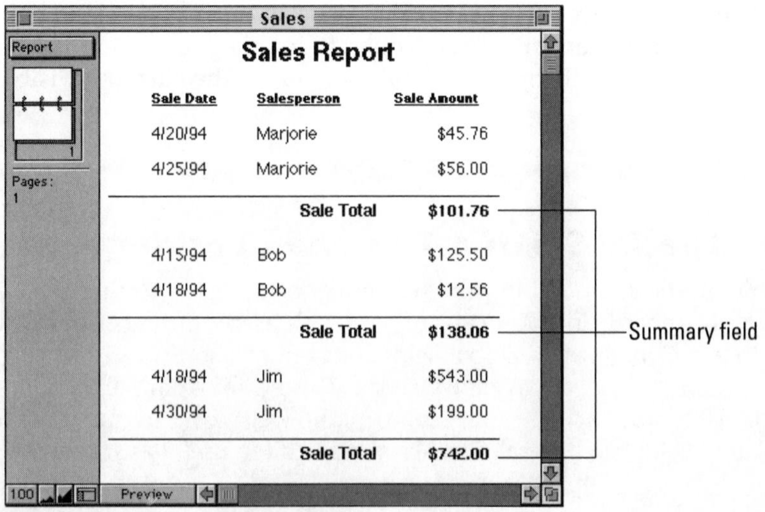

Figure 10-8: A report sorted by a Summary field

To sort by one or more Summary fields, you need to set the "Include summary fields" option in the Sort Records dialog box. Choose Sort from the Mode menu (or press ⌘-S) and then click the "Include summary fields" check box in the Sort Records dialog box. Any Summary fields that are visible in the field list change from being dimmed to being normal, selectable fields, and you can move the desired Summary fields into the Sort Order list. As with other sort fields, you can sort a Summary field in ascending or descending order. However, because you cannot create a value list for a Summary field, you cannot select the "Custom sort" option for such a field. Similarly, you cannot select a different language for a Summary field.

If you want to sort by a Summary field, you also need to include at least one non-Summary field among the sort fields. You should note that although the Summary fields always appear at the bottom of the Sort Order list, they are treated as the *primary* sort fields (that is, they have a higher precedence than non-Summary sort fields).

Unsort: Restoring the Original Record Order

Nothing is forever. If you want to restore the records in a database to their original order — the order in which you entered them — you can easily do so by clicking the Unsort button in the Sort Records dialog box. Records revert to being displayed in the order in which you entered them. (This is the actual order in which records are stored, even after you sort them.)

Remember that you do not need to issue an Unsort command before issuing a new Sort command. Every sort operates on the records in their original order (as you entered them in the database), not on the currently visible order.

Special Sorting Tips and Considerations

Although the examples in this chapter concentrate on sorting the contents of Text and Number fields, you can sort records based on the contents of any field other than a Container or Global field. For example, sorting by date is frequently useful (when you are organizing a check register, for example). And if you were recording harness racing results, you might well want to sort by finish time. Calculation fields, such as sales totals, also are often useful as sort fields.

Here are some additional sorting tips that you may find helpful:

- If you need to sort on a Container field, create an additional field (normally a Text field) that describes or names the picture, movie, or sound in the Container field and then sort on that Text field instead.
- If you sort on a field that has been declared a repeating field, FileMaker bases the sort only on the contents of the first entry in the field.
- When you include a sort in a FileMaker Pro script, you don't need to sort the database before you define the script. Just set sort options and click Done in the Sort Records dialog box. This dismisses the dialog box without sorting but saves the sorting instructions. (However, if you want to be certain that the sort results are as you intended, you may want to perform the sort anyway and then examine the results in Browse mode.)

Summary

- Sorting is the process of arranging a group of records into a specific order. The mechanics of sorting is an important topic in computer science.
- A sort operation is based on the value of one or more fields in the records to be sorted.
- You can use any field type other than a Container or Global field as the basis for a sort.
- Sorting does not change the physical location of records in a database. It merely changes the order in which they are *displayed*. Records are always stored in the order in which you entered them. As a result, you can easily restore the display order of records in a database to the order in which you entered them.
- Sorting is often an important step in preparing a database report.

Using the Spelling Checker

11 CHAPTER

In This Chapter

- Setting spell-checking options
- Checking spelling on command and on the fly
- Installing alternative dictionaries
- Creating, adding words to, and merging user dictionaries

The spelling checker provided with FileMaker Pro 3.0 includes a dictionary that is shared with all other Claris programs that use a spelling checker. The Main Dictionary file is located in the Claris folder, which is inside the System folder of the startup hard disk. This file contains the spellings of approximately 100,000 words.

Of course, no dictionary designed for general use will contain the spellings of all words that are relevant to your business or your life. For example, you are not likely to find company names, people's names, or technical terms in the Main Dictionary. Rather than having the spelling checker flag each of these items as a *questionable spelling* (the term that the spelling checker uses to indicate a word that it does not have in its dictionary), you can create *user dictionaries* that contain other words that are important to you. When you install FileMaker Pro, it creates the first user dictionary for you, which is (not surprisingly) called User Dictionary.

There are few changes introduced in FileMaker Pro 3.0 for spell-checking. Although some menu commands have new names and dialog boxes have new buttons, the basic spell-checking procedures are unchanged.

Setting Spell-Checking Options

FileMaker Pro provides two ways for you to check spelling:

- *You can check spelling on request:* FileMaker Pro examines the current record, set of found records, text selection, or layout only when you choose the appropriate command from the Spelling submenu.
- *You can check spelling on the fly:* As you type, FileMaker Pro automatically checks each word against the words in the current main dictionary and user dictionary.

If you want spelling to be checked on the fly, you have to set an option in the Spelling Options dialog box. The following steps describe how to set spell-checking options:

1. Choose Spelling Options from the Spelling submenu of the Edit menu.

   The Spelling Options dialog box appears, as shown in Figure 11-1.

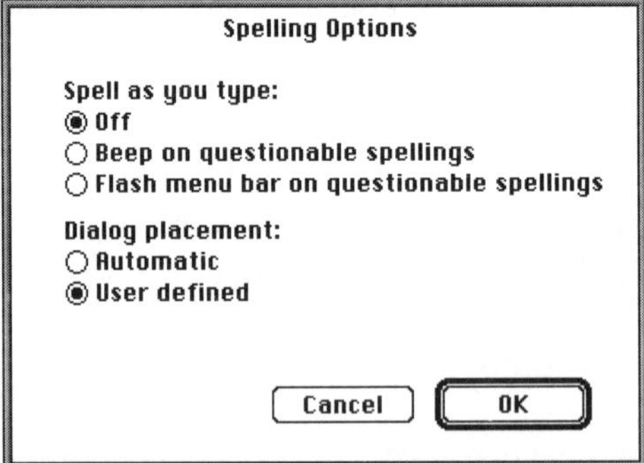

Figure 11-1: The Spelling Options dialog box

2. To initiate on-the-fly spell-checking, click either of these two buttons:

   - Beep on questionable spellings
   - Flash menu bar on questionable spellings

   The advantage of this type of spell-checking is that you can react immediately and correct the errors as the spelling checker discovers them. And you're still free to ignore the beeps or flashes if you prefer to continue typing and make corrections later.

If FileMaker Pro is currently set to check spelling on the fly (as you type), you can switch to checking spelling on request by clicking the Off button.

3. Click the radio button labeled "User defined" in the "Dialog placement" option to specify a preferred location for the Spelling dialog box.

   After checking the box, the next time you spell check your database, you can place the spelling dialog where you want it. It will then be positioned at the new location every time it appears.

— or —

3. Click the Automatic radio button to let FileMaker Pro determine the location for the Spelling dialog box.
4. To save changes made to the spelling options, click OK. (To ignore the changes, click Cancel.)

Checking Your Spelling

Spell checking on request is more commonly used than spell checking on the fly. Therefore it is discussed first (below). However, if you prefer to use the other method, you can skip ahead to the "On-the-Fly Spell Checking" section.

Spell-Checking on Request

By selecting the appropriate command from the Spelling submenu of the Edit menu (see Figure 11-2), you can request that spelling be checked for any of the following:

- Currently selected text
- The current record
- The current set of found (visible) records
- Labels in the current layout

Figure 11-2: The Spelling submenu

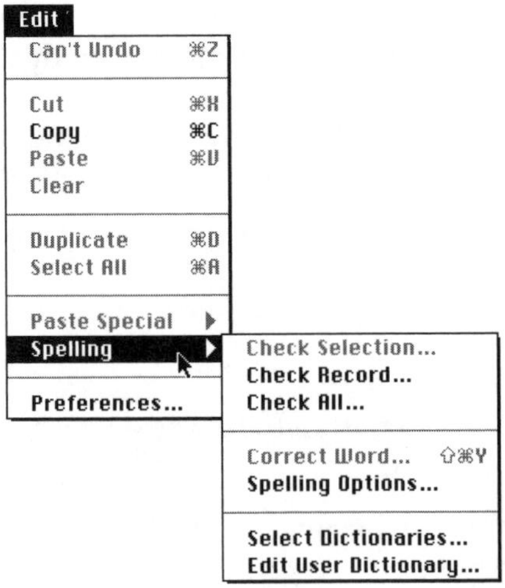

In preparation for a spell-checking session, you need to decide what you want to check and then follow the instructions for that kind of spell checking:

- *To check selected text:* In Browse mode (press ⌘-B), use normal text-selection techniques to select text within a field. The amount of text can be as little as a single word or as much as the entire contents of the field. To begin the spelling check, choose Check Selection from the Spelling submenu of the Edit menu. The Check Selection command is particularly useful when you want to restrict a spell check to a single field rather than examine the entire record.
- *To check the current record:* In Browse mode (press ⌘-B), choose Check Record from the Spelling submenu of the Edit menu. The spelling of all data in all fields is checked. If you've just added a new record, for example, this command enables you to check just that record.
- *To check a subset of records or all visible records:* Issue a Find, Omit, Omit Multiple, or a related command to select a group of records. Or, if you prefer to check all records in the database, choose Find All from the Select menu (or press ⌘-J). Following the find request, the database automatically switches to Browse mode, at which time you can choose Check All from the Spelling submenu of the Edit menu. FileMaker Pro checks the spelling of all data in all fields of the visible (found) records. (For more information on using Find mode and omitting or selecting records, refer to Chapter 9.)
- *To check the current layout:* Select the layout of interest by choosing it from the layout pop-up menu in the upper-left corner of the database window, change to Layout mode (press ⌘-L), and then select Check Layout from the Spelling submenu of the Edit menu. (The Check Layout command appears in

the menu only when you are in Layout mode.) This command is most useful after you've designed a new layout or altered an existing one, and you want to make certain that all field labels and other static text on the layout are spelled correctly.

After you decide what you want to check, proceed with the spell-checking operation as follows:

1. Choose the appropriate command from the Spelling submenu (Check Selection, Check Record, Check All, or Check Layout).

   The Spelling dialog box appears (see Figure 11-3). The spelling checker identifies the first questionable spelling it finds and displays it in the Word box of the Spelling dialog box.

   If you prefer to see questionable words in context (within the sentence or phrase in which each one is embedded), click the tiny triangle in the lower-right corner of the Spelling dialog box. In addition to appearing in the Word box, the word also appears in context at the bottom of the dialog box.

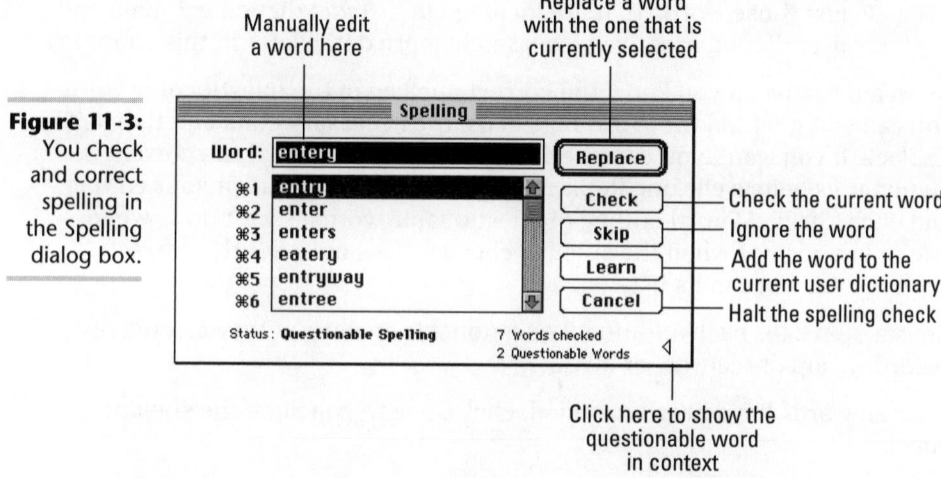

Figure 11-3: You check and correct spelling in the Spelling dialog box.

2. For each questionable spelling that the spelling checker identifies, click one of these buttons:

   - *Replace.* Use Replace to select a replacement word from the list of words that is provided. Either highlight the appropriate word and click Replace, type the word's Command-key equivalent (⌘-1 through ⌘-6), or just double-click the replacement. The questionable word is replaced by the selected word, and the spelling check continues.

Note that in some cases, the spelling checker offers more replacement words than can fit on a single screen. You can use the scroll bar to see the additional word choices. Each time you scroll, the new words are assigned their own Command-key equivalents.

- *Skip*. Click the Skip button to ignore the questionable word here and throughout the rest of text to be examined. You usually use Skip when you know that a word is spelled correctly, but you do not want to add it to the current user dictionary. For example, the last name Lundeen is not in the Main Dictionary file, but, unless it's your last name or the name of an associate with whom you frequently correspond, you probably have no reason to add it to a user dictionary.
- *Learn*. Click Learn to accept the word's spelling and add it to the current user dictionary. If you're certain that a word is spelled correctly and you want it to be known in future spell-checking sessions, click the Learn button. (A *user dictionary* records the spellings of words that you've added with the Learn command. By supporting user dictionaries, the spelling checker is not limited to just those words that are included in its *main* dictionary. Main and user dictionaries are discussed in more detail later in this chapter.)

As an alternative, if you know the correct spelling of the questionable word, you can edit it within the Word box. Make the necessary edits and then click Replace. If you want, you can check the edited word against the current dictionaries before clicking Replace. To check the word, finish your editing and click Check. Manual editing of questionable words is best done when you're in a rush or when the spelling checker does not offer the correct replacement word in its list.

3. Repeat step 2 for each additional questionable spelling in the selected text, record, group of records, or layout.
4. After all words have been examined, click Done to conclude the spelling check.

   Keep in mind that you can click Cancel at any time during a spelling check to immediately halt the process.

If you're working in a password-protected file or in a file in which you don't have access privileges for all fields, you may not be allowed to replace all questionable words. In those cases, the Replace button is labeled Next. Click Next to continue.

On-the-Fly Spell-Checking

If you have set the spell-checking options to notify you of suspected spelling errors as they occur, FileMaker Pro automatically checks each word the moment you press the spacebar or type a punctuation mark (these actions normally signify the completion of a word). You can quickly check the most recent questionable spelling by doing one of the following:

- Choosing Correct Word from the Spelling submenu of the Edit menu
- Pressing Shift-⌘-Y

The normal Spelling dialog box appears (as previously shown in Figure 11-3), providing a list of possible replacements for the questionable word. Respond to the dialog box as you would in on-request spell-checking mode (described previously). After you deal with the word, the dialog box disappears, and you can continue typing.

If you're sure that a flagged word is correct and you have no desire to add it to the current user dictionary (by using the Learn button in the Spelling dialog box), you're free to ignore the spelling checker's beep or flash. Similarly, if you know the correct spelling of a word, making the correction directly in the field is much faster than summoning the Spelling dialog box.

You should note that you cannot rely on on-the-fly spell-checking to catch all errors. For example, if you move the mouse back into a word that has already been checked and edit it but make a spelling error in the process, FileMaker does not notify you that you have made an error. Thus, if you are unsure of your spelling skills, using *both* checking methods is a smart idea: check as you type and then recheck the entire record by choosing the Check Record command.

Installing a Dictionary

When you run a spelling check, you can have only one main and one user dictionary active. However, you can create as many additional user dictionaries as you like.

The Select Dictionaries command enables you to switch between different main and user dictionaries as needs dictate. You can also use this command to let FileMaker Pro know that you've moved one or more dictionaries to a new location on your hard disk. Follow these steps:

1. Launch FileMaker Pro and open a database.

   Unless a database is open, the Edit menu (which contains the Spelling commands) is disabled.

2. From the Mode menu, choose Browse (or press ⌘-B) or Layout (or press ⌘-L).

   The Spelling commands are only available in Browse and Layout modes.

3. Choose Select Dictionaries from the Spelling submenu of the Edit menu.

   The Select Dictionary Type dialog box appears, as shown in Figure 11-4.

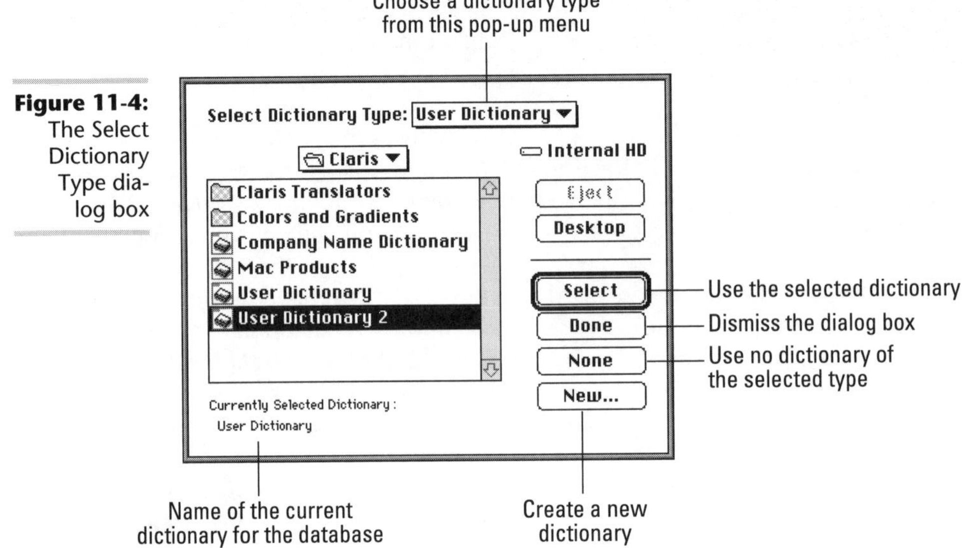

Figure 11-4: The Select Dictionary Type dialog box

4. To install a *main dictionary,* choose Main Dictionary from the pop-up menu at the top of the dialog box. Select a main dictionary from the file list and click Select. (Or click None if you do not want to use a main dictionary.)

   The currently installed main dictionary, if any, is indicated below the file list. Most users leave the main dictionary supplied with FileMaker Pro as the installed one. The only times you might have to install a main dictionary are after you've removed the main dictionary by setting it to None or you've moved it to a different location on disk, or if Claris supplies you with a new main dictionary.

5. To install a *user dictionary*, choose User Dictionary from the pop-up menu at the top of the dialog box. Select the user dictionary you want from the file list and click Select. (Or click None to avoid using a user dictionary.)

   The currently installed user dictionary, if any, is indicated below the file list.

6. If the dialog box does not close automatically, click Done.

   Any user dictionary or main dictionary that you installed is now used rather than the previous one. To return to the main dictionary or user dictionary that you previously used, repeat these steps and select the old dictionary (or dictionaries).

The steps that you need to follow to create a *new* user dictionary are presented in "Creating a User Dictionary," later in this chapter.

Keep in mind that installing a different main dictionary or user dictionary does not globally affect every FileMaker Pro database. Instead, when you install a dictionary, it affects only the *current* database. Every database can have a different main dictionary and user dictionary installed. Whenever you close a file, FileMaker Pro takes note of the last main dictionary and user dictionary installed for the file and automatically makes them available the next time you open the database.

Working with User Dictionaries

As discussed earlier in the chapter, user dictionaries contain spellings of words that you want FileMaker Pro (and any other Claris product that you own) to recognize as being spelled correctly. Although only one user dictionary can be active at a time, you can create as many user dictionaries as you like. This section discusses the procedures that are necessary for working with user dictionaries: creating user dictionaries, adding words to a user dictionary, and merging the contents of two or more user dictionaries.

Creating a User Dictionary

FileMaker Pro automatically creates the first user dictionary for you during the installation process. For many users, this initial dictionary — called User Dictionary — will be the only user dictionary they ever need. Every new "Learned" word automatically gets added to that user dictionary, assuring that the same word encountered in other databases will also be recognized.

Other users, however, may prefer to create several special-purpose user dictionaries instead of simply jamming all their unique words into a single user dictionary. If you dedicate a user dictionary to a special purpose or type of terminology, you may find it easier to maintain. For example, depending on your needs, you could create separate user dictionaries for medical, legal, and insurance terms, and another still that contains the names of companies with which you regularly do business. This approach works best when each of your databases can be serviced by a single user dictionary (just the legal one for database A, just the medical one for database B, and so on). If you find that many databases need to be checked with more than one user dictionary, you're better off combining them into one larger dictionary.

The following steps describe how to create a new user dictionary:

1. Launch FileMaker Pro and open a database.

   Unless a database is open, the Edit menu (which contains the Spelling commands) is disabled.

2. From the Mode menu, choose Browse (or press ⌘-B) or Layout (or press ⌘-L).

   The Spelling commands are only available in Browse and Layout modes.

3. Choose Select Dictionaries from the Spelling submenu of the Edit menu.

   The Select Dictionary Type dialog box appears (as previously shown in Figure 11-4). Make sure the "User Dictionary" is selected in the pop-up menu and the top of the dialog box.

4. Click New to create a new user dictionary.

5. In the file dialog box that appears, enter a name for the dictionary and click Save.

   The new dictionary is created and becomes the current user dictionary.

Whenever you want to use one of the user dictionaries, follow the instructions in the section, "Installing a Dictionary," earlier in this chapter, to make the dictionary of your choice the current user dictionary. In the next section, you will learn to add words to the new dictionary.

Adding Words to a User Dictionary

You can add words to a user dictionary in several ways:

- *Adding words as you go*: As you work with a database and perform on-the-fly or on-request spelling checks, you can click Learn whenever FileMaker Pro finds an important word that it doesn't know. The advantage of this approach is that you add only words that are essential, because, by definition, they have already been encountered at least once in a spell-checking session. The disadvantage is that until you have used FileMaker Pro for a fair amount of time, you may be adding words quite frequently, interrupting the flow of the spelling checks.

- *Manually adding words*: You can use the Edit User Dictionary command in the Spelling submenu to add new words individually. This option enables you to add key terms to a user dictionary without having to wait for them to be encountered in a spell-checking session.

- *Importing a word list*: You also can use the Edit User Dictionary command to import a list of words in Text-Only format that you want to add to a user dictionary *en masse*. This approach makes the most sense when you already have a list of terms prepared, perhaps as a user dictionary that you created in another program. Because such a list can contain many words, this is easily the fastest way to build a user dictionary. To be useful, however, you should carefully screen the contents of the word list beforehand to avoid having to later delete terms that are not needed.

You already know how to use the Learn button to add words to a user dictionary. The following steps describe how to add or remove words manually:

1. Launch FileMaker Pro and open a database.

   Unless a database is open, the Edit menu (which contains the Spelling commands) is disabled.

2. From the Mode menu, choose Browse (or press ⌘-B) or Layout (or press ⌘-L).

   The Spelling commands are only available in Browse and Layout modes.

3. Choose Edit User Dictionary from the Spelling submenu of the Edit menu.

   The User Dictionary dialog box appears and presents a list of the words that the dictionary contains, as shown in Figure 11-5.

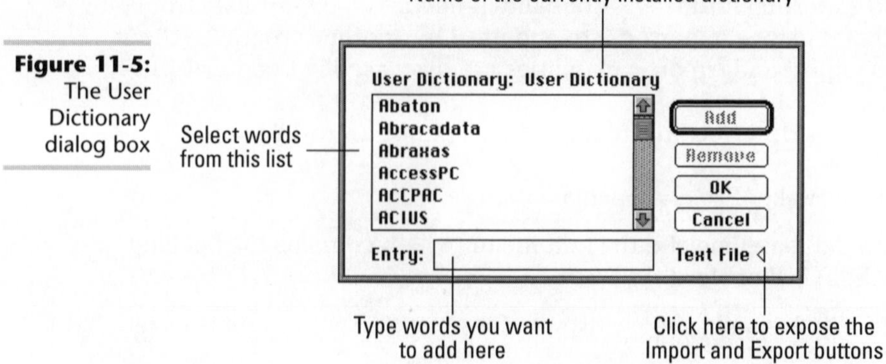

Figure 11-5: The User Dictionary dialog box

4. To add a word to the user dictionary, type the word in the Entry box and click Add.

   If the word already exists in the user or main dictionary, FileMaker Pro informs you. Otherwise, the word is added to the user dictionary.

5. To remove a word from the user dictionary, select the word in the word list and click Remove.

You cannot *edit* words in the user dictionary. The procedure is to remove the old word and then add the replacement (spelled correctly, of course). As an alternative, you can select the misspelled word in the word list, edit it, choose Add, and then use the Remove command to eliminate the original word.

6. Repeat steps 4 and 5 as desired.
7. To accept the additions and deletions, click OK.

— or —

7. To ignore all the changes you've made, click Cancel.

   A dialog box appears, asking if you'd like to "Discard all changes to user dictionary?" To confirm that you want to ignore all changes, click Discard. Otherwise, click Cancel to return to the User Dictionary dialog box.

Another way to add words to a user dictionary is to import a word list. FileMaker Pro can also export the contents of a user dictionary so it can be used in other programs. Whether you are importing or exporting a word list, the files are always in Text-Only format. On import, FileMaker Pro doesn't require that the words be set up in any particular way. As long as every word is separated from the next word by a space, tab, or return character, FileMaker will consider the word for inclusion in the user dictionary. On export, a user dictionary is written as a single, alphabetized paragraph, with every word separated from the next word by a space.

Importing and exporting normally work hand-in-hand. You export data from one program so that it can be imported into and used by another program. (Other FileMaker Pro import and export capabilities are discussed in Chapter 16.)

The following steps describe how to import and export a word list:

1. Launch FileMaker Pro and open a database.

   Unless a database is open, the Edit menu (which contains the Spelling commands) is disabled.

2. From the Mode menu, choose Browse (or press ⌘-B) or Layout (or press ⌘-L).

   The Spelling commands are only available in Browse and Layout modes.

3. Choose Edit User Dictionary from the Spelling submenu of the Edit menu.

   The User Dictionary dialog box appears and presents a list of the words that the dictionary contains.

4. Click the tiny triangle in the lower-right corner of the dialog box.

   The dialog box expands, and Import and Export buttons appear, as shown in Figure 11-6.

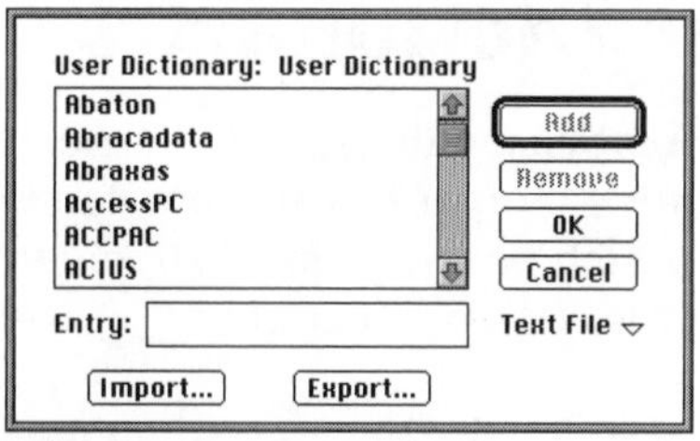

Figure 11-6: The User Dictionary dialog box with importing and exporting enabled

5. To import a word list, click Import, select a text file to import from the file dialog box that appears, and click Open.

   The words in the text file are compared to those in the main and user dictionaries. Any words that are not found are added to the current user dictionary; words that already exist in one of the dictionaries are ignored. When the import is completed, a dialog box notifies you of this fact.

— or —

5. To export a word list, click Export. In the file dialog box that appears, type a name for the file (or accept the one that is suggested), select a destination disk and folder, and click Save.

   The entire contents of the user dictionary are saved as a one-paragraph text file. Each word is separated from the next word by a space. When the export is completed, a dialog box notifies you of this fact.

6. Click OK to dismiss the notification dialog box and click OK a second time to dismiss the User Dictionary dialog box.

Importing Ordinary Word-Processing Documents into a Dictionary

As mentioned in the previous procedure, during an import, FileMaker Pro ignores words that are already contained in its main dictionary or in the current dictionary. Because the program isn't picky about the setup of the word list — just that it's in Text-Only format — you can use this fact to your advantage. You can take *any* word processing document, save a copy of it in Text-Only format, and then import the entire new document into the user dictionary. Any new terms that are encountered will be added to the dictionary; words that are already in the main or user dictionary (the bulk of them, in most cases) will be ignored.

Merging User Dictionaries

Although being able to create as many special-purpose user dictionaries as you like is nice, switching from one dictionary to another can be a pain. And if you aren't keeping careful track of which one you used last, chances are better than average that the wrong dictionary is currently installed.

If your user dictionaries aren't gigantic, you can make life simpler by just merging them into a single user dictionary that you use for most spell-checking sessions. Use the following procedure to merge dictionaries:

1. Begin by creating a new user dictionary to hold the merged user dictionaries. Follow the steps listed in the section, "Creating a User Dictionary," earlier in the chapter.

— or —

1. If you want to merge dictionaries into a user dictionary that already exists, skip directly to step 2.

In this procedure, the new dictionary is referred to as the "primary user dictionary."

2. Choose Select Dictionaries from the Spelling submenu of the Edit menu.

   The Select Dictionary Type dialog box appears (as previously shown in Figure 11-4).

3. Choose User Dictionary from the pop-up menu at the top of the dialog box, select the first user dictionary that you want to merge with the primary user dictionary, and click Select. Then click Done to close the dialog box

   The selected user dictionary becomes the current one.

4. Choose Edit User Dictionary from the Spelling submenu of the Edit menu.

   The User Dictionary dialog box appears (as previously shown in Figure 11-5).

5. Click the tiny triangle at the bottom of the User Dictionary dialog box.

   Import and Export buttons appear.

6. Click Export.

   A standard file dialog box appears.

7. Select an output location and enter a name for the export file.

   After you merge the export file with the primary user dictionary (after completing step 15), you will have no further use for the export file. Although you can save it here to any disk and folder that you choose, you may want to save it to a spot where it's easy to find and delete, such as the *root* (top) level of the startup hard disk or to the Desktop.

8. Click Save.

   The export commences. When the export process is completed, a dialog box appears to notify you of that fact.

9. Click OK to dismiss that dialog box and then click OK again to dismiss the User Dictionary dialog box as well.

10. Choose Select Dictionaries from the Spelling submenu of the Edit menu and then select the primary user dictionary (see step 1) from the Select Dictionary Type dialog box that again appears.

11. Choose Edit User Dictionary from the Spelling submenu of the Edit menu.

    The User Dictionary dialog box appears once again.

12. Click the tiny triangle at the bottom of the User Dictionary dialog box.

    Import and Export buttons appear.

13. Click Import.

    A standard file dialog box appears.

14. Navigate to the disk and folder in which you saved the export file in step 7, select the export file, and click Open.

    The import commences. After FileMaker Pro has successfully merged the two user dictionaries, a dialog box appears to notify you of that fact.

15. Click OK to dismiss the dialog box and then click OK again to dismiss the User Dictionary dialog box as well.

    If you want to merge additional user dictionaries with the primary user dictionary, repeat steps 2 through 15.

If you do any writing about Macintosh products or companies, you may find the user dictionary that's included on the *FileMaker Pro Bible 3.0 Disk* helpful. Mac Dictionary is a user dictionary that contains approximately 300 names of Macintosh companies, products, and computing terms. To install it or merge it with an existing dictionary, follow the instructions presented in this chapter.

Spelling Tips and Tricks

This section examines several easily-mastered tricks for creating useful user dictionaries and working with the spelling checker.

Creating a Spelling List from Existing FileMaker Pro Databases

Having a spelling checker that questions most company names, unusual last names, and technical terms, for example, wastes considerable time. Worse still, it encourages you not to use the spelling checker at all! (This is precisely why most people go "Huh?" when they discover that a database program has a spelling checker. Since databases are often filled with proper nouns, spell-checking sessions can take forever.)

If you have been using FileMaker Pro for a while now, you may have already completed the first step toward creating one or more useful user dictionaries. In an address database (Address Book, for example), you may have collected dozens of company names and people's last names. In an inventory database, you may already have entered the precise spellings of most of the important items that your company sells. A medical records database may contain the names of the majority of diseases that you treat. By using FileMaker Pro's Import/Export command, you can export the contents of these fields and create a text file that you can then import into a user dictionary.

The following steps describe how to create a word list from an existing database:

1. Open the database from which you intend to extract the word list.
2. Choose Export Records from the Import/Export submenu of the File menu.

   A file dialog box appears, as shown in Figure 11-7.

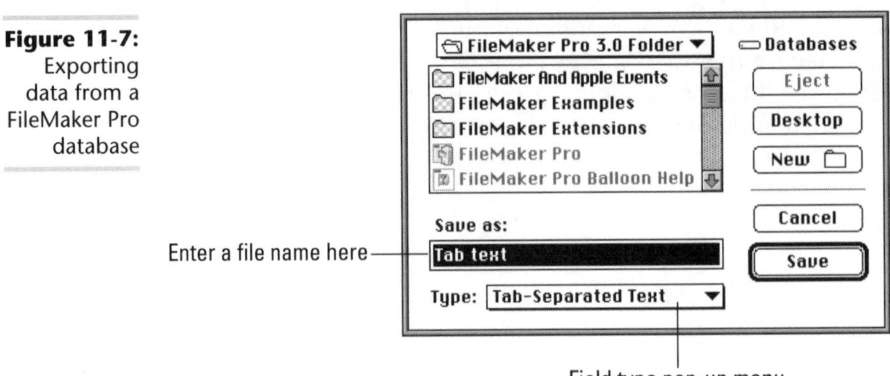

Figure 11-7: Exporting data from a FileMaker Pro database

3. Select a location for the export file, type a file name for it in the Save As box, set the Type to Tab-Separated Text, and click Save.

   The Export Field Order dialog box appears, as shown in Figure 11-8. It works much like the Sort dialog box. The left side contains a list of all fields that have been defined for the database; the right side contains a list of the fields that are currently chosen to be exported (in the order in which they will be exported).

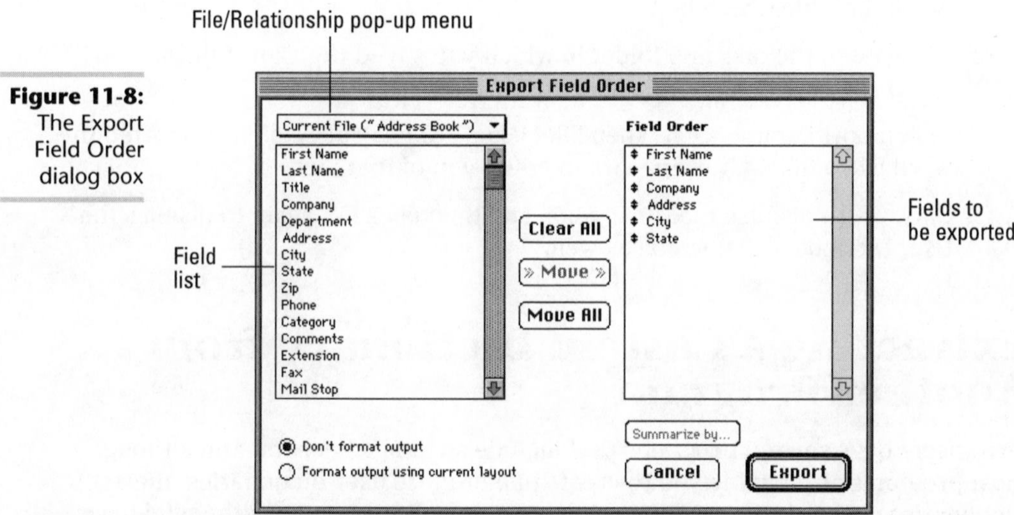

Figure 11-8: The Export Field Order dialog box

4. *Optional:* Because FileMaker Pro databases can be relational, you may have defined one or more relationships between the current database and other databases. You can export fields from a related database by choosing the name of the relationship from the pop-up menu above the field list.

5. Remove unnecessary fields from the Field Order list (on the right) by clicking Clear All or by selecting individual fields and clicking Clear.

6. Add fields to be exported to the Field Order list by selecting them in the left-hand list and clicking Move.

7. Make sure that the "Don't format output" button is selected, and then click Export.

   The export file is created.

8. Choose Select Dictionaries from the Spelling submenu of the Edit menu, and in the Select Dictionary dialog box that appears (as previously shown in Figure 11-4), choose User Dictionary from the pop-up menu at the top of the dialog box, select the appropriate user dictionary from the file list, click Select, and then click Done.

   These actions make the selected user dictionary the one that will receive the word list.

9. Choose Edit User Dictionary from the Spelling submenu of the Edit menu.

   The User Dictionary dialog box appears.

10. Click the tiny triangle at the bottom of the User Dictionary dialog box.

    Import and Export buttons appear at the bottom of the dialog box.

11. Click Import.

    A standard file dialog box appears.

12. Navigate to the disk and folder in which you saved the export file in step 3, select the export file, and click Open.

    The import commences. When FileMaker Pro has successfully imported the word list, a dialog box appears to notify you of that fact.

13. Click OK to dismiss that dialog box and then click OK again to dismiss the User Dictionary dialog box as well.

Extracting a Custom Dictionary from Another Program

Most users have several programs that include spelling checkers. And although most programs also enable you to create one or more user dictionaries, these dictionaries may not be usable by other programs. For example, although I have two custom dictionaries that I developed for use with Microsoft Word, FileMaker Pro cannot read them, and I cannot use the Import command to merge them into another user dictionary. And because these custom dictionaries are not simple text files or any other recognizable format, I can't even open them as normal Word documents. (Like most custom dictionaries, the ones created in Word are stored in a proprietary format that often prevents their contents from being used by other programs.)

In designing its product line, Claris was kind enough to provide the ability to both export and import custom dictionaries as ordinary text files (often called *Text-Only files*). Although many programs enable you to import a word list (usually as a Text-Only file), few programs offer an export option.

But with a special program — CanOpener 2 from Abbott Systems — you can peer into virtually any file and display the text, picture, and sound resources stored in the file. If the word list that is contained in a custom dictionary is readable (as many are), you can copy the list, paste it into a word processing document, and then import it into the current FileMaker Pro user dictionary.

The following steps describe how to extract a word list from a foreign custom dictionary:

1. Launch CanOpener 2, locate the foreign custom dictionary, and open it.

   Be sure that you have selected Text as one of the resources to be displayed, as shown in the top line of Figure 11-9.

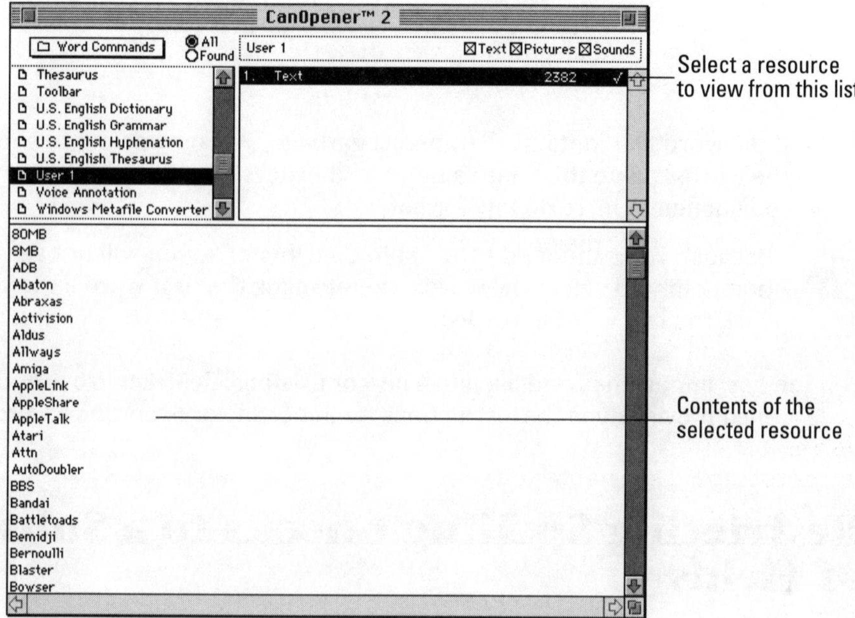

Figure 11-9: A word list stored as a resource

2. Examine each resource that is text.

   If the word list is stored as a text resource, it will look something like the list in the lower part of the dialog box shown in Figure 11-9.

3. Select Save As from the Item menu. In the standard file dialog box that appears (see Figure 11-10), enter a file name in the box labeled Save Text File As, select a location for the file, and click Save.

   The list is saved as a Text-Only file.

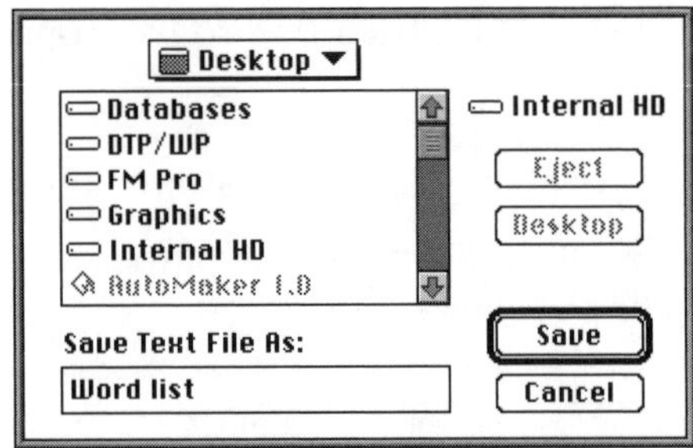

Figure 11-10: Saving a word list as a standard text file

— or —

3. If the word list contains extraneous garbage, you may prefer to simply copy the words, paste them into a new word processing document, and then save the document in Text-Only format.

Because you cannot edit the list in CanOpener 2, you will not see an insertion point. To select the words, double-click the first word and then Shift-click the last word in the list.

You can now import the word list into a new or existing FileMaker Pro user dictionary, as described previously in the instructions for importing or exporting a word list.

Restricting Spelling Checks to a Subset of Fields

Depending on the types of fields that you have created for a database, you may have no desire to check the spelling in *every* field (by using Check Record). Unfortunately, the only other option is to individually select and check one field at a time. Performing this task manually is time consuming. However, you can simplify the process by creating a FileMaker Pro script that selects and checks only the desired fields one-by-one.

Figure 11-11 shows a sample script that checks the contents of a series of fields in a database. When the script executes, it selects the entire contents of the first field (Title) and executes the Check Selection command (from the Spelling submenu of the Edit menu). After the first field is checked, the second field (First Name) is selected, and the same procedure is used to check that field, and so on. Note that this script performs the spelling check for only the current record, and you must click a button (Done, for example) to move from one field to the next.

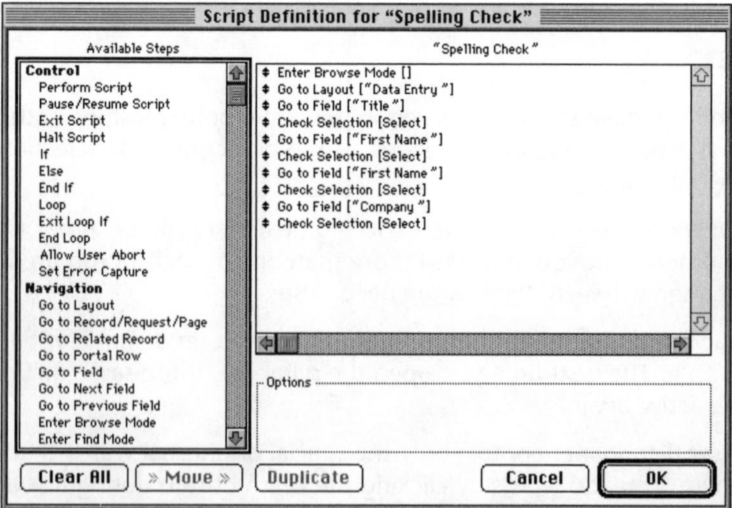

Figure 11-11: Steps for the Spelling Check script

To add more fields to such a script, you simply include additional pairs of Go to Field and Check Selection script steps. Be sure that the "Select entire contents" option is checked for each Check Selection script step.

Summary

- You can have spelling checked as you type, on request, or both. You can check the spelling of any record, group of records, text selection, or set of layout labels.
- Only one main and one user spelling dictionary can be active at any given moment, but you may have more than one of each stored on disk and change between them as the need arises.
- Each database remembers the last main and user dictionary that was used with it. The next time you open the database, those same dictionaries will be active again.
- User dictionaries contain only the special or unusual words that you add to them. You add words by clicking the Learn button during a spelling check, by editing the user dictionary and manually typing the words, or by importing words from a standard text file.
- When FileMaker Pro imports a word list into a user dictionary, it checks each word against the contents of the current main dictionary and user dictionary and ignores words that are already included.
- You can import a user dictionary that was created in another program into FileMaker Pro if the dictionary can be saved as a text file.

Reports 12 CHAPTER

In This Chapter

- Designing a typical report
- Tips for designing attractive, useful reports

Perhaps the main reason that you enter data into a database is so that you can eventually get it back out in an attractive, organized, informative fashion. You've seen how to locate information in a database by using Find mode and how to organize that information with the Sort command. You've even learned about using layouts to view different arrangements of your data. What's been missing up to this point is a discussion of putting all these procedures together to produce something that you can keep and share. When you select, sort, and format a group of records so you can print or view them on-screen, you're creating a report.

Report Design Essentials

A *report* is a summary of the data entered into a database, or an organized, collated view of the data. You don't necessarily have to print a report (you can use Preview mode to view it on-screen), but the process of creating a report is much the same whether you choose to print or not. (You will learn more about printing in Chapter 13.)

Preparing a report involves four steps:

Step 1. *Designing a layout.* Create a layout that displays only the fields that you want to see. Make sure that the layout takes advantage of the available page space and that the data is clearly presented. You use Layout mode to create and modify layouts (as explained in Chapter 6).

Step 2. *Selecting records to include in the report.* You don't always need to show the entire content of a database in a report. Your needs for the report will dictate the particular records to select. You may want to include only records in a given time frame, records associated with certain individuals or organizations, or records with some specific property, such as overdue invoices. Records are selected in Find mode by creating find requests or using related procedures (such as the Omit command).

Step 3. *Sorting the records.* If they have never been sorted, records are presented in the order in which they were entered into the database. For report purposes, records often need to be arranged in some other order so that readers can locate particular records and make sense of the information that the report is designed to present. You arrange records in FileMaker Pro using the Sort command.

Step 4. *Printing.* When designing a report layout, it's important to keep your printing requirements and capabilities in mind (unless you intend to view the report only on-screen). The type of printer you have can affect the layout you use and how information must be arranged within that layout. Finally, certain kinds of information (such as Summary fields) appear only when you display a print preview or print the report.

The following sections provide more information about these four essential steps in the report preparation process.

Designing a Report Layout

When designing a report layout, you should ask yourself these questions:

- *What is the purpose of this report?* This is the key to determining what information to display in the report layout. To begin, you should exclude any fields that are not needed. In a phone directory created from an employee database, for example, you would not want to display information about employees' ages or Social Security numbers — even though that data is routinely collected for the database. If current layouts include extraneous information, you will either have to edit a duplicate of the most appropriate layout or design a new one especially for the report.
- *How much information can — and should — I put on a page?* You should make optimal use of the printed area, but not at the expense of the report's clarity. Allow an adequate amount of white space between records as well as

between fields in each record. It's also important to recognize that when printing or displaying records, FileMaker Pro truncates data that doesn't fit within a field. This is not a problem in Browse mode because the field expands the moment you click in it. In Preview mode or when printing, on the other hand, there is no opportunity to click within fields. You may well have to resize some of the fields so that their data displays completely in the report layout.

- *Is the report layout clear?* A report should be self-explanatory. The recipient of the report should be able to recognize its purpose immediately without having to ask for explanations. Fields and summary sections should be clearly labeled. And don't underestimate the importance of headers and footers for labeling and numbering each report page. The report's purpose can be further reflected in its title, which is normally printed in the header.

Once an appropriate report layout has been created, you can change to that layout at any time by selecting its name from the layouts pop-up menu at the top of the status area. Because creating a report is a multi-step process (described previously), you may want to design a FileMaker Pro script that does the necessary preparatory work, changes to your report layout, and then prints the report for you. (Scripts are discussed in detail in Chapter 15.)

Selecting Records to Include in the Report

Selecting records is perhaps the subtlest part of creating a report. What records do you need to display? Your choice will most likely be based on the content of one or more fields in the database. You may want to choose all records that have a certain value or range of values in a field — for example, all invoice records prepared during the third quarter of the current calendar year.

After you decide which records you want to include in the report, you can create one or more find requests that locate those particular records — and *only* those records. After performing a find operation or using another of FileMaker Pro's related commands (such as Omit), the remaining visible records are referred to as the *found set.* Whether you intend to print your report or just preview it on-screen, the records included in the report are always drawn exclusively from the found set. (Refer to Chapter 9 for more information on finding records and working with found sets.)

Many reports are intended to display every record in the database. To include all records in a report, just choose the Find All command from the Select menu (or press ⌘-J). Find All instantly adds every record to the found set.

Sorting the Found Set

Unless the found set has previously been sorted, the records appear in the order in which they were entered into the database. To create a more meaningful order for the data, you can sort the found set.

You may want to sort on the same fields you used to create the found set. If a field contains names, it is usually best to sort alphabetically (from A to Z). For a sales report in which you want to highlight the performances of your best salespeople, you may want to sort numerically in a descending order (showing highest values first and lowest ones last).

Keep in mind that you can sort by more than one field. In the sales report example, you could sort records first by the salesperson name and then by the amount of each sale. This produces a report in which each salesperson's sales are grouped, with the most prominent sale appearing at the top of the group. (Refer to Chapter 10 for more information on sorting records.)

If you're using a layout that includes at least one sub-summary part, you must sort by the field that you designated when you created the sub-summary; otherwise, the summary information won't appear in the report. Sorting by the specified field has the result of dividing the records into groups based on that field. For example, if the City field was the designated sort field, the report would have separate sections for each city. (For more information on this subject, refer to Chapters 5 and 6.)

Printing or Previewing the Report

Once you have prepared a report, you can admire your work on-screen. You do this by switching to Preview mode (choose Preview from the Mode menu or press ⌘-U). (Sometimes printing is just a waste of paper. Many reports only need to be seen once and then never again. It's often more convenient — and faster — to simply review the report on-screen.)

To produce something that you can use to impress the boss, however, you will probably need to print the report. When designing a report that you intend to print, you should consider the following issues:

- *What type of paper will I be using?* This consideration is especially important when you're working with odd paper sizes or with special stock, such as mailing labels. You want your layout to fit and to print properly on that paper. The paper that you use can dictate the size of the layout body, the distribution of fields in the layout, and whether you will include headers and footers.

- *How much information will the report contain?* Short reports can use large type sizes, while smaller type sizes help conserve paper in longer reports as well as increase the number of fields that can fit across the page. Don't choose type so small that it's difficult to read, though.
- *Do I have all the fields I need?* If you want to summarize information in certain fields across records or within individual records, you may need to define Summary and/or Calculation fields. You can also use a Calculation field to convert data from one format to another format that is more appropriate for your report (see Chapter 14).
- *Which orientation should I use: portrait or landscape?* Because many columnar reports require multiple fields, it's sometimes preferable to print or display the report in landscape mode (that is, sideways) than it is to reorganize and resize the fields so they'll fit in portrait mode. To set the display and printing of the report to landscape or portrait, choose the appropriate orientation icon from the Page Setup dialog box.
- *Is data being fully displayed?* The amount of data that can be displayed in any field in a printed report or in Preview mode is limited to the size of the field on the layout. Before printing, it's a good idea to switch to Preview mode and flip through the report pages. That way, you can quickly determine if some of the fields are too small to display the information that they hold. You can then change their sizes on the layout, as necessary.

Refer to Chapter 13 for instructions on printing from FileMaker Pro.

Report Design Tips

That's all there is to it — presuming, of course, that you started with an appropriate and finely-tuned report layout. If you didn't, you can remedy this situation by diving into the next section, which (in concert with Chapter 6) covers some of the important elements of creating a report layout. Some of the major parts of a report layout can be seen in Figure 12-1.

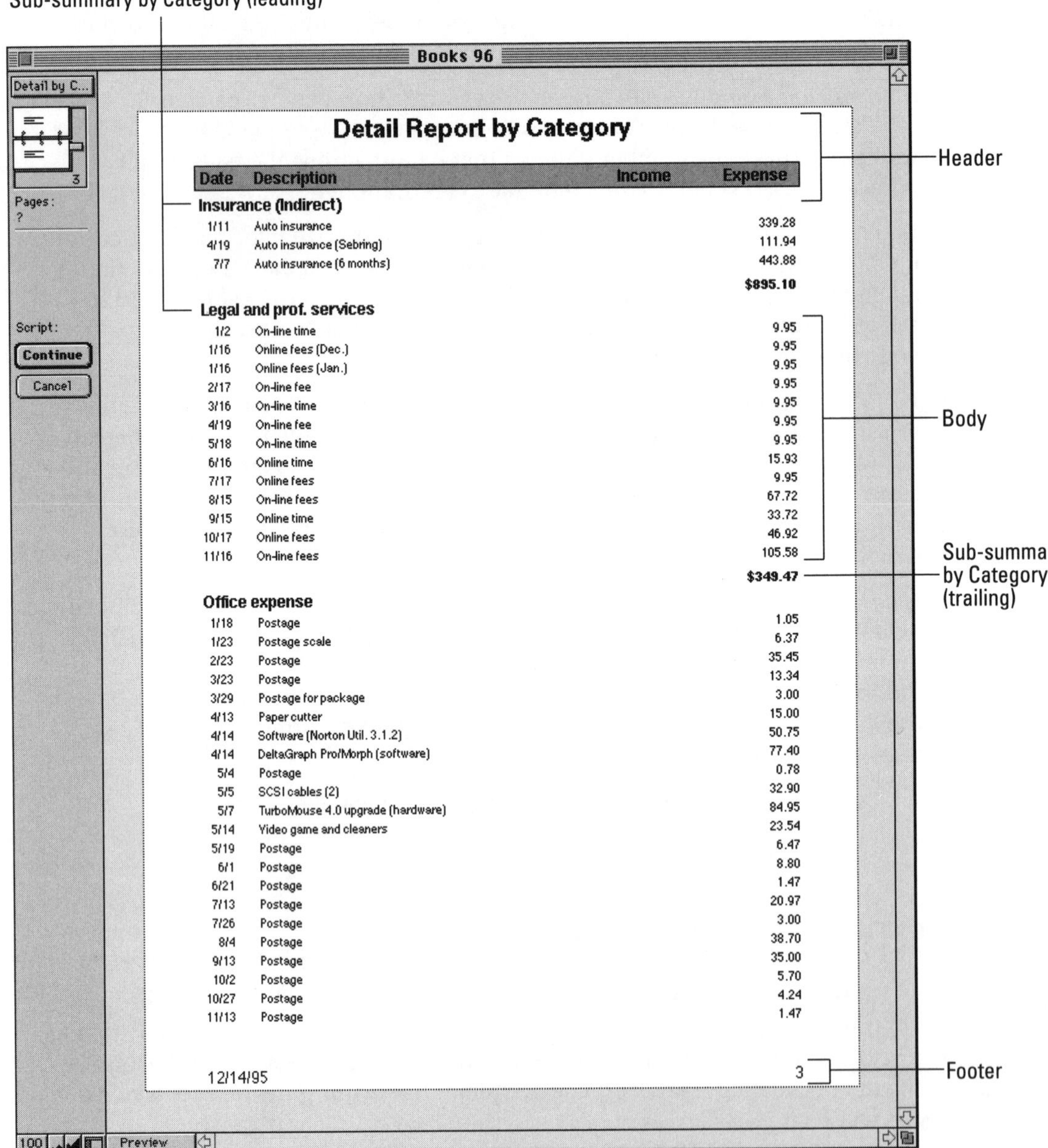

Detail Report by Category

Date	Description	Income	Expense
Insurance (Indirect)			
1/11	Auto insurance		339.28
4/19	Auto insurance (Sebring)		111.94
7/7	Auto insurance (6 months)		443.88
			$895.10
Legal and prof. services			
1/2	On-line time		9.95
1/16	Online fees (Dec.)		9.95
1/16	Online fees (Jan.)		9.95
2/17	On-line fee		9.95
3/16	On-line time		9.95
4/19	On-line fee		9.95
5/18	On-line time		9.95
6/16	Online time		15.93
7/17	Online fees		9.95
8/15	On-line fees		67.72
9/15	Online time		33.72
10/17	Online fees		46.92
11/16	On-line fees		105.58
			$349.47
Office expense			
1/18	Postage		1.05
1/23	Postage scale		6.37
2/23	Postage		35.45
3/23	Postage		13.34
3/29	Postage for package		3.00
4/13	Paper cutter		15.00
4/14	Software (Norton Util. 3.1.2)		50.75
4/14	DeltaGraph Pro/Morph (software)		77.40
5/4	Postage		0.78
5/5	SCSI cables (2)		32.90
5/7	TurboMouse 4.0 upgrade (hardware)		84.95
5/14	Video game and cleaners		23.54
5/19	Postage		6.47
6/1	Postage		8.80
6/21	Postage		1.47
7/13	Postage		20.97
7/26	Postage		3.00
8/4	Postage		38.70
9/13	Postage		35.00
10/2	Postage		5.70
10/27	Postage		4.24
11/13	Postage		1.47

12/14/95 3

Figure 12-1: An example of a report layout, as viewed in Preview mode

Working with Layout Parts

Every layout part that you've defined for your report appears in a particular place when the layout is printed or viewed in Preview mode. Keep the following facts in mind when choosing parts for a report layout:

- A title header (if any) is printed once, at the top of the first page. If you make the title header a full page long, you have effectively created a cover sheet.
- A regular header (if any) prints at the top of every page. If you included a title header, the title header takes the place of the regular header on the first page.
- If a leading grand summary is part of the report, it prints above the body, before the contents of any records are printed. (For more information on grand and sub-summaries, see Chapter 5.)
- All of the found and sorted records are printed in the body of the report. You can exclude the body part from a report if you want to print only summary information. This method is useful for getting total sales information from an invoice database, for example, when you have no interest in seeing the data from individual invoices.
- If you have placed sub-summary parts below the body, each sub-summary prints once for each group of records with the same value in the "When sorted by field" that you used to create the sub-summary. You must sort the database with the "Sort by" field for a sub-summary part to appear. If you like, you can specify a page break before or after a sub-summary, forcing a break after each new group has been printed, for example.
- If the report contains a trailing grand summary, that summary prints below the body once, after the contents of all records are printed.
- A title footer (if any) is printed once, at the bottom of the first page.
- The regular footer (if any) prints at the bottom of every page. If you included a title footer, the title footer takes the place of the regular footer on the first page of the report.

Duplicating a Report Layout

When you design a layout for a report, you can begin in either of two ways. You can start from scratch by just choosing an appropriate predefined layout such as the Columnar Report or Extended Columnar, or you can duplicate and then modify an existing layout. The method you choose will depend on whether you already have a layout that is close to the final report that you envision.

For example, the Want List database on the *Macworld FileMaker Pro 3.0 Bible Disk* successfully reuses a report layout to present two different arrangements of the same data: purchases sorted by catalog number and purchases sorted by purchase date. After creating the first report layout, all that was needed to create the second was to perform the following steps:

1. Create a duplicate of the layout (by choosing Duplicate Layout from the Mode menu or pressing ⌘-D).
2. Edit the title in the header part of the duplicate layout to reflect the new sort order that will be used.
3. Create a duplicate copy of the script that produces the original report, and then modify the duplicate script so it uses the correct sort instructions.
4. Copy the button that is used to execute the original script, edit the button's name, and then attach the new script to the button.

Since many reports are often only a minor variation of another report, you'll find that using this approach enables you to quickly generate loads of informative reports with minimal effort — just the way most of us like it!

Transferring Layouts Between Databases

You may have designed a good layout for a report, but that layout may reside in a different FileMaker Pro database. If you used the same field names in both databases, you can transfer layout elements from the first database to the second.

Follow these steps to move layout elements from one database to another:

1. Open the database that contains the layout elements you want to copy.
2. Choose Layout from the Mode menu (or press ⌘-L).
3. Choose the appropriate layout from the layouts pop-up menu.
4. Choose Select All from the Edit menu (or press ⌘-A), and then choose Copy from the Edit menu (or press ⌘-C).

   All objects on the layout are selected and then copied to the Mac's Clipboard.
5. Open the database in which you want to use the layout.
6. Choose Layout from the Mode menu (or press ⌘-L).
7. Choose New Layout from the Mode menu (or press ⌘-N).

   The New Layout dialog box appears, as shown in Figure 12-2.

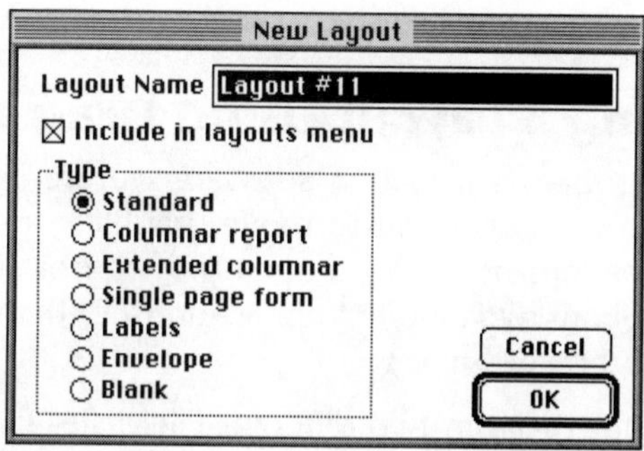

Figure 12-2: The New Layout dialog box

8. Choose the Blank layout type, and click OK.
9. Drag the Body label so that the body is the same length as or longer than the body of the original layout.
10. Choose Paste from the Edit menu (or press ⌘-V).
11. Adjust layout parts and objects to the correct positions and sizes.

Any fields from the first (source) database that don't already exist in the second database are pasted, but are undefined. Because they don't represent real fields, data cannot be entered into them. To assign actual fields to the undefined fields, double-click each one while holding down the ⌘ key. The Specify Field dialog box appears, as shown in Figure 12-3, enabling you to assign an existing field (in this database or a related one) to the undefined field. You can eliminate the fields that you don't care to define by selecting them and pressing Delete. (See Chapter 6 for more information on editing layouts.)

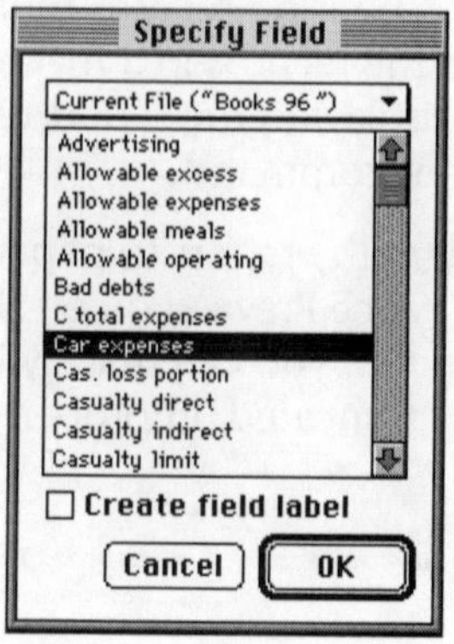

Figure 12-3: Assigning a field name to an undefined field

Duplicating a Layout Using Drag and Drop

FileMaker Pro 3.0 supports a system software feature called drag and drop. Basically, drag and drop enables you to move graphics, text, and data between documents and applications by simply dragging them from one document to the other. (When working with two different applications, both must support drag and drop in order for this to be possible.)

To duplicate a layout that's in two different FileMaker Pro databases, you can drag fields, static text, and graphics from one layout to the other. If Copy and Paste is one step too many for you, give drag and drop a try.

Buttons can also be dragged between layouts, but you will have to redefine the attached scripts.

Summary

- A report is a printed or on-screen copy of a selected group of records sorted in a specific order, arranged in a way that provides information that viewing individual records does not (and cannot).
- The process of preparing a report typically includes selecting or designing an appropriate layout, choosing records to include using Find mode commands, arranging the records in a meaningful fashion with the Sort command, and then displaying the report on-screen with Preview mode or printing it with the Print command.
- Before committing a lengthy report to paper, it's a good idea to examine it first in Preview mode. Since Preview mode shows you *exactly* what a report will look like when printed, you can quickly identify problems — such as field data that is being truncated, improperly aligned header information, and so forth.

Printing 13

CHAPTER

In This Chapter

- Setting page options for various printers
- Previewing a report before (or as an alternative to) printing
- Using the FileMaker Pro Print command
- Avoiding and correcting printing problems

Having mastered the art of designing and producing reports from databases, you are no doubt eager to see your work realized on paper. This chapter takes you through the printing process step by step — from setting up a Macintosh to work with a particular printer through resolving problems that may crop up as you print.

Throughout this chapter, I discuss printing "reports." Although some of the procedures are indeed specific to reports, most can be applied equally to any type of FileMaker document you want to print, such as individual records, script definitions, and field definitions. And many of the printing procedures can be applied to printing documents in other programs, too.

Printing a report involves three basic steps:

Step 1. *Setting Up:* You use Apple's Chooser desk accessory to select the printer that you want to use. After you select a printer, you select print options in the Page Setup dialog box within FileMaker Pro. You can omit the first part of this step if you always use the same printer; frequently, you can omit choosing the print options as well.

Step 2. *Readying a Report for Printing:* With the database open, you select the appropriate layout, find the records that you want to include in the report, and sort the records. You then preview the report to make sure that it will print correctly. (Previewing a report before printing is a good way to save paper.)

Step 3. *Printing:* After you are satisfied with the way a report looks in Preview mode, you send it off to the printer by using the Print command. You can choose from several options to control how a report prints.

If all goes well, the end result of this process is a neatly printed report that contains just the information you need. Unfortunately, things do not always go well, which leads in some cases to a fourth step:

Step 4. *Troubleshooting:* If you don't get the results you want, you need to adopt a systematic approach to isolate and correct the problem.

All Page Setup and Print dialog boxes shown in this chapter are from System 7.5, the current version of Apple's system software. If you are using an earlier version of the system software or have a non-Apple printer, the dialog boxes that *you* see may be slightly different from the ones illustrated here. Many of the Print and Page Setup options, however, will be identical or named similarly to those displayed for Apple print drivers.

If you are upgrading from any recent version of FileMaker Pro, you can safely skip this chapter. The process of printing reports, records, and scripts hasn't changed.

Setting Up

Before printing, you must make the printer known to the Macintosh and use the Page Setup command to enable FileMaker to print correctly.

Selecting a Printer with the Chooser

Depending on your work environment (a stand-alone computer versus a network, for example), many printers may be available to you, but the Mac doesn't know which one you want to use until you tell it. Before you can print anything, whether in FileMaker Pro or any other program, you need to use the Chooser to select the printer that you want to use.

The *Chooser* is a desk accessory, a program you'll find in the Apple menu. The Chooser lets you choose special pieces of software called *print drivers* that your system uses to control different printers. A print driver is a set of instructions that enables the Macintosh to communicate successfully with a printer and enables *you* to get the printer to do what you want it to do: produce documents on paper.

Selecting the Chooser from the Apple menu brings up a desk accessory window that is similar to the window shown in Figure 13-1. (The appearance of the Chooser on your system may be slightly different, depending on the print drivers and the version of the system software that you have installed.)

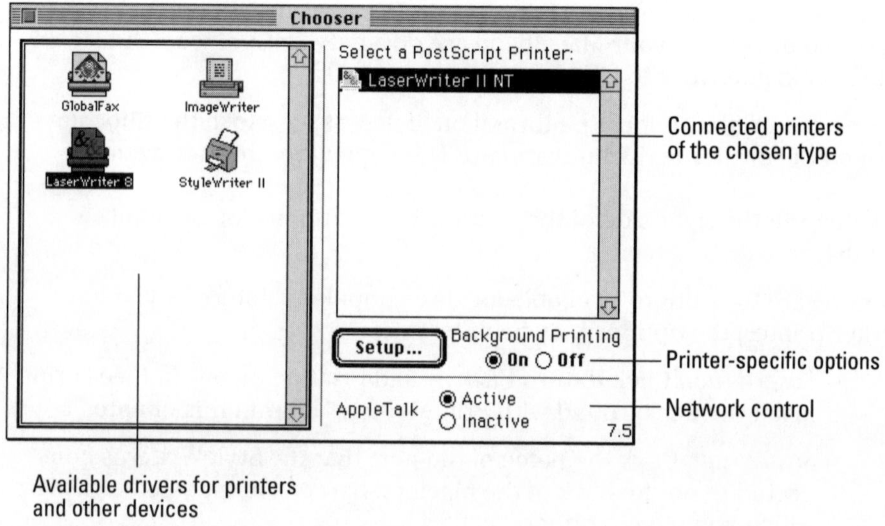

Figure 13-1: The Chooser desk accessory

On the left side of the window, you see icons that represent, among other things, the print drivers that are currently installed on your Mac. You click the icon for the type of printer that you want to use. If you are connected to a network, a list of network zones is also presented. Select a zone to see what printers are currently available.

To the right is an area that contains icons for all printers that can use the selected print driver. (Only printers that are turned on are shown.) After you select a printer, printer-specific options are displayed below this area. Options may include setting the port to which your printer is connected (modem or printer) and turning background printing on or off. AppleTalk control is another common option. *AppleTalk* is a networking system — a way of stringing together computers and peripherals (such as printers) so that they can share information. Many laser printers require the use of AppleTalk.

To select a printer, follow these steps:

1. Select the Chooser from the Apple menu.

   The Chooser window appears.

2. In the left side of the Chooser window, choose the print driver that is appropriate to the printer that you want to use.
3. In the right side of the window, click the icon for the particular printer you wish to use.

   If your Mac is a stand-alone system, you can choose any printer that is connected directly to your Mac. If you are on a network, you can choose any printer on the network to which you have access.

   To select a printer, it must be turned on. If necessary, close the Chooser, turn on the printer and let it warm up. Then open the Chooser again.

4. Click items in the right side of the window to set options for the chosen print driver.

   Following are the options available for three popular printers (if you have another printer, the options may be different):

   - *LaserWriter:* Click to turn Background Printing on or off. (See "Printing in the Background with PrintMonitor" later in this chapter.)
   - *StyleWriter:* Click the name of the port that the StyleWriter is connected to on the back of the Macintosh. (*Ports* are labeled jacks into which you plug peripheral cables.)
   - *ImageWriter:* Click the name of the port that the ImageWriter is connected to on the Macintosh.

5. If the selected printer is directly connected to your Macintosh by a serial cable, click the Inactive button in the AppleTalk section of the window.

   Other than LaserWriters and similar printers, many printers do not require AppleTalk.

— or —

5. If the selected printer is on a network or always requires the AppleTalk option (as Apple LaserWriters do, for example), click the Active button in the AppleTalk section of the window.

   If you're unsure whether your printer requires the AppleTalk option, refer to the printer's documentation.

6. Click the close box in the Chooser window to put your choices into effect and dismiss the window.

   Until you later select a different printer in the Chooser, all future print jobs — regardless of the program you're in — will be directed to the chosen printer.

If Your Print Driver Is Missing

When using the Chooser, you should see an icon for the printer that you want to use. If there is no icon for your printer type, you need to install the appropriate print driver. This software normally comes on a disk with your printer, and the printer's documentation should tell you how to install the software. The following procedure describes this task in general terms; consult the printer documentation for specifics.

To install a manufacturer-provided print driver, follow these steps:

1. Locate the print driver disk that accompanied the printer and insert it into the Macintosh's floppy disk drive.
2. Double-click the disk's icon to open it.
3. Locate the print driver icon for the printer and drag it to the System folder on your startup hard disk.

   If you are running System 7, an alert box appears, informing you that you need to put the driver into the Extensions folder. Click OK to do so.

   — or —

3. If the printer disk comes with an Installer program, use it. The installer's job is to make sure that everything goes where it is supposed to.
4. Turn on the printer, select Chooser from the Apple menu, and choose the newly-installed print driver and your printer.

Drivers for all Apple printers are included with each version of system software. You can install additional Apple drivers by following the directions in your system software manual.

Using Chooser on a Network

If your Mac is connected to a network, you can select any printer that's on the network and currently turned on. For example, when you choose a LaserWriter print driver, you will see the names of all LaserWriters that are on the network. Select whichever one you want to use.

If you are connected to a network that is divided into AppleTalk zones, the Chooser window you see will look somewhat different from the one shown previously in Figure 13-1. An AppleTalk Zones area appears on the left side of the window beneath the installed print drivers. Before selecting the particular printer to which you intend to print, you must select the AppleTalk zone in which the printer is located. As you click a zone name, the names of the printers available in that zone appear in the printer list on the right side of the window.

Using the Page Setup Dialog Box

The first thing that happens when you click the close box in the Chooser window after choosing a printer is that the alert box shown in Figure 13-2 appears, telling you to change Page Setup for all applications that are open. After you click OK to send this alert box away, do as it suggests. This ensures that any differences between the currently chosen print driver and the previous one are taken into account when you print.

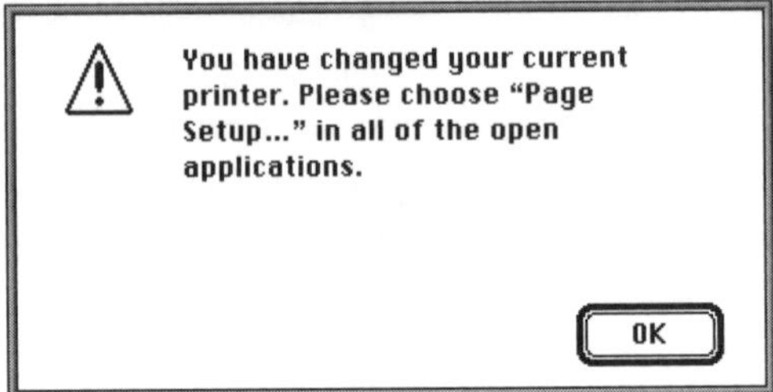

You have changed your current printer. Please choose "Page Setup..." in all of the open applications.
OK

Figure 13-2: This alert appears whenever you select a different printer in the Chooser.

You reach the Page Setup dialog box by choosing Page Setup in the File menu — from FileMaker Pro, from another program, or from the desktop. The Page Setup dialog box contains controls and options that you can use to adapt your printer to the kind of printed output that you want to produce. Different printers present different versions of the Page Setup dialog box. Options that are listed depend on the printer's capabilities and on the kinds of paper that the printer supports.

Page Setup options are *document-specific* rather than global. If you always want to print in landscape mode, for example, you will have to individually set that option for each document. Luckily, however, the most recent Page Setup settings used with a document are stored along with the document when the file is saved.

Using a LaserWriter

Choosing Page Setup when you are working with any laser printer that uses the LaserWriter print driver brings up a dialog box that is similar to the one shown in Figure 13-3. (This is the LaserWriter 8 version of the Page Setup dialog box. If you have an earlier version of the print driver, the dialog box will look different.)

Figure 13-3: The Page Setup dialog box for a LaserWriter

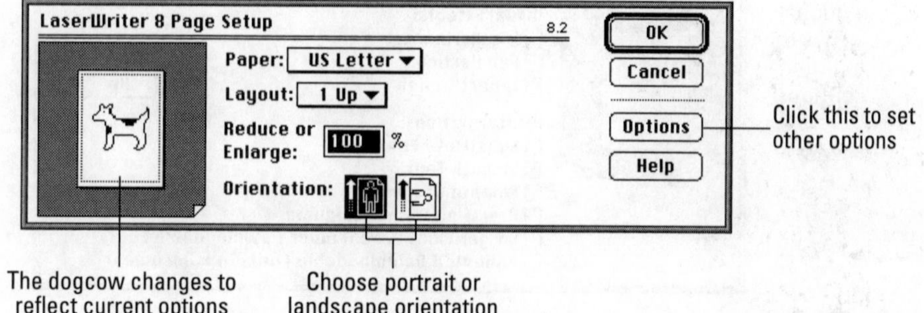

At the top is a pop-up menu that lists the predefined paper sizes you can use with the printer. (A4 and B5 are European standards that are not widely used in the United States and Canada.) The sizes of paper that you can use depend on which printer you choose.

The Layout pop-up menu enables you to print multiple document pages on each page of paper (in a reduced size). Choices include 1 Up (one document page per printed page), 2 Up (two document pages on each printed page), or 4 Up (four document pages on each printed page). For normal printing, choose **1 Up**.

Below the Layout pop-up menu is a text box into which you can enter a magnification factor (Reduce or Enlarge). You may find this option handy if you are having trouble fitting records on a page.

For best results, you should restrict your Reduce or Enlarge choices to values that can be evenly divided by two. Such values work best because most laser printers have resolutions of 300 or 600 dots per inch (dpi). If you scale by an odd factor, the dots will have to be apportioned fractionally, occasionally yielding poor results.

Below the Reduce or Enlarge text box are buttons that control the orientation of the paper. There are two choices: portrait and landscape. Choose the icon on the left for portrait mode, in which text prints in the normal way. Choose the icon on the right for landscape mode, in which text prints across the long dimension of the paper (sideways). Landscape mode, like magnification, is handy for fitting wide records or reports onto a single sheet of paper. You also print envelopes in landscape mode. (Doing so pulls them through the printer lengthwise. Trying to print them in portrait mode frequently results in paper jams.)

Click the Options button to set special printer effects, as shown in Figure 13-4.

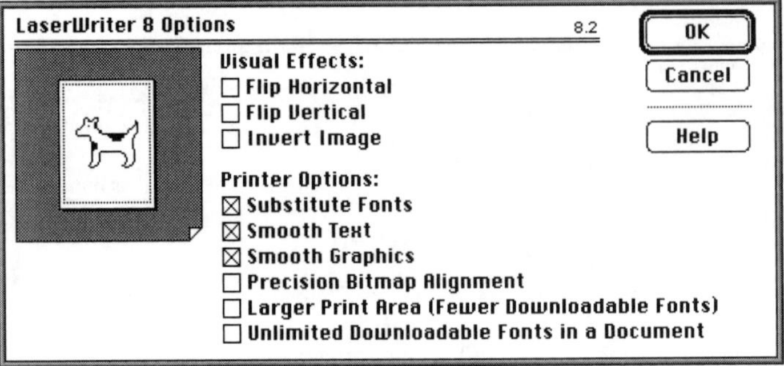

Figure 13-4: Additional LaserWriter printing options

You set most of these options once and never change them, but nothing prevents you from fiddling with them occasionally. Here's how they work:

- *Flip Horizontal:* When this option is checked, the page is inverted left to right, producing a mirror image of the original.
- *Flip Vertical:* Choosing this option inverts the page top to bottom.
- *Invert Image:* This option swaps black to white and white to black. It produces a negative image of the original.
- *Substitute Fonts:* This option enables the Macintosh to supply a different font to the laser printer if the laser version called for in a document isn't available in the system. If this box isn't checked, the Mac will use the *bitmap* version of the font (the one you see on-screen). The text may appear "jaggy," and printing will take longer.
- *Smooth Text:* With this option checked, the Mac applies a special algorithm to text to smooth *jaggies* — those diagonal, staircase-looking edges that mar the appearance of text. Checking this option slows printing a small amount.

- *Smooth Graphics:* This option is similar to Text Smoothing, but it applies to graphics.
- *Precision Bitmap Alignment:* This option attempts to reconcile the mathematical difficulties of printing a 72 dpi bitmap (that is, a screen image) on a 300 dpi printer. In essence, it causes printing at 288 dpi (a 4% reduction).
- *Larger Print Area (Fewer Downloadable Fonts):* This option expands the area available for printing. Laser printers, as a rule, aren't capable of printing all the way to the edge of a page, nor within a certain distance from the top or bottom. Checking this option enlarges the print area, at the expense of printer memory, and hence, decreases the number of fonts that can be used.
- *Unlimited Downloadable Fonts in a Document:* This option enables the Macintosh to supply as many fonts to the printer as the current print job requires. It can slow down printing considerably for documents that use a large number of different fonts in different styles — but that's a design no-no anyway.

After you set all of the Page Setup options for a document, you are ready to print.

At the left side of the initial Page Setup dialog box — as well as the Page Setup Options dialog box — is a small icon of an animal called a *dogcow*. As you set different options, the dogcow shows the effects of your choices.

Moving Up to LaserWriter 8

If you haven't already switched to LaserWriter 8, there are several excellent reasons for doing so. For example, the Print dialog box allows you to select black-and-white, color/grayscale, or calibrated color/grayscale printing. And, unlike earlier versions of the LaserWriter print driver, LaserWriter 8 can display messages (either on-screen or in a detailed printed report) when a PostScript error occurs. LaserWriter 8 can be obtained free from most online information services.

Using a StyleWriter

Choosing Page Setup when you have selected a StyleWriter printer displays a dialog box like the one shown in Figure 13-5.

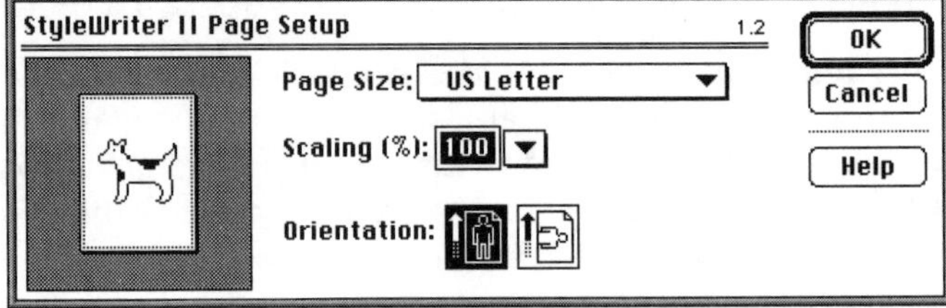

Figure 13-5: The Page Setup dialog box for a StyleWriter

At the top of the dialog box is a Page Size pop-up menu that you use to select the types of paper supported by a StyleWriter (including two envelope styles). In the center is a text box and pop-up menu that you use to set scaling or magnification. You can choose any of the pre-set scaling options from the pop-up menu, or you can type a setting directly into the text box. Acceptable values range from 5 to 999 percent.

At the bottom are a pair of orientation icons. Choose the icon on the left for portrait mode, in which text prints in the usual way. You choose the icon on the right for landscape mode, in which text prints across the long dimension of the paper (sideways). The latter choice is good for fitting wide records or reports onto a single sheet of paper.

Click the OK button to put changes into effect. Click Cancel to dismiss the dialog box without taking action.

Using an ImageWriter

Choosing the Page Setup command when you're using an ImageWriter or another dot-matrix printer that uses the same driver brings up a dialog box shown in Figure 13-6.

ImageWriter 7.0.1
OK
Paper: US Letter
US Legal
Computer Paper
A4 Letter
International Fanfold
Cancel
Orientation
Special Effects: Tall Adjusted
50 % Reduction
No Gaps Between Pages

Figure 13-6: The Page Setup dialog box for an ImageWriter

At the top of this dialog box are radio buttons that you click to indicate the kind of paper you want to use. Note, in particular, the Computer Paper option. Choose this option when you're working with fanfold, tractor-feed paper. This type of paper has perforated, detachable edges with holes in them that guide the paper through the printer.

Below the paper size radio buttons are icons that control the paper's orientation. You have two choices: portrait and landscape. You choose the icon on the left for portrait mode, in which text prints in the usual way. You choose the icon on the right for landscape mode, in which text prints across the long dimension of the paper (sideways). The latter is good for fitting wide records or reports onto a single sheet of paper.

To the right of the paper orientation icons are three check boxes for special printer effects:

- *Tall Adjusted:* Choose this option whenever you are printing graphics. It tells the printer to print the same number of dots per inch horizontally and vertically. If you neglect to choose this option, circles will look like elongated ovals on your printouts, for example.
- *50% Reduction:* This is the only magnification option that is available for an ImageWriter printer. It reduces everything to half its normal size.
- *No Gaps Between Pages:* This option is useful only when you are using continuous feed computer paper. It eliminates top and bottom margins, printing everything on one long sheet. It is especially good for printing banners or spreadsheets in landscape mode.

Click OK to put your changes into effect. Click Cancel to take no action and dismiss the dialog box.

The ImageWriter printer is no longer in production, having been discontinued in favor of the StyleWriter, which is quieter, produces higher-quality printouts, and costs about the same. Even so, many ImageWriters are still in service, and Apple includes print drivers for them with every new release of its system software.

Setting Page Options

No matter what printer you're using — whether it's the latest model or an old standby — you set page options for your printer in the same way. The following procedure describes in general terms how to use the Page Setup dialog box for almost any printer:

1. Open the document that you want to print (a FileMaker Pro database, for example).
2. Choose Page Setup from the File menu.

   A Page Setup dialog box appears that corresponds to the printer you selected in the Chooser.
3. Select the size of paper that you are using (from a pop-up menu or set of radio buttons).

   The standard choice in the United States is US Letter (8 1/2" x 11" paper).
4. Choose the paper orientation.

   Click the left icon, which has an image of an upright torso, to choose portrait mode. Portrait mode is the standard way of printing. Click the right icon, which has an image of a sideways torso, to choose landscape mode. Landscape mode prints sideways on the paper.
5. Select a magnification level to use or leave this option at 100% to print at the standard size.
6. Choose any special printer effects that are relevant to the print job.
7. Click OK.

If you always intend to print information from this document or database on the same kind of paper, in the same orientation, and at the same size, you need to configure Page Setup only once. You do not need to choose it every time you want to print a report. Remember, however, that the Page Setup options you just selected are specific to this document or database; they have no effect on how any other document or database will print.

Readying a Report for Printing

With the preliminaries out of the way, you can get down to brass tacks. Before you can print a report, you need to prepare the report. You learned all about reports in Chapter 12, but you can refresh your memory of the basics by reading the following sections.

Selecting and Sorting

You will seldom print the entire contents of a database. To print many organizational databases, you would hog a printer the whole day and spend most of your time feeding it paper. And you wouldn't be too popular with your coworkers and whoever orders supplies.

Printing only a selection of the information that is contained in a database is much more common than printing the entire database. (Actually, the only reason to print the entire contents of most databases is to have a paper, backup copy of the file's contents in case disaster strikes. Even then, several strategically located disk copies of the database are probably more useful.) The records you choose to print depend on the nature of your report.

Consider this example. Susan is head of sales at a small company, and she has access to a FileMaker Pro database that contains records for every sales transaction. The database includes a field that shows which salesperson is responsible for each transaction. Susan wants to see how Guy — a member of her sales team — has been doing lately.

All Susan needs to do is open the database and issue a find request to locate all records in which Guy's name appears in the Salesperson field. She switches to Find mode and enters **=Guy =Smith** into the Salesperson field on the find request. To restrict things further, she also places **≥1/1/96** in the Date field to limit the search to sales from the current calendar year.

After using Find mode to select a relevant group of records, the next step is to arrange them in a useful order. Susan uses the Sort command to arrange the records in descending order based on the amount of each sale. This sort puts the largest transaction first. Finally, Susan chooses a layout that shows only the information she needs. In this case, she selects a layout that includes a Summary field, one that will show the total of Guy's sales this year (so she won't have to add them manually).

Following are the general steps necessary to prepare a report from a database:

1. Within FileMaker Pro, open the database that contains the information from which you want to prepare a report.
2. Use Find mode to issue one or more find requests to locate the records that you want to use as part of the report.
3. Use the Sort command from the Mode menu (or press ⌘-S) to arrange the found set in a convenient order.
4. From the layout pop-up menu, choose an appropriate layout in which to display the report.
5. Preview or print the report.

Previewing Before Printing

More paper has been wasted because of minor problems with a document's appearance than because of any other problem. Much of this paper waste could be avoided by previewing documents on-screen prior to printing them. Admittedly, checking them isn't always easy (or even possible) in all Macintosh applications. FileMaker Pro, however, has a Preview mode that enables you to see the potential results of any print job.

To switch to Preview mode, choose it from the mode selector pop-up menu or from the Mode menu (or press ⌘-U). You see a view that is similar to Figure 13-7, which shows the Phone Directory layout of the Address Book database in Preview mode.

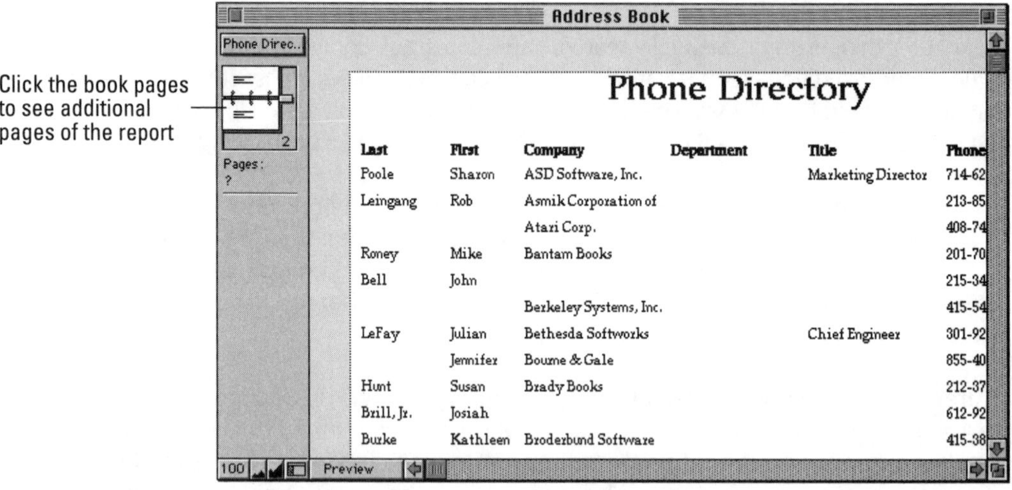

Figure 13-7: An Address Book layout in Preview mode

In this view, output is divided into pages. To see additional pages, click the book icon. Use the scroll bars to move around in the view and check its contents. If you want to find out the total number of pages in the report, drag the bookmark to the bottom of the book icon. (FileMaker Pro doesn't know how many pages the report contains until you perform this action or click through all the book pages.)

If your report looks satisfactory and you want a permanent copy of it, you can print it by choosing Print from the File menu. If problems are detected in Preview mode, you have several options. If the problem is just a case of getting everything to fit, you may be able to cheat by adjusting the scaling or magnification in the Page Setup dialog box. This solution isn't the best choice if you're preparing presentation copies of reports, however.

For more serious Preview problems, you may need to go back to Layout mode and make adjustments. Omitting unnecessary fields is often a good idea — doing so provides more room for relevant data. (Consult Chapter 12 for more information on the art of preparing reports, including tweaking the layout and creating new, report-specific layouts.)

The following steps explain how to use Preview mode and what to do if a report is less than perfect:

1. Prepare a report according to the steps presented in "Selecting and Sorting," earlier in this chapter.
2. Choose Preview mode from the Mode menu (or press ⌘-U).
3. Click the book icon to view the pages of the report.
4. Use the scroll bars to move around on each page if the screen isn't large enough to display the entire page.

   You can also drag the window's size box to increase the viewing area.
5. Review each page carefully to ensure that all data fits without running off the edge. Also check for other problems, such as data within fields that is being truncated.
6. Correct errors in Layout mode or by setting different options in the Page Setup dialog box.

When the report appears satisfactory, you are ready to print.

Printing

Printing should seem like a breeze after all the preparatory work. You accomplish the act of printing a report in FileMaker Pro by choosing the Print command from the File menu. Or, as in most Macintosh programs, you can press ⌘-P to print.

The Print Command

Choosing the Print command (or pressing ⌘-P) displays a Print dialog box. The exact appearance of the dialog box may vary, depending on which printer you have chosen. The following sections examine the Print dialog boxes for the most common printer types.

The Print Command — LaserWriter

When you are using a LaserWriter and choose the Print command, you are presented with a dialog box that is similar to the one shown in Figure 13-8.

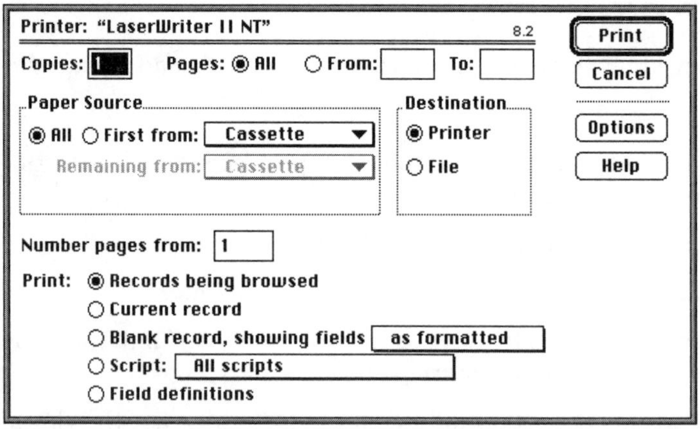

Figure 13-8: The Print dialog box for a LaserWriter

In the upper-left corner is a text box into which you enter the number of copies that you want to print.

Next to the Copies text box are controls for designating which pages to print. Click the radio button of your choice. If you want to print a range of pages rather than the entire report, enter the appropriate numbers in the From and To text boxes (for example, enter **2** in the From box and **4** in the To box to print pages 2 through 4).

Next is a series of radio buttons that control how the print job is performed:

- *Paper Source:* You use this option to designate whether paper will be drawn from the printer's internal paper cassette or fed by hand. The Manual Feed option is not useful for long reports, but you can use it to print a single envelope or piece of letterhead, for example. Envelopes are best fed manually unless you have a special envelope cassette.
- *Destination:* Choose Printer to send the job directly to the printer that you have chosen. Choosing File creates a PostScript file into which the print job is spooled. You can send such a file to a service bureau for printing on a high-end imagesetter. (Note, however, that this is seldom done with a database. Generating print files is more commonly done with illustrations and desktop publishing files.)

You can set three more print options by clicking the Options button:

- *Cover Page:* You use this option to designate whether to include a cover page as part of the print job and whether to place the cover page at the beginning or end of the report. A cover page is useful if you're printing on a network printer and want to make sure that your print job is properly identified. Your user name, the name of the document you're printing, and the number of pages appear on the cover page.
- *Print:* Choose Black & White for text-only reports — it's faster. Choose Color/Grayscale or Calibrated Color/Grayscale if you're including graphics.
- *PostScript Errors:* You can use this option to select one of the following notification methods should an error occur during a print job: No Special Reporting (nothing happens), Summarize on Screen (a dialog box appears), or Print Detailed Report (an error report is sent to the printer).

At the bottom of the dialog box are options that are specific to FileMaker Pro. The "Number pages from" text box enables you to enter the number to use for the first page of the printout. For example, you would enter a number other than 1 if you were preparing one grand document from several smaller reports. In this case, you would let FileMaker Pro know to begin numbering each report section where the previous section left off.

Finally, the Print dialog box has several radio buttons that control exactly what portion of the current FileMaker Pro database prints:

- *Records being browsed:* Prints the current found set in the current sort order.
- *Current record*: Prints only one record — the one currently visible on-screen.
- *Blank record, showing fields:* Prints an empty record. You choose from the pop-up menu to determine what kind of border to put around each field (as formatted in the layout, boxed, or underlined).
- *Script:* Prints a particular script or all scripts. Choose the script you want to print from the pop-up menu. All scripts that are defined for the current database are listed. Choose All Scripts to print all currently defined scripts for the database.
- *Field definitions:* Prints the field definitions for this database.

The latter three print options are excellent tools for documenting a database and its logic.

When you have made your selections in the Print dialog box, click Print to print the material, or click Cancel if you change your mind.

The Print Command — StyleWriter

When you are using a StyleWriter and you choose the Print command, you see the dialog box shown in Figure 13-9.

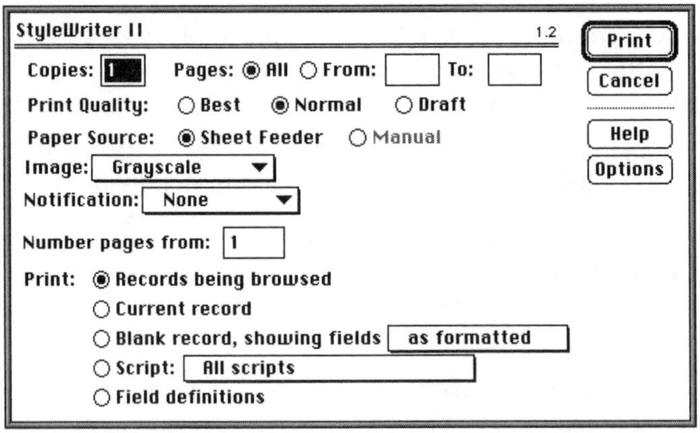

Figure 13-9: The Print dialog box for a StyleWriter

Many options are the same as those shown for the LaserWriter (see "The Print Command — LaserWriter"). In addition, the StyleWriter enables you to set the print quality. You use Best for high quality and Normal for lower quality but speedier printing. The Stylewriter also offers a Draft option that uses a built-in font for very fast printing (but often with strange results).

You can also choose between black-and-white and grayscale printouts and, if you click the Options button, you can instruct the printer to clean its cartridge before the print job commences.

The Print Command — ImageWriter

When you are using an ImageWriter and you choose the Print command, you see the dialog box shown in Figure 13-10.

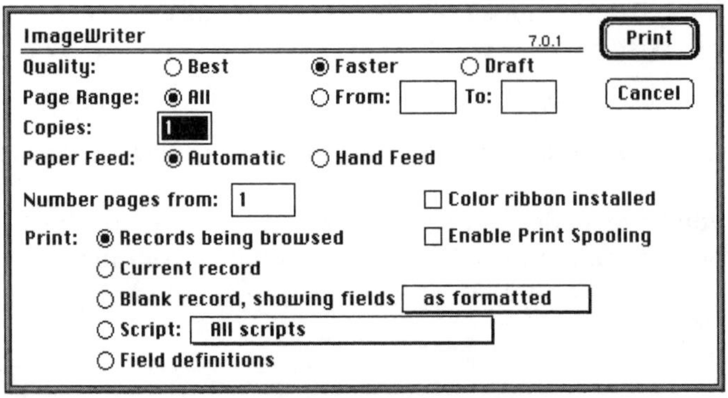

Figure 13-10: The Print dialog box for an ImageWriter

Many options are the same as those shown for the LaserWriter (see "The Print Command — LaserWriter"). In addition, the ImageWriter enables you to set the print quality. You use Best for high quality and Faster for lower quality but speedier printing. The ImageWriter also offers a Draft print quality option. Draft uses a built-in font and is very fast, but it can produce strange results. In general, this setting is not appropriate for most FileMaker Pro documents.

The ImageWriter dialog box also has options that you can use to indicate whether you are using a color ribbon and whether you want the computer to spool documents to memory prior to printing (that is, whether you want the job to print in the background so you can continue to do other work on your Mac).

The Print Procedure

Follow these general steps to print from FileMaker Pro:

1. Choose Print from the File menu (or press ⌘-P).
2. Enter the number of copies to print, if more than one.
3. Select whether to print the entire report or a range of pages.

   If you do not want to print the entire report, enter the first and last page numbers of the range.
4. *Optional:* To include a cover page, click Options and indicate whether it should come at the beginning or end of the print job.
5. Select whether to restrict printing to black-and-white or to print in color or grayscale (by clicking Options in the LaserWriter Print dialog box or by choosing an option from the StyleWriter's Image pop-up menu).
6. Choose the destination for the print job: the chosen printer or a file on disk (LaserWriter).
7. Choose a print quality level (ImageWriter or StyleWriter).
8. Select a paper source.
9. Choose what to print by using the radio button options at the bottom of the dialog box.
10. Click Print.

To cancel a print job as it's being sent to your printer (regardless of the type of printer you are using), press ⌘-period (.). If your print driver supports background printing (a LaserWriter, for example) and you have selected that option in the Chooser, you need to press ⌘-period (.) very quickly — before the print job has spooled to disk. If you aren't fast enough, you can use PrintMonitor (discussed in the next section) to cancel the print job.

Bypassing the Print Dialog Box

As is quite evident in this chapter, using the Print dialog box involves many steps. However, FileMaker Pro also enables you to print without even bringing up the Print dialog box. In this case, all of the Print dialog box's default choices are used.

To bypass the Print dialog box, press Option-⌘-P. An alert box appears briefly, telling you what's to be printed.

Printing in the Background with PrintMonitor

If you're using a laser printer and have chosen to print in the background, you will have occasion to deal with PrintMonitor. This Apple system software utility automatically runs when you send something to the printer and monitors printing while you go on with your work. In System 7, PrintMonitor can be chosen from the Application menu at the far right side of the menu bar. (See your Macintosh owner's manual or your system software manual for more information about the Application menu.) Figure 13-11 shows PrintMonitor in action.

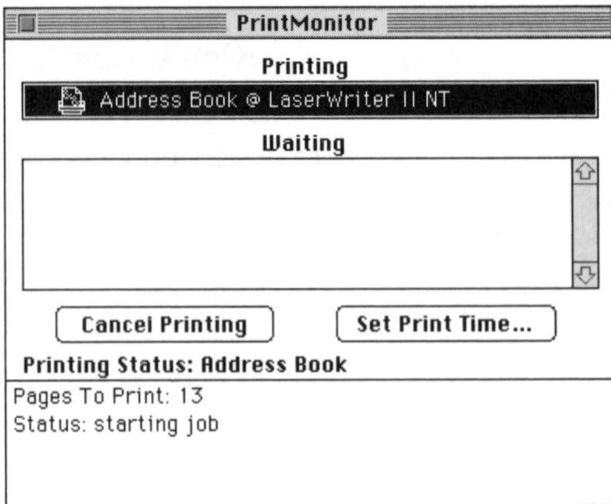

Figure 13-11: PrintMonitor with a job in progress

PrintMonitor is used *only* in conjunction with background printing. Printers that do not have drivers that support background printing must print in the foreground. That is, while a document is printing on such a printer, you must wait for it to finish before regaining control of your Mac.

An area at the top of the PrintMonitor window shows which document is currently being printed, as well as the name of the chosen printer. Below this area is a list of any other documents that are waiting to be printed. If there are many jobs, you can use the scroll bar to examine them and their positions in the list. The two buttons enable you to cancel a print job or set a specific time to have a job printed. Finally, a message area at the bottom of the window tells you what the printer is doing at the moment.

If you have any print jobs waiting, you can drag them into different positions to change the order in which they will be printed. To postpone a job until a specific time, select its name and then click Set Print Time. In the dialog box that appears, enter the time and date that you want the document to be printed. For example, you may want to choose a time when the office is closed if you're in a busy office, have trouble getting access to the network printer, or don't need your printout right away. This option is especially useful if you're printing a very large report. Delaying such a job until after hours shows consideration for the needs of your coworkers and avoids the problems caused by having the only network printer tied up for a long time.

In the Set Print Time dialog box, you can also postpone a job indefinitely. PrintMonitor will hold the job until you choose PrintMonitor from the Application menu again and select Set Print Time. The default time that is presented is always the current time, so you need only click OK to print the job.

Perhaps the most common reason to use PrintMonitor is to cancel a print job. To cancel a background print job with PrintMonitor, follow these steps:

1. Choose PrintMonitor from the Application menu.
2. If the print job isn't the one that is currently printing, click to select the job.
3. Click the Cancel Printing button.

   The Macintosh may take a few seconds to respond.

The recently released LaserWriter 8.3 software includes a new, more powerful version of PrintMonitor that places an icon with your printer's name on the Mac's desktop. Instead of choosing PrintMonitor from the Application menu, you just double-click the new icon. Print jobs can also be initiated by dragging documents onto the icon.

Effective Printing

The preceding information is all you need to know about run-of-the-mill printing. However, the following tips and tricks are useful if you want to get the most out of your printer. What's more, you will likely run into occasional problems. The section on troubleshooting outlines some of the most common problems and provides some solutions to them.

Tips and Tricks

Every type of printer has some quirks. Understanding the more common idiosyncrasies and knowing how to deal with them can not only save you a great deal of grief, but can also help you achieve better results. The following basic hints apply to the most common kinds of printers.

Laser Printers

- *Sunny side up:* Not many people are aware that most laser printer paper (and copier paper, which is the same thing and is frequently used in place of laser paper) has a good side and a so-so side. The paper's manufacturer intends for the paper to be printed only on the good side. You can achieve the best results by making sure that you print on the correct side.

  Sometimes, you cannot easily determine which side is the good side by just looking at the paper. The good side *may* be shinier. A better way to tell is to look at the package in which the paper came. In many cases, you'll see an arrow or some other indicator that shows which side is meant to be printed on. When inserting the paper into your printer, be sure that the correct side is up. (Some printers expect paper to be inserted face up, while others print on the side of the paper that is face down. If you aren't sure which way you should insert paper into your printer, refer to the printer manual.)

- *We be jammin':* Everybody hates paper jams and misfeeds. You can't avoid them all, but you can cut down on their number and frequency. When you load a printer, grasp the paper firmly and "riffle" the edges with your thumb. (Draw your thumb down the edges as if you were flipping through the whole stack of paper.) This action loosens the individual sheets from each other, lessening the chance that two or more pieces of paper will be drawn into the printer together.

- *Fontasies can come true:* A laser printer takes a long time to do two things: construct a font for use in a document and prepare a graphic. You can save time by using only fonts that are built into the printer or are available on a printer's dedicated hard disk. (The printer doesn't have to construct these fonts.) Also, try to limit the number of different text styles that you use. Using too many fonts makes documents print slowly and can, in extreme cases, even crash the system or the printer.

- *You only go 'round once:* Several companies (such as Avery) make special labels for use in laser printers. Resist the temptation to use only a few labels from one sheet and then reuse the sheet later. After a few passes, the extreme heat of the laser printing process can cause the remaining labels to start peeling off the sheet during printing, resulting in no end of expensive trouble. Try to do label printing jobs in large batches and throw away the unused labels from each batch (or find another use for them).
- *Is it just me, or is it warm in here?:* If your printer has been turned off, be sure to allow enough time for it to warm up. If you try to print immediately after you turn it on, you will likely see a message telling you that the printer isn't responding. Give it a minute or so before you try again.

Dot-Matrix Printers

- *Don't be uptight:* When you are using tractor-fed computer paper, make sure that the tension is adjusted correctly between the two feed mechanisms. Too little tension can cause the paper to jam and misfeed; too much tension can tear off the perforated edges and cause another kind of misfeed. Getting the tension exactly right is something of an art.
- *Back in the black:* Use only new ribbons and keep them well inked. Old ribbons can fray, resulting in ugly printouts and possible damage to the print head.

Ink-Jet Printers

- *Ink-a-dink:* Avoid printing long reports that have a large number of graphics. Graphics consume a great deal of expensive ink and take longer to print.
- *Time on my hands:* To speed up printing, limit the number of fonts in the report. You may also want to select a lower print quality for jobs that will not be used for presentations.

Troubleshooting

Things go wrong. Here's some common printing problems and what to do if you encounter them:

- *My printer doesn't do anything:* Is it turned off (the #1 cause of missed print jobs)? Are cable connections snug and secure? With printers such as the StyleWriter and ImageWriter, be sure that the correct port is selected in the Chooser.

- *The laser printer isn't visible in the Chooser:* Is your printer properly hooked up? Again, make sure that all cables are secure and tight. If you are printing to a network laser printer, see if it is connected correctly to the network. Is the printer on-line (turned on) and warmed up? Has the network gone down?
- *The print quality seems poor:* Does your laser printer need more toner, does your StyleWriter need more ink, or does your ImageWriter need a new ribbon? Failure to print dense, even, black tones can be caused by any of these situations. You can temporarily correct this problem on a laser printer by gently rotating the toner cartridge a few times or increasing the print density setting (if the printer has one). With the StyleWriter and ImageWriter, change the Print Quality setting to Best.
- *Laser printing is taking too long:* Is the printer hung up? Try turning off the printer, waiting a few seconds, and then restarting it. You will have to use PrintMonitor to restart the job.

  Occasionally, some print jobs may simply be too complex for your laser printer to handle. Try reprinting them with different print options, printing a smaller set of pages, or turning off background printing. This may help you isolate the cause of the problem.
- *Fields are trailing off the page:* You need to change the magnification, select a new layout, or make layout changes to accommodate the fields. Be sure to use Preview before you print.

Summary

- Before you can print, you need to use the Chooser desk accessory to tell the Mac which printer you want to use. Once a print driver and printer have been selected, all future print jobs will be sent to that printer. If you have just one printer, you will only need to use the Chooser again if you reinstall or update your system software, buy a new printer, or obtain a newer version of your printer's print driver. If you have several printers, you must revisit the Chooser whenever you want to send a job to a different printer.
- In the Page Setup dialog box, you set page options for the document you're about to print. These options include the kind of paper you want to use, the amount of scaling (if any), and whether to employ special effects, such as inversion or printing continuous sheets. Page Setup settings are document-specific and are saved along with the other information contained in the document.
- You can use Preview mode to view a report on-screen. This mode shows how the report will look when you print it. You can correct problems at this stage before you waste time and paper.
- Printing is accomplished via the Print dialog box. You can use it to set the number of copies to print; which pages to print; whether to use color or grays (if your printer can handle them); and exactly what database contents to print, including the current record, the found set, scripts, and field definitions.
- To print directly (without using the Print dialog box), press ⌘-Option-P.
- You can avoid many potential printing problems by setting up a printer correctly before you print. Checking the integrity of all cable connections, loading paper the right way, and restricting the use of fonts and graphics can ensure better results.

Putting FileMaker Pro to Work

This section helps you make more productive use of FileMaker Pro. It explains creating formulas for Calculation fields, automating FileMaker Pro with scripts and buttons, creating and using database templates, and designing help systems for templates.

Calculations and Computations

14

CHAPTER

In This Chapter

- Understanding Calculation fields and their uses
- Creating Calculation fields
- Using algebraic, logical, and other operations in Calculation fields
- Learning about FileMaker Pro's built-in functions

The ability to perform calculations on the contents of database fields gives modern database programs (such as FileMaker Pro) extraordinary power and flexibility. For example, in an invoice database, where each record is an order, you can total all the item prices and compute the sales tax. If the cost of shipping varies according to distance, you can determine how much to charge each order, based on its state of destination. FileMaker Pro offers a variety of computational capabilities to make these and similar tasks easy.

You use a *Calculation field* to perform a specific operation or group of operations on specific data within a record. The operations that you can perform include the standard arithmetic functions, logical operations, and even special operations that perform complex calculations on numbers and text.

In addition to dozens of new FileMaker Pro 3.0 functions that can be used to define Calculation fields, you can now auto-enter data into almost any field type based on the result of a calculation.

About Calculation Fields

Like any field in FileMaker Pro, a Calculation field has two aspects: its definition and the data it contains. The *data* in a Calculation field consists of whatever result is obtained when the field's definition is evaluated. The *definition* specifies, in mathematical form, what manipulations to perform on the contents of one or more other fields in the current record. The results of these manipulations, or operations, are then displayed as the field's contents.

Consider a brief example. Suppose that you have an invoice database that has a field named Merchandise Total. You want to compute the sales tax on this total and display the grand total for the bill (the merchandise total plus the sales tax). You could use Calculation fields for both the sales tax and the grand total, in which case, the field definitions might look like this:

```
Sales Tax = Merchandise Total * .06 [Multiply total by tax rate]

Grand Total = Merchandise Total + Sales Tax [Add tax to total]
```

If the current record shows a Merchandise Total of 23.75, the Sales Tax field would display 1.425, and the Grand Total would display 25.175. Of course, you would want to round this figure off to the nearest cent before presenting a bill. FileMaker Pro enables you to round numbers easily, as you will see shortly.

Calculation fields are similar to Summary fields. There is one important difference, however. Summary formulas are calculated across a *series* of records, while the Calculation field formulas apply only to data in each *individual* record. For example, if you want to compute the total sales for all the invoices issued over a certain span of time, you define a Summary field, but to calculate the merchandise total within an invoice, you use a Calculation field.

Calculation fields can do much more than just add or multiply the contents of other fields. Calculation fields can also manipulate the contents of Text fields and can perform tests on the contents of fields in order to determine which alternative course of action to select.

A formula in a Calculation field can contain several different components: field references, operators, constants, and built-in functions. You should have a basic understanding of these components before you begin creating Calculation fields.

FileMaker Pro 3.0 does not restrict the use of formulas to Calculation fields. Formulas can also be used to validate field data as it is entered or edited, as information to be "auto-entered" into fields, and as components of scripts. For information on using formulas for data validation or auto-entry, see Chapter 5. For details on using formulas in ScriptMaker scripts, refer to Chapter 15.

Available Operations

FileMaker Pro uses operators to specify how to manipulate data items. Operators fall into three broad categories:

- *Arithmetic operators* are used to perform computations on numbers.
- *Logical operators* test to see whether specified conditions are true or false; this information can then be used to determine a course of action.
- *Text operators* work with text, extracting information from it or converting it to another form.

Arithmetic Operations

The arithmetic operators in Table 14-1 perform the basic functions of arithmetic.

Table 14-1
Arithmetic Operators

Operator	*What It Means*
+	The plus sign performs addition. (For example, *2 + 3* yields *5*.)
–	The minus sign performs subtraction. (For example, *3 – 2* yields *1*.)
*	The asterisk indicates multiplication. (For example, *2 * 3* yields *6*.)
/	The slash indicates division. (For example, *3 / 2* yields *1.5*.)
^	The caret indicates exponentiation, raising a number to a power. (For example, *3 ^ 2* yields three to the second power, or *9*.)

Logical Operations

The logical operators perform comparisons. If necessary, you can combine the results into more complex tests. Basically, the logical operators are used to test whether a statement is true or false. Here's an example:

```
1 = 2 [one equals two]
```

This statement is false; one does not equal two.

Here's a more practical example:

```
Bob's Sales > Anne's Sales [Bob's sales exceed Anne's sales]
```

You don't know whether this statement is true because you don't know how much Bob or Anne sold. If Bob's sales equaled 1500 and Anne's sales equaled 1000, then the statement would be true. If the figures were reversed, or if their sales were equal, the statement would be false.

Why should you care? Because you can have a Calculation field perform additional steps that are based on whether a statement is true or false. For example, you might use the following formula in the Calculation field to present a different message (a Text result) depending on which salesperson closed the most sales:

```
If (Bob Sales > Anne Sales, "Nice going, Bob!", "Nice going, Anne!")
```

If Bob's sales totaled more than Anne's sales, the Calculation field displays the true condition for the test (that is, the first message: "Nice going, Bob!"). On the other hand, if Bob's sales were not greater than Anne's, the field displays the false condition for the test (that is, the second message: "Nice going, Anne!"). You will learn more about using logical operators to perform tasks such as this as the chapter progresses. (Pay particular attention to the section on the IF function.)

Table 14-2 lists the logical operators and their meanings.

Table 14-2
Logical Operators

Operator	*What It Means*
=	Means "equals." The test is true if the items on either side of the sign are exactly equal in value. For example, the statement *1 + 1 = 2* is true.
<> or ≠	Means "not equal to." The test is true if the items on the two sides of the sign are not equal in value. For example, *"Bob" <> "Anne"* is true.

Operator	***What It Means***
>	Means "greater than." The test is true if the value of the item at the left of the sign exceeds the value of item to the right. For example, *3 > 2* is true.
<	Means "less than." The test is true if the value of the item at the left of the sign is smaller than the value of the item to the right. For example, *2 < 3* is true.
≤	Means "less than or equal to." For example, *2.9 + 0.1 ≤ 3* is true.
≥	Means "greater than or equal to." For example, *2.9 + 1.5 ≥ 3* is true.
AND	Used to combine the results of two separate tests. The result is true if, and only if, the results of both tests are true. For example, *3 > 2 AND 2 < 3* is true.
OR	Used to combine the results of two separate tests. The result is true if either, or both, of the tests are also true. For example, *3 > 2 OR 2 > 3* is true.
NOT	Used to switch a test's result to its opposite. For example, *NOT 2 > 3* is true.

You can type the less than or equal to (≤), greater than or equal to (≥), and not equal (≠) symbols by pressing Option-<, Option->, and Option-=, respectively.

Text Operations

Table 14-3 lists the three basic text operators.

Table 14-3
Basic Text Operators

Operator	***What It Means***
&	Used to combine (or *concatenate*) two Text fields into one. For example, *"market" & "place" = "marketplace"*.
" "	Used to indicate a text constant. If you enter a text item without quotes, FileMaker Pro assumes that you mean the name of a field. *"Anne" + Last Name = Anne Jones,* if the Last Name field in the current record contains *Jones*.

¶	Used to indicate a paragraph break within a text constant. If you want a constant to have more than one line, you need to use this operator to separate the lines. (The symbol must be enclosed within the quotation marks of the text constant.) For example, *"Anne¶Jones"* yields the following:
	`Anne`
	`Jones`

Creating an Expression

Operators are combined with constants (numeric or text) and field names to create *expressions.* Think of an expression as a mathematical statement. From an earlier example, both of the following are statements:

```
Sales Tax = .06 * Merchandise Total
Grand Total = Merchandise Total + Sales Tax
```

The sales tax rate, *.06*, is a numeric constant; its value does not change. *Merchandise Total* represents the contents of that field in the current record; it may very well change from record to record. If you recall your high school or college algebra, you will recognize Merchandise Total (or any valid field name) as a *variable.* Expressions consist of constants and variables that are separated by operators.

You can build complicated expressions if you wish. For example, consider the following expression:

```
1 + 2 * 3
```

FileMaker Pro evaluates according to the standard algebraic order of operations, which specifies that all multiplications are done *before* any additions. The result for this expression is 7, not 9, which you might expect if all operations were performed strictly in left-to-right order.

To force FileMaker Pro to perform operations in the order that you want, you can use parentheses. Operations within parentheses are performed first, from innermost to outermost. You can nest operations within parentheses to gain further control. For example, the following expression yields 18:

```
((( 1 + 2 ) * 3 ) * 2 )
```

Without parentheses, it would equal 13.

The standard order of operations is as follows:

1. Exponentiation
2. Multiplication and division
3. Addition and subtraction

You also can use parentheses with logical expressions. For example, the following expression is true:

```
(3 > 2 OR 2 > 3) AND 2 > 1
```

Creating a Calculation Field

To create a Calculation field, you decide what type of results you want, determine the necessary expression, and then define the field. After you create the Calculation field in the Define Fields dialog box, you see an additional dialog box that is similar to Figure 14-1.

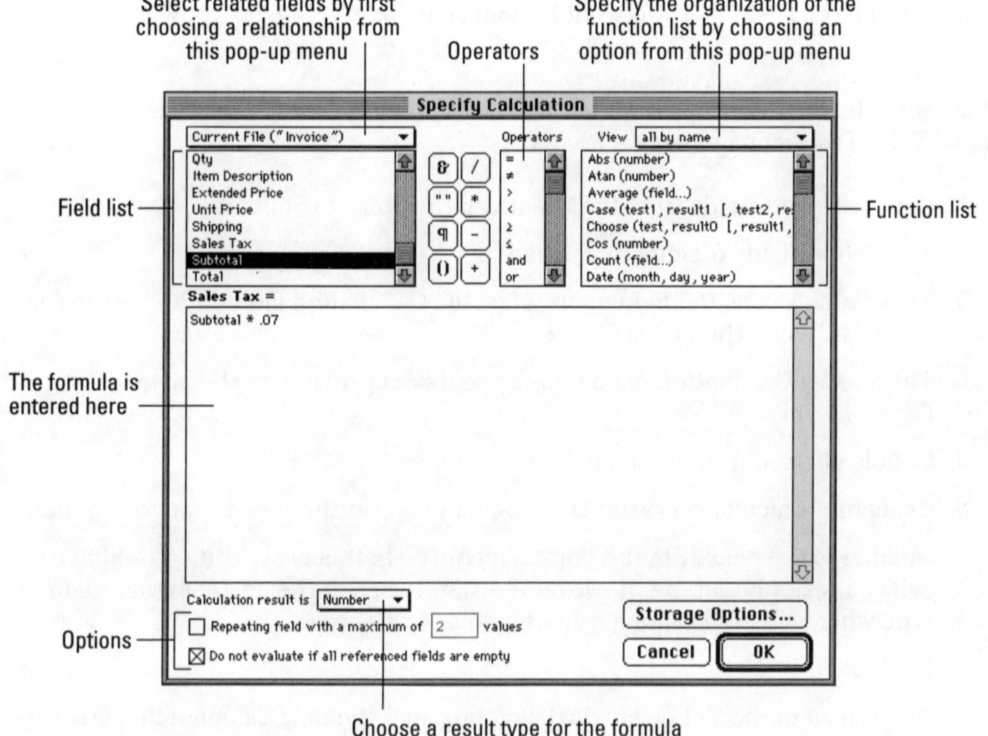

Figure 14-1: Defining a Calculation field

The fields available in the current database appear in a scrolling list at the left. If you want to use fields in a related file in the equation, choose the appropriate relationship from the pop-up menu above the field list.

In the center of the dialog box are the available operators. To the right are the FileMaker Pro functions. You'll learn more about functions in the next section. For now, you only need to know that a *function* is a predefined set of operations that work with specific kinds of data. A function operates on the data, known as the function's *arguments*, and then returns a result.

Beneath these sections is a large blank area. As you create the formula for the Calculation field, it appears in this area. You can type the formula directly or simply choose the appropriate field names, operators, and functions (by clicking or double-clicking them). Below this area, a pop-up menu indicates what type of data the field's result should be. You must select the correct result type. The check boxes and buttons in this section of the dialog box enable you to set storage options for the field, designate it as a repeating field (used in invoice line items, for example), and tell FileMaker Pro what to do if all fields referenced in the formula are empty.

As an example, the following steps show how to define a new Calculation field named Sales Tax that calculates a 7% tax:

1. Choose Define Fields from the File menu (or press ⌘-Shift-D).

   The Define Fields dialog box appears.

2. Type **Sales Tax** as the field name, click the Calculation Field radio button (or press ⌘-C), and then click Create.

   The Specify Calculation dialog box appears (as previously shown in Figure 14-1).

3. Double-click Subtotal in the field list and then type *** .07**.

4. Using the "Calculation result is" pop-up menu, set the result type to Number.

   Number is the default in the pop-up menu, so in this case, you do not have to select a result data type. However, be sure to select the correct result data type when you are creating other Calculation fields.

5. Click OK.

   You return to the Define Fields dialog box, and the new Calculation field appears in the box.

In addition to these two *required* procedures (specifying a formula and setting a result type), there are several options that you can set (shown at the bottom of the Specify Calculation dialog box):

- *Repeating field with a maximum of* [x] *values.* You can define the Calculation field as a repeating field by clicking the first check box. An Extended Price field that multiplies the Item Price by the Quantity Ordered for each line item in an invoice is one example of a repeating Calculation field. When defining a field as repeating, you must also enter the maximum number of times it can repeat within each record.

- *Do not evaluate if all referenced fields are empty.* When checked, this option prevents the calculation of a result for the current record when all fields referenced in the formula have no value.
- *Storage Options.* Click the Storage Options button to display the Storage Options for Field *[field name]* dialog box (see Figure 14-2). This dialog box enables you to turn indexing on or off for the field as well as to instruct FileMaker Pro whether to store the results of the calculations as part of the database.

If you intend to frequently sort by the results of this field or perform find requests using this field as the search criterion, you may want to turn indexing on by clicking the On radio button. If disk space is at a premium or this field must be recalculated often, you may want to click the "Do not store calculation results — calculate only when needed" check box.

Storage Options for Field "Sales Tax"

Indexing and storing the results of a calculation improves performance of some operations like finds at the cost of increased file size and time spent indexing.

Indexing: ( ) On

(•) Off [X] Automatically turn indexing on if needed

[ ] Do not store calculation results -- calculate only when needed

Default language for indexing and sorting text: English

Cancel OK

Figure 14-2: Setting storage options for a Calculation field

You can examine a range of already-defined Calculation fields by looking at the templates and example files that are included with FileMaker Pro. With any of these databases open, choose Define Fields from the File menu (or press ⌘-Shift-D). The dialog box will show the definitions for all of the Calculation fields in the database. If you can't see the entire formula for any field, simply select it and click the Options button.

About FileMaker Pro's Built-In Functions

FileMaker Pro includes dozens of predefined functions that you can use in defining formulas for Calculation fields. The purpose of each of these functions is described in Table 14-4.

The names of the functions that are new in FileMaker Pro 3.0 are shown in **boldface**.

Table 14-4
FileMaker Pro's Built-In Functions

Function Name	*Purpose*
Abs	Calculates the absolute value of an expression
Atan	Calculates the arc tangent of an expression, in radians
Average	Computes the average value of all values in one or more fields
Case	Performs a series of tests and selects one answer (or the default answer, if no test is found to be true)
Choose	Selects one answer from a series
Cos	Calculates the cosine of an expression, in radians
Count	Counts the number of valid, non-empty entries in one or more fields
Date	Converts a numeric value into a valid date
DateToText	Converts a value in a Date field to text
Day	Displays the day of the month, 1 – 31, for a given date
DayName	Displays the weekday name for a given date
DayofWeek	Displays the number of the day within a week, 1 – 7, for a given date
DayofYear	Displays the number of the day within a year, 1 – 366, for a given date
Degrees	Converts a value in radians into degrees
Exact	Returns "true" if two text expressions match exactly (including case)
Exp	Returns the antilog (base *e*) of an expression
Extend	Makes a non-repeating field a repeating field (with the identical value in each place) for use in calculations with other repeating fields
FV	Computes an investment's future value for a given payment amount, interest rate, and number of periods
GetRepetition	Presents the contents of a particular repetition in a repeating field
GetSummary	Calculates the value of a particular Summary field when the database has been sorted by the specified break field
Hour	Displays the number of hours in a time expression
If	Performs a logical test and completes one action if it is true, another if it is false
Int	Returns the integer portion of a numeric value
IsEmpty	Determines whether a value or field is blank

Function Name	*Purpose*
IsValid	Determines whether a related field can be found and contains valid data, and whether a related file can be found
Last	Shows the last valid, non-empty entry in a repeating field
Left	Returns the specified number of characters of a text string, counting from the left
LeftWords	Returns the specified number of words from a text string, counting from the left
Length	Finds the number of characters in a given text string
Ln	Computes the natural (base e) logarithm of an expression
Log	Computes the common (base 10) logarithm of an expression
Lower	Converts a text string to all lowercase
Max	Displays the greatest value among those in specified fields
Middle	Returns the middle portion of a supplied text string, starting at a given position and extending a specified number of characters
MiddleWords	Returns the specified number of words from a text string, counting from the specified starting word
Min	Displays the smallest value among those in specified fields
Minute	Returns the minute portion of a time expression
Mod	Returns the remainder when an expression is divided by a given number
Month	Displays the number of the month in a date expression, within the range 1 – 12
MonthName	Displays the name of month in a date expression
NPV	Finds the net present value of an investment, using values in repeating fields as unequal payment values and the given interest rate
NumToText	Converts a numeric expression to text format
PatternCount	Returns the number of instances of a specified text string found within another text string or field
Pi	Returns the value of the mathematical constant pi
PMT	Calculates a loan payment, using the given principal, interest rate, and term
Position	Scans text for the specified string starting at the given position and returns the location of the first occurrence of the string
Proper	Converts the first letter of each word in the text string to uppercase (used to capitalize names, for example)
PV	Calculates the present value of an investment, using a given payment amount, interest rate, and periods
Radians	Converts a degree value to radians (for use with trigonometric functions)

(continued)

Table 14.4 *(continued)*

Function Name	*Purpose*
Random	Generates a random number
Replace	In a text string, starts at the given position, moves the specified number of places, and replaces the existing text with the specified new text string
Right	Counting from the right, returns a given number of characters in a text expression
RightWords	Returns the specified number of words from a text string, counting from the right
Round	Rounds off a numeric expression to the specified number of decimal places
Seconds	Displays the seconds portion of a time expression
Sign	Examines a numeric expression and returns 1 for positive, – 1 for negative, or 0 for 0
Sin	Computes the sine of an angle, expressed in radians
Sqrt	Computes the square root of a numeric expression (the same as *expression* ^ 0.5)
Status	Displays status information about the current time, operating system in use, version number of FileMaker Pro, name of the selected field, and so on **Note:** There are approximately 30 different status tests.
StDev	Examines all values in any repeating or non-repeating field and gives the sample standard deviation
StDevP	Examines all values in any repeating or non-repeating field and gives the population standard deviation
Substitute	Substitutes one set of characters in a text string for another
Sum	Totals all values in specified fields
Tan	Computes the tangent for a given angle, expressed in radians
TextToDate	Converts a text string into date format
TextToNum	Converts a text string to numeric format, ignoring alphabetic characters
TextToTime	Converts a text string to time format
Time	Converts three given numeric values into a time equivalent
TimeToText	Converts a time value into text format
Today	Returns the current date from the system clock
Trim	Strips the specified text expression of leading and trailing spaces
Truncate	Truncates a number to the specified number of decimal places

Function Name	*Purpose*
Upper	Converts a text expression to all uppercase
WeekofYear	Determines the number of the week in the year, 1 – 52, for the specified date expression
WeekofYearFiscal	Determines the number of the week in the year, 1 – 53, for the specified date expression (in accordance with the particular day that is considered the first day of the week)
WordCount	Returns the total number of words found in a text expression or field
Year	Returns the year part of the specified date expression

The functions can be divided into many categories, but they all work in the same way. A function performs operations on data (the arguments to the function) and then returns a result. The arguments are enclosed in parentheses directly after the function name. For example, in the following expression:

```
Round(Sales Tax, 2)
```

Round is the function name, and Sales Tax and 2 are the arguments.

A function expects certain types of data for each argument: numbers, text, or logical tests. Failure to provide the correct types of arguments will result in errors. For example, although you can choose a Text field as an argument to the Round function, the calculation doesn't make any sense and results in a blank field. The kinds of data expected for each argument appear to the right of the function's name in the Specify Calculation dialog box (previously shown in Figure 14-1).

Functions don't have to be the only component in an expression. They can be combined with constants or references to fields, as shown in the following example:

```
Product Total + Round(Sales Tax, 2)
```

This example shows an expression to define a Grand Total field, obtained by adding the Product Total to the results of rounding off the Sales Tax field's contents to two decimal places.

The following example demonstrates that an expression can also be used as the argument to a function:

```
Round(Product Total * .07, 2)
```

In this example, the Sales Tax field is replaced by an expression that yields the same result. The result of this expression is Sales Tax rounded to two decimal places.

Functions are divided into 11 categories. The following sections provide more details about all of FileMaker Pro's built-in functions. The functions are listed alphabetically within the category to which they belong. In addition to an explanation of each function's purpose and an example of how the function is used, the sections include a statement that shows how to phrase the function and its arguments. (The order for arranging the function and its arguments is called the *syntax* of the function.) Special notes and cautions, as well as references to other, related functions, are included in the explanations of some of the functions.

To use a function in a Calculation field definition, double-click its name in the Function list in the upper-right section of the Specify Calculation dialog box (previously shown in Figure 14-1). Then replace the function's arguments with the appropriate field names or expressions.

If you don't know the specific name of the function you need, click the View pop-up menu in the upper-right corner of the Specify Calculation dialog box. Depending on your selection from this menu, you can view an alphabetical list of all functions (by selecting "all by name"), an alphabetical list of all functions grouped by type (by selecting "all by type"), or just a particular category of functions (by selecting "Text functions," "Logical functions," and so on).

Aggregate (Statistical) Functions

These functions compute statistics on repeating and non-repeating (normal) fields. The result can be either repeating or non-repeating. Although the arguments are often Number fields, Date and Time fields can also be used.

The aggregate functions are as follows:

- Average
- Count
- Max
- Min
- StDev
- StDevP
- Sum

Using Aggregate Functions with Repeating and Non-Repeating Fields

Although aggregate functions are commonly used with repeating fields, FileMaker Pro 3.0 also allows these functions to be used with non-repeating fields, as well as with a mixture of repeating and non-repeating fields. Each aggregate function discussed in this section accepts a single repeating field or series of repeating and/or non-repeating fields as arguments.

Regardless of the result data type chosen (Number or Date, for example), you can optionally specify that the result be a repeating value and display a particular number of repetitions. And even though the aggregate functions commonly take Number fields as their arguments, they can also be applied to Date and Time fields.

Average

Purpose: Computes the average value of all values in the specified field or fields. The fields may be repeating, non-repeating (normal), or a combination of the two, and the result type can be repeating or non-repeating. The average is calculated by adding all the appropriate values together and then dividing by the number of values added. The result is a numeric value or, in the case of a repeating result, a series of numeric values.

Syntax: Average(*field...*)

where *field...* is a list of one or more valid fields containing only numeric values.

Example: Suppose Prices is a repeating field containing the extended price of each item in an order. The following expression displays a message about the cost of these items:

```
"On average, the items you ordered cost $"&NumToText(Average(Prices))
```

If Prices contains 5.00, 10.00, and 30.00, the expression produces the following message:

```
On average, the items you ordered cost $15.00
```

Example: If the non-repeating fields F1, F2, and F3 contain 4, 6, and 8 in a given record, the formula Average(F1, F2, F3) returns 6.

See also: Min, Max, Sum, StDev, StDevP

Count

Purpose: Determines the number of non-blank entries in a repeating field, a series of non-repeating fields, or a mixture of the two field types, returning the result or results as numeric values.

Syntax: Count(*field...*)

where *field...* is a list of one or more valid, non-empty repeating fields of any type, or a series of repeating and/or non-repeating fields.

Example: If the repeating field Prices, formatted to contain up to 10 values, actually contains 5.00, 10.00, and 30.00, then the following expression yields a message about the items ordered:

```
"You ordered " & Count(Prices) & " items. Thank you!"
```

In this case, the expression produces the following message:

```
You ordered 3 items. Thank you!
```

Max

Purpose: Finds the highest, latest, or greatest value among all values in a non-empty repeating field or in a series of non-repeating and/or repeating fields. The result is returned in the appropriate format.

Syntax: Max(*field...*)

where *field...* is a list of one or more non-empty, valid fields of any type, or a series of repeating and/or non-repeating fields.

Example: Suppose that Dates is a repeating field containing dates of orders in an invoice record. Suppose, further, that it contains three values: 03/17/94, 04/18/94, and 05/19/94. In that case, the following expression:

```
"Your last order came on " & Max(Dates)
```

produces this message:

```
Your last order came on 05/19/94
```

See also: Min, Last

Min

Purpose: Finds the lowest, oldest, or smallest value among all values in a non-empty repeating field or in a series of non-repeating and/or repeating fields. The result is returned in the appropriate format.

Syntax: Min(*field...*)

where *field...* is a list of one or more non-empty, valid fields of any type.

Example: If Dates is a repeating field containing three values: 03/16/94, 04/17/94, and 05/18/94, then the following expression:

```
"Your first order came on " & Min(Dates)
```

produces the following message:

```
Your first order came on 03/16/94
```

See also: Last, Max

StDev

Purpose: Computes the standard deviation for all values in a non-empty, numeric repeating field, a series of non-repeating fields, or a mixture of the two field types. The standard deviation gives a measure of how far the values in a sample tend to depart from the average value.

The formula formerly used to calculate StDev in FileMaker Pro 2.1 is the one that is *now* used to calculate StDevP. If you have older FileMaker databases and want them to calculate a *sample* standard deviation, be sure that you use StDev in the formula — rather than StdDevP.

Syntax: StDev(*field...*)

where *field...* is the name of a valid, non-empty repeating field containing numeric data only, or a series of repeating and/or non-repeating fields.

Example: If the repeating field TestScores contains the values 98, 76, and 90, then the expression StDev(TestScores) yields 11.136, the standard deviation of these test scores.

See also: StdDevP

StDevP

Purpose: Computes the *population* standard deviation for all values in a non-empty, numeric repeating field, a series of non-repeating fields, or a mixture of the two field types. The difference between StDev (described previously) and StDevP is that the former is assumed to be based on a sample, whereas the latter is a population statistic (that is, StDevP is not based on a sample).

The formula formerly used to calculate StDev in FileMaker Pro 2.1 is the one that is *now* used to calculate StDevP. If you have older FileMaker databases and want them to calculate a *sample* standard deviation, be sure that StDev is used in the formula — rather than StdDevP.

Syntax: StDevp(*repeating field name*)

where *repeating field name* is the name of a valid, non-empty repeating field containing numeric data only.

Example: If the field TestScores contains the values 98, 76, and 90, then the expression StDev(TestScores) yields 9.09, the population standard deviation of these test scores.

See also: StDev

Sum

Purpose: Adds the contents of each non-blank entry in a numeric repeating field or in a series of non-repeating and/or repeating fields. The result returned is a numeric value.

Syntax: Sum(*field...*)

where *field...* is the name of a valid, non-empty repeating field containing numeric values only, or a series of non-repeating and/or repeating fields.

Example: If the repeating field Prices contains the values 5.00, 10.00, and 30.00, then the following expression:

```
"Your item total is $" & Sum(Prices)
```

produces the following message:

```
Your item total is $45.00
```

See also: Average

Date Functions

Date functions are used to find out various facts about dates entered by the user, to determine the current date from the system clock, and to convert date data into text format.

The date functions are as follows:

- Date
- DateToText
- Day
- DayName
- DayofWeek
- DayofYear
- Month
- MonthName
- Today
- WeekofYear
- WeekofYearFiscal
- Year

Date

Purpose: Determines the calendar date associated with three numbers, interpreted as days, months, and years, computed since January 1, 1 AD.

Syntax: Date(*month, day, year*)

where *month* is the number of the month, *day* is the number of the day, and *year* is the number of the year. (All are numeric expressions.)

Example: In a database, the fields DueMonth, DueDay, and DueYear are used to specify the due date of an invoice. If the fields contain 5, 19, and 1996, then the following expression:

```
"Your invoice was due on " & Date(DueMonth,DueDay,DueYear)
```

produces the following message:

```
Your invoice was due on May 19, 1996
```

The result type for the formula must be set to Date. If it is set to Number, the displayed result is a serial number (728798) rather than the date previously shown.

See also: Day, Month, Year

DateToText

Purpose: Changes the contents of a Date field into text format. The result can then be passed on to another calculation that requires text input, or it can be printed directly. The text result appears in the form MM/DD/YY, so that September 2, 1996, appears as 09/02/96.

Syntax: DateToText (*date*)

where *date* is a Date field or an expression yielding the Date data type.

Example: The following expression defines a Calculation field, with text results, giving an invoice date after the text "The invoice was prepared on":

```
"The Invoice was prepared on " & DateToText(Invoice Date)
```

If the invoice date were October 1, 1996, the field would contain the following message:

```
The Invoice was prepared on 10/01/96
```

See also: TextToDate

Day

Purpose: Returns the number of the day in the month, from 1 to 31, for a specified date. The value returned is numeric.

Syntax: Day(*date*)

where *date* is a valid expression with a date format.

Example: If the field Date contains the value 02/26/96, then the expression Day(Date) returns 26.

See also: Month, Year

DayName

Purpose: Returns a text string with the name of the day of the week for the specified date expression. The text returned is capitalized.

Syntax: DayName(*date*)

where *date* is a valid date.

Example: The following expression could be used as part of a message in a form letter:

```
"We missed you on " & DayName(Appointment Date)
```

If the Appointment Date field in the formula contains 06/23/94, the following message is displayed:

```
We missed you on Thursday
```

See also: MonthName

DayofWeek

Purpose: Returns a number representing the day of the week (from 1 to 7) on which the specified date falls. The number 1 is returned for Monday, 2 for Tuesday, and so on.

Syntax: DayofWeek(*date*)

where *date* is a valid date expression.

Example: If a Birthday field contains 12/16/95, the expression DayofWeek(Birthday) returns 7, which represents Sunday. To display the name of the day rather than a number, you could use the formula DayName(DayofWeek(Birthday)).

See also: DayofYear, WeekofYear

DayofYear

Purpose: Returns the number of days elapsed in the appropriate year since the specified date. The result is a numeric value.

Syntax: DayofYear(*date*)

where *date* is a valid date expression.

Example: Assuming that today is February 9, 1996, the expression DayofYear(Today) returns 40 (since February 9th is the fortieth day of 1996).

Example: The following expression can be used to print a message about the Yuletide holiday:

```
"Only " & NumToText(358 - DayofYear(Today's Date)) & " days until Christmas!"
```

If the Today's Date field contains the value 12/23/96, then the expression produces the following message:

```
Only 2 days until Christmas!
```

See also: DayofWeek, WeekofYear

Month

Purpose: Returns a numeric value in the range 1 through 12, corresponding to the month in the specified date expression.

Syntax: Month(*date*)

where *date* is a valid expression in date format.

Example: If the Date field contains 03/16/96, then the expression Month(Date) yields 3.

See also: Day, Year

MonthName

Purpose: Returns a text value with the proper name of the month in the given date expression. The text returned is capitalized.

Syntax: MonthName(*date*)

where *date* is a valid date expression.

Example: If the field Date contains the value 08/23/65, the following expression:

```
MonthName(Date) & " was a good month! You were born."
```

produces the following message:

```
August was a good month! You were born.
```

See also: DayName

Today

Purpose: Obtains today's date, in proper date format, from the system clock. (To return the correct date, the system clock in the Macintosh must be set correctly.) Note that this function accepts no arguments.

Syntax: Today

Example: Use the Today function in a form letter layout to insert the current date (with the appropriate conversion) as follows:

```
DateToText(Today)
```

WeekofYear

Purpose: Calculates the number of weeks that have elapsed for a specified date in a given year. Fractional weeks at the start or end of a year are treated as full weeks, so possible values can range between 1 and 54. The value returned is in numeric format.

Syntax: WeekofYear(*date*)

where *date* is a valid date expression.

Example: If the Date field contains the value 12/16/95, the expression WeekofYear(Date) returns the value 50.

See also: DayofYear, WeekofYearFiscal

WeekofYearFiscal

Purpose: Calculates the number of weeks that have elapsed for a supplied date in a given year, assuming that the week starts on a particular day. WeekofYearFiscal considers the first week of the year as the first one that contains four or more days — that is, when January 1 falls on a day between Monday and Thursday, that week is considered the first week of the year; otherwise, the next week is considered the first week. The returned numeric value is between 1 and 53.

Syntax: WeekofYearFiscal(*date, starting day*)

where *date* is a valid date expression and *starting day* is a number (1 – 7) that represents the day of the week that is to be treated as the first day of the week (1 is Sunday, 2 is Monday, and so on).

Example: January 1, 1996 fell on a Sunday. If the Date field contains the value 3/12/96, the expression WeekofYearFiscal(Date,1) returns the value 11.

See also: DayofYear, WeekofYear

Year

Purpose: Extracts the year portion of a date expression. The value returned is in numeric format and can be used in calculations.

Syntax: Year(*date*)

where *date* is a valid date expression.

Example: If the Date field contains the value 03/16/1996, then the expression Year(Date) yields the result 1996.

The following expression yields the person's age after this year's birthday:

```
Year(Today) - Year(Birthday)
```

See also: Day, Month

Financial Functions

These functions perform investment-related calculations. They are used to determine loan specifications, how large investments will grow over time, and the amount that investments are worth in constant money. They duplicate functions found on many financial pocket calculators.

The financial functions are as follows:

- FV
- NPV
- PMT
- PV

FV

Purpose: Computes the future value of an investment, based on the provided payment value, interest rate, and number of compounding periods. A numeric value is returned. The result is not the future value of an investment, starting with a certain balance; rather, it is the amount that accrues when equal payments are made over time to an account that bears a particular rate of interest.

Syntax: FV(*payment, rate, periods*)

where *payment* is the amount of each payment, *rate* is the interest rate per period, and *periods* is the number of payment periods.

Example: The following expression:

```
FV(100, .05/12, 360)
```

returns $83,225.86, the value of an account if $100 payments are made each month for 30 years at an annual interest rate of 5% (.05/12).

Payments are assumed to be made at the end of a period. Be sure to give the interest rate per period. Divide the annual rate by 12, as shown in the example, to obtain the monthly rate.

The following formula returns the future value of a continuously compounded investment, assuming a certain starting value:

```
Future Value = Present Value * Exp(Rate * Periods)
```

where Exp indicates the natural antilog of a number.

See also: NPV, PV

NPV

Purpose: Calculates the net present value of a series of unequal payments made regularly to an account bearing fixed interest per period over the life of the payments.

Syntax: NPV(*payment, rate*)

where *payment* is a series of payment values or the name of a valid repeating field containing the numeric value of each payment, and *rate* is a numeric value indicating the interest rate per period.

Example: The following expression yields the profit on the transaction in today's dollars if inflation is assumed to be 3%:

```
NPV(LoanAmt, .03)
```

When the repeating field LoanAmt contains the values –1000, 500, 600, 400, and 700, the result is $1,008.73. Note that the LoanAmt field contains five values that represent an initial loan of $1,000 (expressed as a negative value) and the values for the four annual payments.

See also: FV, PV

PMT

Purpose: Calculates the payment needed to fully amortize a loan, given the loan amount, the interest rate per payment period, and the number of periods.

Syntax: PMT(*principal*, *rate*, *periods*)

where *principal* is a number representing the amount of the loan, *rate* is the interest rate per period, and *periods* is the number of payments.

Example: The following expression:

```
PMT(34100, 10.99/12, 60)
```

yields a payment of 744.55, which is the amount required to finance $34,100 at 10.99% annual interest over 60 months.

PV

Purpose: Calculates the present value of a series of equal payments, made at regular intervals, to an account bearing a fixed rate of interest.

Syntax: PV(*payment*, *rate*, *periods*)

where *payment* is the numeric amount of each payment, *rate* is the interest rate per period, and *periods* is the number of payments.

Example: The following expression:

```
PV(500, .03, 5)
```

yields the value of five annual $500 payments *in today's dollars*, assuming a 3% interest rate — in this case, $2,289.85.

See also: NPV, FV

Logical Functions

In previous versions of FileMaker Pro, If was the only logical function. In FileMaker Pro 3.0, the logical functions are as follows:

- Case
- Choose
- If
- IsEmpty
- IsValid

Case

Purpose: Evaluates a series of expressions and returns the result supplied for the first true expression that is found.

Syntax: Case(*test1, result1 [, test2, result2, default result]...*)

where *test* is any text or numeric expression and *result* is the result that corresponds to the expression.

Example: The Payment field is examined in the following expression:

```
Case(Payment="V", "VISA", Payment="M", "MasterCard", "Other")
```

If the Payment field contains a *V*, the result is VISA. If it contains an *M*, the result is MasterCard. If it contains anything else or is blank, the default result (Other) is returned.

See also: If, Choose

Choose

Purpose: Selects one of a series of results based on an index value.

Syntax: Choose(*expression, result0 [, result1, result2]...*)

where the result of *expression* yields a number (between 0 and the number of the last result specified) that indexes into the result list that follows, and *result* is one or more results. Choose can return text, a number, a date, a time, or a container.

As indicated in its syntax, Choose is a zero-based index. A result of 0 is needed to select the first result in the list.

Example: The following expression returns a random integer (whole number) between 0 and 3:

```
Choose(Int(Random*4), "0","1","2","3")
```

See also: If, Case

If

Purpose: The If function is used when you want to perform one of a set of alternative actions based on the results of a logical test. Normally, the If function is used to choose between two actions; however, you can include If functions within each other to add choices.

The If function works with the other logical operators, such as less than, equals, OR, AND, and NOT. You combine these operators to create a test that is evaluated for each record.

Syntax: If(*Test, Expression1, Expression2*)

where *Test* is a logical or numeric expression yielding a logical or numeric result, *Expression1* is an expression to be evaluated and whose value is assigned to the field if the test is true or is not equal to zero, and *Expression2* is an expression to be evaluated and whose value is assigned to the field if the test is false or is equal to zero.

Example: Consider a simple example:

```
If(Number > 0, "The number is positive.", "The Number is less than or
equal to zero.")
```

If the Number field contains 35, then the expression produces the following text:

```
The number is positive.
```

If the Number field contains –11, the expression produces the following:

```
The number is less than or equal to zero.
```

Remember, the function returns the value of the first expression if the test is true, and it returns the value of the second expression if the test is false.

Again, you can put Ifs inside Ifs (called *nesting*) to add choices. The following example, derived from the first, can handle the additional case where the value in the Number field is equal to zero:

```
If(Number > 0, "The number is positive", If(Number = 0, "The number is
zero", "The number is negative"))
```

The test does not have to be a logical expression. If you use a numeric expression, the first action will be performed if the test result is not zero, and the second action will be performed if the test result is zero.

The values of the two expressions should be the values that you want for the field as a whole, depending on which condition is met. For example, you can use the If function to define a Calculation field that gives the tax rate for mail order shipments. The following expression assigns a tax rate of 6% to shipments within the state if you're shipping from New Mexico; otherwise, the rate is zero:

```
If(State = "NM", .06, 0)
```

If the Calculation field has the name Rate, you can use it in calculations as follows:

```
Tax = Rate * Total
```

Sales tax is then automatically computed and added for in-state shipments and omitted from out-of-state shipments.

IsEmpty

Purpose: Determines whether a particular field or expression is empty. It returns 1 (true) if it is empty or 0 (false) if it is not empty.

Syntax: IsEmpty(*field*)

where *field* is a field name or a text or numeric expression.

Example: The following expression returns 1 if the Last Name field for the current record is blank; otherwise, it returns 0 (false), indicating that the field contains data:

```
IsEmpty(Last Name)
```

See Also: IsValid

IsValid

Purpose: Checks a related file for the presence of a given field. It returns 0 (false) if the field is missing or contains invalid data; otherwise, it returns 1 (true).

Syntax: IsValid(*related field*)

where *related field* is the name of a field in a related file.

Example: The following expression checks for a Customer Number field in the file specified by the relationship named ID:

```
IsValid(ID::Customer Number)
```

A result of 0 (false) is returned if any of the following conditions occur:

- The related file cannot be found.
- The field in the related file does not exist.
- The value contained in the field in the matching record is invalid; that is, it is the wrong data type.

See also: IsEmpty

Numeric Functions

These functions perform a range of standard mathematical computations on numeric fields. Two of the functions, Pi and Random, do not accept arguments.

The numeric functions are as follows:

- Abs
- Exp
- Int
- Mod
- NumToText
- Random
- Round
- Sign
- Sqrt
- Truncate

Abs

Purpose: Returns the absolute value of a numeric expression. This function changes negative values to positive ones and leaves zero and positive values alone.

Syntax: Abs(*expression*)

where *expression* is a numeric expression or the name of a field that contains a numeric value.

Example: If the field Difference contains 125 or –125, then the following expression returns 125:

```
Abs(Difference)
```

See also: Sign

Exp

Purpose: Returns the natural antilog of the given numeric expression. This value is the result obtained when the constant *e* is raised to the power of the expression; *e* is 2.7182818.

Syntax: Exp(*expression*)

where *expression* is a numeric expression or a field that contains a numeric value.

Example: The following expression calculates the number that has base *e* logarithm 2 (which is what is meant by the *antilog* 2):

```
Exp(2)
```

returns 7.389, rounded to three decimal places.

See also: Ln, Log

Int

Purpose: Returns the integer portion of a numeric expression. This portion is the part to the left of the decimal point. The portion to the right, if any, is simply dropped.

Syntax: Int(*expression*)

where *expression* is a numeric expression or a field containing a numeric value.

Example: The expression Int(Pi) is equal to 3.

See also: Round, Truncate

Mod

Purpose: Performs modulo arithmetic, which deals with what remains when a given number or expression is divided by another number.

Syntax: Mod(*expression, divisor*)

where *expression* is a numeric expression or numeric field, indicating the number to be divided; and *divisor* is a numeric expression or numeric field, indicating the number by which to divide.

Example: The following expression is equal to 1, which is the integer remainder when 10 is divided by 3:

```
Mod(10,3)
```

NumToText

Purpose: Changes the contents of a Number field into text format. The result can then be passed on to another calculation that requires text input, or it can be printed directly.

Syntax: NumToText(*number*)

where *number* is a Number field or is a numeric expression.

Example: The following expression shows a field that tells a customer how much an order cost:

```
"Your order came to $" & NumtoText(Grand Total)
```

If the Grand Total field contained 99.95, the expression's value would be as follows:

```
Your order came to $99.95
```

See also: TextToNum

Random

Purpose: This function returns a random value in the range 0 to 1 inclusive. This function takes no arguments.

Syntax: Random

Example: The following expression yields a random integer between 1 and 52 inclusive:

```
Int(52 * Random) + 1
```

Such a number might represent a card drawn from a standard deck of playing cards.

Any of the following conditions causes the generation of a new random number:

- A new record is created.
- The Random function is newly assigned to a formula.
- Data is changed in any of the fields that are referenced by the formula containing the Random function.

Round

Purpose: Rounds off a numeric result to the specified number of decimal places.

Syntax: Round(*expression, places*)

where *expression* is a numeric expression or a field that contains a numeric value, and *places* is a numeric expression that indicates the number of decimal places to retain.

Example: The expression returns the value of Pi to four decimals, or 3.1416:

```
Round(Pi,4)
```

See also: Int, Truncate

Sign

Purpose: Returns one of three values, depending on the value of the expression. If the expression is greater than zero (positive), Sign is equal to 1. If the expression is equal to zero, Sign is also equal to zero. If the expression is less than zero, Sign is equal to –1.

Syntax: Sign(*expression*)

where *expression* is a numeric expression or a field containing a numeric value.

Example: The expression Sign(123) has the value 1.

See also: Abs

Sqrt

Purpose: Returns the square root of the given expression. The square root is the number which, when raised to the second power, equals the original expression.

Syntax: Sqrt(*expression*)

where *expression* is a numeric expression or a field containing a numeric value.

Example: The expression Sqrt(9) is equal to 3.

Other roots can be extracted by using the exponentiation operator (^). The nth root of a number is equal to that number raised to the reciprocal of *n*. Thus, the cube (or third) root of 27 can be calculated using the following expression:

```
27 ^ (1 / 3)
```

Truncate

Purpose: Returns a number that is truncated to the specified number of decimal places. Numbers in additional decimal places (to the right) are dropped, not rounded off.

Syntax: Truncate(*expression*)

where *expression* is a numeric expression or a field containing a numeric value.

Example: The expression Truncate(9.75621,3) returns 9.756. The expression Truncate(9.75621,10) returns 9.75621 (because the additional decimal places do not exist, the original number is returned).

See also: Int, Round

Repeating Functions

Repeating functions enable you to convert a normal field so it can be treated as a repeating field in a calculation, reference a particular repetition in a repeating field, or find the last valid entry in a repeating field.

The repeating functions are as follows:

- Extend
- GetRepetition
- Last

Extend

Purpose: Extends a non-repeating field for use in calculations with repeating fields. Every value in the extended field is identical; that is, the normal value is simply duplicated.

Syntax: Extend(*non-repeating field name*)

where *non-repeating field name* is the name of a valid, single-entry field.

Example: The following expression enables you to calculate series of tax amounts, where Prices is a repeating field and TaxRate is a single field that contains the state sales tax rate:

```
Prices * Extend(TaxRate)
```

GetRepetition

Purpose: Enables you to obtain the value of a specific repetition in a repeating field.

Syntax: GetRepetition(*repeating field name, repetition number*)

where *repeating field name* is the name of a valid, non-empty repeating field of any type and *repetition number* is the number of the specific repetition within the field.

Example: If Prices is a numeric repeating field containing three values, 5.5, 10, and 30, then the expression GetRepetition(2) returns 10.

See also: Last

Last

Purpose: Finds the last valid, non-empty entry in a repeating field. The entry is returned in the appropriate format.

Syntax: Last(*repeating field name*)

where *repeating field name* is the name of a valid, non-empty repeating field of any type.

Example: If Prices is a numeric repeating field containing three values, 5.00, 10.00, and 30.00, then the following expression:

```
"The last item you ordered cost $" & Last(Prices)
```

yields the following result:

```
The last item you ordered cost $30.00
```

See also: GetRepetition

Status Function

The Status function can provide information about the current system on which FileMaker Pro is running, the number of records in the current file, the name of the current user, and more than 30 other useful tidbits. Unlike other function categories, the Status category consists of just one function — but it takes more than 30 preset arguments. The result of the Status function varies with the argument used.

Although you can type the argument to the Status function after choosing Status from the alphabetical function list presented in the Specify Calculation dialog box, it can be difficult to remember the exact spelling and wording of the argument. The easy way to create an expression using the Status function is to choose "Status functions" from the View pop-up menu, and then select the correct argument, as shown in Figure 14-3.

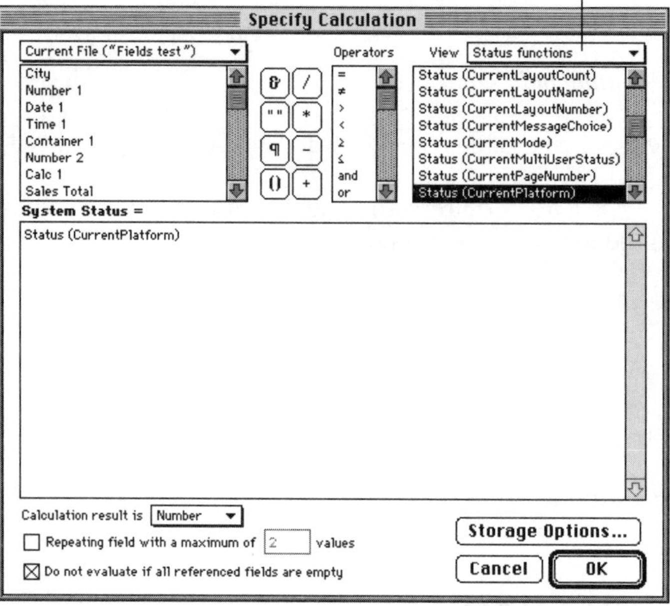

Figure 14-3: Choosing an argument for the Status function

The following section provides a general description of the Status function and its arguments. For a more detailed explanation of the Status function arguments and the meaning of the data they return, choose "Status functions" from FileMaker Pro Help.

Status

Purpose: Performs a check on the state of the database, hardware in use, and so on, and then returns this information in an appropriate form.

Syntax: Status(*status flag*)

where *status flag* is one of the preset arguments supplied by FileMaker Pro 3.0. A given Status function can return a text string, a number, or a date, depending on its purpose. Status functions accept no parameters other than the preset arguments.

Examples:

- Status(CurrentDate) returns the current system date.
- Status(CurrentLayoutCount) returns the number of layouts that are defined for the database.

- Status(CurrentSortStatus) returns a number that indicates whether the database is currently unsorted (0), sorted (1), or semi-sorted (2).

The variations of the Status function are useful as parts of scripts (several, in fact, are *only* useful as parts of scripts). For example, the expression Status(CurrentPlatform) is used to determine whether the database is running on a Macintosh or under Windows. Depending on the result of the Status check, you can have the script execute an AppleScript (if running on a Mac) or do something else (if running under Windows).

Summary Functions

FileMaker Pro 3.0 contains only one summary function: GetSummary. (The GetSummary function was called Summary in FileMaker Pro 2.1.)

GetSummary

Purpose: Returns the values for a particular Summary field when the database is sorted by the break (grouping) field.

Syntax: GetSummary(*summary field, break field*)

where *summary field* is the name of the Summary field, and *break field* is the name of the field that is used to group the records (the "when sorted by" field). The break field can be a Text, Number, Date, Time, or Calculation field.

Example: Suppose you want to see year-to-date sales totals for the individual members of your company's sales force. After the database has been sorted by the Salesperson field, the following expression displays a different value for the Sales Total field for each salesperson in the database:

```
GetSummary(Sales Total,Salesperson)
```

To display a grand total for a Summary field rather than individual subtotals, use the name of the Summary field as both arguments to the function:

```
GetSummary(Sales Total,Sales Total)
```

Text Functions

Text functions are used to compare text strings and to extract pieces of text strings. They can also be used to insert text into a string.

The text functions are as follows:

- Exact
- Left
- LeftWords
- Length
- Lower
- Middle
- MiddleWords
- PatternCount
- Position
- Proper
- Replace
- Right
- RightWords
- Substitute
- TextToDate
- TextToNum
- TextToTime
- Trim
- Upper
- WordCount

Exact

Purpose: Compares two text expressions or fields and determines whether they are exactly the same. The comparison is case sensitive, so capitalization counts. The returned result is a logical value: true if the two strings are exactly the same, false if they are not.

Syntax: Exact(*first text, comparison text*)

where *first text* is a Text field, expression, or constant, and *comparison text* is also a Text field, expression, or constant.

Example: The following expression is true if today's date is February 12, 1996:

```
Exact(DayName(Today), "Monday")
```

To create a text constant — such as *Monday*, in the example — you must surround it with quotation marks.

See also: Position

You can adapt the Exact function to perform a test that *isn't* case sensitive. Use either the Upper or Lower function to convert both text strings to all uppercase or lowercase, as in the following example:

```
Exact(Upper(Field1), Upper(Field2))
```

Left

Purpose: Returns a text result that equals the leftmost part of a given Text field or expression, including only the specified number of characters.

Syntax: Left(*text, number*)

where *text* is a text expression or text from which the leftmost part is to be taken, and *number* is a numeric expression or field specifying how many characters to use.

Example: The expression Left("photocopy", 5) yields "photo."

See also: LeftWords, Right, Middle

LeftWords

Purpose: Returns a text result that equals the leftmost part of a given Text field or expression, including only the specified number of words.

Syntax: LeftWords(*text, number*)

where *text* is a text expression or text from which the leftmost part is to be taken, and *number* is a numeric expression or field specifying how many words to use.

Example: LeftWords("The worst years of your life",2) returns "The worst."

See also: RightWords, MiddleWords, Left

Length

Purpose: Returns a numeric result that indicates the number of characters the specified text contains. When text length is calculated, alphanumeric characters, spaces, numbers, and special characters all contribute to the total.

Syntax: Length(*text*)

where *text* is a text expression, constant, or field that contains a text value.

Example: The expression Length("photocopy") is equal to 9.

See also: Trim

Lower

Purpose: Converts the specified text string into all lowercase letters.

Syntax: Lower(*text*)

where *text* is a text expression, constant, or field containing a text value.

Example: The expression Lower("PrintMonitor") yields "printmonitor."

See also: Upper, Proper

Middle

Purpose: Extracts a specified number of characters out of a given text string, starting at a certain position.

Syntax: Middle(*text, start, number of characters*)

where *text* is a Text field, text constant, or text expression; *start* is a numeric value that indicates where to begin extracting characters; and *number of characters* is a numeric value that indicates the number of characters to use.

Example: The following expression returns the letter Q:

```
Middle("John Q. Public", 6, 1)
```

Remember that *spaces* are characters, too.

See also: Left, Right, MiddleWords

MiddleWords

Purpose: Enables you to extract a consecutive group of words from any text string, regardless of the starting position of the target word group.

Syntax: MiddleWords(*text, starting word, number*)

where *text* is the text expression or text from which the specified portion is to be extracted; *starting word* is a numeric expression or field that contains the number of the first word to be extracted; and *number* is a numeric expression or field specifying how many words to use.

Example: The following expression:

```
MiddleWords("Baby animals must fend for themselves",2,3)
```

returns the following result:

```
animals must fend
```

See also: RightWords, LeftWords, Middle

PatternCount

Purpose: Returns the number of instances that a specified text string is found within another text string or field.

Syntax: PatternCount(*text, pattern*)

where *text* is the text expression or text to be searched, and *pattern* is the particular text string for which you are searching.

Example: The expression PatternCount("You are the apple of my eye","e") returns 5 because there are 5 *e*'s in the text string.

Position

Purpose: Scans a specified text expression in an attempt to locate a particular instance of a search string, starting at a given position, and returns a numeric value equal to the position at which the search string starts within the larger string. If the search string is not found, the result is zero.

Syntax: Position(*text, search string, start, occurrence*)

where *text* is a text constant, field, or expression in which to search; *search string* is the text to search for; *start* is a number that indicates at what character position to begin the search; and *occurrence* is a number, numeric expression, or field containing a number that indicates the particular occurrence of the string you want to find.

Examples: The expression Position("bewitching beauty", "be", 1,1) returns 1; Position("bewitching beauty", "be", 1,2) returns 12, as does Position("bewitching beauty", "be", 10,1).

See also: LeftWords, RightWords, MiddleWords

Proper

Purpose: Returns a text string in which the first letter of each word of the supplied text expression has been capitalized; all others are converted to lowercase.

Syntax: Proper(*text*)

where *text* is a Text field, constant, or expression.

Example: The expression Proper("SURF AND TURF") returns "Surf And Turf."

See also: Upper, Lower

Replace

Purpose: Inserts a specified text string into another text string, starting at a specified position and eliminating a given number of characters. The number of characters replaced need not be equal to the number inserted.

Syntax: Replace(*text, start, size, replacement text*)

where *text* is a Text field, constant, or expression; *start* is a numeric value indicating at what position to begin replacing; *size* is a numeric value that indicates the number of characters to replace; and *replacement text* is a Text field, constant, or expression to insert in the place of the specified characters.

Example: The following expression:

```
Replace("Clinton R. Hicks", 9, 2, "Robert")
```

yields the following result:

```
Clinton Robert Hicks
```

See also: Substitute

Right

Purpose: Starting at the right, extracts the specified number of characters from the specified text expression.

Syntax: Right(*text, number*)

where *text* is a Text field, expression, or constant from which to extract characters, and *number* is a numeric value that indicates how many characters to take.

Example: The expression Right("Rosanna", 4) returns "anna."

See also: Left, Middle, RightWords

RightWords

Purpose: Returns a text result that equals the rightmost part of a specified Text field or expression, including only the specified number of words.

Syntax: RightWords(*text, number*)

where *text* is a text expression or text from which the rightmost part is to be taken, and *number* is a numeric expression or field specifying how many words to use.

Example: The expression RightWords("These are the best days of our lives",5) returns "best days of our lives."

See also: LeftWords, MiddleWords

Substitute

Purpose: Enables you to substitute one text string for another.

Syntax: Substitute(*text, search string, replacement string*)

where *text* is a text expression or Text field, *search string* is the text that is to be replaced, and *replacement string* is the text that is to be used as the replacement.

Example: The expression Substitute("I was actually the walrus","I","He") returns "He was actually the walrus."

See also: Replace

TextToDate

Purpose: Changes a text date value directly into date format. The supplied text must be in the format MM/DD/YYYY for this function to work correctly.

Syntax: TextToDate(*text*)

where *text* is a text constant or text expression in the form MM/DD/YYYY.

Example: The following expression converts a text constant into date format:

```
TextToDate("03/23/1990")
```

This expression yields the following result in date format:

```
03/23/90
```

See also: DateToText, Date

This function and the Date function are the only ways to enter a date constant into a formula that requires a date parameter, such as DayofYear and DayName.

TextToNum

Purpose: Converts the number part of a text expression into numeric format. The alphabetic portion is ignored.

Syntax: TextToNum(*text*)

where *text* is a text constant or a text expression.

Example: The following defines a Calculation field in which non-numeric data such as a dollar sign and commas are stripped from a price:

```
TextToNum(Price)
```

If the information in Price (a Text field) had been entered as $19,995.95, the Calculation field would contain 19995.95.

See also: NumToText

TextToTime

Purpose: Converts a text value or expression into time format. The results can then be passed on to a calculation that requires data in time format.

Syntax: TextToTime(*text*)

where *text* is a text constant or text expression. The data supplied must be in the form HH:MM:SS. Seconds are optional, and AM and PM may be used as suffixes.

Example: The following expression yields 14:15:00:

```
TextToTime("2:15 pm")
```

The formatting of the converted text is initially determined by the result type that you select. If you select Time as the result type, the result returned is 2:15 PM — rather than the military time format used when Text is selected as the result type.

See also: TimeToText, TextToNum

TextToTime and Time are the only ways to enter a time constant into a function or expression that requires data in time format.

Trim

Purpose: Removes leading and trailing spaces from a specified text expression or field.

Syntax: Trim(*text*)

where *text* is a Text field, constant, or expression.

Example: The expression Trim("   Johnny   ") returns "Johnny."

See also: Left, Right, Middle, Position

Some programs and computer systems require a set number of characters per field. Unused spaces in such fields may be padded with blanks. You can use the Trim function to remove these blanks when you import data from such programs and systems.

Upper

Purpose: Converts a given text string into all uppercase.

Syntax: Upper(*text*)

where *text* is a Text field, constant, or expression.

Example: The expression Upper("Honorable") returns "HONORABLE."

See also: Lower, Proper

WordCount

Purpose: Returns the total number of words in a text string.

Syntax: WordCount(*text*)

where *expression* is a Text field or expression.

Example: The expression WordCount(Comments) returns the number of words in the Comments field.

Time Functions

The Time functions are analogous to the Date functions described earlier in this chapter. You can use them to extract pieces from a time expression or to convert number results into valid times — even if the numbers don't fall into the 0 – 60 and 0 – 24 ranges normally required for minutes and hours.

The time functions are as follows:

- Hour
- Minute
- Seconds
- Time
- TimeToText

Hour

Purpose: Extracts the hour part of a time expression or field, yielding a numeric result.

Syntax: Hour(*time*)

where *time* is a Time field or expression.

Example: If Current is a time field containing 12:30 PM, the expression Hour(Current) is equal to 12. If the field contained 12:30 *AM*, on the other hand, the result would be 0.

See also: Minute, Seconds

Minute

Purpose: Extracts the minute part of a time expression or field, yielding a numeric result.

Syntax: Minute(*time*)

where *time* is a Time field or expression.

Example: If Current is a Time field containing 8:23:17, the expression Minute(Current) returns 23.

See also: Hour, Seconds

Seconds

Purpose: Extracts the seconds part of a time expression or field, yielding a numeric result.

Syntax: Seconds(*time*)

where *time* is a Time field or expression.

Example: If Current is a Time field containing 12:30:15 PM, the expression Seconds(Current) yields 15.

See also: Hour, Minute

The Hour, Minute, and Seconds functions can be used together to obtain the decimal equivalent of a time value. You would need to divide the Minute result by 60 and the Seconds result by 3600 as shown in the following expression:

```
Hour(Current) + (Minute(Current) / 60) + (Seconds(Current) / 3600)
```

Time

Purpose: Returns a time value containing the specified number of hours, minutes, and seconds counted from midnight. The function compensates for fractional values, extracting seconds from fractional minutes and minutes from fractional hours.

Syntax: Time(*hours*, *minutes*, *seconds*)

where:

- *hours* is a numeric expression indicating the number of hours
- *minutes* is a numeric expression indicating the number of minutes
- *seconds* is a numeric expression indicating the number of seconds

Example: The expression Time(13, 70, 71) is equal to 2:11:11 PM.

See also: Date

TimeToText

Purpose: Converts a time into text format. The result may be printed directly or used in a text-based expression.

Syntax: TimeToText(*time*)

where *time* is a Time field or an expression yielding a time value.

Example: The following expression extracts the time from a field and prints it along with a message:

```
"Your order was prepared at " & TimeToText(Time Entered)
```

If the Time Entered field contained 02:15:00, the field would read as follows:

```
Your order was prepared at 2:15:00
```

See also: TextToTime

Trigonometric Functions

This group of functions enables you to work with angles, degrees, and other geometric data. Note that the trigonometric functions are designed to work in radians. (There are 2Pi radians in 360 degrees.) You can use the Degrees function to convert radian results into degrees.

The trigonometric functions are as follows:

- Atan
- Cos
- Degrees
- Ln
- Log
- Pi
- Radians
- Sin
- Tan

Atan

Purpose: Returns the arc tangent (in radians) of the specified expression.

Syntax: Atan(*number*)

where *number* is a Number field, numeric expression, or constant.

Example: The expression Atan(Pi) is equal to 1.2626, rounded to four decimal places.

See also: Tan, Degrees

Cos

Purpose: Gives the cosine of the specified expression (assumed to be provided in radians).

Syntax: Cos(*number*)

where *number* is a Number field, numeric expression, or constant — in radians.

Example: The expression Cos(Pi) is equal to –1.

See also: Sin, Degrees

Degrees

Purpose: Converts a value given in radians into degrees. There are 2Pi radians in 360 degrees.

Syntax: Degrees(*number*)

where *number* is a Number field, numeric expression, or constant — in radians.

Example: The expression Degrees(Pi) is equal to 180.

See also: Radians

Ln

Purpose: Returns the natural logarithm of the given numeric expression. The natural logarithm is the number which, when the constant *e* is raised to its power, gives the original number. In calculus, the natural logarithm of a number *x* is said to be the area under the curve Ln evaluated between 1 and *x*.

Syntax: Ln(*number*)

where *number* is a numeric expression or a field containing a numeric value.

Example: The expression Ln(2) has the value 0.693, rounded to three decimals.

See also: Log, Exp

Log

Purpose: Computes the common (base 10) logarithm of the given numeric expression. Raising 10 to this power gives the original number. Thus, the log of 100 is 2, because 10 ^ 2 = 100.

Syntax: Log(*number*)

where *number* is a numeric expression or a field containing a numeric value.

Example: The expression Log(100 * 100) has the value 4.

See also: Ln, Exp

Pi

Purpose: Returns the value of the mathematical constant pi. Pi is defined as the ratio of a circle's circumference to its diameter. It is a transcendental number whose fractional part neither repeats nor terminates. This function takes no arguments.

Syntax: Pi

Example: If R is equal to 2, the following expression is approximately equal to 12.57:

```
Pi * R ^ 2
```

This expression gives the area of a circle with the radius equal to R.

Radians

Purpose: Converts a value in degrees into radians, for use with calculations expecting a value in that form.

Syntax: Radians(*number*)

where *number* is a Number field, constant, or expression containing a value expressed in degrees.

Example: The expression Cos(Radians(45)) is equal to 0.707, rounded to three decimal places.

See also: Degrees

Sin

Purpose: Returns the sine of the given expression, interpreted as an angle expressed in radians.

Syntax: Sin(*number*)

where *number* is a Number field, constant, or expression given in radians.

Example: The expression Sin(Pi) is equal to 0.

See also: Cos

Tan

Purpose: Gives the tangent of the specified angle, assumed to be expressed in radians.

Syntax: Tan(*number*)

where *number* is a numeric field, constant, or expression given in radians.

Example: The expression Tan(Pi) is equal to 0.

See also: Atan

Summary

- FileMaker Pro supports the use of Calculation fields. These fields can perform operations on data in other fields.
- A Calculation field's definition consists of a formula that is made up of mathematical expressions and functions. Calculation fields can combine data from other fields and can also contain constant values.
- An expression consists of one or more operators that join fields or constant values. Database fields are similar to variables in algebra.
- An expression for a Calculation field can include arithmetic, logical, and text operators.
- FileMaker Pro 3.0 includes nearly 100 built-in functions. These functions perform data conversion and date, logical, mathematical, financial, statistical, summary, text, time, and trigonometric calculations. They can also be used to determine the status of important system and database properties.

Automating FileMaker Pro

CHAPTER 15

In This Chapter

- Creating FileMaker Pro scripts
- Understanding script steps
- Assigning scripts to buttons and to the Script menu
- Learning advanced scripting techniques

When most people — particularly new Macintosh owners — see the terms *script* or *scripting*, they think of programming. And when they think of programming, they quickly skip to the next section of the manual, assuming that this is a feature that was not meant for them. Unfortunately, in many cases, they're right. But FileMaker Pro provides an easier, kinder way to create scripts:

- Rather than type scripts in a word processing program or text editor, you design scripts in FileMaker Pro by choosing script steps from a list. Step options are set by clicking buttons and check boxes.
- You can create many scripts simply by executing sort instructions, find requests, and similar commands and then telling FileMaker Pro that you want to use the identical procedures in a script. When you perform these important steps just before creating the script, FileMaker Pro includes them for you as part of the default script. The general philosophy is "Set it up and then save it as a script."

To make it easy to design scripts, FileMaker Pro provides a built-in script-creation utility called ScriptMaker. Using ScriptMaker, you can automate almost any FileMaker Pro function that you usually execute manually by selecting commands from menus. Once defined, a script can be added to the Script menu and/or attached to a button in any layout, making it simple to execute the script any time you like.

Although this chapter is devoted primarily to explaining how to create and use scripts, you can automate FileMaker Pro functions in other ways as well, such as:

- Creating auto-entry fields that are filled in for you whenever a new record is created or a record is edited (refer to Chapter 5)
- Setting a start up script for a database (discussed in Chapter 7)
- Using a macro utility (QuicKeys, for example) to automate functions
- Using Apple Events and AppleScript to enable FileMaker Pro to interact with other programs

If you've upgraded from a previous version of FileMaker Pro, you may have noticed that the scripting capabilities have changed dramatically. In FileMaker Pro 3.0, scripts can now include loops, conditional tests, error control procedures, and steps that support the new relational capabilities. And the number of steps at your disposal has almost doubled since FileMaker Pro 2.1.

Also, in previous versions of FileMaker Pro, you assigned scripts and steps to buttons by choosing Define Button from the Scripts menu. In FileMaker Pro 3.0, you perform these actions by choosing Button from the Format menu.

Using ScriptMaker

The majority of FileMaker Pro scripts are created in ScriptMaker. The commands used in the script are called *steps*. In most cases, the steps duplicate normal FileMaker Pro menu commands. (See the "Script Step Reference" section, later in this chapter, for information about specific steps.) As you read through this chapter, however, you will learn that script steps often are more powerful than the original commands that they represent. For example, you can construct a Clear script step that makes a particular field the active one, selects the entire contents of that field, and then clears its contents. To clear a field without such a script, you must click the field and then manually select its contents (or use the Select All command) before choosing the Clear menu command. Thus, many steps frequently can be reduced to one.

The real power of FileMaker Pro scripts becomes apparent when you design an elaborate sequence of steps to carry out a complex function. With a script, you can be sure that the steps are executed in precisely the same manner each time. If you prefer, the same script can be designed so that the user can select *different* options each time it runs. For example, you could create a Find script that selects a particular group of records (such as all people in the database who are younger than 30) and then displays information about those records in a different layout. With only a minor modification, the same script can be designed so that the find criteria could be changed by the user each time the script is performed. Similarly, a script designed to act on a specific field can be modified so that it simply acts on whatever field happens to be current. In that way, the script can be used with any field in the database.

Creating a script is not a complex process. Here are the basic steps:

1. Open the database for which you want to define a script.

   Scripts are stored with the databases in which they are created.

2. Choose ScriptMaker from the Script menu.

   The Define Scripts dialog box appears, as shown in Figure 15-1.

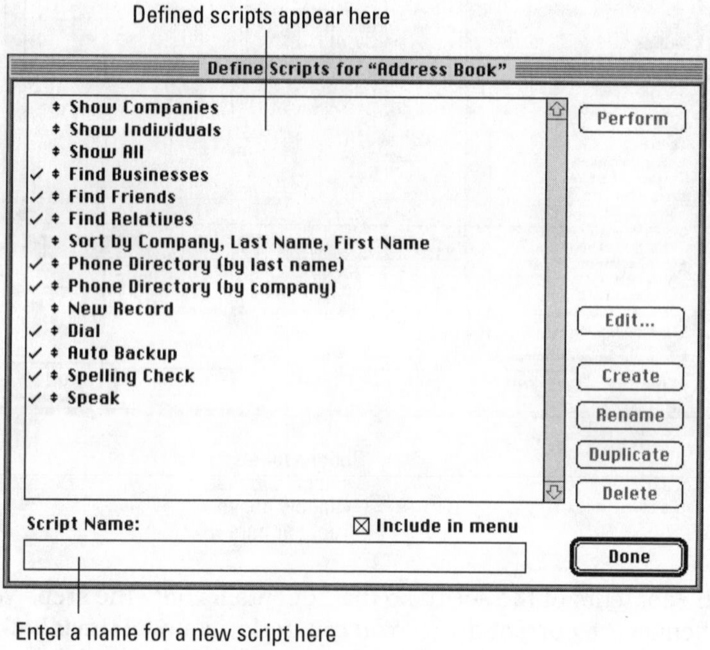

Defined scripts appear here

Figure 15-1: The Define Scripts dialog box

Enter a name for a new script here

3. In the Script Name box, type a name for the script.

   As soon as text is entered in the Script Name box, the Create button becomes available (that is, the button no longer is dimmed).

4. If you do not want to list the script in the Script menu, click to remove the check mark from the "Include in menu" check box.

   You can change the status of this check box at any time during the script-creation or script-editing process. A maximum of 52 scripts can be listed in the Script menu for any database.

5. Click Create.

   The Script Definition dialog box appears, as shown in Figure 15-2. A standard set of script steps, based on FileMaker Pro's best guess of what you might want to do, is listed in the scrolling list on the right side of the dialog box. This is the initial version of the script.

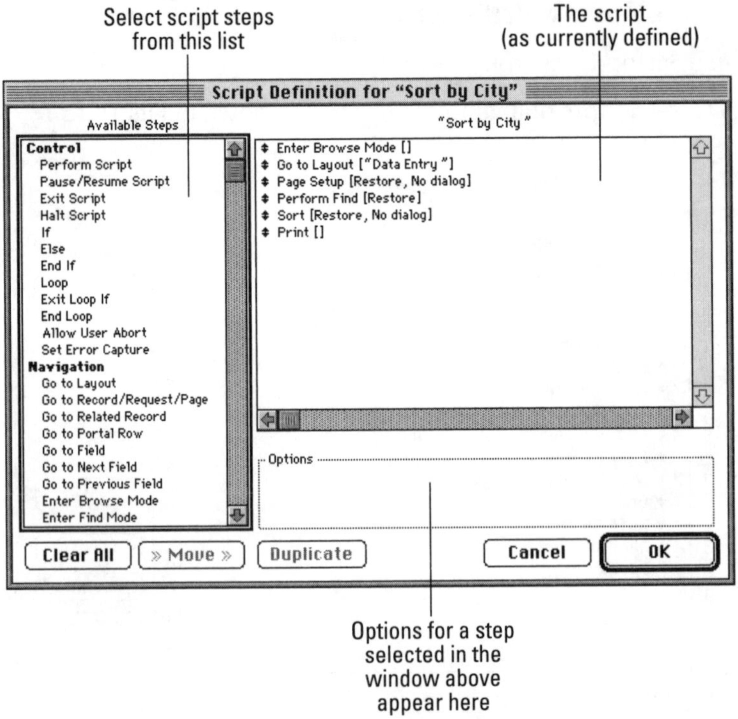

Select script steps from this list

The script (as currently defined)

Script Definition for "Sort by City"

Available Steps

Control
Perform Script
Pause/Resume Script
Exit Script
Halt Script
If
Else
End If
Loop
Exit Loop If
End Loop
Allow User Abort
Set Error Capture
Navigation
Go to Layout
Go to Record/Request/Page
Go to Related Record
Go to Portal Row
Go to Field
Go to Next Field
Go to Previous Field
Enter Browse Mode
Enter Find Mode

"Sort by City"

Enter Browse Mode []
Go to Layout ["Data Entry"]
Page Setup [Restore, No dialog]
Perform Find [Restore]
Sort [Restore, No dialog]
Print []

Options

Clear All | » Move » | Duplicate | Cancel | OK

Options for a step selected in the window above appear here

Figure 15-2: The Script Definition dialog box

6. Edit the contents of the script so that it contains only the steps you need and lists them in the correct order. You can perform any of the following actions:

   - To remove all steps from the script, click Clear All.
   - To remove individual unwanted steps, select them in the current script (in the right side of the dialog box) and then click Clear. (The Clear button replaces the Move button when a step is selected.)

- To add a step to the script, select it in the Available Steps list and then click Move.
- To rearrange the order of steps in the script, click the step you want to relocate and drag it to the desired position.
- To set options for a script step, begin by selecting the step in the script. Options that can be set for the step appear at the bottom of the dialog box.

7. To accept the script definition, click OK. To ignore the changes that you made, click Cancel.

If a script consists of only one step, you may be able to avoid the script-definition process by assigning the step to a button. (See "Attaching a Script to a Button" later in this chapter.)

If you want a permanent record of a script, you can print it by issuing the Print command, clicking the Script radio button in the Print dialog box, and then choosing the script you want to print from the pop-up menu. If you want to print every script for a database, choose "All scripts" from the pop-up menu.

Learning by Example

Learning to script can be facilitated by looking at some examples. In this and other chapters in this book, as well as in the databases included on the *Macworld FileMaker Pro 3.0 Bible Disk*, you'll find plenty of scripts that you can use as starting points. Want to understand an interesting action that you've seen in someone else's database? Choose ScriptMaker from the Script menu, click the script that you want to examine, and then click Edit. You'll see the list of steps that the author of the database selected for the script. (Be aware, however, that some databases — including some that you can buy, those that are available for downloading from popular online services, and a few of the ones on this disk — are protected. Unless you know the necessary password, you may not be allowed to see or modify the scripts.)

Listing Scripts in the Script Menu

As mentioned earlier, if the "Include in menu" check box is checked for a defined script, the script is assigned a place in the Script menu. Up to 52 scripts can be listed in the Script menu. The first 10 such scripts are also listed in the Define Scripts dialog box with a check mark in front of their names. These 10 scripts are special in that they are assigned keyboard shortcuts (⌘-1 through ⌘-0) so that you can also execute them from the keyboard. You can position the scripts that you need to use most often among the first 10 to make them easily accessible.

To change the position of a script in the Define Scripts dialog box, click the double-headed arrow that precedes its name in the script list. The pointer changes to a larger version of the double-headed arrow. Then, while continuing to hold down the mouse button, drag the script up or down in the script list. When the script is in the correct position in the list, release the mouse button. Repeat this process for other scripts that you want to move.

Running a Script

After you finish defining a script, you can execute it in any of several ways:

- Select the name of the script in the Define Scripts dialog box and then click the Perform button.
- Choose the script name from the Script menu (only if "Include in menu" was checked when you defined the script).
- Press the Command-key combination assigned to the script (only if "Include in menu" was checked when you defined the script and if the script is one of the first 10 scripts defined for the database).
- Click a button to which you have attached the script (only if you assigned the script to a button).
- Open the database (only if you defined the script as a startup script that runs automatically each time you open the database) or close the database (only if you defined the script as a closing script that runs automatically each time you close the database). (See Chapter 7 for more information on this option.)

If you need to stop a script in progress, press ⌘-. (period). If a script is paused (by using a Pause step option or the Pause/Resume Script step), you can stop the script by clicking the Cancel button (instead of the Continue button, as you normally would).

Make Your Own Command-Key Equivalents

The first 10 scripts you create that have the "Include in menu" check box checked are automatically assigned a Command-key equivalent (⌘-1 through ⌘-0). You can also use any of these first 10 script slots to create Command-key-equivalent menu commands for which FileMaker Pro does not provide keyboard shortcuts.

For example, you may want to create a one-step script that simply executes the normal Page Setup command (Page Setup [] or Page Setup [Restore]). As long as this script is one of the first 10 scripts added to the Script menu, you can issue its command by pressing its new Command-key equivalent (⌘-3, for example). You can use this trick to add all your frequently used menu commands to the Script menu, such as View As [toggle] (to switch between viewing records normally or as a list), Save a Copy As (to make a backup copy of the current database), and Check Record (to check the spelling of the current record).

As discussed earlier in this chapter, you can assign a script to the Script menu, attach the script to a button, make the script the startup script, or set none of these options. The decision is entirely yours. You can also change a script or button assignment at any time by following the procedures outlined in this chapter. Note that the Perform button can be used with *any* script, regardless of the other ways in which the script can be accessed.

Modifying a Script

FileMaker Pro provides several methods for altering scripts, including renaming, duplicating, deleting, editing, and changing their order. These important script-editing techniques are discussed in the following sections.

Renaming a Script

If you add a script to the Script menu by clicking the "Include in menu" check box in the Define Scripts dialog box (previously shown in Figure 15-1), whatever name you give the script is what appears in the Script menu. (Otherwise, script names are visible only when you are editing scripts, assigning scripts to buttons, or setting a startup action. In such cases, the specific script names aren't nearly as important because they normally are hidden from the user's view.)

Choosing Script Names

When you name or rename a script, it's always best to choose a descriptive name. Although you could follow the same naming conventions that FileMaker Pro uses for layouts (instead of Layout #1, Layout #2, and so on, you could use Script #1, Script #2, and so on), you'll have a miserable time later trying to determine what each script does. On the other hand, there'll be little possible confusion if you name your scripts descriptively — for example, Sort by State, Find Recent Purchases, and Print Aging Report.

Note, too, that there is no practical limit to the length of each script name. Before going overboard, however, and naming a script "Aging Report (designed for an ImageWriter printer in landscape mode) — to be printed only on the last day of the month," keep two things in mind:

- The Define Scripts dialog box does not expand to show all characters in an extremely long script name. FileMaker Pro displays only as much text as fits in the script list; the remainder is shown as ellipses.
- If a long script name is included in the Script menu, the width of the Script menu will expand as much as possible to display the longest script name — an arrangement that can result in a ridiculous-looking pull-down menu. (I have two separate monitors attached to my Mac. When I assigned the long script name described earlier to the Script menu, the resulting pull-down menu extended off my main monitor and halfway onto a nearby two-page display!)

If you decide to change the name, select the script in the Define Scripts dialog box, type a new name in the Script Name text box (or edit the existing name), and then click the Rename button.

Duplicating a Script

Rather than create every new script from scratch, you sometimes will find it easier to edit a copy of an existing script. For example, you may already have created a script that prints a certain report for you. If you want a similar script that displays the report on-screen, just create a duplicate of the script and change the Print step to an Enter Preview Mode step in the duplicate script.

To create a duplicate of a script, follow these steps:

1. From the script list in the Define Scripts dialog box (previously shown in Figure 15-1), select the name of the script that you want to duplicate.

   When selected, the name of the script appears in the Script Name box.

2. Click the Duplicate button.

   A copy of the script is created and is listed as *script name* Copy (for example, Print Sales Report Copy).

3. *Optional:* Change the name of the duplicate script to something more descriptive by selecting the script in the script list, editing its name in the Script Name box, and clicking the Rename button.

4. Click the Edit button and edit the new script as desired.

5. Click Done when you finish working with the script.

Deleting a Script

If you no longer need a script, or if you are approaching the limit of 52 scripts in the Script menu and need to make room for more, you can delete scripts.

To delete a script, follow these steps:

1. In the Define Scripts dialog box, select the name of the script that you want to delete.

2. Click Delete.

3. In the dialog box that appears, click Delete to remove the script or click Cancel if you change your mind.

Editing a Script

Other editing actions that you can perform on a script include adding, removing, or changing the order of steps and replacing previously set options for steps. To change a script's appearance in — or omission from — the Script menu for the database, you can either click the "Include in menu" check box in the Define Scripts dialog box or click the check mark (or space) in front of the script's name. Like other check boxes, this acts as a toggle; each click reverses the state of the option.

If any steps relevant to the Page Setup, Sort, Find, Import, and Export commands are used in a script, their settings are saved as part of the script. If you set the database for landscape printing and include a Page Setup step, for example, that setting is saved with the script. Whenever you edit an existing script that includes a step that performs a Page Setup, Sort, Find, Import, or Export operation, FileMaker Pro presents the dialog box shown in Figure 15-3.

Figure 15-3: You can either keep the previous settings or replace them with the current settings.

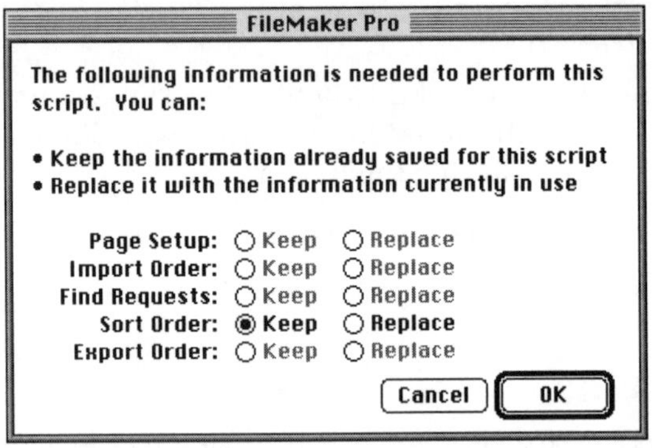

FileMaker Pro

The following information is needed to perform this script. You can:

- Keep the information already saved for this script
- Replace it with the information currently in use

Page Setup: Keep Replace
Import Order: Keep Replace
Find Requests: Keep Replace
Sort Order: Keep Replace
Export Order: Keep Replace

Cancel OK

You use this dialog box to determine whether you want to continue to use the previous settings that were saved with the script (the Keep radio buttons) or replace those settings with the ones that are in effect at the moment (the Replace radio buttons). For example, the Sort Order settings in Figure 15-3 can be kept or replaced. (The other options are dimmed because those steps were not used in the script.) If one of the reasons why you are editing this script is that you just set a different sort order, click the Replace button for Sort Order and then click OK.

Debugging a Script

When a script doesn't do what you intended it to do, you should check several things:

- Are the steps in the proper order?

  A script is not executed en masse — its steps run in the order in which you placed them. If you need to set a printout for Landscape mode, for example, you would place a Page Setup step before the Print step.

- Should you have performed a preparatory action before executing the script?

  If a step acts on a field, for example, you must somehow make the field the current one. If no field is selected, the step does nothing. Use a Specify Field option as part of the step (if one is allowed); include a Go to Field, Go to Next Field, or Go to Previous Field step; or manually select the desired field before running the script.

- Have scripts, layouts, or fields been renamed or deleted?

  Reexamine your scripts in ScriptMaker. If any Perform Script, Go to Layout, or Go to Field step now reads "unknown," it means that the database does not know what script or sub-script it is supposed to perform, the layout to which it is supposed to switch, or the field it is supposed to select. This is often the case when you copy buttons from one database and paste them into another.

- Are you in the proper FileMaker Pro mode?

  Although a script can be *run* from any mode, it cannot operate in Layout mode. For example, a Delete Record/Request step cannot be used to delete a layout. If you're in Layout mode when you execute a script, the script will switch to the mode that the step requires (Browse, Find, or Preview) before continuing.

Script Step Reference

Each element of a script is called a *step*. In this section, the step explanations are presented in the same order in which you'll encounter them in the Available Steps section of the Script Definition dialog box. Figure 15-4 shows the entire set of script steps that are supported by FileMaker Pro 3.0.

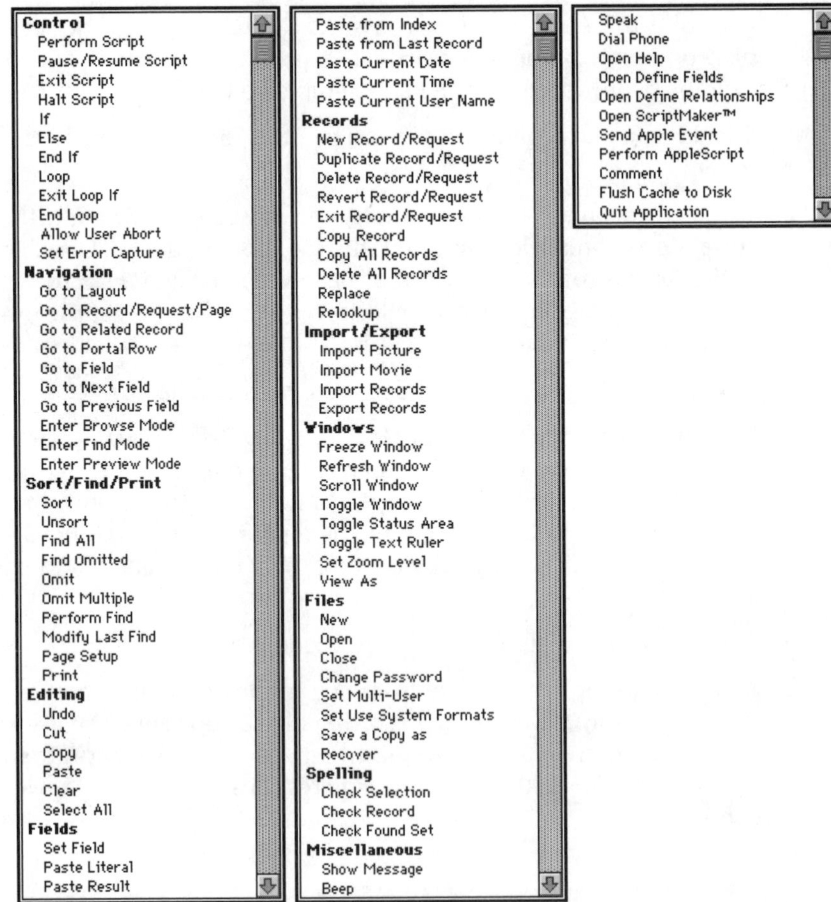

Figure 15-4: Available script steps

The Windows version of FileMaker Pro 3.0 includes several script steps that are not supported by the Macintosh version of the program and vice versa. These steps are related to support for system software features, such as Apple Events and AppleScript (on the Macintosh) and OLE, DDE, and messaging capabilities (Windows). If any of your scripts rely on platform-specific steps, users on the other platform will not be able to run them.

Script Step Options

As you examine the different script steps in ScriptMaker, you'll notice that many of them include options that you can set. The options are individually explained within each step definition (as presented in "Script Step Definitions" in this chapter), but here's a rundown of the effects of the most common step options:

- *Perform without dialog.* Many script steps that normally are performed with an accompanying dialog box (enabling you to select a particular file, for example) can be performed without displaying the dialog box. Set the "Perform without dialog" option when, as part of the script step, you have already specified the file to be opened or other options to be performed, and there is no need to examine or change those options.
- *Specify file.* Click "Specify file" when you always want the current script step to operate on a particular file. This option is often used in conjunction with the "Perform without dialog" option. (Because you have already selected the file, there is no reason to present a file dialog box that enables you to choose a file.)
- *Specify record.* Click "Specify record" when you want the current script step to always operate on a particular record. If you do not click this option, FileMaker Pro assumes that you (or another script step) will make the desired record the active one before this script step is executed.
- *Specify field.* Some script steps operate on the contents of a field. Click "Specify field" if the script should always operate on a particular field. If you do not click this option, FileMaker Pro assumes that you (or another script step) will make the desired field the active one before this script step is executed.

In FileMaker Pro 3.0, you can choose an appropriate field from the current file or from any file for which you have defined a relationship.

- *Select entire contents.* In script steps that deal with field contents (particularly the editing steps, such as Copy, Paste, and Clear), this option causes the entire contents of the chosen field to be selected. Otherwise, only the portion of the field that has been preselected by the user before executing the script will be affected.
- *Restore (import order, sort order, setup options, find requests, and so on).* The wording of the Restore option varies depending on the step to which it is attached. For example, in conjunction with a Sort step, it reads "Restore sort order." Set this option when you want FileMaker Pro to simply execute

whatever settings were in effect for this procedure at the time the script was created. If neither Restore nor "Perform without dialog" is chosen, FileMaker Pro displays the appropriate dialog box when the script step is executed (enabling you to set options as you like).

- *Refresh window.* This option causes the screen to be redrawn when the step is reached.
- *Pause.* This option adds Continue and Cancel buttons to the associated script step. The purpose of this option is to give the user an opportunity to perform an action (entering criteria in a find request or browsing through the report information that is currently displayed, for example) before continuing the current script.
- *Exit after last.* This option is available for relative record-navigation steps (Go to Record/Request/Page). When this option is selected and the script tries to select a record that is outside the range of record numbers (choosing a record before the first record or after the last record in the current browsed set), the step is not performed and the script ends. When this option is not selected, and the script tries to select a record that is outside the range of record numbers, the step is performed on a record that it *can* reach (either the first or last record in the database).
- *On/Off.* Use the On or Off options to toggle a script feature on or off. In many cases, such a script step is used in pairs — the first instance turns on a feature (such as error capture) and a second instance turns it off.

Script Step Definitions

FileMaker Pro 3.0 provides 115 steps that you can use individually or in combination with other steps to form a script. The following sections provide detailed explanations of each step, including the ways in which the available options affect the step. For additional information on a script step, refer to the chapter in which the equivalent menu command is discussed.

Control Script Steps

The following script steps are used to execute subscripts and external scripts, control script execution, provide conditional branching and looping, and enable or disable FileMaker Pro's normal error-handling mechanism.

Perform Script

Purpose: Use Perform Script to execute another script from within the current script. When the execution of the other script concludes, the original script resumes automatically.

Options: Perform sub-scripts

Use the Specify pop-up menu to select the script that you want to perform. The name of every script that is currently defined for the database is listed in this pop-up menu. The final option in the Specify pop-up menu is External Script. Choose External Script if you want to execute a script in another FileMaker Pro database. When an external script is executed, its database is automatically opened in FileMaker Pro, and then the script runs.

Example: Suppose that you have two databases: Invoices and Addresses. You could create a script in Invoices that — using the Perform Script command — executed a find request in Addresses (enabling you to locate a particular customer address or all addresses that include San Francisco in the City field, for example).

Pause/Resume Script

Purpose: Use this script step to pause a script, enabling the user to perform some non-script action during the execution of a script.

Options: Specify

In FileMaker Pro 3.0, a script can be paused indefinitely, for a duration specified by a field value, or for a specific amount of time (as shown in Figure 15-5). When a Pause/Resume Script step is executed, the status area of the document window changes to show Continue and Cancel buttons — indicating that the script has been paused. If Indefinitely (the default choice) is selected, the script will remain paused until the user clicks Continue. If a pause duration is specified (either by the contents of a specific field or by entering a particular pause time), the script will continue either when the user clicks Continue or when the specified time period has elapsed.

Pause/Resume Options
Pause script and wait for user interaction
Indefinitely
For duration given by field value [Specify...]
For duration: [0] hours [0] minutes [0] seconds
[Cancel] [OK]

Figure 15-5: The Pause/Resume Options dialog box

Example: You can alternate Go to Field steps with Pause/Resume Script steps to walk a novice user through a data-entry routine.

Exit Script

Purpose: The Exit Script step is used to immediately end the execution of any subscripts or external scripts, and then resume executing the main script.

Options: none

This script step is particularly useful when executed in conjunction with the If step to test for error conditions or another reason to prematurely end a subscript or external script.

Halt Script

Purpose: When encountered in a script, the Halt Script step immediately ends the execution of the current script, as well as any sub-scripts or external scripts. Like the Exit Script step, a conditional test (an If step) is often used to determine when it is necessary to end the script.

Options: none

If

Purpose: The If step is used to evaluate a calculation (set with the Specify option) and perform a conditional action based on the result. If the calculation evaluates as true (a non-zero result), the additional steps are performed. If the calculation evaluates as false (zero), the remaining steps associated with the If script structure are skipped.

Every If structure must end with an End If step (added automatically by FileMaker Pro). You can specify an additional condition by including an Else step.

Options: Specify

See also: End If, Loop

Else

Purpose: The Else step is used in conjunction with the If step to perform an alternate course of action.

Options: none

Example: The following script moves to Field 1 if the current record contains "Redmond" in the City field (true); otherwise, it moves to Field 2 (false):

```
If ["City = "Redmond""]
 Go to Field ["Field 1"]
Else
 Go to Field ["Field 2"]
End If
```

See also: If, End If, Exit Loop If

End If

Purpose: The End If step ends every If script structure. When you insert an If statement into a script, an End If is automatically added by FileMaker Pro.

Options: none

See also: If, Else

Loop

Purpose: The Loop step is used to repeat a series of script steps. (In the BASIC programming language, loops are performed by combining For/Next, Do/Until, Repeat/While statements, and similar keyword pairs.) An End Loop statement must be placed as the final step in the loop, and it is automatically added by FileMaker Pro.

The loop repeats until the condition specified in an enclosed Exit Loop If or Exit After Last step within the loop is fulfilled.

Options: none

Examples: Here are two ways to exit from a loop. In the first example, the loop is exited after the first 10 records in the database have been processed (the Global field Count is used to keep track of the number of passes made through the loop — one pass per record):

```
Go to Record/Request/Page [First]
Set Field ["Count","0"]
Loop
 … statements to be executed go here …
 Set Field ["Count", "Count + 1"]
 Exit Loop If ["Count = 10"]
End Loop
```

In the second example, the loop automatically ends when the last record in the file is encountered (an Exit Loop If step is unnecessary). The first record to be processed as part of the loop is specified in the first script step. Rather than using a Global field as a counter, the [Next] option (near the bottom of the loop) is used to step through the records:

```
Go to Record/Request/Page [First]
Loop
 … statements to be executed go here …
 Go to Record/Request/Page [Exit after last, Next]
End Loop
```

See also: Exit Loop If, End Loop

Exit Loop If

Purpose: This step specifies the condition that, when tested, determines if a loop has been completed. The calculation is evaluated on each pass through the loop. If the result of the calculation is true (non-zero), the loop is exited; otherwise, another pass is made through the loop.

For an example of how the Exit Loop If step works, see the Loop step (described previously).

Options: Specify the calculation

See also: Loop, End Loop

End Loop

Purpose: The End Loop step is the final step in a Loop structure. When you insert a Loop step into a script, FileMaker Pro automatically adds an End Loop step.

Options: none

See also: Loop, Exit Loop If

Allow User Abort

Purpose: This script step either enables or prevents the user from halting the script to which it is attached. (Scripts can be stopped by pressing ⌘-. [period]). The default setting is On.

Options: On or Off

Examples: In continuous-running demos, it is a good practice to set Allow User Abort to Off and make it the first step in the script. When Allow User Abort is set to Off for such a script, not only do you prevent the script from being halted, but you effectively prevent the user from quitting the program, too.

As another example, if a script contains a critical section that must never be interrupted, you can precede the section by Allow User Abort [Off] and then conclude the section with Allow User Abort [On] — restoring the ability to halt the remainder of the script.

Set Error Capture

Purpose: By default, FileMaker Pro presents alert boxes when an error that it is designed to handle is detected. (This is the equivalent of Set Error Capture [Off].) By adding this step and setting its option to On, you tell FileMaker Pro to suppress all error messages while the script is running — usually because you intend to do the error trapping yourself by using the Status(CurrentError) function.

Options: On or Off

A list of the error codes that Status(CurrentError) generates can be found in the FileMaker Pro Help listing for that function.

Navigation Script Steps

The navigation script steps enable FileMaker Pro to switch to or select a particular layout, record, field, and so on, as well as change to a specific mode (Browse, Find, or Preview).

There are no script steps that change to Layout mode because no script can be executed when FileMaker Pro is in Layout mode.

Go to Layout

Purpose: Use this step to switch to a particular layout that has been created for the current database (which is the same as choosing a specific layout name from the layout pop-up menu in the upper-left corner of the document window).

Options: Refresh screen

The Specify pop-up menu must be used to select the layout that you want to display. In most cases, you will want to change to a particular layout; to do so, choose its name (Menu or Data Entry, for example) from the Specify menu. You can also switch to a layout based on a number in a chosen field. (You *must* specify the field name if you choose this option.)

The Specify pop-up menu also has a special option, called "Original layout," that is useful for ending a script. This option tells FileMaker Pro to switch back to whatever layout was current when the script was executed. For example, a Print Report script could be invoked from a layout named Data Entry. The script might switch to a report layout, print a copy of the report, and then — using the "Original layout" option — end by switching back to the Data Entry layout. The advantage of using "Original layout" rather than specifying the exact layout name (Data Entry, in this case) is that the script conceivably could be invoked from any layout and still return the user to that layout.

Go to Layout is one of the most frequently used script steps. It's not unusual to begin a script with this step (to ensure that the correct layout is displayed, for example). In many databases (such as those found on the *Macworld FileMaker Pro 3.0 Bible Disk*), this step is attached to navigation buttons that display a help or report layout.

Go to Record/Request/Page

Purpose: This step is used to display a particular record in the current found set or to enable the user to select one of these records to display. Go to Record/Request/Page is frequently used to move directly to the first or last record in the database. (Specify 1 to go to the first record, and specify a very high record number — such as 9999 — to go to the last record.) When executed from Find mode, Go to Record/Request/Page displays a find request page instead of a record. When run from Preview mode, Go to Record/Request/Page displays the specified report page.

Options: Specify First, Last, Previous, Next; Specify By Number; Specify By Field Value; Exit after last; Perform without dialog

Depending on the Specify option you select, this step can display the previous, next, first, or last record, request, or page. It can also display a particular record, request, or page (if you choose "By Number"), or it can select a record, request, or page according to the contents of a field that you specify (if you choose "By Field Value").

Records can only be selected from the current found set. If you are using the By Number option to point to a specific record and it is conceivable that the record could be hidden, you will usually want to precede this script step with a find request to ensure that the particular record of interest will indeed be available. If the record to be displayed could be different for each execution of the script, leave the "Perform without dialog" check box unchecked.

When the By Number option is chosen and "Perform without dialog" is *unchecked*, the dialog box in Figure 15-6 appears. The wording changes to reflect the number of records in the found set (that is, the records currently being browsed), the number of find requests, or the pages in the current report.

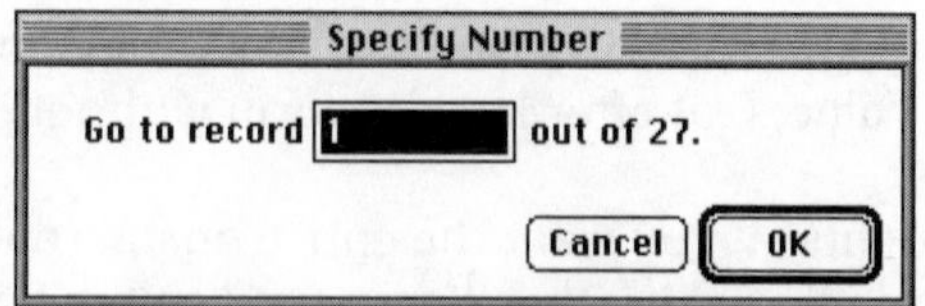

Figure 15-6: The Specify Number dialog box

When "Perform without dialog" *is* checked, no dialog box appears, and the script immediately displays the record, find request, or report page that you've specified.

The "Exit after last" option can be used in conjunction with the Previous or Next option. When chosen, "Exit after last" keeps the script from wrapping around when the last or first record, request, or page is encountered (when Next or Previous is chosen, respectively). This is of special concern when you are using a script to step through the records of a database, for example.

See also: Go to Related Record

Go to Related Record

Purpose: This script step is used to display a record in a related file, based on the current relationship and the field that is presently active. If either a field in a portal or a related field that has been placed directly on the layout is selected, executing the Go to Related Record step displays the matching record from the related database. If the field that defines the relationship is selected, the *first* matching record from the related file is displayed.

Options: Specify relationship, Show only related records

Use the Specify pop-up menu to select a relationship (or define one, if none currently exists). The "Show only related records" option is extremely useful. Choose it to limit the visible records (the found set) in the related file to those that meet the criteria of the relationship.

See also: Go to Record/Request/Page, Go to Portal Row

Go to Portal Row

Purpose: This step enables you to move to a particular row in the active portal. If a portal isn't active, the step is applied to the first portal encountered in the layout's stacking order (that is, the front-most, highest one).

When changing portal rows, this step attempts to keep the same field active (if one is currently active). If no field in the portal is active, the step activates the first field that it can enter.

Options: Select entire contents; Specify First, Last, Next, Previous; Specify By Number; Specify By Field Value; Exit after last; Perform without dialog

Choose "Select entire contents" if you want the entire portal row to be selected, rather than just making a single field active. You must use the Specify pop-up menu to choose a target portal row.

The Next and Previous options include an "Exit after last" option that enables this script step to end if you attempt to select a portal row that is before the first or after the last row. If you do not include this option, the step simply wraps around and goes to the last or first portal row, respectively.

Choose the By Number option to specify a particular portal row by its number. When executed, this step can present a dialog box in which you choose a different row number, or it can go directly to a particular row when "Perform without dialog" is checked.

To choose a portal row based on the current value in a particular field, choose "By field value" and select a field.

See also: Go to Related Record, Go to Field

Go to Field

Purpose: Use this step to go to a particular field in the current layout or in a layout for a related file.

Options: Select/Play, Specify field

When a script includes steps that copy, cut, or paste information, you can use Go to Field to specify the appropriate field for each editing operation. Use the Specify field option to tell FileMaker Pro the field to which you want to go. (You *must* specify a field; otherwise, the script fails at this step.)

Set the Select/Play option if you want to select the contents of a field (usually as a prelude to editing). If you set Select/Play and choose a Container field that contains either a sound or a movie, the sound or movie plays.

See also: Go to Next Field, Go to Previous Field

Go to Next Field

Purpose: Use this step to move to the next field in the current layout. If no field is selected when a Go to Next Field step executes, you move to the first field in the current layout. FileMaker Pro uses the tab order that is set for the layout to determine what the "next" field is.

Options: none

Example: After starting a script with a Go to Field step to set the first field, you could use a series of Go to Next Field steps — each followed by a Pause/Resume Script step — to walk a new user through a data-entry layout. The beginning of the script might look like this:

```
Go to Field ["Last Name"]
Pause/Resume Script
Go to Next Field
Pause/Resume Script
Go to Next Field
```

See also: Go to Previous Field, Go to Field

Go to Previous Field

Purpose: Use this step to move to the preceding field in the current layout. If no field is selected when a Go to Previous Field step executes, you move to the last field in the current layout. FileMaker Pro uses the tab order that is set for the layout to determine what the "previous" field is.

Options: none

See also: Go to Next Field, Go to Field

Enter Browse Mode

Purpose: Regardless of the active mode of the current database, this step switches to Browse mode (which is the same as choosing Browse from the Mode menu or pressing ⌘-B). You use Browse mode to enter and edit data.

Options: Pause

Select the Pause option if you want to temporarily pause the script to enable the user to enter or edit data.

See also: Enter Find Mode, Enter Preview Mode

Enter Find Mode

Purpose: This script step switches the current layout to Find mode, enabling you to execute find requests (which is the same as choosing Find from the Mode menu or pressing ⌘-F).

Options: Restore find requests, Pause

Select “Restore find requests” to start each find request with the criteria that were in effect when the script was created. If you prefer to start the find request from scratch, leave this option unchecked. If additional steps follow Enter Find Mode, you also should select the Pause option — assuming that you want an opportunity to modify the find requests.

See also: Perform Find, Enter Browse Mode, Enter Preview Mode

Enter Preview Mode

Purpose: This step switches the current layout to Preview mode (which is the same as choosing Preview from the Mode menu or pressing ⌘-U).

Options: Pause

Preview mode is often used to display on-screen reports or to examine a layout before printing (commonly called a *print preview* in many Macintosh programs). When the Enter Preview Mode step is followed by other steps, you may want to use the Pause option so that users of the database will have an adequate opportunity to examine the preview.

See also: Print, Enter Find Mode, Enter Browse Mode

Sort/Find/Print Script Steps

The Sort/Find/Print script steps enable you to execute sort, find, and printing commands in scripts, as well as set options for any of these procedures.

Sort

Purpose: Use the Sort step to sort the browsed records in a particular order (which is the same as choosing Sort from the Mode menu or pressing ⌘-S).

Options: Restore sort order, Perform without dialog

If "Restore sort order" is checked, the sort order defaults to the sort instructions that were in effect at the time the script was created. If "Restore sort order" is not checked, the sort order defaults to the most recently executed sort instructions for the database.

If you want to be able to set different sort instructions each time the step executes, make sure that you do *not* check the "Perform without dialog" option. If, on the other hand, the sort instructions will not change from one execution of the script to another, or if you want to keep users from modifying the instructions, check "Perform without dialog."

See also: Unsort

Unsort

Purpose: Use Unsort to restore records to the order in which they were entered into the database (which is the same as clicking the Unsort button in the Sort Records dialog box).

Options: none

Example: This script step is most useful when you have a database with records that were created in a purposeful order but now are sorted in some other order. Records in a checkbook database, for example, normally are created in date order; records in an invoice database are entered in order of invoice number. Unsort restores the records to their original order.

See also: Sort

Find All

Purpose: This step makes all records visible (which is the same as choosing Find All from the Select menu or pressing ⌘-J). Use Find All when you want to work with all records in the database, rather than with just the current found set.

Options: none

See also: Enter Find Mode, Perform Find Request, Modify Last Find, Omit, Omit Multiple, Find Omitted

Find Omitted

Purpose: This step swaps any records that are currently not included in the found set for those that *are* in the found set (which is the same as choosing Find Omitted from the Select menu). The omitted records become visible, and the previously browsed records are hidden. Note that if all records are currently being browsed, this step has no effect.

Options: none

See also: Enter Find Mode, Perform Find Request, Find All, Modify Last Find, Omit, Omit Multiple

Omit

Purpose: This step omits (hides) the current record from the found set (which is the same as choosing Omit from the Select menu or pressing ⌘-M).

Options: none

See also: Enter Find Mode, Perform Find Request, Find All, Modify Last Find, Omit Multiple, Find Omitted

Omit Multiple

Purpose: This step omits (hides) the next *x* consecutive records from the found set (which is the same as choosing Omit Multiple from the Select menu or pressing Shift-⌘-M).

Options: Specify record, Perform without dialog

When an Omit Multiple step executes, a dialog box normally appears (see Figure 15-7) that asks the number of records you want to omit, beginning with the current record.

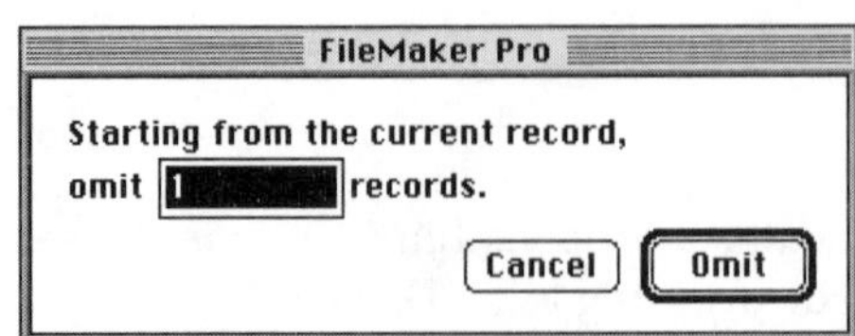

Figure 15-7: This dialog box appears when the Omit Multiple script step executes.

If the "Perform without dialog" option is checked, the step defaults to omitting only the current record, just as though you had used the Omit step described earlier.

The "Specify record" option enables you to set the number of records that you want to omit (as always, beginning with the record that is current at the time the step is performed). If "Perform without dialog" is also selected, the specified number of records are automatically omitted. Otherwise, the normal dialog box appears, and it uses the number of records that you specified as the default entry.

See also: Enter Find Mode, Perform Find Request, Find All, Modify Last Find, Omit, Find Omitted

Perform Find

Purpose: Use this step to execute the current find request or requests (which is the same as clicking the Find button in a find request screen).

Options: Restore find requests

You must already have defined one or more find requests to use this script step. You can do so by using the Enter Find Mode step earlier in the script, by manually setting up the find request (or requests) just before executing the script, or by executing a find request just before creating the script and then checking the "Restore find requests" option.

See also: Find All, Modify Last Find, Enter Find Mode

Modify Last Find

Purpose: This step presents the most recently executed find request, which you can re-execute or use as the basis for a new find request (which is the same as choosing Modify Last Find from the Select menu or pressing ⌘-R).

This script step is always performed by displaying a normal find request on-screen.

Options: none

See also: Enter Find Mode, Perform Find Request, Find All, Omit, Omit Multiple, Find Omitted

Page Setup

Purpose: Use this script step to specify Page Setup options, such as paper size and orientation, for a print job (which is the same as choosing Page Setup from the File menu).

Options: Restore setup options, Perform without dialog

See also: Print

Print

Purpose: Use this step to send data to a printer or other output device (such as a fax-modem) according to the options set in the Print dialog box (which is the same as choosing Print from the File menu or pressing ⌘-P).

Options: Perform without dialog

By default, FileMaker Pro assumes that you want to use the Print options that were in effect when you last printed the database. If you want the chance to specify different Print options each time the script runs, leave the "Perform without dialog" option unchecked. When the script runs, you see the normal FileMaker Pro Print dialog box. On the other hand, if you always want to print with the same set of Print options (or you don't want to give users an opportunity to select other Print options — inappropriate ones that might ruin the print job, for example), click "Perform without dialog."

If special Page Setup options are necessary for a print job to print correctly (such as when you are printing labels on an ImageWriter printer or printing in Landscape mode), you will want to include Page Setup as an earlier script step. Before including either the Print or Page Setup step in a script, start by printing the job correctly. Then, when you enter the Print and Page Setup steps in the script, FileMaker Pro will note the options that are set for these two steps and use those options whenever the script executes.

See also: Page Setup, Enter Preview Mode

Editing Script Steps

The editing script steps enable you to execute standard editing commands within scripts and apply them to selected fields.

Undo

Purpose: This step reverses (undoes) the most recent action performed in the database (which is the same as choosing Undo from the Edit menu or pressing ⌘-Z). The "most recent action" conceivably could be another script step.

Options: none

Not all actions can be undone. Any command associated with deleting records, for example, cannot be reversed. When a command cannot be undone, the Undo command reads Can't Undo, and the Undo script step has no effect.

Cut

Purpose: This step cuts the selected contents of a field to the Clipboard (which is the same as choosing Cut from the Edit menu or pressing ⌘-X). Information that is cut with this step is available for pasting elsewhere in the record, in a different record (enabling you to move existing information from one record to another), or in another program.

Cutting removes the selected text from the field. If your intent is merely to duplicate the information, use the Copy step instead.

Options: Select entire contents, Specify field

Using the options alone or in combination, you can cut the entire contents of the current field ("Select entire contents"), cut the selected contents of a particular field ("Specify field"), or cut the entire contents of a particular field ("Select entire contents" *and* "Specify field").

Like the other editing script steps, Cut must be directed to a specific field in order for it to work. You can use a Go to Field script step to move to a particular field or the "Specify field" option. If you want this step to apply to any field on a layout, you must tab into or click the field before executing the step.

See also: Clear, Copy, Paste

Copy

Purpose: This step copies the selected contents of a field to the Clipboard (which is the same as choosing Copy from the Edit menu or pressing ⌘-C). Information that is copied with this step is available for pasting elsewhere in the record, in a different record (enabling you to duplicate existing information), or in another program.

Options: Select entire contents, Specify field

Using the options alone or in combination, you can copy the entire contents of a field ("Select entire contents"), copy the selected contents of a particular field ("Specify field"), or copy the entire contents of a particular field ("Select entire contents" *and* "Specify field").

See also: Cut, Paste

Paste

Purpose: This script step pastes the current contents of the Clipboard into the current field (which is the same as choosing Paste from the Edit menu or pressing ⌘-V) or into a specified field.

Options: Select entire contents, Paste without style, Specify field

Data can be pasted into a field that is specified as a script step option or into the current field, depending on whether the "Specify field" option is used. Pasted data can replace the entire contents of the field (with "Select entire contents" checked) or can be added to the field at the insertion point (with "Select entire contents" unchecked). If "Paste without style" is checked, any style formatting applied to the text (bold or italic, for example) is ignored. Otherwise, the pasted text includes whatever styles originally were applied to the text.

You should be aware of several common-sense restrictions when you use the Paste step. First, if the Clipboard is empty, nothing is pasted. Second, if the Clipboard contains data that is inappropriate for the selected field (such as a sound, picture, or movie that you are attempting to paste into a Text field), nothing is pasted. Third, if no field is selected in the current layout and a field is not specified as an option for the script step, nothing is pasted.

Because the Clipboard is shared among all Macintosh programs, the material pasted could conceivably come from a program other than FileMaker Pro. For example, you could use a macro utility such as QuicKeys (discussed elsewhere in this chapter) to copy some text in a word processing program and then use the Paste step to transfer a copy of the text to a database field.

The "Link if available" option is for Windows users only. It is grayed out in the Macintosh version of FileMaker Pro 3.0.

See also: Paste Literal, Paste from Last Record, Paste from Index, Paste Current Time, Paste Current Date, Paste Current User, Cut, Copy

Clear

Purpose: The Clear step removes data from the current field (which is the same as choosing Clear from the Edit menu) or removes it from the particular field specified in the script step. Depending on the option selected, this step can delete all the data from a field or only the data that is currently selected.

Options: Select entire contents, Specify field

Clear can be used either on the currently selected field (by leaving the "Specify field" option unchecked) or on a particular field (by clicking "Specify field" and then choosing a field in the current file or in a related file). To clear all data from a field, click the "Select entire contents" check box. To clear only the currently selected data from the field, leave "Select entire contents" unchecked. If the script step does not use the "Select entire contents" option, you must preselect text in the field before executing the script; otherwise, the step has no effect.

Unlike Cut, the Clear step does not save a copy of the data that has been removed — the data is not available for pasting. If you make a mistake, however, you can correct the Clear operation by immediately choosing Undo Clear from the Edit menu.

See also: Cut

Select All

Purpose: The Select All step selects the entire contents of the current field (which is the same as choosing Select All from the Edit menu, pressing ⌘-A, or quadruple-clicking a field). If no field is currently selected, nothing happens.

Options: none

Fields Script Steps

These steps are used to paste or place information of various types into a selected field.

Set Field

Purpose: Use the Set Field step to set the contents of a particular field, based on the result of a calculation. The result of the calculation must be of a type that is appropriate for the target field.

Options: Specify field, Specify the calculation

If the "Specify field" option is not used to select a field to be set, the currently active field (if any) is set. The Specify button is used to create the formula used by the step.

Example: The Set Field step can be used to set the value for a Global field. For example, when using a loop to move through all records in a database and calculate a value, you can create the following Set Field step to initialize the value (held in a Global field named Insurance Total):

```
Set Field ["Insurance Total", "0"]
```

Then you can use the Set Field step again within a loop to update the value in Insurance Total, as follows:

```
Go to Record/Request/Page [First]
Loop
 If ["Insurance = "Yes""]
        Set Field ["Insurance Total","Insurance Total +
Insurance Amount"]
 End If
 Go to Record/Request/Page [Exit after last, Next]
End Loop
```

Thus, if there is a Yes entry in the Insurance field for a record, the value of Insurance Total is updated by adding the amount in the record's Insurance Amount field.

See also: Paste Result

Paste Literal

Purpose: Use this step to paste a specific string (text or number) at the insertion point within the current field. Click Specify to indicate the string that you want to paste.

This script step assumes that you have selected a field and positioned the insertion point before the step is executed. You can do this manually or by choosing the appropriate options for the step.

Options: Select entire contents, Specify field

Paste Literal can be used either on the currently selected field (by leaving the "Specify field" option unchecked) or on a particular field (by clicking "Specify field" and then choosing a field in the current file or in a related file). To replace all data in the field, click the "Select entire contents" check box. To replace only the currently selected data from the field, leave "Select entire contents" unchecked.

See also: Paste

Paste Result

Purpose: This step pastes the result of a calculation (specified as part of the Paste Result step) into a particular field on the current layout in the current record.

Options: Select entire contents, Specify field, Specify the calculation

Click Specify to create the calculation. You can then use the "Specify field" option to choose a field in which to paste the result. If no field is specified, the result is pasted into the active field (if any) on the current layout. If no field is active, or if the target field is not available on the current layout, this step has no effect.

Click "Select entire contents" to replace the entire contents of the target field. If this option is not chosen, only the selected contents of the field are replaced, or the paste is made at the current insertion point. (If there is no current insertion point, the result is pasted at the end of the contents of the target field.)

Both the Paste Result and Set Field steps take the result of a calculation and use it to change the contents of a field. However, there are two notable differences, as follows:

- Paste Result can only change fields that are on the currently selected layout. Set Field doesn't care what layout is active or even if the field has been placed on a layout.
- Set Field automatically replaces the entire contents of the selected field. Paste Result can be directed to replace just the currently selected portion of the target field, or it can insert the result at the current text insertion point.

See also: Set Field

Paste from Index

Purpose: This step enables you to paste information into a field by selecting the data to be pasted from the index for that field (which is the same as choosing the From Index option from the Paste Special submenu of the Edit menu or pressing ⌘-I). When this script step is executed, FileMaker displays the index for the current field (see Figure 15-8) and allows you to select the index entry that you want to paste. This step is very helpful for ensuring the correct spelling and consistent wording of field entries.

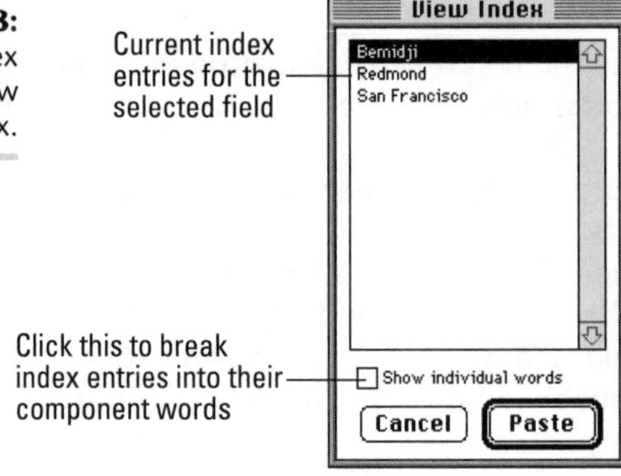

Figure 15-8: The current field's index is presented in the View Index dialog box.

Options: Select entire contents, Specify field

If you do not set the "Specify field" option, FileMaker assumes that you will preselect a field before executing this script step.

The Paste from Index step does nothing if either of the following is true:

- The chosen field doesn't exist in the current layout.
- No index has been created for the field and "automatically turn indexing on if needed" is not part of the field's definition.

See also: Paste

Paste from Last Record

Purpose: This step pastes information from the most recently modified record into the selected field of the current record (which is the same as choosing the From Last Record option from the Paste Special submenu of the Edit menu or pressing ⌘-').

Options: Select entire contents, Specify field

If the field to be used is not set with the "Specify field" option, FileMaker Pro assumes that you will select the field manually or as a previous script step before executing the Paste from Last Record step. Because you generally will want to replace whatever is in the chosen field with the entire contents of that field from the last modified record, the "Select entire contents" option is the one you will most often need to use with this step.

See also: Duplicate Record/Request

Paste Current Date

Purpose: This step pastes today's date (according to your system clock) into the current field (which is the same as choosing the Current Date option from the Paste Special submenu of the Edit menu or pressing ⌘--) or in a field specified as a step option.

Options: Select entire contents, Specify field

The date can be pasted into a field that is specified as a step option or into the current field, depending on whether the "Specify field" option is used. The pasted date can replace the entire contents of the field (with "Select entire contents" checked) or can be added to the field at the insertion point (with "Select entire contents" unchecked). For the step to work, the chosen field must be of a proper type to accept a date.

Example: If you do not already have an auto-entry field that automatically receives the current date when a new record is created or edited, you can use this script step to add a date stamp — such as a step in a data-entry or report-preparation script.

See also: Paste, Paste Current Time

Paste Current Time

Purpose: This step pastes the current time (according to your system clock) into the current field (which is the same as choosing the Current Time option from the Paste Special submenu of the Edit menu or pressing ⌘-;) or in a field specified as a step option.

Options: Select entire contents, Specify field

The time can be pasted into a field that is specified as a step option or into the current field, depending on whether the "Specify field" option is used. The pasted time can replace the entire contents of the field (with "Select entire contents" checked) or can be added to the field at the insertion point (with "Select entire contents" unchecked). For the step to work, the chosen field must be of a proper type to accept a time.

Example: If you do not already have an auto-entry field that automatically receives the current time when a new record is created or edited, you can use this script step to add a time stamp as a step in a data-entry or report-preparation script.

See also: Paste, Paste Current Date

Paste Current User Name

Purpose: This step pastes the name of the current user — according to the setting in the General section of the Preferences dialog box — into the current field (which is the same as choosing Current User Name from the Paste Special submenu of the Edit menu or pressing Shift-⌘-N) or in a field specified as a step option. (See Chapter 7 for instructions on setting or changing the current user name.)

Options: Select entire contents, Specify field

The user name can be pasted into a field that is specified as a step option or into the current field, depending on whether the “Specify field” option is used. The pasted name can replace the entire contents of the field (with “Select entire contents” checked) or can be added to the field at the insertion point (with “Select entire contents” unchecked).

See also: Paste

Records Script Steps

These steps enable you to create, delete, and duplicate records, as well as issue record-related commands.

New Record/Request

Purpose: Use this script step to create a new blank record or find request. When used in Browse mode, this step has the same effect as choosing New Record from the Mode menu (or pressing ⌘-N). When used in Find mode, this step has the same effect as choosing New Request from the Mode menu (or pressing ⌘-N).

Options: none

Example: When scripting a data-entry routine to be used by novice computer users, you might well begin the script with a New Record/Request. In the Address Book database, this single step is attached to the New Record button (in the Data Entry layout) so that users can create additional records easily without having to know the Command key sequence or the menu in which the command is located.

Duplicate Record/Request

Purpose: When executed in Browse mode, this step makes a duplicate of the current record (which is the same as choosing Duplicate Record from the Mode menu or pressing ⌘-D). When executed from Find mode, the step makes a duplicate of the current find request (which is the same as choosing Duplicate Request from the Mode menu or pressing ⌘-D).

Options: none

Example: Making a duplicate record and then editing the duplicate is a common data-entry shortcut for working with records that contain similar information. In a home-expenses database, for example, you undoubtedly would record expenses to the same companies over and over. If the only items that change are the amount and/or payment date, you can save time by finding a previous record for the same company (the electric company, for example), duplicating the old record, and then editing the record by typing the new dollar amount and transaction date.

See also: Paste from Last Record

Delete Record/Request

Purpose: This step is used to delete the current record (which is the same as choosing Delete Record from the Mode menu or pressing ⌘-E) or the current find request (which is the same as choosing Delete Request from the Edit menu or pressing ⌘-E).

Options: Perform without dialog

Select "Perform without dialog" if you don't want the opportunity to confirm the "Permanently delete this ENTIRE record?" query that normally appears. Keep in mind, however, that as with other FileMaker Pro Delete commands, you cannot undo a record deletion.

See also: Delete All Records

Revert Record/Request

Purpose: This step is used to restore the current record or the current find request to its state before you began editing the record (which is the same as choosing Revert Record from the Mode menu) or the find request (which is the same as choosing Revert Request from the Mode menu).

Options: Perform without dialog

Exit Record/Request

Purpose: This step exits the current record (in Browse mode) or find request (in Find mode). It is equivalent to clicking outside of the active record or pressing Enter (to complete a record). Following an Exit Record/Request, field data for the record is updated and no field is currently active.

Options: none

Copy Record

Purpose: This step copies the contents of all eligible fields for the current record to the Clipboard (in tab-delimited format). Graphics and sounds are not copied.

Options: none

When copying a record that contains repeating fields, the repetitions are represented by ASCII 29 — an undefined character.

See also: Copy All Records

Copy All Records

Purpose: This step copies the contents of all eligible fields for all records to the Clipboard in tab-delimited format (which is the same as pressing the Option key while choosing Copy from the Edit menu). Graphics and sounds are not copied.

Options: none

When copying records that contain repeating fields, the repetitions are represented by ASCII 29 — an undefined character.

See also: Copy Record

Delete All Records

Purpose: Use the Delete All Records step (formerly called Delete Found Set) to simultaneously delete all records that are currently being browsed (which is the same as choosing Delete All from the Mode menu).

Options: Perform without dialog

To make sure that this step is performed on the correct set of records, you should first issue appropriate Find commands or use a Find step, such as Perform Find, to select the group of records to be deleted. As with other Delete commands, you cannot undo a Delete All Records step.

See also: Delete Record/Request, Find All, Perform Find, Enter Find Mode, Modify Last Find, Omit, Omit Multiple, Find Omitted

Replace

Purpose: This step enables you to replace the same field in all records being browsed with the contents of the current field, a serial number, or a calculated value (which is the same as choosing Replace from the Mode menu or pressing ⌘-=).

Options: Perform without dialog, Specify field

If you want to automatically use whatever information is in the selected or specified field of the current record, choose "Perform without dialog." If you want to use the Replace step to reserialize the records (assign serial numbers to the chosen field), do not check "Perform without dialog." When the step executes, the dialog box shown in Figure 15-9 appears, enabling you to set a starting serial number and an increment. When the dialog box is on-screen, the user can use Replace to perform the same actions as Reserialize.

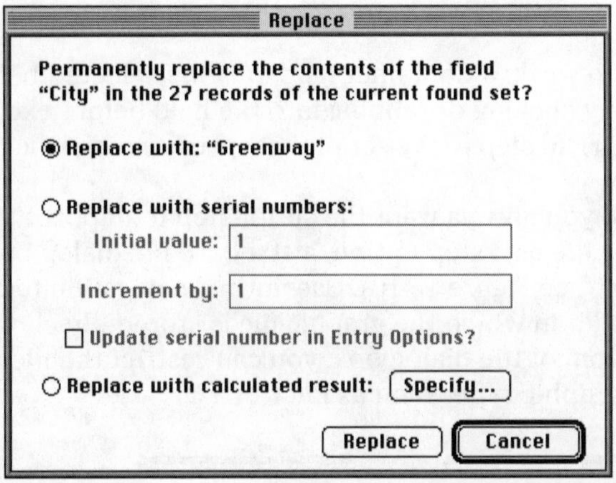

Figure 15-9: This dialog box enables you to set serial-number options, specify a formula to use to calculate replacement values, or simply replace the contents of the current field with a constant in all browsed records.

Replace

Permanently replace the contents of the field "City" in the 27 records of the current found set?

◉ Replace with: "Greenway"

○ Replace with serial numbers:
Initial value: 1
Increment by: 1
☐ Update serial number in Entry Options?

○ Replace with calculated result: Specify...

Replace | Cancel

Example: The Replace step is very useful when you want to ensure consistency in a set of records. For example, you might issue a find request that selects all New York ZIP codes and then use Replace to make sure that all the State fields contain the same information — presumably, New York or NY.

Relookup

Purpose: This step causes a relookup operation to be performed for the currently selected trigger field across all records being browsed (which is the same as choosing Relookup from the Mode menu).

Options: Perform without dialog, Specify field

Use the "Specify field" option to select an eligible trigger field on which to base the relookup operation. If you do not set this option, FileMaker Pro assumes that you will select the field manually before executing the script.

Example: If a database relies on lookups to record customer address data, you could create a Relookup startup script that automatically updates the address information each time that the database is opened.

Import/Export Script Steps

These script steps enable you to export records for use elsewhere and to import pictures, movies, and records into the current database.

Import Picture

Purpose: Use this script step to import a graphic from a disk file into a Container field (which is the same as choosing Import Picture from the Import/Export submenu of the File menu).

Options: Specify file

For Import Picture to work, a Container field must be selected before the step is executed — either by clicking or tabbing into the field before executing the script or by adding a Go to Field step to the script that specifies the name of a Container field.

Click "Specify file" if you always want the script step to import the same picture. If you do not specify a file as a step option, a standard file dialog box appears when the step is executed (see Figure 15-10). Use normal navigation techniques to select the drive and/or folder in which the graphic file is stored. By clicking the Show pop-up menu at the bottom of the dialog box, you can restrict the files displayed to those of a specific graphic type, such as PICT or TIFF.

Figure 15-10: Choose a picture to import from this dialog box.

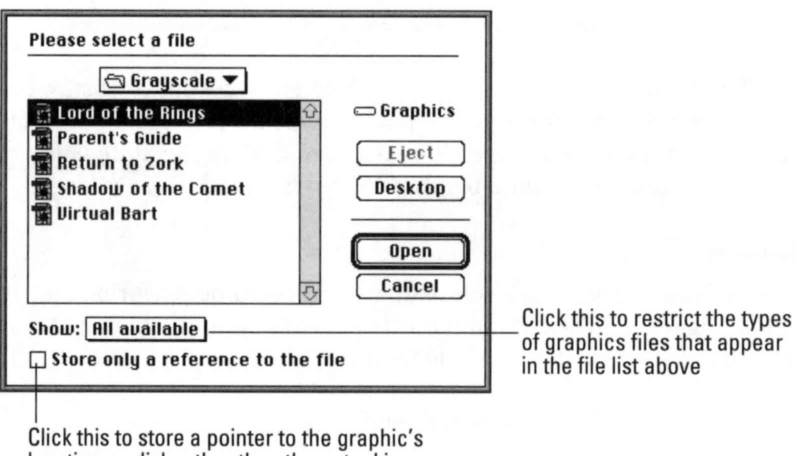

See also: Go to Field, Import Movie

Import Movie

Purpose: This script step is used to import a QuickTime movie into a Container field in the current record (which is the same as choosing Import Movie from the Import/Export submenu of the File menu). When executed, this step displays a dialog box in which you can select a movie file to be imported (see Figure 15-11). If the Show Preview check box in the file dialog is checked, you can see a scene from each movie to help you choose the correct one.

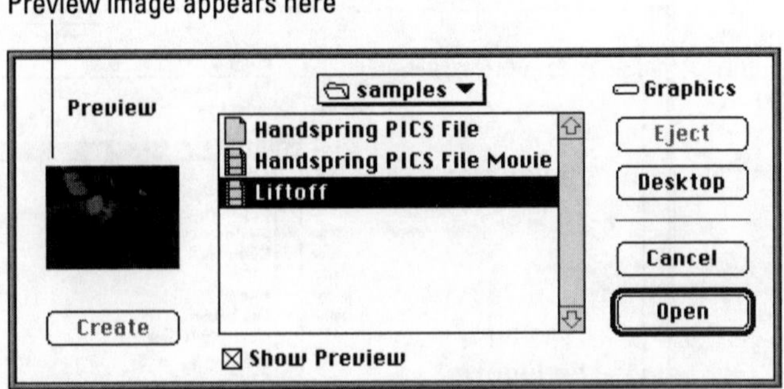

Figure 15-11: Selecting a QuickTime movie to import

Options: none

For Import Movie to work, a Container field must be selected before the step is executed — either by clicking or tabbing into the field before executing the script or by adding a Go to Field step to the script that specifies the name of a Container field. In addition, the QuickTime extension must be active.

See also: Go to Field, Import Picture

Import Records

Purpose: Use the Import Records step to import data into the current database from another FileMaker Pro database or from a compatible data file (which is the same as choosing Import Records from the Import/Export submenu of the File menu).

Options: Restore import order, Perform without dialog, Specify file

Leave all options unchecked to perform an import operation from scratch. When the step executes, FileMaker Pro displays a standard file dialog box from which you select the file to be imported. To make the file list more manageable, you can select a particular file type from the Show pop-up menu at the bottom of the dialog box.

Next, the Import Field Mapping dialog box appears (see Figure 15-12). To execute the import operation, match the fields in the two databases (as explained in Chapter 16), click a radio button to indicate that you want to "Add new records" or "Replace data in current found set," and click OK.

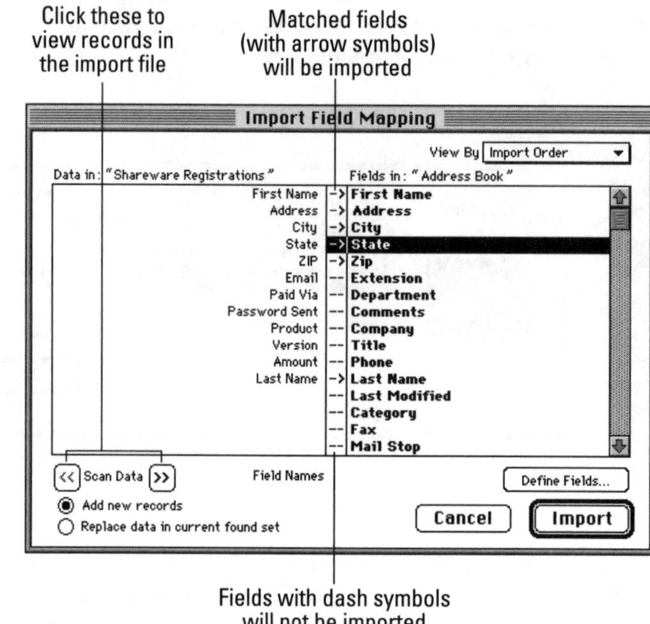

Figure 15-12: The Import Field Mapping dialog box

If you previously selected the import file and the matching fields, you can click the "Restore import order" option to repeat the same import each time.

Example: Suppose that you periodically export new address records to a tab-separated text file called New Addresses. After importing these records into the Address Book database once, you can create a script that uses the Import Records step to import the new records automatically by using the same data file (set "Specify file" to select the New Addresses file) and the same import order ("Restore import order") each time. In this case, you could also add the "Perform without dialog" option because nothing would change that might require user intervention.

See also: Export Records

Export Records

Purpose: Use the Export Records step to export data from the current FileMaker Pro database so that the data can be imported (read) into another FileMaker Pro database or another program (which is the same as choosing Export Records from the Import/Export submenu of the File menu).

Export Records automatically exports data from all records currently being browsed. If you want to limit exports to a subset of records, use find requests or related commands (or script steps) to select those records beforehand. See Chapter 9 for details on finding and selecting records.

Options: Restore export order, Perform without dialog, Specify file

Leave all options unchecked to perform an export from scratch. When the step executes, FileMaker Pro displays a dialog box in which you name the new export data file and select a file type for the file (Tab-Separated Text, for example). Next, the Export Field Order dialog box appears (see Figure 15-13). To execute the export, choose the fields that you want to export, set options (as explained in Chapter 16), and then click OK.

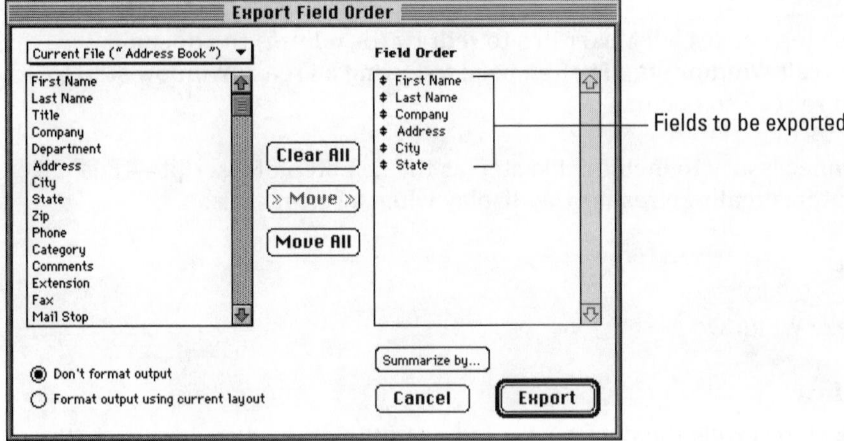

Figure 15-13: The Export Field Order dialog box

If you have performed the export operation before, you can click the "Restore export order" option to repeat the same operation each time.

Example: Suppose that you periodically export new address records to a tab-separated text file called Addresses. After performing this export operation one time, you can create a script that uses the Export Records step to export the new records to the same output file automatically. In this case, you could also add the "Perform without dialog" option because nothing would change that might require user intervention.

See also: Import Records

Windows Script Steps

The windows script steps enable you to control the appearance of the document window.

Freeze Window

Purpose: The Freeze Window step instructs FileMaker Pro to perform the current script without updating information in the document window until either the script ends or a Refresh Window script step is executed.

Options: none

See also: Refresh Window

Refresh Window

Purpose: This step causes FileMaker Pro to redraw (or *refresh*) the document window. A Refresh Window step is often used following a Freeze Window step to force a screen refresh to occur.

It is unnecessary to include this step as the last step of a script — FileMaker Pro automatically refreshes the display when a script ends.

Options: none

See also: Freeze Window

Scroll Window

Purpose: This step scrolls the document window to the desired position or in the indicated direction.

All window scrolling script steps (Home, End, Page Up, Page Down) supported in previous versions of FileMaker Pro have been combined in this new step.

Options: Home, End, Page Up, Page Down; To selection

Choose Home to scroll the document to the top of the window, End to scroll to the bottom of the window, Page Up to scroll up one page, or Page Down to scroll down one page. If you have an Extended keyboard, choosing any of these options has the same effect as pressing the key of the same name.

Choose "To selection" to scroll the window so that the current field is visible.

Unlike most other script step options, you must choose one of the scrolling options.

Toggle Window

Purpose: Depending on the option chosen from the Specify pop-up menu, this step can be used to zoom, unzoom, or maximize the current database document, or to hide the database document window (which is the same as choosing Hide Window from the Window menu).

Options: Maximize, Zoom, Unzoom, Hide

The Specify pop-up menu is not optional for the Toggle Window step; you *must* choose an option. Choose Maximize to expand the document window to the full size of the current display. Choose Zoom to resize the document window to the most recent size and location that has been set for it. Choose Unzoom to return the document to its normal size and position on the screen.

Choosing Hide results in hiding the current database. The name of the database is shown surrounded by parentheses in the Window menu — as in "(Sales)." To make the database visible again, select its name from the Window menu.

Repeated execution of either Zoom or Unzoom has no additional effect — the screen stays zoomed or unzoomed, as appropriate. To reverse the effect of a Toggle Window [Zoom] or a Toggle Window [Unzoom], add the opposite command as a new script step.

Toggle Status Area

Purpose: This step enables you to toggle the state of the *status area* (the section of the document window that contains FileMaker Pro controls, such as the book icon and the Tools palette) or to specifically hide or show the status area. The Toggle version of this step has the same effect as clicking the status area control at the bottom of the document window.

Options: Specify Toggle, Show, or Hide; Lock

To toggle the state of the status area (switching from Hide to Show or from Show to Hide), choose Toggle from the Specify pop-up menu. To switch to a specific state, whether the status area currently is shown or hidden, choose either Hide or Show from the Specify pop-up menu.

Choose the Lock option if you want to prevent the user from changing the display of the status area.

See also: Set Zoom Level

Toggle Text Ruler

Purpose: This step hides or shows the text ruler.

Options: Specify Toggle, Show, or Hide; Refresh screen

Choose Toggle from the Specify menu to switch the state of the text ruler from Hide to Show and vice versa. Choose Show or Hide to set the text ruler to a specific state (regardless of its current state).

Set Zoom Level

Purpose: This step sets the zoom level to any of the normally supported magnification percentages, or instructs FileMaker to zoom the display in or out (using the default zoom increase or decrease).

Options: Lock

Clicking the Lock option grays out the zoom controls in the document window, freezing the display at the chosen zoom level.

In many cases, Set Zoom Level steps are used in pairs — one step (or script) to zoom the screen to a particular level and a second step (or a second script) that restores the window to the original zoom level. Similarly, after locking the zoom level (to prevent the user from changing what you want to show him or her), you must also execute a script step to unlock the zoom level — otherwise, it will continue to be frozen for the database.

By using the Set Zoom Level step in combination with the Scroll Window step, you can display a particular section of a database window at a specific magnification.

See also: Toggle Window

View As

Purpose: This step (formerly called Toggle View-As-List) can be used to specify the way records are displayed (one record per screen or as a continuous scrolling list) or to switch from the current display mode to the other display mode.

There are only two display modes: View as Form and View as List. When browsing records, these commands can be selected from the Select menu.

Options: View as Form, View as List, Toggle

To toggle the manner in which records are displayed (switching from showing one record per screen to showing the records as a list, or vice versa), choose Toggle from the Specify pop-up menu. To set the display mode to a specific state, regardless of the current display mode, choose either View as Form or View as List from the pop-up menu.

Files Script Steps

These steps are used to open, close, and save database files; create new files; and set file-related options.

New

Purpose: This step displays the New Database dialog box, enabling the user to create a new empty file or one based on any of the Claris-supplied templates.

Options: none

Open

Purpose: This step enables the user to select a FileMaker Pro database to be opened (which is the same as choosing Open from the File menu or pressing ⌘-O) or to open a specific database file automatically.

Options: Specify file

If a file is specified, that file is opened when the step executes. If no file is specified, a standard file dialog box appears, enabling you to select a database to open. In either case, a database opened with this script step becomes the current database.

See also: Close

If you intend to perform a script in another database, you don't have to open that other database first. Simply use the Perform Script step, specify that an external script is to be used, and then select the database to open and the particular script you want to perform.

Close

Purpose: This step closes the current file (which is the same as choosing Close from the File menu or pressing ⌘-W) or closes another specific database file.

Options: Specify file

If no options are set, the Close step simply closes the current file. If the "Specify file" option is checked, you can choose a particular file to close (Sales, for example).

Example: The Close step is useful for ending a script that performs a final action for a database. You could, for example, use this step to sort the database in a specific way (to be sure that the database is ready for use the next day) and then close the file. If you have a database that works in conjunction with other databases (see the Callable Help Example folder on the enclosed disk), you can use the Close step to close the other file or files when they're no longer needed. (Closing unnecessary databases frees memory for other FileMaker Pro activities.)

See also: Open, Quit

Change Password

Purpose: When executed, this script step presents the Change Password dialog box shown in Figure 15-14. This dialog box enables the user to change his or her password for the current database.

Figure 15-14: The Change Password dialog box

If no passwords have been defined for the current database (or if they have all been deleted), this script step does nothing.

Options: none

Set Multi-User

Purpose: This step turns the multi-user status for a database on or off (allowing or disallowing network access to the data).

Options: On, Off

Choosing the On option is equivalent to setting Multi-User in the File menu; choosing Off is equivalent to setting Single-User status in the File menu.

If a network protocol has not been chosen in the General section of the Preferences dialog box, setting the Set Multi-User step to On has no effect.

Set Use System Formats

Purpose: Two Macintosh control panels (Date & Time and Numbers) are used to set the default formats for displaying dates, times, and numbers. FileMaker Pro, however, saves its own default settings for displaying dates, times, and numbers as part of each database file. The Set Use System Formats step enables you to choose between using the normal system formats for these entities or the formats that are stored with the database.

Options: On, Off

Choose the On option to use the current system formats. Choose the Off option to use the formats that were saved with the file.

Save a Copy as

Purpose: This step is the same as choosing the Save a Copy As command from the File menu. If no options are set for the Save a Copy as step, the standard save file dialog box appears when the script executes the step (see Figure 15-15). The dialog box enables you (or the current user) to name the copy, determine where on disk the file will be saved, and select the type of copy that is made (a duplicate, a compressed copy, or a clone).

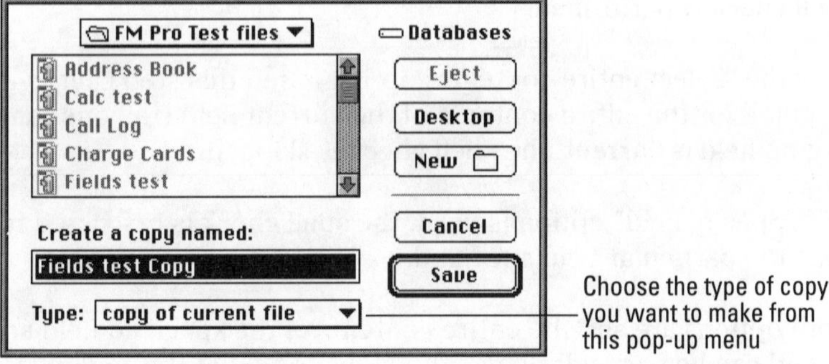

Figure 15-15: Saving a copy of a database

Options: Specify file

Click the "Specify file" option if you always want the file to be saved in a particular location, with the same file name and type.

Example: An example of using the Save a Copy as script step appears in the "Automatic Backups" sidebar in Chapter 2.

Recover

Purpose: The Recover script step performs the same action as choosing Recover from the File menu. Its purpose is to repair damaged database files.

There must be enough free space on the disk to successfully recover the file.

Options: Perform without dialog

Spelling Script Steps

The spelling script steps enable you to check the spelling of a field, an entire record, or the browsed set of records.

Check Selection

Purpose: This step (formerly called Spell Check Selection) uses the spelling checker to examine the selected text in the current field (which is the same as choosing Check Selection from the Spelling submenu of the Edit menu).

Options: Select entire contents, Specify field

With no options set, this step can be used to spell-check selected text in any field of any layout. If no text is selected when the script executes, nothing happens — that is, no spell check is performed.

When only the "Select entire contents" option is set, this step causes a spell check to be executed for the entire contents of the current field (the one that contains the cursor). If no field is current, the spell check is skipped.

If only the "Specify field" option is used, the spell check is restricted to selected text within the particular field specified.

When both options are set, the entire contents of the specified field are checked. This method can be particularly useful for ensuring that the spelling is correct in a long text field (a Comments or Notes field, for example).

See also: Check Record, Check Found Set

Check Record

Purpose: This step (formerly called Spell Check Record) instructs the spelling checker to examine every field in the current record (which is the same as choosing Check Record from the Spelling submenu of the Edit menu).

Options: none

See also: Check Selection, Check Found Set

Check Found Set

Purpose: This step (formerly called Spell Check Found Set) performs a spelling check for every field in all records in the current found set — that is, the records that currently are being browsed. This step is the same as choosing Check All from the Spelling submenu of the Edit menu following a find request.

Options: none

See also: Check Selection, Check Record

Miscellaneous Script Steps

This "catch-all" category includes more than a dozen steps that perform special, less-frequently needed script actions, such as dialing the phone, beeping, displaying messages, and executing AppleScripts.

Show Message

Purpose: This step displays a user-specified message in a dialog box and allows the user to respond by clicking a button. Between one and three captioned buttons can be presented.

Options: Message text, Button captions

Example: The Show Message step can provide data-entry instructions for the user. You might, for instance, attach this step to a Help button. When clicked, an appropriate message could be displayed, such as "Press the Tab key to move from field to field."

In addition, this step can be used to enable a script to take different actions depending on the button that the user clicks — determined by using the Status(CurrentMessageChoice) function. As an example, in the Show Message step that's part of the following script, two buttons were defined (labeled "Once" and "Twice"). The script presents a message to which the user must respond by clicking one of the buttons.

```
Show Message ["How many times should I beep?"]
If ["Status(CurrentMessageChoice) = 1"]
 Beep
Else
 Beep
 Beep
End If
```

If the Once button is clicked [Status(CurrentMessageChoice) = 1], one beep is played; if Twice is clicked, two beeps are heard (see Figure 15-16).

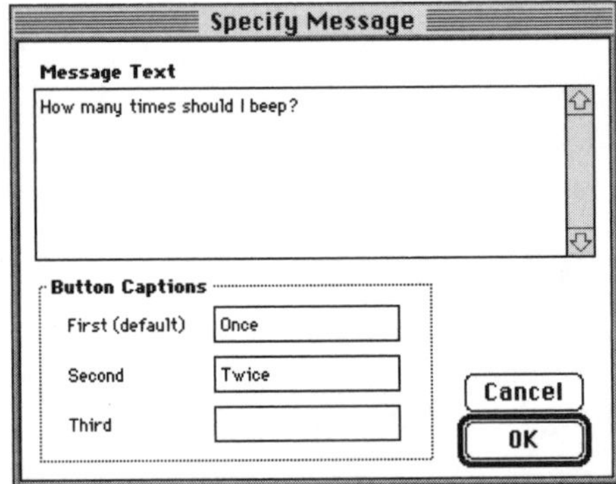

Figure 15-16: Specifying a message and options

To view and use any of the Status functions when defining an If step, choose Status Functions from the View menu in the Specify Calculation dialog box.

Beep

Purpose: This step plays the current sound for the system alert. You can alter the sound that is played by selecting a different alert sound in the Sound control panel. The Beep step is useful for signaling user errors, script errors, and the conclusion of lengthy scripts.

Options: none

Speak

Purpose: If the PlainTalk and Speech Manager system software components are installed on your Mac, you can use this step to speak a text string or the contents of a given field in a voice that you select.

Options: Field value, Text to speak, Use voice, Wait for speech completion before continuing

To speak the contents of a field, click the "Field value" radio button and select the field to be spoken. To make the step speak a particular text string, click the "Text to speak" radio button and enter the text string in the text box.

If you don't want to use the robotic default voice for the speech, choose a voice from the "Use voice" pop-up menu. If you intend to combine several Speak steps in a script, you must select a voice for each step. For all Speak steps in which no voice is chosen, the default voice is used.

The "Wait for speech completion before continuing" option enables you to control the timing of the speech segment. When this option is unchecked, the script continues regardless of whether the speech has been completed.

Dial Phone

Purpose: This step is used to dial phone numbers through an attached modem or the computer's speaker.

Options: Perform without dialog, Specify field, Use Dialing Preferences

Click Specify to set dialing options. The phone number can be taken from a specific field in the current record or be a constant that always dials the same number, regardless of the record that is currently displayed. Click Use Dialing Preferences if you want this step to take user-defined dialing preferences into account. (See Chapter 7 for instructions on setting dialing, modem, and other preferences.)

Open Help

Purpose: This step (formerly called Help) displays the normal FileMaker Pro Help information (which is the same as choosing Help from the Apple menu or pressing ⌘-?).

Options: none

Open Define Fields

Purpose: This step (formerly called Define Fields) displays the Define Fields dialog box for the current database, enabling you to create new fields, edit definitions for existing fields, delete fields, and set and change options for fields (which is the same as choosing Define Fields from the File menu or pressing Shift-⌘-D). See Chapter 5 for more information about defining fields.

Options: none

Open Define Relationships

Purpose: This step displays the Define Relationships dialog box, enabling you to define, delete, or edit relationships between the current database file and others (which is the same as choosing Define Relationships from the File menu).

Options: none

Open ScriptMaker

Purpose: This step presents the Define Scripts dialog box (the opening screen that normally appears when ScriptMaker is chosen from the Script menu). Any steps that appear after the Open ScriptMaker step are not performed.

Options: none

The Open ScriptMaker step is useful when you are modifying or debugging scripts. In addition, if you find yourself frequently popping in and out of ScriptMaker, you can attach this step to a button or add it as one of the first 10 scripts to the Script menu, giving it a Command-key equivalent.

Send Apple Event

Purpose: If you are running System 7 on your Macintosh, you can use the Send Apple Event step to facilitate interaction between FileMaker Pro and other programs.

Options: Specify

Apple Events — a feature of System 7 — enable you to send messages (commands and data) between programs. Although most users will never personally create a script that uses Apple Events, anyone can easily use this script step to launch other programs and documents from FileMaker Pro (discussed in "Using Apple Events," later in this chapter). And if you have QuicKeys (a commercial macro utility from CE Software), you can use this step to execute impressive macros (described in "Using QuicKeys with FileMaker Pro Scripts," later in this chapter).

Perform AppleScript

Purpose: This step is used to send AppleScript commands to another program. The AppleScript commands must either be contained in a designated field on the layout or they can be typed into the Specify AppleScript text box when adding this step to a script.

Options: Specify

When you click the Specify button, the Specify AppleScript dialog box appears. Click the Field value radio button (or the Specify Field button to its right) to choose the field that contains the text of the AppleScript to be performed. If the script is not stored in a field, click the Script text radio button and enter the AppleScript in the text box.

Scripts stored in text fields must be recompiled by FileMaker whenever the script runs. Scripts entered in the text box, on the other hand, are compiled immediately and saved in compiled format. FileMaker always checks for script errors during the compilation process.

To use this script step, the AppleScript system software must be installed on your Macintosh. AppleScript is included as a component of the most recent versions of System 7. It can also be purchased separately.

If the AppleScript has already been created elsewhere (as will usually be the case), you don't have to retype it in FileMaker Pro. Instead, simply open the script in Apple's Script Editor application, copy it, and then paste it into the appropriate field or the text box in the Specify AppleScript dialog box.

Comment

Purpose: Use the Comment step to insert non-executing comments in your scripts. Comment steps make it easy to explain script logic and assumptions — both for your own records and to inform others.

Options: Specify

Click the Specify button to enter the text for the comment.

Flush Cache to Disk

Purpose: This step forces the contents of FileMaker Pro's internal cache to be flushed to disk (rather than waiting for this action to be performed automatically at the designated time).

Options: none

Quit Application

Purpose: This step (formerly called Quit) quits FileMaker Pro and returns the user to the desktop (which is the same as choosing Quit from the File menu or pressing ⌘-Q). Any files that are currently open are saved automatically, if necessary.

Options: none

Example: The Quit Application step can be extremely useful as a final command in a cleanup script. If you always print a report from a particular database as the final activity for the day, for example, you could define a script that does the printing and then ends by quitting FileMaker Pro.

See also: Close

Attaching a Script to a Button

As mentioned in earlier discussions of many of the templates included on the *Macworld FileMaker Pro 3.0 Bible Disk*, you can attach scripts to buttons or icons that you include in a layout. When a button is clicked, the script or script step attached to that button executes instantly — exactly as though you had chosen the script name from the Script menu or clicked Perform in the Define Scripts dialog box.

Buttons frequently are added to layouts to make it easy and convenient for users to perform either simple or complex series of commands. By assigning the Go to Layout step to a button, for example, you can quickly navigate to a particular layout, such as a help screen or a report layout. You can also attach a multi-step script to a button that executes a find request, performs a sort, prints a report, returns to the data entry screen, and then restores the database to its state before the button was clicked. For several examples of buttons, examine the databases in the *Macworld FileMaker Pro 3.0 Bible Disk*.

Although FileMaker-drawn buttons and graphic icons frequently are used as buttons, you can use *any* object as a button (including static text strings, for example).

To attach a script step or a script to a button, follow these steps:

1. Switch to Layout mode. (Choose Layout from the Mode menu, press ⌘-L, or choose Layout from the Mode menu at the bottom of the database window.)
2. Select the object that you want to make into a button.

   When selected, an object has a *handle* (black dot) in each of its corners.
3. Choose Button from the Format menu.

   The Specify Button dialog box appears, as shown in Figure 15-17.

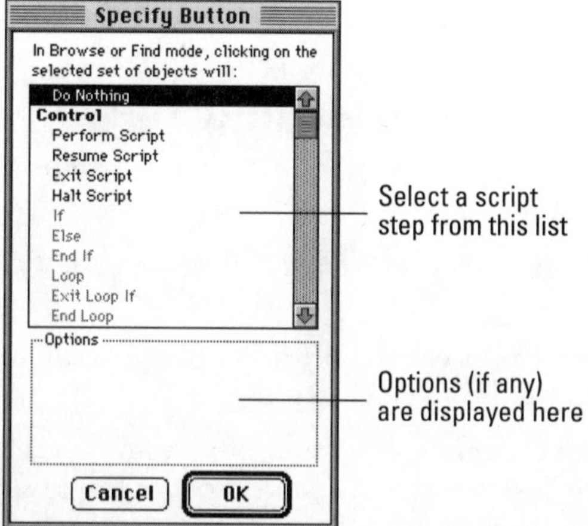

Figure 15-17: The Specify Button dialog box

4. To assign a single script step to the button, select the script step, set any options that appear for that step at the bottom of the dialog box, and then click OK.

— or —

4. To assign a particular script to the button, select Perform Script, select the script to be executed from the Specify pop-up menu that appears in the Options section of the dialog box, and click OK.

There is still more you should know about working with buttons, as follows:

- If you're having trouble identifying the particular objects in a layout that are buttons (as opposed to ordinary graphics, static text, and other objects), change to Layout mode, and choose Buttons from the Show submenu of the Layout menu. Each button will be surrounded by a gray outline.
- When you copy a button in a layout, that button's definition is also copied — that is, any script or script step attached to the button is attached to the copy. If you paste the button into another layout in the same database or a different one, the pasted button will attempt to perform the same function as the original button. You may need to edit the script or script step so that the duplicate now refers to the proper layout, field name, or whatever else the duplicate button references.
- To delete a button that you no longer need, switch to Layout mode, select the button, and then choose Cut or Clear from the Edit menu. Alternatively, you can simply press the Delete key.

NEW TO VERSION 3

To remove a script or script step from a button (undefine it), perform steps 1 through 3 in the previous procedure, select Do Nothing, and click OK.

Scriptmaking Tips

Following are some useful script-making tips passed on by Max Pruden of Claris Technical Support:

- You can use the Go to Record/Request/Page step to go to the last record by specifying a very high record number, such as 9999.
- The Paste Literal step works only if you first specify a target field for the paste by using the Go to Field step.
- When you exit a Sort or Find step, you automatically switch to Browse mode, and the first record in the sort order or found set is displayed. Thus, you don't need to include an Enter Browse Mode step or a Go to Record/Request/Page step to go to the first record.
- Two types of scripts can be executed by the Perform Script step: *internal scripts* (scripts in the current file) and *external scripts* (scripts in other files). When you use Perform Script to execute an external script, you don't need to use the Open step first to open the other database.
- If you want to copy values from Summary fields, use the Refresh screen option with the Enter Browse Mode step.
- If you use the Copy step without setting any options, the step copies the contents of all fields in the layout for the current record (which is the same as the Copy Record step).
- You can use the Toggle Window [Maximize] step to zoom the window to the full size of the current screen. If you don't know the size of the particular monitor that will be used with the database (as when you are distributing or selling your databases to others), this step can be very useful as part of a startup (On Opening) script.
- A script executes in its own database. To perform procedures that affect two files, such as a Copy from one database and a Paste into another, you need two scripts: one in each database. For this example, you would create a script that copies the contents of a field in the current file and include a step to perform an external script (defined in the other database) that selects the appropriate field and then pastes.

What Does This Button Do?

If you're curious about a script step or script that has been assigned to a button, there's a simple way to determine what the step or script does. Just switch to Layout mode, select the button, and choose Button from the Format menu. In the Specify Button dialog box that appears, the step or script that is assigned to the button will be highlighted.

Using Advanced Scripting Procedures

You can create many perfectly functional scripts by selecting single steps and by combining steps for commands with which you are very familiar, such as Go to Layout, Sort, Find, and Print. Some of the steps, step options, and system software features supported by ScriptMaker, however, can add extraordinary flexibility and power to FileMaker Pro. Although you may not immediately be interested in pursuing these power-scripting features, the following sections discuss them.

Decision-Making in Scripts

In previous versions of FileMaker Pro, the If script step enabled you to perform limited decision-making (that is, "If the conditional test *x* is true, perform this step. Otherwise, do nothing."). FileMaker Pro 3.0 extends the decision-making capabilities of scripts by adding Else and End If steps. The End If step marks the end of every If structure. When embedded within an If structure, the Else step allows you to select a second alternative in response to a conditional test, as in the following script:

```
If [x]
 Do this if test x is true
Else
 Do this if test x is false
End If
```

Multiple statements can be included in both the true and false sections of an If structure, and Ifs can be nested within other Ifs.

Using Loops in Scripts

Until now, there has never been a straightforward way to make a script repeat steps — other than by duplicating them. The new support for looping enables you to repeat a sequence of commands a set number of times or until a particular condition has been fulfilled. The three Loop commands are Loop, End Loop, and Exit Loop If.

Environment Considerations

The new Status script steps enable you to determine information about the current state of the database, as well as the environment in which it is being run. Based on the results of the various Status tests, you can use other script steps to change the appearance of the display, branch to appropriate sub-scripts and external scripts (disabling Windows-related steps if the database is being run on a Mac, for example), or display relevant messages. The Status steps will be a boon to any developer who intends to offer cross-platform databases.

Executing Other Scripts from Within a Script

A FileMaker Pro script can be instructed to perform other scripts, known as *sub-scripts*. (In programming parlance, sub-scripts are called *subroutines*.) To allow one script to perform another script (or several other scripts, for that matter), you simply set the "Perform sub-scripts" option when choosing the Perform Script step. After running a sub-script, the original (or calling) script continues from where it left off.

Any script that is executed as part of a Perform Script step — whether it is the object of the step or a sub-script — can be an internal or external script. An *internal script* is a script that is defined within the current database. An *external script* is a script in another database. When you run an external script, FileMaker Pro automatically opens the external database and executes the script. When the external script is completed, control returns to the original script and database, just as it does when a sub-script is performed.

To run an external script, follow these steps:

1. When you define the script, choose Perform Script as one of the steps.
2. With the Perform Script step selected in the script, choose "External script" from the Specify pop-up menu.

   The Specify External Script dialog box appears, as shown in Figure 15-18.

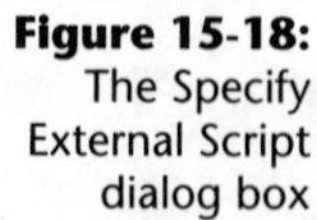
Figure 15-18: The Specify External Script dialog box

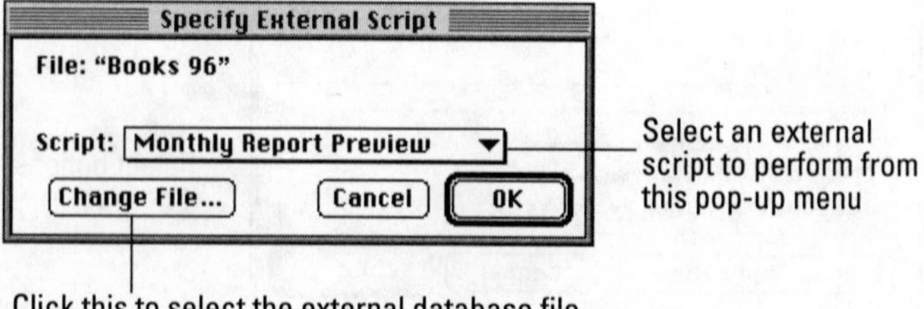

3. Click Change File to select the database that contains the external script you want to execute.

   A standard file dialog box appears.
4. Select the database that contains the external script you want to execute, and click Open.
5. Click the Script pop-up menu, and select the script that you want to perform.
6. Click OK to record your choices.

Using Apple Events

The Send Apple Event script step allows you to send messages from FileMaker Pro to other programs. Although not all programs support the required and Do Script events, most programs should be able to respond to a request to launch or to open a particular document. This section describes how to perform these simple actions from within a FileMaker Pro database.

To create a program or document launcher by using Apple Events, follow these steps:

1. Create a new script, choose the Send Apple Event step, and click Specify.

   The Specify Apple Event dialog box appears, as shown in Figure 15-19.

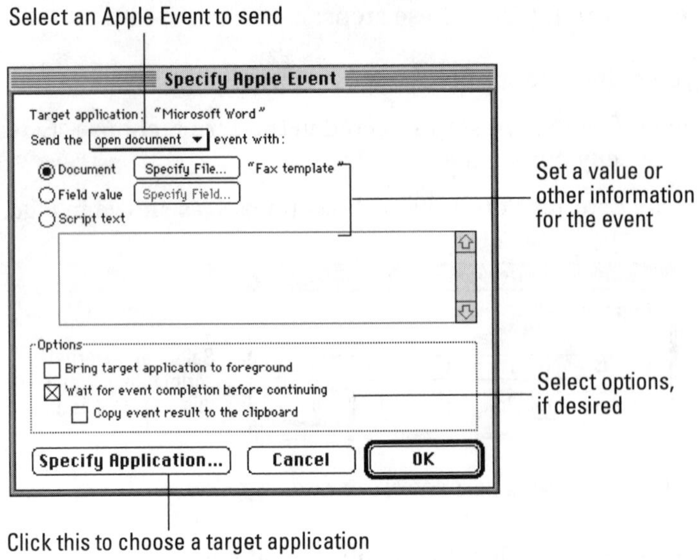

Select an Apple Event to send

Specify Apple Event

Target application: "Microsoft Word"
Send the open document event with:
Document Specify File... "Fax template"
Field value Specify Field...
Script text

Options
Bring target application to foreground
Wait for event completion before continuing
Copy event result to the clipboard

Specify Application... Cancel OK

Set a value or other information for the event

Select options, if desired

Click this to choose a target application

Figure 15-19: The Specify Apple Event dialog box

2. From the Send pop-up menu at the top of the dialog box, choose "Open application."

   A standard file dialog box appears, in which you select the program that you want the script to launch.

— or —

2. From the Send pop-up menu, choose "open document."
3. Click the Specify File button beside the Document radio button to choose a document.
4. At the bottom of the Specify Apple Event dialog box, set any desired options.

   In most cases, you will want to choose "Bring target application to foreground"; otherwise, when the program or document is launched, it may be hidden behind your FileMaker Pro database window.

5. To save the script step settings, click OK.

To learn more about how FileMaker uses Apple Events, check out the Claris database named Apple Events Reference and the many examples in the FileMaker And Apple Events folder that is installed as part of FileMaker Pro 3.0.

After defining a program- or document-launcher script, you can pretty things up by using a screen-capture utility to capture a picture of the program's or document's icon, paste the icon into your FileMaker Pro layout, and then use the Button command in the Format menu to make the icon into a button that launches the script. If you frequently use several utilities while running FileMaker (such as a calculator, clock, and address book, for instance), you can employ this technique to create a string of buttons. Because these button definitions are not specific to one database, you can copy and paste them into any database. As long as the databases are run on your machine, and you don't change the locations of the programs or documents to be launched, the buttons should work fine.

Using QuicKeys with FileMaker Pro Scripts

QuicKeys is a general-purpose macro utility that allows you to automate complex functions in most Macintosh programs, desk accessories, the Finder, and so on. QuicKeys 2 and QuicKeys 3 can work in conjunction with Apple Events. Because FileMaker Pro 3.0 has a Send Apple Event script step, you can use a script to invoke QuicKeys and execute any macro that you have defined. Following are the necessary steps:

1. Select the Send Apple Event script step and click Specify.

   The Specify Apple Event dialog box appears (as previously shown in Figure 15-19).

2. Choose the Other… event.

   The Specify Apple Event dialog box appears.

3. For Event Class and Event ID, enter the following: **QKy2** and **QPNm**. Then click OK.

   Be sure that the capitalization is correct — it must match exactly!

4. If you have QuicKeys 2, click the Specify Application button, and then choose CEIAC in the Extensions folder of your System Folder.

— or —

4. If you have QuicKeys 3, click the Specify Application button and then choose the QuicKeys Toolbox in the Extensions folder of your System Folder.

5. Click the Script text radio button and then type the name of the QuicKeys macro that you want to run.
6. Click OK to finish the step definition.

For example, you could create an Apple Event script that runs a QuicKeys macro called AOL flash, a multi-step macro that runs an America Online flash session (it logs on, sends pending messages, retrieves incoming mail, and then logs off). Because QuicKeys can automate almost any program function, you could also use it to create FileMaker Pro-specific macros — ones that perform a series of field-formatting operations, for example — and then use a Send Apple Event step to activate each macro.

Using AppleScript

Available as part of recent versions of the System 7 system software and also sold separately, AppleScript is an English-based programming language that you can use to integrate Macintosh programs and customize the way your Mac works. Unlike using the scripting feature in FileMaker Pro, using AppleScript really *is* programming.

To execute an AppleScript from within FileMaker Pro, follow these steps:

1. In ScriptMaker's Define Scripts dialog box, specify whether you are creating a new script or editing an existing one. (To create a new script, enter a new name in the Script Name box and click Create. To edit an existing script, select its name in the list box and click Edit.)
2. In the Script Definition dialog box, select the Perform AppleScript step.
3. Click the Specify button.

   The Specify AppleScript dialog box appears, as shown in Figure 15-20.

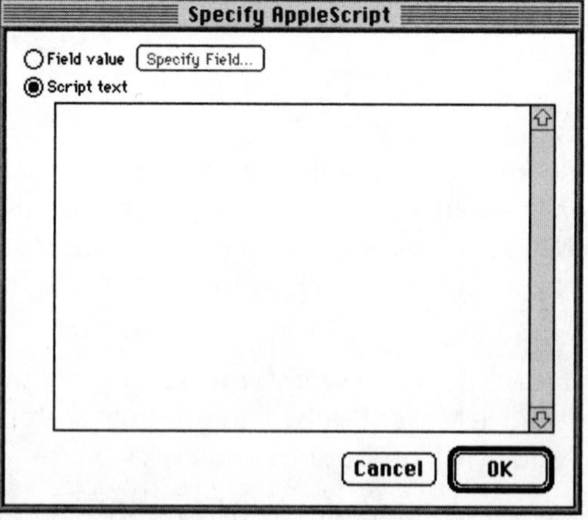

Figure 15-20: The Specify AppleScript dialog box

4. Click Field value, and then click Specify Field.

   The commands in the specified field are compiled each time that FileMaker Pro runs the script.

   –or–

4. Click Script text, and then type the AppleScript commands in the text box.

   The commands are compiled and then stored as part of the database.

5. Finish defining the script, and then click OK.

Summary

- FileMaker Pro provides a built-in script-creation utility called ScriptMaker. Using ScriptMaker, you can automate almost any FileMaker Pro function that you usually execute manually by selecting commands from menus. Once defined, a script can be added to the Script menu and/or attached to a button in any layout, making it simple to execute the script any time you like.
- Rather than type scripts in a word processing program or text editor, you design scripts in FileMaker Pro by choosing script steps from a list. Step options are set by clicking buttons and check boxes.
- You can create many scripts simply by executing sort instructions, find requests, and similar commands and then telling FileMaker Pro that you want to use the identical procedures in a script. When you perform these important steps just before creating the script, FileMaker Pro includes them for you as part of the default script.
- FileMaker Pro 3.0 provides 115 steps that you can use individually or in combination with other steps to form a script.
- You can attach scripts to buttons or icons that you include in a layout. When a button is clicked, the script or script step attached to that button executes instantly — as though you had chosen the script name from the Script menu or clicked Perform in the Define Scripts dialog box.
- Buttons frequently are added to layouts to make it easy and convenient for users to perform either a simple or complex series of commands. By assigning the Go to Layout step to a button, for example, you can quickly navigate to a particular layout, such as a help screen or a report layout. You can also attach a multi-step script to a button that executes a find request, performs a sort, prints a report, returns to the data entry screen, and then restores the database to its state before the button was clicked.

Exchanging Data

CHAPTER 16

In This Chapter

- Understanding file formats
- Importing data from other programs
- Creating a new database by opening a foreign file
- Exporting data from FileMaker Pro
- Working with the Windows version of FileMaker Pro

As nice as it might be, you probably aren't going to spend your entire working life happily curled up inside FileMaker Pro. You likely work with many different applications, and perhaps you even stored your database-type information in some other program before you became a FileMaker Pro user. Wouldn't it be great to be able to move all that data into FileMaker Pro? For example, you may want to transfer your address and phone number data directly to FileMaker. Similarly, you may want to move data from a FileMaker Pro Invoices database to a spreadsheet program so that you can check how you're doing and make predictions.

There are many reasons why you may want to move data. The good news is that you can do so without much trouble, as this chapter explains.

Users of previous versions of FileMaker Pro have little new material to learn concerning importing and exporting data. Be sure, however, to read the section entitled "Opening a Foreign Data File to Create a New Database." It explains how you can open a data file from another program and automatically create a standard FileMaker Pro database to receive the data.

Moving Data to and from Other Places

FileMaker Pro can work with data produced by a variety of other programs. FileMaker Pro can also work with data from other database application programs, such as dBASE. In fact, if the other program can save or export its data in one of half a dozen extremely common formats (such as tab-delimited text), FileMaker Pro can read and use the data. This data exchange is a two-way street: FileMaker produces data that these applications can use, and it can take data from those applications for use in a FileMaker Pro database. The former process is called *exporting*; the latter is called *importing*.

About Importing and Exporting

When you *import* data into FileMaker Pro, you bring that data in from some other program. You can import data from another FileMaker Pro document — even one created on a different type of computer. You can even import data from a remote network source, such as an SQL server. And you can use FileMaker Pro's import capabilities when you want to bring a picture or QuickTime movie data into a database.

When you import data, you can choose to append the new records to your existing file or to use the new data to update existing records. When you import, FileMaker Pro copies data but does not copy layouts or field definitions. In addition, you cannot move new data into Calculation or Summary fields.

You can also make information from a FileMaker Pro database available for use in other applications. You might *export* the current found set of records to a spreadsheet program for further analysis, for example.

Another common use of exporting is to prepare for a mail merge in a word processing program. In FileMaker Pro 3.0, however, you can now perform a mail merge completely within FileMaker. See Chapter 6 for details.

FileMaker Pro cannot export to remote sources, nor can you export data directly into another FileMaker Pro file. Instead of exporting directly into the target application file, you simply export the data to a temporary file and then import it using the target application's procedures to import data. The net effect is the same.

Although FileMaker Pro can work with data from many different applications, its capability is limited by the ways in which these applications store their data. The way that data is stored in an application is called the application's *file format.*

Understanding File Formats

A file format specifies how an application's data is organized and interpreted. You can think of a file format as being a recipe for creating the finished file from its raw data (from the text that you type, for example). The instructions for interpreting a file format must be stored within the application program in which you want to use the data; otherwise, very strange and unsatisfactory results may occur.

FileMaker Pro supports the file formats discussed in the following sections. Note that some formats are for importing data only and that others are solely for export purposes.

Tab-Separated Text

This format is sometimes called ASCII (pronounced *askee*) format, but a few differences exist between tab-separated text and ASCII text. *ASCII* (which stands for American Standard Code for Information Interchange) refers to plain, unformatted text arranged according to an industry-standard coding scheme. In *tab-separated text*, tab characters separate fields in a record, and return characters separate records. Virtually all computer applications can interpret files that are in this format.

Merge

Merge is an export format that you use to create special documents for the data portion of mail merges. Commas separate field values, return characters separate records, and the ASCII character 29 separates repeating fields. In this format, the first record is called the *header*. The header lists the field names contained in the file. Quotation marks surround field data.

Comma-Separated Text

This format is used for BASIC programming and in some applications. Commas separate field values, and return characters separate records. All field values except unformatted numbers are surrounded by quotation marks.

BASIC

This format is similar to comma-separated text but is designed for use with Microsoft's standard BASIC language.

SYLK

SYLK stands for *sy*mbolic *l*in*k* format. This is a spreadsheet format in which data is stored in rows and columns. SYLK can be used by Excel, WingZ, and Resolve, among other spreadsheet applications. Each field is a column, and each record is a row. Returns are output as spaces, and dates and times are output as text within quotation marks. Non-numeric data in a number field is suppressed, and fields are limited to a maximum of 245 characters.

DIF

DIF is another spreadsheet format, used by older applications such as VisiCalc and AppleWorks. Each field is a column, and each record is a row.

WKS

WKS is a spreadsheet format used by Lotus 1-2-3. Each field is a column, and each record is a row.

DBF

DBF is the dBASE III database format. Field names can be no more than 10 characters long, with a maximum of 254 characters per field and 128 fields per record.

Edition File

This format, for use with the Macintosh System 7 Edition Manager (Publish & Subscribe), is an export-only format similar to tab-separated text. When you export data to this format, you're creating an edition file to which other users can subscribe. Exporting in Edition file format is the same as publishing a record in other System 7 programs.

Importing Data from Other Sources

You have several options when you import data from another source. For example, you can combine information stored in several places in one master file (which might contain only selected fields from several similar files). You can also change the order in which records are stored. Although FileMaker Pro normally stores records in the order in which they are entered, it copies records in their sorted order when they are imported. If you import data that includes repeating fields, you can split the latter values into separate records.

Format Selection

When importing data, FileMaker Pro makes it easy to determine whether the import file is in an appropriate format. By default, the Import file dialog box lists only the files that FileMaker Pro understands (based on the XTND translator files that were copied onto your hard disk as part of FileMaker Pro's installation procedure). If the file that you want to import does not appear in the Import file dialog box's list of files, you may need to check the relevant application's documentation to determine what file format it uses. If FileMaker Pro doesn't support the standard file format of your source application, you'll need to have the application output a new data file in a format that FileMaker Pro *can* use. Many applications can output tab- or comma-separated text, for example.

FileMaker Pro supports the following formats for import purposes:

- FileMaker Pro
- Tab-Separated Text
- Comma-Separated Text
- SYLK
- DBF
- DIF
- WKS
- BASIC
- Merge
- ClarisWorks 2.0/3.0
- Data Access Manager

Data Cleanup

Data that you want to import may not be in tiptop shape. You may find, for example, that the match between fields in your source and target files isn't as clean as you had hoped, or that you don't have access to a supported file format. The procedures outlined in the following sections show you how to solve a couple of these problems.

Cleaning Up Data in a Spreadsheet

If you had your Mac for awhile before you bought FileMaker Pro, you probably also had one or more address or contacts files that you created in other programs — address data recorded in the Addresses with Audio HyperCard stack or in a desk accessory, for example. Rather than keep this information spread across a handful of programs and desk accessories, it's usually preferable to put all the data into *one* database, program, or desk accessory. Unfortunately, most of us don't plan for (or count on) the difficulties encountered when trying to create one composite file from two or more separate address files. In particular, the various files are likely to contain different fields. This section discusses some simple procedures you can use to clean up your disparate data before importing it into or exporting it from FileMaker Pro.

Following are two of the most common problems in importing address data:

- Address, phone number, and name fields in the file you want to import are split into two fields (address line 1 and address line 2, area code and phone number, and first name and last name), but the FileMaker Pro database contains only one field for the corresponding items, or vice versa.
- When exported, some ZIP codes may lose their leading zero (for example, 1276 rather than 01276).

Rather than import the data as it is and clean it up in the database afterward, you'll find it more efficient to use a spreadsheet application (such as the one included in ClarisWorks) to make the necessary transformations to the data. To do this, follow these general steps:

1. Export the data from your database, spreadsheet, or address-book program as a tab-delimited ASCII text file.
2. Open the ASCII text file in a spreadsheet program, make the transformations to the data (creating new fields as necessary), and save the revised file as an ASCII text file.
3. Open the FileMaker Pro database into which you intend to import the data.
4. Use the Import Records command to import the tab-separated ASCII text file into the database.

The simplest way to make the transformations in the spreadsheet is to create additional columns on the right side of the spreadsheet. The following text explains how to accomplish this task within the spreadsheet environment of ClarisWorks.

Each new column must contain a formula that combines or converts one or more columns of the original data. Create the appropriate formula, and then use the Fill Down command (⌘-D) to copy the formula into the remaining cells in the column.

The simple spreadsheet shown in Figure 16-1 illustrates the formula needed to convert First Name and Last Name fields into a single Name field. Column A contains first names, column B contains last names, and column C contains the combined first and last names. The formula shown in the entry bar (=A2 & " "& B2) takes the first name in cell A2 (Jody), adds a space (" "), and then adds the last name from cell B2 (Privette) to the end of the text string. As mentioned previously, you use the Fill Down command to copy the formula to all the rest of the cells in column C.

Figure 16-1: A formula to combine first and last names into a single name

Addresses-text - Converted - Co (S

C2 =A2&" "&B2

	A	B	C
1	**First Name**	**Last Name**	**Combined**
2	Jody	Privette	Jody Privette
3	Allyne	Mills	Allyne Mills
4	Melinda	Mongelluzzo	Melinda Mongelluzzo
5	Dave	Terry	Dave Terry
6	Pam	Barnett	Pam Barnett
7	Steven	Stansel	Steven Stansel
8	Abigail	Genuth	Abigail Genuth
9			

100

Suppose you have a database or other address file in which address information is split into two lines or fields and you want to import that data into a file in which Address is only a single line or field. Some addresses in the original file, however, have only one line, while others in the file have two. In Figure 16-2, the equation =IF(B2<>"",A2 & ", " & B2,A2) checks to see whether the address has a second line (B2<>""). If the address has a second line, the formula combines the two portions, separating them with a comma followed by a blank, as in:

251 Rock Road, P.O. Box 116

If the address has no second line, the formula simply copies the first address part (A2) into the cell.

Figure 16-2: A formula to combine two-line addresses into a single address line

File Edit Format Calculate Options View

Addresses-text - Converted - Co (SS)

C2 =IF(B2<>"",A2&", "&B2,A2)

	A	B	C
1	**Address 1**	**Address 2**	**Combined**
2	251 Rock Road	P.O. Box 116	251 Rock Road, P.O. Box 116
3	3885 Bohannon Drive		3885 Bohannon Drive
4	Trade Computer Books Division	Rt. 128	Trade Computer Books Division, Rt. 128
5	1585 Charleston Road		1585 Charleston Road
6	1095 East Duane Avenue, Suite 103		1095 East Duane Avenue, Suite 103
7	2210 Wilshire Blvd.	Suite 277	2210 Wilshire Blvd., Suite 277
8	3724 North 3rd Street	#200	3724 North 3rd Street, #200
9	1050 Walnut Street	Suite 425	1050 Walnut Street, Suite 425
10	217 East 86th Street	Suite 153	217 East 86th Street, Suite 153
11	411 1st Avenue South	Suite 200	411 1st Avenue South, Suite 200
12	112 North Beatty Street		112 North Beatty Street

100

Because ZIP codes are often treated as numbers, the leading zero may disappear when the data is exported, resulting in an improper four-digit code. The lengthy formula =IF(LEN(A2)=4,"0" & A2,NUMTOTEXT(A2)) shown in Figure 16-3 checks to see whether the ZIP code is four digits long (LEN(A2)=4). If the ZIP code contains four digits, a leading zero is appended to the ZIP code ("0" & A2), which then is converted to text. If the ZIP code does not contain four digits, the ZIP code is converted to text and passed through unaltered (NUMTOTEXT(A2)).

Converting ZIP codes to text is necessary to display leading zeros and to handle blank ZIP code fields. If the formula ended simply with A2 rather than NUMTOTEXT(A2), a blank ZIP code would translate as 0 (zero).

Figure 16-3: A formula to check the length of the ZIP code

File Edit Format Calculate Options View

Untitled 4 (SS)

B2 =IF(LEN(A2)=4,"0"&A2,NUMTOTEXT(A2))

	A	B	C	D	E
1	Zip Code	Converted			
2	12874	12874			
3	44039	44039			
4	1759	01759			
5	2390	02390			
6	83301	83301			
7					
8	30032	30032			

100

Converting Return-Delimited Text

Another cleanup problem that you may encounter is data that has been exported in Return-Delimited format. In this format, fields are separated by return characters, and records are separated by two returns. You can convert this format to Tab-Delimited format if you have access to a word processing program that can search for and replace hidden characters, such as the ASCII return and tab characters. Microsoft Word, MacWrite Pro, and ClarisWorks can perform this task, as can other applications.

To convert return-delimited text, follow these steps:

1. Open the return-delimited file in your word processing program.
2. Choose the application's Find/Change command.

   In Microsoft Word, for example, you would choose Replace from the Edit menu.
3. Perform the following change operations:
   - Find all occurrences of two returns (^p^p in Word, for example) and change these characters to something else, such as *XXXX*.

- Find all occurrences of a single return (^p in Word) and change these characters to tabs (^t in Word, for example).
- Find all occurrences of *XXXX* and change these characters to single returns.

4. Save the result as a text file.

   The file is now in Tab-Delimited format.

How to Import

When your data is cleaned up (if cleanup was needed), you're ready to import. To import data into a FileMaker Pro database, follow these steps:

1. Open the destination database file in FileMaker Pro and switch to Browse mode.
2. Choose Import Records from the Import/Export submenu of the File menu.

   The file dialog box shown in Figure 16-4 appears. At the bottom of the dialog box is a Show pop-up menu where you can select the format of the file that you want to import.

Figure 16-4: Choose a file to import from this dialog box.

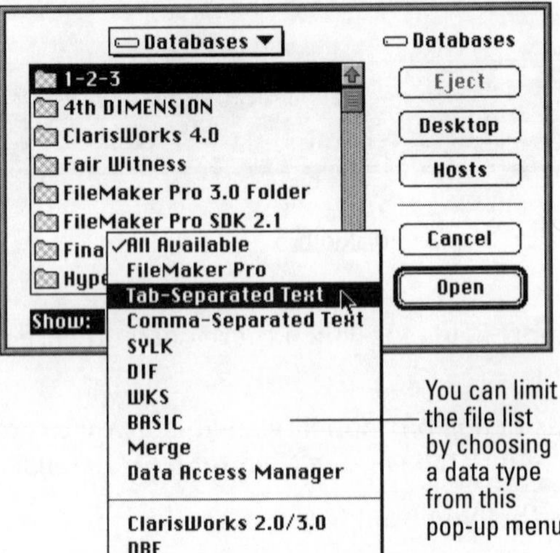

3. *Optional*: To limit the listed files to only those of a particular type, choose the appropriate file format from the Show pop-up menu.

   The default option in the Show pop-up menu is All Available. This tells FileMaker to list in the file dialog box *every* file that it thinks it can read. In most cases, this is fine. However, if you're having a hard time finding the particular file you want to import, you can choose its specific type from the Show pop-up menu.

4. Select the name of the file you want to import.
5. Click Open.

   The Import Field Mapping dialog box appears (see Figure 16-5). The purpose of this dialog box is to match fields in the source file with those in the destination file, as well as to pick the fields you want to import and the ones you want to ignore.

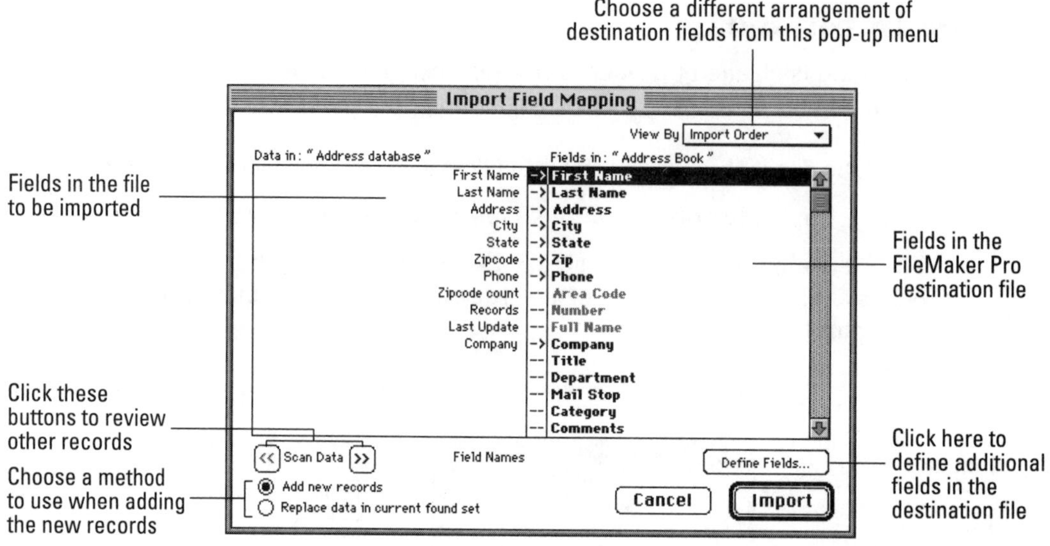

Figure 16-5: The Import Field Mapping dialog box

6. *Optional*: To import fields for which there currently are no matching fields, click Define Fields.

   The Define Fields dialog box appears, enabling you to create the additional fields in the current database. See Chapter 5 for details.

7. Match the fields that you want to import.

   An arrow following a field name in the source file (on the left side of the dialog box) indicates that the field will be imported into the field to the right (in the destination file). If you don't want to import a particular field, click its arrow. The indicator changes to a double dash (- -), showing that the field will not be imported.

   Because fields in the two files can be in any order, it may be necessary for you to manually rearrange them so that they match. You can drag field names in the destination file (on the right side of the dialog box) to change their order.

8. *Optional:* Click the Scan Data buttons to review the matching fields in several records.

   This is mainly a sanity check. By scanning several records, you can assure yourself that the fields do indeed match properly and that you have not omitted an important field or two.

9. Click the appropriate radio button to specify whether you want to add new records or replace data in the current found set.

   The "Add new records" option simply appends the imported records to the destination file, while the "Replace data in current found set" option overwrites the records in the current found set. If you intend to use the latter option, you should first make a backup copy of the destination file.

   The Import command cannot be undone, so a mistake can have serious consequences for your data. Note, too, that if the destination file has fewer records in it than the imported file, the leftover records will not be imported if you use the Replace option.

10. Click Import.

Changing the Field Order When Importing Data

In the upper-right corner of the Import Field Mapping dialog box is a View By pop-up menu that you can use to make it easier to match fields between the two databases. The option that you choose from this menu determines the order of display for the fields in the current database (on the right side of the dialog box). The Matching Names option is particularly useful for quickly selecting all matching field names in the two files. Note, however, that this option only appears when the import file contains a header record that lists the file's field names.

Opening a Foreign Data File to Create a New Database

If you want to directly change an existing file from some other program into a new FileMaker database, you can now do so without first creating the database fields and layouts in FileMaker Pro. That is, you don't need to have a FileMaker Pro database to receive the new data — one can be created on-the-fly for you.

To create a new database from a file in another program, follow these steps:

1. Choose the Open command from the File menu.

   A standard file dialog box appears.

2. From the Show pop-up menu, choose All Available or the specific type of file you want to open.

   The list of file types is identical to the list displayed when you import data using the Import Records command.

3. Select the file and click Open.

   A new file dialog box appears in which you are asked to save the converted file, as shown in Figure 16-6.

CW2-3 Files
Databases
3-column text
3-column text (v1)
Address database
Address database-text
Address worksheet
Eject
Desktop
New
Name converted file:
Address database Converted
Cancel
Save

Figure 16-6: Saving the converted file

4. Accept the proposed name for the converted file or type a new name in the text box. Then click Save.

   The new database is converted to FileMaker Pro format and then opens in a new window. Fields are presented in the default vertical format and are named using the convention f1, f2, f3, and so on. You can now clean up the database by using the Define Fields command to rename and define additional fields, and change the layout as necessary by switching to Layout mode.

Opening a ClarisWorks 2.0, 2.1, or 3.0 database presents you with several special bonuses. Field names and definitions all carry over into the new FileMaker Pro database. Also, if you have defined multiple layouts in the ClarisWorks database, you'll find that they now exist in the FileMaker Pro database as well.

Exporting Data

When you export records, you take FileMaker Pro data and change it to a format that another program can use. The process is virtually the same as importing, except that it operates in reverse.

Format Selection

When you export records, you don't save directly into a document in another application — you simply create a new document that the target application can open. As you do when importing records, you need to determine the file format of the destination program before you export data to be used by that program. You may need to check the relevant application's documentation to determine what file formats it can use. If FileMaker Pro doesn't support the application's standard file format, you'll have to instruct FileMaker to export a new data file in a format that the destination application *can* use. Many Macintosh programs can read tab- or comma-separated text files, for example.

FileMaker Pro supports the following formats for export purposes:

- FileMaker Pro
- Tab-Separated Text
- Comma-Separated Text
- SYLK
- DBF
- DIF
- WKS
- BASIC
- Merge
- Edition File

Data Cleanup

As you do when importing, you may need to clean up your data — either before exporting it or prior to opening it in the destination program. In particular, you may find unnecessary returns and spaces at the end of some records. These unneeded characters are usually the result of careless data entry and can cause trouble in your target file when you export data to it.

As a solution, you can define a new Calculation field for each field to be exported. The definition of this field is a procedure that strips spaces and returns. Use the following definition:

```
If(Position(FieldName, "¶", 1), Trim (Left(FieldName,
Position(FieldName,"¶",1)-1)),Trim(FieldName))
```

Replace "FieldName" with the name of the field that you want to strip. You must define a separate Calculation field for each potential source field. Then export the Calculation fields rather than the originals.

If you use this formula on a field that contains intentional returns (as might be found in a Comments field that contains several paragraphs), the formula truncates the field contents at the end of the first paragraph — effectively deleting all paragraphs that follow.

How to Export

With data cleanup behind you (in the event that cleanup was necessary), you are ready to export the data. Follow these steps to export FileMaker Pro data for use in another application:

1. Open your source FileMaker Pro database.
2. Use Find mode to locate the set of records to export.

   An export always consists only of records in the current found set. You can also use the Sort command to sort these records, if you want.
3. In Browse mode, choose Export Records from the Import/Export submenu of the File menu.

   A standard file dialog box appears, similar in appearance to the dialog box previously shown in Figure 16-4.
4. Type a name for the destination file.

5. Choose a file format for the destination file from the Type pop-up menu.
6. Click Save.

   The Export Field Order dialog box appears, as shown in Figure 16-7.

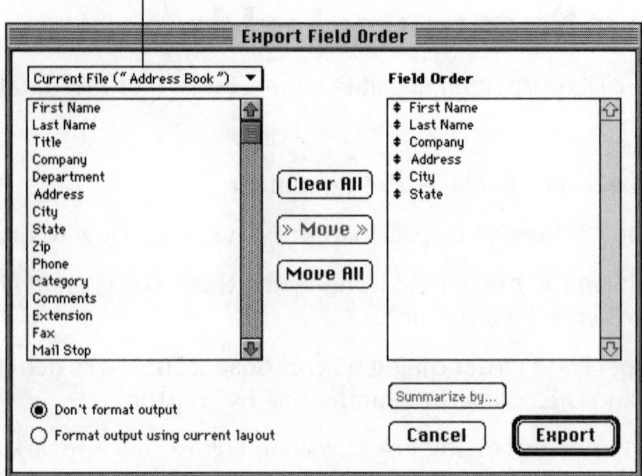

Figure 16-7: The Export Field Order dialog box

7. In the left side of the dialog box, select the fields that you want to export.

   As each field is selected, click the Move button to transfer it to the Field Order section of the dialog box.
8. Drag field names to change the export order of fields, if necessary.

   Click to select the name of the field you want to move and then drag it to a new position in the Field Order list. In most cases, you will want the order of the fields to match the order in which they appear in the destination file (assuming the destination file already exists).
9. Click the appropriate radio button to specify whether you want to format the output.

   Click the "Don't format output" radio button if you want the export to contain unformatted text. Click "Format output using current layout" if you want the data to be formatted to match the number, date, and time formats that you have assigned to the fields in the current layout.
10. Click Export.

    The target data file is created in the chosen format.

If you have defined one or more relationships for the current database, you can also export fields from any of the related files. To view the field names in any related file, just choose the name of the relationship from the pop-up menu at the top of the dialog box. In the export field list, fields from the current file and from related files can be mixed.

Exporting Summary Fields

It's also possible to export summary data from a FileMaker Pro database. The steps are as follows:

1. Open your source FileMaker Pro document.
2. Repeat steps 2 through 6 described previously in "How to Export."
3. Sort the file on the break field that groups the records (that is, the "sub-summary when sorted by" field).
4. In the Export Field Order dialog box, choose a Summary field that you want to export and then click the "Summarize by" button.

   The "Summarize by" dialog box shown in Figure 16-8 appears, listing the fields by which you can summarize the data.

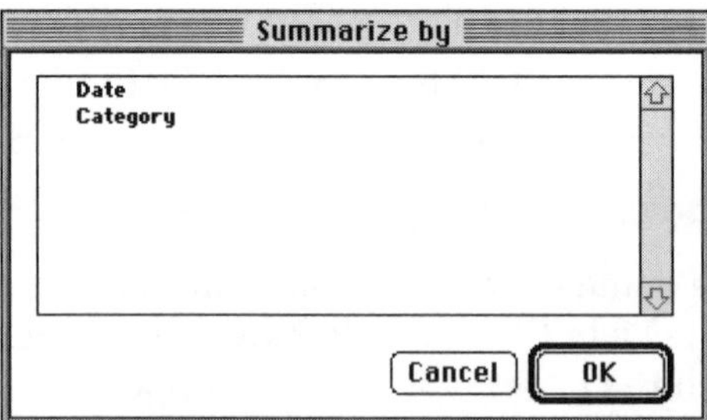

Figure 16-8: The "Summarize by" dialog box

5. Choose one or more of the sort fields that are listed and then click OK.
6. Repeat steps 4 and 5 for any other Summary fields you want to export.
7. Click Export.

Exchanging Data with PCs

Because FileMaker Pro 3.0 also runs under Microsoft Windows 95 and Windows NT 3.51, you can move data to and from PCs as well. Keep two things in mind when you exchange data with a PC. First, you actually have to get the data from your Mac to a PC, and vice versa; and second, you need to understand the differences between the Macintosh and PC versions of FileMaker Pro. The following sections explain both of these concepts.

Moving Data to and from FileMaker Pro for Windows

You can share files between a Mac and a PC in three basic ways: you can use a network (which provides direct access to files), you can use the time-honored "sneaker net" (moving files physically — on floppy disks — between machines), and you can transfer files electronically (using a modem or the serial ports on both computers). Here's how the three methods work:

- *Network*: Setting up a mixed network of Macs and PCs is a task for the experts. You can use AppleShare to make the task easier. For AppleShare, you need something like Farallon's PhoneNet Talk software, with a PhoneNet or Ethernet card for each PC. You can place the FileMaker Pro database files on an AppleShare server, on a host Mac, or on a host PC. FileMaker Pro 3.0 also supports IPX/SPX and TCP/IP networking for multi-user file sharing. (See Chapter 20 for more information about using FileMaker Pro on a network.)
- *Floppy disk*: You need a Macintosh with an Apple SuperDrive drive. (All Macs sold since the late 1980s have these high-density, 1.4MB, floppy drives.) Use PC-formatted floppies to exchange databases between the two types of computers. (A Mac can read PC floppies, but a PC can't read Mac floppies unless it's outfitted with special software.)

  When moving a FileMaker Pro database from a PC to the Mac, you can use the PC Exchange extension to transfer a readable copy of the database to your Mac's hard disk. Or you can use a utility such as DOS Mounter or Access PC to make PC disks visible on the Mac's desktop. When moving files from a Mac to the PC, you can use the same utilities to enable you to transfer a copy of your Mac databases to a PC-formatted floppy. Then just take the floppy over to the PC and load the database into FileMaker Pro for Windows.
- *Serial communications*: You can transfer files by using a modem and the appropriate communications software. Alternatively, you can transfer files directly between the serial ports of the two machines by using a program such as MacLinkPlusPC.

Once you have transfered the files, both the Mac and PC versions of FileMaker Pro can work with the transferred files without any further ado — importing and exporting are unnecessary. You may, however, run into some problems caused by the differences between Macs and PCs, as well as minor differences between the two versions of FileMaker Pro (as explained in the following section).

Understanding the Compatibility Issues

In general, you should watch out for seven potential problem areas when you move a Macintosh FileMaker Pro document to Microsoft Windows (or vice versa):

- Character sets
- Fonts
- File names
- Colors
- Graphics formats
- Printing
- Platform-specific capabilities

Character Sets

Characters with ASCII values 0 through 127 (*low ASCII*) are the same in both systems. Characters with ASCII values greater than 127 (*high ASCII*) may be different, depending on the Windows font you're using. Some Macintosh high-ASCII characters such as the bullet character (Option-8) — do not translate properly in Windows.

Figure 16-9 shows the characters that appear in two supposedly identical fonts on the Mac and the PC (Times, in this case). Only the shaded characters are actually the same; the others are different. Thus, if you enter text with special characters (the *é* characters in *résumé*, for example) on your Mac, you may get unexpected results that require messy (non-automatable) cleanup on the PC.

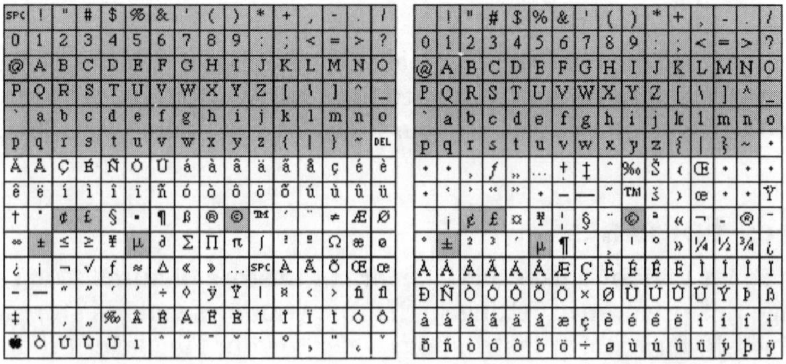

Figure 16-9: The character set for the Times font (Macintosh shown on the left; PC/ Windows shown on the right)

Fonts

TrueType and Adobe fonts are available for both systems. However, you should use the same technology on both computer systems, if you can. Otherwise, you're likely to encounter text-alignment problems in your layouts.

The Macintosh version of FileMaker Pro substitutes PC fonts, as summarized in Table 16-1.

Table 16-1
A Comparison of PC and Macintosh Fonts Used in FileMaker Pro

PC	*Macintosh*
MS Serif	Times
Times New Roman	Times
Times	New York
Tms Rmn	Times
Courier New	Courier
Courier	Monaco

File Names

Macintosh file names can have up to 32 characters, but PC file names under Windows 95 can now contain over 200 characters. You should also note that FileMaker Pro for Windows generally expects database names to end with a FM extension (as in SALES.FM).

Colors

Colors are organized into palettes. FileMaker Pro supports palettes of 8, 16, and 88 colors. Colors are not necessarily mapped the same way on the two systems, so you may see strange color effects on your PC when you open a Mac document.

Graphics Formats

FileMaker Pro for Windows uses a PC file format to store pictures. You can, if you want, change this preference setting so that the Windows version stores graphics in PICT (Macintosh) format. For instructions, refer to your FileMaker Pro for Windows documentation.

Printing

Depending on the print driver you use on your PC, your PC results may differ from your Mac results, even when using the same printer. You may have to create two versions of each report layout: one tailored to the PC and the other for your Macintosh.

Platform-Specific Capabilities

Several capabilities of the two operating systems are platform-specific; that is, they are available only in Windows or only on the Mac. If such features are used in designing a script, the script will not run on the other platform. Some examples of platform-specific capabilities are listed below.

Mac-Specific Features

- Drag and drop
- PlainTalk support
- AppleScript and Apple Events support

Windows-Specific Features

- OLE (Object Linking and Embedding) containers
- Sending electronic mail with optional attachments
- Microsoft Registry support
- DDE messaging

Summary

- You can exchange FileMaker Pro data with other applications and with the Windows version of FileMaker Pro. FileMaker Pro supports a variety of popular file formats.
- FileMaker Pro can import data created in other programs, such as spreadsheets and other database applications.
- You can directly share data with the Windows version of FileMaker Pro, but certain results may differ, especially in terms of fonts, graphics, and colors.

Creating and Using FileMaker Pro Templates

CHAPTER 17

In This Chapter

- Installing new templates
- Saving FileMaker Pro databases as templates

You've already learned a lot about designing and using databases. For some purposes, however, you don't need to go to all the trouble of designing a database from scratch. You may find a template that has been developed by someone else that you can use as is or easily modify to meet your needs. A *template,* in the case of FileMaker Pro, is a predefined and formatted database file into which you can enter your own data. More specifically, a *template* is a database without any records (and, conversely, a *database* is just a template that contains records).

When you install FileMaker Pro 3.0, more than 40 FileMaker Pro templates are copied to your hard disk. You can use any of them by choosing New from the File menu, clicking the button labeled "Create a new file using a template" (in the New Database dialog box), and then choosing a template from the list.

These templates serve two purposes. First, they give you some databases with which you can safely experiment. Second, they are full-featured databases that you may be able to use in your business, home, or school work.

This chapter discusses the techniques and commands you will need to know in order to work with *any* FileMaker Pro template, regardless of where you obtain it — whether you receive it from an online information service, a friend, or a colleague, or purchase it as a commercial product from a member of the Claris Solutions Alliance (see Appendix C). For details on creating your own templates with the intent of giving or selling them to others, see Chapter 21.

Installing a Template

When you obtain a FileMaker Pro template, there are several different methods that the database designers may have provided to enable you to install their templates. Here are some of the most common procedures used to install templates or databases:

- *Run a special installer program.* This method is usually associated only with commercial packages, such as FileMaker Pro. When you run the installer program, you are given an option to install all or selected parts of the software — usually to any disk and folder that you choose.
- *Double-click a self-extracting archive.* To save disk space, templates (and other software) are frequently compressed into one or more self-extracting archives. A self-extracting archive contains compressed copies of the template — conserving disk space and reducing download time (for templates that are distributed through online information services). A self-extracting archive is called *self-extracting* because it includes a built-in file extraction program. When you double-click the icon of a self-extracting archive, a dialog box appears asking where you wish to install the files. After selecting a destination, the files are extracted from the archive, expanded to their normal size, and copied to the destination disk and folder. (The files on the *Macworld FileMaker Pro 3.0 Bible Disk* are all self-extracting archives created with a popular shareware program called Compact Pro.)
- *Extract the templates from a normal archive.* This is a variation of the previous distribution method. Instead of creating self-extracting archives, sometimes normal archives are created. The only difference is that you need a separate file-extraction utility (such as Compact Pro, StuffIt Deluxe, or StuffIt Lite) in order to extract the files. This distribution method (as well as the previous one) is commonly used with templates, programs, and other materials that you'll find on online services, such as CompuServe and America Online.
- *Use the Finder to make a copy of the templates.* Many database templates are distributed as normal, uncompressed files. To install these templates, all you need to do is copy them to your hard disk — just as you would any other file or program.

Reinstalling a Fresh Copy of a Template

Like any other FileMaker Pro database, any changes you make to a template (entering or editing data, changing field definitions, rearranging fields on a layout, and so on) are instantly saved and become a permanent part of the file. Thus, when you are finished experimenting with a new template and are ready to begin entering your own data, you'll want to start with a fresh copy of the template. There are two safe ways you can accomplish this:

- Re-run the installation program, double-click the self-extracting archive, or run the necessary file-extraction utility.
- For templates that are distributed as normal Finder copies, drag a fresh copy of the template from the distribution disk to your hard disk.

As an alternative, it may be simpler to just think ahead. Whenever you receive a template, make a backup copy of the uncompressed templates. When you're through trying it out and are ready to commit your own data to the template, you can use the Finder to make a new copy of the template from your backup copy. This is *always* a good idea.

Saving a Database as a Template

FileMaker Pro templates are also referred to as clones. (These two terms are interchangeable.) A *clone* is an exact copy of a database, but without any records. The clone contains the same field definitions, layouts, buttons, and scripts as the original database. Because all the records have been removed, however, it is in a perfect state to receive fresh data.

There are several instances in which you might want to create a clone of an existing database:

- *To create an archival copy of the structure of an important database — just in case.* Many of us tend to "tweak" a database as we use it: moving fields around, trying out new layouts, and testing additional scripts, for example. Because FileMaker Pro automatically saves *any* change that you make to a database, these little experiments have the potential to wreak havoc — causing scripts to stop functioning, calculation fields to present the wrong results, and so on. If you've created a clone of the original database, you can get back to square one by simply importing the data from your current database into the clone.

- *To begin a new weekly, quarterly, or other time-based database.* Many databases are designed to be used only for a certain period of time and then started over again with new records. For example, I created a database in which I do my bookkeeping. The IRS expects me to turn in an annual 1040 and Schedule C, so I need a fresh copy of this database at the beginning of each year. Another example would be if you were to make a call-tracking database to be used by your department's receptionist to make a permanent record of incoming calls, you might want to start a fresh copy on a more frequent basis (monthly, weekly, or even daily, depending on the call volume).
- *To remove sample records and prepare a commercial or shareware database for your own data.* Some templates — including some of the ones on the *Macworld FileMaker Pro 3.0 Bible Disk* — contain a small set of sample records, enabling you to get a feel for how the database works without having to enter (or risk) your own data. As long as you restrict your experimentation to adding, deleting, and editing records, you can strip out all the sample records by simply making a clone of the database. Then you're ready to begin entering your own data.
- *To enable you to give the template away or sell it.* Unless your records are meant to be used as a sample, you probably don't want to include your personal or business data in a template. Making a clone strips that data out in one easy step.

To make a template or clone from any existing database, use the following procedure:

1. Open the database in FileMaker Pro.
2. Choose Save a Copy As from the File menu.

   A standard file dialog box appears, as shown in Figure 17-1.

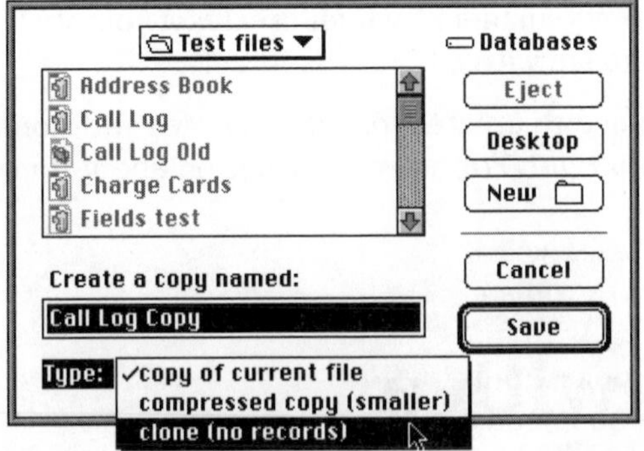

Figure 17-1: A standard file dialog box

3. Choose "clone (no records)" from the Type pop-up menu.
4. Select a destination disk and folder using normal file navigation procedures.
5. Type a name for the clone in the "Create a copy named:" text box.

   If you're saving the file in a *different* folder and/or disk than the one where the current database is stored, you can use the same name as that of the original database. If you're storing it in the *same* folder and/or disk, you will want to use a new name or the default name proposed by FileMaker Pro (*filename* Clone).

   Under no circumstances should you use the same name as the original database when saving the template in the same folder and/or disk location! Doing so replaces your original database with an empty template.

6. Click Save.

   The clone is created but not opened. The original template file remains open in FileMaker Pro. If you want to immediately begin working with the clone, close the original database (choose Close from the File menu or press ⌘-W) and then open the clone (choose Open from the File menu or press ⌘-O).

The other two Save a Copy As options that you can select from the pop-up menu are:

- "copy of current file," which creates a backup copy of the current database with all records intact

- "compressed copy (smaller)," which creates a compressed backup copy of the current database with all records intact

Although they aren't used to create clones, these two additional Save options are very useful in their own right. For more information about these options, see Chapter 2.

Working with a New Template

As mentioned previously in this chapter, the only difference between a database and a template or clone is that the latter contains no records. This presents one immediate problem for many users: When a template is first opened, the database window is likely to be *blank* (as shown in Figure 17-2). Because there are no records, there is nothing for FileMaker Pro to display — other than an empty database window.

Figure 17-2: A blank database window

All that you need to do in order to begin working with the template is choose New Record from the Mode menu (or press ⌘-N). The opening layout immediately appears, and you can get down to business.

Avoiding the Blank Look (in Your Templates and on Users' Faces)

There's nothing so potentially confusing to a new user as a blank screen. To avoid causing a panic, you can make one small modification to your template before handing or selling it to a user: Add a single new record and then close the file. When users open the file, they will see whatever you originally intended them to see, such as a blank data-entry form for record number 1 or an opening menu.

Summary

- There are a number of methods that are used to install FileMaker Pro templates and databases that you obtain from others. The most common methods include running a special installation or file-extraction program, running a separate file-extraction utility, and making a copy from the Finder.
- To adapt a database for use as a template, you clone it by using the Save a Copy As command. The file dialog box has a clone (no records) option that omits records from the new copy. In FileMaker Pro, the terms *template* and *clone* are used interchangeably.
- When working with a clone or template, you may have to create the first record in order to make the various layouts appear.

Documenting and Designing Help Systems for Your Database

18 CHAPTER

In This Chapter

- Deciding what information to include in a help system
- Methods for documenting and providing help information

Do any of the following scenarios sound familiar?

- You've just spent half an hour downloading an interesting-sounding FileMaker Pro template from CompuServe, America Online, or GEnie. You discover that it contains no instructions whatsoever — no Read Me file, no help screens, no descriptive text. Now what?
- Bill, one of your coworkers at XYZ Corp., is on vacation. While he's away, the boss asks whether you can fill in by entering customer orders, printing mailing labels, and generating daily reports. Although you know that Bill accomplishes these tasks with extraordinary ease, using a FileMaker Pro database that he custom-designed, you haven't got a clue as to how he does it.
- A couple of years back, you designed an elaborate database with dozens of scripts and buttons. Recently you realized that, with just a few modifications, you can put the database to work again for a new task. Unfortunately, when you designed the database, documenting how it worked didn't seem very important. Now you can't remember what half the scripts were supposed to do or what that odd field named "Extra" was intended to do. (It's surprising how easily you can forget….)

- You've created a whiz-bang FileMaker Pro template that you think every Mac (or Windows) user will want for their very own. In your rush to share it with the world, you deposit copies of it on half a dozen bulletin boards and ask for a $10 shareware fee. Because you didn't bother to explain how the template works, it doesn't sell as well as you'd hoped, and the people who are sending you the shareware fee are also pestering you with questions.

Of course, not every database needs elaborate documentation. But if you spend a little time creating a simple help system or Read Me file, you can avoid some headaches later on. This chapter discusses appropriate (and sometimes essential) topics that you should include and suggests several different approaches that you can use to create help systems.

Suggested Help Topics

A help system that is carefully thought out anticipates the user's needs. The better you anticipate, the happier the user will be and the less time you will need to spend supporting or explaining the template. Here is a brief list of some material that is appropriate for inclusion in a help system or a Read Me file:

- A description of the purpose of the database
- An explanation of the purpose of each field, the type of data it should contain, and any restrictions and/or validation options that have been set (see Chapter 5 for information on data validation options)
- An explanation of the purpose of each layout, as well as any special preparations that the user must make before using the layout (changing the Page Setup or printer selection, for example)
- An explanation of what each script does and how to execute the script (by selecting it from the Script menu or pressing a button)
- Suggestions for customizing the template (for example, selecting different fonts, changing screen colors, creating new reports and mailing labels, and adding features)

If you want people to treat your template as a serious business product rather than as something you just knocked together in a free moment, you need to make it look like a business product. Documentation and/or a help system is a must!

Choosing Help Topics

The types and quantity of help you provide should be dictated by need and common sense. If you are writing a help system for a database that will only be used by the Accounting Department in your company, for example, you should offer help with common data-entry and report-generation questions that you expect will occur. But since everyone will be using the same version of the database, information about customizing the database may well be avoided.

When deciding the types of help to offer, try to put yourself in the place of a new user. Think about the terms that you've used for field labels that might not be immediately understood. When it could be unclear what type of information should be entered in a field, explain it. (If you're *really* smart, you'll give the database to some other people to test and ask them to tell you what kind of help they need *before* you distribute it to the general public.)

To get more ideas about the types of help to include, you may want to *download* some of the shareware templates that are available on online services such as CompuServe, GEnie, and America Online. You're sure to find several excellent (as well as many quite horrid) examples of help information.

Different Approaches to Presenting Help Information

You can present help information and documentation in several ways. In choosing a method, consider who the intended reader of the information is (you, other developers and technical people, or end users and customers) and how often you expect the reader to refer to the information. For example, creating an elaborate online, context-sensitive help system for information that the reader will probably need to see only once doesn't make much sense.

Approach #1: A Read Me File

Creating a separate Read Me file in a word processing program or text editor is obviously the easiest way to document a template. And having the full text-formatting capabilities of a word processor at your disposal can make the writing go quickly. As an added bonus (only a small one, however), writing the documentation as a separate file can help keep the size and complexity of the template to a minimum.

Arguably, this approach is best for providing information that is usually needed only once, such as installation instructions and minor customization notes, or for when you are creating the database only for your personal use or limited in-house use at your company. In the case of a personal template, if you later decide to share it with others, your notes can form the basis of an in-template help system.

When creating a database to be distributed as shareware, this approach to documentation is certainly better than nothing, but it is definitely *not* the best method. See Approaches 2 and 3, later in this chapter, for more appropriate means of providing help information for shareware.

If you want others to be able to read and print your Read Me file, you should give careful thought to which word processor or text editor you use in creating the file. Obviously, if you write the documentation in an obscure program, you will prevent many people from being able to open and read the file. The following sections offer some suggestions for creating a Read Me file.

SimpleText and Other Text Editors

SimpleText — the successor to TeachText — is a text editor that Apple Computer provides with current versions of the system software. Because everyone has system software installed on their Mac (it's what makes the Mac run), most people will either have SimpleText on their hard disk or have ready access to it on the system software installation disks. And even if SimpleText isn't installed on a user's system, the files created by SimpleText are in Text-Only format, so virtually any word processing program can read them. These reasons are precisely why so many Read Me files are written in SimpleText (or TeachText).

If you intend to distribute a template on online information systems and computer bulletin boards, creating the documentation in SimpleText will also help keep the size of the material small. (No one wants to waste half an hour downloading a few pages of documentation that, because of the format selected, grew to several hundred K. This is a common problem with stand-alone documents, as you will see in the following section.)

Stand-Alone Documents

If the primary method of distribution will be on disk, you can afford the luxury of using a program that can produce stand-alone documents (that is, documents that work just like programs). You don't need a separate program to open them — they're double-clickable!

If you scrounge around online, you're sure to find several utilities of this sort. DOCMaker, a shareware program from Green Mountain Software, is one of the best-known examples. It enables you to create stand-alone documents that include graphics and multiple fonts, styles, and colors (see Figure 18-1). In addition to being able to type and edit text within DOCMaker, you can use it to import text that was created in a variety of popular word processing formats. You can organize DOCMaker documents into chapters, print them, and search them. DOCMaker's only weaknesses are that the documents it creates tend to be large (over 100K) and that the program does not support tabs.

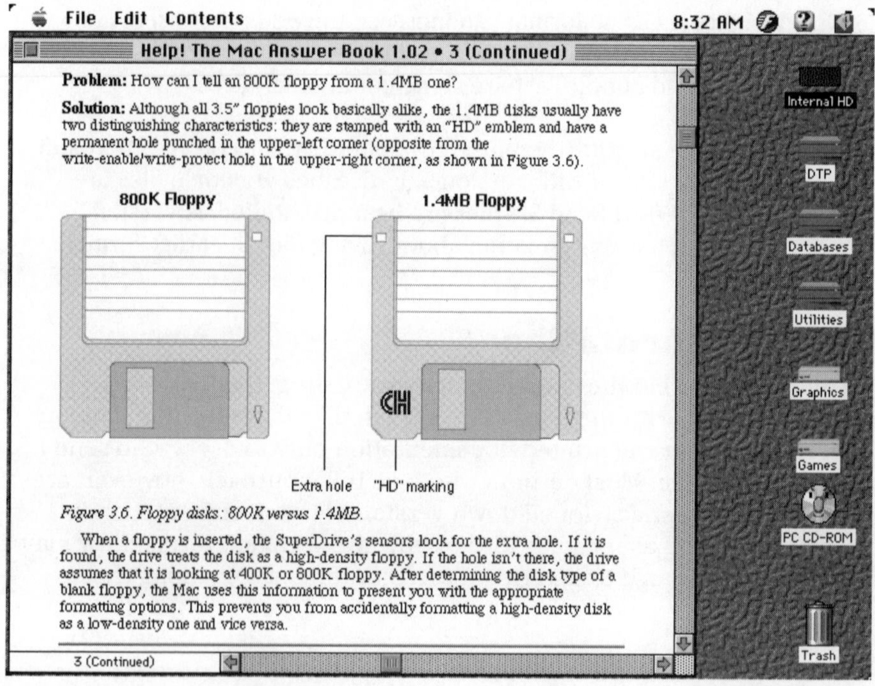

Figure 18-1: A DOCMaker stand-alone document

Several commercial programs are available for converting existing formatted documents into stand-alone documents as well. Two commonly used programs are Common Ground (No Hands Software) and Adobe Acrobat. To use Common Ground, for example, you simply open a document in the word processing, desktop publishing, or other program in which you created it and then, using a special Chooser device supplied with the package, you print the document to disk. In the process, a *reader* is embedded in the final document. The reader enables other users to view the document by just double-clicking it. The advantages of using a program such as Common Ground are that it supports all of the normal formatting, graphics, and fonts and that the process of converting to a stand-alone document is totally painless. However, the size of resulting documents can be enormous.

Word Processing Programs

Using a standard word processing program (Microsoft Word, MacWrite, WriteNow, or WordPerfect, for example) is the least desirable method for creating documentation that will be distributed. (One exception to this general rule is when you develop a template solely for in-house use and everyone in the company uses the same word processing program.) Although many word processing programs can read documents that are created in other word processing programs, the possibility always exists that a sizable number of people will be unable to read the file. Authors who distribute documentation in a word processing format can increase the odds that users can read it by including copies of the documentation in several different formats. Microsoft Word, MacWrite, and SimpleText are some common choices.

Many Macintosh owners have steadfastly refused to upgrade their copy of Microsoft Word to version 6.0 and have stayed with version 5.0/5.1. Since version 6 files are incompatible with version 5, Word Read Me files are best distributed as version 5. Refer to Word's documentation for information about saving files in earlier formats.

Paper-Only Documentation

Of course, you may want to skip the compatibility issues altogether and simply include printed instructions with the template. You can distribute the template on information services but offer the printed documentation only to users who send in the shareware registration fee. Most authors who take this approach, however, are obliged to also include at least a stripped-down version of the documentation in a Read Me file. If you don't give users some idea of how the template works, they may not explore it sufficiently enough to determine whether it does something that's useful for them.

Approach #2: A Help Layout

Another method is to include the documentation or help information in the template itself. The advantages of placing this material in a FileMaker Pro template include the following:

- *No compatibility problems*: Because users need to have a copy of FileMaker Pro in order to use the template, by definition they have all the software they need to read the help text, too.
- *Ready access*: Users who need help don't want to have to hunt for it. When people need help, they usually want it right away. And because Read Me files take up disk space, users frequently toss them into the Trash after reading them, so such files aren't immediately accessible (or they may no longer be accessible at all).

Figure 18-2 shows an example of help text in a FileMaker Pro database. All the help information is contained in a single layout. If the information is too long to fit on a single screen (as it is in this example), users can click the scroll bar to see it all.

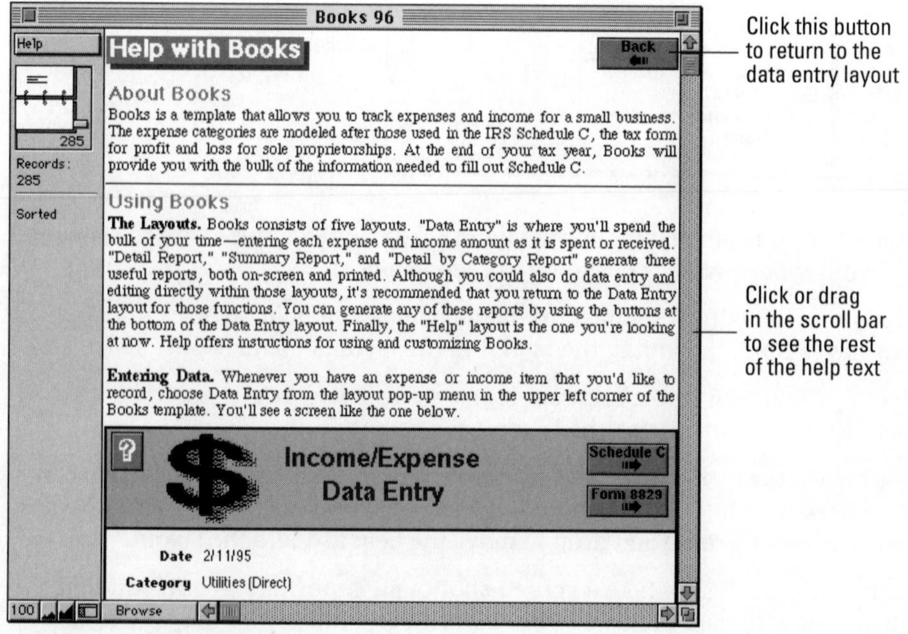

Figure 18-2: Help text as a separate layout

As you can see in the figure, a help layout contains no fields at all. It is constructed entirely of static text and graphics, so you never have to worry about the user inadvertently changing what's on-screen. When this layout is displayed, even if the user clicks the book icon to flip from one record to the next, the help screen doesn't change.

To create a help screen that is similar to the one shown in Figure 18-2, do the following:

1. In a new or existing database, change to Layout mode (choose Layout from the Mode menu or press ⌘-L).
2. Choose New Layout from the Mode menu (or press ⌘-N).

   The New Layout dialog box appears, as shown in Figure 18-3.

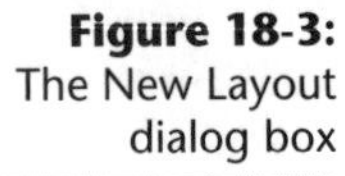

Figure 18-3: The New Layout dialog box

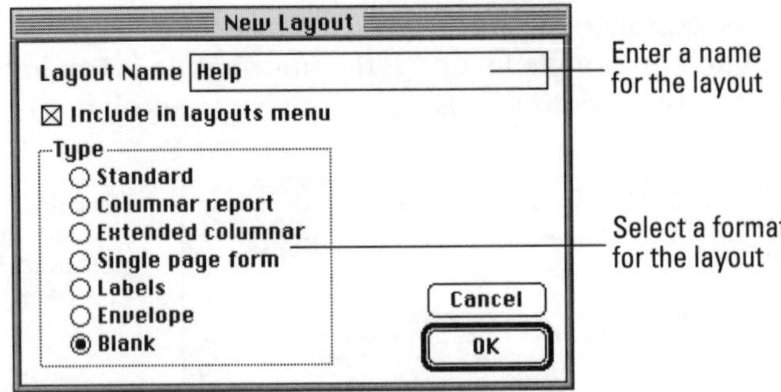

3. Enter an appropriate name for the layout (Help, for example), select Blank as the layout type, and click OK to create the layout.

   Because you usually don't need to display fields in a help layout, choosing Blank saves time. (Including the layout in the layouts menu is optional.)

4. Select the Text tool (the uppercase *A*) from the Tools palette to add text blocks to the layout. Resize the text blocks as necessary.

   If you have already prepared help text in a word processing document, you can copy and paste it into the layout. And if your word processing program supports it, you can also use drag and drop to move the help text into the layout.

   Another approach is to take a screen shot of an important layout, edit and embellish it with callouts using your favorite graphics program, and then paste the image into the help layout. (To take a screen shot, you press Shift-⌘-3.) Figure 18-9, found later in this chapter, shows an example of a screen shot that has been incorporated into a help file.

5. *Optional*: Add graphics by copying them from a graphics program or the Scrapbook desk accessory and then pasting them into the layout.

   You can also import graphics directly into the layout by choosing the Import Picture command from the Import/Export submenu of the File menu. (See Chapter 6 for additional information on adding and importing graphics into a layout.) In addition, some graphics programs, such as the graphics components of ClarisWorks 4.0, support drag and drop. You can use this feature to directly drag graphics onto FileMaker Pro layouts.

6. *Optional*: Create scripts that switch from the help layout to the data entry layout and vice versa (via the Go to Layout script step).

   Although you can place the scripts in the Scripts menu, assigning them to buttons on the layout is more convenient. (See the "Using a Button to Summon Help" sidebar in this chapter.)

As you design the help layout, remember that you can mix fonts, styles, and colors in the same text block. When you are designing for other users, however, getting fancy with font choices doesn't pay. Unless the other users have the same fonts installed on their system, different fonts will be substituted. Also, although you can create the help text as one long text block, you may want to break it into a series of smaller, more manageable chunks. When you use this approach, you can easily intersperse graphics (such as screen captures, illustrations, and clip art) in the text.

Using a Button to Summon Help

To make it easy to move from any layout in the database to your help layout (and back again), you can create buttons for the different layouts. The script that is attached to each navigation button in the database consists of only a single line:

```
Go to layout <x>
```

You replace the <x> with the name of the data entry or help layout. (In the data entry layout, use the name of the help layout. In the help layout, use the name of the data entry layout.) Attach the command to each button by selecting the button on the layout and then choosing Define Button from the Scripts menu. (See Chapter 15 for more information on creating scripts and defining buttons.)

This approach can also be implemented with *multiple* help layouts. In a complex database, you may well want to have separate help screens for providing help with specific functions (such as data entry) performing Find requests and sorts, and printing reports. This serves several purposes. First, it no longer forces the user to scroll through what — in many cases — may be multiple screens of information. Second, it more closely approximates the type of specific, context-appropriate help that users have come to expect from Mac programs. For example, the data entry screen may have separate buttons for data entry and sorting help, while the reports screen could have a single help button that summons help that is specific to preparing a report.

Approach #3: Data Entry Assistance

Setting data validation options makes it easy to assure that users enter only the correct type of information for each field. However, if you want to *really* help them, you can present a custom error message whenever incorrect data is entered for a field. As an example, Figure 18-4 shows how to create a custom message that is displayed if a user neglects to enter a required field in a record. Thus, if you choose the "Display custom message if validation fails" option, you can create a unique, helpful message for any field whose intended contents may not be immediately obvious. (See Chapter 5 for instructions on setting validation options for fields.)

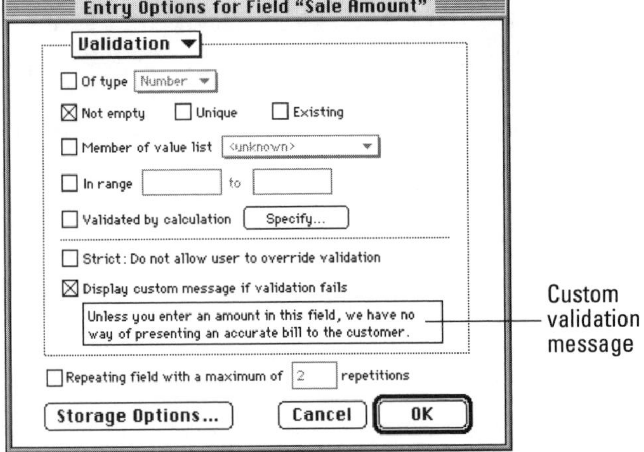

Figure 18-4: You can set the "Display custom message" option to present an alert box whenever a field's validation fails.

If you don't want to tie a custom message to a field's validation options, you can use the new "Show message" script step to present field-related help by attaching the script to a button. To enable users to summon such help, you might place a tiny "?" button at the end of each field and then associate the appropriate message script with each button. Figure 18-5 shows an example of the type of message that might be associated with a Number field help button.

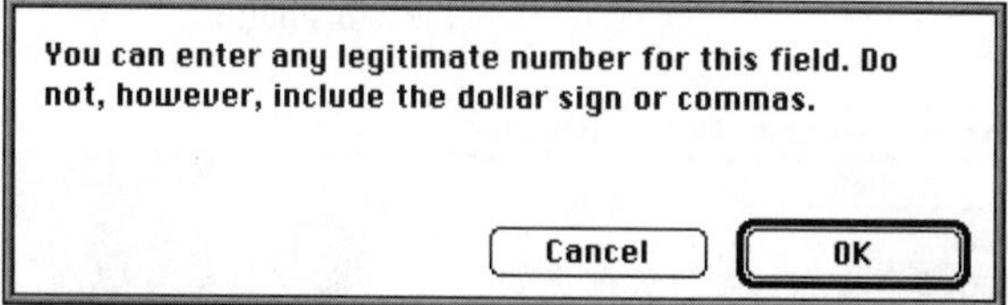
You can enter any legitimate number for this field. Do not, however, include the dollar sign or commas.
Cancel
OK

Figure 18-5: The Show message script step can be used to present custom messages, such as this one.

Approach #4: Script-Guided Help

FileMaker Pro scripts can make your help system much fancier and more helpful. By creating simple scripts and button definitions, you can design a series of help layouts that have the following features:

- *You can page through the help screens.* Each left-arrow and right-arrow button can have an attached script that causes FileMaker to go to the previous or next help layout.
- *You can access the help screens through a menu.* Each button or text string in the help menu can cause a different help layout to be displayed.
- *You can access the help screens through an index.* You can link each index entry to a specific help layout, providing a help system that works in much the same way as FileMaker Pro's help system does.

The *Macworld FileMaker Pro 3.0 Bible Disk* has an example of this type of help system in the folder named Callable Help Example. Instead of forcing the user to jump back and forth between a help layout and other layouts in the database, Callable Help stores the help information in another database file. Because the help information is in a different file, you can view it while you are still working in the main database.

Callable Help is modeled after FileMaker Pro's own help system. Clicking the Help button in the main database (Help Caller, in this example) opens the help database (Books Help, in this example). Figure 18-6 shows the two database files.

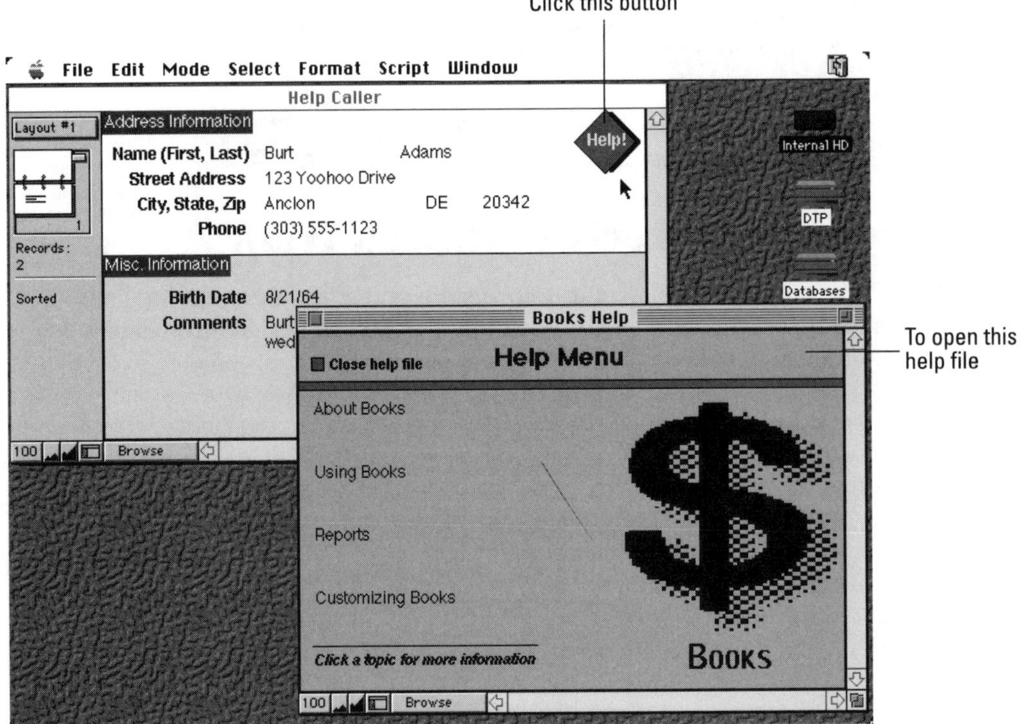

Figure 18-6: The help system consists of two FileMaker Pro databases: the main file (Help Caller) and the help file (Books Help).

You will notice that the help information in Books Help has absolutely nothing to do with the Help Caller database. In fact, it's some help text that I yanked out of one of my own databases and reformatted for this example. Don't let this bother you. What's important is that the files illustrate the mechanics required for you to implement a similar help system of your own.

Here's how the two databases interact. To access help, you simply click the Help button in the main database. Attached to the Help button is a one-line script that reads as follows:

```
Open ["Books Help"]
```

You create the one-line script in ScriptMaker, specifying the name of the help file when you add the Open step to the script (as shown in Figure 18-7). After you create the script, you then use the Button command from the Format menu to link the script to the Help button (with Perform Script *script name*).

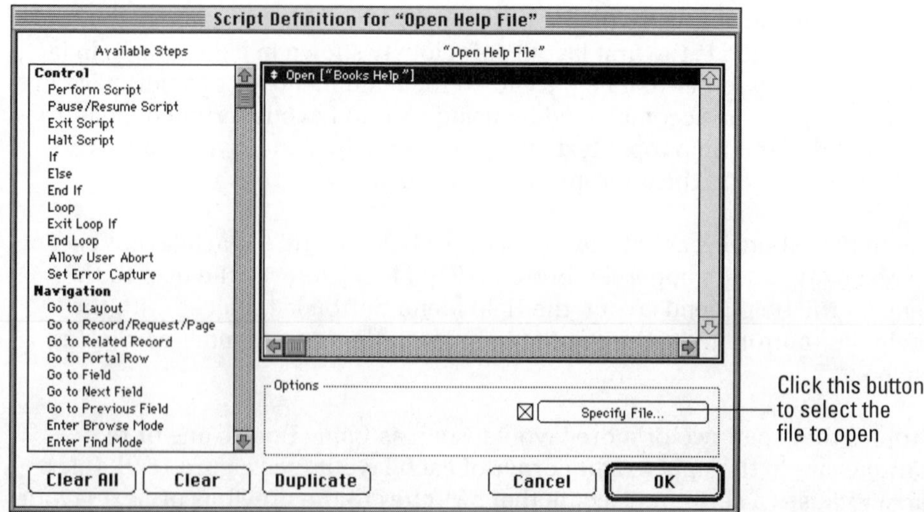

Figure 18-7: Creating the script that opens the help file

When the help file opens, several actions that are set in the preferences for the document automatically occur (see Figure 18-8). The help database displays the first layout (called Help Menu), and then hides the status area (the book pages and Tools palette) by executing the script named "Open Script." (See Chapter 7 for more information on setting Document and General preferences.)

Figure 18-8: Startup actions ("When opening…") are specified in the Document preferences for the database.

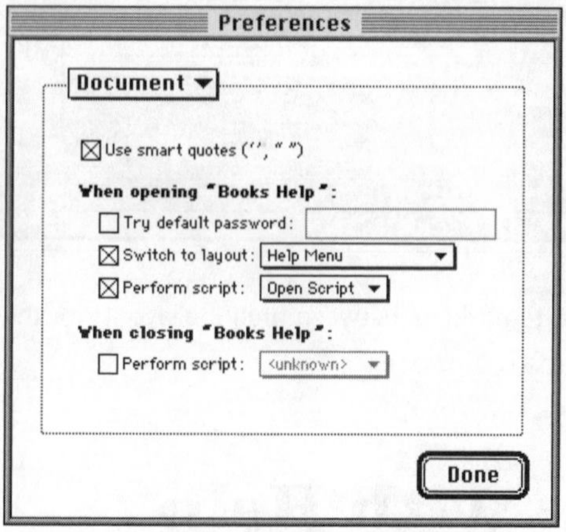

In Books Help, you move to a particular help topic by clicking the name of the topic in the Help Menu, which is the first layout (previously shown in Figure 18-6). In fact, every movement — whether to a help topic, to the main menu, or to a new page in the same help topic — is accomplished by using a Go to Layout script command. Clicking any of the four help topic text strings in the Help Menu layout causes a script to be executed and the appropriate layout to appear.

From one to three buttons are at the top of every help layout. In each layout except the Help Menu layout, the upper-left button (Help Menu) returns the user to the Help menu. In the Help Menu layout, the Help Menu button is replaced with the "Close help file" button, which closes the help file in the same manner as clicking the close box.

In help topics that span two or more layouts, such as Using Books, one or two arrow buttons are in the upper-right corner of each layout (see Figure 18-9). Clicking an arrow causes a script to execute that switches to the previous or next layout for that help topic. As in the FileMaker Pro help system, the number of layouts for a help topic is indicated in the lower-right corner of each layout.

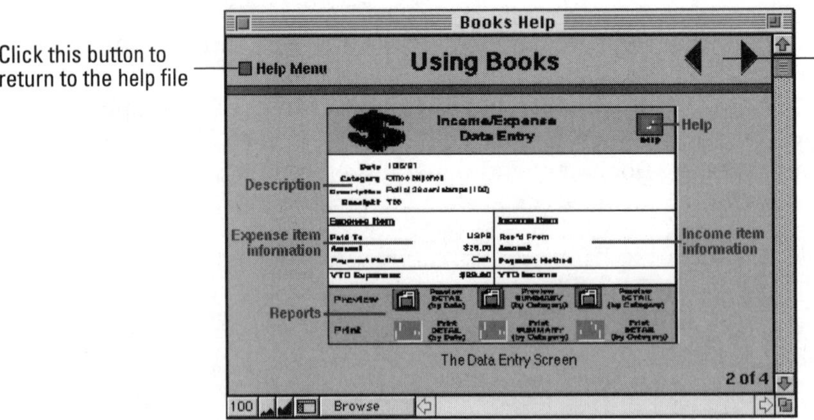

Figure 18-9: Click an arrow to navigate between multiple layouts for the same help topic.

More Help with Help

Regardless of the method you use to incorporate help information into your database, you may find the following tips useful.

Using Headers and Footers in Help Screens

If you want some help information to remain on-screen at all times, put it in the help layout's header or footer. As the user scrolls the window, the header and footer stay in place.

Figure 18-10 shows a help layout from the Apple Events Reference database (found in the FileMaker And Apple Events folder in the FileMaker 3.0 folder) in which both a header and a footer keep critical information on-screen.

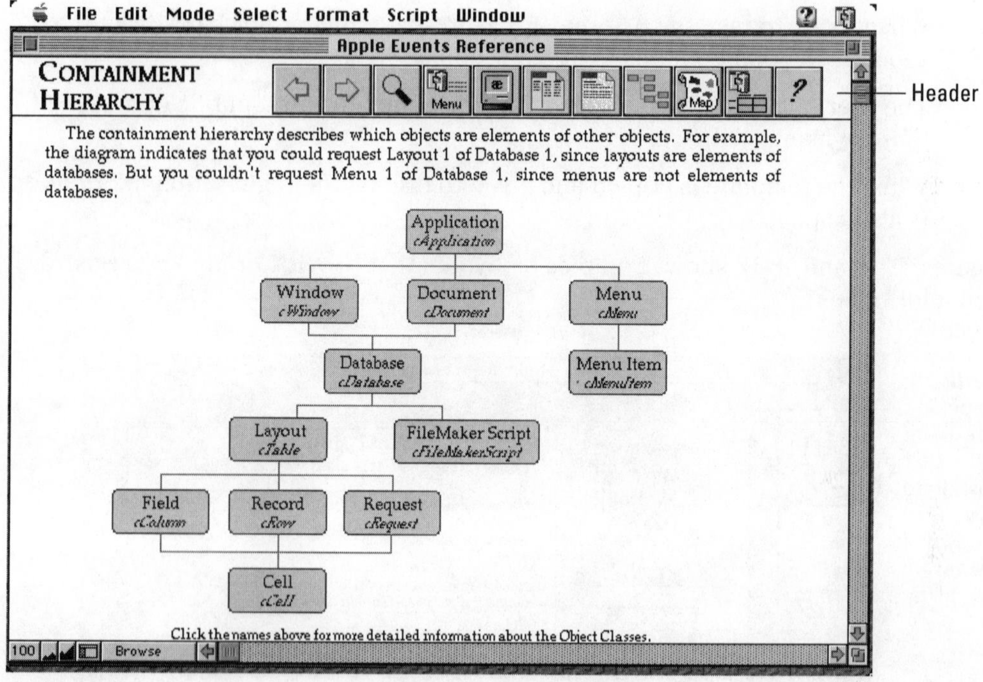

Figure 18-10: You can keep critical help information on-screen by placing it in the header and footer parts.

Riting and Speling

Don't forget that FileMaker Pro also has a built-in spelling checker. You may be a database whiz, but if your documentation or help text is riddled with spelling errors, your skills as a programmer and/or designer may also be questioned. To check spelling for the entire help layout, change to Layout mode, switch to the help screen layout, and choose Check Layout from the Spelling submenu of the Edit menu. See Chapter 11 for more information on using the spelling checker.

Creating a Credits Screen or a Shareware Registration Form

By using the same method that you use to provide in-template help, you can create a credits (or copyright) screen or a shareware registration form for a template. Without such a screen, you are likely to lose credit for the work you've done or miss out on shareware fees that are due you. In the case of a shareware template in particular, you want to make it as convenient as possible for the user to pay for your hard work. Creating the registration form as a separate layout ensures that:

- When ready to pay, the user never has to search his or her hard disk for a separate file that contains your name and address.
- The user is repeatedly reminded that the template is not public domain and that payment is expected.
- When the template is copied and given to others, the registration information is also copied.

Figures 18-11 and 18-12 show examples of layouts that provide credit and registration information.

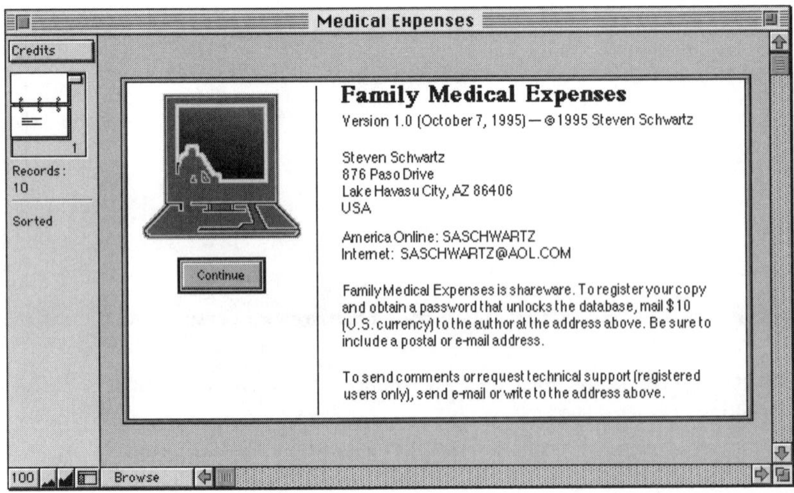

Figure 18-11: This opening screen explains what the user must do to register his or her copy of a shareware template.

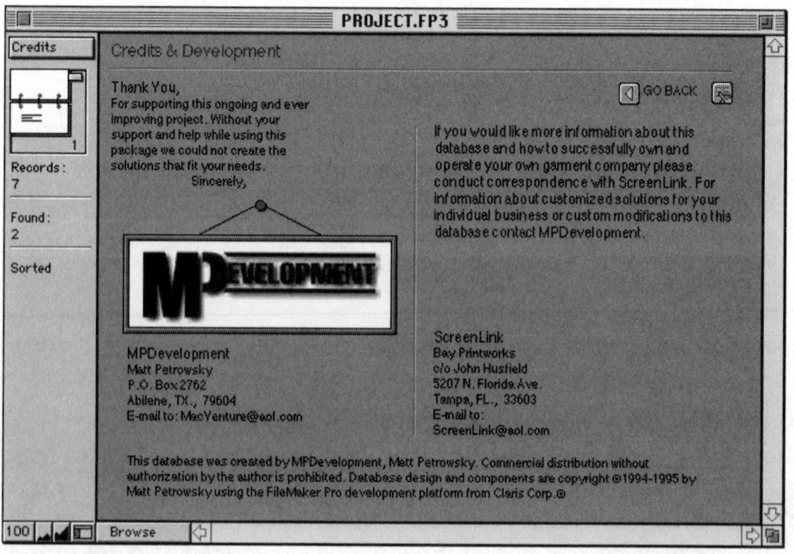

Figure 18-12: An example of a credits screen

Summary

- Even if you don't want to implement a formal help system for your database, you can easily create a Read Me file.
- You can add help, credit or copyright, and shareware registration screens to any database as separate layouts. You can use the Go to Layout script command to switch between any of these screens and the database's main menu or data entry layout.
- When you embed help information in layouts, you can create a single scrolling text screen or break the information into discrete chunks and place it in a series of layouts.
- The "Show message" script step can be attached to buttons and used to display custom help messages. There is also a data validation option that can automatically display a custom message if a field's validation fails — when a user neglects to enter information into a required field, for example.
- You can use text strings as well as graphics objects as buttons. Clicking a text string in a help menu, for example, can cause a specific help layout to display.
- To keep a database as small as possible, you can create a separate help database that the user can display and then dismiss when it is no longer needed. Keeping the help separate from the main database also enables users to view the help at the same time that they are entering data, creating reports, or constructing new layouts.

Part V
Mastering FileMaker Pro

This section will interest more experienced FileMaker Pro users and would-be developers. It discusses using relations and lookups to link databases, and offers tips for creating databases that you'd like to share with (or sell to) others.

Linking Databases: Relationships and Lookups

CHAPTER 19

In This Chapter

- The differences between relationships and lookups
- Defining relationships
- Placing related fields in a layout
- Working with lookups
- Using the Relookup command to update lookup fields

As explained in Chapter 1, FileMaker Pro is now a fully relational database. Any database can draw information from any other *related* database (one with matching data in a key field, such as a customer identification number, a part number, or a Social Security number). This has some important implications for how you can now create databases.

First, many databases will be smaller and easier to maintain than they were in previous versions of FileMaker Pro. Rather than stuff every possible field into each database, you can divide the information among several smaller databases. For example, address information for your customers, clients, or suppliers can be kept in an Address database that is separate from an Invoices database. In that way, a person's address need only be entered once (in the Address database) and then simply referred to by matching a Customer ID field that is included in both the Invoices and Addresses databases. Related data stays in the database in which it is entered — regardless of how many different related files refer to it. When you request data that is in a related file, it is just displayed on-screen rather than being copied into the target database.

Second, you may recall that previous versions of FileMaker Pro provided some relational capabilities through a feature called the lookup. A *lookup* works like a relationship, but instead of merely displaying the related data, it is actually *copied* into the target database. If you already have databases that rely on lookups, you'll be pleased to learn that this feature is still supported in FileMaker Pro 3.0. You can continue using lookups or convert them to relationships. Because lookups are actually preferable in some cases, you should be sure to read the following section of this chapter so you understand the differences between lookups and relationships.

Lookups Versus Relationships

Here's how a lookup works. When an entry is made in a key field in the primary database, a search is done in a secondary database. FileMaker Pro locates the first record that contains a match for the key field, and data is then copied from a selected field in the secondary database into a selected field in the primary database.

For example, suppose you have two databases named Orders and Addresses. Both databases have a Customer ID field. Three lookups are defined as being dependent on the Customer ID field: Name, Mailing Address, and Phone. When a new order is taken, you create a new record in the Orders database and type a number into the Customer ID field. This triggers the three lookups, causing FileMaker Pro to search the Addresses database for a matching Customer ID number. When the ID number is found, the customer's name, address, and phone number are copied into the appropriate fields in the primary database.

Lookups have some drawbacks:

- The looked-up data is physically copied from the secondary database into the primary database, resulting in data duplication and additional storage requirements.
- If the data in the secondary file changes, the primary data does not change unless you execute the lookup again.
- Even if multiple matches exist for the key field, FileMaker only identifies the first match that it finds.

On the other hand, lookups have one feature that's occasionally very useful. Looked-up data that is copied into the primary file will not change unless you trigger the lookup a second time or do a blanket relookup for the found set (described later in "Performing a Relookup"). Sometimes this is exactly what you want. For example, looked-up price information in an invoice shouldn't change when the prices are changed. (You can't pass on an after-the-fact price increase.) Lookups are discussed in the second part of this chapter.

When lookups aren't the answer to your development needs, you can define relationships instead. The advantages of relationships include the following:

- Related data is not copied into the primary file; it's merely referenced. This avoids duplication of data.
- Related data is automatically updated whenever it changes. You don't have to do anything to *trigger* an update.
- In addition to the one-to-one correspondence between records that is offered by lookups, relationships can be one-to-many. By using a general field such as Department as a key field, multiple matching records can be drawn from the related file (all personnel in the Accounting Department, for instance).
- You can define relationships so that there is two-way communication between the files. For example, deletions in the primary file can be carried through to the related file.

Perhaps the easiest way to understand the differences between relationships and lookups is by looking at an example. Figure 19-1 shows three databases used by a hypothetical video rental store to create and print customer invoices.

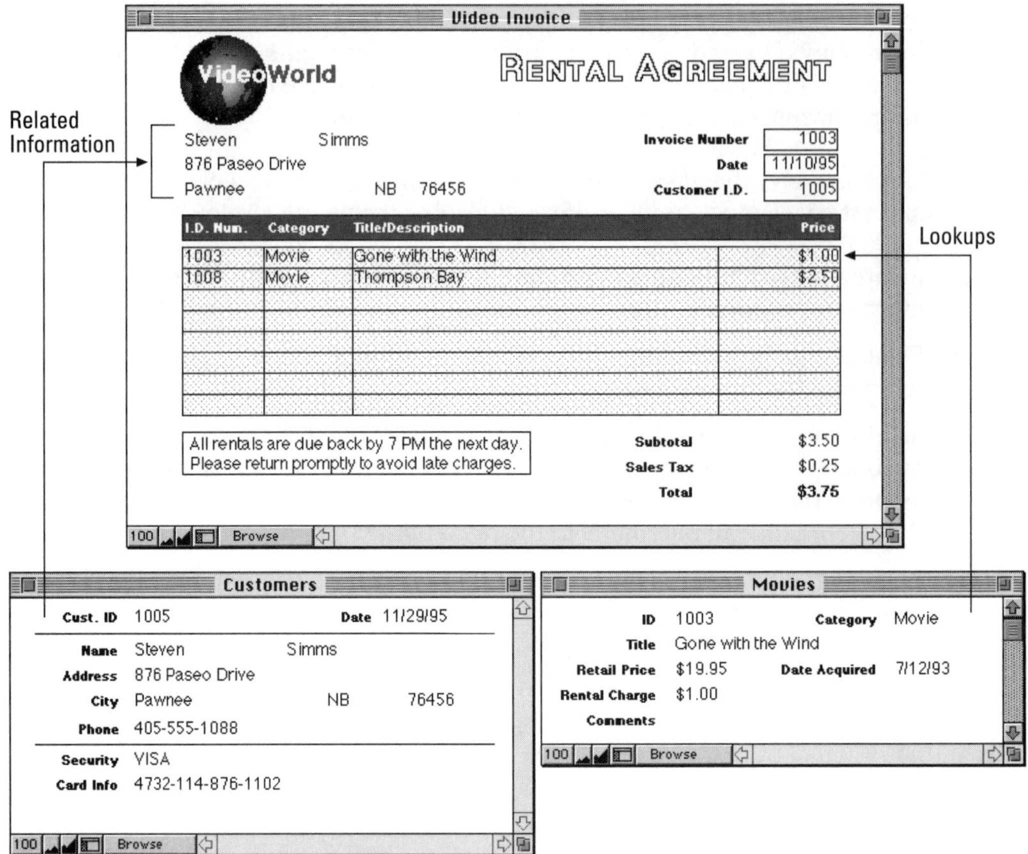

Figure 19-1: Three related databases

In this example, Video Invoice (top) is the main database. When a customer wishes to rent a movie, game, or piece of equipment, a clerk creates a new record in Video Invoice and then completes this form.

The Customers database (bottom left) contains only customer information, such as the name and address, phone number, customer identification number, and security deposit/credit card information. When a customer opens an account with Video World, this information is recorded by the clerk. Similarly, if the customer moves, changes his or her name, or wants to change the security deposit information (switching to a different credit card, for instance), the changes are made in the customer record. As the figure shows, the name and address are displayed in the Video Invoice file as relations. Thus, if a customer's address changes in the

Customers database, the owner can be assured that every invoice for the customer displays the current address (making it easy to locate overdue rentals, if the need arises).

The Movies database (bottom right) contains a separate record for each rental item (movies, video games, and equipment). Each item has a unique identification number, as well as its current rental price. As indicated in the figure, items in the Movies database are copied into each appropriate record in the Video Invoice file via lookups. This makes each invoice line item a permanent entry. When the rental charge for an item changes (because of a sale or a change in policy, for example), only new invoices will reflect the new price. Outstanding invoices will retain their original rental charges — as, of course, they must. (You can't pass along a price increase for items that you rented last week.)

After defining the fields for the three databases and creating layouts for them, it is a simple matter to define the relationships between them.

To define the relationships:

1. In the Video Invoice file, choose Define Relationships from the File menu.

   The Define Relationships dialog box appears.

2. Click New to define the first relationship.

   A standard file dialog box appears.

3. Select the first related file (in this case, Customers) and click Open.

   The Edit Relationship dialog box appears.

4. *Optional:* If you wish, you can change the relationship name.

   By default, the name of the related file is used.

5. Select the pair of fields in the two databases that defines a set of matching records (in this case, Cust. ID and Cust. ID).

   There is no requirement that the matching fields have the same name — although in this instance, they do.

6. *Optional:* To allow the user to delete or create records in the related file (Customers) by making changes in the primary file (Video Invoice), click the appropriate check boxes at the bottom of the dialog box.

7. Click OK to record the first relationship.

8. Repeat steps 2 through 7 to define the relationship with the Movies database. (In this example, the two matching fields are both named ID.)

After the two relationships have been defined, the Define Relationships dialog box looks like Figure 19-2.

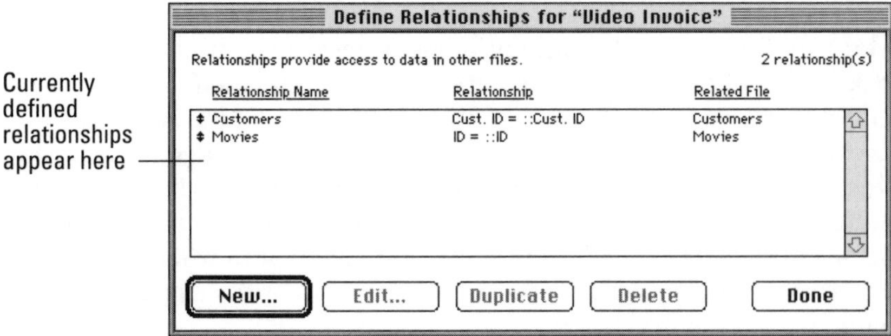

Figure 19-2: The two relationships defined for the Video Invoice database

These steps establish that there are two separate relationships between the Video Invoice database and the Customers and Movies databases, each based on different match fields (Cust. ID and ID, respectively). To specify the fields whose data will be copied to Video Invoice when matches are identified (in the case of rental item lookups) and the fields whose data will merely be displayed in Video Invoice (in the case of the customer name and address relations), options are set for the lookup fields in the Define Fields dialog box and the related fields are placed in a layout for Video Invoice.

The Category, Item Description, and Unit Price fields will be defined as lookups, based on the Movies relationship.

To define these lookup fields:

1. Select the Video Invoice file and choose Define Fields from the File menu.

   The Define Fields dialog box appears.

2. Select the Category field in the field list, and click the Options button.

   The Entry Options dialog box appears.

3. Click the "Looked-up value" radio button.

   The Lookup for Field dialog box appears, as shown in Figure 19-3.

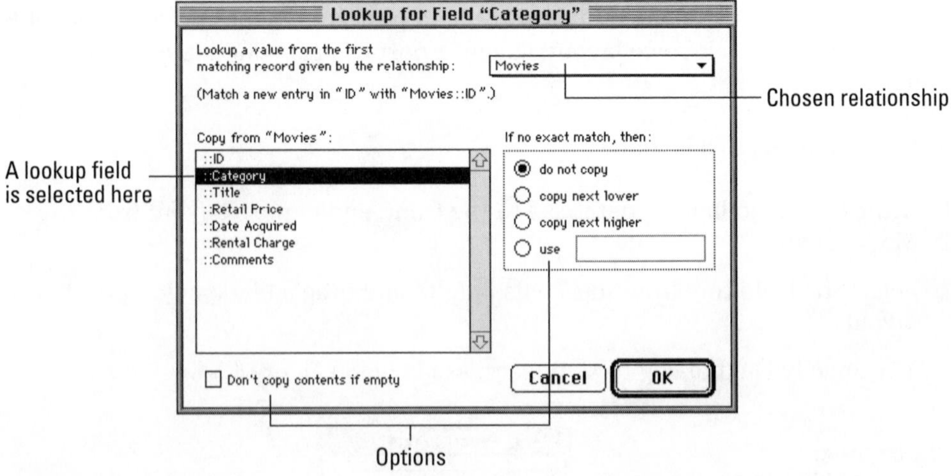

Figure 19-3: Specify a lookup in this dialog box.

4. In the pop-up menu at the top of the dialog box, choose the Movies relationship.
5. In the field list, choose "::Category" as the field to copy from in the Movies database. Then click OK twice to return to the Define Fields dialog box.
6. Repeat steps 2 through 5 to define the lookups for Item Description and Unit Price.

   The fields to copy from the Movies database are Title and Rental Charge, respectively.
7. Click Done to close the Define Fields dialog box.

If you were to examine the Video Invoice file in Layout mode, you'd note that the field names in the line item section of the invoice are unchanged. They still appear as Category, Item Description, and Unit Price, even though they will now be filled in via lookups triggered by typing an item's ID number at the beginning of each invoice line.

Related fields are defined a little differently from lookups. You have two options:

- Place the fields directly on the layout.
- Use the portal tool to draw a rectangle on the layout and then place the fields in the portal.

In this example, we'll place the individual related customer name and address fields directly onto the Video Invoice layout. (Using a portal is explained later in this chapter.)

To add related fields to a layout:

1. Bring the Video Invoice database to the front, and choose Layout from the Mode menu.
2. Select the Field tool from the Tools palette and drag a blank field onto the layout.

   The Specify Field dialog box appears, as shown in Figure 19-4.

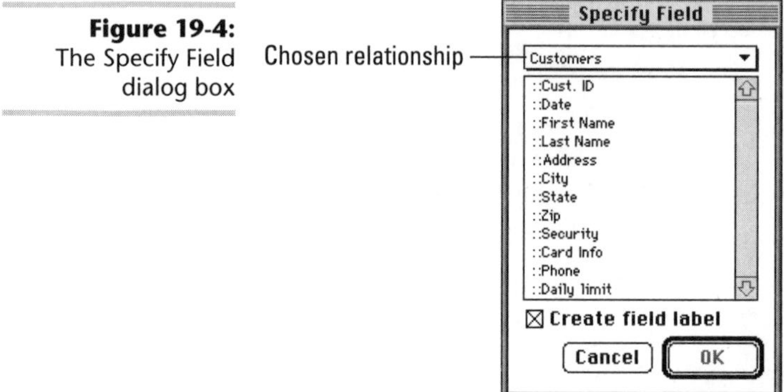

Figure 19-4: The Specify Field dialog box

3. Choose Customers from the pop-up menu at the top of the dialog box.

   This indicates that you are basing the selected field on the Customers relationship previously defined and that you will be choosing a field from the Customers file.
4. Choose the First Name field, click to remove the check mark from the "Create field label" check box, and click OK.

   The field that you just placed on the layout is now labeled "::First Name." The pair of colons that precedes the name indicates that it is a related field.
5. Repeat steps 2 through 4 to create and place additional fields for Last Name, Address, City, State, and Zip. Arrange the fields so they form the address section of the layout (as previously shown in Figure 19-1).

If you were defining one-to-many joins rather than the one-to-one joins used here, you would place the related fields in a *portal* on the layout (drawn with the Portal tool). Related fields in a portal display *all* matches rather than just the first one that is found. For example, you could use a portal to show the names and rental charges of all inventory items of a given type (new movies, for example).

Now that all the necessary fields have been defined and placed in the data entry layout for Video Invoice, here's what happens when a clerk creates a new customer invoice:

- The invoice number and today's date are automatically filled in by FileMaker Pro.
- The clerk asks for the customer's membership number, enters it in the Customer ID field, and presses Tab to move to the first line item.
- The act of tabbing out of the Customer ID field causes FileMaker Pro to search for a matching ID number in the Customers database. When one is found, the customer's name and address information is automatically filled in on the invoice. If a match is not found, the clerk creates a new record in the Customers database for this customer.

If the "Allow creation of related records" check box was checked for this relationship definition, the clerk could enter the name and address information directly on the invoice form — simultaneously generating a new record for the customer in the Customers database.

To make it easy for you to experiment with relationships and lookups, copies of the Video Invoice, Customers, and Movies databases are included on the *Macworld FileMaker Pro 3.0 Bible Disk*. Here are a few additional details concerning the design and use of the three related databases:

- The Video Invoice database has a single layout that is devoted to creating the rental statements that customers receive when they rent movies, games, or video-related equipment (such as VCRs, laser disk players, and video game systems).
- The Customers database contains customer-specific information, including a customer identification number, the date the customer record was created or last modified, name and address data, and information on the security deposit. The deposit information includes the form of the deposit (cash or a specific credit card) and a credit card number (if the deposit was made with a credit card). A unique customer identification number is automatically assigned whenever a new record is created; that is, when this information is taken from a new customer.

The Cust. I.D. field is an auto-entry field. A new serial number is assigned to each record by incrementing the previous record's serial number by 13. The numbers assigned to the sample records are 1013, 1026, 1039, 1052, and 1065. (For more information on creating auto-entry fields, see Chapter 5.)

- The Movies database contains a separate record for every movie, video game, and piece of equipment that the store rents. Every item gets its own identification number which, like Cust. I.D., is automatically assigned when the record is created.

The I.D. field in the Movies database is an auto-entry field. The I.D. numbers begin with 1000, and the number is incremented by 1 for each new record. The numbers assigned to the sample records are 1000 to 1009.

Other information that can be recorded for each movie, game, or piece of equipment includes a category (Movie, Game, or Equipment) that is chosen from a pop-up menu, a title, the retail price, the date acquired, the current daily rental charge, and comments. (Equipment can optionally be identified by a serial number.)

All lookups and relationships are performed from the Video Invoice database. When a customer selects one or more items to rent, the clerk chooses New Record from the Mode menu or presses ⌘-N to create a new rental statement in Video Invoice. A new invoice number is generated by FileMaker Pro, and today's date is automatically entered on the form. Next, the clerk asks for the individual's customer number and enters it in the Customer I.D. field. (If you want to try out the database, you can enter any of the following numbers into this field: 1013, 1026, 1039, 1052, or 1065.)

Customer I.D. is the field that is used to define the relationship with the Customers database. The moment the clerk tabs out of the Customer I.D. field or presses Enter, FileMaker Pro searches the Customers database for a record that contains a match in the Cust. I.D. field. If it finds a match, the customer's name and address information are automatically filled in. On the other hand, if a match is not found, the clerk knows that the customer has an invalid number or that a search of the Customers database must be performed.

After FileMaker Pro has copied the address data onto the form, it automatically positions the cursor in the first I.D. Num. field. When the clerk types the first item's identification number (a movie I.D., for example) and tabs to the next field, this action triggers a lookup. (To assure that a match is found in the sample data, you can enter any number between 1000 and 1009.) FileMaker Pro searches the Movies database for a record that has a matching I.D. When it locates that record, it fills in the rest of the information for that item (category, title, and daily price).

If the customer wants to rent additional items, the clerk enters them in the same manner as the first item was entered. Because the body of the rental agreement is composed of repeating fields, every entry in the I.D. Num. field triggers a lookup for that particular rental item. As the clerk enters items, the subtotal, sales tax, and total are instantly updated. (In this example, the sales tax is set as 7% on all video rental items, so it is calculated by multiplying the subtotal by .07.)

After checking the rental statement to make sure that it contains no errors, the clerk prints out the customer's copy by choosing the Print command from the File menu and selecting "Current record" as the data to be printed.

Whenever the rental price of an item changes (charging less for older movies than for current ones is a common practice), the store owner simply opens the Movies database, locates the record, and then enters the new rental price. Similarly, if a customer moves or loses rental privileges, the owner or a clerk can edit or delete a customer's record in the Customers database.

Among other things, these databases demonstrate the following:

- *A relationship can cause multiple related or lookup fields to be displayed.* When a Customer I.D. is typed into a record in the Video Invoice database, all of the following lookups are triggered: First Name, Last Name, Address, City, State, and Zip.
- *A database can have multiple relationships, each one triggering one or several lookups and/or relations.* The Video Invoice database contains two such fields: Customer I.D. (which displays the customer's name and address) and I.D. Num. (which looks up the category, title, and price information for each rental item).
- *A single database can be linked (via relationships) to multiple databases.* Video Invoice is linked to both the Customers database and the Movies database.
- *When a repeating field is used as a match or key field, every repetition triggers another lookup or relationship.* In Video Invoice, an entry in any of the eight repetitions of I.D. Num. triggers a lookup for that invoice line.
- *When databases are linked by a relationship, you do not have to open the other files before you use them.* As long as the databases have not been moved and the disk is mounted, FileMaker Pro can access data in them.

Going Relational with FileMaker Pro

For end-users and developers who need the functionality afforded by FileMaker Pro's new relational capabilities, there may no longer be a reason to choose another database program. These features make FileMaker Pro a ready match for all but a few very expensive, high-end database management systems.

If you don't think you're ready for relational databases — many of us are very comfortable with FileMaker Pro's flat-file capabilities — there's nothing new you *have* to learn. The relational features are there if you need them and stay out of the way if you don't.

Defining a Relationship

To work with related files in FileMaker Pro, you need to do just two simple things:

- Define the relationship (or relationships).
- Place the related fields in a layout in the current database.

Follow these steps to define a relationship:

1. Choose Define Relationships from the File menu.

   The Define Relationships for "*file name*" dialog box appears (as shown previously in Figure 19-2). If any relationships are already defined for the database, they are listed in this dialog box.

2. Click New.

   A standard file dialog box appears, and you are asked to: "Specify a file to relate to *current database name*."

3. Choose a database file, and click Open.

   The Edit Relationship dialog box appears, as shown in Figure 19-5.

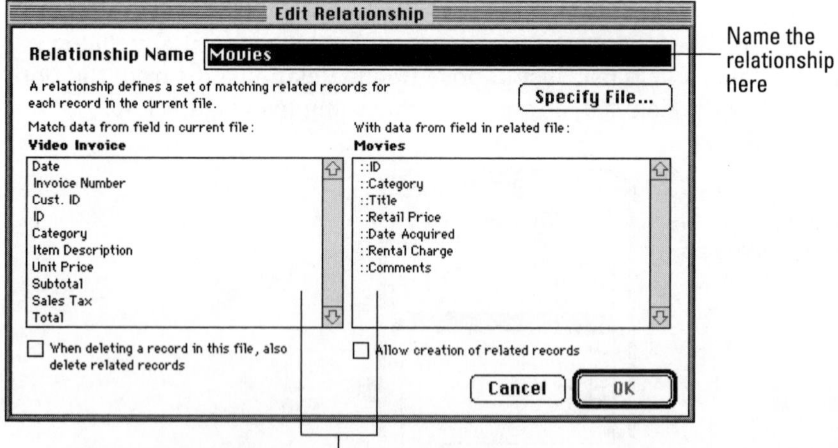

Figure 19-5: The Edit Relationship dialog box

4. Enter a name for the relationship in the Relationship Name box.

   By default, the name of the related file is proposed.

5. Choose a pair of match fields that will define the relationship — one from the left-hand field list (from the current database) and one from the right-hand field list (from the related database).

   When FileMaker Pro later uses the relationship to check for related records, it matches data from the first field with data in the second field.

6. *Optional:* To create a two-way link between the current database and the data in the related file, you can click the check boxes labeled "When deleting a record in this file, also delete related records" and/or "Allow creation of related records."

7. Click OK to save your changes and dismiss the Edit Relationship dialog box. Otherwise, click Cancel to ignore all changes.

8. Repeat steps 2 through 7 for any additional relationships you wish to define.

9. When you are through defining relationships, click Done.

If you later want to *change* a relationship (modifying its name, the match fields, or the options), choose the Define Relationships command from the File menu, select the name of a current relationship in the Define Relationships dialog box, and then click Edit. You can also duplicate or delete existing relationships by clicking the appropriate buttons in the Define Relationships dialog box.

In addition to using the Define Relationships command to specify relationships for a database, you can create them on-the-fly in almost any dialog box that contains a field list. Just choose Define Relationships from the pop-up menu above the field list, as shown in the example in Figure 19-6.

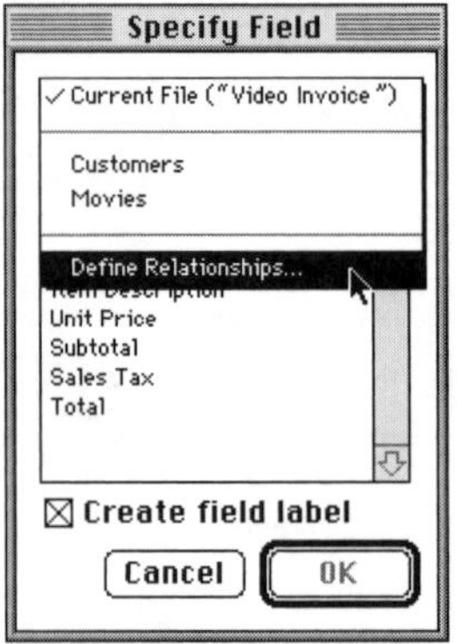

Figure 19-6: Defining a relationship from the Specify Field dialog box

Placing Related Fields in a Layout

There are two ways that you can make data from a related file appear in a layout for the current database:

- Place related fields directly on the layout.
- Create a portal on the layout and then place the related fields in the portal.

The decision concerning which approach is best for a given relationship, however, is not an arbitrary one. If records in the two databases have a one-to-one correspondence with each other (only one customer has the same I.D. number, for example), you should place the related fields directly onto the layout. On the other hand, if you are establishing a one-to-many relationship (you may have many contacts at a particular company, for example), you should place the related fields in a portal. Only a portal can display multiple matching records for the same key field.

Placing Related Fields Directly On the Layout

Follow these steps to place a related field directly onto a layout:

1. Open the database for which a relationship has been defined.
2. Switch to Layout mode by choosing Layout from the Mode menu (or by pressing ⌘-L).

3. From the Layouts pop-up menu, select the name of the layout in which you want to display the related information.
4. Select the Field tool from the Tools palette and drag a field icon onto the layout.

   The Specify Field dialog box appears (as shown previously in Figure 19-6).
5. From the pop-up menu above the field list, select the name of the relationship.

   The field list changes to display only fields that have been defined for the related file (rather than for the current database). The names of related fields are preceded by a pair of colons (for example, "::Last Name").
6. Select the name of the related field that you wish to place on the current layout.
7. If you want a field label to automatically be created for the field, check the "Create field label" check box.
8. Click OK to place the chosen field on the layout, or click Cancel if you've changed your mind.

   The related field appears on the layout. You can now resize it, alter its formatting, or change its position, as necessary.

Placing Related Fields in a Portal

Follow these steps to create and use a portal:

1. Open the database for which a relationship has been defined.
2. Switch to Layout mode by choosing Layout from the Mode menu (or by pressing ⌘-L).
3. From the Layouts pop-up menu, select the name of the layout in which you want to display the related information.
4. Select the Portal tool from the Tools palette, and then click and drag to create the portal. Release the mouse button when the portal is the correct size and shape. (Every portal is a rectangle.)

   Figure 19-7 shows a typical portal. The colored bands in the portal represent rows of records. The name at the bottom is the name of the relationship.

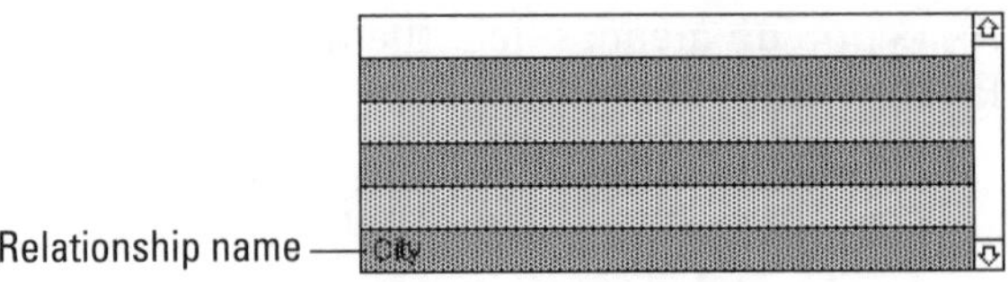

Figure 19-7: A portal (when viewed in Layout mode)

5. Select the Field tool from the Tools palette and drag a field icon into the white top row of the portal.

   The Specify Field dialog box appears (as shown previously in Figure 19-6).

6. From the pop-up menu above the field list, select the name of the relationship.

   The field list changes to display only fields that have been defined for the related file (rather than for the current database). The names of related fields are preceded by a pair of colons (for example, "::Last Name").

7. Select the name of the related field that you wish to place on the current layout.

8. If you want a field label to automatically be created for the field, check the "Create field label" check box.

9. Click OK to place the chosen field on the layout, or click Cancel if you've changed your mind.

10. Repeat steps 5 through 9 to add other related fields to the portal, as required.

Figure 19-8 shows what a portal looks like in Layout mode and in Browse mode. To make it easy to determine which fields are being displayed in the portal, their field labels have been dragged above the portal. As you can see, each related record is displayed on a separate line in the portal. If there are many related records, the scroll bar at the right can be used to view records that are currently off-screen.

First Name	Last Name	Phone
::First Name	::Last Name	::Phone
City		

First Name	Last Name	Phone
Connie	Freeman	408-287-7074
Natalie	Hansen	408-955-0202

Figure 19-8: A portal in Layout mode (left) and Browse mode (right)

Working with Lookups

In order to execute a lookup, you need to have a pair of matching fields in two databases. (As described previously in this chapter, you specify the matching fields by defining a relationship — just as you do when working with related data rather than lookups.) Both fields have to store the same kind of information, such as customer I.D. numbers. In general, the information in the matching fields should be unique.

The moment that you enter or edit information in the field on which the lookup is based, FileMaker Pro automatically performs any lookups that you have associated with that field. Often, only a single lookup is triggered by a field. For example, typing an inventory part number could result in a lookup of the part's price. You can also associate multiple lookups with the same field. Entering an inventory part number could trigger lookups of the part name, color, description, and price, for instance.

Here's an extended example. Suppose that you have two databases that you want to link via lookups. The first is an Orders database. The order form that serves as the main layout for Orders has a field in it called Customer Code. Customer information (including names and addresses) is kept in a separate database called Customers. A unique identification code, which is assigned when a customer first places an order, identifies each record in the Customers database. You define each of the name and address fields in Orders as lookup fields that are triggered by an entry in the Customer Code field.

Whenever a customer calls in a new order, a salesperson creates a new record in Orders and enters the customer's I.D. number into the Customer Code field. FileMaker Pro then checks the Customers database for a record that contains a matching I.D. If it finds a matching I.D., it automatically copies the name and address information for that customer into the current order form. As this example shows, nothing prevents you from defining several lookup fields that are all activated by the same match field — in this case, Customer Code.

Figure 19-9 shows an example of the Lookup for Field "*field name*" dialog box in which you set options for a field that you're defining as a lookup field. To reach this dialog box, choose Define Fields (Shift-⌘-D) and click the Options button. In the Entry Options dialog box that appears, choose Auto Enter from the pop-up menu at the top of the dialog box, and then click the "Looked-up value" radio button. (Clicking the Specify button to the right of "Looked-up value" also works.)

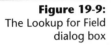

Figure 19-9: The Lookup for Field dialog box

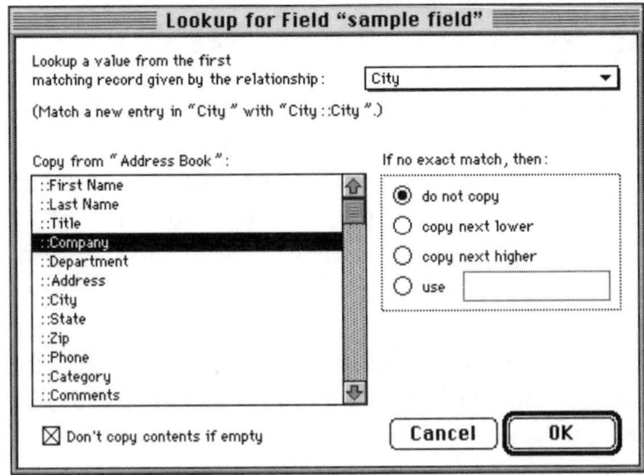

By examining this figure, you can learn several important things about lookups. First, when you define a field as being a lookup field, you need to specify only two pieces of information:

- The name of the relationship on which the lookup is based

  The relationship specifies the names of the two fields to be matched in the databases.

- The field in the lookup file whose contents FileMaker Pro will copy into the current field

Second, the Lookup for Field dialog box enables you to specify what will happen when FileMaker Pro does *not* find a match (see the right-hand side of the dialog box). The default choice is to do nothing ("do not copy"). The next two choices ("copy next lower" and "copy next higher") are often useful when you are performing lookups of numeric values. For example, when you want to determine the amount of postage that is necessary for a package, you could trigger a lookup in a postage rates database by entering a weight in the current database. Because postage is based on full ounces, you would use the "copy next higher" option to take care of any weight that included a fraction of an ounce. Thus, entering **7.4** would return the value for 8 ounces.

The final option ("use") enables you to specify a particular value or text string to enter when FileMaker Pro doesn't find a match. For example, if the lookup is supposed to return a consulting rate and you entered a new consulting code in the trigger field, you could instruct the lookup to return 100 (your usual hourly rate, right?). In the case of missing customer information, you could set this option to copy a message, such as "New Customer" or "Client not found," into the field.

Finally, sometimes FileMaker Pro finds a match, but the field that's to be copied into the current file is blank. You can click the check box for "Don't copy contents if empty" (at the bottom of the dialog box) to indicate what FileMaker Pro should do if it finds a match but the field to be copied is blank. This option is useful if you have hand-entered information into the current file and want to avoid having it replaced by blank data.

Defining Lookup Fields

Follow these steps to define a lookup field in your own database:

1. Open the database in which you want to define one or more lookup fields.
2. Choose Define Fields from the Select menu (or press Shift-⌘-D).

   The Define Fields dialog box appears, as shown in Figure 19-10.

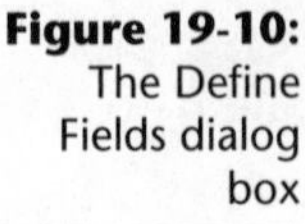

Figure 19-10: The Define Fields dialog box

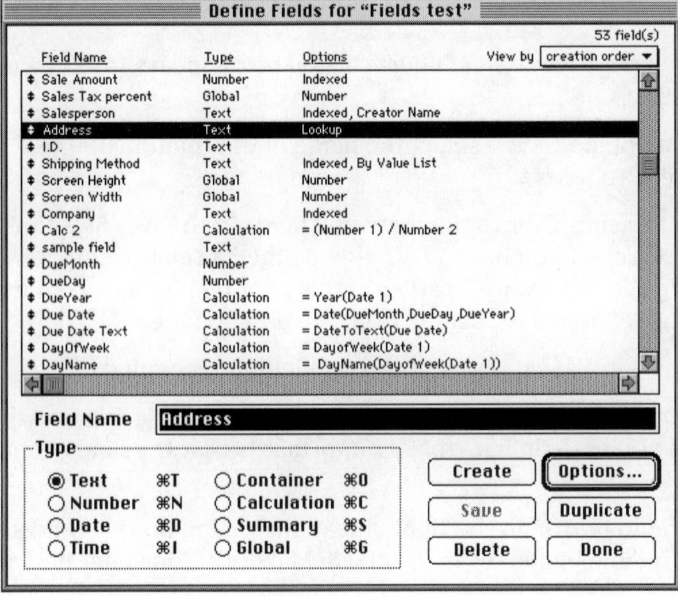

3. In the field list, select the first field that you want to define as a lookup field and then click the Options button.

   The Entry Options for Field "*field name*" dialog box appears, as shown in Figure 19-11.

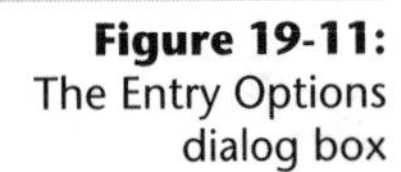

Figure 19-11: The Entry Options dialog box

4. Choose Auto Enter from the pop-up menu at the top of the dialog box.
5. Click the "Looked-up value" radio button (or the Specify button to the right of the radio button).

   The Lookup for Field "*field name*" dialog box appears (as shown previously in Figure 19-9).
6. From the pop-up menu, select the name of the relationship that you want FileMaker Pro to use.

   The relationship defines the matching fields in the two files that will be used for the lookup. If you haven't already defined a relationship (as described in "Defining a Relationship," earlier in this chapter), you can define one now by choosing Define Relationships from the pop-up menu.
7. From the "Copy from" list, choose the field to be copied.

   The name of the chosen field does not need to be the same as the name of the field you're defining. What's important is that the fields contain similar contents.
8. Click a radio button in the right side of the dialog box to indicate how you want to handle instances in which FileMaker Pro does not find an exact match.
   - Select "do not copy" if you want FileMaker Pro to do nothing at all. (This option is the default.)

- Select “copy next lower” or “copy next higher” if you want FileMaker Pro to use the closest value it can find — either lower or higher (numerically or alphabetically). Be sure to use these options only in appropriate instances. (If FileMaker Pro can’t find a matching I.D. number, for example, would you really want it to copy data from the closest I.D. it can find?)
- Select “use” and type a value or text string (up to 254 characters) into the text box to specify default data to be copied into the field.

9. To tell FileMaker not to copy a blank field into the current file, check the “Don’t copy contents if empty” check box.

   Normally, if a lookup is performed and a match is found, FileMaker Pro copies the contents of the appropriate field into the field in the current file. Sometimes, however, the field to be copied from is blank. If the field in the current file already contains data, copying an empty field into it would delete the contents of the current field. Clicking the “Don’t copy contents if empty” option leaves the original data intact.

10. To accept the options that you have set for the lookup field, click OK.

— or —

10. To ignore any changes that you have made to the field definition, click Cancel.

    Either way, you return to the Entry Options dialog box.

11. To accept this field as a lookup field, click OK.

    The Define Fields dialog box appears.

12. When you have finished defining fields and setting field options, click Done.

If you ever want to change a field from a lookup field back to a normal field, choose Define Fields (Shift-⌘-D), select the field in the field list, click Options, and then click any radio button other than the one marked “Looked-up value.” To edit the options for any lookup field, just click the Specify button to the right of “Looked-up value.”

Another Idea for Creating Matching Fields

When FileMaker Pro executes a lookup, it presents data from the first matching record that it finds. If, for example, you use Last Name as the trigger field and the lookup file contains five people who have the last name of Hamilton, FileMaker simply selects the first Hamilton record that it finds. Other Hamiltons in the database would never be located by the lookup. As you can see, a match field should normally contain unique data, such as an I.D. number, Social Security number, or phone number.

Unfortunately, many databases contain no such field. With a little imagination, however, you can create trigger and match fields that are composites of other fields. To do so, you create a Calculation field that concatenates two or more fields (adds them together). In an address database, for example, you could create an I.D. number by combining an individual's last name with the last four digits of his or her phone number (as in "Jones1247"). Although this approach is not guaranteed to produce a unique I.D., the only people you would normally expect to share the same composite number would be members of the same family.

In the file that triggers the lookup, you would need to ask for two pieces of information: the last name (Last Name) and the last four digits of the person's phone number (Last4). The Calculation formula for the I.D. field would read as follows:

```
Last Name & Last4
```

The result type should be set to Text.

Because a matching field must also exist in the lookup file, you could create an I.D. Calculation field by using the following formula:

```
Last Name & Right (Phone, 4)
```

As in the first formula, the result type should also be Text. This formula assumes that you are already collecting a complete phone number (Phone) in the lookup file. The part of the formula that reads "Right (Phone, 4)" tells FileMaker Pro to consider only the last four digits of the phone number. Thus, you do not need to be concerned about whether some phone numbers in the database happen to contain an area code while others do not — nor about whether the phone number was typed with parentheses, dashes, spaces, or as a continuous string — because only the final four characters are used, and they will always be digits.

"Opening" Lookup Files

When FileMaker Pro checks for a match in a related file (whether you are working with lookups or related data), it doesn't actually open the file. The file's name is displayed in the Window menu, surrounded by parentheses to indicate that a link has been established to it. If, for whatever reason, you want to examine the file, you can choose it from the Window menu. The file opens just as it does when you choose Open from the File menu.

The point is that when you are working with lookup or relational fields, you need to open only the file for which the relationship or relationships have been defined. You never need to open the related files themselves unless you have some other reason for opening them (to enter or edit data, for example).

More About Lookups

As you can see, defining and using lookup fields is not difficult. When you are doing so, however, keep the following special features and restrictions in mind:

- *You can use the current file as the lookup file.* That's right. Rather than looking in an external file, you can copy values from other records in the same file. In the Video Invoice database, for example, the lookup field definitions could be changed so that when a Customer I.D. is entered, FileMaker Pro searches Video Invoice (rather than Customers) for a record with a matching Customer I.D. As long as a previous invoice for that customer exists, FileMaker can simply copy the address information from that invoice into the current one. If no match is found, you're talking to a new customer, and you can fill in the information by typing it.
- *When FileMaker Pro is determining whether it has found a match, it compares only the first 20 characters in the trigger and match fields.* Be sure that no I.D. number or text is longer than 20 characters — or that the match doesn't rely on any characters beyond the twentieth. If you have two records that differ only in the twenty-first character or later, FileMaker will simply select the first one of the two that it finds. Also, FileMaker Pro ignores the order of words, capitalization, and punctuation when it is performing the comparison. Thus, it considers "crosby" and "Crosby!" to be the same, just as it considers "Steve Simms" and "Simms, Steve" to be the same. Finally, FileMaker Pro ignores text in Number fields when it is checking for a match (just as it does when *indexing* a Number field).

- *If possible, entries in a match field should be unique.* When FileMaker Pro checks for a match, it simply reports the first one that it finds. If there are several matches, the others will never be used. (This is precisely why it is dangerous in most databases to use Last Name as a match field.) You can avoid duplication in match fields by defining the field as an automatically generated serial number and/or specifying that the field must be unique. (For more information about setting field definition options, see Chapter 5.)
- *You can edit the information in a lookup field just as you can in any other field.* However, a new lookup will occur only when you execute the Relookup command (discussed in the next section) or edit the data in the match field.
- *If possible, avoid selecting a repeating field as one from which you are copying (looking up) data.* FileMaker Pro simply copies the first entry from the repeating field.
- *You may have some older FileMaker Pro databases that rely on lookups.* When you use these old databases with FileMaker Pro 3.0, the secondary files are converted as needed — either when you open and convert the primary file or as the files are referenced while using the primary file. However, a new lookup will occur only when you execute the Relookup command (discussed in the next section) or edit the data in the match field.

During the conversion process, FileMaker Pro 3.0 automatically defines the relationships that were specified by the lookups in the original files.

Performing a Relookup

Sometimes information in your lookup file changes. You update parts descriptions and prices; and contact names, addresses, and phone numbers can change. You can bring any values in the current file up-to-date by simply tabbing or clicking in a match field and then issuing the Relookup command.

As an example, imagine that you have a small mail-order business that sells tropical fish. You create a database called Catalog that can print an on-demand catalog that lists the fish you have on hand and their prices. Catalog performs its lookups by searching an Inventory database that contains description and price information for each type of fish that is currently in stock. As a small, specialized business, prices on particular fish may vary on a daily basis (depending on who your supplier happens to be today or what you recently caught). Whenever a customer requests a catalog, you perform a relookup to make sure that the prices are current.

You need to keep several important things in mind when you are executing a relookup:

- *A relookup is performed for all records that are currently being browsed.* You can restrict the affected records by first selecting a particular record or group of records.
- *Just as each match field in the current file triggers its own lookups, relookups are done only for the current match field (the one that contains the cursor when you choose the Relookup command).* Thus, if a file has several match fields, you can decide to perform a relookup for all or just some of the match fields.
- *You cannot use the Undo command to undo a relookup.* You may want to protect the integrity of the database by using the Save a Copy As command to create a backup of the database before you perform a relookup.

To perform a relookup, follow these steps:

1. Open the database that contains the match field (or fields) and display the appropriate layout.
2. Select the records that you want to affect with the relookup.

   Use normal record selection techniques (such as the Find, Find All, and Omit commands) to select the appropriate records.
3. Tab into or click the first match field.
4. Choose Relookup from the Mode menu.

   The dialog box in Figure 19-12 appears, showing the number of records that are currently being browsed.

Figure 19-12: This dialog box appears when you are performing a relookup.

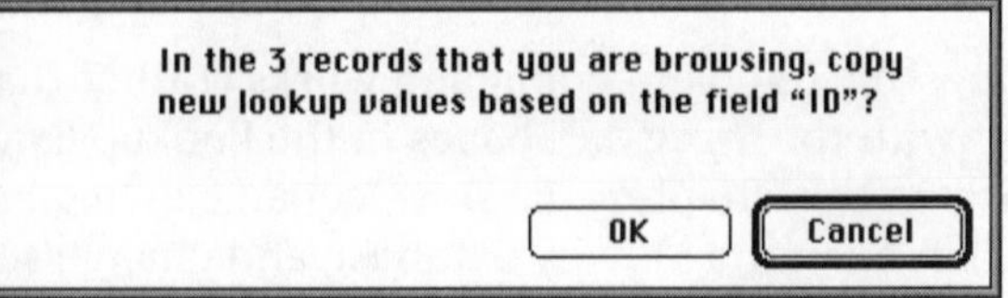
In the 3 records that you are browsing, copy new lookup values based on the field "ID"?
OK
Cancel

5. Click OK to replace the old values with new ones or click Cancel to leave the original values unchanged.
6. If you want to perform a relookup for additional match fields, repeat steps 2 through 5.

Forcing a Relookup for a Single Record

As mentioned previously, a relookup normally affects all records that are currently being browsed, as well as all lookup fields that are associated with the current match field. Sometimes, however, you may want to update only a single record, rather than the entire database or a subset of it. Although you can use find requests to limit browsing to the one record of interest and then choose the Relookup command, there is an easier method that you can use if you are updating only one record.

To perform the equivalent of a single-record relookup, display the appropriate record, select the data in the trigger field, cut it (by choosing Cut from the Edit menu or by pressing ⌘-X), and then immediately paste it back into the same field (by choosing Paste from the Edit menu or by pressing ⌘-V). Remember that editing the contents of a match field always causes a lookup to be performed. Because FileMaker Pro knows only that something has been done to the field, this cut-and-paste procedure forces a lookup to occur. If the data that is looked up has changed, the new values will appear in the lookup fields. (Another way to force a lookup is to delete a single character and then retype it.)

You should always think carefully before executing a relookup. For instance, in an invoice database that pulls price information via a lookup field, performing a relookup on that field would effectively change the amounts due on outstanding invoices! Normal business practices dictate that you would seldom want to do a relookup on such a field.

If you want to see how the Relookup command works (rather than just read about it), you can try it out with the three databases in the Lookup Example folder (discussed previously in this chapter). First, select an existing invoice in the Video Invoice database. Then open the Movies database and change some of the values in the records that are currently being looked up. Finally, follow the relookup procedure previously described.

Summary

- A relationship (a pair of matching fields in two files) must be defined when working with related data and lookups. The names of the match fields in the two databases need not be the same.
- Relational joins can be one-to-one or one-to-many.
- When converting a set of files that are joined together by lookups, the secondary files are converted as needed — either when you open and convert the primary file or as the files are referenced while using the primary file. If you prefer, you can simply open and convert all the files before using the databases.
- By defining a field as a lookup field, you can copy its information from another database file. Related data, on the other hand, is merely referenced; it is not copied into the database.
- To trigger a lookup or to display related data, simply type data into the match field or edit existing data in that field. Then exit the field by pressing Tab or Enter.
- You can have one or many lookup and related fields that are associated with a single match field in the primary database.
- To bring records in the current file up-to-date, you can select the appropriate records and issue the Relookup command. Doing so causes a lookup to be executed for each of the records that are being browsed. (Since *related* data, on the other hand, is always up-to-date, there is no similar command you have to choose.)
- Every relookup is associated with a single match field. Only lookup fields that use that particular match field are affected by the relookup. Thus, if you have multiple match fields, you need to use multiple relookups to bring an entire record up-to-date.

Sharing and Protecting Data

CHAPTER 20

In This Chapter

- Sharing databases with other users on a network
- Protecting a database
- Setting user access privileges
- Opening password-protected databases

Not only is FileMaker Pro network-compatible, but it also includes features that enable it to manage network traffic and to control who sees which databases and who can modify them (regardless of whether the database is on a network or is running in a single-user environment). This chapter explains how to use FileMaker Pro on a network, as well as how to password-protect and assign access privileges to sensitive data.

FileMaker Pro 3.0 adds new network and file protection features that you may want to use, including default passwords that are automatically tried whenever a database is opened and support for TCP/IP networks (enabling you to use FileMaker Pro databases to provide information over the Internet).

Running FileMaker Pro on a Network

Having your personal FileMaker Pro databases at your beck and call is great, but some data — particularly business information — is meant to be shared with others. Back in the old days (before networks), employees spent an inordinate amount of time unnecessarily duplicating and hand-distributing data. When a colleague down the hall needed a copy of your sales spreadsheet, for example, you made a copy of it on disk and carried the disk to his or her desk. Now that all the computer workstations can be linked via the company's network, you can simply share data without physically having to move or copy it. Files can stay right where they are, regardless of whether they're located on your hard disk or on a file server.

Right out of the box, FileMaker Pro 3.0 is a network-ready program. FileMaker Pro databases can be shared among the users of any AppleTalk, MacIPX, or TCP/IP network. Using Farallon PhoneNET Talk network software and a compatible network connector card, PCs can be part of an AppleTalk network, enabling users of Macintosh and Windows versions of FileMaker Pro to share the same databases.

To select a network protocol to use, choose Preferences from the Edit menu and then pick a protocol from the pop-up menu at the bottom of the General section of the Preferences dialog box. (See Chapter 7 for more information about setting preferences.)

Because the software license requires it, and because failure to do so may cause your network to crawl, each user should have his or her own local copy of FileMaker Pro and run that copy when accessing shared databases. (There's an exception to this rule, however, as discussed in the following "FileMaker Pro Server" sidebar.)

FileMaker Pro Server

In May 1994, Claris announced the first version of FileMaker Pro Server, a special server version of FileMaker Pro designed to support up to 100 concurrent licensed FileMaker Pro Macintosh and Windows users over an AppleTalk network. According to a Claris press release: "Network-intensive tasks previously handled locally on a FileMaker Pro network, such as indexing, will be off-loaded to the FileMaker Pro Server, dramatically reducing the amount of data traffic that passes over the network."

Using a newly-designed database engine, Server reportedly is twice as fast as regular FileMaker Pro, yet maintains complete compatibility with FileMaker Pro 2.0 and 2.1 for Mac and Windows.

By the time you read this, FileMaker Pro Server 3.0 should be available. It will be able to host up to 100 databases (up from a maximum of 16 in its previous version) and contains several new features that will make it easier for network administrators to use. FileMaker Pro Server 3.0 will have an estimated street price of $999. Contact Claris or your reseller for information about upgrading from FileMaker Pro Server 2.0 or 2.1.

Hosts and Guests

The person who opens a FileMaker Pro database and then declares it to be a multi-user database becomes the *host* for that database for the current session. (To open a database for sharing, choose Single-User from the File menu. The command changes to Multi-User.) The shared database can be located on your personal hard disk or on any hard disk on the network. (Some networks use special file-sharing software, such as AppleShare from Apple Computer, to enable files to be used by others on the network. Contact your network administrator for details.)

While the database is open, as many as 25 other users on the network can access it. These users are referred to as *guests*. The specific privileges each guest has are determined by the designer of the database or, in some cases, the database administrator.

If the previous host was someone other than you, you will see the changes made by that person, as well as any changes made by guests. Because the host is in charge, only that person's changes to Sort, Find, and Page Setup commands are saved with the file. When you, as the new host, close the database, *your* commands are saved.

The Host Is in Charge

Hosts and guests have different privileges and responsibilities. Following are some guidelines for being a host:

- Any lookup files required by the database must be opened by the host.
- To avoid bringing the network to a standstill, the host should try to avoid running additional programs while he or she is serving as host.
- Only the host can define fields, change the order of layouts, save copies of the file, define groups, set access privileges, or change the database back to single-user status.

As you can see, the host is in charge of the big stuff: making certain that the database is ready to use, ensuring that his or her personal computer is not overburdened, and making major changes to the structure of the database. Reserving these major privileges for the host makes good sense. If any of these actions were available to all users, no one would be able to get any work done. Imagine trying to enter a new record while the fields in a key layout were simultaneously being shifted around by several individuals.

In point of fact, if the host attempts any of these actions, FileMaker Pro automatically asks all guests to close the file. After the host completes the necessary changes and reopens the database as multi-user, guests can reopen the file and resume their work.

When you — as host — finish using the file and want to close it, you can choose Close, Quit, or Multi-User from the File menu. If any guests are using the database, FileMaker Pro asks that you notify them, requesting that they close the database as well.

To close a database (as a host), follow these steps:

1. Choose Multi-User, Close (⌘-W), or Quit (⌘-Q) from the File menu.

   If any guests are using the database, the Ask dialog box appears on the your screen, as shown in Figure 20-1.

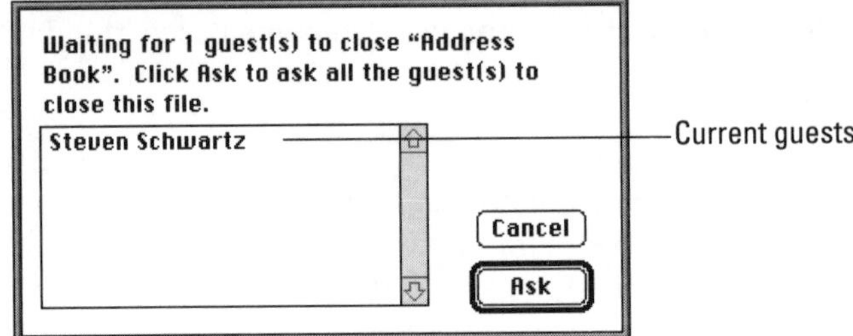

Figure 20-1: The Ask dialog box

2. Click Ask to send each guest a message asking them to close the file.

   A message appears on each guest's screen (see Figure 20-2), stating that the host wants to close the file and that guests must relinquish access to it.

   To acknowledge the message, guests click the OK button.

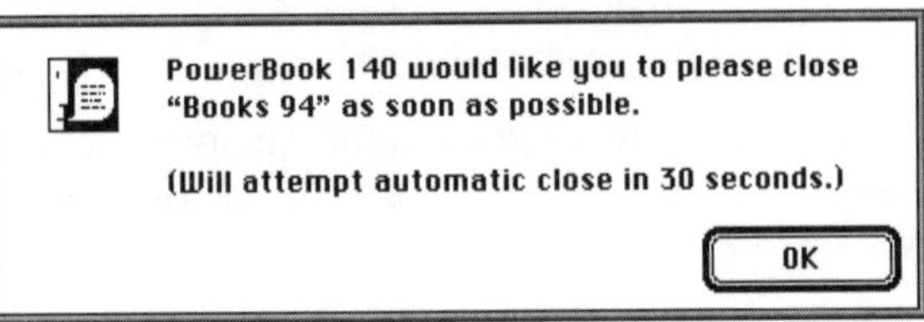

Figure 20-2: This message appears on guests' screens. While displayed, the message counts down to zero.

   After 30 seconds, FileMaker Pro automatically attempts to close the file.

   If the file can be closed safely, FileMaker does so, regardless of whether guests have responded to the message. If the file cannot be closed safely, it remains open.

Setting a File as Single-User or Multi-User

When a host changes the status of a file from multi-user to single-user, or vice versa, that new status is saved along with the other database settings. If, for example, a host closes a file while it is still set as multi-user, the next time the file is opened, the file is automatically marked as sharable and is ready to receive guests. On the other hand, if the file is set to single-user status when it is closed, the next host — whoever that might be — must reset the file to multi-user (assuming that the file is still meant to be shared).

Guest Activities

To open a shared (multi-user) database as a guest, choose Open from the File menu (or press ⌘-O), click the Hosts button in the file dialog box that appears, and then choose a file and click Open. Only files that have been opened by a host appear in the file list. (FileMaker Pro also has a keyboard shortcut that you can use to go directly to the Hosts dialog box: Option-⌘-O.)

If your network is divided into zones, the zones will be listed in a separate section at the bottom of the Hosts dialog box. In that case, you first must select a zone and then choose one of the shared files that appear at the top of the dialog box.

To specify a local TCP/IP host, click Local Hosts and then choose one from the hosts shown in the upper list. To specify a host outside of your local TCP/IP area, click Specify Host. In the dialog box that appears, enter a domain name or an IP address. You can add this host to the lower list by clicking "Permanently add entry to Host list." (This feature enables you to easily connect to the same database again later — without having to search for the domain name or address.)

Forcing FileMaker Pro to Check Again

If you're certain that a particular file has been opened as multi-user, but you don't see it in the file list for the appropriate network zone, press the Option key as you click the zone name. This action allows FileMaker Pro more time to check for shared files.

Each guest may perform any action on the database that his or her privileges allow. At a minimum, each guest can browse the file (they can examine records, but cannot change data in them). Other normal activities, such as editing, adding, and deleting records, also may be permitted. For details, see "Protecting Databases and Setting Access Privileges," later in this chapter.

Notes on Cross-Platform Database Sharing

As mentioned earlier in this chapter, both Macs and PCs can share FileMaker Pro databases on a network. In general, any typical task (such as entering and editing data, creating and deleting records, and sorting or issuing find requests) can be performed on either platform (Mac or Windows). Data, graphics, and other elements that appear on one machine also appear on the other. In addition, the program commands used to work with databases are the same whether the user is running the Macintosh or Windows version of FileMaker Pro. However, there are a few important differences:

- Platform-specific tasks can be performed only on the appropriate platform. A Windows user, for example, cannot execute a script that relies on Apple Events or AppleScript.
- Fonts occasionally can pose a problem. Common fonts, such as Times and Helvetica, are mapped to compatible fonts when viewed on a different platform from the one on which the database was created. Unusual fonts may not translate so well and can cause field labels to spill over into fields or wrap to a new line, for example.
- Special symbols used in entering data or creating layout text can produce unusual or unexpected results when viewed on the other platform.
- File-naming conventions differ between the two platforms.

For information concerning other differences between the Mac and Windows versions of FileMaker Pro, as well as the mechanics of sharing databases between these two platforms *without* a network, see Chapter 16.

Protecting Databases and Setting Access Privileges

Some databases are designed to be shared equally by all users on a network. It is not uncommon for a department to have a shared business-contacts database, for example. Allowing such a database to be shared can save considerable time and energy compared to having every department member maintain her or his own version of a contacts file.

Not all company information, however, is intended to be shared among all employees or even all members of the same department. A database that contains employee salary information, for example, may well be available only to members of the accounting department. And within that database, certain layouts and data may properly be modified or viewed only by the head of the department.

Other information often is meant for no one other than the person who designed the database in which it is stored. A manager, for example, may create a database that he uses to record comments about employee performance. Although the contents of this file may be extremely useful when the manager writes his annual employee evaluations, this highly sensitive information is not meant for public consumption; neither is the information intended to be viewed or edited by anyone else in the company.

FileMaker Pro anticipates the need for security and for assigning different types of privileges to different users. To this end, you can create passwords for databases, create groups, and associate access privileges and database resources with specific groups. The following information may help you better understand how these elements interact and how they are used:

- *Passwords and privileges.* Each password is associated with a particular set of *privileges* (what users can or cannot do with the database). Without a password, users can be prevented from even opening the file or can be granted minimal privileges, such as only viewing the data.
- *Groups and resources.* All group members are assigned passwords, which restrict the privileges of members of that group. Groups also can be associated with particular database *resources* (layouts and fields). You can prevent group members from seeing a sensitive report layout, for example, or stop them from modifying data in certain fields.

Creating Passwords

The purpose of creating passwords is to restrict the types of activities that a user can perform on a database. (Examples of activities include browsing, adding, deleting, and editing records.) The *master password* — normally held by the database designer or database administrator — provides complete access to the file, enabling the password holder to perform any desired design activity, including creating or changing layouts and editing scripts. The master password is also required when a user wants to set or change the access privileges of other individuals or groups who use the database.

The database designer or administrator may also create additional passwords that allow fewer privileges. Depending on the content of a database, you may want to create a password that allows the user only to view the data (browse records), for example. This access is the minimum access any user can be given and is available to anyone who is able to open the database. You can also set privileges for users who have no password or have forgotten their passwords (described later in this section).

To create passwords for a database, follow these steps:

1. Open the database for which you want to create passwords.

   Every database must have its own passwords. There is no command with which you can create a "universal" password that works with all of your databases.

2. Choose Define Passwords from the Access Privileges submenu of the File menu.

   The Define Passwords dialog box appears, as shown in Figure 20-3.

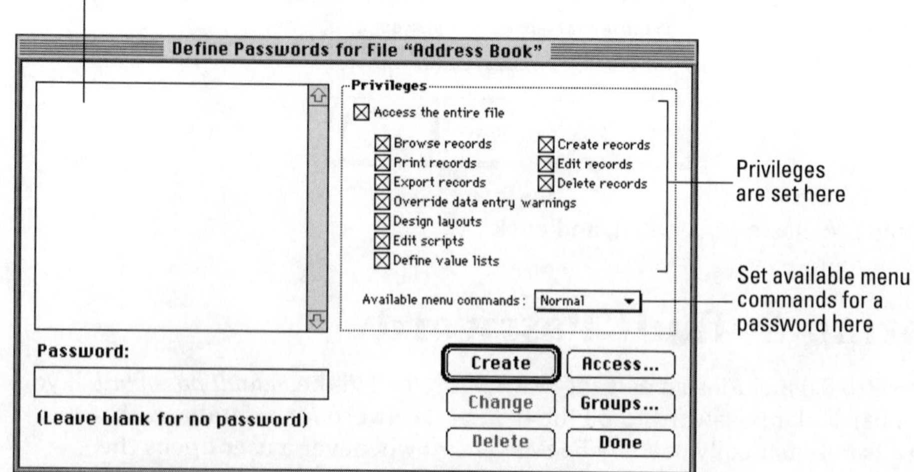

Figure 20-3: The Define Passwords dialog box

3. If you have not yet created a master password for this database, do so now as follows:

   In the Privileges section of the Define Passwords dialog box, check the box labeled "Access the entire file." Type a new password in the Password box, and then click Create.

4. *Optional:* To specify the menus that the users with the current password will see, choose an option (Normal, Editing Only, or None) from the Available menu commands pop-up menu.

5. If this is the only password you want to create at this time, click Done.

   — or —

5. Create the next password by typing it in the Password box, set privileges to be associated with the password by clicking check boxes, and then click Create.

6. Click Done to save the new passwords for the file.

   Before closing the Define Passwords dialog box, FileMaker Pro makes sure that you know the master password (and hence, have the right to assign and modify passwords) by displaying the dialog box shown in Figure 20-4.

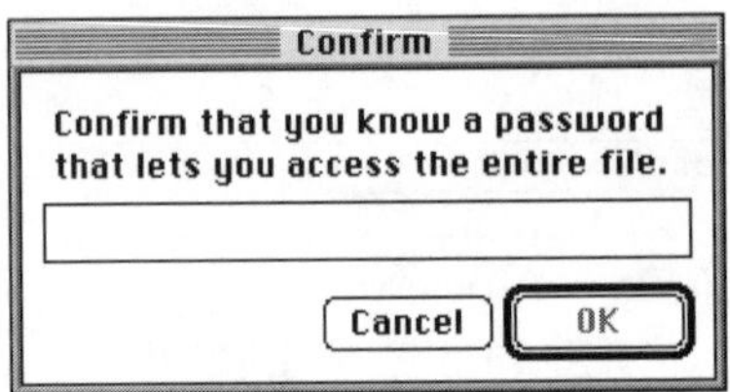

Figure 20-4: Enter the master password in this dialog box.

7. Type the master password, and click OK.

Creating Default Passwords

FileMaker Pro 3.0 includes an elegant new feature called the *default password*. If you declare a particular password to be the default password for a database, that password is automatically used by FileMaker Pro whenever a user opens the database. No password dialog box appears, and the privileges associated with the default password are automatically set.

In previous versions of FileMaker Pro, if you wanted to set a basic password — one that everyone could use to open the database with only minimal privileges — the best you could do was to create a blank password (using the "No password" option, as discussed in the "Passwords for Shareware Templates" sidebar).

If you set a default password, you should have a backup that allows you to enter the "master" password. Because you don't get the opportunity with the default password, you would not be able to make any changes as a normal user. You can make the password dialog reappear if you change your password.

Any password that has been defined for a database can be set as the default password. To establish a default password, follow these steps:

1. Open the database for which you want to set a default password.
2. If an appropriate password doesn't already exist, create a password as previously instructed in "Creating Passwords."
3. Choose Preferences from the Edit menu.

   The Preferences dialog box appears, as shown in Figure 20-5.

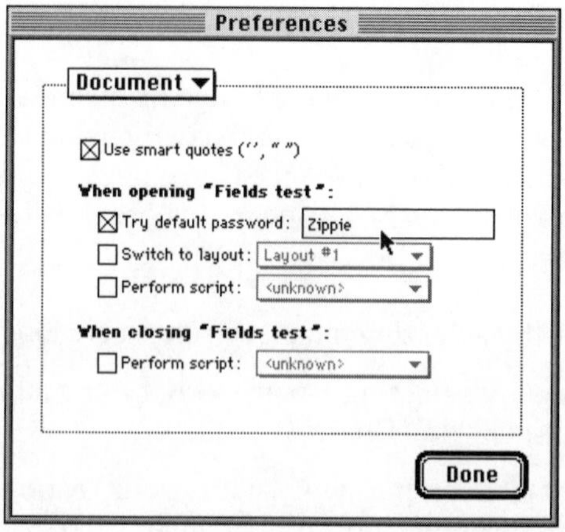

Figure 20-5: Setting a default password for a database

4. Choose Document from the pop-up menu at the top of the Preferences dialog box.

5. In the "When opening" section of the dialog box, click the "Try default password" check box. Then type the password in the text box to the right.

6. Click Done to save your changes and close the dialog box.

In all future sessions — regardless of who is using the database — the default password will automatically be invoked when the database is opened. You can eliminate a default password by returning to the Preferences dialog box and removing the check mark from the "Try default password" check box.

Passing Out Passwords

When the database designer or administrator hands out the passwords, the distribution is handled on a group basis (see "Creating and Deleting Groups," later in this chapter). If the major groups are defined as departments, for example, the administrator is responsible for ensuring that every salesperson receives the same password. By distributing the passwords, the administrator is defining the group membership.

The group names, as well as their very existence, are of no concern to employees; only the person with the master password ever actually *sees* the group names. All users know is that they have a password that gives them particular rights — not whether others also have the same password and privileges. Individuals with any password other than the master password have the Change Password command displayed in the File menu rather than the Access Privileges submenu, which only the administrator can use to view and change passwords, groups, and access privileges.

Modifying Passwords

If you have the master password, you can change or delete any password for the database. To alter a password, open the database by using the master password, and choose Define Passwords from the Access Privileges submenu of the File menu. When the Define Passwords dialog box appears (as previously shown in Figure 20-3), you can do the following:

- *Delete a password* by selecting a password and clicking Delete.
- *Change a password* by selecting a password, typing a new password in the Password box, and clicking Change.

After deleting or altering passwords, it is your responsibility to let the affected individuals know about the changes.

Even if you do not have the master password for a database, you can change any password that has been assigned to *you*. For details, see "Changing a Password" later in this chapter.

Passwords for Shareware Templates

One handy use for passwords is when you are developing shareware or commercial templates that you intend to sell to others. Before distributing the templates, you can create several levels of passwords that address different customer needs. Following are some examples:

- *No password:* Create a blank password with limited privileges (browse records, print/export records, and edit records, for example). This technique allows a prospective customer to examine the database, print reports, and so on, but he or she is restricted to using the records you included in the database.
- *Default password:* FileMaker Pro 3.0 allows you to set a default password for any database that will automatically be tried whenever the database is opened. (The user never even sees a dialog box asking for a password.) By using this approach, you can set privileges for the database and keep the user from having to deal with the annoying prompt for a password that accompanies the "no password" setting described in the previous point.
- *Second-level password:* In addition to the privileges available when no password or a default password is used, this password can allow a user to create and delete records. Offer to provide this password in exchange for a basic shareware fee. If they like your product, most customers will prefer this option.

- *Master-level password:* Check the "Access the entire file" option when specifying privileges for this password. This password gives customers complete freedom to modify the template as they see fit, as well as the ability to remove the password protection. Because it is the equivalent of selling the code for a computer program, you will usually want to offer this master password for a much higher fee. (Recognize, of course, that giving a user full access means that he or she has more opportunity to revise your scripts or to use the template in ways that you never intended, which can lead to support nightmares.)

Unless you see a reason to restrict access to certain layouts or fields, you probably don't need to create groups (described in the next section, "Creating and Deleting Groups").

Creating and Deleting Groups

After you define passwords, the next step is to define groups and assign at least one password to each group. Because each password has specific privileges associated with it, you can be sure that all members of the group have identical privileges.

You are not *required* to create groups. If you simply want to prevent anyone else from opening a database that you designed, for example, all you need to do is create a master password with full access privileges. In this case, groups would serve no purpose.

Each group is a cohesive class of users. Group membership can be based on employee rank, departments in your company, or anything else you like. In most cases, "need to know" is the most critical factor in determining group membership. The key thing to remember is that in addition to sharing a password, members of any given group have the same privileges in the database and can work with the same layouts and fields.

To define a group, follow these steps:

1. If the database is not open, open it now and supply the master password when you are asked for it.

   Only a person who knows the master password can create or modify groups.

2. Choose Define Groups from the Access Privileges submenu of the File menu.

   The Define Groups dialog box appears, as shown in Figure 20-6.

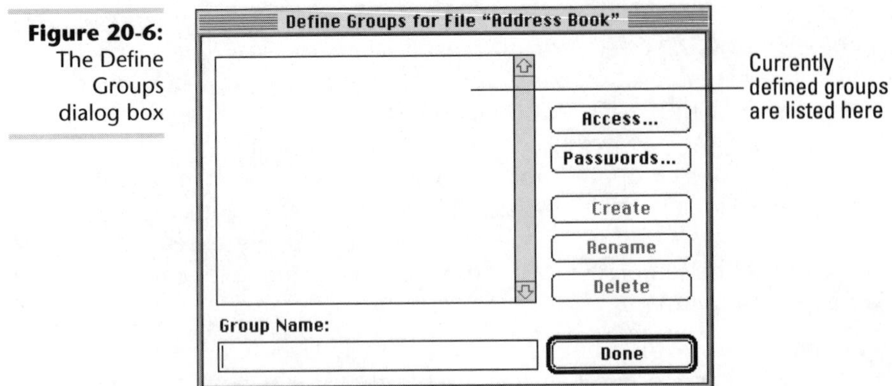

Figure 20-6: The Define Groups dialog box

3. Type a name for the group in the Group Name box, and click Create.
4. To associate privileges and resources with the group name, click Access.

   The Access Privileges dialog box appears, as shown in Figure 20-7.

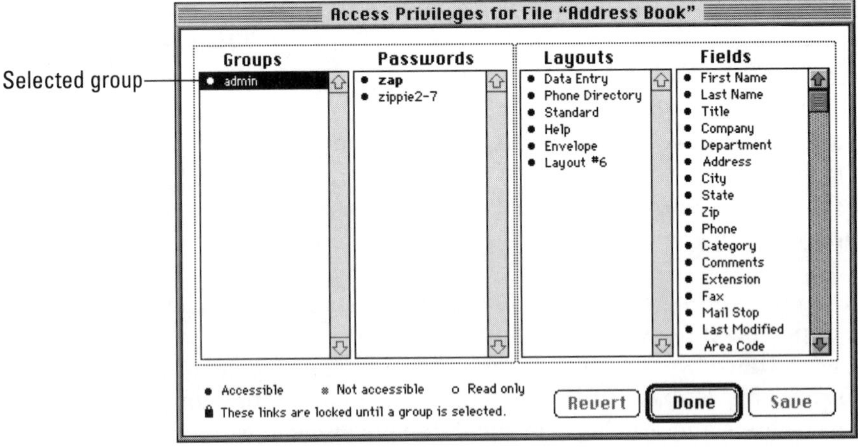

Figure 20-7: The Access Privileges dialog box

5. Select the current group in the Groups column.
6. In the Passwords column, click the bullet next to each password that you want to associate with the group.

   Whatever privileges were assigned to the selected passwords are now associated with that group.

   A solid bullet beside a password means that the password is associated with the currently selected group. A dimmed bullet means that the password is *not* associated with the currently selected group.

You can assign multiple passwords to one group, as well as associate multiple groups with the same password, if you like.

7. To restrict access to particular layouts or fields, click the bullets that precede them in the Layouts and Fields columns.

   A solid bullet means that the resource is accessible to the currently selected group. An open bullet means that the resource can be read but not altered by the group. A dimmed bullet means that the resource is not accessible by the group. (If a user attempts to display an inaccessible layout or a layout that contains an inaccessible field, FileMaker Pro covers the entire layout and displays the message "Access Denied.")

8. Click Save to save the current settings, or click Revert to restore the original settings.

9. If you want to set passwords and resource privileges for other groups, select another group and repeat steps 5 through 8; otherwise, click Done to return to the Define Groups dialog box.

10. When you finish defining groups in the Define Groups dialog box, click Done to save your changes and return to the database.

You can delete any group by selecting the group's name in the Define Groups dialog box and then clicking Delete. Before you delete groups for a database that is currently being shared, however, other users must close the file. When you choose Define Groups from the Access Privileges submenu of the File menu, the Ask dialog box appears immediately if other people are using the file (as previously shown in Figure 20-1). Click Ask, wait until the other users close the file or until FileMaker Pro closes it, and then delete the group.

Setting, Changing, and Examining Access Privileges

FileMaker Pro provides another method of setting, changing, and examining the relationships between assigned passwords, groups, and database resources. If you have the master password, you can choose Overview from the Access Privileges submenu of the File menu. The Access Privileges dialog box appears, as previously shown in Figure 20-7. (This is the same dialog box that appears when you set group privileges, as described in the previous section.)

If you examine the various dialog boxes that appear when you choose a command from the Access Privileges submenu, you'll notice that you can click buttons that take you to any step in the protection-specification process: working with passwords, creating groups, or selecting available resources.

Another Use for the Access Privileges Dialog Box

Regardless of how you reach the Access Privileges dialog box, you can also use it for the following tasks:

- Determining which fields are displayed in any layout
- Determining all layouts in which a specific field appears

To see the fields used in a particular layout, select the layout name in the Layouts column of the dialog box. As shown in the following figure, all fields that appear in the selected layout are preceded by a solid bullet in the Fields column. To see all layouts that display a particular field, select the field in the Fields column. Associated layouts are preceded by a solid bullet.

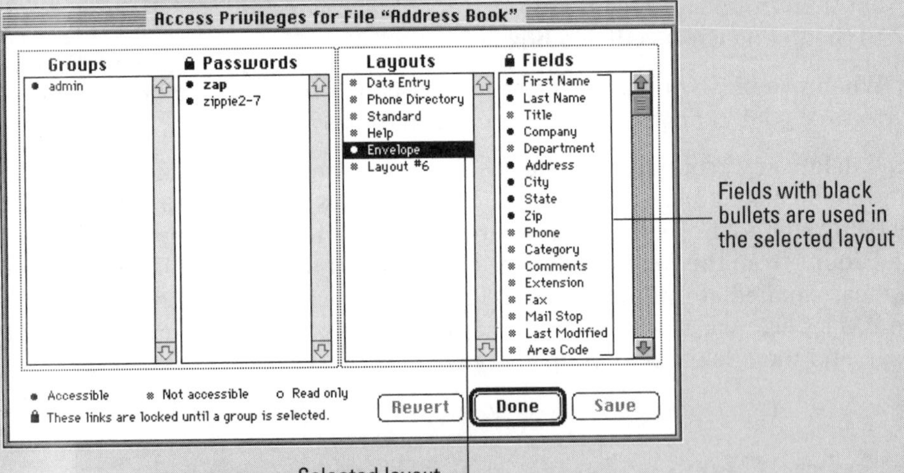

This information can make it easier for you to assign resources to different groups. In the Address Book database shown in the figure, for example, you may want to keep a certain group from seeing the contents of a particular field. If you click the field in the Fields column, you can quickly determine which layouts use that field and, hence, will be dimmed when a user from that group attempts to display those layouts. If the group members *must* see or work with a layout that currently includes a restricted field, you can modify the layout by removing the field, or you can make a new version of the layout that does not include the field.

Using a Protected File

When you attempt to open a password-protected database — whether that database is on a network or only on your personal computer — you immediately see the dialog box shown in Figure 20-8. As you type, the characters are shown as bullets in the dialog box. This extra bit of security keeps passersby from taking a gander at your password. If you make a mistake while typing the password, just press the Delete key to remove the incorrect characters and then retype them.

Figure 20-8: Entering a password

When you finish, click OK, or press Return or Enter. If the password is correct, the database opens, and you are assigned the access privileges that are associated with the password.

If you type the password incorrectly (or are simply entering a guess), FileMaker Pro displays a dialog box to inform you that the password is incorrect. If you click the OK button in this dialog box, the original password dialog box reappears (refer to Figure 20-8), and you can try again. If you don't know or remember the password, click Cancel. FileMaker Pro remains open, and you can select a different database with which to work.

Opening a Database Without a Password

If the person who assigned passwords also created a no-password option that enables users to open the database without having a password, a slightly different version of the password dialog box appears (see Figure 20-9). If you don't have a password, you can open the database merely by clicking OK or by pressing Return or Enter. As with actual passwords, a no-password user also has specific access privileges that have been assigned by the database designer or administrator.

File "Address Book"
Password
(Leave blank for limited access)
Cancel
OK
This means that the database can be opened without a password

Figure 20-9: A password dialog box with a "no password" option

If you have assigned a default password to the database (as described in "Creating Default Passwords," earlier in this chapter), *no* password dialog box appears. Instead, FileMaker Pro transparently uses the default password for you (or any other user) and opens the database with the specific privileges that were associated with that password.

Changing a Password

After using any password other than the master password to open a database, you'll notice that the Access Privileges submenu of the File menu has been replaced by a new command: Change Password. Although you cannot alter your access privileges for the file, you can change your password whenever you want.

To change a password, follow theses steps:

1. Choose Change Password from the File menu.

   The Change Password dialog box appears, as shown in Figure 20-10.

Figure 20-10: The Change Password dialog box

Change Password
Old password:
New password:
Confirm new password:
Cancel OK

2. Type your current password in the "Old password" box.
3. Press the Tab key, and type the new password in the "New password" box.
4. Press the Tab key, and type the new password a second time (to verify it) in the "Confirm new password" box.
5. Click OK to save the new password.

Although security experts suggest that you change your password regularly, this FileMaker Pro procedure has one big drawback. When you change a password for yourself, *you also are changing it for everyone else who uses the same password* — that is, all members of the group or groups to which the password has been assigned. It is your responsibility to see that all affected users of the database are informed of the password change.

Unless you are the sole user of a particular password, a better approach is to simply leave password changes to the database administrator. Because that person has complete access to the database and can view or alter passwords at any time (even if a user has already changed the password), the administrator is in a perfect position to handle this task. And because the administrator also knows which users share each password, he or she can make sure that the new password is communicated only to the right people.

Summary

- If you are working on an AppleTalk, MacIPX, or TCP/IP network, FileMaker Pro databases can be shared among users. Up to 25 users (plus the host) can simultaneously open and work in any shared database. Unless you have FileMaker Pro Server, however, each user should have his or her own copy of FileMaker Pro.
- The first person to open a database for sharing during a computing session is called the *host*. Although guests (other users) can view and edit data in the file, only the host's Page Setup, Find, and Sort changes are saved when the file is closed. The host is also responsible for closing the database.
- If they are on the same network, users of the Windows version of FileMaker Pro can share their databases with Mac users, and vice versa.
- To protect a database or assign different privileges to different classes of users, you can assign passwords to the database, define groups that are associated with each password, and limit access to particular resources (layouts and fields).

Developing Databases for Others

CHAPTER 21

In This Chapter

- Tips for enhancing templates that are meant for general distribution
- Using passwords to restrict access to template features
- Using FileMaker Pro SDK to create templates that run as stand-alone programs

No database is an island. . . Actually, this statement is only sometimes true. You will create plenty of databases that are only for your personal use — a home or business financial database or one that contains information about friends and business associates, for example. At times, however, you will want to share your examples of database wizardry with friends, colleagues, or the public at large. Here are a few examples:

- *Sharing in-house business templates:* Your company doesn't have a network, so employees can't access a central shared database. However, when someone in the company constructs a database that might be useful to other people in your department or to the company as a whole, you can distribute the template to everyone who needs it.

  Let's say as a Sales Associate, John creates a contact database that he uses to track sales leads, make follow-up calls, and record his successes and failures with each customer. The department decides to standardize by providing a copy of the template to all of their salespeople so they can install it on their own computers.

- *Sharing with friends:* Sam's club has an ongoing membership drive. Because several people on the membership committee use FileMaker Pro, Sam creates a template to record information about each prospective or new member and then passes the template out to the other people on the committee. Each month, the members hand Sam a disk that contains a current copy of their version of the database. Sam clicks a button on the template that executes a script that identifies records that have been added or modified during the past 30 days and exports those records to a file. Sam then opens his master copy of the database and imports the records.

- *Sharing with the world:* After you develop a database to organize the contents of your wine cellar, record the results of your biweekly gambling treks to Atlantic City, or track your huge music CD and cassette collection, you may decide that the database is too good to keep to yourself. Because you're a member of an online information service (such as America Online, CompuServe, or GEnie), you decide to offer the template to others. Depending on your personal philosophy or degree of entrepreneurial spirit, you can post the template as *freeware* (free to anyone who wants it) or *shareware* (software for which you request a fee from all users who decide to keep it).

FileMaker Pro provides two means of sharing templates. The usual method is to use the Save A Copy As command to create a clone of the finished database, stripping it of all records. Each user has access to the scripts and layouts you have painstakingly created, but your personal data stays with you.

The second approach is reserved for members of the Claris Solutions Alliance — third-party developers of commercial templates, add-ons, and training materials that are based on Claris products. Claris offers a special product called FileMaker Pro SDK (Solutions Distribution Kit). Database templates that have been processed by SDK can be run as *stand-alone programs;* that is, the templates can be used on any Mac or PC, even one that does not have a copy of FileMaker Pro installed on it. For anyone developing commercial templates, SDK provides the enormous benefit of vastly expanding the potential market for the templates. Instead of being able to address only the needs of other individuals who already own FileMaker Pro — or who can be convinced to buy a copy of the program so they can use your template — you can provide ready-made database solutions to anyone who has a computer.

About the Claris Solutions Alliance

Members of the Claris Solutions Alliance include consultants, companies, and individual developers who offer commercial solutions to Claris customers. They provide such products and services as contract programming and database development, specialized and mass-market templates, and training programs and materials. You can learn more about the Claris Solutions Alliance by requesting a membership directory from Claris. See Appendix D for information on obtaining a free copy of the directory.

Chapter 17 introduced you to the procedures for creating a database template. This chapter carries the discussion further by doing the following:

- Suggesting techniques that you can use to improve the user interface for your templates
- Showing how to protect the structure of a template
- Explaining methods of restricting access to certain template features (for example, distributing templates with some key features disabled as a way of encouraging users to send in the shareware fee to obtain full access to features)

Creating Shareable Templates

Regardless of whether you are using the regular version of FileMaker Pro or FileMaker Pro SDK to create templates, you can use the following techniques and strategies to improve the appearance, functionality, and marketability of your work:

- Simplify the interface with menus
- Include buttons and scripts to handle common functions
- Design for monitors of various sizes and color display capabilities
- Distribute shareware templates as demos or with selected sets of features disabled

Simplify the Interface by Using Menus

For any database that contains more than just a simple data entry layout, providing a menu to guide users to the different parts of the database is often a good idea. Menus can be particularly helpful for ensuring that computer novices and individuals who are unfamiliar with the database can easily find their way around and can reach the functions that they need to use at any given moment.

Menus are most useful when the database is divided into several different modes, each associated with a particular layout or set of layouts. In a parts inventory database, for example, you may have separate layouts for entering parts sales; generating order forms when the inventory for a part drops below a critical level; and printing a status report that shows the optimal number, number on hand, and reorder level for every part. A simple menu that has three choices (Sales Entry, Order Parts, and Status Report) can help any user move directly to the section of interest.

Of course, the more logical sections your database contains, the more helpful (and appropriate) a menu can be. In databases that include dozens of layouts, you can create additional submenu screens as needed. For example, if you have created layouts for half a dozen different types of reports and labels, you may want to design separate Report and Label menus, placing each set of menus on a separate layout. (Don't *overdo* menu nesting of this sort, however. Although additional menus are helpful to novices and new users, the added time and button-clicking required to navigate through unnecessary menu layers can get old very quickly.)

Figure 21-1 shows a menu created as a separate layout in the New Buttons FM database. In this example, clicking any of the three buttons carries the user to a different layout in the database. Separate layouts are devoted to blank buttons, over-sized (large) buttons, and navigational buttons. (New Buttons FM is included on the *Macworld FileMaker Pro 3.0 Bible Disk.*) This same type of menu could enable users to select from several types of reports or to switch between several primary database functions, such as executing a find request, generating mailing labels, or opening an associated database.

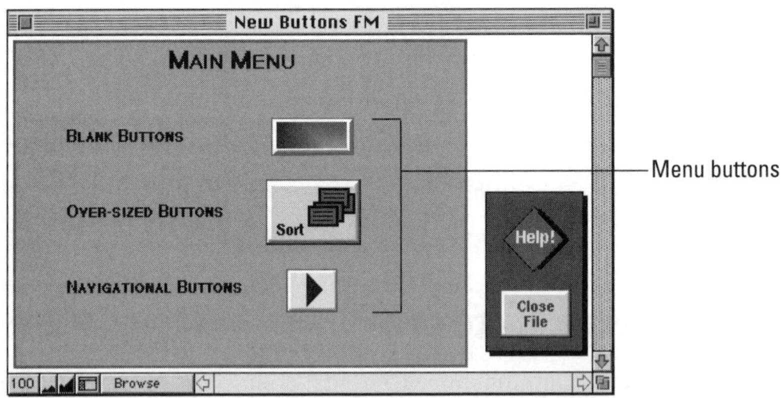

Figure 21-1: A menu created in its own dedicated layout

In the Address Book database, the menu is incorporated into the Data Entry layout (see Figure 21-2). Because users spend the majority of their time in this layout, the menu palette enables them to simply click a button to perform a variety of functions that are related to data entry. Several of the buttons duplicate menu commands in order to help novice users execute commands without having to remember the menu in which the command is located.

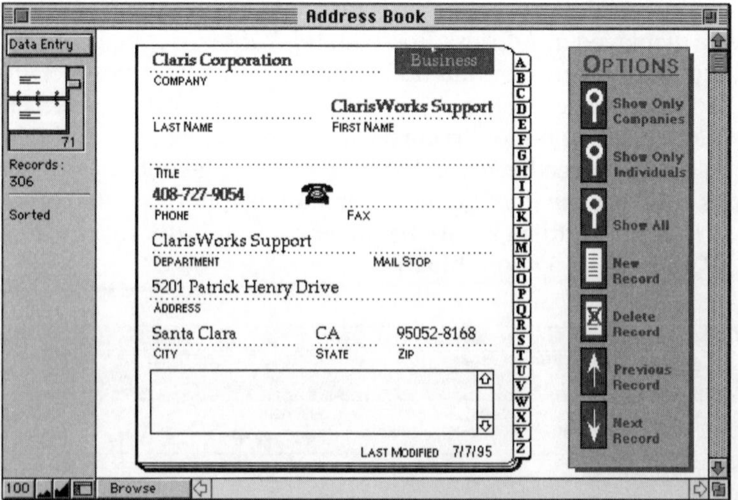

Figure 21-2: A menu palette

Creating a Main Menu

If you want to use a main menu to control access to the different parts of a database, you can set the menu layout to be displayed automatically whenever the database is opened. To accomplish this, choose Preferences from the Edit menu, choose Document from the pop-up menu, and then in the section labeled "When opening '*database name*'," click the check box marked "Switch to layout" and choose the name of your menu layout from the pop-up menu. To save the new Preference setting, click the Done button. From this point on, anyone who opens the database will immediately see the menu rather than the last layout used (the normal FileMaker Pro default).

The menu at the bottom of the database shown in Figure 21-3 is a variation of the menu palette displayed in Address Book. Instead of restricting itself to data-entry functions, it presents all major functions that a user may want to perform with the database, including selecting important subgroups, generating on-screen and printed reports, clearing out old records, and summoning help. Although this type of menu could easily have been created as a separate layout (as was the one for New Buttons FM), placing it in the most common layout (Data Entry) eliminates the necessity of having to add an additional layer of complexity to a full-featured database. (Parsimony is a good thing!)

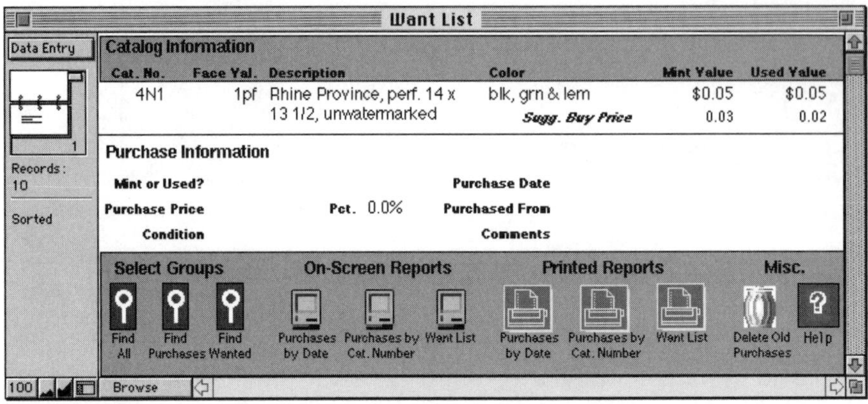

Figure 21-3: A menu incorporated into an existing layout

Avoid Button Clutter

After you understand how easily you can assign actions to buttons (as the step-by-step instructions in this section explain), you may be tempted to go button crazy. If you check the bulletin boards and online information services, you'll find many templates that have layouts that contain two or even three full rows of buttons. Just as using a dozen fonts in a document can make a desktop publishing effort look like a ransom note, presenting too many buttons in one place can slow the user down (because finding the correct button for a function is difficult). Bad programming...

If you really need that many icons, either find a logical way to group them by function (as was done in the Want List database in Figure 21-3) or think seriously about creating a *series* of menu layouts rather than just a single menu.

Creating a Navigation Menu

As mentioned throughout this book, buttons — such as those used in the menu examples — gain their functionality by having ScriptMaker scripts or a script step attached to them. The following series of steps explains how to design a navigation menu like the one used by the New Buttons FM database.

To create a navigation menu, do the following:

1. Open the database and switch to Layout mode (by choosing Layout from the Mode menu or by pressing ⌘-L).
2. Create a new layout to hold the menu by choosing New Layout from the Mode menu (or by pressing ⌘-N).

   — or —

2. If you like, you can create the menu as part of an *existing* layout (as previously shown in Figures 21-2 and 21-3). If you decide to do so, go directly to step 3.
3. Use the Button tool to create text buttons. If you prefer graphic buttons, you can paste, import, or draw the graphics in FileMaker Pro that will serve as the buttons.
4. Arrange the buttons on the layout as desired.
5. Select a button by clicking it once and then choose Button from the Format menu.

   The Specify Button dialog box appears, as shown in Figure 21-4.

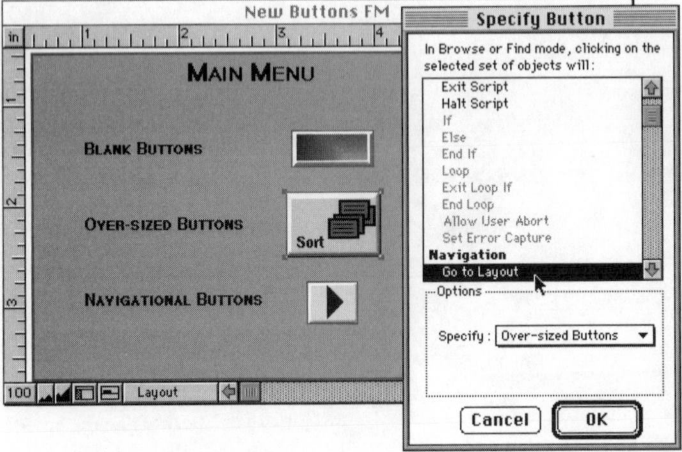

Figure 21-4: Defining a button

6. Choose the Go to Layout step from the scrolling list and, from the Specify pop-up menu at the bottom of the dialog box, select the layout that you want to go to.
7. Repeat steps 5 and 6 for each menu button that you want to define, selecting a different layout to go to for each button.
8. If you haven't already done so, name the menu layout by choosing Layout Setup from the Mode menu and typing a name in the Layout Name text box (see Figure 21-5). Click OK.

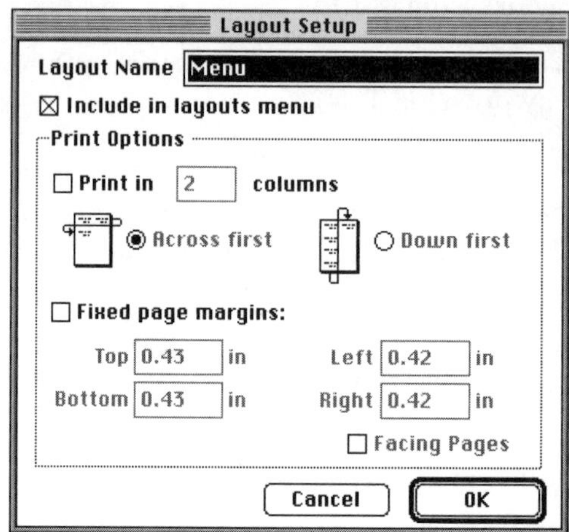

Figure 21-5: Naming a layout

9. *Optional:* If you always want the menu layout to immediately appear when you open the database, see the "Creating a Main Menu" sidebar, earlier in this chapter.

Providing Instant Access via Buttons and Scripts

Anything that increases ease of use simultaneously increases the worth of your templates. Why ask users to do things the hard way (manually selecting various sets of sort instructions, for example), when you can create scripts and buttons that will accomplish these tasks for them when they choose a command from the Script menu or click a button?

Think carefully about how others will want to use your template. If you know that many users will perform common sort procedures, focus on specific subgroups, or generate the same kinds of reports, you should create layouts and appropriate scripts to automate these elements.

To make the scripts accessible, assign them to buttons, list them in the Script menu, or do both. (See Chapter 15 for more information on creating scripts and defining buttons.)

Label Those Buttons!

Although the Mac is a graphically-oriented computer and icons are a common part of its user interface, you may frequently be tempted to design buttons as unlabeled icons. Resist at all costs! Although the meaning of a button may be obvious to you, it may not be apparent to other people who will use your database or template. (A new Macintosh user may not even understand the use of a question mark as a Help button.)

When you are designing a template for others, you should avoid anything that slows people down by causing them to guess what you had in mind, search for the help file, or reach for a manual. As the examples in Figures 21-1 through 21-3 clearly show, adding a label to a button takes little screen space.

Not All Buttons Must Be Icons

Although buttons are cool and lend a professional appearance to most databases, not everyone is a graphics wizard. Nor is everyone an icon lover. In FileMaker Pro, *any* object can be a button.

In Layout mode, you can use the Button tool to create 3-D buttons with standard text labels. The following figure shows an example of a text button. You can use normal editing procedures to change the size of the button, as well as the font, style, size, and color of the button text.

SORT

Consider Color and Screen Space

Fortunately, the days of sterile-looking *monochrome* (black-and-white) monitors are almost gone. Adding color to layouts can make them more attractive, easier on the eyes, and more pleasant to use. Unfortunately, many Macs that have monochrome displays (such as the Mac Plus, SE, Classics, Portable, and several models of the PowerBook) are still in use. In addition, the sizes and shapes of monitors and built-in displays vary. When creating templates, you want to accommodate as large an audience as possible. To do so, you need to make two important decisions:

- Should you support color, monochrome, or both?
- Should the templates fit on the smallest possible screen, be optimized for one standard size of display, or be offered in several sizes?

Color

You can safely include color in a template in two ways:

- Select colors that contrast appropriately regardless of whether users display them on a color, grayscale, or monochrome monitor.
- Provide two versions of the template: one color and one monochrome.

If you want to support all monitor types simultaneously, do the design work in color. After you create a layout, use the Monitors control panel to change the display to the Black & White setting (see Figure 21-6). Make sure that the chosen colors do not obscure any text and that the text and other elements are still clearly visible when you're doing data entry or viewing reports. If you discover problems, use Monitors to switch back to the original color setting, make changes, and pop back into Black & White mode to see how the new colors work out. After finalizing your color choices, you may want to make an additional check by using Monitors to cycle through all the Colors and Grays settings that are available.

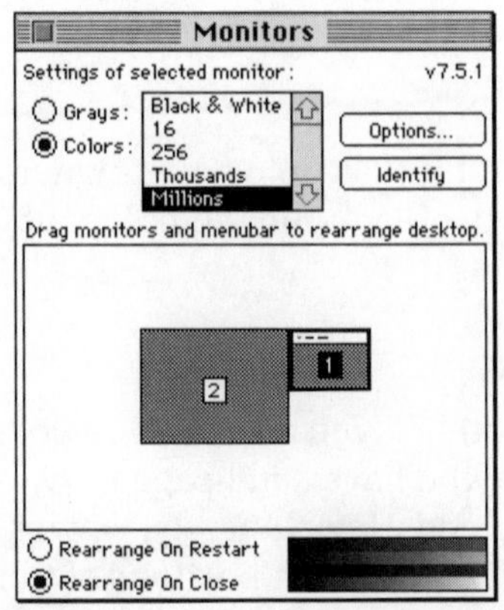

Figure 21-6: To display the Monitors control panel, choose Control Panels from the Apple menu and then select Monitors.

Normally, the monitor and display card can show the same number of grays as they can colors. When switching from colors to grays, the display card simply substitutes an equivalent gray shade for each color that you have used. As a result, if a display is readable and attractive in color, it should be equally readable and attractive in grayscale.

Because different users will have different display cards that govern the number of colors they can see, you may simply settle for handling only a few of the most basic monitor and display card combinations. Monochrome, 8-bit color, and grayscale will cover most of your potential audience, so you can reduce the amount of "colorization" work that you have to do by supporting only two Monitors settings: 256 colors and Black & White. Or, if you want to avoid this hassle entirely, you can simply supply two different versions of the template — one optimized for 256 colors and another for black and white.

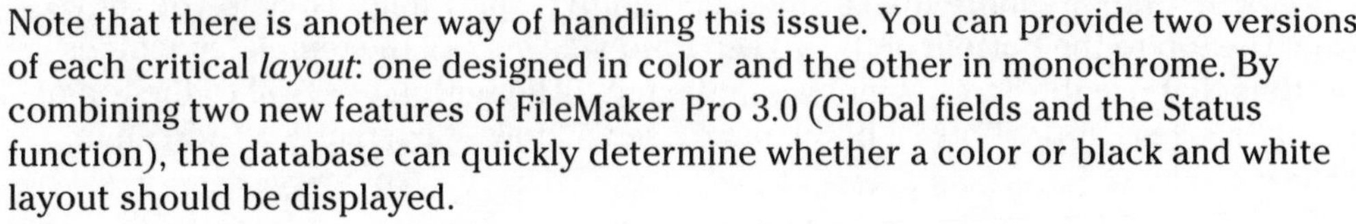

Note that there is another way of handling this issue. You can provide two versions of each critical *layout*: one designed in color and the other in monochrome. By combining two new features of FileMaker Pro 3.0 (Global fields and the Status function), the database can quickly determine whether a color or black and white layout should be displayed.

Use a Global field to record the user's preference (color versus black and white) and include an IF step in your scripts to display the correct layout, as in the following code sample:

```
If ["Status(CurrentScreenDepth) ≥ 8"]
 Go to Layout ["Layout #2-color"]
Else
 Go to Layout ["Layout #2-B & W"]
End If
```

If the screen depth is set to 8-bit (256 colors) or higher, the color version of the layout is shown; otherwise, the black-and-white layout is shown.

Screen Real Estate

When you are designing for others, you also need to consider the sizes of their displays. For example, users who have a full-page or two-page display commonly design layouts that fill the screen. Unfortunately, when such templates are opened on a Mac Classic or a PowerBook, significant portions of the window will be off-screen.

As with color templates, you have several options:

- Restrict the template dimensions to fit the smallest screen size that you want to support.
- Assume that a user who has a small screen will be willing to scroll to reach parts of any layout that are off-screen.
- Provide several versions of the template, each optimized for a particular display.
- Divide a large layout into several smaller ones and switch between the different layouts using menus or buttons.

Database Associates Inc. uses an interesting approach in their commercial template named AddressTrak (shown in Figure 21-7) that you may want to use in some large templates. Programmed for a standard 13-inch monitor, AddressTrak contains some layouts that require more than a single screen to display fully. To help you move from the top to the bottom of the screen (and vice versa), the template includes buttons that use the Scroll Window script step. (The button to scroll to the top of the database is at the bottom of the database window — currently off-screen in Figure 21-7).

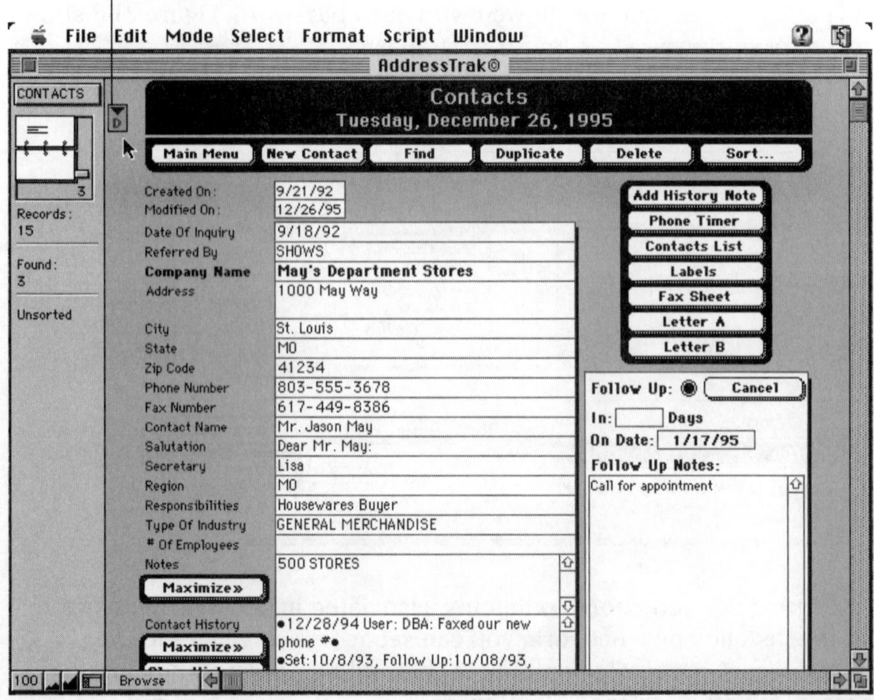

Figure 21-7: The Contacts layout from AddressTrak

If you just want to expand the window to completely fill whatever screen the user has, you can use the following step in an opening script:

```
Toggle Window [Maximize]
```

Protecting a Template

When you design a template for in-house use, you may want to prevent others from changing it. For example, regardless of whether the person who is changing the locations of fields in a data layout is an expert or a novice who selected Layout mode by mistake, you may want to prevent changes to the field locations or formatting. Similarly, if a database contains sensitive information, such as salaries, you may want to prevent other users from accessing the database at all or restrict who has access rights to such layouts.

By choosing the Access Privileges command from the File menu, the designer of any FileMaker Pro database can set passwords, define specific groups of users for the database, and set privileges that are allowed with each password. Figure 21-8 shows the basic process of setting a password for a database.

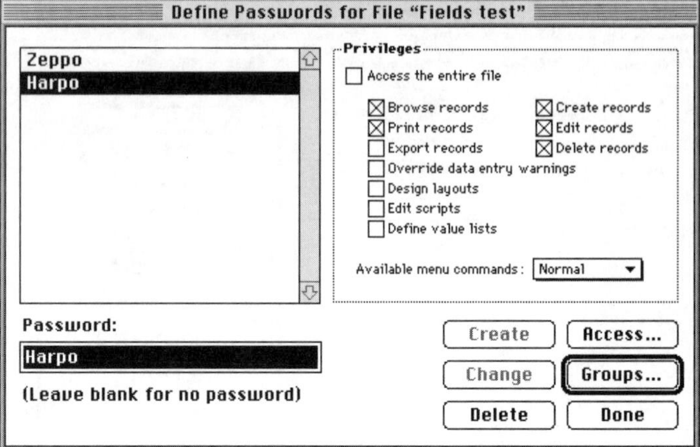

Figure 21-8: Setting access privileges

Although access privileges are more commonly associated in people's minds with products that are installed on a network, you can set access privileges for *any* FileMaker Pro database — including databases that will be run on stand-alone Macs. For more information, refer to Chapter 20.

In addition to protecting the template from unwanted changes, you can restrict access to certain features when you create a demo or shareware version of a template. To restrict access, you assign one or more passwords for the database, each limiting the particular features that are available to the user (as shown previously in Figure 21-8). By taking this approach, you give users an added incentive to buy the full version or to pay the requested shareware fee.

For example, you could define three different passwords for a database. At the lowest level, access could be limited to basic features, allowing users to only browse and edit the sample records included in the database. This level of access provides the equivalent of a demo, giving the user a feel for the database's capabilities but not enabling any of its real functionality. This password could be supplied in the documentation included in the version of the template or set as a default password that would automatically (and transparently) be used by FileMaker Pro every time the database was opened. (For instructions on setting a default password, see Chapter 20.)

As an alternative, FileMaker Pro also allows you to define a "no password" password. To do this, you simply leave the password box (previously shown in Figure 21-8) blank, select privileges, and then click Create. When new users open the file, they can leave the Password text box blank and be granted access to the minimal privileges that you assigned to this condition. This approach, however, is not as elegant as using a default password, as previously described.

Figure 21-8 also shows another Privileges option — Editing Only — that was introduced in FileMaker Pro 3.0. By choosing Editing Only from the "Available menu commands" pop-up menu, you can simultaneously restrict users to Browse mode and allow them to only edit existing records and execute scripts.

On receipt of a basic shareware fee, you can supply a second password that enables the user to print and export records, create new records, delete records, and override data entry warnings. Assuming that the user is happy with the way that the database is designed (as you hope they will be), this level of functionality will be all the person requires. For an additional charge, you could offer a master password that enables the user to also modify the structure of the database (changing and designing layouts, as well as editing scripts). Advanced users may want to take advantage of this ultimate password so they can freely customize and modify the template in ways that make it more useful to them.

FileMaker Pro provides an additional level of protection that can sometimes be useful. By defining *groups* (collections of users who share the same password), you can restrict access to particular fields and layouts. In making a demo, for example, you could use this feature to keep users from ever seeing certain reports. For more information on creating groups, see Chapter 20.

One of my own shareware templates — Family Medical Expenses — is included on the *Macworld FileMaker Pro 3.0 Bible Disk*. It illustrates yet another approach to creating shareware templates.

Family Medical Expenses already contains a small set of sample records. Users can freely try out any basic operation in the template (executing scripts, viewing and printing reports, and replacing the sample data). However, they cannot add new records, modify or create scripts, or change the layouts. After the shareware fee is received, the user is sent the master password — enabling her or him to remove the password protection from the template and change the template in any way that is desired. This approach to "crippling" a shareware template has the advantage of leaving all functions intact while still giving the user an important reason for sending the shareware fee.

Using FileMaker Pro SDK

As mentioned at the beginning of this chapter, FileMaker Pro SDK (Solutions Distribution Kit) is a special programming tool that compiles FileMaker Pro templates, changing them into stand-alone programs. If you intend to create commercial templates, using FileMaker Pro SDK offers several direct benefits when compared to creating normal FileMaker Pro templates:

- *It increases the size of the potential market.* To use a normal template, an individual must already own or be willing to buy FileMaker Pro. When you are selling an expensive vertical-market database (such as a video store rentals database), customers may consider the cost of a copy of FileMaker Pro to be a drop in the bucket. When you are attempting to sell an inexpensive, general-purpose template, on the other hand, you cannot expect customers to shoulder the cost of a program just so they can use the template.
- *It protects your investment while preventing tampering.* Providing an unprotected FileMaker Pro template to customers is tantamount to handing them the source code for your product. If you have used special techniques to create the template, SDK keeps them safe from prying eyes and prevents customers from inadvertently or deliberately modifying the way the template works.

When you become a member of the Claris Solutions Alliance, you are eligible to purchase the SDK CD-ROM from Claris. With it, you can produce royalty-free, stand-alone FileMaker Pro databases that will run on the Mac or in Microsoft Windows.

Summary

- Templates that are "good enough" for you may not be good enough to market commercially or to give to others. You need to consider many factors when you are designing templates for distribution.
- When developing a template for the widest possible audience, you can easily add features that enhance ease-of-use and enable it to be used on a variety of monitors and display cards.
- Shareware and demo templates can use FileMaker Pro's password feature to restrict access to parts or features of the template.
- If you are interested in becoming a commercial template developer, you should investigate the possibility of joining the Claris Solutions Alliance and purchasing a copy of FileMaker Pro SDK.

Appendixes

Part VI

This section presents important ancillary material for FileMaker Pro users. The appendixes include an extensive glossary, keyboard command shortcuts, resources you can turn to for additional information, and how to install and use the programs and templates on the *Macworld FileMaker Pro 3 Bible* disk.

Using the Macworld FileMaker Pro 3 Bible Disk

This books includes a high-density (1.4MB) Macintosh disk that contains an assortment of hand-picked, ready-to-run FileMaker Pro database templates, utilities, and demos. The material is stored on the floppy as a group of self-extracting archives created with Compact Pro (from Cyclos). When you double-click any archive, you are given an opportunity to choose a destination disk (usually a hard disk) where you want to expand the files. The files are automatically extracted from the archive and copied to the location that you've chosen on the destination disk.

To use the *Macworld FileMaker Pro 3 Bible* disk, you need the following:

- A high-density floppy drive (also known as an Apple SuperDrive)
- Almost 3MB of free hard disk space (if you want to extract all the files)

Extracting the Files

To extract files from the *Macworld FileMaker Pro 3 Bible* disk, do the following:

1. Insert the *Macworld FileMaker Pro 3 Bible* disk into the Macintosh's floppy drive.

   The disk window appears, as shown in Figure A-1. The archives are stored in two folders. The Author Contributions folder contains all files that were discussed in the examples presented in this book. The Other Contributions folder contains freeware and shareware templates, demos, and utilities.

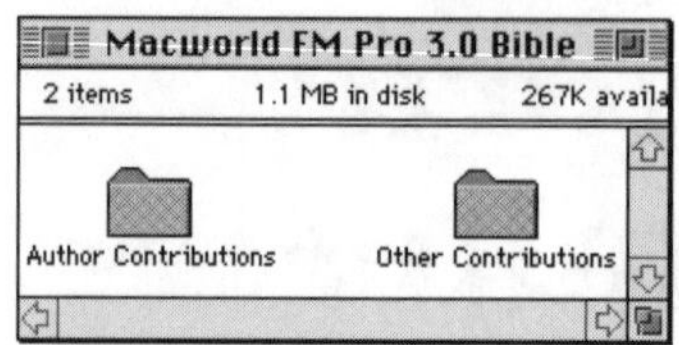

Figure A-1: The contents of the disk

2. Open either folder and locate the archive you want.

   The disk contains eight separate archives. The contents of the various archives are described later in this appendix.

3. Double-click the archive's icon.

   The extraction program launches. The Select Destination Folder dialog box appears, as shown in Figure A-2.

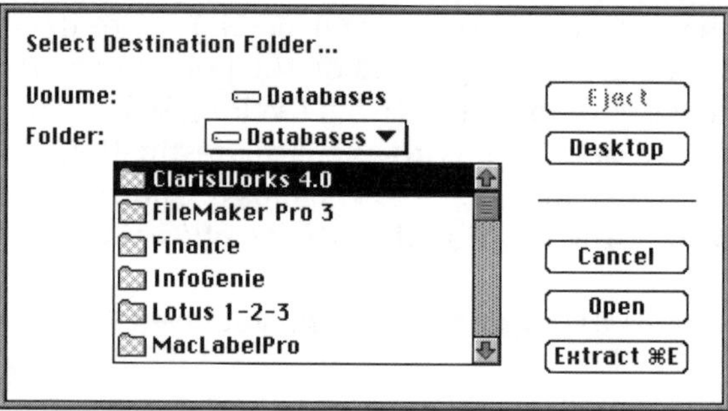

Figure A-2: Select a location for the extracted files.

4. Use normal navigation procedures to select the disk and folder where you want to copy the contents of the archive.

Be sure to select a disk other than the *Macworld FileMaker Pro 3 Bible* disk — a hard disk, for example. Treat the *Macworld FileMaker Pro 3 Bible* disk as you would treat any master disk. If you ever need to reinstall any of the software, you can use the original disk to do so.

5. Click the Extract button.

   The Extracting dialog box appears, as shown in Figure A-3. The files are extracted one-by-one from the archive and then are copied to the destination disk and folder that you selected in step 4.

Extracting: Address Book–Graphics

Files remaining to be extracted: 14 Stop

Compacted by Compact Pro™ AutoExtractor™ © 1992 Bill Goodman

Figure A-3: This dialog box shows the name of each file as it is extracted from the archive.

When all files have been extracted, the extraction program automatically quits and you are returned to the desktop.

To extract the contents of additional archives, repeat steps 2 through 5.

Disk Contents

The material on the *Macworld FileMaker Pro 3 Bible* disk is divided into two categories:

- **Author Contributions**: Templates, databases, examples, and other materials created by the author especially for this book.
- **Other Contributions**: A folder that contains working demos of commercial database templates, freeware templates, shareware templates, and a shareware database utility program.

Tables A-1 and A-2 provide brief descriptions of what you'll find on the disk.

Table A-1
Contents of the Author Contributions Archive

File name(s)	*Description*
Author Contributions Docs	DOCMaker stand-alone document that explains how to use the templates and other materials in this folder
Address Book folder	Address Book template and supporting graphics
Callable Help Example	Shows how to call a Help database from another database
Find Examples	Database that shows how to create find requests
Mac Dictionary	Special user dictionary (spelling) with more than 300 Macintosh company names, product names, and industry terms
New Buttons	Menu-driven database containing buttons that you can use in your own templates
Relational Example	Three related databases that illustrate relationships and lookups
Summary Field Tester	Test file that you can use to see how different Summary field functions work
Want List	Template for recording stamp purchases and "wants" — easily modified for use with other collectibles

Table A-2
Contents of the Other Contributions Folder

File name(s)	*Description*
Addresstrak	Demo of personal information management database
AscTech Timing Tool	Tests speed differences between FileMaker Pro and FileMaker Pro Server (freeware)
Family Medical Expenses	Shareware template for tracking annual medical expenditures
FMP 3.0 Error Codes	Listing of all FileMaker Pro 3.0 error codes for those who want to trap errors (freeware)
INFOMaker	Shareware utility for converting file formats
Room Schedule	Freeware template for room scheduling
The Report Card	Demo of grade-tracking and reporting database for school systems

Note that the contributed software (found in the Other Contributions folder) often includes documentation that explains how to use and install the necessary files. In general, you can use Apple's SimpleText or TeachText programs, or any other word processing program, to read the documentation. Be sure to look through the documentation before using any of the programs.

Protecting the Originals

Because FileMaker Pro automatically saves any changes that you make to a database or template, making a backup copy of any template before you use it the first time is always a good idea. All files on the *Macworld FileMaker Pro 3 Bible* disk are stored as archives and cannot be run until after you have extracted them, so you don't have to worry about inadvertently changing the originals. If you need additional unaltered copies of any file, you can simply extract another copy from the master disk.

Floppy disks, however, occasionally develop errors that make them partially or totally unusable. The *Macworld FileMaker Pro 3 Bible* disk can be copied, so you may want to make a backup copy of the disk, extract files from the backup, and put the original disk away for safekeeping.

About Shareware and Freeware

If you're new to computing, the concept of shareware is probably new to you. *Shareware* programs or templates are computer products that you can "try before you buy." If you like the software, you're requested to send a fee to the author of the program. In order to ensure the widest possible distribution of shareware, the authors frequently post copies of their masterpieces on computer information services (such as CompuServe and America Online) and the Internet, enabling users everywhere to download the programs, try them out, and decide for themselves whether the programs are useful.

Shareware is distributed on the honor system. Shareware authors are trusting you to do the right thing. That is, if you decide to keep and use their program or template, you should send them the small fee that's requested. If you decide that the program is not for you, on the other hand, you should remove it from your hard disk. Usually, shareware authors encourage you to share their programs with your friends and colleagues. See each program's documentation for any special distribution instructions that the authors may have included.

Freeware, on the other hand, comes with few strings attached. No fee is requested for keeping and using a freeware program or template, but you must abide by the author's distribution instructions. For example, the author may allow you to give a copy of the program or template to friends on the condition that you make sure that the copy has not been altered in any way and that it contains all the original files — including the documentation.

Keyboard Shortcuts

APPENDIX

B

This appendix contains keyboard equivalents for FileMaker Pro commands and actions. These commands are organized according to the various kinds of tasks that you may want to perform. Note that the tables in this appendix do not contain *all* the commands that the program offers; they merely list the commands for which there are keyboard shortcuts.

Table B-1
General Commands

Command	*Key*	*Menu*	*Comments*
Cancel any operation	⌘-Period (.)		
Clear	Clear		
Close	⌘-W	File	You can also click the close box on the document window
Define Fields	Shift-⌘-D	File	
Help	⌘-?	Apple or Balloon Help	
Network Access	⌘-Option-O		You can also click Host in the Open dialog box
Open	⌘-O	File	
Print	⌘-P	File	
Print direct	⌘-Option-P		Bypasses the Print dialog box
Quit	⌘-Q	File	

Table B-2
Mode-Selection Commands

Command	*Key*	*Menu*	*Comments*
Browse	⌘-B	Mode	You can also choose this command from the Mode pop-up menu
Find	⌘-F	Mode	You can also choose this command from the Mode pop-up menu
Layout	⌘-L	Mode	You can also choose this command from the Mode pop-up menu
Preview	⌘-U	Mode	You can also choose this command from the Mode pop-up menu

Table B-3
Window Control Commands

Command	*Key*	*Menu*	*Comments*
Resize window	Shift-⌘-Z		
Scroll to top of current record or preview page	Home		
Scroll to bottom of current record or preview page	End		
Scroll up one page in current record	Page Up		
Scroll down one page in current record	Page Down		
Scroll to first record with View as List option checked	Home		
Scroll to last record with View as List option checked	End		
Scroll up one page	Page Up		
Scroll down one page	Page Down		
Select a record by number	Esc		
Status area (toggle on and off)	⌘-Option-S		You can also click the Status Area control

Table B-4
Layout Mode Commands

Command	*Key*	*Menu*	*Comments*
Align	⌘-K	Arrange	
AutoGrid	⌘-Y	Arrange	Works as an on/off toggle
Resize an object with AutoGrid on	⌘-drag a handle while resizing		Allows object sizes other than those provided by the grid
Align to Grid off	⌘-drag the object		Allows object dragging while positioning in other locations than those provided by the grid
Bring Forward	Shift-⌘-F	Arrange	
Bring to Front	Shift-⌘-Option-F	Arrange	
Constrain lines to vertical/horizontal	Shift-drag as drawn		
Constrain lines to 45-degree angles	Shift-drag as drawn		
Constrain ovals to circles and rectangles to squares (as drawn or resized)	Option-drag		
Constrain resizing to vertical/horizontal	Shift-drag a handle		
Date format	Option-double-click a Date field		Same as choosing Date from the Format menu
Delete Layout	⌘-E	Mode	
Display object's format	Option-double-click the object		See also specific object and field types listed in this table
Drag selected layout part past an object	Option-drag		
Duplicate Selection	⌘-D (or Option-drag the object)	Edit	
Field borders	⌘-Option-B	Format	
Field format	⌘-Option-F	Format	

(continued)

Table B-4 *(continued)*

Command	*Key*	*Menu*	*Comments*
Graphic format	Option-double-click a Container field or graphic object		Same as choosing Graphic from the Format menu
Group	⌘-G	Arrange	
Lock	⌘-H	Arrange	
Merge Field	⌘-M	Edit➪Paste Special	
Move selected object one pixel	Arrow keys		Moves in the direction of the arrow key
New Layout	⌘-N	Mode	
Number format	Option-double-click a Number field		Same as choosing Number from the Format menu
Redefine field on layout	Command-double-click the field		
Reorder selected layout part	Shift-drag the part		
Reorient part labels	⌘-click the label		
Reset default format based on current object	⌘-click the object		
Select All	⌘-A	Edit	
Select objects by type	⌘-Option-A		An object must be selected first
Send Backward	Shift-⌘-J	Arrange	
Send to Back	Shift-⌘-Option-J	Arrange	
Set Alignment	Shift-⌘-K	Arrange	
Sliding/Printing	Option-⌘-T	Format	
Square the object being resized	Option-drag a handle		
Text format	Option-double-click a Text field or label		Same as choosing Text from the Format menu
Time format	Option-double-click a Time field		Same as choosing Time from the Format menu

Command	*Key*	*Menu*	*Comments*
T-Squares	⌘-T	Show	Works as an on/off toggle
Ungroup	Shift-⌘-G	Arrange	
Unlock	Shift-⌘-H	Arrange	

Table B-5
Text Formatting Commands

Command	*Key*	*Menu*	*Comments*
Align Center	⌘-\	Format➪Align Text	Can also be chosen from the text ruler bar
Align Full	Shift-⌘-\	Format➪Align Text	Can also be chosen from the text ruler bar
Align Left	⌘-[	Format➪Align Text	Can also be chosen from the text ruler bar
Align Right	⌘-]	Format➪Align Text	Can also be chosen from the text ruler bar
Bold	Shift-⌘-B	Format➪Style	Can also be chosen from the text ruler bar
Italic	Shift-⌘-I	Format➪Style	Can also be chosen from the text ruler bar
Outline	Shift-⌘-O	Format➪Style	
Plain	Shift-⌘-P	Format➪Style	
Next larger point size	⌘->	Format➪Size	
Next smaller point size	⌘-<	Format➪Size	
One point larger	⌘-Option->	Format➪Size➪Custom	
One point smaller	⌘-Option-<	Format➪Size➪Custom	
Select All	⌘-A	Edit	
Shadow	Shift-⌘-S	Format➪Style	
Subscript	Shift-⌘-- (hyphen)	Format➪Style	
Superscript	Shift-⌘-+	Format➪Style	
Underline	Shift-⌘-U	Format➪Style	Can also be chosen from the text ruler bar

Table B-6
Data Entry and Editing Commands

Command	*Key*	*Menu*	*Comments*
Clear	Clear	Edit	
Copy	⌘-C	Edit	
Correct Word	Shift-⌘-Y	Edit➪Spelling	Option to "Spell as you type" must be on
Cut	⌘-X	Edit	
Delete next character	del		Extended keyboard only
Delete next word	Option-del		Extended keyboard only
Delete previous character	Delete (or Backspace)		
Delete previous word	Option-Delete		
Enter a tab character	Option-Tab		
Next field	Tab		
Nonbreaking space	Option-spacebar		
Paste	⌘-V	Edit	
Paste Current Date	⌘-- (hyphen)	Edit➪Paste Special	
Paste Current Time	⌘-;	Edit➪Paste Special	
Paste Current User Name	Shift-⌘-N	Edit➪Paste Special	
Paste without text style	⌘-Option-V		
Paste From Index	⌘-I	Edit➪Paste Special	
Paste From Last Record	⌘-'	Edit➪Paste Special	
Paste From Last Record and move to next field	Shift-⌘-'		
Previous field	Shift-Tab or Option-Tab		
Select All	⌘-A	Edit	
Undo	⌘-Z	Edit	

Table B-7
Commands for Working with Records

Command	*Key*	*Menu*	*Comments*
Copy found set	⌘-Option-C		
Delete Record or Find Request	⌘-E	Mode	Command is mode-specific
Delete immediately	⌘-Option-E		Bypass confirmation dialog box
Duplicate Record or Find Request	⌘-D	Mode	Command is mode-specific
Find All	⌘-J	Select	
New Record or Request	⌘-N	Mode	Command is mode-specific
Next record, request, or layout	⌘-Tab		Command is mode-specific
Omit	⌘-M	Select	
Omit Multiple	Shift-⌘-M	Select	
Previous record, request, or layout	Shift-⌘-Tab or ⌘-Option-Tab		Command is mode-specific
Modify Last Find	⌘-R	Select	
Replace	⌘-=	Mode	
Sort	⌘-S	Mode	

Appendix C

Resources

In addition to using this book and the material that came with your copy of FileMaker Pro, you can turn to many other resources for more information about the product. These resources can help you accomplish any of the following:

- Learn new database programming techniques and tricks
- Work around or discover solutions to problems that you have encountered in using FileMaker Pro
- Find out about upcoming versions of FileMaker Pro, as well as utilities that enhance the program
- Purchase ready-to-run FileMaker Pro templates that are designed for your particular business
- Hire a specialist to create a database template especially for you
- Try out free and inexpensive templates

Technical Support and General Help

If you need help with a problem that isn't explained in this book or in the *FileMaker Pro User's Guide,* the best source of information is the Claris Technical Support Department (408-727-9054 for Macintosh questions; 408-727-9004 for Windows questions). Have your FileMaker Pro serial number handy when you call.

If you have a fax machine or fax modem, you can obtain a wealth of technical information, troubleshooting notes, and programming tips by calling the Claris FAX AnswerLine. Dial 800-800-8954 from a touch-tone phone and request that a catalog of document listings be faxed to you. After you receive the catalog, you can call the same number to request that as many as five additional documents be faxed to you. (If you need more than five, you can make multiple calls.) Although the FAX AnswerLine is impersonal when you compare it to speaking with a live technical support representative, it does provide answers to many common (and not-so-common) FileMaker Pro questions. And, best of all, it's completely free!

If you have a modem inside your Macintosh or one connected to it, you can get in touch with Claris in several other ways. The company maintains technical support accounts on several major information services, including CompuServe (76004,1614), AppleLink (CLARIS.TECH), and America Online (Keyword: CLARIS; e-mail: CLARIS). If you search the special interest group sections offered by these information services, you will also find freeware, shareware, and demo versions of FileMaker Pro templates that you can download to your Mac and try out; sections devoted exclusively to troubleshooting and programming tips; and scores of dedicated users who — if you ask nicely — may be able to offer a solution to your FileMaker Pro problem *du jour.*

If you have Internet access and a Web browser, you may wish to visit Claris' World Wide Web site. Claris Web's home page is located at http://www.claris.com.

Design Tips and Programming Tricks

In 1995, an enterprising FileMaker Pro developer named Matt Petrowsky decided that the best way to spread the word about FileMaker Pro was to use it in a manner that Claris never intended — to publish and distribute an electronic magazine called *FileMaker Pro ISO* (Interactive Support Online). Dedicated to FileMaker Pro topics, this gorgeous monthly database (shown in Figure C-1) contains scads of excellent design and programming tips. Each issue also includes a bonus: an unprotected database that you can take apart and learn new FileMaker techniques.

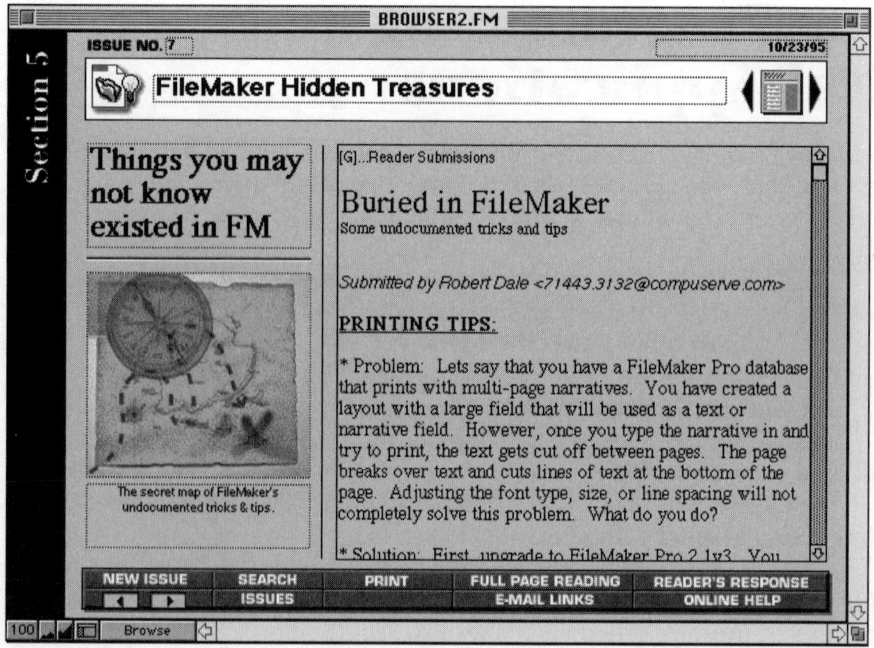

Figure C-1: FileMaker Pro ISO

At this time, first-year subscriptions to *FileMaker Pro ISO* are being offered for free. You will receive the biweekly releases for one complete year from the date of subscription. To start your subscription, e-mail the following information to <ISOeZine@aol.com>:

- Your full name
- Your e-mail address of preference
- Your physical mailing address
- Your FileMaker proficiency level (Beginner, Intermediate, Advanced)

Custom Programming and Vertical Applications

Because FileMaker Pro is such a popular database program, you probably won't be surprised to learn that some individuals and companies make their living by providing after-market materials, such as database templates, custom programming, and training materials.

Claris publishes a guide to third-party companies who provide FileMaker Pro solutions and who support other Claris products. You can obtain up to five free copies of the *Claris Solutions Alliance Directory* from Claris by calling 408-727-8227, and you can purchase additional copies for a nominal fee.

If your intent is to provide some FileMaker Pro solutions of your own, you can currently join the Claris Solutions Alliance (CSA) program for an annual fee of $249 by calling the same phone number.

If you join the CSA, you're also entitled to buy a copy of a marvelous Claris development product called FileMaker Pro SDK (Solutions Development Kit). This modified version of FileMaker Pro (for both Mac and Windows) enables you to create stand-alone, royalty-free FileMaker Pro databases. This means that you can distribute your FileMaker Pro solutions to any Mac or PC user — regardless of whether they have their own copy of FileMaker Pro.

Publishing FileMaker Pro Databases on the World Wide Web

If you're running a Web server, you can publish your FileMaker Pro databases on the World Wide Web. And guests can add to and access data in your files regardless of whether they have a copy of FileMaker Pro! For information on this exciting new use for FileMaker Pro, visit the Claris Web site at `http://www.claris.com` and download the article entitled "Publish Your Database on the Web" by Kevin Jundt. (The article was originally published in the October 1995 issue of the *Claris TechInfo Journal*.)

Web FM

When you're ready to explore the possibilities of publishing FileMaker Pro databases on your Web server, you'll want to check out Web Broadcasting Company's Web site at `http://www.macweb.com/webfm/` and download a demo copy of WEB FM 2.0. In combination with WebSTAR server software, WEB FM enables you to put a Web interface on your existing FileMaker Pro 3.0 databases as well as add form and database processing features to your Web server.

WEB FM requires no CGI (common gateway interface) programming. You just create a HTML form with input fields that use the same names as the fields in your FileMaker Pro database. If you don't have a Web server and aren't interested in setting one up, Web Broadcasting can also host the database for you on its server, for an additional fee.

News Sources

MacWEEK — published 48 times per year — is the only major Macintosh-industry newspaper. *MacWEEK* is unquestionably the best source of up-to-the-minute news about Macintosh software and hardware — whether still in the development stage or recently released — and it also provides information concerning corporate doings, changes in Apple's system software, and so on. It's a "must-have" for individuals who want to keep up with the goings-on in the Macintosh world.

Subscriptions to *MacWEEK* are free to qualified candidates (*MacWEEK* determines who qualifies), or you can purchase a subscription for $125 per year ($225 for Canada/Mexico; $350 international). To obtain a subscription application, contact:

Customer Service Department
MacWEEK
c/o JCI
P.O. Box 1766
Riverton, NJ 08077-7366
609-786-8230

Magazines: An Additional Source for Tips

Several good computer magazines occasionally provide FileMaker Pro tips and techniques. In addition to featuring in-depth reviews of new versions of programs (such as FileMaker Pro), they sometimes publish user tips and feature articles that explain how to get more out of your copy of FileMaker Pro.

Macworld and *MacUser* magazines focus primarily on the needs of business users. *Macintosh Home Journal* caters more to novice users and the needs of individuals who have Macs at home. You should be able to pick up a copy of any of these magazines at a local newsstand, or you can contact the magazines directly for subscription information at the following addresses:

Macworld
Subscription Department
P.O. Box 51666
Boulder, CO 80321-1666
(800-288-6848 in U.S.; 303-447-9330 outside the U.S.)

MacUser
P.O. Box 56986
Boulder, CO 80322-6986
(800-627-2247 in U.S./Canada; 303-447-9330 all other countries)

Macintosh Home Journal
P.O. Box 468
Mt. Morris, IL 61054
(800-800-6542)

Glossary

While this book assumes that you're familiar with the basics of operating a Macintosh (using the mouse, choosing menu commands, selecting objects and text, and printing), everyone can use a little help now and then. This glossary includes definitions of some additional common terms that you may run into while using FileMaker Pro and reading this book.

access privileges

Activities that a user can perform when using a particular password.

alert box

A program or system software dialog box that notifies you that something important has occurred or is about to happen.

algorithm

A series of steps for accomplishing a specific task.

alias

A System 7 stand-in for a program, file, folder, or disk. Double-clicking an alias results in the same action that would occur if you double-clicked the original icon.

alphanumeric data

Information consisting of letters of the alphabet, numbers, or a mixture of the two (for example, *1911 Oak Street*).

Apple Events

Messages sent between applications that enable the applications to interact.

Apple menu

The menu at the far left side of the menu bar. Under System 6, the Apple menu was reserved for desk accessories (small programs that you could use while you were running another program). Under System 7, you can place almost anything in the Apple menu, including frequently used programs, documents, folders, control panels, and *aliases* (stand-ins for programs, documents, folders, or disks).

AppleScript

A System 7 programming language from Apple Computer.

Application menu

Found at the upper right corner of the menu bar (System 7 only), this menu lists all programs that are currently running and enables you to freely switch from one program to another. The top half of the Application menu enables you to temporarily hide some or all of the programs, relieving some of the Desktop clutter.

archive

A compressed copy of one or more files. Archives can be created to save disk space, to reduce the time it takes to transmit (upload) and receive (download) the files by modem, or to serve simply as a backup copy (a personal safety net).

argument

A value supplied to a function, from which the function's value is calculated.

arrow keys

Keys on a standard keyboard that, when pressed, move the insertion point within or between fields.

ascending sort

A sorting order that starts with the smallest (or oldest) value and ends with the largest (or most recent) value. For numbers, values begin with the smallest value and proceed in numerical order. For text, values start with *A* and go through *Z*. Dates and times are sorted in chronological order. In fields that contain mixed data types (text, numbers, and characters), numbers come first.

ASCII

American Standard Code for Information Interchange. A code that associates a numerical value (0 through 255) with a character or control code.

auto-entered value

A value, text string, date, calculation, or other item that is automatically entered into a particular field when a new record is created. Auto-entry options are used to set a default entry for a field.

auto-entry field

A database field that FileMaker Pro automatically fills in for each new record.

auto-incrementing field

A field that is automatically filled in by the database program when you create a new record. The entry in the field is based on an increment over the contents of that field in the previous record. This feature is very useful for generating new invoice numbers, check numbers, record numbers, and so on.

Avery

A manufacturer of specialized stock for printing a wide variety of labels, including labels for floppy disks, address labels, and so on.

backup (noun)

An exact copy of a file.

back up (verb)

To create a duplicate of one or more files.

balloon help

When the mouse pointer is passed over a program or system software object, menu item, or icon that has help information attached to it, a cartoon-style help balloon appears (System 7 only). To turn balloon help on or off, choose the appropriate command from the Balloon Help menu in the upper right corner of the menu bar.

bitmap

A collection of individual picture elements (pixels or dots) that together constitute a graphic item.

body

A layout part that contains the main record information.

book

An icon in the status area. In Browse mode, you use the book to flip through database records.

Boolean

A type of algebra in which expressions are evaluated for their truth value. Results are either true or false.

browsed records

Those records in a FileMaker Pro database that are currently visible (not hidden).

button

An object in a FileMaker Pro database layout that has a script attached to it. Clicking the button makes the script action or actions occur. In dialog boxes, you click buttons to select, confirm, or cancel an action.

cache

An area in the computer's memory that is set aside for temporarily storing data that is on its way to and from a disk. Using a cache can greatly speed up operation because RAM is much faster to access than a disk.

Calculation field

A field type that is used to generate within-record computations. Formulas in Calculation fields can reference other fields, use FileMaker Pro's built-in functions, and contain constants.

check box

A small box that is associated with an option in a dialog box. Clicking the box changes the state of the option from selected to deselected (and vice versa). Normally, you can choose multiple check boxes.

Chooser

The control panel that you use to select a printer or other "printing" device (such as a fax modem) and, in some cases, to set options for that device.

click

To press the mouse button once and then immediately release it.

Clipboard

An area in the Mac's memory that is used to store the most recently copied (⌘-C) or cut (⌘-X) object or text string. The contents of the Clipboard can be pasted (⌘-V) into other locations on the same document, another document, or even in another application.

clone (or template)

An exact copy of a database — including all layouts, field definitions, and scripts — but *without* records. A template (also called a clone by FileMaker Pro) is used as the basis for a new database.

close box

The tiny box in the upper left corner of some windows that, when clicked, closes or dismisses the window and any document that it contains.

conditional test

A logical test that — when executed — causes a script to take a particular course, depending on the result of the test. The IF function and script step are used to implement conditional testing in FileMaker Pro.

constant

A value that does not change. Pi, *e*, and 274 are all examples of constants.

Container field

Fields of this type can be used to store graphics, QuickTime movies, or sound clips. In the Windows version of FileMaker Pro, container fields can also store OLE objects.

cosine

For a right (90-degree) triangle, the ratio of an adjacent side to the hypotenuse (the side opposite the 90-degree angle) for one of the other two angles.

crash

The cessation of functioning by a computer or a program. Signs that a computer has crashed include system crash dialog boxes (which contain a bomb symbol), as well as keyboard and mouse lock-ups.

current field

The database field that is presently selected (by tabbing or clicking into the field). Only the current field can be modified.

current record

The record that is presently selected. Only the current record can be modified.

database

An organized collection of information, normally with one central topic.

database program (or database management program)

A program for entering, editing, and otherwise managing data records.

data-entry keys

Keys on a standard keyboard that, when pressed, add data at the insertion point.

data validation

User-specified criteria that instruct the database program to check a particular field's contents for allowable and unacceptable data. Validation criteria can include range checking and required fields, for example.

default

The initial, "factory setting" for a changeable value. This setting determines how an option behaves if you never change the setting.

default value

A common value that is automatically entered in a field when you create a new record. Using a default value saves typing time and ensures that information is entered consistently.

descending sort

A sorting order that starts with the largest (or most recent) value and ends with the least (or oldest) value. An alphabetic sort in descending order begins with *Z*.

Desktop

The main work area on the Macintosh.

dialog box

A special type of window that programs and the system software use to present information or to enable you to make choices.

dimmed command

A menu command that cannot presently be selected — usually because it is irrelevant to the current operation. Dimmed items are also referred to as *grayed-out* and can appear in dialog boxes, as well as in menus.

dogcow

An icon in the LaserWriter Page Setup dialog box that demonstrates the combined effects of selected options.

dot matrix

A type of printer technology in which a print head that has many pins, each corresponding to one picture element (pixel or dot), is passed rapidly over a page, hammering out an impression through a ribbon.

double-click

To press the mouse button twice in rapid succession.

download

To elect to receive a file (usually via a modem and phone line) from an information service, a bulletin board system, or another user's computer.

downloading

The process of using a modem to retrieve a program or document file from an online information service, a bulletin board system, or another user's computer.

drag

To hold down the mouse button while moving the mouse pointer.

drag and drop

Applications that support Apple's drag and drop technology enable you to freely drag text and graphics from one document to another, as well as between different applications. In essence, drag and drop is simply a direct way of accomplishing a copy and paste operation, without using the Mac's Clipboard as an intermediary.

emergency quit command

A keyboard command (⌘-Option-Esc) that you can use to force a program to quit. You can sometimes use this command of last resort to escape from a program that has locked up or crashed.

export

To move a copy of selected data from one program to another. To ensure compatibility with the program that will receive the data, most programs that export data can write it in a number of different file formats.

expression

A mathematical statement that consists of one or more operators (such as + or *) that join two or more variables or constants.

external script

A script in another database that is executed with the Perform Script step. When an external script is performed in this manner, the database that contains the script automatically opens first.

Fat Binary

A version of an application that is designed so that it will run correctly on any type of Macintosh, including the new Power Macs.

field

Fields are the building blocks of which records are composed. Each database field is meant to store one particular type of information, such as a Social Security number or a birth date.

field type

Set in the Define Fields dialog box, a field type specifies the type of information that a particular field is intended to collect and display. Some common field types are text, numeric, date, time, and picture. The main reason for declaring field types is to enable the database program to screen for invalid data so that it can warn you if you have, for example, entered text in a numeric field.

file

Any named, ordered collection of information that is stored on disk. Programs, documents, and system software components (such as the Finder) are examples of files.

file dialog box

Any dialog box that is designed to enable file-handling tasks, such as opening, saving, importing, and exporting files. Unlike most dialog boxes, file dialog boxes frequently have no title.

file format

A standard specification for the way data is stored and interpreted.

Find

A command for locating a record or group of records based on criteria that you establish. For example, you may want to find the address record for Ames Corporation or identify the records of all salespeople who earned more than $40,000 last year. Most database programs enable you to set multiple criteria when performing a find request.

flat-file database

A flat-file database normally consists of a single file. Every field that is necessary has to be in that file.

folder

A holder of documents, applications, and other folders on the desktop. A folder is the equivalent of a directory or subdirectory on a PC system.

found set

The remaining visible (or browsed) records following a find procedure, such as a find request, Omit command, or Omit Multiple command.

freeware

Programs or templates that are offered to users free of charge.

function

An operation performed on a value that yields a unique result for that value. The function of two different values can be the same, but the function of a given value can never differ from the original result.

Global field

A Global field is used to hold the same value for all records in the database. It can also be used to temporarily store script results.

grayscale

Objects and text are displayed in shades of gray rather than in color. As with color, most grayscale displays can support multiple numbers of gray shades (4, 16, and 256, for example).

group

A set of objects in a layout to which you have applied the Group command so that you can treat them as a single entity rather than as a collection of objects.

guest

Any user who opens a shared database after the host has opened it.

handle

A black dot that appears at the corners of an object when it is selected (only in Layout mode). You can drag the handles to change the size of an object.

header

A special first record that is frequently included as part of an export file. The header identifies (by name) all the fields that are present in the file and indicates the order in which they can be found.

hierarchical menu (also pop-up menu, submenu)

A secondary menu that pops up when a menu command is selected.

high ASCII

Any ASCII character with a value higher than 127; the upper half of the ASCII character set. Special symbols and foreign language characters are high ASCII.

host

The user who first opens a database and sets its status to multiuser, enabling other users on the network to share that database. In subsequent sessions, other users may become the host.

import

To bring data from another program into the current program. Importing saves you the effort of needlessly retyping data. FileMaker Pro, for example, can read any tab-delimited text file — regardless of what program actually created the file.

index

FileMaker Pro maintains an internal list of data that covers the contents of every selected Text, Number, Date, Time, and Calculation field. Indexes are responsible for the speed with which FileMaker Pro executes find requests. In previous versions of the program, indexing was automatically performed for every appropriate field type. In FileMaker Pro 3.0, indexing is an option that must be turned on individually for the desired fields.

inkjet

A type of printer technology in which ink is forced at high pressure onto the page. Inkjet printers are frequently inexpensive, while being able to match the resolution and quality of many laser printers. The biggest drawback of inkjet printers is their speed (or—more precisely—their lack of it).

insertion point

A blinking vertical line that indicates the point at which the next typed, pasted, or imported data will appear.

installer

A special program provided to enable users to easily copy a program, templates, and supporting files to their hard disk.

internal script

A script that is contained in and executed from the current database.

invalid data

Information that does not adhere to the specific format for a given field or that falls outside the acceptable range of values for that field. This term also refers to data of the wrong type, such as character data in a numeric field.

keyboard shortcut

Keys that you press to execute a program or system command, as an alternative to selecting a command from a menu. It is also called a *keyboard equivalent* and a *Command-key equivalent.*

laser printing

A type of printer technology in which laser light creates an image of a page on a rotating drum, magnetizing the drum. Toner particles adhere to the magnetized drum and are then transferred onto paper, where they are fused at high heat. This technology works like a conventional photocopier.

layout

In FileMaker Pro, a particular arrangement of fields, graphics, and static text. Unlimited layouts can be designed for each database, each with a different purpose. For example, some layouts may be used for data entry and others for generating printed or on-screen reports. You can use a layout for viewing records, entering data, and generating printed and on-screen reports. A database can have multiple layouts.

layout parts

The major sections in a database layout. Depending on the purpose of the layout, it may contain a body, header, footer, and summary parts, for example.

list view

Using the View as List command, you can display records in a continuous scrolling list rather than one record per screen.

lookup

A field option that instructs FileMaker Pro to search an external database for a record that contains a match to the data entered in the current database. If a match is found, data from another field in the external database is automatically copied into a field in the current database. For example, entering an inventory part number in one database can trigger a lookup of a price and description for that part in another database.

lookup field

A field in the current database into which data will be copied when a lookup is triggered.

lookup file

The database in which data is looked up (in response to data being entered or edited in the trigger field in the current file).

low ASCII

Any ASCII character with a value less than or equal to 127; the lower half of the ASCII character set. Ordinary letters and numbers are low ASCII.

mail merge

Combining address and other personal or business information (usually from a database) with a form letter (usually created in a word processing program) to generate a series of "personalized" letters. (You can also generate a merge directly within a FileMaker Pro 3.0 layout.)

master password

A special password that provides complete access to a database, including permission to change the design of the database, set or change passwords and access privileges, and establish or change groups.

match fields

The fields in the two files that are compared. These fields define the relationship between the files.

menu

A list of choices, presented by a program, from which you can select an action. Menus appear when you click menu titles in the menu bar. You choose commands by dragging through the menu and releasing the mouse button while a command is highlighted.

menu bar

In a program or at the Desktop, the horizontal strip at the top of the screen that contains the menu titles.

merge

The process of combining information from a database with a text document, such as for a form letter (also known as a *mail merge*).

modal dialog box

Any dialog box that you need to respond to before you can continue working.

mode

A state of a FileMaker Pro database in which you can perform only one global type of activity. The four modes are Browse, Find, Layout, and Preview.

modeless dialog box

A dialog box that you can leave open while you attend to other work; it does not require an immediate response or dismissal.

modifier key

A key or keys that, when pressed in combination with a letter, number, or punctuation key, changes the meaning of the second key. When you are typing text, for example, the Shift and Option keys frequently act as modifier keys. On a Macintosh keyboard, modifier keys include Shift, Option, ⌘, and — on some keyboards — Control.

monochrome

Refers to a two-color display (usually black-and-white).

mouse pointer

An on-screen indicator that moves in response to movements that you make with the mouse or another pointing device. The mouse pointer changes its shape to reflect the activity that you are performing.

omit

To temporarily remove a record from a found set, hiding it from view.

open

To load a copy of a document from disk into a program. You can also open desktop windows for disks and folders by double-clicking the icon that represents them.

operator

A symbol indicating that a certain mathematical process should be performed on the entities surrounding the operator symbol. Both + and > are examples of operators.

order of operations

Refers to the way in which algebraic expressions are evaluated. Exponents are done first, then multiplication and division, then addition and subtraction. Including parentheses in an expression can alter the order of operations.

password

A string of characters that a user must type when opening a protected FileMaker Pro database. Different passwords often are associated with different privileges, specifying what a user can or cannot do with the database.

platform

A particular computer/operating system combination. The Mac/System 7 and PC/Windows are two common platforms, both of which are compatible with FileMaker Pro.

pop-up menu (or hierarchical menu)

A menu in which one or more menu items contain a submenu.

portal

A rectangular area on a layout created with the Portal tool; used to display multiple records from a related file.

preferences

Program-specific or document-specific settings that you use to govern how certain aspects of a program behave.

Preview

A FileMaker Pro mode that enables the user to see what a printed report or other document will look like prior to committing it to paper.

print driver

A software program that is used to control a specific printer. Macintosh print drivers are accessed in the Chooser.

PrintMonitor

A special Apple program that watches over and controls background laser print jobs.

questionable spelling

The term that FileMaker Pro's spelling checker uses to identify a word that is not contained in the current main or user dictionaries.

QuicKeys

A macro utility from CE Software that enables users to automate many functions in most programs. When you use the Send Apple Event script step, QuicKeys macros that access other programs can be executed from within FileMaker Pro.

QuickTime

An Apple system extension that enables you to play moving picture and sound data on any Macintosh (requires System 6.0.8 or higher).

radio button

In dialog boxes, buttons that present a series of mutually-exclusive options or settings (for example, enabling or disabling background printing).

RAM

Random Access Memory. The memory that the Mac uses to run programs, use desk accessories, temporarily store data, and so on.

range checking

A database program feature that prevents input errors by making certain that each entry in a particular field is within acceptable ranges. For example, entries for student grades might have to be between 0 and 4.

Read Me file

A text file that provides information about a program or template. Manufacturers of commercial programs often include a Read Me file on disk to inform users about important topics that are not covered in the program's manual. Although you do not have to name the file Read Me, such a file name encourages users to open the file and examine its contents.

reader

A separate utility program that enables the contents of a document to be read, regardless of whether or not the user has his or her own copy of the program in which the document was created. A reader typically provides the user only with "read" privileges; that is, it can read documents created with a particular program, but does not allow users to "write" (create new documents of that type).

record

The basic unit of every database. All databases are composed of records, each storing information for a single entity, such as a person, catalog item, video tape, or recipe.

relational database program

A program in which shared key fields link information in multiple database files, enabling you to generate reports and display information based on data from more than one database.

Relookup

A Mode menu command that causes all lookups for a database to be executed again (for every record currently being browsed). Choosing this command ensures that all lookup fields contain current data.

repeating field

A field option that enables a single field to store and display multiple values.

report

A copy of selected information from a database, consisting of specified records in a certain layout, presented in a particular sort order.

required field (not empty)

A field that must be filled in before finalizing the information for the record. The record is checked for completeness only when you press Enter; attempt to switch to a different record, layout, or mode; close the database; or try to quit FileMaker Pro while the database is still open.

reset switch

A hardware switch or button that causes the Mac to go through its startup sequence. (See the owner's manual for the availability and location of the switch or button.)

resources

In a FileMaker Pro database, these are the layouts and the fields. When defining access privileges associated with a particular group, the database designer or administrator can prevent users from modifying or even seeing particular resources.

root

The top or highest level of any disk. When a disk icon is first opened, the root is the part of the disk that you first see.

save

To store a current copy of a document on disk.

script

A user-defined sequence of commands and actions that automates FileMaker Pro tasks. A script consists of one or more commands associated with a specific database that FileMaker will execute automatically or when instructed by the user to do so.

ScriptMaker

The FileMaker Pro component that you use to design scripts.

scroll arrow

The arrow icon at either end of a scroll bar. When you click the arrow, the window's contents move in the opposite direction of the arrow.

scroll bar

A rectangular bar along the right side or bottom edge of a window. Clicking or dragging in a scroll bar changes your view of the window's contents. Document windows and large text fields often have scroll bars.

scroll box

The box in a scroll bar. The position of the scroll box indicates the position of what is in the window relative to the entire document.

SCSI (pronounced "skuzzy")

Small Computer Systems Interface. Enables devices, such as hard disks, CD-ROM drives, tape drives, and scanners, to be connected in series to the Macintosh.

search criteria

Information used as a reference in search operations.

self-extracting archive

One or more compressed files that contain a built-in file extraction program. When a user double-clicks the icon of a self-extracting archive, a file dialog box appears that enables the user to select a destination disk and folder for the expanded (normal) files.

shareware

Programs or templates that are distributed to users on the honor system. If you decide to keep the program or template, you send the author the requested fee.

Shut Down

A command in the Special menu that you use to shut down the Mac and devices that are connected to it.

sine

For a right (90-degree) triangle, the ratio of the opposite side to the hypotenuse for one of the other two angles.

size box

A box in the lower right corner of some windows. Dragging the size box changes the size of the window.

sort

To rearrange database records in a different order than the one in which they were originally entered. Most database programs can simultaneously sort on multiple fields. The more powerful database programs enable you to specify *key* or *index* fields — special sort fields that are automatically maintained by the program. Indexes are particularly useful for very large databases, where a normal sort would be extremely time consuming.

sort order

The order in which a field is sorted. Every FileMaker Pro database field can be sorted in one of three sort orders: ascending, descending, or according to the field's value list (if one has been defined).

source code

In a computer program, source code is the set of instructions that makes a program do what it was intended to do. The instructions are in a human-readable form (usually in a programming language such as Pascal, C, BASIC, FORTRAN, or assembly language). In a FileMaker Pro template, script definitions and Apple Event instructions may be considered the equivalent of source code.

stand-alone document

A document that contains its own reader and, hence, does not require the user to own any specific program in which to open and read the document. The document *is* a program.

stand-alone program

After FileMaker Pro SDK is used to compile a template, it becomes a stand-alone program. It can be run on any Mac, and it does not require that a copy of FileMaker Pro be installed.

status area

The area on the immediate left of the database window. In Browse mode, the status area contains controls that enable you to select a different layout, navigate among records, change the magnification (zoom), and show or hide the status area. Information on the current state of the database (such as whether it is sorted, the number of records being browsed, and the current record number) is also displayed in the status area.

step

A single action set for a FileMaker Pro script.

sub-script

Any FileMaker Pro script that is performed by another script.

summary field

A type of field used to summarize the information in the same field across many records.

System file

A critical component of the system software, located in the System Folder on the startup disk.

system software

Software that supports application programs by managing system resources, such as memory and input/output devices.

tangent

In a right (90-degree) triangle, the ratio of the opposite side to the adjacent side for one of the two other angles.

template (or stationery document)

A partially completed document that serves as a starting point for other documents. In a word processing program, for example, you might make a memo template that contains appropriate headers and text formatting, making it simple for you to create each new memo without unnecessarily having to retype basic text. The equivalent document in FileMaker Pro is known as a *clone* and is created using the Save a Copy As command.

text box (or text-edit box)

A rectangular area in a dialog box or program that presents information that you can edit. A common example is the space provided for a file name in Open and Save dialog boxes.

text file (also called text-only file)

A file saved without formatting (a single font and no style or size options). The usual purpose of creating a pure text file is to enable it to be read by other programs or other types of computers.

text-only file

A document that contains only simple text — no formatting. Most text editors, such as SimpleText, automatically save documents in this format. You can usually create such files by using the word processing program's Save As command and choosing Text-Only as the format. The point of creating a text-only file is to assure that the greatest number of people will own at least one program that can read the file.

title bar

The horizontal bar at the top of a window that shows the name of the window's contents. You can move the window by dragging its title bar.

trigger field

A field in the current database that, when data is entered or modified, initiates a lookup.

uncompressing (or decompressing)

To shorten the length of time required to download files from an information service, a special utility program is often used to compress the files (making them smaller). Uncompressing the files restores them to their original size and format.

unique field

A field that can contain only data that is not duplicated in any other record.

user name

A unique name assigned to a Macintosh, normally used to distinguish that Macintosh from others on a network.

value list

A list of acceptable choices or values that have been defined and are associated with a field. Using value lists can help speed data entry and ensure the consistency of information. Value lists can be displayed as pop-up lists, pop-up menus, radio buttons, or check boxes.

variable

A value in an expression that may change, usually indicated by a letter or name. A field can be considered to be a variable, because its contents may change from record to record.

windoid

A tiny, special-purpose window that is typically provided as a user-control tool. The Size tool is an example of a windoid.

zoom

Changing the magnification level or view of the database by enlarging or reducing all elements on a layout.

zoom box

A tiny box in the upper right corner of some windows. Click the zoom box to expand the window to its maximum size. A second click returns the window to its original size.

Index

• Symbols •

• A •

• B •

• D •

• E •

• F •

• G •

• H •

• I •

• J •

• K •

• L •

• M •

• N •

• Q •

• R •

• S •

• T •

• U •

• V •

• W •

• Y •

• Z •

7/29/96

The Fun & Easy Way™ to learn about computers and more!

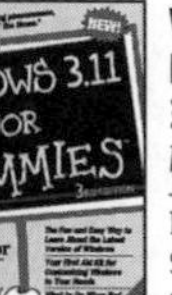

Windows® 3.11 For Dummies®, 3rd Edition
by Andy Rathbone

ISBN: 1-56884-370-4
$16.95 USA/
$22.95 Canada

SUPER STAR

Mutual Funds For Dummies™
by Eric Tyson

ISBN: 1-56884-226-0
$16.99 USA/
$22.99 Canada

SUPER STAR

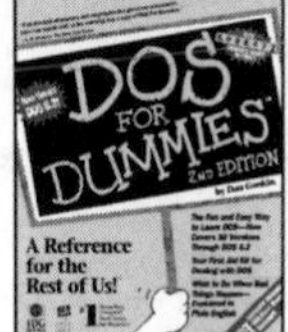

DOS FOR DUMMIES
2ND EDITION
A Reference for the Rest of Us!

DOS For Dummies®, 2nd Edition
by Dan Gookin

ISBN: 1-878058-75-4
$16.95 USA/
$22.95 Canada

SUPER STAR

The Internet For Dummies®, 2nd Edition
by John Levine & Carol Baroudi

ISBN: 1-56884-222-8
$19.99 USA/
$26.99 Canada

Personal Finance For Dummies™
by Eric Tyson

ISBN: 1-56884-150-7
$16.95 USA/
$22.95 Canada

SUPER STAR

PCs FOR DUMMIES
2ND EDITION
A Reference for the Rest of Us!

PCs For Dummies®, 3rd Edition
by Dan Gookin & Andy Rathbone

ISBN: 1-56884-904-4
$16.99 USA/
$22.99 Canada

VIII FINALIST

MACS FOR DUMMIES
3RD EDITION
A Reference for the Rest of Us!

Macs® For Dummies®, 3rd Edition
by David Pogue

ISBN: 1-56884-239-2
$19.99 USA/
$26.99 Canada

SUPER STAR

THE SAT I FOR DUMMIES
A Reference for the Rest of Us!

The SAT® I For Dummies™
by Suzee Vlk

ISBN: 1-56884-213-9
$14.99 USA/
$20.99 Canada

ere's a complete listing of IDG Books' *...For Dummies®* titles

itle	Author	ISBN	Price
TABASE			
ccess 2 For Dummies®	by Scott Palmer	ISBN: 1-56884-090-X	$19.95 USA/$26.95 Canada
ccess Programming For Dummies®	by Rob Krumm	ISBN: 1-56884-091-8	$19.95 USA/$26.95 Canada
pproach 3 For Windows® For Dummies®	by Doug Lowe	ISBN: 1-56884-233-3	$19.99 USA/$26.99 Canada
3ASE For DOS For Dummies®	by Scott Palmer & Michael Stabler	ISBN: 1-56884-188-4	$19.95 USA/$26.95 Canada
3ASE For Windows® For Dummies®	by Scott Palmer	ISBN: 1-56884-179-5	$19.95 USA/$26.95 Canada
3ASE 5 For Windows® Programming For Dummies®	by Ted Coombs & Jason Coombs	ISBN: 1-56884-215-5	$19.99 USA/$26.99 Canada
oxPro 2.6 For Windows® For Dummies®	by John Kaufeld	ISBN: 1-56884-187-6	$19.95 USA/$26.95 Canada
ıradox 5 For Windows® For Dummies®	by John Kaufeld	ISBN: 1-56884-185-X	$19.95 USA/$26.95 Canada
SKTOP PUBLISHING/ILLUSTRATION/GRAPHICS			
orelDRAW! 5 For Dummies®	by Deke McClelland	ISBN: 1-56884-157-4	$19.95 USA/$26.95 Canada
orelDRAW! For Dummies®	by Deke McClelland	ISBN: 1-56884-042-X	$19.95 USA/$26.95 Canada
esktop Publishing & Design For Dummies®	by Roger C. Parker	ISBN: 1-56884-234-1	$19.99 USA/$26.99 Canada
arvard Graphics 2 For Windows® For Dummies®	by Roger C. Parker	ISBN: 1-56884-092-6	$19.95 USA/$26.95 Canada
ageMaker 5 For Macs® For Dummies®	by Galen Gruman & Deke McClelland	ISBN: 1-56884-178-7	$19.95 USA/$26.95 Canada
ageMaker 5 For Windows® For Dummies®	by Deke McClelland & Galen Gruman	ISBN: 1-56884-160-4	$19.95 USA/$26.95 Canada
hotoshop 3 For Macs® For Dummies®	by Deke McClelland	ISBN: 1-56884-208-2	$19.99 USA/$26.99 Canada
uarkXPress 3.3 For Dummies®	by Galen Gruman & Barbara Assadi	ISBN: 1-56884-217-1	$19.99 USA/$26.99 Canada
NANCE/PERSONAL FINANCE/TEST TAKING REFERENCE			
veryday Math For Dummies™	by Charles Seiter	ISBN: 1-56884-248-1	$14.99 USA/$22.99 Canada
ersonal Finance For Dummies™ For Canadians	by Eric Tyson & Tony Martin	ISBN: 1-56884-378-X	$18.99 USA/$24.99 Canada
uickBooks 3 For Dummies®	by Stephen L. Nelson	ISBN: 1-56884-227-9	$19.99 USA/$26.99 Canada
uicken 8 For DOS For Dummies®, 2nd Edition	by Stephen L. Nelson	ISBN: 1-56884-210-4	$19.95 USA/$26.95 Canada
uicken 5 For Macs® For Dummies®	by Stephen L. Nelson	ISBN: 1-56884-211-2	$19.95 USA/$26.95 Canada
uicken 4 For Windows® For Dummies®, 2nd Edition	by Stephen L. Nelson	ISBN: 1-56884-209-0	$19.95 USA/$26.95 Canada
axes For Dummies,™ 1995 Edition	by Eric Tyson & David J. Silverman	ISBN: 1-56884-220-1	$14.99 USA/$20.99 Canada
he GMAT® For Dummies™	by Suzee Vlk, Series Editor	ISBN: 1-56884-376-3	$14.99 USA/$20.99 Canada
he GRE® For Dummies™	by Suzee Vlk, Series Editor	ISBN: 1-56884-375-5	$14.99 USA/$20.99 Canada
ime Management For Dummies™	by Jeffrey J. Mayer	ISBN: 1-56884-360-7	$16.99 USA/$22.99 Canada
urboTax For Windows® For Dummies®	by Gail A. Helsel, CPA	ISBN: 1-56884-228-7	$19.99 USA/$26.99 Canada
OUPWARE/INTEGRATED			
larisWorks For Macs® For Dummies®	by Frank Higgins	ISBN: 1-56884-363-1	$19.99 USA/$26.99 Canada
otus Notes For Dummies®	by Pat Freeland & Stephen Londergan	ISBN: 1-56884-212-0	$19.95 USA/$26.95 Canada
licrosoft® Office 4 For Windows® For Dummies®	by Roger C. Parker	ISBN: 1-56884-183-3	$19.95 USA/$26.95 Canada
licrosoft® Works 3 For Windows® For Dummies®	by David C. Kay	ISBN: 1-56884-214-7	$19.99 USA/$26.99 Canada
martSuite 3 For Dummies®	by Jan Weingarten & John Weingarten	ISBN: 1-56884-367-4	$19.99 USA/$26.99 Canada
TERNET/COMMUNICATIONS/NETWORKING			
merica Online® For Dummies®, 2nd Edition	by John Kaufeld	ISBN: 1-56884-933-8	$19.99 USA/$26.99 Canada
ompuServe For Dummies®, 2nd Edition	by Wallace Wang	ISBN: 1-56884-937-0	$19.99 USA/$26.99 Canada
odems For Dummies®, 2nd Edition	by Tina Rathbone	ISBN: 1-56884-223-6	$19.99 USA/$26.99 Canada
IORE Internet For Dummies®	by John R. Levine & Margaret Levine Young	ISBN: 1-56884-164-7	$19.95 USA/$26.95 Canada
ORE Modems & On-line Services For Dummies®	by Tina Rathbone	ISBN: 1-56884-365-8	$19.99 USA/$26.99 Canada
osaic For Dummies®, Windows Edition	by David Angell & Brent Heslop	ISBN: 1-56884-242-2	$19.99 USA/$26.99 Canada
etWare For Dummies®, 2nd Edition	by Ed Tittel, Deni Connor & Earl Follis	ISBN: 1-56884-369-0	$19.99 USA/$26.99 Canada
etworking For Dummies®	by Doug Lowe	ISBN: 1-56884-079-9	$19.95 USA/$26.95 Canada
ROCOMM PLUS 2 For Windows® For Dummies®	by Wallace Wang	ISBN: 1-56884-219-8	$19.99 USA/$26.99 Canada
CP/IP For Dummies®	by Marshall Wilensky & Candace Leiden	ISBN: 1-56884-241-4	$19.99 USA/$26.99 Canada

rosoft and Windows are registered trademarks of Microsoft Corporation. Mac is a registered trademark of Apple Computer. SAT is a registered trademark of the College Entrance Examination Board. GMAT is a registered trademark of the Graduate nagement Admission Council. GRE is a registered trademark of the Educational Testing Service. America Online is a registered trademark of America Online, Inc. The "...For Dummies Book Series" logo, the IDG Books Worldwide logos, Dummies Press, I The Fun & Easy Way are trademarks, and ---- For Dummies and ... For Dummies are registered trademarks under exclusive license to IDG Books Worldwide, Inc., from International Data Group, Inc.

lastic requests & educational orders please cational Sales at 1. 800. 434. 2086

FOR MORE INFO OR TO ORDER, PLEASE CALL ▸ 800. 762. 2974

For volume discounts & special orders please call Corporate Sales, at 415. 655. 3000

The Internet For Macs® For Dummies®, 2nd Edition	by Charles Seiter	ISBN: 1-56884-371-2	$19.99 USA/$26.99 Canad
The Internet For Macs® For Dummies® Starter Kit	by Charles Seiter	ISBN: 1-56884-244-9	$29.99 USA/$39.99 Canad
The Internet For Macs® For Dummies® Starter Kit Bestseller Edition	by Charles Seiter	ISBN: 1-56884-245-7	$39.99 USA/$54.99 Canad
The Internet For Windows® For Dummies® Starter Kit	by John R. Levine & Margaret Levine Young	ISBN: 1-56884-237-6	$34.99 USA/$44.99 Canad
The Internet For Windows® For Dummies® Starter Kit, Bestseller Edition	by John R. Levine & Margaret Levine Young	ISBN: 1-56884-246-5	$39.99 USA/$54.99 Canad
MACINTOSH			
Mac® Programming For Dummies®	by Dan Parks Sydow	ISBN: 1-56884-173-6	$19.95 USA/$26.95 Canad
Macintosh® System 7.5 For Dummies®	by Bob LeVitus	ISBN: 1-56884-197-3	$19.95 USA/$26.95 Canad
MORE Macs® For Dummies®	by David Pogue	ISBN: 1-56884-087-X	$19.95 USA/$26.95 Canad
PageMaker 5 For Macs® For Dummies®	by Galen Gruman & Deke McClelland	ISBN: 1-56884-178-7	$19.95 USA/$26.95 Canad
QuarkXPress 3.3 For Dummies®	by Galen Gruman & Barbara Assadi	ISBN: 1-56884-217-1	$19.99 USA/$26.99 Canad
Upgrading and Fixing Macs® For Dummies®	by Kearney Rietmann & Frank Higgins	ISBN: 1-56884-189-2	$19.95 USA/$26.95 Canad
MULTIMEDIA			
Multimedia & CD-ROMs For Dummies®, 2nd Edition	by Andy Rathbone	ISBN: 1-56884-907-9	$19.99 USA/$26.99 Canad
Multimedia & CD-ROMs For Dummies®, Interactive Multimedia Value Pack, 2nd Edition	by Andy Rathbone	ISBN: 1-56884-909-5	$29.99 USA/$39.99 Canad
OPERATING SYSTEMS:			
DOS			
MORE DOS For Dummies®	by Dan Gookin	ISBN: 1-56884-046-2	$19.95 USA/$26.95 Canad
OS/2® Warp For Dummies®, 2nd Edition	by Andy Rathbone	ISBN: 1-56884-205-8	$19.99 USA/$26.99 Canad
UNIX			
MORE UNIX® For Dummies®	by John R. Levine & Margaret Levine Young	ISBN: 1-56884-361-5	$19.99 USA/$26.99 Canad
UNIX® For Dummies®	by John R. Levine & Margaret Levine Young	ISBN: 1-878058-58-4	$19.95 USA/$26.95 Canad
WINDOWS			
MORE Windows® For Dummies®, 2nd Edition	by Andy Rathbone	ISBN: 1-56884-048-9	$19.95 USA/$26.95 Canad
Windows® 95 For Dummies®	by Andy Rathbone	ISBN: 1-56884-240-6	$19.99 USA/$26.99 Canad
PCS/HARDWARE			
Illustrated Computer Dictionary For Dummies®, 2nd Edition	by Dan Gookin & Wallace Wang	ISBN: 1-56884-218-X	$12.95 USA/$16.95 Canad
Upgrading and Fixing PCs For Dummies®, 2nd Edition	by Andy Rathbone	ISBN: 1-56884-903-6	$19.99 USA/$26.99 Canad
PRESENTATION/AUTOCAD			
AutoCAD For Dummies®	by Bud Smith	ISBN: 1-56884-191-4	$19.95 USA/$26.95 Canad
PowerPoint 4 For Windows® For Dummies®	by Doug Lowe	ISBN: 1-56884-161-2	$16.99 USA/$22.99 Canad
PROGRAMMING			
Borland C++ For Dummies®	by Michael Hyman	ISBN: 1-56884-162-0	$19.95 USA/$26.95 Canad
C For Dummies®, Volume 1	by Dan Gookin	ISBN: 1-878058-78-9	$19.95 USA/$26.95 Canad
C++ For Dummies®	by Stephen R. Davis	ISBN: 1-56884-163-9	$19.95 USA/$26.95 Canad
Delphi Programming For Dummies®	by Neil Rubenking	ISBN: 1-56884-200-7	$19.99 USA/$26.99 Canad
Mac® Programming For Dummies®	by Dan Parks Sydow	ISBN: 1-56884-173-6	$19.95 USA/$26.95 Canad
PowerBuilder 4 Programming For Dummies®	by Ted Coombs & Jason Coombs	ISBN: 1-56884-325-9	$19.99 USA/$26.99 Canad
QBasic Programming For Dummies®	by Douglas Hergert	ISBN: 1-56884-093-4	$19.95 USA/$26.95 Canad
Visual Basic 3 For Dummies®	by Wallace Wang	ISBN: 1-56884-076-4	$19.95 USA/$26.95 Canad
Visual Basic "X" For Dummies®	by Wallace Wang	ISBN: 1-56884-230-9	$19.99 USA/$26.99 Canad
Visual C++ 2 For Dummies®	by Michael Hyman & Bob Arnson	ISBN: 1-56884-328-3	$19.99 USA/$26.99 Canad
Windows® 95 Programming For Dummies®	by S. Randy Davis	ISBN: 1-56884-327-5	$19.99 USA/$26.99 Canad
SPREADSHEET			
1-2-3 For Dummies®	by Greg Harvey	ISBN: 1-878058-60-6	$16.95 USA/$22.95 Canad
1-2-3 For Windows® 5 For Dummies®, 2nd Edition	by John Walkenbach	ISBN: 1-56884-216-3	$16.95 USA/$22.95 Canad
Excel 5 For Macs® For Dummies®	by Greg Harvey	ISBN: 1-56884-186-8	$19.95 USA/$26.95 Canad
Excel For Dummies®, 2nd Edition	by Greg Harvey	ISBN: 1-56884-050-0	$16.95 USA/$22.95 Canad
MORE 1-2-3 For DOS For Dummies®	by John Weingarten	ISBN: 1-56884-224-4	$19.99 USA/$26.99 Canad
MORE Excel 5 For Windows® For Dummies®	by Greg Harvey	ISBN: 1-56884-207-4	$19.95 USA/$26.95 Canad
Quattro Pro 6 For Windows® For Dummies®	by John Walkenbach	ISBN: 1-56884-174-4	$19.95 USA/$26.95 Canad
Quattro Pro For DOS For Dummies®	by John Walkenbach	ISBN: 1-56884-023-3	$16.95 USA/$22.95 Canad
UTILITIES			
Norton Utilities 8 For Dummies®	by Beth Slick	ISBN: 1-56884-166-3	$19.95 USA/$26.95 Canad
VCRS/CAMCORDERS			
VCRs & Camcorders For Dummies™	by Gordon McComb & Andy Rathbone	ISBN: 1-56884-229-5	$14.99 USA/$20.99 Canad
WORD PROCESSING			
Ami Pro For Dummies®	by Jim Meade	ISBN: 1-56884-049-7	$19.95 USA/$26.95 Canad
MORE Word For Windows® 6 For Dummies®	by Doug Lowe	ISBN: 1-56884-165-5	$19.95 USA/$26.95 Canad
MORE WordPerfect® 6 For Windows® For Dummies®	by Margaret Levine Young & David C. Kay	ISBN: 1-56884-206-6	$19.95 USA/$26.95 Canad
MORE WordPerfect® 6 For DOS For Dummies®	by Wallace Wang, edited by Dan Gookin	ISBN: 1-56884-047-0	$19.95 USA/$26.95 Canad
Word 6 For Macs® For Dummies®	by Dan Gookin	ISBN: 1-56884-190-6	$19.95 USA/$26.95 Canad
Word For Windows® 6 For Dummies®	by Dan Gookin	ISBN: 1-56884-075-6	$16.95 USA/$22.95 Canad
Word For Windows® For Dummies®	by Dan Gookin & Ray Werner	ISBN: 1-878058-86-X	$16.95 USA/$22.95 Canad
WordPerfect® 6 For DOS For Dummies®	by Dan Gookin	ISBN: 1-878058-77-0	$16.95 USA/$22.95 Canad
WordPerfect® 6.1 For Windows® For Dummies®, 2nd Edition	by Margaret Levine Young & David Kay	ISBN: 1-56884-243-0	$16.95 USA/$22.95 Canad
WordPerfect® For Dummies®	by Dan Gookin	ISBN: 1-878058-52-5	$16.95 USA/$22.95 Canad

Windows is a registered trademark of Microsoft Corporation. Mac is a registered trademark of Apple Computer. OS/2 is a registered trademark of IBM. UNIX is a registered trademark of AT&T. WordPerfect is a registered trademark of Novell. The "...For Dummies Book Series" logo, the IDG Books Worldwide logos, Dummies Press, and The Fun & Easy Way are trademarks, and ---- For Dummies and ... For Dummies are registered trademarks under exclusive license to IDG Books Worldwide, Inc., from International Data Group, Inc.

For scholastic requests & educational orders please call Educational Sales at 1. 800. 434. 2086

FOR MORE INFO OR TO ORDER, PLEASE CALL ▸ 800 762 2974

For volume discounts & special orders p Corporate Sales, at 415. 655. 3000

Fun, Fast, & Cheap!™

'he Internet For Macs® For Dummies® Quick Reference
'y Charles Seiter

5BN:1-56884-967-2
9.99 USA/$12.99 Canada

Windows® 95 For Dummies® Quick Reference
by Greg Harvey

ISBN: 1-56884-964-8
$9.99 USA/$12.99 Canada

Photoshop 3 For Macs® For Dummies® Quick Reference
by Deke McClelland

ISBN: 1-56884-968-0
$9.99 USA/$12.99 Canada

WordPerfect® For DOS For Dummies® Quick Reference
by Greg Harvey

ISBN: 1-56884-009-8
$8.95 USA/$12.95 Canada

Title	Author	ISBN	Price
'ATABASE			
Access 2 For Dummies® Quick Reference	by Stuart J. Stuple	ISBN: 1-56884-167-1	$8.95 USA/$11.95 Canada
:BASE 5 For DOS For Dummies® Quick Reference	by Barrie Sosinsky	ISBN: 1-56884-954-0	$9.99 USA/$12.99 Canada
:BASE 5 For Windows® For Dummies® Quick Reference	by Stuart J. Stuple	ISBN: 1-56884-953-2	$9.99 USA/$12.99 Canada
'aradox 5 For Windows® For Dummies® Quick Reference	by Scott Palmer	ISBN: 1-56884-960-5	$9.99 USA/$12.99 Canada
'ESKTOP PUBLISHING/ILLUSTRATION/GRAPHICS			
CorelDRAW! 5 For Dummies® Quick Reference	by Raymond E. Werner	ISBN: 1-56884-952-4	$9.99 USA/$12.99 Canada
Harvard Graphics For Windows® For Dummies® Quick Reference	by Raymond E. Werner	ISBN: 1-56884-962-1	$9.99 USA/$12.99 Canada
Photoshop 3 For Macs® For Dummies® Quick Reference	by Deke McClelland	ISBN: 1-56884-968-0	$9.99 USA/$12.99 Canada
'INANCE/PERSONAL FINANCE			
Quicken 4 For Windows® For Dummies® Quick Reference	by Stephen L. Nelson	ISBN: 1-56884-950-8	$9.95 USA/$12.95 Canada
'ROUPWARE/INTEGRATED			
Microsoft® Office 4 For Windows® For Dummies® Quick Reference	by Doug Lowe	ISBN: 1-56884-958-3	$9.99 USA/$12.99 Canada
Microsoft® Works 3 For Windows® For Dummies® Quick Reference	by Michael Partington	ISBN: 1-56884-959-1	$9.99 USA/$12.99 Canada
'TERNET/COMMUNICATIONS/NETWORKING			
The Internet For Dummies® Quick Reference	by John R. Levine & Margaret Levine Young	ISBN: 1-56884-168-X	$8.95 USA/$11.95 Canada
'ACINTOSH			
Macintosh® System 7.5 For Dummies® Quick Reference	by Stuart J. Stuple	ISBN: 1-56884-956-7	$9.99 USA/$12.99 Canada
'PERATING SYSTEMS:			
'OS			
DOS For Dummies® Quick Reference	by Greg Harvey	ISBN: 1-56884-007-1	$8.95 USA/$11.95 Canada
'NIX			
UNIX® For Dummies® Quick Reference	by John R. Levine & Margaret Levine Young	ISBN: 1-56884-094-2	$8.95 USA/$11.95 Canada
'INDOWS			
Windows® 3.1 For Dummies® Quick Reference, 2nd Edition	by Greg Harvey	ISBN: 1-56884-951-6	$8.95 USA/$11.95 Canada
'Cs/HARDWARE			
Memory Management For Dummies® Quick Reference	by Doug Lowe	ISBN: 1-56884-362-3	$9.99 USA/$12.99 Canada
'RESENTATION/AUTOCAD			
AutoCAD For Dummies® Quick Reference	by Ellen Finkelstein	ISBN: 1-56884-198-1	$9.95 USA/$12.95 Canada
'PREADSHEET			
1-2-3 For Dummies® Quick Reference	by John Walkenbach	ISBN: 1-56884-027-6	$8.95 USA/$11.95 Canada
1-2-3 For Windows® 5 For Dummies® Quick Reference	by John Walkenbach	ISBN: 1-56884-957-5	$9.95 USA/$12.95 Canada
Excel For Windows® For Dummies® Quick Reference, 2nd Edition	by John Walkenbach	ISBN: 1-56884-096-9	$8.95 USA/$11.95 Canada
Quattro Pro 6 For Windows® For Dummies® Quick Reference	by Stuart J. Stuple	ISBN: 1-56884-172-8	$9.95 USA/$12.95 Canada
'ORD PROCESSING			
Word For Windows® 6 For Dummies® Quick Reference	by George Lynch	ISBN: 1-56884-095-0	$8.95 USA/$11.95 Canada
Word For Windows® For Dummies® Quick Reference	by George Lynch	ISBN: 1-56884-029-2	$8.95 USA/$11.95 Canada
WordPerfect® 6.1 For Windows® For Dummies® Quick Reference, 2nd Edition	by Greg Harvey	ISBN: 1-56884-966-4	$9.99 USA/$12.99/Canada

rosoft and Windows are registered trademarks of Microsoft Corporation. Mac and Macintosh are registered trademarks of Apple Computer. UNIX is a registered trademark of AT&T. WordPerfect is a registered trademark of Novell. The "...For Dummies Book ies" logo, the IDG Books Worldwide logos, Dummies Press, The Fun & Easy Way, and Fun, Fast, & Cheap! are trademarks, and ---- For Dummies and ... For Dummies are registered trademarks under exclusive license to IDG Books Worldwide, Inc., from rnational Data Group, Inc.

'lastic requests & educational orders please :ational Sales at 1. 800. 434. 2086

FOR MORE INFO OR TO ORDER, PLEASE CALL ▸ 800 . 762 . 2974

For volume discounts & special orders please call Corporate Sales, at 415. 655. 3000

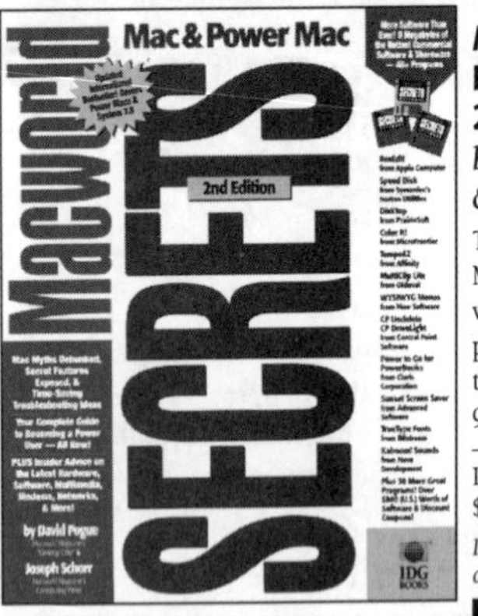

Macworld® Mac® & Power Mac SECRETS™, 2nd Edition
by David Pogue & Joseph Schorr

HOT!

This is the definitive Mac reference for those who want to become power users! Includes three disks with 9MB of software!

ISBN: 1-56884-175-2
$39.95 USA/$54.95 Canada

Includes 3 disks chock full of software.

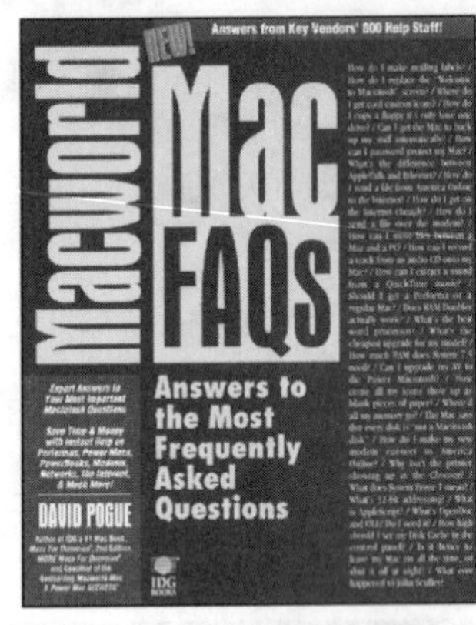

Macworld® Mac® FAQs™
by David Pogue

HOT!

Written by the hottest Macintosh author around, David Pogue, *Macworld Mac FAQs* gives users the ultimate Mac reference. Hundreds of Mac questions and answers side-by-side, right at your fingertips, and organized into six easy-to-reference sections with lots of sidebars and diagrams.

ISBN: 1-56884-480-8
$19.99 USA/$26.99 Canada

Macworld® System 7.5 Bible, 3rd Edition
by Lon Poole

ISBN: 1-56884-098-5
$29.95 USA/$39.95 Canada

Macworld® ClarisWorks 3.0 Companion, 3rd Edition
by Steven A. Schwartz

ISBN: 1-56884-481-6
$24.99 USA/$34.99 Canada

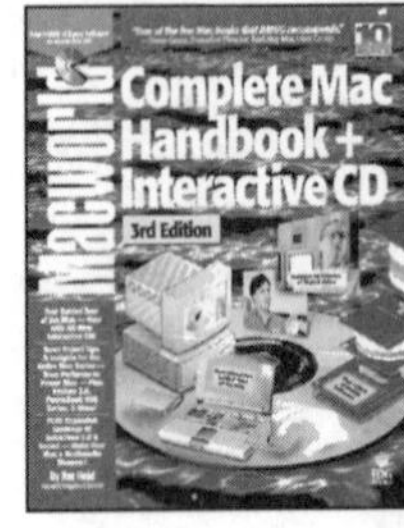

Macworld® Complete Mac® Handbook Plus Interactive CD, 3rd Edition
by Jim Heid

ISBN: 1-56884-192-2
$39.95 USA/$54.95 Cana

Includes an interactive CD-RO

Macworld® Ultimate Mac® CD-ROM
by Jim Heid

ISBN: 1-56884-477-8
$19.99 USA/$26.99 Canada

CD-ROM includes version 2.0 of QuickTime, and over 65 MB of the best shareware, freeware, fonts, sounds, and more!

Macworld® Networking Bible, 2nd Edition
by Dave Kosiur & Joel M. Snyder

ISBN: 1-56884-194-9
$29.95 USA/$39.95 Canada

Macworld® Photoshop 3 Bible, 2nd Edition
by Deke McClelland

ISBN: 1-56884-158-2
$39.95 USA/$54.95 Cana

Includes stunning CD-ROM with add-ons, digitized photos and more.

NEW!

Macworld® Photoshop 2.5 Bible
by Deke McClelland

ISBN: 1-56884-022-5
$29.95 USA/$39.95 Canada

Macworld® FreeHand 4 Bible
by Deke McClelland

ISBN: 1-56884-170-1
$29.95 USA/$39.95 Canada

Macworld® Illustrator 5.0/5.5 Bible
by Ted Alspach

ISBN: 1-56884-097-7
$39.95 USA/$54.95 Cana

Includes CD-ROM with QuickTime tutorials.

Mac is a registered trademark of Apple Computer. Macworld is a registered trademark of International Data Group, Inc. ----SECRETS, and ----FAQs are trademarks under exclusive license to IDG Books Worldwide, Inc., from International Data Group, Inc.

For scholastic requests & educational orders please call Educational Sales at 1. 800. 434. 2086

FOR MORE INFO OR TO ORDER, PLEASE CALL ▸ 800 762 2974

For volume discounts & special orders Corporate Sales, at 415. 655. 3000

"*Macworld Complete Mac Handbook Plus CD* covered everything I could think of and more!"

Peter Tsakiris, New York, NY

"Very useful for PageMaker beginners and veterans alike—contains a wealth of tips and tricks to make you a faster, more powerful PageMaker user."

Paul Brainerd, President and founder, Aldus Corporation

"Thanks for the best computer book I've ever read—*Photoshop 2.5 Bible*. Best $30 I ever spent. I *love* the detailed index....Yours blows them all out of the water. This is a great book. We must enlighten the masses!"

Kevin Lisankie, Chicago, Illinois

"*Macworld Guide to ClarisWorks 2* is the easiest computer book to read that I have ever found!"

Steven Hanson, Lutz, FL

"...thanks to the *Macworld Excel 5 Companion,* 2nd Edition occupying a permanent position next to my computer, I'll be able to tap more of Excel's power."

Lauren Black, Lab Director, Macworld Magazine

Macworld® QuarkXPress 3.2/3.3 Bible
by Barbara Assadi & Galen Gruman

ISBN: 1-878058-85-1
$39.95 USA/$52.95 Canada

Includes disk with QuarkXPress XTensions and scripts.

Macworld® PageMaker 5 Bible
by Craig Danuloff

ISBN: 1-878058-84-3
$39.95 USA/$52.95 Canada

Includes 2 disks with PageMaker utilities, clip art, and more.

Macworld® FileMaker Pro 2.0/2.1 Bible
by Steven A. Schwartz

ISBN: 1-56884-201-5
$34.95 USA/$46.95 Canada

Includes disk with ready-to-run data bases.

Macworld® Word 6 Companion, 2nd Edition
by Jim Heid

ISBN: 1-56884-082-9
$24.95 USA/$34.95 Canada

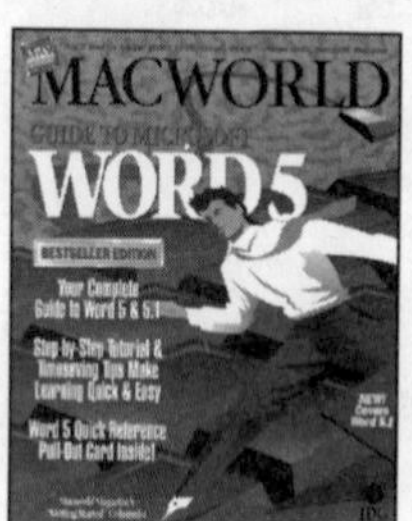

Macworld® Guide To Microsoft® Word 5/5.1
by Jim Heid

ISBN: 1-878058-39-8
$22.95 USA/$29.95 Canada

Macworld® ClarisWorks 2.0/2.1 Companion, 2nd Edition
by Steven A. Schwartz

ISBN: 1-56884-180-9
$24.95 USA/$34.95 Canada

Macworld® Guide To Microsoft® Works 3
by Barrie Sosinsky

ISBN: 1-878058-42-8
$22.95 USA/$29.95 Canada

Macworld® Excel 5 Companion, 2nd Edition
by Chris Van Buren & David Maguiness

ISBN: 1-56884-081-0
$24.95 USA/$34.95 Canada

Macworld® Guide To Microsoft® Excel 4
by David Maguiness

ISBN: 1-878058-40-1
$22.95 USA/$29.95 Canada

crosoft is a registered trademark of Microsoft Corporation. Macworld is a registered trademark of International Data Group, Inc.

Order Center: **(800) 762-2974** (8 a.m.–6 p.m., EST, weekdays)

Quantity	ISBN	Title	Price	Total

Shipping & Handling Charges

	Description	First book	Each additional book	Total
Domestic	Normal	$4.50	$1.50	$
	Two Day Air	$8.50	$2.50	$
	Overnight	$18.00	$3.00	$
International	Surface	$8.00	$8.00	$
	Airmail	$16.00	$16.00	$
	DHL Air	$17.00	$17.00	$

*For large quantities call for shipping & handling charges.
**Prices are subject to change without notice.

Ship to:

Name ____________________

Company ____________________

Address ____________________

City/State/Zip ____________________

Daytime Phone ____________________

Payment: ☐ Check to IDG Books Worldwide (US Funds Only)
☐ VISA ☐ MasterCard ☐ American Express

Card # ____________________ Expires __________

Signature ____________________

Subtotal __________

CA residents add applicable sales tax __________

IN, MA, and MD residents add 5% sales tax __________

IL residents add 6.25% sales tax __________

RI residents add 7% sales tax __________

TX residents add 8.25% sales tax __________

Shipping __________

Total __________

Please send this order form to:

IDG Books Worldwide, Inc.
Attn: Order Entry Dept.
7260 Shadeland Station, Suite 100
Indianapolis, IN 46256

Allow up to 3 weeks for delivery.
Thank you!

IDG BOOKS WORLDWIDE, INC. END-USER LICENSE AGREEMENT

Read This. You should carefully read these terms and conditions before opening the software packet(s) included with this book ("Book"). This is a license agreement ("Agreement") between you and IDG Books Worldwide, Inc. ("IDGB"). By opening the accompanying software packet(s), you acknowledge that you have read and accept the following terms and conditions. If you do not agree and do not want to be bound by such terms and conditions, promptly return the Book and the unopened software packet(s) to the place you obtained them for a full refund.

1. **License Grant.** IDGB grants to you (either an individual or entity) a nonexclusive license to use one copy of the enclosed software program(s) (collectively, the "Software") solely for your own personal or business purposes on a single computer (whether a standard computer or a workstation component of a multi-user network). The Software is in use on a computer when it is loaded into temporary memory (i.e., RAM) or installed into permanent memory (e.g., hard disk, CD-ROM or other storage device). IDGB reserves all rights not expressly granted herein.

2. **Ownership.** IDGB is the owner of all right, title and interest, including copyright, in and to the compilation of the Software recorded on the disk(s)/CD-ROM. Copyright to the individual programs on the disk(s)/CD-ROM is owned by the author or other authorized copyright owner of each program. Ownership of the Software and all proprietary rights relating thereto remain with IDGB and its licensors.

3. **Restrictions On Use and Transfer.**

   (a) You may only (i) make one copy of the Software for backup or archival purposes, or (ii) transfer the Software to a single hard disk, provided that you keep the original for backup or archival purposes. You may not (i) rent or lease the Software, (ii) copy or reproduce the Software through a LAN or other network system or through any computer subscriber system or bulletin-board system, or (iii) modify, adapt or create derivative works based on the Software.

   (b) You may not reverse engineer, decompile, or disassemble the Software. You may transfer the Software and user documentation on a permanent basis, provided that the transferee agrees to accept the terms and conditions of this Agreement and you retain no copies. If the Software is an update or has been updated, any transfer must include the most recent update and all prior versions.

4. **Restrictions on Use of Individual Programs.** You must follow the individual requirements and restrictions detailed for each individual program in Appendix A of this Book. These limitations are contained in the individual license agreements recorded on the disk(s)/CD-ROM. These restrictions include a requirement that after using the program for the period of time specified in its text, the user must pay a registration fee or discontinue use. By opening the Software packet(s), you will be agreeing to abide by the licenses and restrictions for these individual programs. None of the material on this disk(s) or listed in this Book may ever be distributed, in original or modified form, for commercial purposes.

5. **Limited Warranty.** IDGB warrants that the Software and disk(s)/CD-ROM are free from defects in materials and workmanship under normal use for a period of sixty (60) days from the date of purchase of this Book. If IDGB receives notification within the warranty period of defects in materials or workmanship, IDGB will replace the defective disk(s)/CD-ROM.

IDGB AND THE AUTHOR OF THE BOOK DISCLAIM ALL OTHER WARRANTIES, EXPRESS OR IMPLIED, INCLUDING WITHOUT LIMITATION IMPLIED WARRANTIES OF MERCHANTABILITY AND FITNESS FOR A PARTICULAR PURPOSE, WITH RESPECT TO THE SOFTWARE, THE PROGRAMS, THE SOURCE CODE CONTAINED THEREIN, AND/OR THE TECHNIQUES DESCRIBED IN THIS BOOK. IDGB DOES NOT WARRANT THAT THE FUNCTIONS CONTAINED IN THE SOFTWARE WILL MEET YOUR REQUIREMENTS OR THAT THE OPERATION OF THE SOFTWARE WILL BE ERROR FREE.

This limited warranty gives you specific legal rights, and you may have other rights which vary from jurisdiction to jurisdiction.

6. **Remedies.**

   (a) IDGB's entire liability and your exclusive remedy for defects in materials and workmanship shall be limited to replacement of the Software, which is returned to IDGB at the address set forth below with a copy of your receipt. This Limited Warranty is void if failure of the Software has resulted from accident, abuse, or misapplication. Any replacement Software will be warranted for the remainder of the original warranty period or thirty (30) days, whichever is longer.

   (b) In no event shall IDGB or the author be liable for any damages whatsoever (including without limitation damages for loss of business profits, business interruption, loss of business information, or any other pecuniary loss) arising out of the use of or inability to use the Book or the Software, even if IDGB has been advised of the possibility of such damages.

(c) Because some jurisdictions do not allow the exclusion or limitation of liability for consequential or incidental damages, the above limitation or exclusion may not apply to you.

7. **U.S. Government Restricted Rights.** Use, duplication, or disclosure of the Software by the U.S. Government is subject to restrictions stated in paragraph (c) (1) (ii) of the Rights in Technical Data and Computer Software clause of DFARS 252.227-7013, and in subparagraphs (a) through (d) of the Commercial Computer—Restricted Rights clause at FAR 52.227-19, and in similar clauses in the NASA FAR supplement, when applicable.

8. **General.** This Agreement constitutes the entire understanding of the parties, and revokes and supersedes all prior agreements, oral or written, between them and may not be modified or amended except in a writing signed by both parties hereto which specifically refers to this Agreement. This Agreement shall take precedence over any other documents that may be in conflict herewith. If any one or more provisions contained in this Agreement are held by any court or tribunal to be invalid, illegal or otherwise unenforceable, each and every other provision shall remain in full force and effect.

Alternate Disk Format Available. The enclosed disk is provided in 3 1/2" 1.44MB, high-density format. If you have a low-density drive, and you cannot arrange to transfer the data to the disk size you need, you can obtain the programs on a 3-1/2" 720K low-density disk by writing to the following address: Disk Fulfillment Department, Attn: *Macworld FileMaker Pro 3 Bible*, IDG Books Worldwide, Inc., 7260 Shadeland Station, Indianapolis, IN 46256, or call 1-800-762-2974. Please specify the size of disk you need and allow 3 to 4 weeks for delivery.

Disk Instructions

This book includes a high-density (1.4MB) Macintosh disk that contains an assortment of hand-picked, ready-to-run FileMaker Pro database templates, utilities, and demos. (See Appendix A for a detailed description of the contents.) To use the *Macworld FileMaker Pro 3 Bible* disk, you need the following:

- A high-density floppy drive (also known as an Apple SuperDrive)
- Almost 3MB of free hard disk space (if you want to extract all the files)

Extracting the Files

To extract files from the *Macworld FileMaker Pro 3 Bible* disk, do the following:

1. Insert the *Macworld FileMaker Pro 3 Bible* disk into the Macintosh's floppy drive. The disk window appears. The archives are stored in two folders. The Author Contributions folder contains all files that were discussed in the examples presented in this book. The Other Contributions folder contains freeware and shareware templates, demos, and utilities.
2. Open either folder and locate the archive you want. The disk contain eight separate archives. The contents of the various archives are described in Appendix A.
3. Double-click the archive's icon. The extraction program launches. The Select Destination Folder dialog box appears.
4. Use normal navigation procedures to select the disk and folder where you want to copy the contents of the archive.

Be sure to select a disk other than the *Macworld FileMaker Pro 3 Bible* disk — a hard disk, for example. Treat the *Macworld FileMaker Pro 3 Bible* disk as you would treat any master disk. If you ever need to reinstall any of the software, you can use the original disk to do so.

5. Click the Extract button. The Extracting dialog box appears. The files are extracted one-by-one from the archive and then are copied to the destination disk and folder that you selected in step 4.

When all files have been extracted, the extraction program automatically quits and 'ou are returned to the desktop.

'xtract the contents of additional archives, repeat steps 2 through 5.